Principles of Accounting, Volume 2: Managerial Accounting

SENIOR CONTRIBUTING AUTHORS
MITCHELL FRANKLIN, LE MOYNE COLLEGE (FINANCIAL ACCOUNTING)
PATTY GRAYBEAL, UNIVERSITY OF MICHIGAN-DEARBORN (MANAGERIAL ACCOUNTING)
DIXON COOPER, OUACHITA BAPTIST UNIVERSITY

ISBN: 978-1-947172-60-9

OpenStax
Rice University
6100 Main Street MS-375
Houston, Texas 77005

To learn more about OpenStax, visit https://openstax.org.
Individual print copies and bulk orders can be purchased through our website.

©2019 Rice University. Textbook content produced by OpenStax is licensed under a Creative Commons Attribution Non-Commercial ShareAlike 4.0 International License (CC BY-NC-SA 4.0). Under this license, any user of this textbook or the textbook contents herein can share, remix, and build upon the content for noncommercial purposes only. Any adaptations must be shared under the same type of license. In any case of sharing the original or adapted material, whether in whole or in part, the user must provide proper attribution as follows:

- If you noncommercially redistribute this textbook in a digital format (including but not limited to PDF and HTML), then you must retain on every page the following attribution:
  "Access for free at openstax.org."
- If you noncommercially redistribute this textbook in a print format, then you must include on every physical page the following attribution:
  "Access for free at openstax.org."
- If you noncommercially redistribute part of this textbook, then you must retain in every digital format page view (including but not limited to PDF and HTML) and on every physical printed page the following attribution:
  "Access for free at openstax.org."
- If you use this textbook as a bibliographic reference, please include
  https://openstax.org/details/books/principles-managerial-accounting in your citation.

For questions regarding this licensing, please contact support@openstax.org.

Trademarks
The OpenStax name, OpenStax logo, OpenStax book covers, OpenStax CNX name, OpenStax CNX logo, OpenStax Tutor name, Openstax Tutor logo, Connexions name, Connexions logo, Rice University name, and Rice University logo are not subject to the license and may not be reproduced without the prior and express written consent of Rice University. XANEDU and the XanEdu Logo are trademarks of Xanedu Publishing, Inc. The XANEDU mark is registered in the United States, Canada, and the European Union. These trademarks may not be used without the prior and express written consent of XanEdu Publishing, Inc.

HARDCOVER BOOK ISBN-13	978-1-947172-60-9
PAPERBACK BOOK ISBN-13	978-0-9986257-8-2
B&W PAPERBACK BOOK ISBN-13	978-1-59399-595-9
DIGITAL VERSION ISBN-13	978-1-947172-59-3

10 9 8 7 6 5 4 3 2 1

Printed by
XanEdu
4750 Venture Drive, Suite 400
Ann Arbor, MI 48108
800-562-2147
www.xanedu.com

OpenStax

OpenStax provides free, peer-reviewed, openly licensed textbooks for introductory college and Advanced Placement® courses and low-cost, personalized courseware that helps students learn. A nonprofit ed tech initiative based at Rice University, we're committed to helping students access the tools they need to complete their courses and meet their educational goals.

Rice University

OpenStax, OpenStax CNX, and OpenStax Tutor are initiatives of Rice University. As a leading research university with a distinctive commitment to undergraduate education, Rice University aspires to path-breaking research, unsurpassed teaching, and contributions to the betterment of our world. It seeks to fulfill this mission by cultivating a diverse community of learning and discovery that produces leaders across the spectrum of human endeavor.

Philanthropic Support

OpenStax is grateful for our generous philanthropic partners, who support our vision to improve educational opportunities for all learners.

Laura and John Arnold Foundation	The Maxfield Foundation
Arthur and Carlyse Ciocca Charitable Foundation	Burt and Deedee McMurtry
Ann and John Doerr	Michelson 20MM Foundation
Bill & Melinda Gates Foundation	National Science Foundation
Girard Foundation	The Open Society Foundations
Google Inc.	Jumee Yhu and David E. Park III
The William and Flora Hewlett Foundation	Brian D. Patterson USA-International Foundation
Rusty and John Jaggers	The Bill and Stephanie Sick Fund
The Calvin K. Kazanjian Economics Foundation	Robin and Sandy Stuart Foundation
Charles Koch Foundation	The Stuart Family Foundation
Leon Lowenstein Foundation, Inc.	Tammy and Guillermo Treviño

TABLE OF CONTENTS

Preface 1

1 Accounting as a Tool for Managers 11

    1.1 Define Managerial Accounting and Identify the Three Primary Responsibilities of Management 12
    1.2 Distinguish between Financial and Managerial Accounting 21
    1.3 Explain the Primary Roles and Skills Required of Managerial Accountants 28
    1.4 Describe the Role of the Institute of Management Accountants and the Use of Ethical Standards 38
    1.5 Describe Trends in Today's Business Environment and Analyze Their Impact on Accounting 43

2 Building Blocks of Managerial Accounting 69

    2.1 Distinguish between Merchandising, Manufacturing, and Service Organizations 70
    2.2 Identify and Apply Basic Cost Behavior Patterns 83
    2.3 Estimate a Variable and Fixed Cost Equation and Predict Future Costs 100

3 Cost-Volume-Profit Analysis 127

    3.1 Explain Contribution Margin and Calculate Contribution Margin per Unit, Contribution Margin Ratio, and Total Contribution Margin 128
    3.2 Calculate a Break-Even Point in Units and Dollars 135
    3.3 Perform Break-Even Sensitivity Analysis for a Single Product Under Changing Business Situations 147
    3.4 Perform Break-Even Sensitivity Analysis for a Multi-Product Environment Under Changing Business Situations 154
    3.5 Calculate and Interpret a Company's Margin of Safety and Operating Leverage 158

4 Job Order Costing 185

    4.1 Distinguish between Job Order Costing and Process Costing 186
    4.2 Describe and Identify the Three Major Components of Product Costs under Job Order Costing 194
    4.3 Use the Job Order Costing Method to Trace the Flow of Product Costs through the Inventory Accounts 207
    4.4 Compute a Predetermined Overhead Rate and Apply Overhead to Production 213
    4.5 Compute the Cost of a Job Using Job Order Costing 217
    4.6 Determine and Dispose of Underapplied or Overapplied Overhead 220
    4.7 Prepare Journal Entries for a Job Order Cost System 223
    4.8 Explain How a Job Order Cost System Applies to a Nonmanufacturing Environment 226

5 Process Costing 251

5.1 Compare and Contrast Job Order Costing and Process Costing   252
5.2 Explain and Identify Conversion Costs   262
5.3 Explain and Compute Equivalent Units and Total Cost of Production in an Initial Processing Stage   264
5.4 Explain and Compute Equivalent Units and Total Cost of Production in a Subsequent Processing Stage   268
5.5 Prepare Journal Entries for a Process Costing System   271

6 Activity-Based, Variable, and Absorption Costing   293

6.1 Calculate Predetermined Overhead and Total Cost under the Traditional Allocation Method   294
6.2 Describe and Identify Cost Drivers   299
6.3 Calculate Activity-Based Product Costs   302
6.4 Compare and Contrast Traditional and Activity-Based Costing Systems   310
6.5 Compare and Contrast Variable and Absorption Costing   313

7 Budgeting   347

7.1 Describe How and Why Managers Use Budgets   348
7.2 Prepare Operating Budgets   357
7.3 Prepare Financial Budgets   365
7.4 Prepare Flexible Budgets   374
7.5 Explain How Budgets Are Used to Evaluate Goals   378

8 Standard Costs and Variances   405

8.1 Explain How and Why a Standard Cost Is Developed   406
8.2 Compute and Evaluate Materials Variances   411
8.3 Compute and Evaluate Labor Variances   416
8.4 Compute and Evaluate Overhead Variances   421
8.5 Describe How Companies Use Variance Analysis   429

9 Responsibility Accounting and Decentralization   457

9.1 Differentiate between Centralized and Decentralized Management   458
9.2 Describe How Decision-Making Differs between Centralized and Decentralized Environments   464
9.3 Describe the Types of Responsibility Centers   467
9.4 Describe the Effects of Various Decisions on Performance Evaluation of Responsibility Centers   481

10 Short-Term Decision Making   513

10.1 Identify Relevant Information for Decision-Making   514

10.2 Evaluate and Determine Whether to Accept or Reject a Special Order   521
10.3 Evaluate and Determine Whether to Make or Buy a Component   524
10.4 Evaluate and Determine Whether to Keep or Discontinue a Segment or Product   528
10.5 Evaluate and Determine Whether to Sell or Process Further   532
10.6 Evaluate and Determine How to Make Decisions When Resources Are Constrained   536

11 Capital Budgeting Decisions   565

11.1 Describe Capital Investment Decisions and How They Are Applied   566
11.2 Evaluate the Payback and Accounting Rate of Return in Capital Investment Decisions   570
11.3 Explain the Time Value of Money and Calculate Present and Future Values of Lump Sums and Annuities   577
11.4 Use Discounted Cash Flow Models to Make Capital Investment Decisions   585
11.5 Compare and Contrast Non-Time Value-Based Methods and Time Value-Based Methods in Capital Investment Decisions   594

12 Balanced Scorecard and Other Performance Measures   619

12.1 Explain the Importance of Performance Measurement   620
12.2 Identify the Characteristics of an Effective Performance Measure   626
12.3 Evaluate an Operating Segment or a Project Using Return on Investment, Residual Income, and Economic Value Added   629
12.4 Describe the Balanced Scorecard and Explain How It Is Used   638

13 Sustainability Reporting   663

13.1 Describe Sustainability and the Way It Creates Business Value   664
13.2 Identify User Needs for Information   681
13.3 Discuss Examples of Major Sustainability Initiatives   686
13.4 Future Issues in Sustainability   691

A Financial Statement Analysis   701

B Time Value of Money   713

C Suggested Resources   717

Index   733

Preface

Welcome to *Principles of Accounting*, an OpenStax resource. This textbook was written to increase student access to high-quality learning materials, maintaining highest standards of academic rigor at little to no cost.

About OpenStax

OpenStax is a nonprofit based at Rice University, and it's our mission to improve student access to education. Our first openly licensed college textbook was published in 2012, and our library has since scaled to over 30 books for college and AP® courses used by hundreds of thousands of students. OpenStax Tutor, our low-cost personalized learning tool, is being used in college courses throughout the country. Through our partnerships with philanthropic foundations and our alliance with other educational resource organizations, OpenStax is breaking down the most common barriers to learning and empowering students and instructors to succeed.

About OpenStax resources

Customization

Principles of Accounting is licensed under a Creative Commons Attribution-NonCommercial-ShareAlike 4.0 International (CC BY-NC-SA) license, which means that you can distribute, remix, and build upon the content, as long as you provide attribution to OpenStax and its content contributors, do not use the content for commercial purposes, and distribute the content under the same CC BY-NC-SA license.

Because our books are openly licensed, you are free to use the entire book or pick and choose the sections that are most relevant to the needs of your course. Feel free to remix the content by assigning your students certain chapters and sections in your syllabus, in the order that you prefer. You can even provide a direct link in your syllabus to the sections in the web view of your book.

Instructors also have the option of creating a customized version of their OpenStax book. The custom version can be made available to students in low-cost print or digital form through their campus bookstore. Visit the Instructor Resources section of your book page on openstax.org for more information.

Art attribution in *Principles of Accounting*

In *Principles of Accounting*, most art contains attribution to its title, creator or rights holder, host platform, and license within the caption. Because the art is openly licensed, anyone may reuse the art as long as they provide the same attribution to its original source.

To maximize readability and content flow, some art does not include attribution in the text. If you reuse art from this text that does not have attribution provided, use the following attribution: Copyright Rice University, OpenStax, under CC BY-NC-SA 4.0 license.

Errata

All OpenStax textbooks undergo a rigorous review process. However, like any professional-grade textbook, errors sometimes occur. Since our books are web based, we can make updates periodically when deemed pedagogically necessary. If you have a correction to suggest, submit it through the link on your book page on openstax.org. Subject matter experts review all errata suggestions. OpenStax is committed to remaining transparent about all updates, so you will also find a list of past errata changes on your book page on openstax.org.

Format

You can access this textbook for free in web view or PDF through openstax.org, and for a low cost in print.

About *Principles of Accounting*

Principles of Accounting is designed to meet the scope and sequence requirements of a two-semester accounting course that covers the fundamentals of financial and managerial accounting. This book is specifically designed to appeal to both accounting and non-accounting majors, exposing students to the core concepts of accounting in familiar ways to build a strong foundation that can be applied across business fields. Each chapter opens with a relatable real-life scenario for today's college student. Thoughtfully designed examples are presented throughout each chapter, allowing students to build on emerging accounting knowledge. Concepts are further reinforced through applicable connections to more detailed business processes. Students are immersed in the "why" as well as the "how" aspects of accounting in order to reinforce concepts and promote comprehension over rote memorization.

Coverage and scope

Our *Principles of Accounting* textbook adheres to the scope and sequence requirements of accounting courses nationwide. We have endeavored to make the core concepts and practical applications of accounting engaging, relevant, and accessible to students.

Principles of Accounting, Volume 1: Financial Accounting

Chapter 1: The Role of Accounting in Society

Chapter 2: Introduction to Financial Statements

Chapter 3: Analyzing and Recording Transactions

Chapter 4: The Adjustment Process

Chapter 5: Completing the Accounting Cycle

Chapter 6: Merchandising Transactions

Chapter 7: Accounting Information Systems

Chapter 8: Fraud, Internal Controls, and Cash

Chapter 9: Accounting for Receivables

Chapter 10: Inventory

Chapter 11: Long-Term Assets

Chapter 12: Current Liabilities

Chapter 13: Long-Term Liabilities

Chapter 14: Corporation Accounting

Chapter 15: Partnership Accounting

Chapter 16: Statement of Cash Flows

Principles of Accounting, Volume 2: Managerial Accounting

Chapter 1: Accounting as a Tool for Managers

Chapter 2: Building Blocks of Managerial Accounting

Chapter 3: Cost-Volume-Profit Analysis

Chapter 4: Job Order Costing

Chapter 5: Process Costing

Chapter 6: Activity-Based, Variable, and Absorption Costing

Chapter 7: Budgeting

Chapter 8: Standard Costs and Variances

Chapter 9: Responsibility Accounting and Decentralization

Chapter 10: Short-Term Decision-Making

Chapter 11: Capital Budgeting Decisions

Chapter 12: Balanced Scorecard and Other Performance Measures

Chapter 13: Sustainability Reporting

Engaging feature boxes

Throughout *Principles of Accounting*, you will find features that engage students by taking selected topics a step further.

- **Your Turn.** This feature provides students an opportunity to apply covered concepts.
- **Concepts in Practice.** This feature takes students beyond mechanics and illustrates the utility of a given concept for accountants and non-accountants. We encourage instructors to reference these as part of their in-class lectures and assessments to provide easily relatable applications.
- **Think It Through.** This scenario-based feature puts students in the role of decision-maker. With topics ranging from ethical dilemmas to conflicting analytical results, the purpose of this feature is to teach students that in the real world not every question has just one answer.
- **Continuing Application at Work.** This feature follows an individual company or segment of an industry and examines how businesspeople conduct the decision-making process in different situations. It allows students to see how concepts build on each other.
- **Ethical Considerations.** This feature illustrates the ethical implication of decisions, how accounting concepts are applied to real-life examples, and how financial and managerial decisions can impact many stakeholders.
- **IFRS Connection.** This feature presents the differences and similarities between U.S. GAAP and IFRS, helping students understand how accounting concepts and rules between countries may vary and thus affect financial reporting and decision-making.
- **Link to Learning.** This feature provides a very brief introduction to online resources and videos that are pertinent to students' exploration of the topic at hand.

Pedagogical features that reinforce key concepts

- **Learning Objectives.** Each chapter is organized into sections based on clear and comprehensive learning objectives that help guide students on what they can expect to learn. After completing the modules and assessments, students should be able to demonstrate mastery of the learning objectives.
- **Summaries.** Designed to support both students and instructors, section summaries distill the information in each module down to key, concise points.
- **Key Terms.** Key terms are bolded the first time that they are used and are followed by a definition in context. Definitions of key terms are also listed in the glossary, which appears at the end of the chapter.

Assessments to test comprehension and practice skills

An assortment of assessment types are provided in this text to allow for practice and self-assessment throughout the course of study.

- **Multiple Choice**. are basic review questions that test comprehension.
- **Questions** include brief, open-response questions to test comprehension.
- **Exercises** (Sets A and B) are application Application questions that require a combination of quantitative and analytical skills.
- **Problems** (Sets A and B) are advanced Advanced activities that allow students to demonstrate learning and application of multiple learning objectives and skills concurrently in one set of facts. Problems are designed to assess higher levels of Bloom's taxonomy.
- **Thought Provokers** are open-ended questions, often with more than one acceptable response, designed to stretch students intellectually.

Effective art program

Our art program is designed to enhance students' understanding of concepts through clear and effective presentations of financial materials and diagrams.

JOURNAL			
Date	**Account**	**Debit**	**Credit**
	Cost of Goods Sold	25,000	
	Finished Goods Inventory		25,000
	To record the cost of products sold		

Figure 1   Journal Entry.

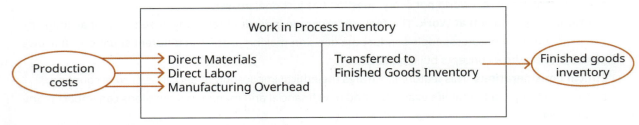

Figure 2   Work in Process Inventory T-Account.

WHICHARD & KLEIN, LLP
Income Statement
For the Year Ended December 31, 2019

Service Revenue	$412,000
Operating Expenses	
Salaries	210,000
Office Expense	35,000
Office Equipment	9,000
Administrative Salaries	45,000
Utilities	11,000
Miscellaneous	7,500
Total Operating Expenses	317,500
Operating Income	$ 94,500

Figure 3   Income Statement.

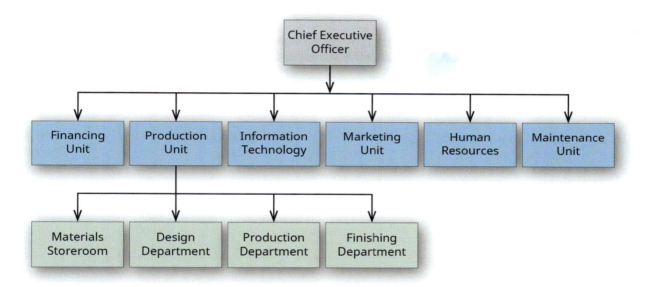

Figure 4   Organizational Chart.

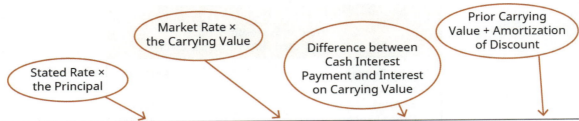

Year	Cash Interest Payment	Interest on Carrying Value	Amortization of Discount	Carrying value
Jan. 1 Year 1				91,800
Dec. 31 Year 1	5,000	6,426	1,426	93,226
Dec. 31 Year 2	5,000	6,526	1,526	94,752
Dec. 31 Year 3	5,000	6,633	1,633	96,384
Dec. 31 Year 4	5,000	6,747	1,747	98,131
Dec. 31 Year 5	5,000	6,869	1,869	100,000

Figure 5 Cash Interest Payment.

GENERAL LEDGER					
Cash					Account No. 101
Date	Item	Ref.	Debit	Credit	Balance
2019					
Jan. 3	Cash for common stock		20,000		20,000
Jan. 9	Payment from client		4,000		24,000
Jan. 12	Utility bill			300	23,700
Jan. 14	Dividends payment			100	23,600
Jan. 17	Cash for services		2,800		26,400
Jan. 18	Paid cash for equipment			3,500	22,900
Jan. 20	Paid employee salaries			3,600	19,300
Jan. 23	Customer payment		5,500		24,800

Figure 6 General Ledger.

Additional resources

Student and instructor resources

We've compiled additional resources for both students and instructors, including Getting Started Guides, an instructor solution guide, and companion presentation slides. Instructor resources require a verified instructor account, which you can apply for when you log in or create your account on openstax.org. Instructor and student resources are typically available within a few months after the book's initial publication. Take advantage of these resources to supplement your OpenStax book.

Community Hubs

OpenStax partners with the Institute for the Study of Knowledge Management in Education (ISKME) to offer Community Hubs on OER Commons—a platform for instructors to share community-created resources that support OpenStax books, free of charge. Through our Community Hubs, instructors can upload their own materials or download resources to use in their own courses, including additional ancillaries, teaching material, multimedia, and relevant course content. We encourage instructors to join the hubs for the subjects most relevant to your teaching and research as an opportunity both to enrich your courses and to engage with other faculty.

To reach the Community Hubs, visit www.oercommons.org/hubs/OpenStax.

Technology partners

As allies in making high-quality learning materials accessible, our technology partners offer optional low-cost tools that are integrated with OpenStax books. To access the technology options for your text, visit your book page on openstax.org.

About the authors

Senior contributing authors

Mitchell Franklin, Le Moyne College (Financial Accounting)

Mitchell Franklin (PhD, CPA) is an Associate Professor and Director of the Undergraduate and Graduate Accounting Programs at Le Moyne College's Madden School of Business. His research interests include the impact of tax law on policy, and innovative education in both financial accounting and taxation, with articles published in journals including *Issues in Accounting Education, Advances in Accounting Education, Tax Notes, Journal of Taxation*, and *The CPA Journal and Tax Adviser*. He teaches introductory and advanced courses in individual and corporate taxation as well as financial accounting. Prior to joining Le Moyne College, he served on the faculty at Syracuse University.

Patty Graybeal, University of Michigan-Dearborn (Managerial Accounting)

Patty Graybeal received her BBA from Radford University and her MACCT and PhD from Virginia Tech. She teaches undergraduate and graduate courses in financial, managerial, governmental, and international accounting. She has published scholarly articles on performance plans and compensation structures, as well as bankruptcy prediction, and she currently focuses on pedagogical issues related to instructional methods and resources that enhance student academic success. Prior to UM-Dearborn, she was on the faculty at Wake Forest University, George Mason University, and Virginia Tech. She brings significant real-world experience to the classroom from her prior work in healthcare administration and her current work with the auto industry.

Dixon Cooper, Ouachita Baptist University

Dixon Cooper received his BBA in Accounting and MS in Taxation from the University of North Texas. He has taught undergraduate and graduate courses in accounting, finance, and economics. In addition to his academic activities, he served for approximately fifteen years as an author/editor for the AICPA's continuing education program and maintained a tax compliance and financial services practice. He also has several years of experience in public accounting and consulting. Prior to teaching at Ouachita Baptist University, he was a faculty member at the University of North Texas, Texas Christian University Austin College, and the University of Arkansas.

Contributing authors

LuAnn Bean, Florida Institute of Technology

Ian Burt, Niagara University

Shana Carr, San Diego City College

David T. Collins, Bellarmine University

Shawna Coram, Florida State College at Jacksonville

Kenneth Creech, Briar Cliff University

Alan Czyzewski, Indiana State University

Michael Gauci, Florida Atlantic University

Cindy Greenman, Embry-Riddle Aeronautical University

Michael Haselkorn, Bentley University

Christine Irujo, Westfield State University

Cynthia Johnson, University of Arkansas at Little Rock

Cynthia Khanlarian, North Carolina Agricultural and Technical State University

Terri Lukshaitis, Ferris State University

Debra Luna, Southwest University

Bill Nantz, Houston Community College

Tatyana Pashnyak, Bainbridge State College

Brian Pusateri, University of Scranton

Ellen Rackas, Muhlenberg College

Marianne Rexer, Wilkes University

Roslyn Roberts, California State University, Sacramento

Rebecca Rosner, Long Island University

Jeffrey J. Sabolish, University of Michigan-Flint

Jason E. Swartzlander, Bluffton University

Diane Tanner, University of North Florida

Mark M. Ulrich, Queensborough Community College

Janis Weber, University of Louisiana Monroe

Linda Williams, Tidewater Community College

Darryl Woolley, University of Idaho

Reviewers

Janice Akao, Butler Community College

Chandra D. Arthur, Cuyahoga Community College

Kwadwo Asare, Bryant University

Dereck Barr-Pulliam, University of Wisconsin–Madison

John Bedient, Albion College

Debra Benson, Kennesaw State University

Amy Bourne, Oregon State University

Stacy Boyer-Davis, Northern Michigan University

Dena Breece, Methodist University

Lawrence Chui, University of St. Thomas, Minnesota

Sandra Cohen, Columbia College Chicago

Bryan Coleman, Assumption College

Sue Cooper, Salisbury University

Constance Crawford, Ramapo College of New Jersey

Cori O. Crews, Valdosta State University

Annette Davis, Glendale Community College

Ronald de Ramon, Rockland Community College

Julie Dilling, Moraine Park Technical College

Terry Elliott, Morehead State University

Jim Emig, Villanova University

Darius Fatemi, Northern Kentucky University

Rhonda Gilreath, Tiffin University

Alan Glazer, Franklin & Marshall College

Marina Grau, Houston Community College

Amber Gray, Adrian College

Jeffry Haber, Iona College

Michelle Hagadorn, Roanoke College

Regina Ivory Butts, Fort Valley State University

Simone Keize, Broward College

Christine Kloezeman, California State University, Los Angeles

Lauri L. Kremer, Lycoming College

W. Eric Lee, University of Northern Iowa

Julie G. Lindsey, University of Phoenix

Jennifer Mack, Lindenwood University

Suneel Maheshwari, Indiana University of Pennsylvania

Richard Mandau, Piedmont Technical College

Josephine Mathias, Mercer County Community College

Ermira Mazziotta, Muhlenberg College

Karen B. McCarron, Georgia Gwinnett College

Michelle A. McFeaters, Grove City College

Britton McKay, Georgia Southern University

Christopher McNamara, Finger Lakes Community College

Glenn McQueary, Houston Community College

Tammy Metzke, Milwaukee Area Technical College

Stacey Mirinaviciene, Keuka College

Eleonor Moore, Kirtland Community College

Hassan Niazi, Northern State University

Felicia Olagbemi, Colorado State University-Global Campus

Suzanne Owens, Colorado Mesa University

Jenice Prather-Kinsey, University of Alabama at Birmingham

Tom Prieto, College of the Canyons

Atul Rai, Wichita State University

Kevin Raiford, College of Southern Nevada

Dave Repp, Strayer University

Patrick Rogan, Cosumnes River College

John Rossi, Moravian College

Angela Seidel, Saint Francis University

Margaret Shackell, Cornell University

Debra Sinclair, University of South Florida St. Petersburg

Mohsen Souissi, Fayetteville State University

Zivia Sweeney, University of Southern California

Tim Swenson, Sullivan University

Hai Ta, Niagara University

Andress Walker, Ventura County Community College District

Teresa Walker, Greensboro College

Roland Warfield, Seton Hill University

Michael Wiggins, Georgia Southern University

Joseph Winter, Niagara University

David Ziebart, University of Kentucky

1 Accounting as a Tool for Managers

Figure 1.1 Business Honor Society Student Meeting. (credit: modification of "Group of People Sitting Near Table" by Christina Morillo/Pexels, Pexels license / Public Domain)

Chapter Outline

1.1 Define Managerial Accounting and Identify the Three Primary Responsibilities of Management

1.2 Distinguish between Financial and Managerial Accounting

1.3 Explain the Primary Roles and Skills Required of Managerial Accountants

1.4 Describe the Role of the Institute of Management Accountants and the Use of Ethical Standards

1.5 Describe Trends in Today's Business Environment and Analyze Their Impact on Accounting

Why It Matters

You have been elected as the coordinator of committees for your school's business honor society. In essence, this makes you the manager of all the committees. This is a new position that was created because the committees have never been evaluated for their effectiveness within the organization. Your job in this position is to ensure that the committees—such as recruiting, fundraising, community service, professional activities, and regional and national conference presentations—are operating within the goals put forth in the society's mission statements, as well as to assess the effectiveness and efficiency of each committee in meeting the organization's goals. Your starting point is to understand the overriding mission—the strategic direction and purpose—of the society. Next, you want to understand how each committee fits into the strategic goal of the society and then identify the separate goals of each committee. Once you understand the purpose and goal of each committee, it will be necessary to know how each committee is going about meeting its goals. Last, you will evaluate each committee to see if the goals are being met.

Notice that in performing your role as the coordinator of committees, you will need financial information, such as budgets and financial statements, along with other nonfinancial information, for example, the society's mission statement, each committee's strategy statement, and records of their activities and meetings. To help assess how well the honor society and its committees are meeting their goals, you need more information than can be obtained from simply looking at the various financial documents assembled by each committee within the organization. The same is true in any business organization. Managers and other internal decision makers need more information than is available in the basic financial statements: they need information generated by the managerial accounting system.

1.1 Define Managerial Accounting and Identify the Three Primary Responsibilities of Management

Financial accounting process provides a useful level of detail for external users, such as investors and creditors, but it does not provide enough detailed information for the types of decisions made in the day-to-day operation of the business or for the types of decisions that guide the company long term. **Managerial accounting** is the process that allows decision makers to set and evaluate business goals by determining what information they need to make a particular decision and how to analyze and communicate this information. Let's explore the role of managerial accounting in several different organizations and at different levels of the organization, and then examine the primary responsibilities of management.

Three friends who are recent graduates from business school, Alex, Hana, and Gillian, have each just begun their first postgraduation jobs. They meet for lunch and discuss what each of their jobs entails. Alex has taken a position as a market analyst for a Fortune 500 company that operates in the shipping industry. Her first assignment is to suggest and evaluate ways the company can increase the revenue from shipping contracts by 10 percent for the year. Before tackling this project, she has a number of questions. What is the purpose of this analysis? What type of information does she need? Where would she find this information? Can she get it from a basic income statement and balance sheet? How will she know if her suggestions for pricing are creating more shipping contracts and helping to meet the company's goal? She begins with an analysis of the company's top fifty customers, including the prices they pay, discounts offered, discounts applied, frequency of shipments, and so on, to determine if there are price adjustments that need to be made to attract those customers to use the company's shipping services more frequently.

Hana has a position in the human resources department of a pharmaceutical company and is asked to research and analyze a new trend in compensation in which employers are forgoing raises to employees and are instead giving large bonuses for meeting certain goals. Her task is to ascertain if this new idea would be appropriate for her company. Her questions are similar to Alex's. What information does she need? Where would she find this information? How would she determine the impact of this type of change on the business? If implemented, what information would she need to assess the success of the plan?

Gillian is working in the supply chain area of a major manufacturer that produces the various mirrors found on cars and trucks. Her first assignment is to determine whether it is more cost effective and efficient for her company to make or purchase a bracket used in the assembly of the mirrors. Her questions are also similar to her friends' questions. Why is the company considering this decision? What information does she need? Where would she find this information? Would choosing the option with the lowest cost be the correct choice?

The women are surprised by how similar their questions are despite how different their jobs are. They each are assigned tasks that require them to use various forms of information from many different sources to answer an important question for their respective companies. Table 1.1 provides possible answers to each of the questions posed in these scenarios.

Managerial Accounting and Various Business Roles

Questions	Possible Answers
Alex, Marketing Analyst	
What is the purpose of this analysis?	To determine a better way to price their services
What type of information does she need?	Financial and nonfinancial information, such as the number of contracts per client
Where would she find this information?	Financial statements, customer contracts, competitor information, and customer surveys
Can she get it from a basic income statement and balance sheet?	No, she would need to use many other sources of information
How will she know if her suggestions for pricing are creating more shipping contracts and helping to meet the company's goal?	By using a means to evaluate the success, such as by comparing the number of contracts received from each company before the new pricing structure with the number received after the pricing change of contracts
Hana, Human Resources	
What information does she need?	Financial and nonfinancial information, such as how other companies have implemented this idea, including the amount of the bonus and the types of measures on which the bonus was measured
Where would she find this information?	Mostly from internal company sources, such as employee performance records, but also from industry and competitor sources
How would she determine the impact of this type of change on the business?	Perform surveys to determine the effect of the bonus method on employee morale and employee turnover; she could determine the effect on gross revenue of annual bonuses versus annual raises
If implemented, what information would she need to assess the success of the plan?	Measuring employee turnover; evaluating employee satisfaction after the change; assessing whether the performance measures being used to determine the bonus were measures that truly impacted the company in a positive manner
Gillian, Supply Chain	
Why is the company considering this decision?	Management likely wants to minimize costs, and this particular part is one they believe may be more cost effective to buy than to make

Table 1.1

Managerial Accounting and Various Business Roles

Questions	Possible Answers
What information does she need?	She needs the cost to buy the part as well as all the costs that would be incurred to make the part; whether her company has the ability (capacity) to make the part; the quality of the part if they buy it compared to if they make it; the ability of a supplier of the part to deliver on time
Where would she find this information?	She would find the information from internal records about production costs, from cost details provided by the external producer, and from industry reports on the quality of production from the external supplier
Would choosing the option with the lowest cost be the correct choice?	The lowest-cost option may not be the best choice if the quality is subpar, if the part is not delivered in a timely manner and thus throws off or slows production, or if the use of a purchased part will affect the relationship between the company and the car manufacturer to whom the mirror is ultimately sold

Table 1.1

The questions the women have and the answers they require show that there are many types of information that a company needs to make business decisions. Although none of these individuals is given the title of manager, they need information to help provide management with the information necessary to make decisions to move the company forward with its strategic plan. The scenarios of the three women are not unique. These types of questions occur every day in businesses across the world.

Some decisions will be more clearly appropriate for higher-level management. For example, Lynx Boating Company produces three different lines of boats (sport boats, pontoon boats, and large cruisers). All three boat lines are profitable, but the pontoon boat line seems to be less profitable than the other two types of boats. Management may want to consider abandoning the pontoon line and using that additional capacity to produce one of the other more profitable lines. They would need detailed financial information in order to make such a decision.

LINK TO LEARNING

This short video goes inside a manufacturing process (https://openstax.org/l/50Manufacturing) to show you how machines, people, planning, implementation, efficiency, and costs interact to arrive at a finished product.

Service organizations also face decisions that require more detailed information than is available in financial accounting statements. A company's financial statements aggregate information for the company as a whole, but for most managerial decisions, information must be gathered in a timely manner at a product, customer, or division level. For example, the management of City Hospital is considering the purchase of four new magnetic resonance imaging (MRI) machines that scan three times faster than their current machines and thus would allow the hospital's imaging department to evaluate eight additional patients each day. Each machine costs $425,000 and will last five years before needing to be replaced. Would this be a wise investment for City Hospital? Hospital management would need the appropriate information to assess the alternatives in order to make this decision. Throughout your study of managerial accounting, you will learn about the types of information needed to make these decisions, as well as techniques for analyzing this information. First, it is important to understand the various roles managers play in the organization in order to understand the types of information and the level of detail that are needed. Most of the job responsibilities of a manager fit into one of three categories: planning, controlling, or evaluating.

The model in Figure 1.2 sums up the three primary responsibilities of management and the managerial accountant's role in the process. As you can see from the model, the function of accomplishing an entity's mission statement is a circular, ongoing process.

Figure 1.2 The Process of Adhering to the Mission Statement. (attribution: Copyright Rice University, OpenStax, under CC BY-NC-SA 4.0 license)

Planning

One of the first items on a new company's agenda is the creation of a **mission statement**. A mission statement is a short statement of a company's purpose and focus. This statement should be broad enough that it will encompass future growth and changes of the company. Table 1.2 contains the mission statement of three different types of companies: a manufacturer, an e-commerce company, and a service company.

Sample Mission Statements

Company	Mission Statement
Dow Chemical	"To passionately create innovation for our stakeholders at the intersection of chemistry, biology, and physics."[1]
Starbucks	"To inspire and nurture the human spirit—one person, one cup, and one neighborhood at a time."[2]

Table 1.2

---

1 "Mission and Vision." DOW. https://www.dow.com/en-us/about-dow/our-company/mission-and-vision

Sample Mission Statements

Company	Mission Statement
Google	"Our mission is to organize the world's information and make it universally accessible and useful."[3]

Table 1.2

Once the mission of the company has been determined, the company can begin the process of setting **goals**, or what the company expects to accomplish over time, and **objectives**, or the targets that need to be met in order to meet the company's goals. This is known as **planning**. Planning occurs at all levels of an organization and can cover various periods of time. One type of planning, called **strategic planning**, involves setting priorities and determining how to allocate corporate resources to help an organization accomplish both short-term and long-term goals. For example, one hotel may want to be the low-price, no-frills, clean alternative, while another may decide to be the superior quality, high-price luxury hotel with many amenities. Obviously, to be successful, either of these businesses must determine the goals necessary to meet their particular strategy.

Typically, a strategic plan will span any number of years an organization chooses (three, five, seven, or even ten years), and often companies will have multiple strategic plans, such as one for three years, one for five years, and one for ten years. Given the time length involved in many plans, the organization also needs to factor in the potential effects of changes in their senior executive leadership and the composition of the board of directors.

What types of objectives are part of a strategic plan? Strategic objectives should be diverse and will vary from company to company and from industry to industry, but some general goals can include maximizing market share, increasing short-term profits, increasing innovation, offering the best value for the cost, maintaining commitment to community programs, and exceeding environmental protection mandates.

From a managerial accounting perspective, planning involves determining steps or actions to meet the strategic or other goals of the company. For example, Daryn's Dairy, a major producer of organic dairy products in the Midwest, has made increasing the market share of its products one of its strategic goals. However, to be truly effective, the goals need to be defined specifically. For example, the goals might be stated in terms of percentage growth, both annually and in terms of the number of markets addressed in their growth projections.

Also, Daryn's planning process would include the steps the company plans to use to implement to increase market share. These plans may include current-year plans, five-year plans, and ten-year plans.

The current-year plan may be to sell the company's products in 10 percent more stores in the states in which it currently operates. The five-year plan may be to sell the products internationally in three countries, and the ten-year plan may be to acquire their chief competitor and, thus, their customers. Each of these plans will require outlining specific steps to reach these goals and communicating those steps to the employees who will carry out or have an impact on reaching these goals and implementing these plans.

Planning can involve financial and nonfinancial processes and measures. One planning tool discussed in Budgeting is the budgeting process, which requires management to assess the resources—for example, time,

---

2 "Our Starbucks Mission Statement." Starbucks. https://www.starbucks.com/about-us/company-information/mission-statement
3 "About." Google. https://www.google.com/about/

money, and number and type of employees needed—to meet current-year objectives. Budgeting often includes both financial data, such as worker pay rates, and nonfinancial data, such as the number of customers an employee can serve in a given time period.

A retail company can plan for the expected sales volume, a hospital can plan for the number of x-rays they expect to administer, a law firm can plan the hours expected for the various types of legal services they perform, a manufacturing firm can plan for the level of quality expected in each item produced, and a utility company can plan for the level of air pollutants that are acceptable. Notice that in each of these examples, the aspect of the business that is being planned and evaluated is a qualitative (nonfinancial) factor or characteristic. In your study of managerial accounting, you will learn about many situations in which both financial and nonfinancial data or information are equally relevant. However, the qualitative aspects are typically not quantified in dollars but evaluated using some other standards, such as customers served or students advised.

While these functions are initially stated in qualitative terms, most of these items would at some point be translated into a dollar value or dollar effect. In each of these examples, the managerial accounting function would help to determine the variables that would help appropriately measure the desired goal as well as plan how to quantify these measures. However, measures are only useful if tracked and used to determine their effectiveness. This is known as the control function of management.

Controlling

To measure whether plans are meeting objectives or goals, management must put in place ways to assess success or lack of success. **Controlling** involves the monitoring of the planning objectives that were put into place. For example, if you have a retail store and you have a plan to minimize shoplifting, you can implement a control, such as antitheft tags that trigger an alarm when someone removes them from the store. You could also install in the ceilings cameras that provide a different view of customers shopping and therefore may catch a thief more easily or clearly. The antitheft tags and cameras serve as your controls against shoplifting.

Managerial accounting is a useful tool in the management control function. Managerial accounting helps determine the appropriate controls for measuring the success of a plan. There are many types of controls that a company can use. Some controls can be in the form of financial measures, such as the ratio for inventory turnover, which is a measure of inventory control and is defined as Cost of Goods Sold ÷ Average Inventory, or in the form of a performance measure, such as decreasing production costs by 10 percent to help guide or control the decisions made by managers. Other controls can be physical controls, such as fingerprint identification or password protection. Essentially, the controlling function in management involves helping to coordinate the day-to-day activities of a business so that these activities lead to meeting corporate goals.

Without controls, it is very unlikely a plan would be successful, and it would be difficult to know if your plan was a success. Consider the plan by Daryn's Dairy to increase market share. The plan for the first year was to increase market share by selling the company's products in 10 percent more stores in the states in which the company already operates. How will the company implement this plan? The implementation, or carrying out, of the plan will require the company to put controls in place to measure which new stores are successfully selling the company's products, which products are being sold the most, what the sales volume and dollar value of the new stores are, and whether the sales in these new stores are affecting the volume of sales in current stores. Without this information, the company would not know if the plan is reaching the desired result of increased market share.

The control function helps to determine the courses of action that are taken in the implementation of a plan by helping to define and administer the steps of the plan. Essentially, the control function facilitates coordination of the plan within the organization. It is through the system of controls that the actual results of decisions made in implementing a plan can be identified and measured. Managerial accounting not only helps to determine and design control measures, it also assists by providing performance reports and control reports that focus on variances between the planned objective performance and the actual performance. Control is achieved through effective feedback, or information that is used to assess a process. Feedback allows management to evaluate the results, determine whether progress is being made, or determine whether corrective measures need to be taken. This evaluation is in the next management function.

Evaluating

Managers must ultimately determine whether the company has met the goals set in the planning phase. **Evaluating**, also called *assessing* or *analyzing*, involves comparing actual results against expected results, and it can occur at the product, department, division, and company levels. When there are deviations from the stated objectives, managers must decide what modifications are needed.

The controls that were put into place to coordinate the implementation of a particular company plan must be evaluated so that success can be measured, or corrective action can be taken. Consider Daryn's Dairy's one-year plan to increase market share by selling products in 10 percent more stores in the states in which the company currently operates. Suppose one of the controls put into place is to measure the sales in the current stores to determine if selling the company's products in new stores is adding new sales or merely moving sales from existing stores. This control measure, same-store sales, must be evaluated to determine the effect of the decision to expand the selling of products within the state. This control measure will be evaluated by comparing sales in the current year in those stores to sales from the prior year in those same stores. The results of this evaluation will help guide management in their decision to move forward with their plan, to modify the plan, or to scrap the plan.

As discussed previously, not all evaluations will involve quantitative or financial measures. In expanding market share, the company wants to maintain or improve its reputation with customers and does not want the planned increased availability or easier access to their products to decrease customer perceptions of the products or the company. They could use customer surveys to evaluate the perceived effect on the company's reputation as a result of implementing this one-year plan. However, there are many ways that companies can evaluate various controls. In addition to the financial gauges, organizations are now measuring efficiencies, customer development, employee retention, and sustainability.

Managers spend their time in various stages of planning, controlling, and evaluating. Generally, higher-level managers spend more time on planning, whereas lower-level managers spend more time on evaluating. At any level, managers work closely with the managerial accounting team to help in each of these stages. Managerial accountants help determine whether plans are measurable, what controls should be implemented to carry out a plan, and what are the proper means of evaluation of those controls. This would include the type of feedback necessary for management to assess the results of their plans and actions. Management accountants generate the reports and information needed to assess the results of the various evaluations, and they help interpret the results.

To put this in context, think about how you will spend your weekend. First, you are the manager of your own time. You must plan based on your workload and on how much time you will spend studying, exercising, sleeping, and meeting with friends. You then control how your plan is implemented by setting self-imposed or possibly group meeting–imposed deadlines, and last, you evaluate how well you carried out your plan by gathering more data—such as grades on assignments, personal fulfillment, and number of hours of sleep—to determine if you met your plans (goals). Not planning, controlling, and evaluating often results in less-than-desirable outcomes, such as late assignments, too little sleep, or bad grades. In this scenario, you did not need a separate managerial accountant to help you with these functions, because you could manage planning, controlling, and evaluating on your own. However, in the business world, most businesses will have both managers and managerial accountants. Table 1.3 illustrates some examples.

Relating Managerial Accounting Functions to Various Business Majors

	Sales	**Human Resources**	**Logistics**
Planning	What are our expected sales for each product in each geographic region? How much should be budgeted for salaries and commissions for our salespeople?	How much should we budget for salary and wage increases for the year? How much should we plan to spend on safety and training for the year?	Should we invest in radio-frequency identification (RFID) processors to enable computer tracking of inventory? How much raw material should be ordered and delivered to ensure timely delivery of our finished products to our customers?
Controlling	Are we meeting expected sales growth in each region? Are each of the salespeople meeting their sales projections?	Is our projected budget for wages and salaries sufficient? Are we meeting our safety and training goals?	Are our products being delivered to our customers in a timely manner, and at what cost? Are we dealing with stock-outs in inventory? If so, what is that costing us?
Evaluating	How do our actual sales compare to our forecasted or budgeted sales? What sales promotions are our competitors offering, and what effect is it having on our market share?	Would it be cheaper to hire temporary employees to get through our "busy" season or to pay our current employees for overtime?	What are the cost differences in starting our own delivery service versus continuing to use other carriers? Should we outsource the manufacturing of a component part or continue to make it ourselves? What are the price differences?

Table 1.3

YOUR TURN

Evaluating On-Campus versus Off-Campus Living

The principal purpose of managerial accounting is to deliver information useful for management decision-making. Many of the techniques used in managerial accounting are useful for decisions in your everyday life. In choosing whether to live on campus or off campus, how might you use planning, controlling, and evaluating in your decision-making process? What types of financial and nonfinancial information might you need?

Solution

Planning:

- Creating a list of financial and nonfinancial goals to be accomplished in your next year in college
- Determining how much each alternative will cost, including utilities, food, and transportation, and creating a budget

Controlling:

- Using an expense recording app to monitor your expenses
- Monitoring the effectiveness of your study time as reflected in your grades
- Monitoring your physical health to measure if your living arrangements are conducive to staying healthy

Evaluating:

- Assessing the effectiveness of your living arrangements by measuring your grades, bank account, and general happiness

Financial:

- Cost of staying in dorm versus the cost of an apartment or house
- Estimate of differences in other costs, such as utilities, food, and additional transportation

Nonfinancial:

- Convenience of location of dorm versus apartment or house
- Quality of living experience including number of roommates, ability to have own room, study environment differences
- Length of rental term of dorm versus apartment or house
- Where you plan to live in the summer, what you plan to do during that time

THINK IT THROUGH

US Small Business Administration

Many students who study managerial accounting will work for a small business, and some may even own a small business. In order to operate a small business, you need an understanding of managerial accounting, among other skills. The US Small Business Administration is an agency within the federal government that has the sole purpose of supporting small businesses. You can find a plethora of information on their website, https://www.sba.gov/.

1. What are some of the steps in creating a small business?
2. What are the top ten reasons given for a business failure?
3. How could an understanding of managerial accounting help a small business owner?

1.2 Distinguish between Financial and Managerial Accounting

Now that you have a basic understanding of managerial accounting, consider how it is similar to and different from financial accounting. After completing a financial accounting class, many students do not look forward to another semester of debits, credits, and journal entries. Thankfully, managerial accounting is much different from financial accounting. Also known as *management accounting* or *cost accounting*, managerial accounting provides information to managers and other users within the company in order to make more informed decisions. The overriding roles of managers (planning, controlling, and evaluating) lead to the distinction between financial and managerial accounting. The main objective of management accounting is to provide useful information to managers to assist them in the planning, controlling, and evaluating roles.

Unlike managerial accounting, financial accounting is governed by rules set out by the **Financial Accounting Standards Board (FASB)**, an independent board made up of accounting professionals who determine and publicize the standards of financial accounting and reporting in the United States. Larger, publicly traded companies are also governed by the US Securities and Exchange Commission (SEC), in the form of the **generally accepted accounting principles (GAAP)**, the common set of rules, standards, and procedures that publicly traded companies must follow when they are composing their financial statements.

Financial accounting provides information to enable stockholders, creditors, and other stakeholders to make informed decisions. This information can be used to evaluate and make decisions for an individual company or to compare two or more companies. However, the information provided by financial accounting is primarily historical and therefore is not sufficient and is often synthesized too late to be overly useful to management. Managerial accounting has a more specific focus, and the information is more detailed and timelier. Managerial accounting is not governed by GAAP, so there is unending flexibility in the types of reports and information gathered. Managerial accountants regularly calculate and manage "what-if" scenarios to help managers make decisions and plan for future business needs. Thus, managerial accounting focuses more on the future, while financial accounting focuses on reporting what has already happened. In addition, managerial accounting uses nonfinancial data, whereas financial accounting relies solely on financial data.

For example, Daryn's Dairy makes many different organic dairy products. Daryn's managers need to track their costs for certain jobs. One of the company's top-selling ice creams is their seasonal variety; a new flavor is introduced every three months and sold for only a six-month period. The cost of these specialty ice creams is different from the cost of the standard flavors for reasons such as the unique or expensive ingredients and the specialty packaging. Daryn wants to compare the costs involved in making the specialty ice cream and those involved in making the standard flavors of ice cream. This analysis will require that Daryn track not only the cost of materials that go into the product, but also the labor hours and cost of the labor, plus other costs, known as overhead costs (rent, electricity, insurance, etc.), that are incurred in producing the various ice creams. Once the total costs for both the specialty ice cream and the standard flavored ice cream are known, the cost per unit can be determined for each type. These types of analyses help a company evaluate how to set pricing, evaluate the need for new or substitute ingredients, manage product additions and deletions, and make many other decisions. Figure 1.3 shows an example of a materials cost analysis by Daryn's Dairy used to compare the materials cost for producing 500 gallons of their best-selling standard flavor—vanilla—with one of their specialty ice creams—Very Berry Biscotti.

Ingredients	STANDARD VANILLA ICE CREAM (500-gallon batch)			SPECIALTY BERRY BISCOTTI ICE CREAM (500-gallon batch)		
	Quantity	Total Cost	Per Gallon Cost	Quantity	Total Cost	Per Gallon Cost
Cream	140 gal	$500	$1.00	160 gal	$500	$1.00
Milk	312 gal	250	0.50	300 gal	250	0.50
Sugar	750 lbs	200	0.40	725 lbs	200	0.40
Vanilla flavoring	3.25 gal	150	0.30	3.25 gal	150	0.30
Vanilla beans	200 lbs	300	0.60			
Berries				500 lbs	400	0.80
Biscotti crumbles				250 lbs	275	0.55
Total		$1,400	$2.80		$1,775	$3.55

Figure 1.3 Material Cost Analysis. Daryn's Dairy materials cost comparison analysis between best-selling standard vanilla ice cream and Very Berry Biscotti, a limited-edition specialty ice cream. (attribution: Copyright Rice University, OpenStax, under CC BY-NC-SA 4.0 license)

Financial and Managerial Accounting Comparative

Managerial and financial accounting are used by every business, and there are important differences in their reporting functions. Those differences are detailed in Figure 1.4.

COMMUNICATION THROUGH REPORTING	FINANCIAL ACCOUNTING	MANAGERIAL ACCOUNTING
Users of reports	External users: stockholders, creditors, regulators	Internal users: managers, officers, and other employees
Types of reports	Financial statements: balance sheet, income statement, cash-flow statement, etc.	Internal reports: job cost sheet, cost of goods manufactured, production cost report, etc.
Frequency of reports	Quarterly; annually	As frequently as needed
Purpose of reports	Helps those external users make decisions: credit terms, investment, and other decisions	Assists the internal users in the planning and control decision-making process
Focus of reports	Pertains to company as a whole Uses GAAP structure Composed from a multitude or combination of other more individual data	Pertains to departments, sections of the business Very detailed reporting No GAAP constraints
Nature of reports	Monetary	Monetary and nonmonetary information
Verification of reports	Audited by CPA	No independent audits

Figure 1.4 Comparing Reports between Financial and Managerial Accounting. (attribution: Copyright Rice University, OpenStax, under CC BY-NC-SA 4.0 license)

Users of Reports

The information generated from the reports of financial accountants tends to be used primarily by **external users**, including the creditors, tax authorities and regulators, investors, customers, competitors, and others outside the company, who rely on the financial statements and annual reports to access information about a company in order to make more informed decisions. Since these external people do not have access to the documents and records used to produce the financial statements, they depend on Generally Applied Accounting Principles (GAAP). These outside users also depend greatly on the preparation of audits that are done by public accounting firms, under the guidelines and standards of either the American Institute of Certified Public Accountants (AICPA), the US Securities and Exchange Commission (SEC), or the Public Company Accounting Oversight Board (PCAOB).

Managerial accounting information is gathered and reported for a more specific purpose for **internal users**, those inside the company or organization who are responsible for managing the company's business interests and executing decisions. These internal users may include management at all levels in all departments, owners, and other employees. For example, in the budget development process, a company such as Tesla may want to project the costs of producing a new line of automobiles. The managerial accountants could create a budget to estimate the costs, such as parts and labor, and after the manufacturing process has begun, they can measure the actual costs, thus determining if they are over or under their budgeted amounts. Although outside parties might be interested in this information, companies like Tesla, Microsoft, and Boeing spend significant amounts of time and money to keep their proprietary information secret. Therefore, these internal budget reports are only available to the appropriate users. While you can find a cost of goods sold schedule in the financial statements of publicly traded companies, it is difficult for outside parties to break it down in order to identify the individual costs of products and services.

LINK TO LEARNING

Investopedia is considered to be the largest Internet financial education resource in the world. There are many short, helpful videos that explain various concepts of managerial accounting. Watch this video explaining managerial accounting and how useful it can be to many different types of managers (https://openstax.org/l/50ManageAccount) to learn more.

Types of Reports

Financial accounting information is communicated through reporting, such as the financial statements. The financial statements typically include a balance sheet, income statement, cash flow statement, retained earnings statement, and footnotes. Managerial accounting information is communicated through reporting as well. However, the reports are more detailed and more specific and can be customized. One example of a managerial accounting report is a budget analysis (variance report) as shown in Figure 1.5. Other reports can include cost of goods manufactured, job order cost sheets, and production reports. Since managerial accounting is not governed by GAAP or other constraints, it is important for the creator of the reports to disclose all assumptions used to make the report. Since the reports are used internally, and not typically released to the general public, the presentation of any assumptions does not have to follow any industry-wide guidelines. Each organization is free to structure its reports in the format that organizes its information in the best way for it.

BUDGET ANALYSIS			
	Actual	Budgeted	Variance
Sales	$ 500,000	$ 490,000	$ 10,000
Cost of Goods Sold	(320,000)	(290,000)	(30,000)
Gross Margin	180,000	200,000	(20,000)
Selling & Administrative Expenses	(75,000)	(90,000)	15,000
Net Income	105,000	110,000	(5,000)

Figure 1.5 Example of a Budget (Variance) Analysis. (attribution: Copyright Rice University, OpenStax, under CC BY-NC-SA 4.0 license)

This type of analysis helps management to evaluate how effective they were at carrying out the plans and meeting the goals of the corporation. You will see many examples of reports and analyses that can be used as tools to help management make decisions.

> ## THINK IT THROUGH
>
> ### Projection Error
>
> You are working as the accountant in the special projects and budgets area of Sturm, Ruger & Company, a law firm that currently specializes in bankruptcy law. In order to serve their customers better and more efficiently, the company is trying to decide whether or not to expand its services and offer credit counseling, credit monitoring, credit rebuilding, and identity protection services. The president comes to you and asks for some sales and revenue projections. He would like the projections in three days' time so that he can present the results to the board at the annual meeting.
>
> You work tirelessly for two straight days compiling projections of sales and revenues to prepare the reports. The report is provided to the president just before the board is to arrive.
>
> When you return to your office, you start clearing away some of the materials that you used in your report, and you discover an error that makes all of your projections significantly overstated. You ask the president's administrative assistant if the president has presented the report to the board, and you find that he had mentioned it but not given the full report as of yet.
>
> What would you do?
>
> - What are the ethical concerns in this matter?
> - What would be the results of telling the president of your error?
> - What would be the results of *not* telling the president of your error?

Frequency of Reports

The financial statements are typically generated quarterly and annually, although some entities also require monthly statements. Much work is involved in creating the financial statements, and any adjustments to accounts must be made before the statements can be produced. A physical count inventory must be done to adjust the inventory and cost of goods sold accounts, depreciation must be calculated and entered, all prepaid asset accounts must be reviewed for adjustments, and so forth. The annual reports are not finalized for several weeks after the year-end, because they are based on historical data; for a company that is traded on one of the major or regional stock exchanges, it must have an audit of the financial statements conducted by an independent certified public accountant. This audit cannot be completed until after the end of the company's fiscal year, because the auditors need access to all of the information for the company for that year. For companies that are privately held, an audit is not normally required. However, potential lenders might require an independent audit.

Conversely, managers can quickly attain managerial accounting information. No external, independent auditors are needed, and it is not necessary to wait until the year-end. Projections and estimates are adequate. Managers should understand that in order to obtain information quickly, they must accept less precision in the reporting. While there are several reports that are created on a regular basis (e.g., budgets and variance reports), many management reports are produced on an as-needed basis.

Purpose of Reports

The general purpose of financial statement reporting is to provide information about the results of operations, financial position, and cash flows of an organization. This data is useful to a wide range of users in order to make economic decisions. The purpose of the reporting done by management accountants is more specific to internal users. Management accountants make available the information that could assist companies in increasing their performance and profitability. Unlike financial reports, management reporting centers on components of the business. By dividing the business into smaller sections, a company is able to get into the details and analyze the smallest segments of the business.

An understanding of managerial accounting will assist anyone in the business world in determining and understanding product costs, analyzing break-even points, and budgeting for expenses and future growth (which will be covered in other parts of this course). As a manager, chief executive officer, or owner, you need to have information available at hand to answer these types of questions:

- Are my profits higher this quarter over last quarter?
- Do I have enough cash flow to pay my employees?
- Are my jobs priced correctly?
- Are my products priced correctly in order for me to make the profit I need to make?
- Who are my most productive and least productive employees?

In the world of business, information is power; stated simply, the more you know, typically, the better your decisions can be. Managerial accounting delivers data-driven feedback for these decisions that can assist in improving decision-making over the long term. Business managers can leverage this powerful tool in order to make their businesses more successful, because management accounting adds value to common business decision-making. All of this readily available information can lead to great improvements for any business.

Focus of Reports

Because financial accounting typically focuses on the company as a whole, external users of this information choose to invest or loan money to the entire company, not to a department or division within the company. Therefore, the global focus of financial accounting is understandable.

However, the focus of management accounting is typically different. Managerial reporting is more focused on divisions, departments, or any component of a business, down to individuals. The mid-level and lower-level managers are typically responsible for smaller subsets within the company.

Managers need accounting reports that deal specifically with their division and their specific activities. For instance, production managers are responsible for their specific area and the results within their division. Accordingly, these production managers need information about results achieved in their division, as well as individual results of departments within the division. The company can be broken into segments based on what managers need—for example, geographic location, product line, customer demographics (e.g., gender, age, race), or any of a variety of other divisions.

Nature of Reports

Both financial reports and managerial reports use **monetary accounting information**, or information relating to money or currency. Financial reports use data from the accounting system that is gathered from the reporting of transactions in the form of journal entries and then aggregated into financial statements. This information is monetary in nature. Managerial accounting uses some of the same financial information as financial accounting, but much of that information will be broken down to a more detailed level. For example, in financial reporting, net sales are needed for the income statement. In managerial accounting, the quantity and dollar value of the sales of each product are likely more useful. In addition, managerial accounting uses a significant amount of **nonmonetary accounting information**, such as quantity of material, number of employees, number of hours worked, and so forth, which does not relate to money or currency.

Verification of Reports

Financial reports rely on structure. They are generated using accepted principles that are enforced through a vast set of rules and guidelines, also known as GAAP. As mentioned previously, companies that are publicly traded are required to have their financial statements audited on an annual basis, and companies that are not publicly traded also may be required to have their financial statements audited by their creditors. The information generated by the management accountants is intended for internal use by the company's divisions, departments, or both. There are no rules, guidelines, or principles to follow. Managerial accounting is much more flexible, so the design of the managerial accounting system is difficult to standardize, and standardization is unnecessary. It depends on the nature of the industry. Different companies (even different managers within the same company) require different information. The most important issue is whether the reporting is useful for the planning, controlling, and evaluation purposes.

YOUR TURN

Daryn's Dairy

Figure 1.6 Assorted Ice Cream Flavors. (credit: "Assorted Ice Creams" by "jeshoots"/Pexel, CC0)

Suppose you have been hired by Daryn's Dairy as a market analyst. Your first assignment is to evaluate the sales of various standard and specialty ice creams within the Midwest region where Daryn's Dairy operates. You also need to determine the best-selling flavors of ice cream in other regions of the United States as well as the selling patterns of the flavors. For example, do some flavors sell better than others at different times of the year, or are some top sellers sold as limited-edition flavors? Remember that one of the strategic goals of the company is to increase market share, and the first step in meeting this goal is to sell their product in 10 percent more stores within their current market, so your research will help upper-level management carry out the company's goals. Where would you gather the information? What type of information would you need? Where would you find this information? How would the company determine the impact of this type of change on the business? If implemented, what information would you need to assess the success of the plan?

Solution

Answers will vary. Sample answer:

Where would you gather the information? Where would you find this information?

- Current company sales information would be obtained from internal company reports and records that detail the sale of each type of ice cream including volume, cost, price, and profit per flavor.
- Sales of ice cream from other companies may be more difficult to obtain, but the footnotes and supplemental information to the annual reports of those companies being analyzed, as well as industry trade journals, would likely be good sources of information.

What types of information would you need?

- Some of the types of information that would be needed would be the volume of sales of each flavor (number of gallons), how long each flavor has been sold, whether seasonal or limited-edition flavors are produced and sold only once or are on a rotating basis, the size of the market being examined (number of households), whether the other companies sell similar products (organic, all natural, etc.), the median income of consumers or other information to assess the consumers' willingness to pay for organic products, and so forth.

How would Daryn's Dairy determine the impact of this type of change on the business?

- Management would evaluate the cost to expand into new stores in their current market compared to the potential revenues from selling their products in those stores in order to assess the ability of the potential expansion to generate a profit for the company.

If implemented, what information would Daryn's Dairy need to assess the success of the plan?

- Management would measure the profitability of selling any new products, expanding into new stores in their current market, or both to determine if the implementation of the plan was a success. If the plan is a success and the company is generating profits, the company will continue to figure out ways to improve efficiency and profitability. If the plan is not a success, the company will determine the reasons (cost to produce too high, sales price too high, volume too low, etc.) and make a new plan.

1.3 Explain the Primary Roles and Skills Required of Managerial Accountants

It is clear that management accountants must have a solid foundation in accounting, in both financial and managerial accounting, but other than accounting skills, what makes good managerial accountants?

- They must have knowledge of the business in which they are working. **Commercial awareness** is knowing how a business is run and how it is influenced by the external environment and knowing and understanding the overall industry within which the business is operating.
- **Collaboration**, which involves working in cross-functional teams and earning the trust and respect of colleagues in order to complete a task, is vital to improving managerial accounting talents. They should be "team players."
- Management accountants should have **effective communication** skills that allow them to convey

accounting information in both written and oral forms in a way that the intended audience can understand. Being able to gather the data quickly and accurately is important, but the data is meaningless if it is not presented in an intuitive style that the audience can understand.
- Strong technology skills are also essential. These skills include not only accounting and reporting software but also other programs that would assist in automating processes, improving efficiencies, and adding value to the company. For many companies, additional software and accompanying technology are often needed for both their financial and managerial accounting functions. For example, *enterprise resource planning* (ERP) systems often play a major role in the creation of comprehensive accounting systems. This additional support is often provided by outside suppliers such as Hyperion, Cognos, Sage, SAP, PeopleSoft, and Oracle.
- Managerial accountants must possess extensive analytical skills. They must regularly work with financial analysts and management personnel to find ways to reduce expenses and analyze budgets. These skills include the ability to envision, verbalize, conceptualize, or solve both multifaceted and simplistic problems by making choices that make sense with the given information.
- Managerial accountants must have ethics and values. They should be an example to others and encourage them to follow internal control practices and procedures. Ethics is discussed in more detail in Describe the role of the Institute of Management Accountants and the use of ethical standards.

Managers at all levels make many different types of decisions every day, but to make most decisions, they need specific information. Some information is easily obtainable, and some is not. Managers do not always know what information they need or what is available, and they need to know if the decisions they make are having the desired outcome and meeting specific goals.

To this point, we've described *managerial accounting* as a process. The following definition considers it a profession. Management accountants are the individuals who help management with this information. The Institute of Management Accountants (IMA) defines management accounting as "a profession that involves partnering in management decision making, devising planning and performance management systems, and providing expertise in financial reporting and control to assist management in the formulation and implementation of an organization's strategy."[4]

The IMA also reports that nearly 75 percent of financial professionals work in business as management accountants in positions such as financial analysts, accounting managers, controllers, and chief financial officers.[5] These professionals have a significant impact on businesses through influencing the decision-making process and business strategy.

Management accountants work at various levels of the organization, from the project level to the division level to the controller and chief financial officer. Often, management accountants work where they are needed and not necessarily at corporate headquarters. They tend to be hands-on in the decision-making process. They need many types of information to inform the many decisions they must make.

---

4 "Management Accounting Careers." Institute of Management Accountants. https://www.imanet.org/students/management-accounting-careers?ssopc=1
5 "Management Accounting Careers." Institute of Management Accountants. https://www.imanet.org/students/management-accounting-careers?ssopc=1

CONTINUING APPLICATION AT WORK

Who Uses Managerial Accounting?

When most people think of an accounting job, they think of someone who does taxes or who puts together financial statements. However, almost all jobs use accounting information, particularly managerial accounting information. Table 1.4 shows how certain professions might use managerial accounting information. Can you think of other examples?

Use of Managerial Accounting Information

Profession	How They Use Managerial Accounting in Their Industry
Engineer	Properly track and report the use of resources involved in an engineering project; measure and communicate costs of a project and its outcomes
Mayor	Put together a budget, a planning and control mechanism that plays an important role in every government
Nurse	Track operating or service costing per patient, or per unit
Mechanic	Use job costing to figure total costs and overall profitability on each job
Retail store manager	Forecast inventory needs, review profit margins, and track sales margins on individual products as well as entire stores
Restaurant owner	Calculate the cost of serving a single table by estimating the cost of the food plus time of server, keep food costs under control through inventory tracking
Architect	Track direct and indirect costs for each job; track profitability per job
Farmer	Calculate yields per field, analyze fertilizer and seeding rates, and control waste

Table 1.4

Organizational Structure

Most companies have an organizational chart that displays the configuration and the delegation of authority in the decision-making processes (Figure 1.7). The structure helps define roles and responsibilities. The organizational charts provide guidance to employees and other stakeholders by outlining the official reporting affiliations that direct the workflow within the organization. If the company is particularly efficient, it also will include contact information within the chart. This is a convenient directory to circulate among employees. It helps them find a particular person in a certain position, or determine whom to speak to about certain areas within the company, or even identify a specific person's supervisor to report positive or negative work behavior.

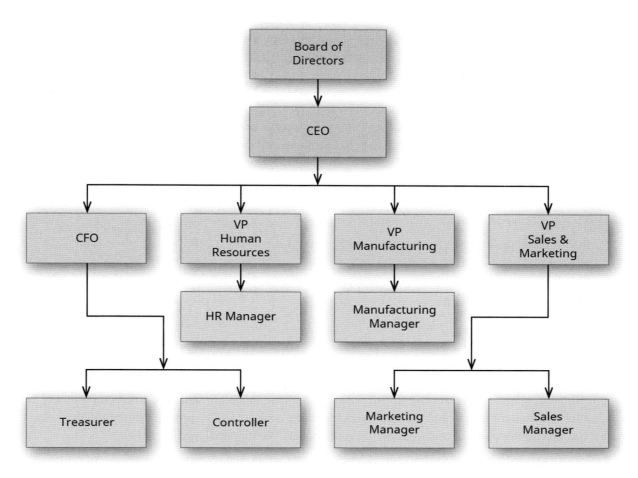

Figure 1.7 Sample Organizational Chart. (attribution: Copyright Rice University, OpenStax, under CC BY-NC-SA 4.0 license)

Stockholders of a company are the owners; however, they elect a **board of directors** to manage that company for them. The board selects the officers who will implement the policies and strategic goals that the board has set in place. The **chief executive officer (CEO)** is the corporation officer who has the overall responsibility for the management of the company. The person overseeing all of the accounting and finance concerns is the **chief financial officer (CFO)**. This individual is in charge of the financial planning and record-keeping of the organization and reports to the CEO. The **controller** is responsible for the accounting side of the business (accounting records, financial statements, tax returns, and internal reports) and reports to the CFO. Also reporting to the CFO is the **treasurer**, who is in control of the finance side of the business (cash position, corporation funds). An additional area that sometimes falls under the control of the CFO is the internal audit staff. Internal auditors supply independent assurance that a company's internal control processes are effective. However, there is strong support for keeping the internal audit staff outside of the CFO, because of a possible conflict of interest.

THINK IT THROUGH

Managing Cash Flow

Assume you are the managerial accountant at Anchor Head Brewery, a Midwest craft brewery that distributes nationwide. Its year-end is December 31. Because of poor cash flow management, the CFO has some concerns about having enough cash to be able to pay the tax bill that is expected. In early December, the purchasing department bought excess hops, barley, malt, oats, and yeast in anticipation of brewing more beer for the holiday and Super Bowl seasons. In order to decrease the company's net income, thereby reducing their taxable income, the CFO tells you to enter the purchase of this inventory as part of the "Supplies Expense" in the current year.

1. In which account should these materials be recorded?
2. How should you reply to this request?
3. Should you bring this matter to another executive officer?

Careers

The field of managerial accounting, or corporate accounting, is composed of the financial and accounting responsibilities required to operate any type of business. Managerial accountants are employed within organizations to monitor costs, sales, budgets, and spending; conduct audits; predict future requirements; and aid the executive leaders of the organization with financial decision-making.

Figure 1.8 lists approximate salaries for several financial and managerial accounting employment positions. In reviewing the salary information, be aware that there are often major variances in salaries based on geographical locations. For example, a cost accountant manager in San Francisco, California, would typically be paid significantly more than an accountant in a similar position in Fayetteville, Arkansas. However, the cost of living, especially housing costs, in San Francisco is also significantly higher than the cost of living in Fayetteville.

Source: "40 Top Paying Accounting Jobs." *Accounting Degrees Review*. https://www.accounting-degree.org/top-paying-accounting-jobs/

Figure 1.8 Accounting Position Salaries. Salaries are shown for some entry-level and advanced-level jobs available with an accounting degree. (attribution: Copyright Rice University, OpenStax, under CC BY-NC-SA 4.0 license)

Managerial accountants find employment opportunities in a wide variety of settings and industries. Professionals in this discipline are in high demand from public and private companies, government agencies, and not-for-profit entities (NFPs). Some areas of management accounting are versatile to any sector (corporate, government, or NFP).

- A **financial analyst** assists in preparing budgets, tracking actual costs, examining task performance, scrutinizing different types of variances, and supporting other management personnel in organizing forecasts and projections.
- A **budget analyst** arranges and manages the master budget and compares master budget projections to actual results. This individual must be vastly aware of all operations in the budget and work closely with the rest of the accounting staff as well as management personnel.
- An **internal auditor** typically reports to high-level executives within the company. An internal auditor is often called on to investigate budget variances, industrial sabotage, poor work quality, fraud, and theft. He or she also safeguards the internal controls and confirms they are working and effective.
- A **cash-management accountant** has responsibilities that include transferring monies between accounts, monitoring deposits and payments, reconciling cash balances, creating and tracking cash forecasts, and performing all other cash-related financial processes.

Other areas of managerial accounting are specific to the sector in which accountants work. For example, the area of cost accounting is more specific to the corporate or manufacturing sector. These **cost accountants** amass large sums of data, checking for accuracy and then formulating the cost of raw materials, work in process, finished goods, labor, overhead, and other associated manufacturing costs.

Governmental entities also use accounting to communicate with their constituents. **Government agencies** include all levels of government, federal, state, county, and city, including military, law enforcement, airports, and school systems. Government accountants deal with budgets, auditing, and payroll, the same as all other managerial accountants. However, they must follow a different set of accounting rules called the Governmental Accounting Standards Board (GASB).

Nonprofit (not-for-profit) organizations are tax-exempt organizations that serve their communities in a variety of areas, such as religion, education, social services, health care, and the arts. Managerial accountants in this area are most often focused on budgets. The biggest difference between a corporate budget analyst and a nonprofit budget analyst is that the nonprofit analyst works the budget backward, compared to the corporate analyst. For example, if a corporation was selling widgets, its budget would start with a sales forecast of how many widgets the company thinks it can sell. This gives the company a forecast of how much it can spend on expenses and fixed assets. The nonprofit budget analysts often start with the expenses. They forecast how much the expenses will be in order to continue to offer their service to the community. From there, they then adjust how much they will need to obtain through fundraising, donations, grants, or other sources to meet their expenses.

YOUR TURN

Career Planning

All companies need to plan ahead in order to continuously move forward. Their top management must take into consideration where they want the company to be in the next three to five years. Just like a company, you also need to consider where you want to be in three to five years, and you need to start taking strides now to accomplish what it is you need to in order to get there (Figure 1.9).

Figure 1.9 Career Planning. (attribution: Copyright Rice University, OpenStax, under CC BY-NC-SA 4.0 license)

Answer the following:

1. What job would you like to be doing in three to five years? What is your plan for getting there? Identify five to ten steps needed.
2. Do you have a specific company you would like to be working for in the next three to five years?

What are the reasons you want to work for them?
3. In order to acquire the position you want, at the company you want, you need a résumé. Your résumé is like the company report of "you." It needs to offer reliable information about your experiences and achievements. What are the basic elements of a résumé, and how will you provide reassurance that the information on your résumé is trustworthy?

Solution

Answers will vary. Sample answer:

1. I would like to own my own home remodeling company. Steps to get there include the following:
    A. complete double major in business and building construction
    B. in the summers before graduation, work for a local handyman franchise
    C. after graduation, work for a home builder as a project manager
    D. while working, save money for five years to be used to start my own company
    E. put together a business plan
    F. start my own business six years after graduation
2. I would like to work for a national home builder such as Pulte or Toll Brothers. Ideally, I would have an internship with one of them during college. I would like to work for a national builder or a large regional builder because they already have a good business model and I could learn how that works.
3. My résumé needs to contain my education information such as the degree and my majors as well as classes that are pertinent to my career. It should also indicate all of my work experience and any particular skills or certifications I have achieved, such as Eagle Scout. An example of how this information may be presented on a résumé can be seen in Figure 1.10.

Bobby Builder
123 SeeSaw Lane
Anywhere, USA 54321
555-555-5555

Education:

Unique University
Bachelor of Science, Building Construction, May 2019   GPA 3.7
Bachelor of Business Administration, May 2018   GPA 3.5

Experience:

Construction Assistant. Your Town Construction and Landscaping. Summers 2017–2019
- Completed repairs for household issues including plumbing, electrical, wood rot, and painting
- Constructed decks, patios, custom cabinetry
- Installed wood floors
- Interacted with clients including scheduling and planning

Road Crew Worker. Department of Transportation. Summer 2017
- Flagged traffic

Busser. The Restaurant. June 2015–May 2017
- Cleared tables, stocked supplies in busy diner
- Assisted waitstaff as needed in delivering meals, refilling drinks and greeting tables

Awards & Accomplishments:

Treasurer, Building Construction Club. 2017–2018
Management Student Award. 2018
Eagle Scout

Figure 1.10 Sample Résumé. (attribution: Copyright Rice University, OpenStax, under CC BY-NC-SA 4.0 license)

Certifications

There are many distinct accounting certifications that accountants can earn in order to improve their careers, attain promotions, and acquire raises in their pay. The certifications are somewhat different from each other and focused toward different career paths. Many accountants have more than one of these credentials to diversify their paths.

The **Certified Public Accountant (CPA)** is considered the top tier in accounting certifications. Many companies or positions require CPA certification. For example, most employees at accounting firms earn a CPA certificate within the first few of years of graduation. Some positions, such as controller or CFO, often require CPA certification. In the United States, each state has different educational and experience requirements in order to obtain the CPA. The certification requires passing the four-part CPA exam as well. This is administered by the American Institute of Certified Public Accountants (AICPA). There are four parts to the exam: Financial Accounting and Reporting (FAR), Auditing and Attestation (AUD), Regulation (REG), and Business Environment and Concepts (BEC). Each part is graded on a 100-point scale. A score of seventy-five or greater must be achieved in order to pass each section. The exams can be intimidating, as it is a difficult process to go through. As of 2017, the AICPA reported a pass rate of less than 50 percent, which may contribute to its high regard around the world. After passing the CPA exam, candidates must work for one year under the supervision of a licensed CPA before their own license is approved by a state regulatory agency. Those certified in public accounting work in all areas of accounting. However, do not assume that being a CPA is the only way to secure an excellent position in accounting.

The **Certified Management Accountant (CMA)** is another top-tiered certification for accountants. The CMA title identifies the individual as a specialist in corporate accounting management. The CMA has some overlap with the CPA, but the CPA is focused more on compliance, tax, and controls. CMAs favor financial analytics, budgeting, and strategic assessment. This certification requires the minimum of a bachelor's degree from an accredited college or university, two years of work experience, and successfully passing both parts of the exam. Part one of the exam covers financial reporting, planning, performance, and controls. Part two focuses on financial decision-making. The exam is administered by the IMA and has a 50 percent passing rate globally.

Not as popular in the United States as the CPA, the **Certified Financial Analyst (CFA)** certification is more in demand throughout Europe and Asia. This certification prepares accountants for a career in the finance and investment domains. Requirements of this credential include a bachelor's degree or four years' worth of experience, plus passing all three sections of the exam. The exam is administered by the CFA Institute. There are three separate exams, each one taking up to six hours to complete. The exams must be completed in succession. This credential is considered one of the more rigorous ones to obtain, with a passing rate of less than 45 percent.

The **Enrolled Agent (EA)** credential focuses on a career in taxation, whether it is working in tax preparation for the public, internally for a corporation, or for the government at the Internal Revenue Service (IRS). The EA certification was created by the IRS to signify significant knowledge of the US tax code and the ability to apply the concepts of that code. Enrolled agents have the privilege of being able to sign tax returns as paid preparers, and they are able to represent their clients in front of the IRS. The EA certification can be obtained by passing a three-part exam covering all types of individual and business tax returns. Once the certification is obtained, enrolled agents must follow strict ethical standards and complete 72 hours of continuing education courses every three years.

The **Certified Internal Auditor (CIA)** is a credential offered by the Institute of Internal Auditors (IIA) and is one of the only certifications that is accepted worldwide. CIAs tend to be employed in auditing areas within government agencies, banking, finance, or corporations. They examine financial documents to investigate deficiencies in internal controls. Requirements for this certification include a bachelor's degree, two years of work experience in a related field, and passing the three sections of the examination. Also required are providing character references, following a code of ethics, and continuing education.

The **Certified Fraud Examiner (CFE)** certification signifies proven proficiency in fraud prevention, detection, and deterrence. CFEs are instructed in how to identify the red flags that may indicate fraudulent actions. The designation is awarded by the Association of Certified Fraud Examiners (ACFE) after applicants have met the following requirements: bachelor's degree, two years of work-related experience, moral character references, and the passing of four separate exams.

The **Certified Government Auditing Professional (CGAP)** designation is exclusively for auditors employed throughout the public sector (federal, state, local) and is offered by the IIA. Requirements for this credential are the same as for the CIA. The exam has 115 multiple-choice questions and covers four areas focusing on proficiency in generally accepted government auditing standards (GAGAS).

These certifications lead to different job responsibilities and different career paths. As indicated, each of the certifications requires varying degrees of education and has exams that are unique to that particular certification. All of these certifications also require a certain number of hours of continuing education in order to keep the certification active. This ensures that the certificate holder is up to date on changes in the field. There are always many opportunities throughout the year to obtain continuing education credits through seminars, webinars, symposiums, and online and in-person classes.

> **LINK TO LEARNING**
>
> Accounting.com has an application that will help to acquaint you with the different opportunities available, skill sets that may be required, and different salaries for accounting careers. See the Careers in Accounting report (https://openstax.org/l/50AccountCareer) for more information.

1.4 Describe the Role of the Institute of Management Accountants and the Use of Ethical Standards

As you've learned, unlike the specific rules set forth by GAAP and the SEC that govern financial accounting, managerial accounting does not have specific rules and is considered flexible, as the reporting stays internal and does not need to follow external rules. Managers of a business need detailed information in a timely manner. This means that a managerial accountant needs to understand many detailed aspects of how the company operates in addition to financial accounting methods, because the framework of typical management reports often comes from the financial statements. However, the reports can be individualized and customized to the information the manager is seeking. Each company has different strategies, timing, and needs for information.

The **Institute of Management Accountants (IMA)**, the professional organization for management accountants, provides research, education, a means of knowledge sharing, and practice development to its members. The IMA also issues the Certified Management Accountant (CMA) certification to those accountants who meet the educational requirements, pass the rigorous two-part exam, and maintain continuing professional education requirements. The CMA exam covers essential managerial accounting topics as well as topics on economics and finance. Many accountants hold both CMA and CPA certifications.

Business Ethics

The IMA also develops standards and principles to help management accountants deal with ethical challenges.

Trust is an important cornerstone of business interactions, both internal and external. When there is a lack of trust, it changes how decisions are made. Trust develops when there are good ethics: when people know right from wrong. Consider these three questions as put forth by the Institute of Business Ethics: (1) Do I mind others knowing what I have done? (2) Who does my decision affect or hurt? (3) Would my decision be considered fair to those affected? These questions can help evaluate the ethics of a decision.

Ethics is more than simply obeying laws; it involves doing the right thing as well as the legal thing. Many companies have a code of conduct to help guide their employees. For example, Google has a code of ethics that they expect all of their employees and board members to follow. Failing to do so can cause termination of employment. The preface of the code includes "Don't be evil." They use that to show all employees and other shareholders within Google that they are serious about ethics—that trust and respect are essential in providing a great service to their customers.

The IMA has its own Statement of Ethical Professional Practice for its members. Managerial accountants should never commit acts that violate the standards of ethics, and they should never ignore such deeds by others within their companies. Many other professional organizations, across many different professions, have codes of ethics. For example, there are codes of ethics for the AICPA, ACFE, Financial Executives International, American Marketing Association, National Society of Professional Engineers, and the American Nurses Association.

ETHICAL CONSIDERATIONS

Institute of Management Accountants (IMA) Ethical Standards

Four standards of ethical conduct in management accountants' professional activities were developed by the Institute of Management Accountants. The four standards are competence, confidentiality, integrity, and credibility. Credibility is a key standard that is based on an accountant communicating information with fairness and objectivity, disclosing all information that is relevant to the intended users understanding, and disclosing "delays or deficiencies in information, timeliness, processing, or internal controls in conformance with organization policy and/or applicable law."[6]

Often, when we think of unethical behavior, we imagine large-scale scenarios involving tens of thousands of dollars or more, but ethical issues are more likely faced on a small scale. For example, suppose you work for an organization that makes and sells virtual reality headsets. Because of competition, your company has decreased their forecasted sales for next year by 20 percent over the current year. In a meeting, the CEO expressed concern over the effect of the decreased sales on the bonuses of upper-level executives, since their bonus is tied to meeting income projections. The vice president of marketing suggested in the meeting that if the company simply continued to produce the same number of headsets as they had in the previous year, income levels may still be achieved in order for the bonuses to be awarded. This would involve the company producing excess inventory with hopes of selling them, in order to achieve income levels sufficiently adequate to be able to pay bonuses to executives. While a conflict of interest might not be intuitively obvious, the company (and thus its managerial accountants) has an obligation to many stakeholders such as investors, creditors, employees and the community. The obligation of a corporation to these stakeholders depends

---

6 Institute of Management Accountants. "Standards of Ethical Conduct for Management Accountants." AccountingVerse. https://www.accountingverse.com/managerial-accounting/introduction/code-of-ethics.html

somewhat on the stakeholder. For example, the primary obligation to a creditor may be to make timely payments, the obligation to the community may be to minimize negative environmental impact. Most stakeholders to not have access to internal information or decisions and thus rely on management to be ethical in their decision-making. The company may indeed be able to sell all that it produces, but given the forecasted drop in sales, producing the same number of units as during the current year will likely lead to unsellable inventory, the need to sell the units at a significant discount in order to dispose of them, or both. Following the recommendation to produce more than forecasted sales might hurt the value of the company's stock, which could hurt many categories of stakeholders who depend on the accountants and financial analysts to protect their financial interests.

In addition to managing production and inventory, a budget and the entire budget process have an impact on managerial decision-making. Suppose you are the manager of the research department of a pharmaceutical company. Your budget includes the costs for various types of training for your staff. Because of the amount of time spent in development of a highly promising medication to treat diabetes, your staff has not had time to complete as much training during the current year as you had allowed for in the budget. You are concerned that if you do not use the training money, your training budget will be decreased in the next budget cycle. To prevent this from happening, you arrange for several online training sessions for your staff. These training sessions are on the basics of laboratory safety. All of your staff is very experienced and current on this topic and can likely go straight to the course completion quiz and complete it in a matter of minutes without actually watching any of the ten modules. What would encourage a manager to schedule and spend money on training that is not useful for the employees? While it is expected to stay within the budget, many managers will spend any "excess" amounts remaining in the budget at the end of the fiscal year. This practice is known as "use it or lose it." Managers do this to avoid having their budgets cut in the next fiscal year. Stated simply, management spends everything in their budget regardless of the value added or the necessity. This is not ethical behavior and is usually the result of a budgetary process that needs to be modified so that the possibility of being able to pad the budget is removed or at least minimized.

All employees within a company are expected to act ethically within their business actions. This can sometimes be difficult when the company itself almost promotes the idea of unethical actions. For example, Wells Fargo started offering incentives to their employees who succeeded in selling to current customers other services and products that the bank had to offer. This incentive created an unethical culture. Employees manufactured fake accounts, credit cards, and other services in order to qualify for the bonuses. In the end, 5,300 employees lost their jobs, and everyone learned a lesson on creating proper incentives. Executives who aspire to run an ethical company can do so, if they change reward systems from "pay for performance" to more holistic values. Examples of proper incentives include attendance rewards, merit rewards, team bonuses, overall profit sharing, and stock options.

LINK TO LEARNING

Most, if not all, major corporations have a code of ethics or a code of conduct. Read Google's Code of Conduct (https://openstax.org/l/50GoogleCode) and consider the following questions:

- What is the basic foundation for their code of conduct? What do you think it means?
- After reading their document, has it changed your opinion of the company?

- Do you think having a code of ethics or a code of conduct really matters?

Ethics Legislation

In response to several corporate scandals, the United States Congress passed the **Sarbanes-Oxley Act of 2002 (SOX)**, also known as the "public company accounting reform." It is a federal law (http://www.soxlaw.com/) that was a far-reaching reform of business practices. Its focus is primarily on public accounting firms that act as auditors of publicly traded corporations. The act intended to protect investors by enhancing the accuracy and reliability of corporate financial statements and disclosures. Thousands of corporations now must confirm that their accounting processes comply with SOX. The act itself is fairly detailed, but the most significant issues for compliance are as follows:

- Section 302. The CEO and CFO must review all financial reports and sign the report.
- Section 404. All financial reports must be audited on an annual basis and must be accompanied by an internal control audit.
- Section 806. **Whistleblowers**, or those who provide evidence of fraud, are afforded special protections.
- Section 906. The criminal penalties for a fraudulent financial report are increased from pre-SOX. Penalties can be up to $5 million in fines and up to 25 years in prison.

> **LINK TO LEARNING**
>
> The Sarbanes-Oxley Act has been in place for many years now and has its champions and its critics. Read this 2017 article from Accounting Today on the benefits and negative impacts of the act (https://openstax.org/l/50SOAcctToday) to learn more. This article from ConnectUS discusses the benefits and negative impacts (https://openstax.org/l/50SOConnectUS) as well.

Individuals who work throughout the accounting profession have a significant responsibility to the general public. Financial accountants deliver information about companies that the public uses to make major financial decisions. There must be a level of trust and confidence in the ethical behavior of these accountants. Just like others in the business world, accountants are confronted endlessly with ethical dilemmas. A high standard of ethical behavior is expected of those employed in a profession. While ethical codes are helpful guidelines, the rationale to act ethically must originate from within oneself, from personal morals and values. There are steps that can provide an outline for examining ethical issues:

1. Recognize the ethical issue at hand and those involved (employees, creditors, vendors, and community).
2. Establish the facts of the situation (who, what, where, when, and how).
3. Recognize the competing values related to the issue (confidentiality and conflict of interest).
4. Determine alternative courses of action (do not limit yourself).
5. Evaluate each course of action and how each relates to the values in step 3.
6. Recognize the possible consequences of each course of action and how each affects those involved in step 1.
7. Make a decision, and take a course of action.

8. Evaluate the decision. (Is the issue solved? Did it create other issues?)

ETHICAL CONSIDERATIONS

Ethical Dilemma

You are about to sign a new client to a very large contract worth over $900,000. Your supervisor is under a lot of pressure to increase sales. He calls you into his office and tells you his future with the company is in jeopardy, and he asks you to include the revenue for the new contract in the sales figures for the quarter that ends today. You know the contract is a certainty, but the client is out of town and cannot possibly sign for at least a week. Use the eight steps in examining an ethical situation to determine how you would react to this situation.

One of the issues with ethics is that what one person, community, or even country considers unethical or wrong may not be problematic for another person, community, or country, who see it as a way of doing business. For example, **bribery** in the world of business happens when an organization or representative of an organization gives money or other financial benefits to another individual, business, or official in order to gain favor or to manipulate a business decision. Bribery in the United States is illegal. However, in Russia or China, a bribe is sometimes one cost of doing business, so it is part of their culture and completely ordinary.

The **Foreign Corrupt Practices Act (FCPA)** was implemented in 1977 in the aftermath of disclosures of bribery of foreign bureaucrats by more than 400 US corporations. The law is broken down into two parts: the antibribery section and the accounting section. The antibribery section specifically prohibits payments to foreign government officials to aid in attaining or retaining business. This provision applies to all US persons and foreign firms acting within the United States. It also requires corporations that are listed in the United States to converge their accounting records with certain accounting provisions. These include making and keeping records that fairly represent the transactions of the company and maintaining an acceptable system of internal controls. Companies doing business outside the United States are obligated to follow this law and dedicate resources to its compliance.

The accounting section of the FCPA requires a company to have good internal controls so a slush fund to pay bribes cannot be created and maintained. A *slush fund* is a cash account that is often created for illegal activities or payments that are not typically recorded on the books.

More details on the SOX and the FCPA are covered in such courses as auditing, intermediate accounting, cost accounting, and business law.

YOUR TURN

Logistics Analyst

As a corporate accountant, it is very important to understand both financial and managerial aspects of the company and industry in which you are working. In order to assist management in their roles of planning, controlling, and evaluating, an accountant needs to be aware not only of GAAP but also of the products or services offered by the company, the processes by which those products or services are produced, and pertinent facts about suppliers, customers, and competitors. Not having this knowledge not only makes it more difficult for the corporate or managerial accountant to perform any assigned duties, but there is also an ethical responsibility to be knowledgeable in order to offer assistance, analysis, or recommendations to management or customers.

Assume you have been hired by Triumph Motorcycles as a new logistics analyst. In this position, you will carry out such tasks as obtaining and analyzing information about your company's goods or services; monitoring the production, service, and information processes and flow; and looking for ways to improve efficiency of operations.

How would you go about obtaining the knowledge and understanding you will need to work for this company? How would financial and managerial accounting concepts help you in understanding the company and the industry as a whole?

Solution

Answers will vary. Sample answer:

Ways to learn about the company and industry include the company website, press or news releases, industry trade journals, company internal documents such as procedure manuals and job descriptions, and conversations or interviews with fellow employees at various levels of the organization. The more knowledge you have regarding financial and managerial accounting, the better you can link the operations of the organizations to financial results and the more easily you can ascertain both efficiencies and inefficiencies in the organization.

1.5 Describe Trends in Today's Business Environment and Analyze Their Impact on Accounting

The business environment never rests. Regulations are always changing, global competition continues to increase, and technology provides continual disruption. Management accounting is always evolving due to changes in the business environment. The types of information needed and obtainable have changed significantly over time.

Many areas of employment are impacting businesses and the managerial accounting function today. For example, more than 60 percent of workers in the United States are employed within service industries, such as government agencies, marketing firms, accounting firms, and airlines. The health-care and social service industries have doubled in size. However, as the number of service jobs has increased, the number of manufacturing jobs, as a percentage of all jobs, has been decreasing.[7] One of the primary reasons for the decline in manufacturing jobs is automation and other technological changes.

How are service industries different from manufacturing organizations? The fundamental difference is the product they sell. The service company, such as a marketing, legal, or consulting firm, produces **intangible goods**, meaning that the product has no physical substance. Manufacturing companies produce **tangible goods**, which customers can handle and see. This leads to another significant difference between manufacturing companies and service firms: inventory. Service firms, unlike manufacturing, do not have large

---

7   Dr. Patricia Buckley. "Geographic Trends in Manufacturing Job Creation: Something Old, Something New." *Deloitte Insight*. September 25, 2017. https://www2.deloitte.com/insights/us/en/economy/behind-the-numbers/geographic-trends-in-manufacturing-job-creation.html

inventories, because there is no tangible product. Manufacturing will have inventories of raw materials, of goods that are in the process of being produced and goods that have been completed but not yet sold. Managerial accountants must track all of this information for manufacturing companies. However, managerial accountants are still needed within service-based firms to track time, materials, and overhead. For example, Boeing Company is a manufacturer of airplanes. Their accountants must track several different types of inventory categories, direct labor, and overhead costs, among other things. One of Boeing's customers, Delta Air Lines, is a service-based company. The managerial accountants for the airline also are responsible for following costs, but their reports are targeted toward industry-specific measures such as operating margins, revenue from passenger miles, load factors, and passenger yield, among others.

Much of managerial accounting focuses on manufacturing. However, the techniques used for cost accounting for manufacturing companies also can be applied to service-based organizations. The former would develop a cost of goods manufactured schedule, and the latter would need a cost of service schedule. The structure of the reports is principally the same, but section headings would reflect the type of organization.

Technology

Business entities always look for ways to leverage technology. Any type of technology that can increase production, reduce costs, or increase safety will attract attention from the business world. There are many areas of technology that businesses have used already, but to continue reaping those benefits, these companies need to adjust quickly with the ever-advancing business technology.

Companies have the ability to integrate many of their business processes through **enterprise resource planning (ERP)** systems, which help companies streamline their operations and help management respond quickly to change. Although they are expensive, these systems help alleviate the complications that arise from business systems that do not coordinate with one another. For example, a company may have many different individual systems for each function: human resources may have a system to track employees' insurance benefits, training, and retirement programs, while payroll may have a program that tracks employees' earnings, taxes, deductions, and direct deposit information. Much of the information human resources and payroll collect is the same. Having one system with different silos is much more efficient than having two separate systems. Management must be aware of and adapt to whichever type of system that the business has—either one ERP or several independent systems that may not coordinate information (Figure 1.11).

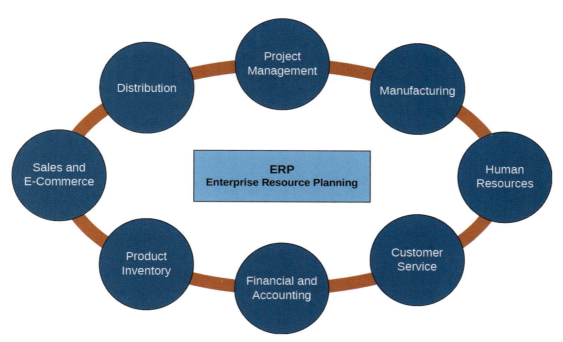

Figure 1.11 Eight Primary Components of Enterprise Resource Planning (ERP). The diagram shows the role of ERP in streamlining a business by coordinating the various components of that business. (attribution: Copyright Rice University, OpenStax, under CC BY-NC-SA 4.0 license)

Businesses have been on the forefront of advancing technology. As computer systems developed throughout the twentieth century, they brought with them the potential for many benefits, but the business world needed to adapt and transform their infrastructure. Over the last forty years, tangible assets (buildings, machinery, and vehicles) have declined from 80 percent of a company's value to 15 percent, while intangible assets (trademarks, patents, and competencies) are now at an average of 85 percent of a company's value. It can be difficult to put a value on some of the intangible assets, but it is not hard to realize they do have worth. JetBlue has the number one brand loyalty of all North American airlines. Apple has built a kingdom around brand loyalty. Intangible assets can give a company a competitive edge, entice consumers, and protect the organization's brain trust.

Technological advances can directly affect managerial accounting reports, through estimates of overhead costs. Historically, overhead was typically calculated on the basis of relatively straightforward relationships, such as direct labor costs or direct labor hours. With the advancements through automation, in many instances, direct labor costs are much lower and no longer relevant in computing overhead costs. **Automation** is a method of using systems such as computers or robots to operate different processes and machinery to improve efficiencies and lower direct labor costs. Companies use automation to remove the complex, superfluous stages from a process in order to streamline the practice. In essence, labor is being traded for machine production. Such industries as auto production are excellent examples. This exchange of direct labor for greater costs in overhead for such factors as machinery depreciation will be addressed in Job Order Costing and Process Costing on calculating production costs.

LINK TO LEARNING

Automation has changed the production of automobiles over the last 100 years. This 100-second video from Ford Motor Company on automation (https://openstax.org/l/50Ford) demonstrates this concept.

With the growth of the Internet and the speed by which information is shared, businesses can now communicate with employees from around the world within seconds. This has made outsourcing common in certain sectors. **Outsourcing** is hiring workers outside of the company who perform their tasks inside or outside of the country. Most of the exported jobs have gone to less-developed countries, where there are lower labor costs. Outsourcing saves the company money on labor and overhead costs and has become a major trend over the past several years. More and more organizations, both large and small, are now using outsourcing as a way of growing their entities without adding additional labor and overhead costs. Outsourcing allows a company to focus on its own competencies and hire those outside sources to handle other duties.

Another technology that is quickly becoming widespread is **radio-frequency identification (RFID)**. This technology uses electromagnetic fields to routinely identify and trace inventory tags that have been attached to objects. The tags contain information that has been stored by electronic means. The RFID tags can made into many shapes and sizes and enclosed in many different materials. These tiny devices have advantages over the common bar code. They do not need to be positioned precisely over the scanner and cannot be manipulated like barcodes. This technology has been used for many years in identifying and tracking lost pets, but it was considered too expensive for more extensive use in industry. With the advancements over the last several years, RFID devices are now seen as "throwaway" control devices. One company recently signed a contract to sell 500 million RFID tags at a cost of about ten cents per device. Other current uses include antitheft tags attached to merchandise, credit card chips, and heavy-duty transponders used in shipping containers. New uses being investigated include RFID chips in passports, food, and people.

THINK IT THROUGH

Outsourcing

With the increase in global businesses and competition, there has been an increased focus on outsourcing in order to reduce costs. As you've learned, outsourcing involves hiring an outside company to provide services or products rather than having them produced internally.

For example, you are the vice president of operations for a manufacturing firm. Other firms similar to yours have outsourced some of the product assembly. You estimate that you could save a significant amount of money on wages and benefits, as you would let go approximately ten workers if you outsource. Would you outsource? Why or why not?

Lean Practices

All companies want to be successful. This requires continuously trying to improve the function of the organization. A **lean business model** is one in which a company strives to eliminate waste in its products, services, and processes, while still fulfilling the company's mission. This type of model was originally implemented by the Japanese automaker, Toyota Motor Corporation, soon after the end of World War II. The implications of an organization adopting a lean business model can be overall business improvement, but a lean business model can be difficult to implement because it often requires all systems and procedures that an organization follows to be readjusted and coordinated. Managerial accounting plays a vital role in the success and implementation of a lean business model by providing accurate cost and performance evaluation information. Entities must comprehend the nature and sources of costs and develop systems that encapsulate costs accurately. The better an organization is at controlling costs, the more it can improve its overall financial performance. **Continuous improvement** is the manufacturing process that rejects the ideas of "good enough." It is an ongoing effort to improve processes, products, services, and practices. This philosophy has led organizations to adopt practices such as total quality management, just-in-time manufacturing, and Lean Six Sigma. The fundamental ideas of all of these involve continuous improvement; they differ only in focus.

Total quality management (TQM) concentrates on quality improvement and applies this benchmark to all aspects of business activities. In TQM, management and employees look to reveal waste and errors, streamline the supply chain, improve customer relations, and confirm that employees are informed and properly trained. The objective of TQM is continuous improvement by concentrating on systematic problem-solving and customer service. Scientific methods are used to study what succeeds and what does not, and then the best practices are implemented throughout the organization.

However, the pursuit of total quality will cost the company money. With the help of management accountants, companies can track these costs and forecast whether or not the improvements will eventually save the organization money down the road.

Just-in-time (JIT) manufacturing is an inventory system that companies use to increase efficiency and decrease waste by receiving goods only as they are needed within the production process, thereby reducing warehousing costs. This method requires accurate forecasting. Managerial accountants work together with purchasing and production schedulers in keeping the flow of materials accurate and efficient.

This method was initiated by Toyota Motor Corporation, and it has expanded to many other manufacturing organizations throughout the world. Toyota set the example by controlling their inventory levels by relying on their supply chain to deliver the raw materials it needed to build their cars. The parts arrived just as they were needed, not before or after.

One major advantage of JIT manufacturing is reducing costs by eradicating warehouse storage needs. Organizations, in turn, tend to spend less money on raw materials because of a reduction in spoilage and waste. Another advantage is that companies can easily move from the assembly of one product to the assembly of another.

Disadvantages of JIT manufacturing start with its complexity. In moving from a traditional manufacturing approach to a JIT approach, management must reconfigure the entire flow of the production process, from the initial use of the raw materials to the output of the final finished good. Another disadvantage of JIT manufacturing is that it makes organizations more susceptible to disruptions in the supply chain. If a supplier of raw materials has a labor strike, weather problems, a breakdown of machinery, or some other catastrophe and cannot deliver the materials on time, that one supplier can shut down an entire production process and delay delivery of finished goods. An example of this occurred in 2011 after a tsunami and earthquake hit Japan and disrupted production at a critical supplier of auto parts. General Motors (GM) facilities in the United States announced they would have to shut down assembly plants where they could not continue production without the parts from Japan.

Lean Six Sigma (LSS) is a quality control program that depends on a combined effort of many team members to enhance performance by analytically removing waste and diminishing variations between products. The *lean* component of LSS is the concept that anything that is not needed in a product or service, or any unnecessary steps that exist, add cost to the product or service and therefore should be considered waste and eliminated. The *Six Sigma* component of LSS has to do with the elimination of defects. Essentially, as a company becomes leaner, it should also be able to reduce defects in manufacturing or in providing a service. Fewer defects add to cost savings through the need for fewer reworked products, fewer repeat service calls, and therefore, more satisfied customers. It was developed by Motorola in 1986 and emphasized cycle-time improvement and the reduction of defects. This process has shown to be a powerful way of improving business efficiency and effectiveness. As organizations continue to modify and update their processes for optimal productivity, they must be flexible. As of 2017, LSS had developed into a business management way of thinking that focused on customer needs, customer retention, and improvement of business products and services. There are many establishments, including Motorola, that now do LSS training. There are certifications including white belt, yellow belt, green belt, black belt, and master black belt. The belts signify an employee's knowledge regarding LSS. For example, a white belt understands the terminology, structure, and idea of LSS and reports issues to green or black belts. A green belt typically manages LSS projects, and a master black belt works with upper-level management to find the areas in the business where LSS needs to be implemented, leads several LSS teams, and oversees implementation of those projects.

Kaizen (Japanese for *change for the better*) is another process that is often linked to Six Sigma (Figure 1.12). The two concepts are often used together for process improvements, as they both are designed for continuous improvement by eliminating waste and increasing efficiencies. The concept of *kaizen* comes from an ancient Japanese philosophy that involves continuously working toward perfection in all areas of one's life. It was adopted in the business world after World War II in an effort to rebuild Japan. It centers on making small, day-to-day changes that develop into major improvements over time. The key behind the success of kaizen comes from requiring all employees—from the CEO at the top, all the way down to the shop-floor janitors—to participate by making recommendations to improve the organization. From the start of the process, it must be well defined that all recommendations are appreciated and that there will be no adverse results for participating. Workers, instead, should be rewarded for any modifications that advance the workplace. Employees become more self-assured and invested when they help improve the company.

Figure 1.12 Kaizen Board Showing Kaizen Process and Some Related Tactics. (credit left: modification of "Woman Standing in Front of Sitting People" by "rawpixel.com"/Pexels, Pexels license / Public Domain; right: modification of "A few kaizen tactics" by Sacha Chua/Flickr, CC BY 2.0)

Another lean practice, the **theory of constraints (TOC)**, involves recognizing and removing bottlenecks within the value chain that may be limiting an organization's profitability. This philosophy, developed by Dr. Eliyahu M. Goldratt, is a valuable instrument for improving the flaws in processes. The main goal of this methodology is to remove obstructions, or constraints, which are referred to as "bottlenecks." There are several types of bottlenecks that organizations must deal with endlessly. One example occurs at the grocery store when it is crowded and there are only three checkout lanes open but ten people in each line. Obviously, the bottleneck is created by having too few checkout lanes open. The bottleneck can be mitigated by opening more checkout lanes. Other examples are listed in Table 1.5.

Examples of Constraints

Bottleneck	Examples
Physical	Employee resources, limited space, equipment resources
Policy	Procedures, regulations, contracts
Culture	"It's the way we've always done it"
Market	Size of the market, demand for product, nature of competition

Table 1.5

There are five steps in the cycle of continuous improvement under TOC:

1. Identify the system constraint.
2. Decide how best to exploit the constraint and make quick changes using existing resources.
3. Subordinate everything else to the process to ensure alignment with and support of the needs of the constraint.
4. Elevate the system's constraint, and determine if the constraint has shifted to another area in the process.
5. Repeat the process.

This is a continuous cycle; therefore, once a bottleneck is solved, the next bottleneck should be addressed immediately (Figure 1.13).

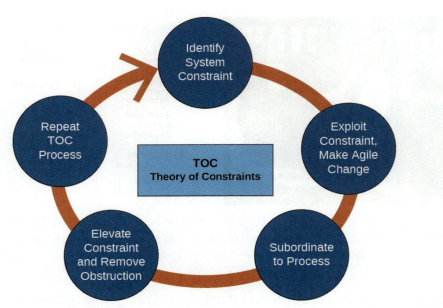

Figure 1.13 Five Focusing Steps of the Theory of Constraints in Its Cyclical Process. (attribution: Copyright Rice University, OpenStax, under CC BY-NC-SA 4.0 license)

Balanced Scorecard

The **balanced scorecard (BSC)** approach uses both financial and nonfinancial measures in evaluating all attributes of the organization's procedures. This approach differs from the traditional approach of only using financial measures to evaluate a company. While financial measures are essential, they are only a portion of what needs to be evaluated. The balanced scorecard focuses on both high-level and low-level measures, using the company's own strategic plan. This method assesses the organization in four separate perspectives:

- Financial. The financial measures are the major focus of the BSC—but not the only measures. This perspective asks questions like whether the organization is making money or whether the stockholders are pleased.
- Customer. The BSC also evaluates how the organization is perceived, from the customer's perspective. This measures customer satisfaction, new customer growth, and market share.
- Internal process. The internal procedures and processes perspective observes how smoothly things are running. This perspective will examine quality, efficiency, and waste as they relate directly to the products or services.
- Learning and growth/capacity. This area evaluates the entity and its performance from the standpoint of human capital, infrastructure, culture, technology, and other areas. Are employees collaborating and sharing information? Does everyone have access to the latest trends in training and continuing education in their areas?

The main advantage of this approach is that it offers organizations a way to see the cause-and-effect in the objectives. For example, if an organization would like to make more money in order to pay higher dividends to its stockholders, the organization will need to increase market share, improve customer satisfaction, or grow its customer base. In order to make customers happier or gain new customers, the organization could try to reduce defects and increase overall quality of the products; to accomplish that, the organization could retrain or offer new training to its employees.

Globalization

The development of business through international influence or extending social and cultural aspects around the world is known as **globalization**. It has expanded our competitive borders, giving customers more alternatives. Customers can order an item from another country with the click of a button and have that item delivered in a few days or less. How has globalization affected companies? Not only must they choose between ordering goods or components globally, but they must decide in which countries to sell their goods, and in which companies they may be able to establish factories.

Globalization affects management accountants in several ways. Companies need real-time, accurate information to make good decisions, so more timely and accurate information is needed. As companies expand globally, managers need to know the cost of operating internationally, as well as the laws, rules, and customs. Globalization also can expose companies to improvements in running a business.

Debates continue as to the positive and negative consequences of globalization in all of its contexts. The advantages of globalization include helping developing countries in creating jobs, developing industries, differentiating and expanding their markets, and bettering their standard of living for their citizens. Some believe the expansion of pop culture around the globe to be an advantage of cultural globalization. It has multiplied the interchange of ideas, music, art, language, and cultural ideals. On the other side of the debate, one common criticism of globalization is that it has enhanced wealth disparity and, further, that organizations of the Western world have benefited much more than those anywhere else. There is also the argument that globalization is improving standards of living worldwide as industrialization is expanding, but it is causing global warming and climate change, due to the greenhouse gases the factories emit. Additionally, in some areas it has led to the abuse and misuse of natural resources and caused other detrimental consequences.

How do these various globalization debates affect businesses? A successful company must be profitable to stay in business, but profitability is not the single key to success. A successful company must also consider the environment in which it operates—culturally, socially, environmentally, and economically—which requires companies to evolve and adjust as each of these environments changes. This evolution means that companies must continually evaluate themselves and their impact on all of their stakeholders, which include investors, creditors, management, employees, customers, governments, and, either directly or indirectly, the world. What companies used as measures of success forty years ago are different from the measures used twenty years ago, and those are different from those that are used today and still different from what will be needed in the future. Management accounting is the area in which many of these changing measures are either generated or evaluated. Such measures not only evaluate the cost effectiveness of products or services, but determine the best way to evaluate and reward employees and evaluate the cost-benefit of environmental protections, the impact of automation versus outsourcing, and the cost of training and educating employees.

ETHICAL CONSIDERATIONS

Global Ethics

In an article in *Business 2 Community*, Kate Gerasimova draws on her experience within the Russian and American business environments to discuss the role of ethics in global business endeavors. Ethics are the principles, and the values that underlie them, that allow us to determine what is right and wrong. According to Gerasimova, ethics fall into three categories: "code and compliance, destiny and values, and social outreach."[8] In the global business context, she also emphasizes the importance of respecting differences in values held by coworkers, communicating honestly in business dealings, and building trust. To assist in the application of the organization's ethical approach to doing business in a different culture, it needs to develop a set of "core values as the basis for global policies and decision-making."[9] Gerasimova notes that organizations also need to consider that "clients and coworkers may have a different perspective on ethics and proper behavior than those to which you are accustomed." To address the different perspectives, an organization should train its employees to be culturally sensitive while balancing the need for rules and policies with the ability for employees to be flexible and to use their imagination.

Social Responsibility and Sustainability

What is **sustainability**, and what does it have to do with businesses? The United Nations definition is "the ability to meet the needs of the present without compromising the ability of future generations to meet their own needs."[10] Usually, sustainability is viewed as having three components: economic, social, and environmental. Obviously, a business cannot continue into the future unless it is economically sound; however, if it maintains its economic status by depleting too many natural resources or paying illegal wages, then that company is not practicing good social responsibility.

Corporate social responsibility (CSR) is an organization's programs that evaluate and take responsibility for the organization's effects on environmental and social welfare. There are many aspects of corporate social responsibility, including the types, locations, and wages of the labor employed; the ways in which renewable and nonrenewable resources are utilized; how charitable organizations or local areas in which the company operates are helped; and setting corporate employee policies such as maternity and paternity leave that promote family well-being. Although the causes and cures of climate change are open to discussion, most will agree that everyone, including corporations, should do their part to avoid further damage and improve any negative impact on the environment.

CONCEPTS IN PRACTICE

Corporate Social Responsibility at New Belgium Brewing

As New Belgium Brewing Company states on their website: "We're New Belgium and we pollute. There. We said it. We are not perfect and we know it." But New Belgium Brewing has become a leader in sustainability. They preach it in every aspect of the company: production, marketing, employees, and customers. The company makes the point that being energy efficient is not only being environmentally responsible, it is being financially responsible through their "internal energy efficiency tax." The company uses many different metrics to track and improve its impact on the environment. For example,

---

8   Kate Gerasimova. "The Critical Role of Ethics and Culture in Business Globalization." *Business to Community*. September 29, 2016. https://www.business2community.com/strategy/critical-role-ethics-culture-business-globalization-01667737
9   Kate Gerasimova. "The Critical Role of Ethics and Culture in Business Globalization." *Business to Community*. September 29, 2016. https://www.business2community.com/strategy/critical-role-ethics-culture-business-globalization-01667737
10 "Sustainable Development." General Assembly of the United Nations. http://www.un.org/en/ga/president/65/issues/sustdev.shtml

> the company measures its energy usage and taxes itself on energy consumption and then saves those internal tax dollars to implement further energy savings by installing new processes and techniques. They divert 99.9 percent of the waste from their brewery away from landfills. The company makes enough in recycling revenues to pay four salaries. These are just a few ways in which New Belgium Brewing faces the challenges of social responsibility. Read more at http://www.newbelgium.com/Sustainability/Environmental-Metrics.

In late 2016, the Paris Agreement (Paris Accord) brought together nations for the common cause of combatting climate change. There were 197 nations in attendance, and until recently, all 197 ratified or agreed to the effort. It requires all partners to pursue specific endeavors to keep the global temperature rise to 2 degrees Celsius above that of preindustrial levels. This would be accomplished by voluntarily reducing greenhouse gas emissions. In early 2017, US President Donald Trump announced that the United States would withdraw from the agreement. At that time, only Syria and Nicaragua were holdouts. Since then, both have signed the agreement, leaving the United States now as the lone holdout, although it will take several years for the formal withdrawal. In spite of the president's announcement, there have been representatives from cities, states, corporations, and universities around the United States that have pledged to continue with the agreement and meet the greenhouse gas emission targets as set out in the Paris Accord. Many of the corporations who have promised to move forward with reducing greenhouse gases have expressed that the Paris Accord expands markets for groundbreaking clean technologies and that it creates employment opportunities alongside economic growth.

In terms of managerial accounting, sustainable business practices create many issues. Organizations need to decide what elements will be measured. For example, minimizing electricity consumption, maximizing employee safety, or reducing greenhouse gases may be the biggest issue of concern for a company. Then, the company needs to determine ways of measurement that make sense regarding those items. Companies are becoming more aware of their impact on the world, and many are creating social responsibility reports in addition to their annual reports. This type of reporting requires different types of information and analysis than the typical financial measures gathered by companies. This is sometimes referred to as the *triple bottom line*, as it assesses an organization's performance not only relating to the profit, but also relating to the world and its people, and will be covered in Sustainability Reporting.

YOUR TURN

Zaley's Machining Division

Zaley is an aerospace manufacturing firm in the southwest United States. They manufacture several products used in the aviation and aerospace industry. The company has been steadily growing over the past ten years in both sales and personnel. The engineering and design team uses computerized aided drafting (CAD) to design the various products that are produced by the machining division.

The machining division recently implemented significant technological improvements by installing an advanced technique using hard-metal and aluminum high-speed machining. The following managers are involved with the machining division:

- Alex Freedman, technical specialist (supervises all computer programs)
- Emma Vlovski, sales manager (supervises all sales agents)
- Kayla McClaughley, cost accounting director (supervises all cost accountants)
- Mwangi Kori, lead test engineer (oversees all new-product testing and design)
- Torek Sanchez, production director (supervises all manufacturing employees)

Each of these managers needs information to make decisions needed to carry out the respective jobs.

Think about what might be involved in the job of each of these managers and the types of decisions they may be required to make in order to meet the goals of the company. What information would be needed by each of the managers?

Solution

Answers will vary. Sample answer:

- Alex Freeman, technical specialist (supervises all computer programs), needs information on the hours and type of usage possibly by department or by individual to ascertain if the equipment is being used effectively or if the programs used by the company are appropriate or additions or deletions need to be made. In addition, this information is needed to address how much and what type of staffing he needs in his department.
- Emma Vlovski, sales manager (supervises all sales agents), would want information about the level and type of sales for the company as a whole as well as for the individual sales agents. She would want to know which products are selling well, which ones are not, which sales agents are being the most successful, and why they are more successful than the others. Emma would also want information on how the agents are compensated, as this may be tied to the sales agent's efforts to meet sales goals.
- Kayla McClaughley, cost accounting director (supervises all cost accountants), would want to know what tasks the cost accountants perform, how much time they spend on these tasks, and whether there are any redundancies in workload so that improvements in efficiency can be made. If any of the accountants has certifications such as CPA or CMA, she would want to know if they are keeping their certifications current through continuing professional education.
- Mwangi Kori, lead test engineer (oversees all new-product testing and design), would need information on the efficiency and effectiveness of each of the products tested, including success and failure rates. She would want information on how well the policies and procedures for design changes are being followed and if those policies and procedures need updating or rewriting.
- Thomas Sanchez, production director (supervises all manufacturing employees), would want information on hours worked, pay rates, and training (past and ongoing) for the manufacturing employees. She would also want information on how each individual employee performs his or her role in the manufacturing environment. For example, are there particular employees who have fewer defects or down time in their part of the process than others?

🔑 Key Terms

automation method of using systems such as computers or robots to operate different processes, and machinery to improve efficiencies and lower direct labor costs

balanced scorecard tool used to evaluate performance using qualitative and nonqualitative measures

board of directors group of individuals elected by the shareholders of a company with the role of placing management, supervising management, and making key decisions on major issues of the company

bribery when an organization or representative of an organization gives money or other financial benefits to another individual, business, or official in order to gain favor or to manipulate a business decision

budget analyst someone who arranges and manages the master budget and compares master budget projections to actual results

cash-management accountant someone with responsibilities that include transferring monies between accounts, monitoring deposits and payments, reconciling cash balances, creating and tracking cash forecasts, and performing all other cash-related financial processes

Certified Financial Analyst (CFA) certification for a career in the finance and investment domains; requirements include a bachelor's degree or four years' experience and passing all three sections of the exam

Certified Fraud Examiner (CFE) signifies proven proficiency in fraud prevention, detection, and deterrence; requirements include bachelor's degree, two years of work-related experience, moral character references, and passing of four separate exams

Certified Government Auditing Professional (CGAP) designation exclusively for auditors employed throughout the public sector (federal, state, local); requirements are the same as for the CIA, but with a different exam

Certified Internal Auditor (CIA) credential offered by the Institute of Internal Auditors (IIA) and one of the only certifications accepted worldwide; requirements include a bachelor's degree, two years of work experience in a related field, and passing the three sections of the examination

Certified Management Accountant (CMA) certification for a specialist in corporate accounting management, including financial analytics, budgeting, and strategic assessment; requires a bachelor's degree, two years of work experience, and successfully passing both parts of the exam

Certified Public Accountant (CPA) top tier in accounting certifications; in the United States, each state has different educational and experience requirements, and certification requires passing the four-part CPA administered by the American Institute of Certified Public Accountants (AICPA)

chief executive officer (CEO) executive within a company with the highest ranking title who has the overall responsibility for the management of a company; reports to the board of directors

chief financial officer (CFO) corporation officer who reports to the CEO and oversees all of the accounting and finance concerns of a company

collaboration working in cross-functional teams and earning the trust and respect of colleagues in order to complete a task

commercial awareness knowing how a business is run and how it is influenced by the external environment, and knowing and understanding the overall industry within which the business is operating

continuous improvement ongoing effort to improve processes, products, services, and practices

controller financial officer of a corporation reporting to the CFO who is responsible for an organization's accounting records, financial statements, tax returns, and internal reporting

controlling monitoring of the planning objectives that were put into place

corporate social responsibility (CSR) actions that firms take to assume responsibility for their impact on the environment and social well-being

cost accountant employee who amasses large sums of data, checking for accuracy and then formulating the cost of raw materials, work in process, finished goods, labor, overhead, and other associated manufacturing costs

effective communication conveying information in both written and oral forms in a way that the intended audience can understand

Enrolled Agent (EA) credential focusing on a career in taxation; created by the IRS to signify significant knowledge of the US tax code and the ability to apply the concepts of that code

enterprise resource planning (ERP) system that helps a company streamline its operations and helps management respond quickly to change

evaluating comparing actual results against the planned results

external user someone who relies on the financial statements and annual reports to access information about a company in order to make more informed decisions (e.g., creditor, tax authority and regulator, investor, customer, competitor, and others)

Financial Accounting Standards Board (FASB) independent, nonprofit organization that sets financial accounting and reporting standards for both public and private sector businesses in the United States that use Generally Accepted Accounting Principles (GAAP)

financial analyst someone who assists in preparing budgets and tracking actual costs, and performs other tasks that support other management personnel in organizing forecasts and projections

Foreign Corrupt Practices Act (FCPA) law that specifically prohibits payments to foreign government officials to aid in attaining or retaining business and requires a company to have good internal controls so a slush fund to pay bribes cannot be created and maintained

generally accepted accounting principles (GAAP) common set of rules, standards, and procedures that publicly traded companies must follow when composing their financial statements

globalization development of business through international influence, or extending social and cultural aspects around the world

goal what a company expects to accomplish over time

government agency found at all levels of government: federal, state, county, city, and so on; includes military, law enforcement, airports, and school systems

Institute of Management Accountants (IMA) professional organization for management accountants that provides research, education, a means of knowledge sharing, and practice development to its members

intangible good good with financial value but no physical presence; examples include copyrights, patents, goodwill, and trademarks

internal auditor employee of an organization whose job is to provide an independent and objective evaluation of the company's accounting and operational activities

internal user someone inside the company or organization who is responsible for managing the company's business interests and executing decisions (e.g., all levels of management, owner, and other employees)

just-in-time (JIT) manufacturing inventory system that companies use to increase efficiency and decrease waste by receiving goods only as they are needed within the production process, thereby reducing warehousing costs

kaizen another process that is often linked to Six Sigma and is designed for continuous improvement by eliminating waste and increasing efficiencies; a Japanese word meaning *change for the better*

lean business model one in which a company strives to eliminate waste in its products, services, and processes, while still fulfilling the company's mission

Lean Six Sigma (LSS) quality control program that depends on a combined effort of many team members to enhance performance by analytically removing waste and diminishing variations between products

managerial accounting process that allows decision makers to set and evaluate business goals by determining what information they need to make a particular decision and how to analyze and communicate this information

mission statement short statement of a company's purpose and focus

monetary accounting information relating to money or currency

nonmonetary accounting information not relating to money or currency, such as the quantity of materials, number of employees, number of hours worked, and so forth

nonprofit (not-for-profit) organization tax-exempt organization that serves its community in a variety of areas

objective target that needs to be met in order to meet company goals

outsourcing act of using another company to provide goods or services that your company requires

planning process of setting goals and objectives

radio-frequency identification (RFID) technology that uses electromagnetic fields to routinely identify and trace inventory tags that have been attached to objects

Sarbanes-Oxley Act (SOX) federal law that regulates business practices; intended to protect investors by enhancing the accuracy and reliability of corporate financial statements and disclosures through governance guidelines including sanctions for criminal conduct

strategic planning setting priorities and determining how to allocate corporate resources to help an organization accomplish short-term and long-term goals

sustainability meeting the needs of the present generation without compromising the ability of future generations to meet their own needs by being aware of current economic, social, and environmental impacts

tangible good physical good that customers can handle and see

theory of constraints (TOC) process of recognizing and removing bottlenecks within the value chain that may be limiting an organization's profitability

total quality management (TQM) process in which management and employees look to reveal waste and errors, streamline the supply chain, improve customer relations, and confirm that employees are informed and properly trained

treasurer financial officer of a corporation reporting to the CFO who is in control of the finance side of the business (cash position, corporation funds)

whistleblower someone who provides evidence of fraud

 Summary

1.1 Define Managerial Accounting and Identify the Three Primary Responsibilities of Management

- The purpose of managerial accounting is to supply financial and nonfinancial information to the organization's management and other internal decision makers.
- Most of the job responsibilities of a manager fit into one of three categories: planning, controlling, and evaluating.
- Planning involves setting goals and forming the plans to achieve those goals.
- Controlling involves the day-to-day activities. Its purpose is to help in planning functions and to facilitate coordination within the organization.
- Evaluation determines whether plans are being followed and whether progress is being made as planned toward the fulfillment of organizational goals and objectives. It also involves taking corrective measures in case of deviations identified in the course of action.

1.2 Distinguish between Financial and Managerial Accounting

- Managerial accounting provides information to managers and other users within the company. It has a specific focus, and the information is detailed and timely.
- Financial accounting follows the guidelines of the GAAP, set in place by the FASB and, in many cases, by the SEC. Managerial accounting is much more flexible and does not have to follow specific rules or guidelines.
- There are seven key differences between managerial accounting and financial accounting: users, types of reports produced, frequency of producing the reports, purpose of the information produced, focus of the reporting information, nature of the original information used to produce the reports, and verification of the data used to create the reports.

1.3 Explain the Primary Roles and Skills Required of Managerial Accountants

- Essential skills for managerial accountants include commercial awareness, collaboration, effective communication skills, strong technology talents, extensive analytical abilities, and elevated ethical values.
- Management accountants work with individuals at all levels of an organization from the CEO to the shop floor workers.
- There are many different career paths management accountants can take to work in corporations, government entities, service firms, or nonprofit organizations.
- There are numerous certifications that accountants can earn to improve their careers and set themselves apart from their peers.

1.4 Describe the Role of the Institute of Management Accountants and the Use of Ethical Standards

- Many professional organizations share resources, such as education, research, and practice development, with their members. They also enforce a code of ethics for their members.
- All employees within a company are expected to act ethically within their business actions. This can sometimes be difficult when the company almost promotes the idea of unethical actions.
- In response to several corporate scandals, the United States Congress passed the Sarbanes-Oxley Act of 2002 (SOX).
- Ethical codes can be helpful guidelines, but the rationale to act ethically must originate from within oneself, from personal morals and values. There are steps that provide an outline for examining ethical issues.
- One of the issues with ethics is that what one person, community, or even country considers unethical or wrong, another person, community, or country may have no problem with and see it as just a way of doing business.
- The Foreign Corrupt Practices Act of 1977 specifically prohibits payments to foreign government officials to aid in attaining or retaining business. This provision applies to all US persons and foreign firms acting within the United States.

1.5 Describe Trends in Today's Business Environment and Analyze Their Impact on Accounting

- Business regulations are always being altered, global competition continues to increase, and technology provides continual disruption. Management accounting must keep up with the changes in the business environment.
- The fundamental difference between manufacturing organizations and service-based firms is whether the organizations produce a tangible product.
- Business entities have been in the lead for using technology, but they must continue to adjust quickly with the ever-advancing business technology.
- ERP systems help companies streamline their operations and help management respond quickly to change.

- Lean manufacturing, which was started in Japan by automakers, is now a widely used practice that attempts to increase productivity and eliminate waste.
- The philosophy of continuous improvement has led organizations to adopt practices such as TQM, JIT manufacturing, and LSS.
- The balanced scorecard approach uses both financial and nonfinancial measures in evaluating all attributes of the organization's procedures.
- Globalization has expanded competitive borders, giving customers and companies more alternatives.
- Many companies have started to assess their corporation not only on financial profits, but also on their corporate social responsibility.

Multiple Choice

1. LO 1.1 The managers of an organization are responsible for performing several broad functions. They are _____.
   A. planning, controlling, and selling
   B. directing, controlling, and evaluating
   C. planning, evaluating, and manufacturing
   D. planning, controlling, and evaluating

2. LO 1.1 Management accountants help the management of an organization in their planning function through _____.
   A. monitoring anti-theft systems
   B. strategic planning
   C. evaluating costs
   D. analyzing profits

3. LO 1.1 Which of the following is a primary aspect of the evaluating function within an organization?
   A. comparing actual results against expected results for products, departments, divisions, or the company as a whole
   B. reviewing only the quantitative or financial results of the company
   C. setting goals
   D. putting controls in place for the upcoming year

4. LO 1.1 During the control function, the measurements taken of the performance must be accurate enough to see _____.
   A. only positive results
   B. deviations and variances
   C. the primary focus
   D. only the negative results

5. LO 1.1 Which of the following is **false** regarding strategic planning?
   A. It is the sole responsibility of supervisors.
   B. It will span many years.
   C. It should include both short-term and long-term goals.
   D. Strategic objectives will be diverse and vary from company to company.

6. LO 1.2 Managerial accounting produces information:
   A. to meet the needs of external users
   B. that is often focused on the future
   C. to meet the needs of investors
   D. that follows the rules of GAAP

7. LO 1.2 Management accounting:
   A. emphasizes special-purpose information
   B. relates to the company as a whole
   C. is limited to strictly cost figures
   D. is controlled by GAAP

8. LO 1.2 Internal users of accounting information would *not* include _____.
   A. managers
   B. employees
   C. creditors
   D. officers

9. LO 1.2 External users of accounting information would include _____.
   A. employees
   B. managers
   C. investors
   D. supervisors

10. LO 1.2 Which of the following statements is **incorrect**?
   A. The practice of management accounting is fairly flexible.
   B. The information gathered from management accounting is not required by law.
   C. Management accounting focuses mainly on the internal user.
   D. Reports produced using management accounting must follow GAAP.

11. LO 1.3 The stockholders of a company are:
   A. the owners
   B. policy setters
   C. responsible and liable for the financial well-being of the company
   D. operating within the company as independent shareholders

12. LO 1.3 The controller of a corporation:
   A. reports to the CFO and is in charge of the finance side of the business
   B. reports to the CFO and is in charge of the accounting side of the business
   C. reports to the CEO and implements all cash policies
   D. reports to the board of directors

13. LO 1.3 The Certified Financial Analyst (CFA) certification:
   A. only requires a high school diploma
   B. is administered by the AICPA
   C. consists of three separate exams that must be taken in succession
   D. is the most popular certification among accountants in the United States

14. LO 1.3 The Certified Management Accountant (CMA) certification:
   A. signifies someone specializing in tax accounting
   B. requires an associate's degree and four years of work experience
   C. includes a two-part exam, education requirements, and a work experience requirement
   D. is offered to managers who take special courses in accounting

15. LO 1.3 Which of the following terms means the ability to work in cross-functional teams in order to complete a task?
   A. supervisory skills
   B. conceptualization
   C. collaboration
   D. resource planning

16. LO 1.3 Which of the following terms means knowing how a business is run and how it is influenced by external forces, and knowing and understanding the overall industry?
   A. commercial awareness
   B. conceptualization
   C. collaboration
   D. imagination

17. LO 1.4 What is the law that protects investors from fraudulent financial accounting activity?
   A. FASB
   B. SACS
   C. SOX
   D. CPAS

18. LO 1.4 What year was the Sarbanes-Oxley Act enacted?
   A. 2007
   B. 1992
   C. 1997
   D. 2002

19. LO 1.4 When a representative of an organization gives money to another business official in order to gain favor and/or manipulate a business decision, this is known as _____.
   A. whistleblowing
   B. bribery
   C. buyer debits
   D. face value

20. LO 1.4 The law that specifically prohibits payments to foreign officials in order to attain business is knowns as _____.
   A. FCPA
   B. AICPA
   C. SOX
   D. IFRS

21. **LO** 1.4 Which of the following is *not* a step in the outline for examining ethical issues?
    A. Establish the facts of the situation.
    B. Evaluate each course of action.
    C. Make a decision.
    D. Confirm decision with FASB.

22. **LO** 1.5 Which of the following is *not* an objective used in the balanced scorecard approach?
    A. Customer
    B. Financial
    C. Vendor
    D. Learning and growth

23. **LO** 1.5 Which of the following is *not* true regarding continuous improvement?
    A. It applies to both service and manufacturing companies.
    B. It is used to reduce performance costs.
    C. It rejects the idea of "good enough."
    D. It can be applied only to improve processes and products but not services and practices.

24. **LO** 1.5 A company's attempts to utilize sustainable business practices with regard to its employees, the environment, and society are known as _____.
    A. a balanced scorecard
    B. corporate social responsibility
    C. total quality management
    D. value chain

25. **LO** 1.5 A process that is often linked to Six Sigma and is designed toward continuous improvement by eliminating waste is _____.
    A. kamikaze
    B. value chain
    C. total quality management
    D. kaizen

26. **LO** 1.5 An inventory system that organizations use to increase efficiency and decrease waste is _____.
    A. corporate social responsibility
    B. just-in-time manufacturing
    C. total quality management
    D. Lean Six Sigma

27. **LO** 1.5 A quality control program that depends on multiple team members for removing waste and diminishing defects within products is _____.
    A. kaizen
    B. total quality management
    C. Lean Six Sigma
    D. a balanced scorecard

Questions

1. LO 1.1 Carlita believes an important part of the planning process for managers is being sure to position the company to achieve its goals. She thinks that positioning is an extensive concept and can depend on the right information and that managerial accountants assist in positioning the company. Is she correct? Explain.

2. LO 1.1 What are some activities and tasks a manager might perform when engaging in the controlling function of management responsibilities?

3. LO 1.1 If there are deviations from the stated goals and objectives, what steps can managers take to get back on track? Provide at least two specific examples.

4. LO 1.1 Explain how managerial accountants help managers plan, control, and evaluate.

5. LO 1.1 How do the subject matter of reports and the verification of reports differ between financial accounting and managerial accounting?

6. LO 1.2 What is the purpose of management accounting?

7. LO 1.2 Who are the primary users of the information gathered by managerial accountants?

8. LO 1.2 What are the key differences between financial accounting and managerial accounting?

9. LO 1.3 Other than accounting skills, what six qualities must be prevalent in a managerial accountant?

10. LO 1.3 Explain how having more than one of the accounting credentials would be beneficial to an accounting career.

11. LO 1.3 Briefly discuss the chain of command for someone being hired into an organization as a staff managerial accountant.

12. LO 1.3 According to the information available at http://www.accounting.com/careers/, what are six different areas of accounting on which you can focus your career?

13. LO 1.3 According to the information on management accounting available at http://www.accounting.com/careers/, what are some areas of specialization?

14. LO 1.3 Go to http://www.accounting.com/careers/ and look up your state to find projected job growth and projected salaries.

15. LO 1.4 What other professional business organizations have a code of ethics?

16. LO 1.4 How can having a bonus system based purely on sales goals create an environment that encourages unethical behavior?

17. LO 1.4 What led to the United States Congress passing the public accounting reform act called Sarbanes-Oxley?

18. LO 1.5 What is an enterprise resource planning (ERP) system? What are the principal benefits of such a system?

19. LO 1.5 Describe what is meant by the term "balanced" in the term *balanced scorecard method*.

20. LO 1.5 What is corporate social responsibility, and who are the stakeholders?

Exercise Set A

EA1. LO 1.2 Indicate whether each statement describes financial accounting or managerial accounting.
  A. The information is directed at external users who are making decisions pertaining to investing, extending credit, and other decisions.
  B. The principal users are the organization's managers.
  C. The key focus is on the entity as a whole.
  D. The rules and principles are very flexible.
  E. The information gathered is usually available after an independent audit has been completed.

EA2. LO 1.2 Identify the following as True or False:
  A. Managerial accounting reports must comply with the rules set in place by the FASB.
  B. Financial accounting reports are typically general-purpose reports.
  C. Financial accounting reports pertain to the entity as a whole, whereas managerial accounting focuses more on subunits of the organization.
  D. The main users of the financial accounting information are the internal users.
  E. Managerial reports are prepared on an as-needed basis.
  F. Financial accounting reports often must be audited at least annually by an independent auditor.

EA3. LO 1.2 Define each of these users of accounting information as an internal user of external user:
  A. Management
  B. Employees
  C. Investors
  D. Creditors
  E. Customers
  F. Tax authorities

EA4. LO 1.2 Discuss what information would be most useful for these users of accounting information:
  A. Management
  B. Employees
  C. Investors
  D. Creditors
  E. Customers
  F. Tax authorities

EA5. LO 1.3 Taylor Speedy has prepared the following list of statements about managerial accounting, financial accounting, and the functions of management. Identify each statement as true or false.
  A. Financial accounting centers on providing information to internal users.
  B. Staff positions are directly involved in the company's primary revenue-generating activities.
  C. Preparation of budgets is part of financial accounting.
  D. Managerial accounting applies only to merchandising and manufacturing companies.
  E. Both managerial accounting and financial accounting deal with many of the same economic events.

EA6. LO 1.3 Match the term with the description:

A. Certified Public Accountant	i. Specialist in corporate accounting management; favors financial analytics, budgeting, and strategic domains
B. Certified Financial Analyst	ii. Considered the top tier in accounting certifications; must pass a four-part exam, with education and work experience requirements
C. Certified Management Accountant	iii. Designation that is exclusively for auditors of the public sector
D. Certified Internal Auditor	iv. Credential for auditors who work within organizations and is one of a few that is accepted worldwide
E. Certified Fraud Examiner	v. Certification for those with a career in finance and investment areas
F. Certified Government Auditing Professional	vi. Designation that proves proficiency in fraud prevention, detection, and deterrence

EA7. LO 1.4 After the passage of the Sarbanes-Oxley Act in 2002, many new responsibilities were put into place for organizations and their management. What are the four significant issues that were addressed by the act and its provisions as presented in this chapter? How does the act and its various requirements help deter fraudulent activity?

EA8. LO 1.4 Indicate whether each of the following statements is true or false.
A. Bribery in the world of business typically happens when an organization or representative of an organization gives financial benefits to an official to gain favor or manipulate a business decision.
B. The Foreign Corrupt Practices Act was implemented in the aftermath of disclosures that businesses were violating the IMA Code of Ethics.
C. Managers are required to follow specific rules issued by the IMA for internal financial reporting.
D. Ethics is more than obeying laws.
E. The Sarbanes-Oxley Act addressed public company accounting reform.

EA9. LO 1.5 Match each lean business method to the best description:

A. Just-in-time manufacturing	i. The focus is on quality throughout the entire process.
B. Continuous improvements	ii. Inventory is attained or produced only as needed.
C. Total quality management	iii. A combined effort of team members is used to eliminate waste and defects.
D. Lean Six Sigma	iv. All managers and employees are always looking for ways to improve operations.

EA10. LO 1.5 For each of the activities listed, choose the manufacturing concept that applies: (i) just-in-time inventory, (ii) continuous improvement, or (iii) total quality management.
   A. A company receives inventory daily based on customer orders.
   B. Manufacturing factories have been arranged in such a fashion to reduce inefficiencies.
   C. Companies organize customer focus groups in order to look at customer needs and expectations.
   D. The entire production process is standardized and written down with procedures.
   E. Each customer receives a survey of satisfaction with their product.
   F. All orders are complete and shipped within three business days.

EA11. LO 1.5 Look up the definitions for the following terms:
   A. Budget (Budgeting)
   B. Capital budget (Capital Budgeting Decisions)
   C. Balanced scorecard (Balanced Scorecard and Other Performance Measures)
   D. Break-Even point (Cost Volume Profit Analysis)

Provide examples of how each of these terms is used in your own life and how using these practices is useful.

Exercise Set B

EB1. LO 1.2 Indicate whether the statement describes reporting by the financial accounting function or the managerial accounting function of an organization.
   A. The users of the report are managers who need a daily summary of work done each shift.
   B. The report is a job cost sheet for jobs completed in a 24-hour period.
   C. The annual report is released each year on the company's website.
   D. The report is audited by the company's certified public accountant firm.
   E. The report is prepared every day because the customer service manager needs information about inventory ready to be shipped to customers.

EB2. LO 1.2 Identify the following as true or false:
   A. Financial accounting reports are *not* released to external users.
   B. Managerial accounting reports are *not* used by employees inside the organization.
   C. Managerial accounting reports include only monetary information.
   D. Financial accounting reports are monetary in nature.
   E. If a result of a company's operations is nonmonetary in nature, it must be converted to monetary units for managerial reporting.
   F. Tax authorities and government regulatory agencies are external users of financial information.

EB3. LO 1.2 Companies need to report both monetary and nonmonetary data and information.
   A. Define these two terms and provide examples of each.
   B. Discuss what sources are available that provide companies with both types of data and information.

EB4. LO 1.3 Marvin has been thinking about the fields of managerial and financial accounting and the functions of management within an organization. He has the following list of statements to understand. Identify them as true or false.
   A. Managerial accounting reports are prepared only quarterly and annually.
   B. Financial accounting reports are general-purpose reports.
   C. Managerial accounting reports pertain to subunits of the business.
   D. Managerial accounting reports must comply with GAAP.
   E. The company treasurer reports directly to the vice president of operations.

EB5. LO 1.3 Match the term with the description.

A. Chief Executive Officer	i. has responsibilities that include transferring monies between accounts and monitoring deposits
B. Chief Financial Officer	ii. the corporation officer who has the overall responsibility of the management of a company
C. Enrolled Agent	iii. a corporate officer who reports to the chief executive officer and oversees all of the accounting and finance concerns of a company
D. Cash Management Accountant	iv. the financial officer of a corporation reporting to the chief financial officer who is responsible for the accounting records and financial statements
E. Controller	v. credential focusing on a career in taxation created by the IRS to signify significant knowledge of the US tax code
F. Financial Analyst	vi. Someone who assists in preparing budgets, tracking actual costs and performs other tasks that support other management personnel in organizing forecasts and projections

EB6. LO 1.4 The Foreign Corrupt Practices Act (FCPA) was implemented in 1977. Why was it enacted, and what are its major provisions?

EB7. LO 1.4 Indicate whether each of the following statements is true or false.
   A. Section 302 of Sarbanes-Oxley requires the CEO and CFO to review all financial reports and sign the reports.
   B. One of the three questions put forth by the Institute of Business Ethics is "Do I mind others knowing what I have done?"
   C. Ethical issues may be faced on a small scale, such as making a business decision to produce excess inventory for the sole purpose of trying to influence managers' bonuses.
   D. A manager who spends excess budgeted funds remaining at the end of a fiscal year on unnecessary expenditures thinking that it is better to "use it than lose it" is acting ethically.
   E. The Foreign Corrupt Practices Act was implemented in 2001 to protect investors by enhancing the accuracy and reliability of corporate financial statements and disclosures.

Thought Provokers

TP1. LO 1.1 Table 1.3 shows how different areas within the business world use the information from managerial accountants. Think of the ways that the events coordinator for the United Way (a nonprofit charitable organization) would use each area (planning, controlling, and evaluation).

TP2. LO 1.1 There are individuals who are under the impression that managerial accounting provides services mainly for manufacturing organizations. Are they correct? Explain.

TP3. LO 1.3 Think about the organization chart in Figure 1.7. Describe ways in which each of the accounting and managerial functions might overlap and complement each other.

TP4. LO 1.4 Controversy tends to surround the topic of whistleblowers. For example, should they be considered heroes or traitors? Many pro-whistleblowing policies have been enacted by the federal government to allow these individuals to reap significant monetary rewards for coming forward and giving information about behaviors and actions such as corporate fraud and unethical deeds. Many corporate whistleblowers face negative consequences of their actions, such as reassignment, revenge, and hate crimes, and are seen as traitors (e.g., Edward Snowden and Gina Gray). Yet Sherron Watkins and Cynthia Cooper were celebrated as heroes. Look up the stories of Sherron Watkins and Cynthia Cooper. Why do you think that some whistleblowers are vilified and others made to be heroes?

2 Building Blocks of Managerial Accounting

Figure 2.1 Building Blocks of Managerial Accounting. How costs behave and how managers can estimate future costs are the building blocks of managerial accounting. (credit: modification of "Blocks" by "Hey Paul"/Flickr, CC BY 2.0)

Chapter Outline

LO 2.1 Distinguish between Merchandising, Manufacturing, and Service Organizations

LO 2.2 Identify and Apply Basic Cost Behavior Patterns

LO 2.3 Estimate a Variable and Fixed Cost Equation and Predict Future Costs

Why It Matters

Many 16-year-olds in the United States eagerly anticipate having a car of their own and the freedom that comes from having their own means of transportation. For many, this means not having to bum a ride from a friend, take a bus, hire Uber or Lyft, or worse, borrow the parents' car. However, as appealing as having one's own set of wheels sounds, it comes with an array of costs that many young drivers do not anticipate. Some of the costs associated with buying and owning a car are fixed, and some vary with the level of activity. For example, a driver pays car payments and insurance premiums every month whether or not the car is driven, but the cost of maintenance and gas can be controlled by driving less. A driver cannot control the price of gasoline or the mechanic's hourly wage but can control how much of each is used each month.

Just as car owners incur a variety of costs—fixed, variable, controllable, and uncontrollable—businesses incur these types of costs as well. The goal of managerial accountants is to use this cost information to assist management in both long- and short-term decision-making. Managerial accounting follows standards and best practices for reporting cost data that are less formal than those used for financial accounting. This means management often has the discretion to determine how costs are used internally.

Since businesses collect and analyze cost data for internal use, there may be distinct differences among businesses in how they estimate and treat certain costs. What does not change, regardless of how cost data is used, are generally agreed upon cost classifications managers use for decision-making. In short, most businesses incur the same *type* of costs, but how each firm classifies and manages these costs can vary widely.

2.1 Distinguish between Merchandising, Manufacturing, and Service Organizations

Most businesses can be classified into one or more of these three categories: manufacturing, merchandising, or service. Stated in broad terms, manufacturing firms typically produce a product that is then sold to a merchandising entity (a retailer) For example, Proctor and Gamble produces a variety of shampoos that it sells to retailers, such as Walmart, Target, or Walgreens. A service entity provides a service such as accounting or legal services or cable television and internet connections.

Some companies combine aspects of two or all three of these categories within a single business. If it chooses, the same company can both produce and market its products directly to consumers. For example, Nike produces products that it directly sells to consumers and products that it sells to retailers. An example of a company that fits all three categories is Apple, which produces phones, sells them directly to consumers, and also provides services, such as extended warranties.

Regardless of whether a business is a manufacturer of products, a retailer selling to the customer, a service provider, or some combination , all businesses set goals and have strategic plans that guide their operations. Strategic plans look very different from one company to another. For example, a retailer such as Walmart may have a strategic plan that focuses on increasing same store sales. Facebook's strategic plan may focus on increasing subscribers and attracting new advertisers. An accounting firm may have long-term goals to open offices in neighboring cities in order to serve more clients. Although the goals differ, the process all companies use to achieve their goals is the same. First, they must develop a plan for how they will achieve the goal, and then management will gather, analyze, and use information regarding costs to make decisions, implement plans, and achieve goals.

Table 2.1 lists examples of these costs. Some of these are similar across different types of businesses; others are unique to a particular business.

	Costs
Type of Business	**Costs Incurred**
Manufacturing Business	• Direct labor • Plant and equipment • Manufacturing overhead • Raw materials
Merchandising Business	• Lease on retail space • Merchandise inventory • Retail sales staff

Table 2.1 Some costs, such as raw materials, are unique to a particular type of business. Other costs, such as billing and collections, are common to most businesses, regardless of the type.

Costs	
Type of Business	**Costs Incurred**
Service Business	• Billing and collections • Computer network equipment • Professional staff

Table 2.1 Some costs, such as raw materials, are unique to a particular type of business. Other costs, such as billing and collections, are common to most businesses, regardless of the type.

Knowing the basic characteristics of each cost category is important to understanding how businesses measure, classify, and control costs.

Merchandising Organizations

A merchandising firm is one of the most common types of businesses. A **merchandising firm** is a business that purchases finished products and resells them to consumers. Consider your local grocery store or retail clothing store. Both of these are merchandising firms. Often, merchandising firms are referred to as *resellers* or *retailers* since they are in the business of reselling a product to the consumer at a profit.

Think about purchasing toothpaste from your local drug store. The drug store purchases tens of thousands of tubes of toothpaste from a wholesale distributor or manufacturer in order to get a better per-tube cost. Then, they add their mark-up (or profit margin) to the toothpaste and offer it for sale to you. The drug store did not manufacture the toothpaste; instead, they are reselling a toothpaste that they purchased. Virtually all of your daily purchases are made from merchandising firms such as Walmart, Target, Macy's, Walgreens, and AutoZone.

Merchandising firms account for their costs in a different way from other types of business organizations. To understand merchandising costs, Figure 2.2 shows a simplified income statement for a merchandising firm:

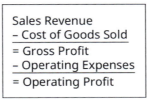

Figure 2.2 Simplified Income Statement for a Merchandising Firm. (attribution: Copyright Rice University, OpenStax, under CC BY-NC-SA 4.0 license)

This simplified income statement demonstrates how merchandising firms account for their sales cycle or process. *Sales revenue* is the income generated from the sale of finished goods to consumers rather than from the manufacture of goods or provision of services. Since a merchandising firm has to purchase goods for resale, they account for this cost as *cost of goods sold*—what it cost them to acquire the goods that are then sold to the customer. The difference between what the drug store paid for the toothpaste and the revenue generated by selling the toothpaste to consumers is their *gross profit*. However, in order to generate sales revenue, merchandising firms incur expenses related to the process of operating their business and selling the merchandise. These costs are called *operating expenses*, and the business must deduct them from the gross profit to determine the *operating profit*. (Note that while the terms "operating profit" and "operating income" are often used interchangeably, in real-world interactions you should confirm exactly what the user means in using those terms.) Operating expenses incurred by a merchandising firm include insurance, marketing, administrative salaries, and rent.

Figure 2.3 Shopping Mall. Merchandising firms must identify and manage their costs to remain competitive and attract customers to their business. (credit: "stairs shopping mall" by "jarmoluk"/Pixabay, CC0)

CONCEPTS IN PRACTICE

Balancing Revenue and Expenses

Plum Crazy is a small boutique selling the latest in fashion trends. They purchase clothing and fashion accessories from several distributors and manufacturers for resale. In 2017, they reported these revenue and expenses:

Rent	$12,000	Sales revenue	$150,000
Advertising	4,000	Cost of goods sold	60,000
Utilities	1,500	Supplies	3,000
Salaries and wages	35,000	Miscellaneous	1,200

Before examining the income statement, let's look at Cost of Goods Sold in more detail. Merchandising companies have to account for inventory, a topic covered in Inventory (http://cnx.org/content/m67888/latest/) . As you recall, merchandising companies carry inventory from one period to another. When they prepare their income statement, a crucial step is identifying the actual cost of goods that were sold for the period. For Plum Crazy, their Cost of Goods Sold was calculated as shown in Figure 2.4.

PLUM CRAZY
Cost of Goods Sold
For the Year Ended December 31, 2017

Beginning Merchandise Inventory	$ 23,500
+ Purchases	115,000
Goods Available for Sale	138,500
– Ending Merchandise Inventory	(78,500)
Cost of Goods Sold	$ 60,000

Figure 2.4 Plum Crazy's Cost of Goods Sold Statement. (attribution: Copyright Rice University, OpenStax, under CC BY-NC-SA 4.0 license)

Once the calculation of the Cost of Goods Sold has been completed, Plum Crazy can now construct their income statement, which would appear as shown in Figure 2.5.

PLUM CRAZY
Income Statement
For the Year Ended December 31, 2017

Sales Revenue		$150,000
Cost of Goods Sold		60,000
Gross Profit		90,000
Advertising	$ 4,000	
Rent	12,000	
Salaries and Wages	35,000	
Supplies	3,000	
Utilities	1,500	
Miscellaneous	1,200	
Operating Expenses	56,700	56,700
Net Income		$ 33,300

Figure 2.5 Plum Crazy's Income Statement. (attribution: Copyright Rice University, OpenStax, under CC BY-NC-SA 4.0 license)

Since merchandising firms must pass the cost of goods on to the consumer to earn a profit, they are extremely cost sensitive. Large merchandising businesses like Walmart, Target, and Best Buy manage costs by buying in bulk and negotiating with manufacturers and suppliers to drive the per-unit cost.

CONTINUING APPLICATION AT WORK

Introduction to the Gearhead Outfitters Story

Gearhead Outfitters, founded by Ted Herget in 1997 in Jonesboro, AR, is a retail chain which sells outdoor gear for men, women, and children. The company's inventory includes clothing, footwear for hiking and running, camping gear, backpacks, and accessories, by brands such as The North Face, Birkenstock, Wolverine, Yeti, Altra, Mizuno, and Patagonia. Ted fell in love with the outdoor lifestyle while working as a ski instructor in Colorado and wanted to bring that feeling back home to Arkansas. And so, Gearhead was born in a small downtown location in Jonesboro. The company has had great success over the years, expanding to numerous locations in Ted's home state, as well as Louisiana, Oklahoma, and Missouri.

While Ted knew his industry when starting Gearhead, like many entrepreneurs he faced regulatory and financial issues which were new to him. Several of these issues were related to accounting and the wealth of decision-making information which accounting systems provide.

For example, measuring revenue and expenses, providing information about cash flow to potential lenders, analyzing whether profit and positive cash flow is sustainable to allow for expansion, and managing inventory levels. Accounting, or the preparation of financial statements (balance sheet, income statement, and statement of cash flows), provides the mechanism for business owners such as Ted to make fundamentally sound business decisions.

LINK TO LEARNING

Walmart is inarguably a retail giant, but how did the company become so successful? Read the article about how low costs have allowed Walmart to keep prices low while still making a large profit (https://openstax.org/l/50Walmart) to learn more.

Manufacturing Organizations

A **manufacturing organization** is a business that uses parts, components, or raw materials to produce finished goods (Figure 2.6). These finished goods are sold either directly to the consumer or to other manufacturing firms that use them as a component part to produce a finished product. For example, Diehard manufactures automobile batteries that are sold directly to consumers by retail outlets such as AutoZone, Costco, and Advance Auto. However, these batteries are also sold to automobile manufacturers such as Ford, Chevrolet, or Toyota to be installed in cars during the manufacturing process. Regardless of who the final consumer of the final product is, Diehard must control its costs so that the sale of batteries generates revenue sufficient to keep the organization profitable.

Figure 2.6 Manufacturing firms apply direct labor to raw materials in order to produce the finished goods purchased from retailers. (credit: "work manufactures" by "dodaning0"/Pixabay, CC0)

Manufacturing firms are more complex organizations than merchandising firms and therefore have a larger variety of costs to control. For example, a merchandising firm may purchase furniture to sell to consumers, whereas a manufacturing firm must acquire raw materials such as lumber, paint, hardware, glue, and varnish that they transform into furniture. The manufacturer incurs additional costs, such as direct labor, to convert the raw materials into furniture. Operating a physical plant where the production process takes place also generates costs. Some of these costs are tied directly to production, while others are general expenses necessary to operate the business. Because the manufacturing process can be highly complex, manufacturing firms constantly evaluate their production processes to determine where cost savings are possible.

CONCEPTS IN PRACTICE

Cost Control

Controlling costs is an integral function of all managers, but companies often hire personnel to specifically oversee cost control. As you've learned, controlling costs is vital in all industries, but at Hilton Hotels, they translate this into the position of Cost Controller. Here is an excerpt from one of Hilton's recent job postings.

Position Title: Cost Controller

Job Description: "A Cost Controller will work with all Heads of Departments to effectively control all products that enter and exit the hotel."[1]

> **Job Requirements:**
>
> "As Cost Controller, you will work with all Heads of Departments to effectively control all products that enter and exit the hotel. Specifically, you will be responsible for performing the following tasks to the highest standards:
>
> - Review the daily intake of products into the hotel and ensure accurate pricing and quantity of goods received
> - Control the stores by ensuring accuracy of inventory and stock control and the pricing of goods received
> - Alert relevant parties of slow-moving goods and goods nearing expiry dates to reduce waste and alter product purchasing to accommodate
> - Manage cost reporting on a weekly basis
> - Attend finance meetings, as required
> - Maintain good communication and working relationships with all hotel areas
> - Act in accordance with fire, health and safety regulations and follow the correct procedures when required"[2]
>
> As you can see, the individual in this position will interact with others across the organization to find ways to control costs for the benefit of the company. Some of the benefits of cost control include:
>
> - Lowering overall company expenses, thereby increasing net income.
> - Freeing up financial resources for investment in research & development of new or improved products, goods, or services
> - Providing funding for employee development and training, benefits, and bonuses
> - Allowing corporate earnings to be used to support humanitarian and charitable causes

Manufacturing organizations account for costs in a way that is similar to that of merchandising firms. However, as you will learn, there is a significant difference in the calculation of cost of goods sold. Figure 2.7 shows a simplification of the income statement for a manufacturing firm:

```
Sales
– Cost of Goods Sold
= Gross Profit
– Operating Expenses
= Operating Profit
```

Figure 2.7 Simplified Income Statement for a Manufacturing Firm. (attribution: Copyright Rice University, OpenStax, under CC BY-NC-SA 4.0 license)

At first it appears that there is no difference between the income statements of the merchandising firm and the manufacturing firm. However, the difference is in how these two types of firms account for the cost of goods sold. Merchandising firms determine their cost of goods sold by accounting for both existing inventory and new purchases, as shown in the Plum Crazy example. It is typically easy for merchandising firms to calculate their costs because they know exactly what they paid for their merchandise.

---

1 Hilton. "Cost Controller: Job Description." Hosco. https://www.hosco.com/en/job/hilton-istanbul-bomonti-hotel-conference-center/cost-controller

2 Hilton. "Cost Controller: Job Description." Hosco. https://www.hosco.com/en/job/hilton-istanbul-bomonti-hotel-conference-center/cost-controller

Unlike merchandising firms, manufacturing firms must calculate their cost of goods sold based on how much they manufacture and how much it costs them to manufacture those goods. This requires manufacturing firms to prepare an additional statement before they can prepare their income statement. This additional statement is the *Cost of Goods Manufactured* statement. Once the cost of goods manufactured is calculated, the cost is then incorporated into the manufacturing firm's income statement to calculate its cost of goods sold.

One thing manufacturing firms must consider in their cost of goods manufactured is that, at any given time, they have products at varying levels of production: some are finished and others are still process. The cost of goods manufactured statement measures the cost of the goods actually finished during the period, whether or not they were started during that period.

Before examining the typical manufacturing firm's process to track cost of goods manufactured, you need basic definitions of three terms in the schedule of Costs of Goods Manufactured: direct materials, direct labor, and manufacturing overhead. **Direct materials** are the components used in the production process whose costs can be identified on a per item-produced basis. For example, if you are producing cars, the engine would be a direct material item. The direct material cost would be the cost of one engine. **Direct labor** represents production labor costs that can be identified on a per item-produced basis. Referring to the car production example, assume that the engines are placed in the car by individuals rather than by an automated process. The direct labor cost would be the amount of labor in hours multiplied by the hourly labor cost. **Manufacturing overhead** generally includes those costs incurred in the production process that are not economically feasible to measure as direct material or direct labor costs. Examples include the department manager's salary, the production factory's utilities, or glue used to attach rubber molding in the auto production process. Since there are so many possible costs that can be classified as manufacturing overhead, they tend to be grouped and then allocated in a predetermined manner to the production process.

Figure 2.8 is an example of the calculation of the Cost of Goods Manufactured for Koeller Manufacturing. It demonstrates the relationship between cost of goods manufactured and cost of goods in progress and includes the three main types of manufacturing costs.

KOELLER MANUFACTURING
Schedule of Cost of Goods Manufactured
For the Month Ended March 31, 2017

Work in Process Inventory (beginning balance)		$ 75,000
Current Manufacturing Costs:		
Direct Material	$15,000	
Direct Labor	25,000	
Manufacturing Overhead	23,000	
Total Manufacturing Costs		63,000
Total Cost of Work in Process		138,000
– Work in Process, ending balance		43,000
Cost of Goods Manufactured		$ 95,000

Figure 2.8 Koeller Manufacturing's Cost of Goods Manufactured. (attribution: Copyright Rice University, OpenStax, under CC BY-NC-SA 4.0 license)

As you can see, the manufacturing firm takes into account its work-in-process (WIP) inventory as well as the costs incurred during the current period to finish not only the units that were in the beginning WIP inventory, but also a portion of any production that was started but not finished during the month. Notice that the current manufacturing costs, or the additional costs incurred during the month, include direct materials, direct labor, and manufacturing overhead. Direct materials are calculated as

> Materials Inventory (beginning balance)
> + Net Material Purchases
> = Materials Available for Use
> − Materials Inventory (ending balance)
> = Direct Materials Used in Production

All of these costs are carefully tracked and classified because the cost of manufacturing is a vital component of the schedule of cost of goods sold. To continue with the example, Koeller Manufacturing calculated that the cost of goods sold was $95,000, which is carried through to the Schedule of Cost of Goods Sold (Figure 2.9).

KOELLER MANUFACTURING
Schedule of Cost of Goods Sold
For the Month Ended March 31, 2017

Beginning Finished Goods Inventory	$ 65,000
+ Cost of Goods Manufactured	95,000
Goods Available for Sale	160,000
− Ending Finished Goods Inventory	58,000
Cost of Goods Sold	$102,000

Figure 2.9 Koeller Manufacturing's Cost of Goods Sold. (attribution: Copyright Rice University, OpenStax, under CC BY-NC-SA 4.0 license)

Now when Koeller Manufacturing prepares its income statement, the simplified statement will appear as shown in Figure 2.10.

KOELLER MANUFACTURING
Income Statement
For the Month Ended March 31, 2017

Sales	$214,000
− Cost of Goods Sold	102,000
Gross Profit	112,000
− Operating Expenses	80,000
Operating Income	$ 32,000

Figure 2.10 Koeller Manufacturing's Income Statement. (attribution: Copyright Rice University, OpenStax, under CC BY-NC-SA 4.0 license)

So, even though the income statements for the merchandising firm and the manufacturing firm appear very similar at first glance, there are many more costs to be captured by the manufacturing firm. Figure 2.11 compares and contrasts the methods merchandising and manufacturing firms use to calculate the cost of goods sold in their income statement.

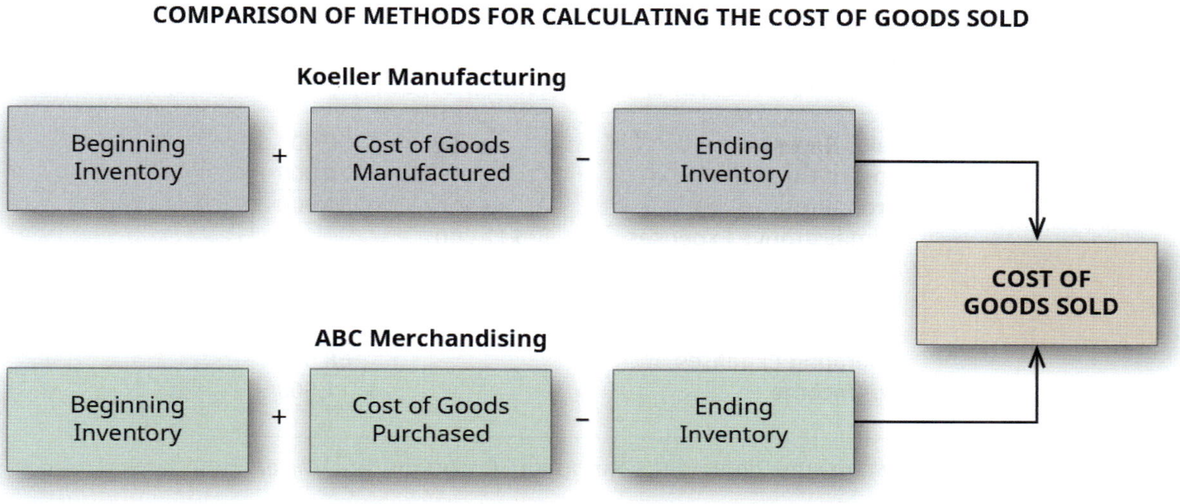

COMPARISON OF METHODS FOR CALCULATING THE COST OF GOODS SOLD

Koeller Manufacturing

Beginning Inventory + Cost of Goods Manufactured − Ending Inventory = **COST OF GOODS SOLD**

ABC Merchandising

Beginning Inventory + Cost of Goods Purchased − Ending Inventory = **COST OF GOODS SOLD**

Figure 2.11 Merchandising firms consider the cost of goods purchased, and manufacturing firms consider the cost of goods manufactured in order to determine the cost of goods sold. (attribution: Copyright Rice University, OpenStax, under CC BY-NC-SA 4.0 license)

CONCEPTS IN PRACTICE

Calculating Cost of Goods Sold in Manufacturing

Just Desserts is a bakery that produces and sells cakes and pies to grocery stores for resale. Although they are a small manufacturer, they incur many of the costs of a much larger organization. In 2017, they reported these revenue and expenses:

Office rent	$20,000	Sales revenue	$150,000
Office utilities	1,500	Cost of goods sold	70,000
Administrative salaries	35,000	Administrative expenses	12,000

Their income statement is shown in Figure 2.12.

JUST DESSERTS
Income Statement
For the Year Ended December 31, 2017

Sales Revenue		$150,000
Cost of Goods Sold		70,000
Gross Profit		80,000
Administrative Expenses	$12,000	
Administrative Salaries	35,000	
Office Utilities	1,500	
Office Rent	20,000	
Operating Expenses		68,500
Net Income		$ 11,500

Figure 2.12 Just Desserts' Income Statement. (attribution: Copyright Rice University, OpenStax, under CC BY-NC-SA 4.0 license)

You'll learn more about the flow of manufacturing costs in Identify and Apply Basic Cost Behavior Patterns. For now, recognize that, unlike a merchandising firm, calculating cost of goods sold in manufacturing firms can be a complex task for management.

Service Organizations

A **service organization** is a business that earns revenue by providing **intangible products**, those that have no physical substance. The service industry is a vital sector of the U.S. economy, providing 65% of the U.S. private-sector gross domestic product and more than 79% of U.S. private-sector jobs.[3] If **tangible products**, physical goods that customers can handle and see, are provided by a service organization, they are considered ancillary sources of revenue. Large service organizations such as airlines, insurance companies, and hospitals incur a variety of costs in the provision of their services. Costs such as labor, supplies, equipment, advertising, and facility maintenance can quickly spiral out of control if management is not careful. Therefore, although their cost drivers are sometimes not as complex as those of other types of firms, cost identification and control are every bit as important in the service industry.

For example, consider the services that a law firm provides its clients. What clients pay for are services such as representation in legal proceedings, contract negotiations, and preparation of wills. Although the true value of these services is not contained in their physical form, they are of value to the client and the source of revenue to the firm. The managing partners in the firm must be as cost conscious as their counterparts in merchandising and manufacturing firms. Accounting for costs in service firms differs from merchandising and manufacturing firms in that they do not purchase or produce goods. For example, consider a medical practice. Although some services provided are tangible products, such as medications or medical devices, the primary benefits the physicians provide their patients are the intangible services that are comprised of his or her knowledge, experience, and expertise.

---

3 John Ward. "The Services Sector: How Best to Measure It?" International Trade Administration. Oct. 2010. https://2016.trade.gov/publications/ita-newsletter/1010/services-sector-how-best-to-measure-it.asp. "United States GDP from Private Services Producing Industries." Trading Economics / U.S. Bureau of Economic Analysis. July 2018. https://tradingeconomics.com/united-states/gdp-from-services. "Employment in Services (% of Total Employment) (Modeled ILO Estimate)." International Labour Organization, ILOSTAT database. The World Bank. Sept. 2018. https://data.worldbank.org/indicator/SL.SRV.EMPL.ZS.

This OpenStax book is available for free at http://cnx.org/content/col25479/1.11

Service providers have some costs (or revenue) derived from tangible goods that must be taken into account when pricing their services, but their largest cost categories are more likely to be administrative and personnel costs rather than product costs.

> Service Revenue
> − Operating Expenses
> = Operating Profit

For example, Whichard & Klein, LLP, is a full-service accounting firm with their primary offices in Baltimore, Maryland. With two senior partners and a small staff of accountants and payroll specialists, the majority of the costs they incur are related to personnel. The value of the accounting and payroll services they provide to their clients is intangible in comparison to goods sold by a merchandiser or produced by a manufacturer but has value and is the primary source of revenue for the firm. At the end of 2019, Whichard and Klein reported the following revenue and expenses:

Revenue from services provided	$412,000	Utilities	$11,000
Accounting personnel salaries	210,000	Miscellaneous expenses	7,500
Office expense	35,000	Administrative salaries	45,000
Office equipment	9,000		

Their Income Statement for the period is shown in Figure 2.13.

WHICHARD & KLEIN, LLP
Income Statement
For the Year Ended December 31, 2019

Service Revenue	$412,000
Operating Expenses	
Salaries	210,000
Office Expense	35,000
Office Equipment	9,000
Administrative Salaries	45,000
Utilities	11,000
Miscellaneous	7,500
Total Operating Expenses	317,500
Operating Income	$ 94,500

Figure 2.13 Whichard & Klein's Income Statement. (attribution: Copyright Rice University, OpenStax, under CC BY-NC-SA 4.0 license)

The bulk of the expenses incurred by Whichard & Klein are in personnel and administrative/office costs, which are very common among businesses that have services as their primary source of revenue.

CONCEPTS IN PRACTICE

Revenue and Expenses for a Law Office

The revenue and expenses for a law firm illustrate how the income statement for a service firm differs from that of a merchandising or manufacturing firm.

Welch & Graham is a well-established law firm that provides legal services in the areas of criminal law, real estate transactions, and personal injury. The firm employs several attorneys, paralegals, and office support staff. In 2017, they reported the following revenue and expenses:

Office rent	$ 20,000	Paralegal salaries	$ 100,000
Office utilities	12,500	Service revenue	1,500,000
Administrative salaries	150,000	Office expenses	12,000
Attorneys' salaries	750,000		

Their income statement is shown in Figure 2.14.

WELCH & GRAHAM, ATTORNEYS AT LAW
Income Statement
For the Year Ended December 31, 2017

Service Revenue		$1,500,000
Operating Expenses		
Administrative Salaries	$ 150,000	
Attorney Salaries	750,000	
Office Expenses	12,000	
Office Rent	20,000	
Paralegal Salaries	100,000	
Office Utilities Expenses	12,500	
Total Operating Expenses		1,044,500
Net Income		$ 455,500

Figure 2.14 Welch & Graham's Income Statement. (attribution: Copyright Rice University, OpenStax, under CC BY-NC-SA 4.0 license)

As you can see, the majority of the costs incurred by the law firm are personnel related. They may also incur costs from equipment and materials such computer networks, phone and switchboard equipment, rent, insurance, and law library materials necessary to support the practice, but these costs represent a much smaller percentage of total cost than the administrative and personnel costs.

THINK IT THROUGH

Expanding a Business

Margo is the owner of a small retail business that sells gifts and home decorating accessories. Her business is well established, and she is now considering taking over additional retail space to expand her business to include gourmet foods and gift baskets. Based on customer feedback, she is confident that there is a demand for these items, but she is unsure how large that demand really is. Expanding her business this way will require that she incur not only new costs but also increases in existing costs.

Margo has asked for your help in identifying the impact of her decision to expand in terms of her costs. When discussing these cost increases, be sure to specifically identify those costs that are directly tied to her products and that would be considered overhead expenses.

2.2 Identify and Apply Basic Cost Behavior Patterns

Now that we have identified the three key types of businesses, let's identify cost behaviors and apply them to the business environment. In managerial accounting, different companies use the term *cost* in different ways depending on how they will use the cost information. Different decisions require different costs classified in different ways. For instance, a manager may need cost information to plan for the coming year or to make decisions about expanding or discontinuing a product or service. In practice, the classification of costs changes as the use of the cost data changes. In fact, a single cost, such as rent, may be classified by one company as a fixed cost, by another company as a committed cost, and by even another company as a period cost. Understanding different cost classifications and how certain costs can be used in different ways is critical to managerial accounting.

ETHICAL CONSIDERATIONS

Institute of Management Accountants and Certified Management Accountant Certification

Managerial accountants provide businesses with clear and direct insight into the monetary effects of any particular operational action under consideration. They are expected to report financial information in a transparent and ethical fashion. The Institute of Management Accountants (IMA) offers the Certified Management Accountant (CMA) certification. IMA members and CMAs agree to uphold a set of ethical principles that includes honesty, fairness, objectivity, and responsibility. Any managerial accountant, even if not an IMA member or certified CMA, should act in accordance with these principles and encourage coworkers to follow ethical principles for reporting financial results and monetary effects of financial decisions related to their organization. The IMA Committee on Ethics encourages organizations and individuals to adopt, promote, and execute business practices consistent with high ethical standards.[4]

Major Cost Behavior Patterns

Any discussion of costs begins with the understanding that most costs will be classified in one of three ways: fixed costs, variable costs, or mixed costs. The costs that don't fall into one of these three categories are hybrid costs, which are examined only briefly because they are addressed in more advanced accounting courses. Because fixed and variable costs are the foundation of all other cost classifications, understanding whether a cost is a fixed cost or a variable cost is very important.

Fixed versus Variable Costs

A **fixed cost** is an unavoidable operating expense that does not change in total over the short term, even if a

---

4 "Ethics Center." Institute of Management Accountants. https://www.imanet.org/career-resources/ethics-center?ssopc=1

business experiences variation in its level of activity. Table 2.2 illustrates the types of fixed costs for merchandising, service, and manufacturing organizations.

Examples of Fixed Costs

Type of Business	Fixed Cost
Merchandising	Rent, insurance, managers' salaries
Manufacturing	Property taxes, insurance, equipment leases
Service	Rent, straight-line depreciation, administrative salaries, and insurance

Table 2.2

We have established that fixed costs do not change in total as the level of activity changes, but what about fixed costs on a *per-unit* basis? Let's examine Tony's screen-printing company to illustrate how costs can remain fixed in total but change on a per-unit basis.

Tony operates a screen-printing company, specializing in custom T-shirts. One of his fixed costs is his monthly rent of $1,000. Regardless of whether he produces and sells any T-shirts, he is obligated under his lease to pay $1,000 per month. However, he can consider this fixed cost on a per-unit basis, as shown in Figure 2.15.

Monthly Rent	Number of T-Shirts Manufactured	Average Rent Cost per T-Shirt
$1,000	200	$5.00
1,000	400	2.50
1,000	600	1.67

Figure 2.15 Individual Rent Cost per T-Shirt Produced. (attribution: Copyright Rice University, OpenStax, under CC BY-NC-SA 4.0 license)

Tony's information illustrates that, despite the unchanging fixed cost of rent, as the level of activity increases, the per-unit fixed cost falls. In other words, fixed costs remain fixed in total but can increase or decrease on a per-unit basis.

Two specialized types of fixed costs are committed fixed costs and discretionary fixed costs. These classifications are generally used for long-range planning purposes and are covered in upper-level managerial accounting courses, so they are only briefly described here.

Committed fixed costs are fixed costs that typically cannot be eliminated if the company is going to continue to function. An example would be the lease of factory equipment for a production company.

Discretionary fixed costs generally are fixed costs that can be incurred during some periods and postponed during other periods but which cannot normally be eliminated permanently. Examples could include advertising campaigns and employee training. Both of these costs could potentially be postponed temporarily, but the company would probably incur negative effects if the costs were permanently eliminated. These classifications are generally used for long-range planning purposes.

In addition to understanding fixed costs, it is critical to understand variable costs, the second fundamental cost classification. A **variable cost** is one that varies in direct proportion to the level of activity within the business. Typical costs that are classified as variable costs are the cost of raw materials used to produce a product, labor applied directly to the production of the product, and overhead expenses that change based upon activity. For each variable cost, there is some activity that drives the variable cost up or down. A **cost driver** is defined as any activity that causes the organization to incur a variable cost. Examples of cost drivers are direct labor hours, machine hours, units produced, and units sold. Table 2.3 provides examples of variable costs and their associated cost drivers.

Variable Costs and Associated Cost Drivers

	Variable Cost	Cost Driver
Merchandising	Total monthly hourly wages for sales staff	Hours business is open during month
Manufacturing	Direct materials used to produce one unit of product	Number of units produced
Service	Cost of laundering linens and towels	Number of hotel rooms occupied

Table 2.3

Unlike fixed costs that remain fixed in total but change on a per-unit basis, variable costs remain the same per unit, but change in total relative to the level of activity in the business. Revisiting Tony's T-Shirts, Figure 2.16 shows how the variable cost of ink behaves as the level of activity changes.

Cost of Ink per T-Shirt	Number of T-Shirts Produced	Total Variable Cost of Ink
$0.15	2,000	$300
0.15	4,000	600
0.15	6,000	900

Figure 2.16 Variable Costs per Unit. (attribution: Copyright Rice University, OpenStax, under CC BY-NC-SA 4.0 license)

As Figure 2.16 shows, the variable cost per unit (per T-shirt) does not change as the number of T-shirts produced increases or decreases. However, the variable costs change in total as the number of units produced increases or decreases. In short, total variable costs rise and fall as the level of activity (the cost driver) rises and falls.

Distinguishing between fixed and variable costs is critical because the **total cost** is the sum of all fixed costs (the **total fixed costs**) and all variable costs (the **total variable costs**). For every unit produced, every customer served, or every hotel room rented, for example, managers can determine their total costs both per unit of activity and in total by combining their fixed and variable costs together. The graphic in Figure 2.17 illustrates the concept of total costs.

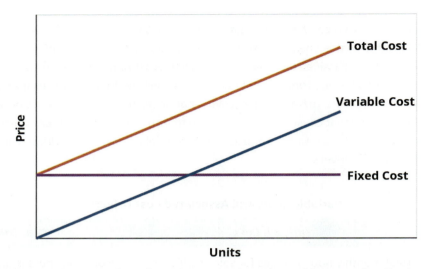

Figure 2.17 Total Cost as the Sum of Total Fixed Costs and Total Variable Costs. (attribution: Copyright Rice University, OpenStax, under CC BY-NC-SA 4.0 license)

Remember that the reason that organizations take the time and effort to classify costs as either fixed or variable is to be able to control costs. When they classify costs properly, managers can use cost data to make decisions and plan for the future of the business.

CONCEPTS IN PRACTICE

Boeing[5]

If you've ever flown on an airplane, there's a good chance you know Boeing. The Boeing Company generates around $90 billion each year from selling thousands of airplanes to commercial and military customers around the world. It employs around 200,000 people, and it's indirectly responsible for more than a million jobs through its suppliers, contractors, regulators, and others. Its main assembly line in Everett, WA, is housed in the largest building in the world, a colossal facility that covers nearly a half-trillion cubic feet. Boeing is, simply put, a massive enterprise.

And yet, Boeing's managers know the exact cost of everything the company uses to produce its airplanes: every propeller, flap, seat belt, welder, computer programmer, and so forth. Moreover, they know how those costs would change if they produced more airplanes or fewer. They also know the price at which they sold each plane and the profit the company made on each sale. Boeing's executives expect their managers to know this information, in real time, if the company is to remain profitable.

---

5   Attribution: Modification of work by Sharon Kioko and Justin Marlowe. "Cost Analysis." *Financial Strategy for Public Managers*. CC BY 4.0. https://press.rebus.community/financialstrategy/chapter/cost-analysis/

Link between Business Decision and Cost Information Utilized

Decision	Cost Information
Discontinue a product line	Variable costs, overhead directly tied to product, potential reduction in fixed costs
Add second production shift	Labor costs, cost of fringe benefits, potential overhead increases (utilities, security personnel)
Open additional retail outlets	Fixed costs, variable operating costs, potential increases in administrative expenses at corporate headquarters

Table 2.4

Average Fixed Costs versus Average Variable Costs

Another way management may want to consider their costs is as average costs. Under this approach, managers can calculate both average fixed and average variable costs. **Average fixed cost (AFC)** is the total fixed costs divided by the total number of units produced, which results in a per-unit cost. The formula is:

$$\text{Average Fixed Cost (AFC)} = \frac{\text{Total Fixed Costs}}{\text{Total Number of Units Produced}}$$

To show how a company would use AFC to make business decisions, consider Carolina Yachts, a company that manufactures sportfishing boats that are sold to consumers through a network of marinas and boat dealerships. Carolina Yachts produces 625 boats per year, and their total annual fixed costs are $1,560,000. If they want to determine an average fixed cost per unit, they will find it using the formula for AFC:

$$\text{AFC} = \frac{\$1,560,000}{625} = \$2,496 \text{ per boat}$$

When they produce 625 boats, Carolina Yachts has an AFC of $2,496 per boat. What happens to the AFC if they increase or decrease the number of boats produced? Figure 2.18 shows the AFC for different numbers of boats.

Number of Boats Produced	Total Fixed Costs	Average Fixed Cost (per boat)
500	$1,560,000	$3,120
625	1,560,000	2,496
700	1,560,000	2,229

Figure 2.18 Average Fixed Costs for Carolina Yachts. (attribution: Copyright Rice University, OpenStax, under CC BY-NC-SA 4.0 license)

We see that total fixed costs remain unchanged, but the average fixed cost per unit goes up and down with the number of boats produced. As more units are produced, the fixed costs are spread out over more units, making the fixed cost per unit fall. Likewise, as fewer boats are manufactured, the average fixed costs per unit rises. We can use a similar approach with variable costs.

Average variable cost (AVC) is the total variable costs divided by the total number of units produced, which results in a per-unit cost. Like ATC, we can use this formula:

$$\text{Average Variable Cost (AVC)} = \frac{\text{Total Variable Costs}}{\text{Total Number of Units Produced}}$$

To demonstrate AVC, let's return to Carolina Yachts, which incurs total variable costs of $6,875,000 when they produce 625 boats per year. They can express this as an average variable cost per unit:

$$\text{AVC} = \frac{\$6,875,000}{625} = \$11,000 \text{ per boat}$$

Because average variable costs are the average of all costs that change with production levels on a per-unit basis and include both direct materials and direct labor, managers often use AVC to determine if production should continue or not in the short run. As long as the price Carolina Yachts receives for their boats is greater than the per-unit AVC, they know that they are not only covering the variable cost of production, but each boat is making a contribution toward covering fixed costs. If, at any point, the average variable cost per boat rises to the point that the price no longer covers the AVC, Carolina Yachts may consider halting production until the variable costs fall again.

These changes in variable costs per unit could be caused by circumstances beyond their control, such as a shortage of raw materials or an increase in shipping costs due to high gas prices. In any case, average variable cost can be useful for managers to get a big picture look at their variable costs per unit.

LINK TO LEARNING

Watch the video from Khan Academy that uses the scenario of computer programming to teach fixed, variable, and marginal cost (https://openstax.org/l/50costing) to learn more.

Mixed Costs and Stepped Costs

Not all costs can be classified as purely fixed or purely variable. **Mixed costs** are those that have both a fixed and variable component. It is important, however, to be able to separate mixed costs into their fixed and variable components because, typically, in the short run, we can only change variable costs but not most fixed costs. To examine how these mixed costs actually work, consider the Ocean Breeze hotel.

The Ocean Breeze is located in a resort area where the county assesses an occupancy tax that has both a fixed and a variable component. Ocean Breeze pays $2,000 per month, regardless of the number of rooms rented. Even if it does not rent a single room during the month, Ocean Breeze still must remit this tax to the county. The hotel treats this $2,000 as a fixed cost. However, for every night that a room is rented, Ocean Breeze must remit an additional tax amount of $5.00 per room per night. As a result, the occupancy tax is a mixed cost. Figure 2.19 further illustrates how this mixed cost behaves.

Number of Rooms Rented per Month (Cost Driver)	Fixed Cost Component ($2,000 per month)	Variable Cost Component ($5 per room)	Total Cost (Fixed + Variable)
0	$2,000	$ 0	$2,000
60	2,000	300	2,300
85	2,000	425	2,425
100	2,000	500	2,500

Figure 2.19 Mixed Costs Example for Ocean Breeze. (attribution: Copyright Rice University, OpenStax, under CC BY-NC-SA 4.0 license)

Notice that Ocean Breeze cannot control the fixed portion of this cost and that it remains fixed in total, regardless of the activity level. On the other hand, the variable component is fixed per unit, but changes in total based upon the level of activity. The fixed portion of this cost plus the variable portion of this cost combine to make the total cost. As a result, the formula for total cost looks like this:

$$Y = a + bx$$

where Y is the total mixed cost, a is the fixed cost, b is the variable cost per unit, and x is the level of activity.

Graphically, mixed costs can be explained as shown in Figure 2.20.

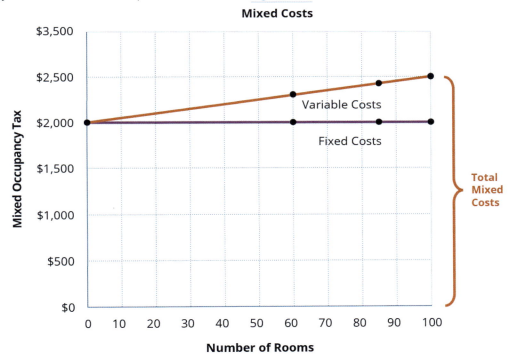

Figure 2.20 Ocean Breeze's Mixed Cost Graph. (attribution: Copyright Rice University, OpenStax, under CC BY-NC-SA 4.0 license)

The graph shows that mixed costs are typically both fixed and linear in nature. In other words, they will often have an initial cost, in Ocean Breeze's case, the $2,000 fixed component of the occupancy tax, and a variable component, the $5 per night occupancy tax. Note that the Ocean Breeze mixed cost graph starts at an initial

$2,000 for the fixed component and then increases by $5 for each night their rooms are occupied.

Some costs behave less linearly. A cost that changes with the level of activity but is not linear is classified as a **stepped cost**. Step costs remain constant at a fixed amount over a range of activity. The range over which these costs remain unchanged (fixed) is referred to as the **relevant range**, which is defined as a specific activity level that is bounded by a minimum and maximum amount. Within this relevant range, managers can predict revenue or cost levels. Then, at certain points, the step costs increase to a higher amount. Both fixed and variable costs can take on this stair-step behavior. For instance, wages often act as a stepped variable cost when employees are paid a flat salary and a commission or when the company pays overtime. Further, when additional machinery or equipment is placed into service, businesses will see their fixed costs stepped up. The "trigger" for a cost to step up is the relevant range. Graphically, step costs appear like stair steps (Figure 2.21).

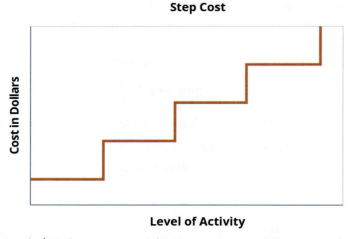

Figure 2.21 Step Cost Graph. (attribution: Copyright Rice University, OpenStax, under CC BY-NC-SA 4.0 license)

For example, suppose a quality inspector can inspect a maximum of 80 units in a regular 8-hour shift and his salary is a fixed cost. Then the relevant range for QA inspection is from 0–80 units per shift. If demand for these units increases and more than 80 inspections are needed per shift, the relevant range has been exceeded and the business will have one of two choices:

(1) Pay the quality inspector overtime in order to have the additional units inspected. This overtime will "step up" the variable cost per unit. The advantage to handling the increased cost in this way is that when demand falls, the cost can quickly be "stepped down" again. Because these types of step costs can be adjusted quickly and often, they are often still treated as variable costs for planning purposes.

(2) "Step up" fixed costs. If the company hires a second quality inspector, they would be stepping up their fixed costs. In effect, they will double the relevant range to allow for a maximum of 160 inspections per shift, assuming the second QA inspector can inspect an additional 80 units per shift. The down side to this approach is that once the new QA inspector is hired, if demand falls again, the company will be incurring fixed costs that are unnecessary. For this reason, adding salaried personnel to address a short-term increase in demand is not a decision most businesses make.

Step costs are best explained in the context of a business experiencing increases in activity beyond the relevant range. As an example, let's return to Tony's T-Shirts.

Tony's cost of operations and the associated relevant ranges are shown in Table 2.5.

Tony's T-Shirts Cost Options

	Cost	Type of Cost	Relevant Range
Lease on Screen-Printing Machine	$2,000 per month	Fixed	0–2,000 T-shirts per month
Employee	$10 per hour	Variable	20 shirts per hour
Tony's Salary	$2,500 per month	Fixed	N/A
Screen-Printing Ink	$0.25 per shirt	Variable	N/A
Building Rent	$1,500 per month	Fixed	2 screen-printing machines and 2 employees

Table 2.5

As you can see, Tony has both fixed and variable costs associated with his business. His one screen-printing machine can only produce 2,000 T-shirts per month and his current employee can produce 20 shirts per hour (160 per 8-hour work day). The space that Tony leases is large enough that he could add an additional screen-printing machine and 1 additional employee. If he expands beyond that, he will need to lease a larger space, and presumably his rent would increase at that point. It is easy for Tony to predict his costs as long as he operates within the relevant ranges by applying the total cost equation $Y = a + bx$. So, for Tony, as long as he produces 2,000 or fewer T-shirts, his total cost will be found by $Y = \$6,000 + \$0.75x$, where the variable cost of $0.75 is the $0.25 cost of the ink per shirt and $0.50 per shirt for labor ($10 per hour wage/20 shirts per hour). As soon as his production passes the 2,000 T-shirts that his one employee and one machine can handle, he will have to add a second employee and lease a second screen-printing machine. In other words, his fixed costs will rise from $6,000 to $8,000, and his variable cost per T-shirt will rise from $0.75 to $1.25 (ink plus 2 workers). Thus, his new cost equation is $Y = \$8,000 + \$1.25x$ until he "steps up" again and adds a third machine *and* moves to a new location with a presumably higher rent. Let's take a look at this in chart form to better illustrate the "step" in cost Tony will experience as he steps past 2,000 T-shirts.

Tony's cost information is shown in the chart for volume between 500 and 4,000 shirts.

Number of T-Shirts	Total Cost (rounded)
500	$ 6,375
750	6,563
1,000	6,750
1,250	6,938
1,500	7,125
1,750	7,313
2,000	7,500
2,250	10,813
2,500	11,125
2,750	11,438
3,000	11,750
3,250	12,063
3,500	12,375
3,750	12,688

When presented graphically, notice what happens when Tony steps outside of his original relevant range and has to add a second employee and a second screen-printing machine:

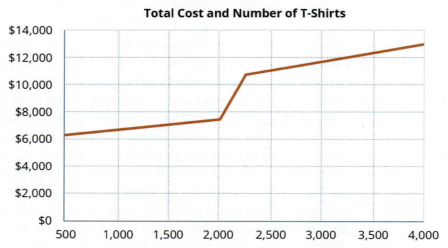

Figure 2.22 Stepped Variable Costs for Tony's T-Shirts. (attribution: Copyright Rice University, OpenStax, under CC BY-NC-SA 4.0 license)

It is important to remember that even though Tony's costs stepped up when he exceeded his original capacity (relevant range), the *behavior* of the costs did not change. His fixed costs still remained fixed in total and his total variable cost rose as the number of T-shirts he produced rose. Table 2.6 summarizes how costs behave within their relevant ranges.

Summary of Fixed and Variable Cost Behaviors

Cost	In Total	Per Unit
Variable Cost	Changes in response to the level of activity	Remains fixed per unit regardless of the level of activity
Fixed Cost	Does not change with the level of activity, within the relevant range, but does change when the relevant range changes	Changes based upon activity within the relevant range: increased activity decreases per-unit cost; decreased activity increases per-unit cost

Table 2.6

Product versus Period Costs

Many businesses can make decisions by dividing their costs into fixed and variable costs, but there are some business decisions that require grouping costs differently. Sometimes companies need to consider how those costs are reported in the financial statements. At other times, companies group costs based on functions within the business. For example, a business would group administrative and selling expenses by the period (monthly or quarterly) so that they can be reported on an Income Statement. However, a manufacturing firm may carry product costs such as materials from one period to the other in order to have the costs "travel" with the units being produced. It is possible that both the selling and administrative costs and materials costs have both fixed and variable components. As a result, it may be necessary to analyze some fixed costs together with some variable costs. Ultimately, businesses strategically group costs in order to make them more useful for decision-making and planning. Two of the broadest and most common grouping of costs are product costs and period costs.

Product costs are all those associated with the acquisition or production of goods and products. When products are purchased for resale, the cost of goods is recorded as an asset on the company's balance sheet. It is not until the products are sold that they become an expense on the income statement. By moving product costs to the expense account for the cost of goods sold, they are easily matched to the sales revenue income account. For example, Bert's Bikes is a bicycle retailer who purchases bikes from several wholesale distributors and manufacturers. When Bert purchases bicycles for resale, he places the cost of the bikes into his inventory account, because that is what those bikes are—his inventory available for sale. It is not until someone purchases a bike that it creates sales revenue, and in order to fulfill the requirements of double-entry accounting, he must match that income with an expense: the cost of goods sold (Figure 2.23).

JOURNAL			
Date	Account	Debit	Credit
	Cost of Goods Sold Finished Goods Inventory *To record the cost of products sold*	25,000	25,000

Figure 2.23 Journal Entry for Cost of Goods Sold. Product costs are collected in the finished goods inventory, where they remain until the goods are sold. (attribution: Copyright Rice University, OpenStax, under CC BY-NC-SA 4.0 license)

Some product costs have both a fixed and variable component. For example, Bert purchases 10 bikes for $100 each. The distributor charges $10 per bike for shipping for 1 to 10 bikes but $8 per bike for 11 to 20 bikes. This shipping cost is fixed per unit but varies in total. If Bert wants to save money and control his cost of goods sold, he can order an 11th bike and drop his shipping cost by $2 per bike. It is important for Bert to know what is fixed and what is variable so that he can control his costs as much as possible.

What about the costs Bert incurs that are not product costs? **Period costs** are simply all of the expenses that are not product costs, such as all selling and administrative expenses. It is important to remember that period costs are treated as expenses in the period in which they occur. In other words, they follow the rules of accrual accounting practice by recognizing the cost (expense) in the period in which they occur regardless of when the cash changes hands. For example, Bert pays his business insurance in January of each year. Bert's annual insurance premium is $10,800, which is $900 per month. Each month, Bert will recognize 1/12 of this insurance cost as an expense in the period in which it is incurred (Figure 2.24).

JOURNAL			
Date	Account	Debit	Credit
	Insurance Expense	900	
	Prepaid Insurance		900
	To recognize current period insurance expense		

Figure 2.24 Journal Entry for Insurance Expense. Bert applies 1/12 of the prepaid insurance premium per month to the expense account in order to match period costs with period revenues. (attribution: Copyright Rice University, OpenStax, under CC BY-NC-SA 4.0 license)

Why is it so important for Bert to know which costs are product costs and which are period costs? Bert may have little control over his product costs, but he maintains a great deal of control over many of his period costs. For this reason, it is important that Bert be able to identify his period costs and then determine which of them are fixed and which are variable. Remember that fixed costs are fixed over the relevant range, but variable costs change with the level of activity. If Bert wants to control his costs to make his bike business more profitable, he must be able to differentiate between the costs he can and cannot control.

Just like a merchandising business such as Bert's Bikes, manufacturers also classify their costs as either product costs or period costs. For a manufacturing business, product costs are the costs associated with making the product, and period costs are all other costs. For the purposes of external reporting, separating costs into period and product costs is not all that is necessary. However, for management decision-making activities, refinement of the types of product costs is helpful.

In a manufacturing firm, the need for management to be aware of the types of costs that make up the cost of a product is of paramount importance. Let's look at Carolina Yachts again and examine how they can classify the product costs associated with building their sportfishing boats. Just like automobiles, every year, Carolina Yachts makes changes to their boats, introducing new models to their product line. When the engineers begin to redesign boats for the next year, they must be careful not to make changes that would drive the selling price of their boats too high, making them less attractive to the customer. The engineers need to know exactly what the addition of another feature will do to the cost of production. It is not enough for them to get total product cost data; instead, they need specific information about the three classes of product costs: materials, labor, and overhead.

As you've learned, direct materials are the raw materials and component parts that are directly economically traceable to a unit of production.

Table 2.7 provides some examples of direct materials.

Examples of Direct Materials

Manufacturing Business	Product	Direct Materials
Bakery	Birthday cakes	Flour, sugar, eggs, milk
Automobile manufacturer	Cars	Glass, steel, tires, carpet
Furniture manufacturer	Recliners	Wood, fabric, cotton batting

Table 2.7

In each of the examples, managers are able to trace the cost of the materials directly to a specific unit (cake, car, or chair) produced. Since the amount of direct materials required will change based on the number of units produced, direct materials are almost always classified as a variable cost. They remain fixed per unit of production but change in total based on the level of activity within the business.

It takes more than materials for Carolina Yachts to build a boat. It requires the application of labor to the raw materials and component parts. You've also learned that direct labor is the work of the employees who are directly involved in the production of goods or services. In fact, for many industries, the largest cost incurred in the production process is labor. For Carolina Yachts, their direct labor would include the wages paid to the carpenters, painters, electricians, and welders who build the boats. Like direct materials, direct labor is typically treated as a variable cost because it varies with the level of activity. However, there are some companies that pay a flat weekly or monthly salary for production workers, and for these employees, their compensation could be classified as a fixed cost. For example, many auto mechanics are now paid a flat weekly or monthly salary.

While in the example Carolina Yachts is dependent upon direct labor, the production process for companies in many industries is moving from human labor to a more automated production process. For these companies, direct labor in these industries is becoming less significant. For an example, you can research the current production process for the automobile industry.

The third major classification of product costs for a manufacturing business is overhead. Manufacturing overhead (sometimes referred to as *factory overhead*) includes all of the costs that a manufacturing business incurs, other than the variable costs of direct materials and direct labor required to build products. These overhead costs are not directly attributable to a specific unit of production, but they are incurred to support the production of goods. Some of the items included in manufacturing overhead include supervisor salaries, depreciation on the factory, maintenance, insurance, and utilities. It is important to note that manufacturing overhead does not include any of the selling or administrative functions of a business. For Carolina Yachts, costs like the sales, marketing, CEO, and clerical staff salaries will not be included in the calculation of manufacturing overhead costs but will instead be allocated to selling and administrative expenses.

As you have learned, much of the power of managerial accounting is its ability to break costs down into the smallest possible trackable unit. This also applies to manufacturing overhead. In many cases, businesses have a need to further refine their overhead costs and will track indirect labor and indirect materials.

When labor costs are incurred but are not directly involved in the active conversion of materials into finished products, they are classified as **indirect labor** costs. For example, Carolina Yachts has production supervisors who oversee the manufacturing process but do not actively participate in the construction of the boats. Their wages generally support the production process but cannot be traced back to a single unit. For this reason, the production supervisors' salary would be classified as indirect labor. Similar to direct labor, on a product or department basis, indirect labor, such as the supervisor's salary, is often treated as a fixed cost, assuming that it does not vary with the level of activity or number of units produced. However, if you are considering the supervisor's salary cost on a per unit of production basis, then it could be considered a variable cost.

Similarly, not all materials used in the production process can be traced back to a specific unit of production. When this is the case, they are classified as **indirect material** costs. Although needed to produce the product, these indirect material costs are not traceable to a *specific* unit of production. For Carolina Yachts, their indirect materials include supplies like tools, glue, wax, and cleaning supplies. These materials are required to build a boat, but management cannot easily track how much of a bottle of glue they use or how often they use a particular drill to build a specific boat. These indirect materials and their associated cost represent a small fraction of the total materials needed to complete a unit of production. Like direct materials, indirect materials are classified as a variable cost since they vary with the level of production. Table 2.8 provides some examples of manufacturing costs and their classifications.

Examples of Classifications of Manufacturing Costs

Cost	Classification	Fixed or Variable
Production supervisor salary	Indirect labor	Fixed
Raw materials used in production	Direct materials	Variable
Wages of production employees	Direct labor	Variable
Straight-line depreciation on factory equipment	General manufacturing overhead	Fixed
Glue and adhesives	Indirect materials	Variable

Table 2.8

Prime Costs versus Conversion Costs

In certain production environments, once a business has separated the costs of the product into direct materials, direct labor, and overhead, the costs can then be gathered into two broader categories: prime costs and conversion costs. **Prime costs** are the direct material expenses and direct labor costs, while **conversion costs** are direct labor and general factory overhead combined. Please note that these two categories of costs are examples of cost categories where a particular cost can be included in both. In this case, direct labor is included in both prime costs and conversion costs.

These cost classifications are common in businesses that produce large quantities of an item that is then packaged into smaller, sellable quantities such as soft drinks or cereal. In these types of production environments, it easier to lump the costs of direct labor and overhead into one category, since these costs are what are needed to convert raw materials into a finished product. This method of costing is termed *process costing* and is covered in Process Costing.

Although it seems as if there are many classifications or labels associated with costs, remember that the purpose of cost classification is to assist managers in the decision-making process. Since this type of data is not used for external reporting purposes, it is important to understand that (1) a single cost can have many different labels; (2) the terms are used independently, not simultaneously; and (3) each classification is important to understand in order to make business decisions. Figure 2.25 uses some example costs to demonstrate these principles.

Cost	Fixed	Variable	Mixed	Step	Period	Product DM	DL	OH	Prime	Conversion
Rent on production facility	√							OH		√
Plant supervisor salary	√							OH		√
Raw materials		√				DM			√	
Administrative salaries	√				√					
Commissioned sales staff		√	√		√					
Delivery truck			√		√					
Advertising	√				√					
Plant utilities			√					OH		√
Income tax		√		√	√					

Figure 2.25 Classification Based on Cost Function. Costs can fall into more than one category, sometimes making the process of cost identification complex. DM, direct materials; DL, direct labor; OH, overhead. (attribution: Copyright Rice University, OpenStax, under CC BY-NC-SA 4.0 license)

Effects of Changes in Activity Level on Unit Costs and Total Costs

We have spent considerable time identifying and describing the various ways that businesses categorize costs. However, categorization itself is not enough. It is important not only to understand the categorization of costs but to understand the relationships between changes in activity levels and the changes in costs in total. It is worth repeating that when a cost is considered to be fixed, that cost is only fixed for the relevant range. Once the boundary of the relevant range has been reached or moved beyond, fixed costs will change and then remain fixed for the new relevant range. Remember that, within a relevant range of activity, where the relevant range refers to a specific activity level that is bounded by a minimum and maximum amount, total fixed costs are constant, but costs change on a per-unit basis. Let's examine an example that demonstrates how changes in activity can affect costs.

ETHICAL CONSIDERATIONS

Cost Accounting Helps Reduce Fraud and Promotes Ethical Behavior

Managerial and related cost accounting systems assist managers in making ethical and sound business decisions. Managerial accountants implement accounting reporting systems to minimize or prevent fraud and promote ethical decision-making. For example, tracking changes in costing activity and ensuring that activity remains in a relevant range, helps ensure that an organization's business activity is properly bounded within a reasonable range of expense. If the minimum or maximum expense range is

> exceeded, this can indicate that management is acting without authority or is pursuing unauthorized activities. Excessive costs may even be a red flag that possible fraud is occurring. Cost accounting helps ensure that financial costs are within an acceptable range and helps an organization make reliable forward-looking financial decisions.

Comprehensive Example of the Effect on Changes in Activity Level on Costs

Pat is planning a three-day ski trip on his spring break after he works on a Habitat for Humanity project in Dallas. The costs for the trip are as follows:

Car rental (up to five passengers)	$200
Condo rental (up to five occupants)	400
Gasoline	120
Food (per day)	40
Lift tickets (per day)	30

He is considering his costs for the trip if he goes alone, or if he takes one, two, three, or four friends. However, before he can begin his analysis, he needs to consider the characteristics of the costs. Some of the costs will stay the same no matter how many people go, and some of the costs will fluctuate, based on the number of participants.

Those costs that do not change are the fixed costs. Once you incur a fixed cost, it does not change within a given range. For example, Pat can take up to five people in one car, so the cost of the car is fixed for up to five people. However, if he took more friends, then he would need more cars. The condo rental and the gasoline expenses would also be considered fixed costs, because they are not going to change in the reference range.

The costs that do change as the number of participants change are the variable costs. The food and lift ticket expenses are examples of variable costs, since they fluctuate based upon the number of participants and the number of days of activities.

In analyzing the costs, Pat also needs to consider the total costs and average costs. The analysis will calculate the average fixed costs, the total fixed costs, the average variable costs, and the total variable costs.

In the analysis of total costs versus average costs, both total and average fixed costs will stay the same and total and average variable costs will change. Here are the total fixed costs:

Car rental	$200
Condo	400
Gasoline	120
Total fixed costs	$720

The total fixed costs for the trip will be $720.00, no matter whether Pat goes alone or takes up to 4 friends. However, the average fixed costs will be the total fixed costs divided by the number of participants. The average fixed cost could range from $720 (720/1) to $144 (720/5).

Here are the variable costs:

Food (per day)	$40
Lift tickets (per day)	30
Average variable cost (per day)	$70

The average variable cost will be $70.00 per person per day, no matter how many people go on the trip. However, the total variable costs will range from $70.00, if Pat goes alone, to $350.00, if five people go. Figure 2.26 shows the relationships of the various costs, based on the number of participants.

Number of Skiers	Average Variable Cost	Total Variable Cost	Total Fixed Cost	Average Fixed Cost	Average Cost per Skier
1	$210	$ 210	$720	$720	$930
2	210	420	720	360	570
3	210	630	720	240	450
4	210	840	720	180	390
5	210	1,050	720	144	354

Figure 2.26 Comprehensive Ski Trip Cost Classification. (attribution: Copyright Rice University, OpenStax, under CC BY-NC-SA 4.0 license)

Looking at this analysis, it is clear that, if there is an activity that you think that you cannot afford, it can become less expensive if you are creative in your cost-sharing techniques.

YOUR TURN

Spring Break Trip Planning

Margo is planning an 8-day spring break trip from Atlanta, Georgia, to Tampa, Florida, leaving on Sunday and returning the following Sunday. She has located a condominium on the beach and has put a deposit down on the unit. The rental company has a maximum occupancy for the condominium of seven adults. There is an amusement park that she plans to visit. She is going to use her parents' car, an SUV that can carry up to six people and their luggage. The SUV can travel an average of 20 miles per gallon, the total distance is approximately 1,250 miles (550 miles each way plus driving around Tampa every day), and the average price of gas is $3 per gallon. A season pass for an amusement park she wants to visit is $168 per person. Margo estimates spending $40 per day per person for food. She estimates the costs for the trip as follows:

Condo Rental	$1,400
Gasoline	188
Food (per person per day)	40
Amusement Park Season Pass (per person)	168

Now that she has cost estimates, she is trying to decide how many of her friends she wants to invite. Since the car can only seat six people, Marg made a list of five other girls to invite. Use her data to answer the following questions and fill out the cost table:

1. What are the total variable costs for the trip?
2. What are the average variable costs for the trip?

3. What are the total fixed costs for the trip?
4. What are the average fixed costs for the trip?
5. What are the average costs per person for the trip?
6. What would the trip cost Margo if she were to go alone?

Number of People, Including Margo	Total Variable Cost	Average Variable Cost	Total Fixed Cost	Average Fixed Cost	Average Cost per Person
1					
2					
3					
4					
5					
6					

7. What additional costs would be incurred if a seventh girl was invited on the trip? Would this be a wise decision (from a cost perspective)? Why or why not?
8. Which cost will *not* be affected if a seventh girl was invited on the trip?

Solution

Number of People, Including Margo	Total Variable Cost	Average Variable Cost	Total Fixed Cost	Average Fixed Cost	Average Cost per Person
1	$488	$488	$1,588	$1,588	$2,076
2	976	488	1,588	794	1,282
3	1,464	488	1,588	529	1,017
4	1,952	488	1,588	397	885
5	2,440	488	1,588	318	806
6	2,928	488	1,588	265	753

Answers will vary. All responses should recognize that there is no room in the car for the seventh girl and her luggage, although the condominium will accommodate the extra person. This means they will have to either find a larger vehicle and incur higher gas expenses or take a second car, which will at least double the fixed gas cost.

2.3 Estimate a Variable and Fixed Cost Equation and Predict Future Costs

Sometimes, a business will need to use cost estimation techniques, particularly in the case of mixed costs, so that they can separate the fixed and variable components, since only the variable components change in the short run. Estimation is also useful for using current data to predict the effects of future changes in production on total costs. Three estimation techniques that can be used include the scatter graph, the high-low method, and regression analysis. Here we will demonstrate the scatter graph and the high-low methods (you will learn the regression analysis technique in advanced managerial accounting courses.

Functions of Cost Equations

The cost equation is a linear equation that takes into consideration total fixed costs, the fixed component of mixed costs, and variable cost per unit. Cost equations can use past data to determine patterns of past costs that can then project future costs, or they can use estimated or expected future data to estimate future costs. Recall the mixed cost equation:

$$Y = a + bx$$

where Y is the total mixed cost, a is the fixed cost, b is the variable cost per unit, and x is the level of activity.

Let's take a more in-depth look at the cost equation by examining the costs incurred by Eagle Electronics in the manufacture of home security systems, as shown in Table 2.9.

Cost Information for Eagle Electronics

Cost Incurred	Fixed or Variable	Cost
Lease on manufacturing equipment	Fixed	$50,000 per year
Supervisor salary	Fixed	$75,000 per year
Direct materials	Variable	$50 per unit
Direct labor	Variable	$20 per unit

Table 2.9

By applying the cost equation, Eagle Electronics can predict its costs at any level of activity (x) as follows:

1. Determine total fixed costs: $50,000 + $75,000 = $125,000
2. Determine variable costs per unit: $50 + $20 = $70
3. Complete the cost equation: $Y = \$125{,}000 + \$70x$

Using this equation, Eagle Electronics can now predict its total costs (Y) for any given level of activity (x), as in Figure 2.27:

Units Produced	Cost Equation	Total Costs
5,000	Y = $125,000 + ($70 × 5,000)	$475,000
8,000	Y = $125,000 + ($70 × 8,000)	685,000
12,000	Y = $125,000 + ($70 × 12,000)	965,000

Figure 2.27 Total Cost Estimation for Various Production Levels. (attribution: Copyright Rice University, OpenStax, under CC BY-NC-SA 4.0 license)

When using this approach, Eagle Electronics must be certain that it is only predicting costs for its relevant range. For example, if they must hire a second supervisor in order to produce 12,000 units, they must go back and adjust the total fixed costs used in the equation. Likewise, if variable costs per unit change, these must also be adjusted.

This same approach can be used to predict costs for service and merchandising firms, as shown by examining the costs incurred by J&L Accounting to prepare a corporate income tax return, shown in Table 2.10.

Cost Information for J&L Accounting

Cost Incurred	Fixed or Variable	Cost
Building rent	Fixed	$1,000 per month
Direct labor (for CPAs)	Variable	$250 per tax return
Secretarial staff	Fixed	$2,000 per month
Accounting clerks	Variable	$100 per return

Table 2.10

J&L wants to predict their total costs if they complete 25 corporate tax returns in the month of February.

1. Determine total fixed costs: $1,000 + $2,000 = $3,000
2. Determine variable costs per tax return: $250 + $100 = $350
3. Complete the cost equation: Y = $3,000 + $350x

Using this equation, J&L can now predict its total costs (Y) for the month of February when they anticipate preparing 25 corporate tax returns:

$$Y = \$3{,}000 + (\$350 \times 25)$$
$$Y = \$3{,}000 + \$8{,}750$$
$$Y = \$11{,}750$$

J&L can now use this predicted total cost figure of $11,750 to make decisions regarding how much to charge clients or how much cash they need to cover expenses. Again, J&L must be careful to try not to predict costs outside of the relevant range without adjusting the corresponding total cost components.

J&L can make predictions for their costs because they have the data they need, but what happens when a business wants to estimate total costs but has not collected data regarding per-unit costs? This is the case for the managers at the Beach Inn, a small hotel on the coast of South Carolina. They know what their costs were for June, but now they want to predict their costs for July. They have gathered the information in Figure 2.28.

Cost Incurred	Fixed or Variable	June Costs
Insurance	Fixed	$ 700
Loan Payment	Fixed	2,500
Front Desk Staff	Variable	3,800
Cleaning Staff	Variable	2,500
Laundry Service	Variable	1,200

Figure 2.28 Monthly Total Cost Detail for Beach Inn. (attribution: Copyright Rice University, OpenStax, under CC BY-NC-SA 4.0 license)

In June, they had an occupancy of 75 nights. For the Beach Inn, occupancy (rooms rented) is the cost driver. Since they know what is driving their costs, they can determine their per-unit variable costs in order to forecast future costs:

$$\frac{\text{Front Desk Staff}}{75 \text{ nights}} = \frac{\$3{,}800}{75} = \$50.67 \text{ variable front desk staff costs per night}$$

$$\frac{\text{Cleaning Staff}}{75 \text{ nights}} = \frac{\$2{,}500}{75} = \$33.33 \text{ variable cleaning staff costs per night}$$

$$\frac{\text{Laundry Service}}{75 \text{ nights}} = \frac{\$1{,}200}{75} = \$16.00 \text{ variable laundry service costs per night}$$

Now, the Beach Inn can apply the cost equation in order to forecast total costs for any number of nights, within the relevant range.

1. Determine total fixed costs: $700 + $2,500 = $3,200
2. Determine variable costs per night of occupancy: $50.67 + $33.33 + $16.00 = $100
3. Complete the cost equation: Y = $3,200 + $100x

Using this equation, the Beach Inn can now predict its total costs (Y) for the month of July, when they anticipate an occupancy of 93 nights.

$$Y = \$3{,}200 + (\$100 \times 93)$$
$$Y = \$3{,}200 + \$9{,}300$$
$$Y = \$12{,}500$$

In all three examples, managers used cost data they have collected to forecast future costs at various activity levels.

YOUR TURN

Waymaker Furniture

Waymaker Furniture has collected cost information from its production process and now wants to predict costs for various levels of activity. They plan to use the cost equation to formulate these predictions. Information gathered from March is presented in Table 2.11.

March Cost Information for Waymaker Furniture

Cost Incurred	Fixed or Variable	March Cost
Plant supervisor salary	Fixed	$12,000 per month
Lumber (direct materials)	Variable	$75,000 total
Production worker wages	Variable	$11.00 per hour
Machine maintenance	Variable	$5.00 per unit produced
Lease on factory	Fixed	$15,000 per month

Table 2.11

In March, Waymaker produced 1,000 units and used 2,000 hours of production labor.

Using this information and the cost equation, predict Waymaker's total costs for the levels of production in Table 2.12.

Waymaker's Levels of Production

Month	Activity Level
April	1,500 units
May	2,000 units
June	2,500 units

Table 2.12

Solution

Total Fixed Cost = $12,000 + $15,000 = $27,000. Direct Materials per Unit = $75,000 / 1,000 Units = $75 per unit. Direct Labor per Hour = $11.00. Machine Maintenance = $5.00 per unit. Total Variable Cost per Unit = $75 + $11 + $5 = $91 per unit.

Month	Activity Level	VC per Unit	Total VC	Fixed Cost	Total Cost
April	1,500 Units	$91	$136,500	$27,000	$163,500
May	2,000 Units	91	182,000	27,000	209,000
June	2,500 Units	91	227,500	27,000	254,500

Demonstration of the Scatter Graph Method to Calculate Future Costs at Varying Activity Levels

One of the assumptions that managers must make in order to use the cost equation is that the relationship between activity and costs is linear. In other words, costs rise in direct proportion to activity. A diagnostic tool that is used to verify this assumption is a scatter graph.

A **scatter graph** shows plots of points that represent actual costs incurred for various levels of activity. Once the scatter graph is constructed, we draw a line (often referred to as a *trend line*) that appears to best fit the pattern of dots. Because the trend line is somewhat subjective, the scatter graph is often used as a preliminary tool to explore the possibility that the relationship between cost and activity is generally a linear relationship. When interpreting a scatter graph, it is important to remember that different people would likely draw different lines, which would lead to different estimations of fixed and variable costs. No one person's line and cost estimates would necessarily be right or wrong compared to another; they would just be different. After using a scatter graph to determine whether cost and activity have a linear relationship, managers often move on to more precise processes for cost estimation, such as the high-low method or least-squares regression analysis.

To demonstrate how a company would use a scatter graph, let's turn to the data for Regent Airlines, which operates a fleet of regional jets serving the northeast United States. The Federal Aviation Administration establishes guidelines for routine aircraft maintenance based upon the number of flight hours. As a result, Regent finds that its maintenance costs vary from month to month with the number of flight hours, as depicted in Figure 2.29.

Month	Activity Level (Flight Hours)	Maintenance Costs
January	21,000	$84,000
February	23,000	90,000
March	14,000	70,500
April	17,000	75,000
May	10,000	64,500
June	19,000	78,000

Figure 2.29 Monthly Maintenance Cost and Activity Detail for Regent Airlines. (attribution: Copyright Rice University, OpenStax, under CC BY-NC-SA 4.0 license)

When creating the scatter graph, each point will represent a pair of activity and cost values. Maintenance costs are plotted on the vertical axis (Y), while flight hours are plotted on the horizontal axis (X). For instance, one point will represent 21,000 hours and $84,000 in costs. The next point on the graph will represent 23,000 hours and $90,000 in costs, and so forth, until all of the pairs of data have been plotted. Finally, a trend line is added to the chart in order to assist managers in seeing if there is a positive, negative, or zero relationship between the activity level and cost. Figure 2.30 shows a scatter graph for Regent Airlines.

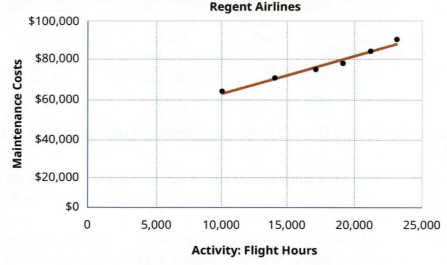

Figure 2.30 Scatter Graph of Maintenance Costs for Regent Airline. (attribution: Copyright Rice University, OpenStax, under CC BY-NC-SA 4.0 license)

In scatter graphs, cost is considered the dependent variable because cost *depends* upon the level of activity. The activity is considered the independent variable since it is the cause of the variation in costs. Regent's scatter graph shows a positive relationship between flight hours and maintenance costs because, as flight hours increase, maintenance costs also increase. This is referred to as a positive linear relationship or a linear cost behavior.

Will all cost and activity relationships be linear? Only when there is a relationship between the activity and that particular cost. What if, instead, the cost of snow removal for the runways is plotted against flight hours? Suppose the snow removal costs are as listed in Table 2.13.

Snow Removal Costs

Month	Activity Level: Flight Hours	Snow Removal Costs
January	21,000	$40,000
February	23,000	50,000
March	14,000	8,000
April	17,000	0
May	10,000	0
June	19,000	0

Table 2.13

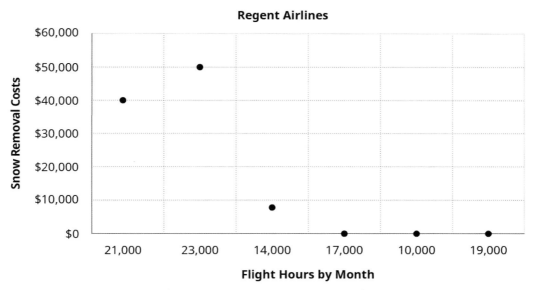

Figure 2.31 Scatter Graph of Snow Removal Costs for Regent Airlines. (attribution: Copyright Rice University, OpenStax, under CC BY-NC-SA 4.0 license)

As you can see from the scatter graph, there is really not a linear relationship between how many flight hours are flown and the costs of snow removal. This makes sense as snow removal costs are linked to the amount of snow and the number of flights taking off and landing but not to how many hours the planes fly.

Using a scatter graph to determine if this linear relationship exists is an essential first step in cost behavior analysis. If the scatter graph reveals a linear cost behavior, then managers can proceed with a more sophisticated analyses to separate mixed costs into their fixed and variable components. However, if this linear relationship is not present, then other methods of analysis are not appropriate. Let's examine the cost data from Regent Airline using the high-low method.

Demonstration of the High-Low Method to Calculate Future Costs at Varying Activity Levels

As you've learned, the purpose of identifying costs is to control them, and managers regularly use past costs to predict future costs. Since we know that variable costs change with the level of activity, we can conclude that there is *usually* a positive relationship between cost and activity: As one rises, so does the other. Ideally, this can be confirmed on a scatter graph. One of the simplest ways to analyze costs is to use the **high-low method**, a technique for separating the fixed and variable cost components of mixed costs. Using the highest and lowest levels of activity and their associated costs, we are able to estimate the variable cost components of mixed costs.

Once we have established that there is linear cost behavior, we can equate variable costs with the slope of the line, expressed as the rise of the line over the run. The steeper the slope of the line, the faster costs rise in response to a change in activity. Recall from the scatter graph that costs are the dependent Y variable and activity is the independent X variable. By examining the change in Y relative to the change in X, we can predict cost:

$$\text{Variable Cost} = \frac{\text{Rise of the line}}{\text{Run of the line}} = \frac{Y_2 - Y_1}{X_2 - X_1}$$

where Y_2 is the total cost at the highest level of activity; Y_1 is the total cost at the lowest level of activity; X_2 is the number of units, labor hours, etc., at the highest level of activity; and X_1 is the number of units, labor hours, etc., at the lowest level of activity.

Using the maintenance cost data from Regent Airlines shown in Figure 2.32, we will examine how this method works in practice.

Month	Activity Level (Flight Hours)	Maintenance Costs
January	21,000	$84,000
February	23,000	90,000
March	14,000	70,500
April	17,000	75,000
May	10,000	64,500
June	19,000	78,000

Figure 2.32 Monthly Maintenance Cost and Activity Detail for Regent Airlines. (attribution: Copyright Rice University, OpenStax, under CC BY-NC-SA 4.0 license)

The first step in analyzing mixed costs with the high-low method is to identify the periods with the highest and lowest levels of activity. In this case, it would be February and May, as shown in Figure 2.33. We always choose the highest and lowest activity and the costs that correspond with those levels of activity, even if they are not the highest and lowest costs.

	Activity Level (Flight Hours)	Cost (Maintenance Costs)
Highest level (February)	23,000	$90,000
Lowest level (May)	10,000	64,500

Figure 2.33 High–Low Data Points for Regent Airlines Maintenance Costs. (attribution: Copyright Rice University, OpenStax, under CC BY-NC-SA 4.0 license)

We are now able to estimate the variable costs by dividing the difference between the costs of the high and the low periods by the change in activity using this formula:

$$\text{Variable Cost} = \frac{\text{Change in Cost}}{\text{Change in Activity}} = \frac{\text{Cost at the high activity level} - \text{Cost at the low activity level}}{\text{Highest activity level} - \text{Lowest activity level}}$$

For Regent Airlines, this is:

$$\text{Variable Cost} = \frac{\$90{,}000 - \$64{,}500}{23{,}000 - 10{,}000} = \$1.96 \text{ per flight hour}$$

Having determined that the variable cost per flight-hour is $1.96, we can now determine the amount of fixed costs. We can determine these fixed costs by taking the total costs at *either* the high or the low level of activity and subtracting this variable component. You will recall that total cost = fixed costs + variable costs, so the fixed cost component for Regent Airlines can be isolated as shown:

$$\text{Fixed cost} = \text{total cost} - \text{variable cost}$$
$$\text{Fixed cost} = \$90{,}000 - (23{,}000 \times \$1.96)$$
$$\text{Fixed cost} = \$44{,}920$$

Notice that if we had chosen the other data point, the low cost and activity, we would still get the same fixed cost of $44,920 = [$64,500 − (10,000 × $1.96)].

Now that we have isolated both the fixed and the variable components, we can express Regent Airlines' cost of maintenance using the total cost equation:

$$Y = \$44{,}920 + \$1.96x$$

where Y is total cost and x is flight hours.

Because we confirmed that the relationship between cost and activity at Regent exhibits linear cost behavior on the scatter graph, this equation allows managers at Regent Airlines to conclude that for every one unit increase in activity, there will be a corresponding rise in variable cost of $1.96. When put into practice, the managers at Regent Airlines can now predict their total costs at any level of activity, as shown in Figure 2.34.

Activity Level (Flight Hours)	Fixed Costs	Variable Cost at $1.96 per hour	Total Costs
10,000	$44,920	$19,600	$64,520
20,000	44,920	39,200	84,120
30,000	44,920	58,800	103,720
40,000	44,920	78,400	123,320

Figure 2.34 Predictions of Total Cost and Cost Components at Different Levels of Activity for Regent Airlines. (attribution: Copyright Rice University, OpenStax, under CC BY-NC-SA 4.0 license)

Although managers frequently use this method, it is not the most accurate approach to predicting future costs because it is based on only two pieces of cost data: the highest and the lowest levels of activity. Actual costs can vary significantly from these estimates, especially when the high or low activity levels are not representative of the usual level of activity within the business. For a more accurate model, the least-squares regression method would be used to separate mixed costs into their fixed and variable components. The least-squares regression method is a statistical technique that may be used to estimate the total cost at the given level of activity based on past cost data. Least-squares regression minimizes the errors of trying to fit a line between the data points and thus fits the line more closely to all the data points.

Understanding the various labels used for costs is the first step toward using costs to evaluate business decisions. You will learn more about these various labels and how they are applied in decision-making processes as you continue your study of managerial accounting in this course.

Key Terms

average fixed cost (AFC) total fixed costs divided by the total number of units produced, which results in a per-unit cost

average variable cost (AVC) total variable costs divided by the total number of units produced, which results in a per-unit cost

conversion costs total of labor and overhead for a product; the costs that "convert" the direct material into the finished product

cost driver activity that is the reason for the increase or decrease of another cost; examples include labor hours incurred, labor costs paid, amounts of materials used in production, units produced, or any other activity that has a cause-and-effect relationship with incurred costs

direct labor labor directly related to the manufacturing of the product or the production of a service

direct materials materials used in the manufacturing process that can be traced directly to the product

fixed cost unavoidable operating expense that does not change in total, regardless of the level of activity

high-low method technique for separating the fixed and variable cost components of mixed costs

indirect labor labor not directly involved in the active conversion of materials into finished products or the provision of services

indirect materials materials used in production but not efficiently traceable to a specific unit of production

intangible good good with financial value but no physical presence; examples include copyrights, patents, goodwill, and trademarks

manufacturing organization business that uses parts, components, or raw materials to produce finished goods

manufacturing overhead costs incurred in the production process that are not economically feasible to measure as direct material or direct labor costs; examples include indirect material, indirect labor, utilities, and depreciation

merchandising firm business that purchases finished products and resells them to consumers

mixed costs expenses that have a fixed component and a variable component

period costs typically related to a particular time period instead of attached to the production of an asset; treated as an expense in the period incurred (examples include many sales and administrative expenses)

prime costs direct material expenses and direct labor costs

product costs all expenses required to manufacture the product: direct materials, direct labor, and manufacturing overhead

relevant range quantitative range of units that can be produced based on the company's current productive assets; for example, if a company has sufficient fixed assets to produce up to 10,000 units of product, the relevant range would be between 0 and 10,000 units

scatter graph plot of pairs of numerical data that represents actual costs incurred for various levels of activity, with one variable on each axis, used to determine whether there is a relationship between them

service organization business that earns revenue primarily by providing an intangible product

stepped cost one that changes with the level of activity but will remain constant within a relevant range

tangible good physical good that customers can handle and see

total cost sum of all fixed and all variable costs

total fixed costs sum of all fixed costs

total variable costs sum of all variable costs

variable cost one that varies in direct proportion to the level of activity within the business

Summary

2.1 Distinguish between Merchandising, Manufacturing, and Service Organizations
- Merchandising, manufacturing, and service organizations differ in what they provide to consumers; however, all three types of firms must control costs in order to remain profitable. The type of costs they incur is primarily determined by the product/good, or service they provide.
- As the type of organization differs, so does the way they account for costs. Some of these differences are reflected in the income statement.

2.2 Identify and Apply Basic Cost Behavior Patterns
- Costs can be broadly classified as either fixed or variable costs. However, in order for managers to manage effectively, these two cost classifications are often further expanded to include mixed, step, prime, and conversion costs.
- For manufacturing firms, it is essential that they differentiate among direct materials, direct labor, and manufacturing overhead in order to identify and manage their total product costs.
- For planning purposes, managers must be careful to consider the relevant range because it is only within this relevant range that total fixed costs remain constant.

2.3 Estimate a Variable and Fixed Cost Equation and Predict Future Costs
- In order to make business decisions, managers can utilize past cost data to predict future costs employing three methods: scatter graphs, the high-low method, and least-squares regression analysis.
- Scatter graphs are used as a diagnostic tool to determine if the relationship between activity and cost is a linear relationship.
- Both the high-low method and the least-squares regression method separate mixed costs into their fixed and variable components to allow managers to predict future costs from historical costs.

Multiple Choice

1. LO 2.1 Which of the following is the primary source of revenue for a service business?
   A. the production of products from raw materials
   B. the purchase and resale of finished products
   C. providing intangible goods and services
   D. the sale of raw materials to manufacturing firms

2. LO 2.1 Which of the following is the primary source of revenue for a merchandising business?
   A. the production of products from raw materials
   B. the purchase and resale of finished products
   C. the provision of intangible goods and services
   D. the sale of raw materials to manufacturing firms

3. LO 2.1 Which of the following is the primary source of revenue for a manufacturing business?
   A. the production of products from raw materials
   B. the purchase and resale of finished products
   C. the provision of intangible goods and services
   D. both the provision of services and the sale of finished goods

4. LO 2.1 Which of the following represents the components of the income statement for a service business?
　A. Sales Revenue – Cost of Goods Sold = gross profit
　B. Service Revenue – Operating Expenses = operating income
　C. Sales Revenue – Cost of Goods Manufactured = gross profit
　D. Service Revenue – Cost of Goods Purchased = gross profit

5. LO 2.1 Which of the following represents the components of the income statement for a manufacturing business?
　A. Sales Revenue – Cost of Goods Sold = gross profit
　B. Service Revenue – Operating Expenses = gross profit
　C. Service Revenue – Cost of Goods Manufactured = gross profit
　D. Sales Revenue – Cost of Goods Manufactured = gross profit

6. LO 2.1 Which of the following represents the components of the income statement for a merchandising business?
　A. Sales Revenue – Cost of Goods Sold = gross profit
　B. Service Revenue – Operating Expenses = gross profit
　C. Sales Revenue – Cost of Goods Manufactured = gross profit
　D. Service Revenue – Cost of Goods Purchased = gross profit

7. LO 2.2 Conversion costs include all of the following *except*:
　A. wages of production workers
　B. depreciation on factory equipment
　C. factory utilities
　D. direct materials purchased

8. LO 2.2 Which of the following is *not* considered a product cost?
　A. direct materials
　B. direct labor
　C. indirect materials
　D. selling expense

9. LO 2.2 Fixed costs are expenses that _____.
　A. vary in response to changes in activity level
　B. remain constant on a per-unit basis
　C. increase on a per-unit basis as activity increases
　D. remain constant as activity changes

10. LO 2.2 Variable costs are expenses that _____.
　A. remain constant on a per-unit basis but change in total based on activity level
　B. remain constant on a per-unit basis and remain constant in total regardless of activity level
　C. decrease on a per-unit basis as activity level increases
　D. remain constant in total regardless of activity level within a relevant range

11. LO 2.2 Total costs for ABC Distributing are $250,000 when the activity level is 10,000 units. If variable costs are $5 per unit, what are their fixed costs?
　A. $240,000
　B. $200,000
　C. $260,000
　D. Their fixed costs cannot be determined from the information presented.

12. LO 2.2 Which of the following would not be classified as manufacturing overhead?
  A. indirect materials
  B. indirect labor
  C. direct labor
  D. property taxes on factory

13. LO 2.2 Which of the following are prime costs?
  A. indirect materials, indirect labor, and direct labor
  B. direct labor, indirect materials, and indirect labor
  C. direct labor and indirect labor
  D. direct labor and direct materials

14. LO 2.2 Which of the following statements is true regarding average fixed costs?
  A. Average fixed costs per unit remain fixed regardless of level of activity.
  B. Average fixed costs per unit rise as the level of activity rises.
  C. Average fixed costs per unit fall as the level of activity rises.
  D. Average fixed costs per unit cannot be determined.

15. LO 2.3 The high-low method and least-squares regression are used by managers to _____.
  A. decide whether to make or buy a component part
  B. minimize corporate tax liability
  C. maximize output
  D. estimate costs

16. LO 2.3 Which of the following methods of cost estimation relies on only two data points?
  A. the high-low method
  B. account analysis
  C. least-squares regression
  D. SWOT analysis.

17. LO 2.3 In the cost equation $Y = a + bx$, Y represents which of the following?
  A. fixed costs
  B. variable costs
  C. total costs
  D. units of production

18. LO 2.3 A scatter graph is used to test the assumption that the relationship between cost and activity level is _____.
  A. curvilinear
  B. cyclical
  C. unpredictable
  D. linear

Questions

1. LO 2.1 Identify the three primary classifications of businesses and explain the differences among the three.

2. LO 2.1 Explain how the income statement of a manufacturing company differs from the income statement of a merchandising company.

3. LO 2.1 Walsh & Coggins, a professional accounting firm, collects cost information about the services they provide to their clients. Describe the types of cost data they would collect and explain the importance of analyzing this cost data.

4. LO 2.1 Lizzy's is a retail clothing store, specializing in formal wear for weddings. They purchase their clothing for resale from specialty distributors and manufacturers. Recently the owners of Lizzy's have noted an increased interest in costume jewelry and fashion accessories among their clientele. If the owners of Lizzy's decide to expand their business to include these products, what cost data would they need to collect and analyze prior to expanding the business?

5. LO 2.2 Identify and describe the three types of product costs in a manufacturing firm.

6. LO 2.2 Explain the difference between a period cost and a product cost.

7. LO 2.2 Explain the concept of relevant range and how it affects total fixed costs.

8. LO 2.2 Explain the differences among fixed costs, variable costs, and mixed costs.

9. LO 2.2 Explain the difference between prime costs and conversion costs.

10. LO 2.3 Explain how a scatter graph is used to identify and measure cost behavior.

11. LO 2.3 Explain the components of the total cost equation and describe how each of the components can be used by management for decision-making.

12. LO 2.3 Explain how the high-low method is used for cost estimation. What, if any, are the limitations of this approach to cost estimation?

Exercise Set A

EA1. LO 2.1 Magio Company manufactures kitchen equipment used in hospitals. They distribute their products directly to the customer and, for the year ending 2019, they reported the these revenues and expenses. Use this information to construct an income statement for the year 2019.

Sales revenue	$985,000
Cost of goods sold	489,000
Operating expenses	245,000

EA2. LO 2.1 Park and West, LLC, provides consulting services to retail merchandisers in the Midwest. In 2019, they generated $720,000 in service revenue. Their total cost (fixed and variable) per client was $2,500 and they served 115 clients during the year. If operating expenses for the year were $302,000 what was their net income?

EA3. LO 2.1 Canine Couture is a specialty dog clothing boutique that sells clothing and clothing accessories for dogs. In 2019, they had gross revenue from sales totaling $86,500. Their operating expenses for this same period were $27,500. If their Cost of Goods Sold (COGS) was 24% of gross revenue, what was their net operating income for the year?

EA4. LO 2.2 Hicks Contracting collects and analyzes cost data in order to track the cost of installing decks on new home construction jobs. The following are some of the costs that they incur. Classify these costs as fixed or variable costs and as product or period costs.
  A. Lumber used to construct decks ($12.00 per square foot)
  B. Carpenter labor used to construct decks ($10 per hour)
  C. Construction supervisor salary ($45,000 per year)
  D. Depreciation on tools and equipment ($6,000 per year)
  E. Selling and administrative expenses ($35,000 per year)
  F. Rent on corporate office space ($34,000 per year)
  G. Nails, glue, and other materials required to construct deck (varies per job)

EA5. LO 2.2 Rose Company has a relevant range of production between 10,000 and 25,000 units. The following cost data represents average cost per unit for 15,000 units of production.

	Average Cost per Unit
Direct materials	$12
Direct labor	10
Indirect materials	2
Fixed manufacturing overhead	4
Variable manufacturing overhead	3
Fixed selling and administrative expenses	8
Variable sales commissions	25

Using the cost data from Rose Company, answer the following questions:
  A. If 10,000 units are produced, what is the variable cost per unit?
  B. If 18,000 units are produced, what is the variable cost per unit?
  C. If 21,000 units are produced, what are the total variable costs?
  D. If 11,000 units are produced, what are the total variable costs?
  E. If 19,000 units are produced, what are the total manufacturing overhead costs incurred?
  F. If 23,000 units are produced, what are the total manufacturing overhead costs incurred?
  G. If 19,000 units are produced, what are the per unit manufacturing overhead costs incurred?
  H. If 25,000 units are produced, what are the per unit manufacturing overhead costs incurred?

EA6. LO 2.2 Carr Company provides human resource consulting services to small- and medium-sized companies. Last year, Carr provided services to 700 clients. Total fixed costs were $159,000 with total variable costs of $87,500. Based on this information, complete this chart:

	500 Clients	800 Clients	900 Clients
Total costs			
Fixed costs	?	?	?
Variable costs	?	?	?
Total costs	?	?	?
Cost per client			
Fixed cost	?	?	?
Variable cost	?	?	?
Total cost per client	?	?	?

EA7. LO 2.2 Western Trucking operates a fleet of delivery trucks. The fixed expenses to operate the fleet are $79,900 in March and rose to $93,120 in April. It costs Western Trucking $0.15 per mile in variable costs. In March, the delivery trucks were driven a total of 85,000 miles, and in April, they were driven a total of 96,000 miles. Using this information, answer the following:

A. What were the total costs to operate the fleet in March and April, respectively?
B. What were the cost per mile to operate the fleet in March and April, respectively?

EA8. LO 2.2 Suppose that a company has fixed costs of $18 per unit and variable costs $9 per unit when 15,000 units are produced. What are the fixed costs per unit when 12,000 units are produced?

EA9. LO 2.3 The cost data for Evencoat Paint for the year 2019 is as follows:

Month	Gallons of Paint Produced	Equipment Maintenance Expenses
January	110,000	$70,700
February	68,000	66,800
March	71,000	67,000
April	77,000	68,100
May	95,000	69,200
June	101,000	70,300
July	125,000	70,400
August	95,000	68,900
September	95,000	69,500
October	89,000	68,600
November	128,000	72,800
December	122,000	71,450

A. Using the high-low method, express the company's maintenance costs as an equation where x represents the gallons of paint produced. Then estimate the fixed and variable costs.
B. Predict the maintenance costs if 90,000 gallons of paint are produced.
C. Predict the maintenance costs if 81,000 gallons of paint are produced.
D. Using Excel, create a scatter graph of the cost data and explain the relationship between gallons of paint produced and equipment maintenance expenses.

Chapter 2 Building Blocks of Managerial Accounting

EA10. LO 2.3 This cost data from Hickory Furniture is for the year 2017.

Month	Number of Tables Produced	Factory Utility Expenses
January	550	$2,063
February	710	2,663
March	650	2,438
April	470	1,823
May	512	1,920
June	625	2,344
July	805	3,019
August	750	2,813
September	675	2,531
October	525	1,969
November	875	3,281
December	685	2,569

A. Using the high-low method, express the company's utility costs as an equation where X represents number of tables produced.
B. Predict the utility costs if 800 tables are produced.
C. Predict the utility costs if 600 tables are produced.
D. Using Excel, create a scatter graph of the cost data and explain the relationship between number of tables produced and utility expenses.

EA11. LO 2.3 Markson and Sons leases a copy machine with terms that include a fixed fee each month plus a charge for each copy made. Markson made 9,000 copies and paid a total of $480 in January. In April, they paid $320 for 5,000 copies. What is the variable cost per copy if Markson uses the high-low method to analyze costs?

EA12. LO 2.3 Markson and Sons leases a copy machine with terms that include a fixed fee each month of $500 plus a charge for each copy made. The company uses the high-low method to analyze costs. If Markson paid $360 for 5,000 copies and $280 for 3,000 copies, how much would Markson pay if it made 7,500 copies?

Exercise Set B

EB1. LO 2.1 Winterfell Products manufactures electrical switches for the aerospace industry. For the year ending 2019, they reported these revenues and expenses. Use this information to construct an income statement for the year 2019.

Sales revenue	$865,000
Cost of goods sold	354,000
Operating expenses	315,000

EB2. LO 2.1 CPK & Associates is a mid-size legal firm, specializing in closings and real estate law in the south. In 2019, they generated $945,000 in sales revenue. Their expenses related to this year's revenue are shown:

Operating expenses (including salaries)	$312,000
Cost of services	
Total cost per client	1,750
Clients served in 2019	225

Based on the information provided for the year, what was their net operating income?

EB3. LO 2.1 Flip or Flop is a retail shop selling a wide variety of sandals and beach footwear. In 2019, they had gross revenue from sales totaling $93,200. Their operating expenses for this same period were $34,000. If their Cost of Goods Sold (COGS) was 21% of gross revenue, what was their net operating income for the year?

EB4. Roper Furniture manufactures office furniture and tracks cost data across their process. The following are some of the costs that they incur. Classify these costs as fixed or variable costs, and as product costs or period costs.

- A. Wood used to produce desks ($125.00 per desk)
- B. Production labor used to produce desks ($15 per hour)
- C. Production supervisor salary ($45,000 per year)
- D. Depreciation on factory equipment ($60,000 per year)
- E. Selling and administrative expenses ($45,000 per year)
- F. Rent on corporate office ($44,000 per year)
- G. Nails, glue, and other materials required to produce desks (varies per desk)
- H. Utilities expenses for production facility
- I. Sales staff commission (5% of gross sales)

EB5. LO 2.2 Baxter Company has a relevant range of production between 15,000 and 30,000 units. The following cost data represents average variable costs per unit for 25,000 units of production.

	Average Cost per Unit
Direct materials	$10
Direct labor	9
Indirect materials	3
Fixed manufacturing overhead	6
Variable manufacturing overhead	2
Fixed selling and administrative expenses	8
Variable sales commissions	14

Using the costs data from Rose Company, answer the following questions:

- A. If 15,000 units are produced, what is the variable cost per unit?
- B. If 28,000 units are produced, what is the variable cost per unit?
- C. If 21,000 units are produced, what are the total variable costs?
- D. If 29,000 units are produced, what are the total variable costs?
- E. If 17,000 units are produced, what are the total manufacturing overhead costs incurred?
- F. If 23,000 units are produced, what are the total manufacturing overhead costs incurred?
- G. If 30,000 units are produced, what are the per unit manufacturing overhead costs incurred?
- H. If 15,000 units are produced, what are the per unit manufacturing overhead costs incurred?

EB6. LO 2.2 Sanchez & Vukmin, LLP, is a full-service accounting firm located near Chicago, Illinois. Last year, Sanchez provided tax preparation services to 500 clients. Total fixed costs were $265,000 with total variable costs of $180,000. Based on this information, complete this chart.

	500 Clients	800 Clients	900 Clients
Total costs			
Fixed costs	?	?	?
Variable costs	?	?	?
Total costs	?	?	?
Cost per client			
Fixed cost	?	?	?
Variable cost	?	?	?
Total cost per client	?	?	?

EB7. LO 2.2 Case Airlines provides charter airline services. The fixed expenses to operate the company's aircraft are $377,300 in January and $378,880 in February. It costs Case Airlines $0.45 per mile in variable costs. In January, Case aircraft flew a total of 385,000 miles, and in February, Case aircraft flew a total of 296,000 miles. Using this information, answer the following:

A. What were the total costs to operate the aircraft in January and February, respectively?
B. What were the total costs per mile to operate the fleet in January and February, respectively?

EB8. LO 2.2 Suppose that a company has fixed costs of $11 per unit and variable costs $6 per unit when 11,000 units are produced. What are the fixed costs per unit when 20,000 units are produced?

EB9. LO 2.3 The cost data for BC Billing Solutions for the year 2020 is as follows:

Month	Invoices Processed	Overtime Wages
January	12,000	$7,760
February	8,000	6,800
March	1,000	6,000
April	7,000	6,100
May	5,000	6,200
June	10,000	7,300
July	11,000	7,400
August	9,000	6,900
September	5,000	6,500
October	9,000	6,600
November	8,000	6,800
December	11,000	7,450

A. Using the high-low method, express the company's overtime wages as an equation where x represents number of invoices processed. Assume BC has monthly fixed costs of $3,800.
B. Predict the overtime wages if 9,000 invoices are processed.
C. Predict the overtime wages if 6,500 invoices are processed.
D. Using Excel, create a scatter graph of the cost data and explain the relationship between the number of invoices processed and overtime wage expense.

EB10. LO 2.3 This cost data from Hickory Furniture is for the year 2017.

Month	Number of Chairs Produced	Factory Utility Expenses
January	425	$1,659
February	510	1,964
March	625	2,406
April	725	2,791
May	685	2,637
June	575	2,214
July	510	1,964
August	810	3,119
September	700	2,695
October	650	2,503
November	875	3,369
December	680	2,618

A. Using the high-low method, express the factory utility expenses as an equation where x represents number of chairs produced.
B. Predict the utility costs if 900 chairs are produced.
C. Predict the utility costs if 750 chairs are produced.
D. Using Excel, create a scatter graph of the cost data and explain the relationship between number of chairs processed and utility expenses.

EB11. LO 2.3 Able Transport operates a tour bus that they lease with terms that involve a fixed fee each month plus a charge for each mile driven. Able Transport drove the tour bus 4,000 miles and paid a total of $1,250 in March. In April, they paid $970 for 3,000 miles. What is the variable cost per mile if Able Transport uses the high-low method to analyze costs?

EB12. LO 2.3 Able Transport operates a tour bus that they lease with terms that involve a fixed fee each month plus a charge for each mile driven. Able Transport drove the bus 7,000 miles and paid a total of $1,360 in June. In October, Able Transport paid $1,280 for the 5,000 miles driven. If Able Transport uses the high-low method to analyze costs, how much would Able Transport pay in December, if they drove 6,000 miles?

Problem Set A

PA1. LO 2.1 Ballentine Manufacturing produces and sells lawnmowers through a national dealership network. They purchase raw materials from a variety of suppliers, and all manufacturing and assembly work is performed at their plant outside of Kansas City, Missouri. They recorded these costs for the year ending December 31, 2017. Construct an income statement for Ballentine Manufacturing to reflect their net income for 2017.

Administrative and selling expenses	$ 425,000
Cost of goods sold	1,400,000
Rent on corporate headquarters	75,000
Marketing and advertising	400,000
Sales revenue	2,700,000
Straight-line depreciation on office equipment	100,000

PA2. LO 2.1 Tom West is a land surveyor who operates a small surveying company, performing surveys for both residential and commercial clients. He has a staff of surveyors and engineers who are employed by the firm. For the year ending December 31, 2017, he reported these income and expenses. Using this information, construct an income statement to reflect his net income for 2017.

Service income	$850,000
Surveyor salary	124,000
Supplies and materials	32,000
Utilities	14,000
Office rent	24,000
Administrative expenses	115,000

PA3. LO 2.1 Just Beachy is a retail business located on the coast of Florida where it sells a variety of beach apparel, T-shirts, and beach-related souvenir items. They purchase all of their inventory from wholesalers and distributors. For the year ending December 31, 2017, they reported these revenues and expenses. Using this information, prepare an income statement for Just Beachy for 2017.

Sales revenue	$685,000
Building rent	48,000
Advertising	50,000
Sales staff salaries	85,000
Cost of goods sold	315,000
Utilities	23,000
Supplies	9,000

PA4. LO 2.2 Listed as follows are various costs found in businesses. Classify each cost as a fixed or variable cost, and as a product and/or period cost.
- A. Wages of administrative staff
- B. Shipping costs on merchandise sold
- C. Wages of workers assembling computers
- D. Cost of lease on factory equipment
- E. Insurance on factory
- F. Direct materials used in production of lamps
- G. Supervisor salary, factory
- H. Advertising costs
- I. Property taxes, factory
- J. Health insurance cost for company executives
- K. Rent on factory

PA5. **LO 2.2** Wachowski Company reported these cost data for the year 2017.

Factory maintenance costs	$ 90,000
Direct labor, wages	352,000
Direct labor, health insurance	32,000
Indirect labor, health insurance	15,000
Health insurance for production supervisor	6,500
Administrative costs	55,000
Rental of office space for administrative staff	17,500
Sales commissions	52,500
Direct material	1,230,000
Indirect materials	632,000
Advertising expense	39,000
Depreciation on factory building	62,000
Indirect labor, wages	70,000
Production supervisor's salary	32,000

Use the data to complete the following table.

Total prime costs	
Total manufacturing overhead costs	
Total conversion costs	
Total product costs	
Total period costs	

PA6. **LO 2.3** Carolina Yachts builds custom yachts in its production factory in South Carolina. Once complete, these yachts must be shipped to the dealership. They have collected this shipping cost data:

Month	Yachts Shipped	Shipping Cost
January	6	$11,650
February	4	9,100
March	3	7,825
April	8	14,200
May	2	6,550
June	7	12,925
July	5	10,375

A. Prepare a scatter graph of the shipping data. Plot cost on the vertical axis and yachts shipped on the horizontal axis. Is the relationship between shipping costs and unit shipped approximately linear? Draw a straight line through the scatter graph.

B. Using the high-low method, create the cost formula for Carolina Yachts' shipping costs.

C. The least-squares regression method was used and the analysis resulted in this cost equation: $Y = 4,000 + 1,275x$. Comment on the accuracy of your high-low method estimation.

D. What would you estimate shipping costs to be if Carolina Yachts shipped 10 yachts in a single month? Use the cost formula you obtained in part B. Comment on how accurately this is reflected by the scatter graph you constructed.

E. What factors other than number of yachts shipped do you think could affect Carolina Yachts' shipping expense? Explain.

Problem Set B

PB1. LO 2.1 Hicks Products produces and sells patio furniture through a national dealership network. They purchase raw materials from a variety of suppliers and all manufacturing, and assembly work is performed at their plant outside of Cleveland, Ohio. They recorded these costs for the year ending December 31, 2017. Construct an income statement for Hicks Products, to reflect their net income for 2017.

Sales revenue	$3,100,000
Straight-line depreciation on office equipment	90,000
Advertising and marketing expense	625,000
Administrative salaries	136,000
Cost of goods sold	1,700,000
Rent on corporate headquarters	65,000

PB2. LO 2.1 Conner & Scheer, Attorneys at Law, provide a wide range of legal services for their clients. They employ several paralegal and administrative support staff in order to provide high-quality legal services at competitive prices. For the year ending December 31, 2017, the firm reported these income and expenses. Using this information, construct an income statement to reflect the firm's net income for 2017.

Service revenue	$2,250,000
Paralegal salaries	215,000
Supplies and materials	42,000
Utilities	26,000
Office rent	58,000
Administrative expenses	195,000
Attorney salaries	925,000

PB3. LO 2.1 Puzzles, Pranks & Games is a retail business selling children's toys and games as well as a wide selection of jigsaw puzzles and accessories. They purchase their inventory from local and national wholesale suppliers. For the year ending December 31, 2017, they reported these revenues and expenses. Using this information, prepare an income statement for Puzzles, Pranks & Games for 2017.

Sales revenue	$415,000
Rent	24,000
Advertising	13,000
Sales staff salaries	45,000
Cost of goods sold	210,000
Utilities	11,000
Supplies	4,000

PB4. LO 2.2 Pocket Umbrella, Inc, is considering producing a new type of umbrella. This new pocket-sized umbrella would fit into a coat pocket or purse. Classify the following costs of this new product as direct materials, direct labor, manufacturing overhead, or selling and administrative.[6]
   A. Cost of advertising the product
   B. Fabric used to make the umbrellas
   C. Maintenance of cutting machines used to cut the umbrella fabric so it will fit the umbrella frame
   D. Wages of workers who assemble the product
   E. President's salary
   F. The salary of the supervisor of the people who assemble the product
   G. Wages of the product tester who stands in a shower to make sure the umbrellas do not leak
   H. Cost of market research survey
   I. Salary of the company's sales managers
   J. Depreciation of administrative office building

PB5. Using the costs listed in the previous problem, classify the costs as either product costs or period costs.

PB6. LO 2.3 Gadell Farms produces venison sausage that is distributed to grocery stores throughout the Southeast. They have collected this shipping cost data:

Month	Tons Produced	Packaging Cost
January	6	$1,700
February	4	2,000
March	3	2,100
April	8	2,700
May	2	1,602
June	7	1,900
July	5	2,300

   A. Prepare a scatter graph of the shipping data. Plot cost on the vertical axis and tons produced on the horizontal axis. Is the relationship between packaging costs and tons produced approximately linear? Draw a straight line through the scatter graph.
   B. Using the high-low method, estimate the cost formula for Gadell Farms' packaging costs.
   C. The least-squares regression method was used and the analysis resulted in this cost equation: $Y = 1650 + 78.57x$. Comment on the accuracy of your high-low method estimation.
   D. What would you estimate packaging costs to be if Gadell Farms shipped 10 tons in a single month? Use the cost formula you obtained in part B. Comment on how accurately this is reflected by the scatter graph you constructed.
   E. What factors other than number of tons produced do you think could affect Gadell Farm's packaging expense? Explain.

---

6 Attribution: Modification of work by Roger Hermanson, James Edwards, and Michael Maher. *Accounting Principles: A Business Perspective.* 2011, CC BY. Source: Available at https://open.umn.edu/opentextbooks/textbooks/383.

Thought Provokers

TP1. LO 2.1 In a team of two or three students, interview the manager/owner of a local business. In this interview, ask the manager/owner the following questions:
   A. Does the business collect and use cost information to make decisions?
   B. Does it have a specialist in cost estimation who works with this cost data? If not, who is responsible for the collection of cost information? Be as specific as possible.
   C. What type of cost information does the business collect and how is each type of information used?
   D. How important does the owner/manager believe cost information is to the success of the business?

Then, write a report to the instructor summarizing the results of the interview.

Content of the memo must include

- date of the interview,
- the name and title of the person interviewed,
- name and location of the business,
- type of business (service, merchandising, manufacturing) and brief description of the goods/services provided by the business, and
- responses to questions A–D.

TP2. LO 2.2 This list contains costs that various organizations incur; they fall into three categories: direct materials (DM), direct labor (DL), or overhead (OH).[7]
   A. Classify each of these items as direct materials, direct labor, or overhead.
      i. Glue used to attach labels to bottles containing a patented medicine.
      ii. Compressed air used in operating paint sprayers for Student Painters, a company that paints houses and apartments.
      iii. Insurance on a factory building and equipment.
      iv. A production department supervisor's salary.
      v. Rent on factory machinery.
      vi. Iron ore in a steel mill.
      vii. Oil, gasoline, and grease for forklift trucks in a manufacturing company's warehouse.
      viii. Services of painters in building construction.
      ix. Cutting oils used in machining operations.
      x. Cost of paper towels in a factory employees' washroom.
      xi. Payroll taxes and fringe benefits related to direct labor.
      xii. The plant electricians' salaries.
      xiii. Crude oil to an oil refinery.
      xiv. Copy editor's salary in a book publishing company.
   B. Assume your classifications could be challenged in a court case. Indicate to your attorneys which of your answers for part a might be successfully disputed by the opposing attorneys and why. In which answers are you completely confident?

---

7 Attribution: Modification of work by Roger Hermanson, James Edwards, and Michael Maher. *Accounting Principles: A Business Perspective*. 2011, CC BY. Source: Available at https://open.umn.edu/opentextbooks/textbooks/383.

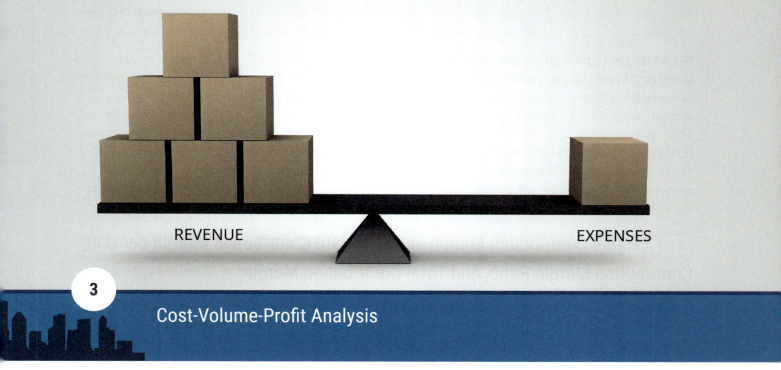

3 Cost-Volume-Profit Analysis

Figure 3.1 Balancing Cost, Volume, and Profit. Managers employ cost-volume-profit (CVP) analysis to determine the sales level at which they break even or balance their revenue with their expenses. (credit: modification of "Balance Swing Equality" by "Mediamodifier"/Pixabay, CC0)

Chapter Outline

LO 3.1 Explain Contribution Margin and Calculate Contribution Margin per Unit, Contribution Margin Ratio, and Total Contribution Margin

LO 3.2 Calculate a Break-Even Point in Units and Dollars

LO 3.3 Perform Break-Even Sensitivity Analysis for a Single Product Under Changing Business Situations

LO 3.4 Perform Break-Even Sensitivity Analysis for a Multi-Product Environment Under Changing Business Situations

LO 3.5 Calculate and Interpret a Company's Margin of Safety and Operating Leverage

Why It Matters

As president of the Accounting Club, you are working on a fundraiser selling T-shirts on campus. You have gotten quotes from several suppliers ranging from $8 to $10 per shirt and now have to select a vendor. The prices vary based on whether the T-shirts have pockets, have long sleeves or short sleeves, and are printed on one side or both. You are confident that you can sell them for $15 each. However, the college charges clubs a $100 "student sale" fee, and your T-shirt sales must cover this cost and still net the club enough money to pay for your spring trip

In addition, several of the vendors will give volume discounts—the more shirts you purchase, the less each shirt costs. In short, you need to know exactly which style of T-shirt, vendor, and quantity will allow you to reach your desired net income and cover your fixed expense of $100. You decide on a short-sleeve shirt with a pocket that costs $10 each and that you can sell for $15.

This $5 per shirt "gross profit" will first go toward covering the $100 student sale fee. That means you will have to sell 20 shirts to pay the fee ($100/$5 = 20 shirts). After selling the first 20 shirts, the $5 profit will be available to start paying for the cost of the trip. Your faculty advisor has calculated that the trip will cost $125 per student, and you have 6 people signed up for the trip. This means the sale will need to generate an additional $750 from the sale (6 students × $125). At $5 per shirt you will need to sell 150 shirts to cover the student costs ($750/$5). So, you will need to sell a total of 170 shirts: 20 to cover your fixed cost of $100 and an additional 150 to cover the student's cost of the trip ($750). What you have just completed is a cost-volume-profit analysis. In this chapter, we will explore how managers can use this type of analysis to make a wide range of decisions about their business operations.

3.1 Explain Contribution Margin and Calculate Contribution Margin per Unit, Contribution Margin Ratio, and Total Contribution Margin

Before examining contribution margins, let's review some key concepts: fixed costs, relevant range, variable costs, and contribution margin. Fixed costs are those costs that will not change within a given range of production. For example, in the current case, the fixed costs will be the student sales fee of $100. No matter how many shirts the club produces within the relevant range, the fee will be locked in at $100. The **relevant range** is the anticipated production activity level. Fixed costs remain constant within a relevant range. If production levels exceed expectations, then additional fixed costs will be required.

For example, assume that the students are going to lease vans from their university's motor pool to drive to their conference. A university van will hold eight passengers, at a cost of $200 per van. If they send one to eight participants, the fixed cost for the van would be $200. If they send nine to sixteen students, the fixed cost would be $400 because they will need two vans. We would consider the relevant range to be between one and eight passengers, and the fixed cost in this range would be $200. If they exceed the initial relevant range, the fixed costs would increase to $400 for nine to sixteen passengers.

Variable costs are those costs that vary per unit of production. Direct materials are often typical variable costs, because you normally use more direct materials when you produce more items. In our example, if the students sold 100 shirts, assuming an individual variable cost per shirt of $10, the total variable costs would be $1,000 (100 × $10). If they sold 250 shirts, again assuming an individual variable cost per shirt of $10, then the total variable costs would $2,500 (250 × $10).

Contribution margin is the amount by which a product's selling price exceeds its total variable cost per unit. This difference between the sales price and the per unit variable cost is called the contribution margin because it is the per unit contribution toward covering the fixed costs. It typically is calculated by comparing the sales revenue generated by the sale of one item versus the variable cost of the item:

$$\text{Contribution Margin} = \text{Sales} - \text{Variable Costs}$$

In our example, the sales revenue from one shirt is $15 and the variable cost of one shirt is $10, so the individual contribution margin is $5. This $5 contribution margin is assumed to first cover fixed costs first and then realized as profit.

As you will see, it is not just small operations, such as the accounting club scenario provided in Why It Matters, that benefit from cost-volume-profit (CVP) analysis. At some point, all businesses find themselves asking the same basic questions: How many units must be sold in order to reach a desired income level? How much will each unit cost? How much of the sales price from each unit will help cover our fixed costs? For example, Starbucks faces these same questions every day, only on a larger scale. When they introduce new menu items, such as seasonal specialty drinks, they must determine the fixed and variable costs associated with each item.

Adding menu items may not only increase their fixed costs in the short run (via advertising and promotions) but will bring new variable costs. Starbucks needs to price these drinks in a way that covers the variable costs per unit and additional fixed costs and contributes to overall net income. Regardless of how large or small the enterprise, understanding how fixed costs, variable costs, and volume are related to income is vital for sound decision-making.

Figure 3.2 Starbucks. Large corporations like Starbucks use cost-volume-profit analysis to make decisions about their products and services to ensure that they are maximizing their revenues. (credit: modification of "StarbucksVaughanMills" by "Raysonho"/Wikimedia Commons, CC0)

Understanding how to use fixed costs, variable costs, and sales in CVP analyses requires an understanding of the term margin. You may have heard that restaurants and grocery stores have very low margins, while jewelry stores and furniture stores have very high margins. What does "margin" mean? In the broadest terms, margin is the difference between a product or service's selling price and its cost of production. Recall the accounting club's T-shirt sale. The difference between the sales price per T-shirt and the purchase price of the T-shirts was the accounting club's margin:

Sales Price	$15
Cost per T-shirt	10
Margin	$ 5

Recall that Building Blocks of Managerial Accounting explained the characteristics of fixed and variable costs and introduced the basics of cost behavior. Let's now apply these behaviors to the concept of contribution margin. The company will use this "margin" to cover fixed expenses and hopefully to provide a profit. Let's begin by examining contribution margin on a per unit basis.

Unit Contribution Margin

When the contribution margin is calculated on a per unit basis, it is referred to as the contribution margin per unit or unit contribution margin. You can find the contribution margin per unit using the equation shown in image.

> **Per Unit Sales Price – Variable Cost per Unit = Contribution Margin per Unit**

It is important to note that this unit contribution margin can be calculated either in dollars or as a percentage.

To demonstrate this principle, let's consider the costs and revenues of Hicks Manufacturing, a small company that manufactures and sells birdbaths to specialty retailers.

Hicks Manufacturing sells its Blue Jay Model for $1100 and incurs variable costs of $20 per unit. In order to calculate their per unit contribution margin, we use the formula in image to determine that on a *per unit* basis, their contribution margin is:

HICKS MANUFACTURING
Blue Jay Model
For Year Ended December 31, 2019

Sales Price per Unit	$100
– Variable Cost per Unit	20
= Contribution Margin per Unit	$ 80

This means that for every Blue Jay model they sell, they will have $80 to *contribute* toward covering fixed costs, such as rent, insurance, and manager salaries. But Hicks Manufacturing manufactures and sells more than one model of birdbath. They also sell a Cardinal Model for $75, and these birdbaths incur variable costs of $15 per unit. For the Cardinal Model, their contribution margin on a per unit basis is the $75 sales price less the $15 per unit variable costs is as follows:

HICKS MANUFACTURING
Cardinal Model
For Year Ended December 31, 2019

Sales Price per Unit	$75
– Variable Cost per Unit	15
= Contribution Margin per Unit	$60

This demonstrates that, for every Cardinal model they sell, they will have $60 to *contribute* toward covering fixed costs and, if there is any left, toward profit. Every product that a company manufactures or every service a company provides will have a unique contribution margin per unit. In these examples, the contribution margin per unit was calculated in dollars per unit, but another way to calculate contribution margin is as a ratio (percentage).

Contribution Margin Ratio

The **contribution margin ratio** is the percentage of a unit's selling price that exceeds total unit variable costs. In other words, contribution margin is expressed as a percentage of sales price and is calculated using this formula:

$$\text{Contribution Margin Ratio} = \frac{\text{Contribution Margin per Unit}}{\text{Sales Price per Unit}}$$

For Hicks Manufacturing and their Blue Jay Model, the contribution margin ratio will be

$$\frac{\$80 \text{ Contribution Margin per Unit}}{\$100 \text{ Sales Price per Unit}} = 0.80$$

At a contribution margin ratio of 80%, approximately $0.80 of each sales dollar generated by the sale of a Blue Jay Model is available to cover fixed expenses and contribute to profit. The contribution margin ratio for the birdbath implies that, for every $1 generated by the sale of a Blue Jay Model, they have $0.80 that contributes to fixed costs and profit. Thus, 20% of each sales dollar represents the variable cost of the item and 80% of the sales dollar is margin. Just as each product or service has its own contribution margin on a per unit basis, each has a unique contribution margin ratio. Although this process is extremely useful for analyzing the profitability of a single product, good, or service, managers also need to see the "big picture" and will examine contribution margin in total across all products, goods, or services.

YOUR TURN

Margin at the Kiosk

You rent a kiosk in the mall for $300 a month and use it to sell T-shirts with college logos from colleges and universities all over the world. You sell each T-shirt for $25, and your cost for each shirt is $15. You also pay your sales person a commission of $0.50 per T-shirt sold in addition to a salary of $400 per month. Construct a contribution margin income statement for two different months: in one month, assume 100 T-shirts are sold, and in the other, assume 200 T-shirts are sold.

Solution

Pertinent information		Contribution margin income statement 100 units sold		Contribution margin income statement 200 units sold	
Sales price per unit	$25	Sales revenue	$2,500	Sales revenue	$5,000
Variable costs:		Variable costs per unit ($15 + 0.50) x 100 units	1,550	Variable costs per unit ($15 + 0.50) x 200 units	3,100
Per shirt cost	15	Contribution margin	950	Contribution margin	1,900
Per shirt commission	0.50	Fixed costs	700	Fixed costs	700
Fixed costs:		Net operating income	$250	Net operating income	$1,200
Kiosk rental	300				
Salary	400				

Total Contribution Margin

This "big picture" is gained by calculating **total contribution margin**—the total amount by which total sales exceed total variable costs. We calculate total contribution margin by multiplying per unit contribution margin by sales volume or number of units sold. This approach allows managers to determine how much profit a company is making before paying its fixed expenses. For Hicks Manufacturing, if the managers want to determine how much their Blue Jay Model contributes to the overall profitability of the company, they can calculate total contribution margin as follows:

HICKS MANUFACTURING
Blue Jay Model
For Month Ended April, 2019

Units Sold	450
Contribution Margin per Unit	x$ 80
Total Contribution Margin	$36,000

For the month of April, sales from the Blue Jay Model contributed $36,000 toward fixed costs. Looking at contribution margin in total allows managers to evaluate whether a particular product is profitable and how the sales revenue from that product contributes to the overall profitability of the company. In fact, we can create a specialized income statement called a contribution margin income statement to determine how changes in sales volume impact the bottom line.

To illustrate how this form of income statement can be used, contribution margin income statements for Hicks Manufacturing are shown for the months of April and May.

In April, Hicks sold 500 Blue Jay Models at $100 per unit, which resulted in the operating income shown on the contribution margin income statement:

HICKS MANUFACTURING
Contribution Margin Income Statement
For Month Ended April, 2019

Sales (500 units at $100 per unit)	$50,000
Variable Cost (500 units at $20 per unit)	10,000
Contribution Margin	40,000
Fixed Costs	23,000
Operating Income	$17,000

In May, 750 of the Blue Jay models were sold as shown on the contribution margin income statement. When comparing the two statements, take note of what changed and what remained the same from April to May.

HICKS MANUFACTURING
Contribution Margin Income Statement
For Month Ended May, 2019

Sales (750 units at $100 per unit)	$75,000
Variable Cost (750 units at $20 per unit)	15,000
Contribution Margin	60,000
Fixed Costs	23,000
Operating Income	$37,000

Using this contribution margin format makes it easy to see the impact of changing sales volume on operating income. Fixed costs remained unchanged; however, as more units are produced and sold, more of the per-unit sales price is available to contribute to the company's net income.

Before going further, let's note several key points about CVP and the contribution margin income statement. First, the contribution margin income statement is used for *internal* purposes and is not shared with external stakeholders. Secondly, in this specialized income statement, when "*operating* income" is shown, it actually refers to "net operating income" *without regard to income taxes*. Companies can also consider taxes when performing a CVP analysis to project both net operating income and net income. (The preparation of contribution margin income statements with regard to taxes is covered in advanced accounting courses; here, we will consider net income as net operating income without regard to taxes.)

Regardless of whether contribution margin is calculated on a per-unit basis, calculated as a ratio, or incorporated into an income statement, all three express how much sales revenue is available to cover fixed expenses and contribute to profit. Let's examine how all three approaches convey the same financial performance, although represented somewhat differently.

You will recall that the per-unit contribution margin was $80 for a Hicks Blue Jay birdbath. When Hicks sold 500 units, each unit contributed $80 to fixed expenses and profit, which can be verified from April's income statement:

April Total Contribution Margin	$40,000
Per Unit Contribution Margin	$ 80

$$\frac{\text{Total Contribution Margin}}{\text{Per Unit Contribution Margin}} = \text{Number of Units Sold} = \frac{\$40{,}000}{80} = 500 \text{ units}$$

Now, let's use May's Contribution Margin Income Statement as previously calculated to verify the contribution margin based on the contribution margin ratio previously calculated, which was 80%, by applying this formula:

$$\text{Total Sales} \times \text{Contribution Margin Ratio} = \text{Total Contribution Margin}$$

May Total Sales	$75,000
Contribution Margin Ratio	80%

$75,000 × 0.80 = $60,000

Regardless of how contribution margin is expressed, it provides critical information for managers. Understanding how each product, good, or service contributes to the organization's profitability allows managers to make decisions such as which product lines they should expand or which might be discontinued. When allocating scarce resources, the contribution margin will help them focus on those products or services with the highest margin, thereby maximizing profits.

The Evolution of Cost-Volume-Profit Relationships

The CVP relationships of many organizations have become more complex recently because many labor-intensive jobs have been replaced by or supplemented with technology, changing both fixed and variable costs. For those organizations that are still labor-intensive, the labor costs tend to be variable costs, since at higher levels of activity there will be a demand for more labor usage. For example, assuming one worker is needed for every 50 customers per hour, we might need two workers for an average sales season, but during the Thanksgiving and Christmas season, the store might experience 250 customers per hour and thus would need five workers.

However, the growing trend in many segments of the economy is to convert labor-intensive enterprises (primarily variable costs) to operations heavily dependent on equipment or technology (primarily fixed costs). For example, in retail, many functions that were previously performed by people are now performed by machines or software, such as the self-checkout counters in stores such as Walmart, Costco, and Lowe's. Since machine and software costs are often depreciated or amortized, these costs tend to be the same or fixed, no matter the level of activity within a given relevant range.

In China, completely unmanned grocery stores have been created that use facial recognition for accessing the store. Patrons will shop, bag the purchased items, leave the store, and be billed based on what they put in their bags. Along with managing the purchasing process, inventory is maintained by sensors that let managers know when they need to restock an item.

In the United States, similar labor-saving processes have been developed, such as the ability to order groceries or fast food online and have it ready when the customer arrives. Another major innovation affecting labor costs is the development of driverless cars and trucks (primarily fixed costs), which will have a major impact on the number of taxi and truck drivers in the future (primarily variable costs). Do these labor-saving processes change the cost structure for the company? Are variable costs decreased? What about fixed costs? Let's look at this in more detail.

When ordering food through an app, there is no need to have an employee take the order, but someone still needs to prepare the food and package it for the customer. The variable costs associated with the wages of order takers will likely decrease, but the fixed costs associated with additional technology to allow for online ordering will likely increase. When grocery customers place their orders online, this not only requires increased fixed costs for the new technology, but it can also increase variable labor costs, as employees are needed to fill customers' online orders. Many stores may move cashier positions to online order fulfillment rather than hiring additional employees. Other stores may have employees fill online grocery orders during slow or downtimes.

Using driverless cars and trucks decreases the variable costs tied to the wages of the drivers but requires a major investment in fixed-cost assets—the autonomous vehicles—and companies would need to charge prices that allowed them to recoup their expensive investments in the technology as well as make a profit. Alternatively, companies that rely on shipping and delivery companies that use driverless technology may be faced with an increase in transportation or shipping costs (variable costs). These costs may be higher because technology is often more expensive when it is new than it will be in the future, when it is easier and more cost effective to produce and also more accessible. A good example of the change in cost of a new technological innovation over time is the personal computer, which was very expensive when it was first developed but has decreased in cost significantly since that time. The same will likely happen over time with the cost of creating and using driverless transportation.

You might wonder why a company would trade variable costs for fixed costs. One reason might be to meet company goals, such as gaining market share. Other reasons include being a leader in the use of innovation and improving efficiencies. If a company uses the latest technology, such as online ordering and delivery, this may help the company attract a new type of customer or create loyalty with longstanding customers. In addition, although fixed costs are riskier because they exist regardless of the sales level, once those fixed costs are met, profits grow. All of these new trends result in changes in the composition of fixed and variable costs for a company and it is this composition that helps determine a company's profit.

As you will learn in future chapters, in order for businesses to remain profitable, it is important for managers to understand how to measure and manage fixed and variable costs for decision-making. In this chapter, we begin examining the relationship among sales volume, fixed costs, variable costs, and profit in decision-making. We will discuss how to use the concepts of fixed and variable costs and their relationship to profit to determine the sales needed to break even or to reach a desired profit. You will also learn how to plan for changes in selling price or costs, whether a single product, multiple products, or services are involved.

THINK IT THROUGH

Deciding Between Orders

You are evaluating orders from two new customers, but you will only be able to accept one of the orders without increasing your fixed costs. Management has directed you to choose the one that is most profitable for the company. Customer A is ordering 500 units and is willing to pay $200 per unit, and these units have a contribution margin of $60 per unit. Customer B is ordering 1,000 units and is willing to pay $140 per unit, and these units have a contribution margin ratio of 40%. Which order do you select and why?

LINK TO LEARNING

Watch this video from Investopedia reviewing the concept of contribution margin (https://openstax.org/l/50ContMargin) to learn more. Keep in mind that contribution margin per sale first contributes to meeting fixed costs and then to profit.

3.2 Calculate a Break-Even Point in Units and Dollars

In Building Blocks of Managerial Accounting, you learned how to determine and recognize the fixed and variable components of costs, and now you have learned about contribution margin. Those concepts can be used together to conduct cost-volume-profit (CVP) analysis, which is a method used by companies to determine what will occur financially if selling prices change, costs (either fixed or variable) change, or sales/production volume changes.

It is important, first, to make several assumptions about operations in order to understand CVP analysis and the associated contribution margin income statement. However, while the following assumptions are typical in CVP analysis, there can be exceptions. For example, while we typically assume that the sales price will remain the same, there might be exceptions where a quantity discount might be allowed. Our CVP analysis will be based on these assumptions:

- Costs are linear and can clearly be designated as either fixed or variable. In other words, fixed costs remain fixed in total over the relevant range and variable costs remain fixed on a per-unit basis. For example, if a company has the capability of producing up to 1,000 units a month of a product given its current resources, the relevant range would be 0 to 1,000. If they decided that they wanted to produce 1,800 units a month, they would have to secure additional production capacity. While they might be able to add an extra production shift and then produce 1,800 units a month without buying an additional machine that would increase production capacity to 2,000 units a month, companies often have to buy additional production equipment to increase their relevant range. In this example, the production capacity between 1,800 and 2,000 would be an expense that currently would not provide additional contribution toward fixed costs.
- Selling price per unit remains constant and does not increase or decrease based on volume (i.e., customers are not given discounts based on quantity purchased).
- In the case of manufacturing businesses, inventory does not change because we make the assumption that all units produced are sold.
- In the case of a company that sells multiple products, the sales mix remains constant. For example, if we are a beverage supplier, we might assume that our beverage sales are 3 units of coffee pods and two units of tea bags.

Using these assumptions, we can begin our discussion of CVP analysis with the break-even point.

Basics of the Break-Even Point

The **break-even point** is the dollar amount (total sales dollars) or production level (total units produced) at which the company has recovered all variable and fixed costs. In other words, no profit or loss occurs at break-even because Total Cost = Total Revenue. Figure 3.3 illustrates the components of the break-even point:

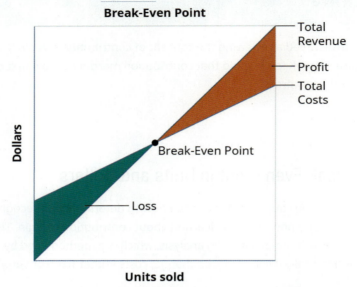

Figure 3.3   Break-Even Point. (attribution: Copyright Rice University, OpenStax, under CC BY-NC-SA 4.0 license)

The basic theory illustrated in Figure 3.3 is that, because of the existence of fixed costs in most production processes, in the first stages of production and subsequent sale of the products, the company will realize a loss. For example, assume that in an extreme case the company has fixed costs of $20,000, a sales price of $400 per unit and variable costs of $250 per unit, and it sells no units. It would realize a loss of $20,000 (the fixed costs) since it recognized no revenue or variable costs. This loss explains why the company's cost graph recognized costs (in this example, $20,000) even though there were no sales. If it subsequently sells units, the loss would be reduced by $150 (the contribution margin) for each unit sold. This relationship will be continued until we reach the break-even point, where total revenue equals total costs. Once we reach the break-even point for each unit sold the company will realize an increase in profits of $150.

For each additional unit sold, the loss typically is lessened until it reaches the break-even point. At this stage, the company is theoretically realizing neither a profit nor a loss. After the next sale beyond the break-even point, the company will begin to make a profit, and the profit will continue to increase as more units are sold. While there are exceptions and complications that could be incorporated, these are the general guidelines for break-even analysis.

As you can imagine, the concept of the break-even point applies to every business endeavor—manufacturing, retail, and service. Because of its universal applicability, it is a critical concept to managers, business owners, and accountants. When a company first starts out, it is important for the owners to know when their sales will be sufficient to cover all of their fixed costs and begin to generate a profit for the business. Larger companies may look at the break-even point when investing in new machinery, plants, or equipment in order to predict how long it will take for their sales volume to cover new or additional fixed costs. Since the break-even point represents that point where the company is neither losing nor making money, managers need to make decisions that will help the company reach and *exceed* this point as quickly as possible. No business can operate for very long below break-even. Eventually the company will suffer losses so great that they are forced to close their doors.

> ### ETHICAL CONSIDERATIONS
>
> #### Break-Even Analysis and Profitability
>
> The first step in determining the viability of the business decision to sell a product or provide a service is analyzing the true cost of the product or service and the timeline of payment for the product or service. Ethical managers need an estimate of a product or service's cost and related revenue streams to evaluate the chance of reaching the break-even point.
>
> Determining an accurate price for a product or service requires a detailed analysis of both the cost and how the cost changes as the volume increases. This analysis includes the timing of both costs and receipts for payment, as well as how these costs will be financed. An example is an IT service contract for a corporation where the costs will be frontloaded. When costs or activities are frontloaded, a greater proportion of the costs or activities occur in an earlier stage of the project. An IT service contract is typically employee cost intensive and requires an estimate of at least 120 days of employee costs before a payment will be received for the costs incurred. An IT service contract for $100,000 in monthly services with a 30% profit margin will require 4 months of upfront financing of $280,000 balanced over the four months before a single payment is received.
>
> The overall profit at a specific point in time requires a careful determination of all of the costs associated with creating and selling the product or providing the service. An ethical managerial accountant will provide a realistic cost estimate, regardless of management's desire to sell a product or provide a service. What might be a lucrative product on its face needs additional analysis provided by the managerial accountant.

To illustrate the concept of break-even, we will return to Hicks Manufacturing and look at the Blue Jay birdbath they manufacture and sell.

> ### LINK TO LEARNING
>
> Watch this [video of an example of performing the first steps of cost-volume-profit analysis (https://openstax.org/l/50CVPanalysis)](https://openstax.org/l/50CVPanalysis) to learn more.

Sales Where Operating Income Is $0

Hicks Manufacturing is interested in finding out the point at which they break even selling their Blue Jay Model birdbath. They will break even when the operating income is $0. The operating income is determined by subtracting the total variable and fixed costs from the sales revenue generated by an enterprise. In other words, the managers at Hicks want to know how many Blue Jay birdbaths they will need to sell in order to cover their fixed expenses and break even. Information on this product is:

HICKS MANUFACTURING
Blue Jay Model
For Year Ended December 31, 2019

Sales Price per Unit	$ 100
Variable Cost per Unit	20
Contribution Margin per Unit	80
Total Fixed Cost per Month	$18,000

In order to find their break-even point, we will use the contribution margin for the Blue Jay and determine how many contribution margins we need in order to cover the fixed expenses, as shown in the formula in Figure 3.4.

$$\text{Break-Even Point in Units:} \frac{\text{Total Fixed Costs}}{\text{Contribution Margin per Unit}}$$

Figure 3.4 Break-Even Point in Units. (attribution: Copyright Rice University, OpenStax, under CC BY-NC-SA 4.0 license)

Applying this to Hicks calculates as:

$$\frac{\$18,000}{\$80} = 225 \text{ units}$$

What this tells us is that Hicks must sell 225 Blue Jay Model birdbaths in order to cover their fixed expenses. In other words, they will not begin to show a profit until they sell the 226th unit. This is illustrated in their contribution margin income statement.

HICKS MANUFACTURING
Contribution Margin Income Statement
For Year Ended December 31, 2019

Sales (225 units at $100 per return)	$22,500
Variable Cost (225 units at $20 per return)	4,500
Contribution Margin	18,000
Fixed Costs	18,000
Operating Income	$ 0

The break-even point for Hicks Manufacturing at a sales volume of $22,500 (225 units) is shown graphically in Figure 3.5.

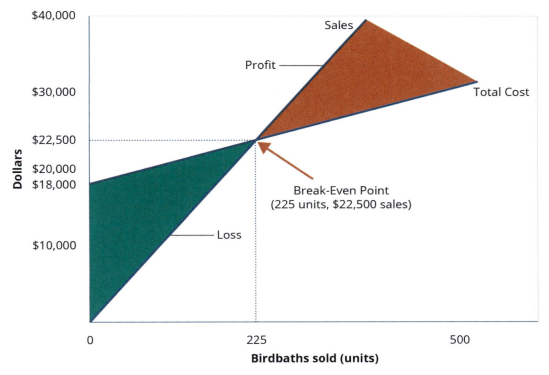

Figure 3.5 Hicks Manufacturing Break-Even Point for 225 Units. (attribution: Copyright Rice University, OpenStax, under CC BY-NC-SA 4.0 license)

As you can see, when Hicks sells 225 Blue Jay Model birdbaths, they will make no profit, but will not suffer a loss because all of their fixed expenses are covered. However, what happens when they do not sell 225 units? If that happens, their operating income is negative.

Sales Where Operating Income Is Negative

In a recent month, local flooding caused Hicks to close for several days, reducing the number of units they could ship and sell from 225 units to 175 units. The information in Figure 3.6 reflects this drop in sales.

HICKS MANUFACTURING Contribution Margin Income Statement For Year Ended December 31, 2019	
Sales (175 units at $100 per unit)	$17,500
Variable Cost (175 units at $20 per unit)	3,500
Contribution Margin	14,000
Fixed Costs	18,000
Operating Income	$ (4,000)

Figure 3.6 Hicks Manufacturing Contribution Margin Income Statement. (attribution: Copyright Rice University, OpenStax, under CC BY-NC-SA 4.0 license)

At 175 units ($17,500 in sales), Hicks does not generate enough sales revenue to cover their fixed expenses and they suffer a loss of $4,000. They did not reach the break-even point of 225 units.

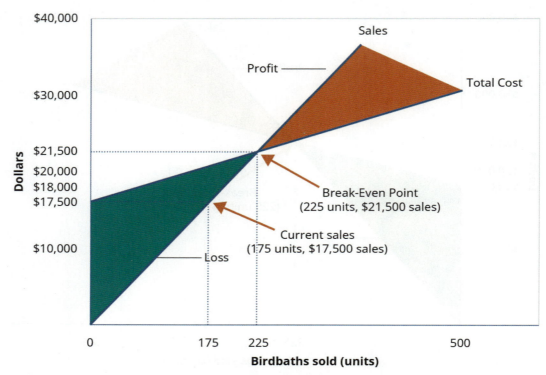

Figure 3.7 Hicks Manufacturing Break-Even Point for 175 Units. (attribution: Copyright Rice University, OpenStax, under CC BY-NC-SA 4.0 license)

Sales Where Operating Income Is Positive

What happens when Hicks has a busy month and sells 300 Blue Jay birdbaths? We have already established that the contribution margin from 225 units will put them at break-even. When sales exceed the break-even point the unit contribution margin from the additional units will go toward profit. This is reflected on their income statement.

HICKS MANUFACTURING Contribution Margin Income Statement For Year Ended December 31, 2019	
Sales (300 units at $100 per unit)	$30,000
Variable Cost (300 units at $20 per unit)	6,000
Contribution Margin	24,000
Fixed Costs	18,000
Operating Income	$ 6,000

Again, looking at the graph for break-even (Figure 3.8), you will see that their sales have moved them beyond the point where total revenue is equal to total cost and into the profit area of the graph.

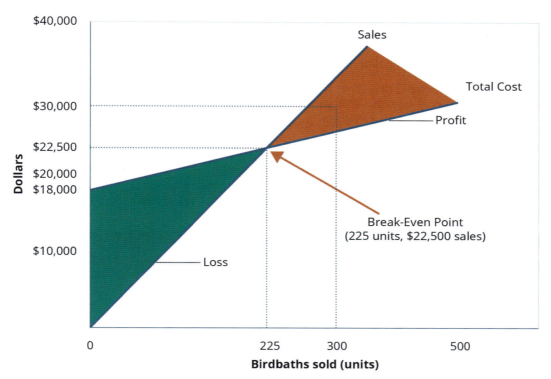

Figure 3.8 Hicks Manufacturing Break-Even Point for 300 Units. (attribution: Copyright Rice University, OpenStax, under CC BY-NC-SA 4.0 license)

Hicks Manufacturing can use the information from these different scenarios to inform many of their decisions about operations, such as sales goals.

However, using the contribution margin per unit is not the only way to determine a break-even point. Recall that we were able to determine a contribution margin expressed in dollars by finding the contribution margin ratio. We can apply that contribution margin ratio to the break-even analysis to determine the break-even point in dollars. For example, we know that Hicks had $18,000 in fixed costs and a contribution margin ratio of 80% for the Blue Jay model. We will use this ratio (Figure 3.9) to calculate the break-even point in dollars.

$$\text{Break-Even Point in Dollars} = \frac{\text{Fixed Costs}}{\text{Contribution Margin Ratio}}$$

Figure 3.9 Break-Even Point in Dollars. (attribution: Copyright Rice University, OpenStax, under CC BY-NC-SA 4.0 license)

Applying the formula to Hicks gives this calculation:

$$\frac{\$18,000}{0.80} = \$22,500$$

Hicks Manufacturing will have to generate $22,500 in monthly sales in order to cover all of their fixed costs. In order for us to verify that Hicks' break-even point is $22,500 (or 225 units) we will look again at the contribution margin income statement at break-even:

HICKS MANUFACTURING
Contribution Margin Income Statement
For Year Ended December 31, 2019

Sales (225 units at $100 per unit)	$22,500
Variable Cost (225 units at $20 per unit)	4,500
Contribution Margin	18,000
Fixed Costs	18,000
Operating Income	$ 0

By knowing at what level sales are sufficient to cover fixed expenses is critical, but companies want to be able to make a profit and can use this break-even analysis to help them.

THINK IT THROUGH

The Cost of a Haircut

You are the manager of a hair salon and want to know how many ladies' haircuts your salon needs to sell in a month in order to cover the fixed costs of running the salon. You have determined that, at the current price of $35 per haircut, you have $20 in variable costs associated with each cut. These variable costs include stylist wages, hair product, and shop supplies. Your fixed costs are $3,000 per month. You perform a break-even analysis on a per-unit basis and discover the following:

Sales price per service	$ 35
Variable cost per service	20
Contribution margin per service	15
Break-even (in services)	200

You have 4 stylists plus yourself working in the salon and are open 6 days per week. Considering the break-even point and the number of available stylists, will the salon ever break even? If it does, what will need to happen? What can be done to achieve the break-even point?

Examples of the Effects of Variable and Fixed Costs in Determining the Break-Even Point

Companies typically do not want to simply break even, as they are in business to make a profit. Break-even analysis also can help companies determine the level of sales (in dollars or in units) that is needed to make a desired profit. The process for factoring a desired level of profit into a break-even analysis is to add the desired level of profit to the fixed costs and then calculate a new break-even point. We know that Hicks Manufacturing breaks even at 225 Blue Jay birdbaths, but what if they have a target profit for the month of July? They can simply add that target to their fixed costs. By calculating a target profit, they will produce and (hopefully) sell enough bird baths to cover both fixed costs and the target profit.

If Hicks wants to earn $16,000 in profit in the month of May, we can calculate their new break-even point as follows:

$$\text{Target Profit} = \frac{\text{Fixed costs} + \text{desired profit}}{\text{Contribution margin per unit}} = \frac{\$18{,}000 + \$16{,}000}{\$80} = 425 \text{ units}$$

We have already established that the $18,000 in fixed costs is covered at the 225 units mark, so an additional 200 units will cover the desired profit (200 units × $80 per unit contribution margin = $16,000). Alternatively, we can calculate this in terms of dollars by using the contribution margin ratio.

$$\text{Target Profit} = \frac{\text{Fixed costs} + \text{desired profit}}{\text{Contribution margin ratio}} = \frac{\$18{,}000 + \$16{,}000}{0.80} = \$42{,}500$$

As done previously, we can confirm this calculation using the contribution margin income statement:

Sales (425 units at $100 per unit)	$42,500
Variable Costs (425 units at $20 per unit)	8,500
Contribution Margin	34,000
Fixed Costs	18,000
Operating Income (loss)	$16,000

Note that the example calculations ignored income taxes, which implies we were finding target operating income. However, companies may want to determine what level of sales would generate a desired after-tax profit. To find the break-even point at a desired after-tax profit, we simply need to convert the desired after-tax profit to the desired pre-tax profit, also referred to as operating income, and then follow through as in the example. Suppose Hicks wants to earn $24,000 after-taxes, what level of sales (units and dollars) would be needed to meet that goal? First, the after-tax profit needs to be converted to a pre-tax desired profit:

$$\text{Pre-tax desired profit} = \frac{\text{After-tax profit}}{(1 - \text{tax rate})}$$

If the tax rate for Hicks is 40%, then the $24,000 after-tax profit is equal to a pre-tax profit of $40,000:

$$\$40{,}000 = \frac{\$24{,}000}{(1 - 0.40)}$$

The tax rate indicates the amount of tax expense that will result from any profits and 1 – tax rate indicates the amount remaining after taking out tax expense. The concept is similar to buying an item on sale. If an item costs $80 and is on sale for 40% off, then the amount being paid for the item is 60% of the sale price, or $48 ($80 × 60%). Another way to find this involves two steps. First find the discount ($80 × 40% = $32) and then subtract the discount from the sales price ($80 – $32 = $48).

Taxes and profit work in a similar fashion. If we know the profit before tax is $100,000 and the tax rate is 30%, then tax expenses are $100,000 × 30% = $30,000. This means the after-tax income is $100,000 – $30,000 = $70,000. However, in most break-even situations, as well as other decision-making areas, the desired after-tax profit is known, and the pre-tax profit must be determined by dividing the after-tax profit by 1 – tax rate.

To demonstrate the combination of both a profit and the after-tax effects and subsequent calculations, let's return to the Hicks Manufacturing example. Let's assume that we want to calculate the target volume in units and revenue that Hicks must sell to generate an after-tax return of $24,000, assuming the same fixed costs of $18,000.

Since we earlier determined $24,000 after-tax equals $40,000 before-tax if the tax rate is 40%, we simply use the break-even at a desired profit formula to determine the target sales.

$$\text{Target sales} = \frac{(\text{Fixed costs} + \text{Desired profit})}{\text{Contribution margin per unit}} = \frac{(\$18{,}000 + \$40{,}000)}{\$80} = 725 \text{ units}$$

This calculation demonstrates that Hicks would need to sell 725 units at $100 a unit to generate $72,500 in sales to earn $24,000 in after-tax profits.

Alternatively, target sales in sales dollars could have been calculated using the contribution margin ratio:

$$\text{Target sales} = \frac{\text{(Fixed costs + Desired profit)}}{\text{Contribution margin per unit}} = \frac{(\$18,000 + \$40,000)}{0.80} = \$72,500$$

Once again, the contribution margin income statement proves the sales and profit relationships.

Sales (725 units x $100 per unit)	$ 72,500
Variable costs (725 units x $20 per unit)	(14,500)
Contribution margin	$ 58,000
Fixed costs	(18,000)
Pre-tax profit	$ 40,000
Income tax expense (40%)	(16,000)
After-tax profit	$ 24,000

Thus, to calculate break-even point at a particular after-tax income, the only additional step is to convert after-tax income to pre-tax income prior to utilizing the break-even formula. It is good to understand the impact of taxes on break-even analysis as companies will often want to plan based on the after-tax effects of a decision as the after-tax portion of income is the only part of income that will be available for future use.

Application of Break-Even Concepts for a Service Organization

Because break-even analysis is applicable to any business enterprise, we can apply these same principles to a service organization. For example, Marshall & Hirito is a mid-sized accounting firm that provides a wide range of accounting services to its clients but relies heavily on personal income tax preparation for much of its revenue. They have analyzed the cost to the firm associated with preparing these returns. They have determined the following cost structure for the preparation of a standard 1040A Individual Income Tax Return:

Charge to Client (sales price per return)	$400
Variable Cost per Return	150

They have fixed costs of $14,000 per month associated with the salaries of the accountants who are responsible for preparing the *Form 1040A*. In order to determine their break-even point, they first determine the contribution margin for the *Form 1040A* as shown:

Sales Price per Return	$400
Variable Cost per Return	150
Contribution Margin per Return	250

Now they can calculate their break-even point:

$$\text{Break-Even Point in Units} = \frac{\text{Total fixed costs}}{\text{Contribution margin per unit}} = \frac{\$14,000}{\$250} = 56 \text{ returns}$$

Remember, this is the break-even point in units (the number of tax returns) but they can also find a break-even point expressed in dollars by using the contribution margin ratio. First, they find the contribution margin ratio. Then, they use the ratio to calculate the break-even point in dollars:

$$\text{Break-Even Point in Dollars} = \frac{\text{Fixed costs}}{\text{Contribution margin ratio}} = \frac{\$14,000}{0.625} = \$22,400$$

We can confirm these figures by preparing a contribution margin income statement:

MARSHALL & SON, CPAs
Contribution Margin Income Statement
For Year Ended December 31, 2019

Sales (56 at $400 per return)	$22,400
Variable Costs (56 at $150 per return)	8,400
Contribution Margin	14,000
Fixed costs	14,000
Operating Income (loss)	$ 0

Therefore, as long as Marshall & Hirito prepares 56 *Form 1040* income tax returns, they will earn no profit but also incur no loss. What if Marshall & Hirito has a target monthly profit of $10,000? They can use the break-even analysis process to determine how many returns they will need to prepare in order to cover their fixed expenses and reach their target profit:

$$\text{Target Profit} = \frac{\text{Fixed costs} + \text{desired profit}}{\text{Contribution margin per unit}} = \frac{\$14{,}000 + \$10{,}000}{\$250} = 96 \text{ returns}$$

They will need to prepare 96 returns during the month in order to realize a $10,000 profit. Expressing this in dollars instead of units requires that we use the contribution margin ratio as shown:

$$\text{Target Profit} = \frac{\text{Fixed costs} + \text{desired profit}}{\text{Contribution margin per unit}} = \frac{\$14{,}000 + \$10{,}000}{0.625} = \$38{,}400$$

Marshall & Hirito now knows that, in order to cover the fixed costs associated with this service, they must generate $38,400 in revenue. Once again, let's verify this by constructing a contribution margin income statement:

MARSHALL & SON, CPAs
Contribution Margin Income Statement
For Year Ended December 31, 2019

Sales (96 at $400 per return)	$38,400
Variable Costs (96 at $150 per return)	14,400
Contribution Margin	24,000
Fixed Costs	14,000
Operating Income (loss)	$10,000

As you can see, the $38,400 in revenue will not only cover the $14,000 in fixed costs, but will supply Marshall & Hirito with the $10,000 in profit (net income) they desire.

As you've learned, break-even can be calculated using either contribution margin per unit or the contribution margin ratio. Now that you have seen this process, let's look at an example of these two concepts presented together to illustrate how either method will provide the same financial results.

Suppose that Channing's Chairs designs, builds, and sells unique ergonomic desk chairs for home and business. Their bestselling chair is the Spine Saver. Figure 3.10 illustrates how Channing could determine the break-even point in sales dollars using either the contribution margin per unit or the contribution margin ratio.

Sales Price per Unit	Cost per Unit	Contribution Margin per Unit	Fixed Costs	Fixed Costs/ Contribution Margin per Unit	Break-Even in Units	Break Even in Dollars
$1,250	$850	$400	$16,800	$16,800/$400	42	42 x $1,250 = $52,500

Contribution Margin per Unit ($1,250 – 850)	Contribution Margin Ratio (CM/Sales or $400 ÷ $1,250)	Break-Even in Sales Dollars (FC ÷ CM or $16,800 ÷ 0.32)	Break-Even in Units (Break Even Sales ÷ Unit Selling Price or $52,500 ÷ $1,250)
$400	32%	$52,500	42 Units

Figure 3.10 Channing's Break-Even Point. (attribution: Copyright Rice University, OpenStax, under CC BY-NC-SA 4.0 license)

Note that in either scenario, the break-even point is the same in dollars and units, regardless of approach. Thus, you can always find the break-even point (or a desired profit) in units and then convert it to sales by multiplying by the selling price per unit. Alternatively, you can find the break-even point in sales dollars and then find the number of units by dividing by the selling price per unit.

YOUR TURN

College Creations

College Creations, Inc (CC), builds a loft that is easily adaptable to most dorm rooms or apartments and can be assembled into a variety of configurations. Each loft is sold for $500, and the cost to produce one loft is $300, including all parts and labor. CC has fixed costs of $100,000.

A. What happens if CC produces nothing?
B. Now, assume CC produces and sells one unit (loft). What are their financial results?
C. Now, what do you think would happen if they produced and sold 501 units?
D. How many units would CC need to sell in order to break even?
E. How many units would CC need to sell if they wanted to have a pretax profit of $50,000?

Solution

A. If they produce nothing, they will still incur fixed costs of $100,000. They will suffer a net loss of $100,000.

B. If they sell one unit, they will have a net loss of $99,800.

Sales revenue	$ 500
Variable cost per unit	300
Contribution margin	200
Fixed costs	100,000
Operating income (loss)	$ (99,800)

C. If they produce 501 units, they will have operating income of $200 as shown:

Sales revenue (501 units at $500)	$250,500
Variable cost per unit (501 units at $300)	150,300
Contribution margin	100,200
Fixed costs	100,000
Operating income (loss)	$ 200

D. Break-even can be determined by FC/CM per unit: $100,000 ÷ $200 = 500. Five hundred lofts must be sold to break even.

E. The desired profit can be treated like a fixed cost, and the target profit would be (FC + Desired Profit)/CM or ($100,000 + $50,000) ÷ $200 = 750. Seven hundred fifty lofts need to be sold to reach a desired income of $50,000. Another way to have found this is to know that, after fixed costs are met, the $200 per unit contribution margin will go toward profit. The desired profit of $50,000 ÷ $200 per unit contribution margin = 250. This means that 250 additional units must be sold. To break even requires 500 units to be sold, and to reach the desired profit of $50,000 requires an additional 250 units, for a total of 750 units.

3.3 Perform Break-Even Sensitivity Analysis for a Single Product Under Changing Business Situations

Finding the break-even point or the sales necessary to meet a desired profit is very useful to a business, but cost-volume-profit analysis also can be used to conduct a **sensitivity analysis**, which shows what will happen if the sales price, units sold, variable cost per unit, or fixed costs change. Companies use this type of analysis to consider possible scenarios that assist them in planning.

LINK TO LEARNING

Watch this video that shows what happens if one or more of the variables in a break-even analysis is changed (https://openstax.org/l/50BrkEvenChange) to learn more.

The Effects on Break-Even under Changing Business Conditions

Circumstances often change within a company, within an industry, or even within the economy that impact the decision-making of an organization. Sometimes, these effects are sudden and unexpected, for example, if a hurricane destroyed the factory of a company's major supplier; other times, they occur more slowly, such as when union negotiations affect your labor costs. In either of these situations, costs to the company will be affected. Using CVP analysis, the company can predict how these changes will affect profits.

Changing a Single Variable

To demonstrate the effects of changing any one of these variables, consider Back Door Café, a small coffee shop that roasts its own beans to make espresso drinks and gourmet coffee. They also sell a variety of baked goods and T-shirts with their logo on them. They track their costs carefully and use CVP analysis to make sure that their sales cover their fixed costs and provide a reasonable level of profit for the owners.

Change in Sales Price

The owner of Back Door has one of her employees conduct a survey of the other coffee shops in the area and finds that they are charging $0.75 more for espresso drinks. As a result, the owner wants to determine what would happen to operating income if she increased her price by just $0.50 and sales remained constant, so she performs the following analysis:

Price Change Analysis		
	With Current Price	**With New Price**
Sales Price per Unit	$ 3.75	$ 4.25
Variable Cost per Unit	$ 1.50	$ 1.50
Contribution Margin per Unit	$ 2.25	$ 2.75
Fixed Costs	$2,475	$2,475
Break-even (in units)	1,100	900
Break-Even (in dollars)	$4,125	$3,825
Contribution Margin Income Statement **Current Price versus New Price**		
Unit Sales, Expected	1,500	1,500
Sales	$5,625	$6,375
Variable Costs	2,250	2,250
Contribution Margin	$3,375	$4,125
Fixed Costs	2,475	2,475
Net Income	$ 900	$1,650

The only variable that has changed is the $0.50 increase in the price of their espresso drinks, but the net operating income will increase by $750. Another way to think of this increase in income is that, if the sales price increases by $0.50 per expresso drink and the estimated sales are 1,500 units, then this will result in an increase in overall contribution margin of $750. Moreover, since all of the fixed costs were met by the lower sales price, all of this $750 goes to profit. Again, this is assuming the higher sales price does not decrease the number of units sold. Since the other coffee shops will still be priced higher than Back Door, the owner believes that there will not be a decrease in sales volume.

When making this adjustment to their sales price, Back Door Café is engaging in **target pricing**, a process in which a company uses market analysis and production information to determine the maximum price customers are willing to pay for a good or service in addition to the markup percentage. If the good can be produced at a cost that allows both the desired profit percentage as well as deliver the good at a price acceptable to the customer, then the company should proceed with the product; otherwise, the company will not achieve its desired profit goals.

Change in Variable Cost

In March, the owner of Back Door receives a letter from her cups supplier informing her that there is a $0.05 price increase due to higher material prices. Assume that the example uses the original $3.75 per unit sales price. The owner wants to know what would happen to net operating income if she absorbs the cost increase, so she performs the following analysis:

	Variable Cost Change Analysis	
	With Current Price	With Increased Variable Cost
Sales Price per Unit	$ 3.75	$ 3.75
Variable Cost per Unit	$ 1.50	$ 1.55
Contribution Margin per Unit	$ 2.25	$ 2.20
Fixed Costs	$2,475	$ 2,475
Break-even in Units	1,100	1,125
Break-even in Dollars	$4,125	$4,218.75
	Monthly Contribution Margin Income Statement **Current Variable Costs versus Increased Variable Costs**	
Unit Sales, Expected	1,500	1,500
Sales	$5,625	$ 5,625
Variable Costs	2,250	2,325
Contribution Margin	$3,375	$ 3,300
Fixed Costs	2,475	2,475
Net Income	$ 900	$ 825

She is surprised to see that just a $0.05 increase in variable costs (cups) will reduce her net income by $75. The owner may decide that she is fine with the lower income, but if she wants to maintain her income, she will need to find a new cup supplier, reduce other costs, or pass the price increase on to her customers. Because the increase in the cost of the cups was a variable cost, the impact on net income can be seen by taking the increase in cost per unit, $0.05, and multiplying that by the units expected to be sold, 1,500, to see the impact on the contribution margin, which in this case would be a decrease of $75. This also means a decrease in net income of $75.

Change in Fixed Cost

Back Door Café's lease is coming up for renewal. The owner calls the landlord to indicate that she wants to renew her lease for another 5 years. The landlord is happy to hear she will continue renting from him but informs her that the rent will increase $225 per month. She is not certain that she can afford an additional $225 per month and tells him she needs to look at her numbers and will call him back. She pulls out her CVP spreadsheet and adjusts her monthly fixed costs upwards by $225. Assume that the example uses the original $3.75 per unit sales price. The results of her analysis of the impact of the rent increase on her annual net income are:

Fixed Cost Change Analysis		
	With Current Price	With Increased Fixed Cost
Sales Price per Unit	$ 3.75	$ 3.75
Variable Cost per Unit	$ 1.50	$ 1.50
Contribution Margin per Unit	$ 2.25	$ 2.25
Fixed Costs	$2,475	$2,700
Break-even in Units	1,100	1,200
Break-even in Dollars	$4,125	$4,500
Monthly Contribution Margin Income Statement **Current Fixed Costs versus Increased Fixed Costs**		
Unit Sales, Expected	1,500	1,500
Sales	$5,625	$5,625
Variable Costs	2,250	2,250
Contribution Margin	$3,375	$3,375
Fixed Costs	2,475	2,700
Net Income	$ 900	$ 675

Because the rent increase is a change in a fixed cost, the contribution margin per unit remains the same. However, the break-even point in both units and dollars increase because more units of contribution are needed to cover the $225 monthly increase in fixed costs. If the owner of the Back Door agrees to the increase in rent for the new lease, she will likely look for ways to increase the contribution margin per unit to offset this increase in fixed costs.

In each of the prior examples, only one variable was changed—sales volume, variable costs, or fixed costs. There are some generalizations that can be made regarding how a change in any one of these variables affects the break-even point. These generalizations are summarized in Table 3.1.

Generalizations Regarding Changes in Break-Even Point from a Change in One Variable

Condition	Result
Sales Price Increases	Break-Even Point Decreases (Contribution Margin is Higher, Need Fewer Sales to Break Even)
Sales Price Decreases	Break-Even Point Increases (Contribution Margin is Lower, Need More Sales to Break Even)
Variable Costs Increase	Break-Even Point Increases (Contribution Margin is Lower, Need More Sales to Break Even)
Variable Costs Decrease	Break-Even Point Decreases (Contribution Margin is Higher, Need Fewer Sales to Break Even)

Table 3.1

Generalizations Regarding Changes in Break-Even Point from a Change in One Variable

Condition	Result
Fixed Costs Increase	Break-Even Point Increases (Contribution Margin Does Not Change, but Need More Sales to Meet Fixed Costs)
Fixed Costs Decrease	Break-Even Point Decreases (Contribution Margin Does Not Change, but Need Fewer Sales to Meet Fixed Costs)

Table 3.1

LINK TO LEARNING

Watch this video that walks through, step by step, how to calculate break even in units and dollars and at a desired profit or sales level (https://openstax.org/l/50BreakEven$) to learn more.

Changing Multiple Variables

We have analyzed situations in which one variable changes, but often, more than one change will occur at a time. For example, a company may need to lower its selling price to compete, but they may also be able to lower certain variable costs by switching suppliers.

Suppose Back Door Café has the opportunity to purchase a new espresso machine that will reduce the amount of coffee beans required for an espresso drink by putting the beans under higher pressure. The new machine will cost $15,000, but it will decrease the variable cost per cup by $0.05. The owner wants to see what the effect will be on the net operating income and break-even point if she purchases the new machine. She has arranged financing for the new machine and the monthly payment will increase her fixed costs by $400 per month. When she conducts this analysis, she gets the following results:

Variable Cost and Fixed Cost Change Analysis		
	With Current Price	With Decreased VC and Increased FC
Sales Price per Unit	$ 3.75	$ 3.75
Variable Cost per Unit	$ 1.50	$ 1.45
Contribution Margin per Unit	$ 2.25	$ 2.30
Fixed Costs	$ 2,475	$ 2,875
Break-even in Units	1,100	1,250
Break-even in Dollars	$4,125.00	$4,687.50
Monthly Contribution Margin Income Statement **Current Fixed Costs versus Increased Fixed Costs**		
Unit Sales, Expected	1,500	1,500
Sales	$ 5,625	$ 5,625
Variable Costs	2,250	2,175
Contribution Margin	$ 3,375	$ 3,450
Fixed Costs	2,475	2,875
Net Income	$ 900	$ 575

Looking at the "what-if" analysis, we see that the contribution margin per unit increases because of the $0.05 reduction in variable cost per unit. As a result, she has a higher total contribution margin available to cover fixed expenses. This is good, because the monthly payment on the espresso machine represents an increased fixed cost. Even though the contribution margin ratio increases, it is not enough to totally offset the increase in fixed costs, and her monthly break-even point has risen from $4,125.00 to $4,687.50. If the new break-even point in units is a realistic number (within the relevant range), then she would decide to purchase the new machine because, once it has been paid for, her break-even point will fall and her net income will rise. Performing this analysis is an effective way for managers and business owners to look into the future, so to speak, and see what impact business decisions will have on their financial position.

Let's look at another option the owner of the Back Door Café has to consider when making the decision about this new machine. What would happen if she purchased the new machine to realize the variable cost savings and also raised her price by just $0.20? She feels confident that such a small price increase will go virtually unnoticed by her customers but may help her offset the increase in fixed costs. She runs the analysis as follows:

Selling price, variable cost, and fixed cost change analysis			
	With Current Price	With decreased VC and increased FC	With increased SP, decreased VC, and increased FC
Sales price per unit	$ 3.75	$ 3.75	$ 3.95
Variable cost per unit	$ 1.50	$ 1.45	$ 1.45
Contribution margin per unit	$ 2.25	$ 2.30	$ 2.50
Fixed costs	$ 2,475	$ 2,875	$ 2,875
Break-even in units	1,100	1,250	1,150
Break-even in dollars	$4,125.00	$4,687.50	$4,542.50
Monthly contribution margin income statement			
Unit sales, expected	1,500	1,500	1,500
Sales	$ 5,625	$ 5,625	$ 5,925
Variable costs	2,250	2,175	2,175
Contribution margin	$ 3,375	$ 3,450	$ 3,750
Fixed costs	2,475	2,875	2,875
Net income	$ 900	$ 575	$ 875

The analysis shows the expected result: an increase in the per-unit contribution margin, a decrease in the break-even point, and an increase in the net operating income. She has changed three variables in her costs—sales price, variable cost, and fixed cost. In fact, the small price increase almost gets her back to the net operating income she realized before the purchase of the new expresso machine.

By now, you should begin to understand why CVP analysis is such a powerful tool. The owner of Back Door Café can run an unlimited number of these what-if scenarios until she meets the financial goals for her company. There are very few tools in managerial accounting as powerful and meaningful as a cost-volume-profit analysis.

CONCEPTS IN PRACTICE

Value Menus

In January 2018, McDonald's brought back its $1 value menu. After discontinuing its popular Dollar Menu six years previously, the new version has a list of items priced not only at $1, but at $2 and $3 as well. How can McDonald's afford to offer menu items at this discounted price? Volume! Although the margin on each unit is very small, the food chain hopes to make up the difference in quantity. They also hope that consumers will add higher priced (and higher margin) items to their orders.[1] The strategy is not without its risks, however, as rising food or labor costs could put franchisees in a position where the value pricing does not cover their product costs. Rivals Taco Bell and Dunkin' Donuts have aggressively marketed their value menus, making it almost impossible for McDonald's to ignore the growing trend among consumers for "value pricing." Watch this video (https://openstax.org/l/50BrkEvenChange1) to see what McDonald's is offering consumers.

3.4 Perform Break-Even Sensitivity Analysis for a Multi-Product Environment Under Changing Business Situations

Up to this point in our CVP analysis, we have assumed that a company only sells one product, but we know that, realistically, this is not the case. Most companies operate in a **multi-product environment**, in which they sell different products, manufacture different products, or offer different types of services. Companies price each one of their products or services differently, and the costs associated with each of those products or services vary as well. In addition, companies have limited resources, such as time and labor, and must decide which products to sell or produce and in what quantities, or which services to offer in order to be the most profitable. These profitability considerations are often what contributes substance to a sales mix decision

The Basics of Break-Even Analysis in a Multi-Product Environment

In order to perform a break-even analysis for a company that sells multiple products or provides multiple services, it is important to understand the concept of a sales mix. A **sales mix** represents the relative proportions of the products that a company sells—in other words, the percentage of the company's total revenue that comes from product A, product B, product C, and so forth. Sales mix is important to business owners and managers because they seek to have a mix that maximizes profit, since not all products have the same profit margin. Companies can maximize their profits if they are able to achieve a sales mix that is heavy with high-margin products, goods, or services. If a company focuses on a sales mix heavy with low-margin items, overall company profitability will often suffer.

Performing a break-even analysis for these multi-product businesses is more complex because each product has a different selling price, a different variable cost, and, ultimately, a different contribution margin. We must also proceed under the assumption that the sales mix remains constant; if it does change, the CVP analysis must be revised to reflect the change in sales mix. For the sake of clarity, we will also assume that all costs are companywide costs, and each product contributes toward covering these companywide costs.

THINK IT THROUGH

Selling Subs

You are the manager of a sub shop located near a college campus. The college has recently added a fast-food style café to the student center, which has reduced the number of students eating at your restaurant. Your highest margin items are drinks (a contribution margin of approximately 90%) and vegetarian subs (a contribution margin of approximately 75%). How can you use CVP analysis to help you compete with the college's café? What would you suggest as possible ways to increase business while maintaining target income levels?

Calculating Break-Even Analysis in a Multi-Product Environment

When a company sells more than one product or provides more than one service, break-even analysis is more

---

1 Zlati Meyer. "McDonald's Hope Customers Buck Up Thursday to New Dollar Menu." *USA Today*. January 3, 2018. https://www.usatoday.com/story/money/2018/01/03/mcdonalds-hopes-customers-buck-up-thursday-new-dollar-menu/996350001/

complex because not all of the products sell for the same price or have the same costs associated with them: Each product has its own margin. Consequently, the break-even point in a multi-product environment depends on the mix of products sold. Further, when the mix of products changes, so does the break-even point. If demand shifts and customers purchase more low-margin products, then the break-even point rises. Conversely, if customers purchase more high-margin products, the break-even point falls. In fact, even if total sales dollars remain unchanged, the break-even point can change based on the sales mix. Let's look at an example of how break-even analysis works in a multi-product environment.

In multi-product CVP analysis, the company's sales mix is viewed as a **composite unit**, a selection of discrete products associated together in proportion to the sales mix. The composite unit is not sold to customers but is a concept used to calculate a combined contribution margin, which is then used to estimate the break-even point. Think of a composite unit as a virtual basket of fruit that contains the proportion of individual fruits equal to the company's sales mix. If we purchased these items individually to make the fruit basket, each one would have a separate price and a different contribution margin. This is how a composite unit works in CVP analysis. We calculate the contribution margins of all of the component parts of the composite unit and then use the total to calculate the break-even point. It is important to note that fixed costs are allocated among the various components (products) that make up this composite unit. Should a product be eliminated from the composite unit or sales mix, the fixed costs must be re-allocated among the remaining products.

If we use the fruit basket as an example, we can look at the individual fruits that make up the basket: apples, oranges, bananas, and pears. We see that each individual fruit has a selling price and a cost. Each fruit has its own contribution margin. But how would we determine the contribution margin for a composite of fruit, or in other words, for our basket of fruit?

For our particular baskets, we will use 5 apples, 3 oranges, 2 bananas, and 1 pear. This means that our product mix is 5:3:2:1, as shown in Figure 3.11.

Fruit	Number of Units	Selling Price per Unit	Total Selling Price	Cost per Unit	Total Cost	Contribution Margin
Apple	5	$0.60	$3.00	$0.25	$1.25	$1.75
Orange	3	1.00	3.00	0.75	2.25	0.75
Banana	2	0.80	1.60	0.50	1.00	0.60
Pear	1	1.90	1.90	1.50	1.50	0.40
Total			$9.50		$6.00	$3.50

Figure 3.11 Contribution Margin Based on Product Mix. (attribution: Copyright Rice University, OpenStax, under CC BY-NC-SA 4.0 license)

Notice that the composite contribution margin is based on the number of units of each item that is included in the composite item. If we change the composition of the basket, then the composite contribution margin would change even though contribution margin of the individual items would not change. For example, if we only include 4 apples, the contribution margin of a single apple is still $0.35, but the contribution margin of the apples in the basket is $1.40, not $1.75 as it is when 5 apples are included in the basket. Let's look at an additional example and see how we find the break-even point for a composite good.

We will consider West Brothers for an example of a multi-product break-even analysis. West Brothers manufactures and sells 3 types of house siding: restoration vinyl, architectural vinyl, and builder grade vinyl, each with its own sales price, variable cost, and contribution margin, as shown:

	Sales Price per Square Foot	Variable Cost per Square Foot
Builder Grade	$6.25	$3.25
Architectural	7.75	4.50
Restoration	9.25	6.25

The sales mix for West Brothers is 5 ft^2 of builder grade to 3 ft^2 of architectural grade to 2 ft^2 of restoration grade vinyl (a ratio of 5:3:2). This sales mix represents one composite unit, and the selling price of one composite unit is:

5 ft^2 of Builder Grade at $6.25	$31.25
3 ft^2 of Architectural at $7.75	23.25
2 ft^2 of Restoration at $9.25	18.50
Selling Price of 1 Composite Unit	$73.00

West Brothers' fixed costs are $145,000 per year, and the variable costs for one composite unit are:

5 ft^2 of Builder Grade at $3.25	$16.25
3 ft^2 of Architectural at $4.50	13.50
2 ft^2 of Restoration at $6.25	12.50
Variable Costs of 1 Composite Unit	$42.25

We will calculate the contribution margin of a composite unit for West Brothers using the same formula as before:

$$\text{Selling Price per Composite Unit} - \text{Variable Cost per Composite Unit} = \text{Contribution Margin per Composite Unit}$$

Applying the formula, we determine that $73 − $42.25 = 30.75. We then use the contribution margin per composite unit to determine West Brothers' break-even point:

$$\text{Break-Even Point per Composite Unit} = \frac{\text{Total fixed costs}}{\text{Contribution margin per composite unit}} = \frac{\$145{,}000}{\$30.75} = 4{,}715.45 \text{ composite units}$$

West Brothers will break even when it sells 4,715.45 (or 4,716 since it can't sell a partial unit) composite units. To determine how many of each product West Brothers needs to sell, we apply their sales mix ratio (5:3:2) to the break-even quantity as follows:

Builder Grade	5 × 4,715.45	23,577
Architectural	3 × 4,715.45	14,146
Restoration	2 × 4,715.45	9,431
Total Units		47,154

Using a forecasted or estimated contribution margin income statement, we can verify that the quantities listed will place West Brothers at break-even.

WEST BROTHERS
Forecasted Contribution Margin
Income Statement at Break-Even
For Month Ended December 31, 2019

Sales	
Builder grade (23,577 at $6.25)	$147,358
Architectural (14,146 at $7.75)	109,634
Restoration (9,431 at $9.25)	87,236
Total Sales	344,228
Variable Costs	
Builder Grade (23,577 at $3.25)	76,626
Architectural (14,146 at $4.50)	63,659
Restoration (9,431 at $9.25)	58,943
Total Variable Costs	199,228
Contribution Margin	145,000
Fixed Costs	145,000
Net Income	0

West Brothers can use this CVP analysis for a wide range of business decisions and for planning purposes. Remember, however, that if the sales mix changes from its current ratio, then the break-even point will change. For planning purposes, West Brothers can change the sales mix, sales price, or variable cost of one or more of the products in the composite unit and perform a "what-if" analysis.

YOUR TURN

Margins in the Sales Mix

The sales mix of a company selling two products, A and B, is 3:1. The per-unit variable costs is $4 for Product A and $5 for Product B. Product A sells for $10 and product B sells for $9. Fixed costs for the company are $220,000.

A. What is the contribution margin per composite unit?
B. What is the break-even point in composite units?
C. How many units of product A and product B will the company sell at the break-even point?

Solution

A.

Product	Sales Price per Unit	Variable Cost per Unit	Contribution Margin per Unit
A	$8	$5	$3
B	9	5	4

B.

Sales Price	Variable Cost	Contribution Margin
$33	$20	$13

Break-even per composite unit = 15,385.

C.

	Number of units per product		
	A	3 × 15,385	46,155
	B	1 × 15,385	15,385
	Sales		
		Product A	$369,231
		Product B	$138,462
		Total sales	$507,692
	Variable costs		
		Product A	$230,769
		Product B	$ 76,923
		Total variable costs	$307,692
	Contribution margin		$200,000
	Fixed costs		$200,000
	Net Income		$ 0

3.5 Calculate and Interpret a Company's Margin of Safety and Operating Leverage

Our discussion of CVP analysis has focused on the sales necessary to break even or to reach a desired profit, but two other concepts are useful regarding our break-even sales. Those concepts are margin of safety and operating leverage.

Margin of Safety

A company's **margin of safety** is the difference between its current sales and its break-even sales. The margin of safety tells the company how much they could lose in sales before the company begins to lose money, or, in other words, before the company falls below the break-even point. The higher the margin of safety is, the lower the risk is of not breaking even or incurring a loss. In order to calculate margin of safety, we use the following formula:

> **Margin of Safety in Dollars = Total Budgeted (or actual sales) – Break-Even Sales**

Let's look at Manteo Machine, a company that machines parts that are then sold and used in the manufacture of farm equipment. For their core product, the break-even analysis is as follows:

Sales Price per Unit	$ 90
Variable Cost per Unit	$ 40
Contribution Margin per Unit	$ 50
Fixed Costs	$ 85,000
Break-Even (in units)	1700
Contribution Margin per Unit	$ 50
Selling Price per Unit	$ 90
Contribution Margin Ratio	55.55%
Break-Even (in dollars)	$151,786

Interpreting this information tells Manteo Machine that, when sales equal $153,000, they will be at the break-even point. However, as soon as sales fall below this figure, they will have negative net operating income. They have decided that they want a margin of safety of $10,000. They can add this as if it were a fixed cost (very much the same way we added target profit earlier) and then find a new break-even point that includes a $10,000 margin of safety. If they approached it from this perspective, their new break-even would appear as follows:

Sales Price per Unit	$ 90
Variable Cost per Unit	$ 40
Contribution Margin per Unit	$ 50
Fixed Costs + Margin of Safety	$ 95,000
Break-Even (in units)	1900
Contribution Margin per Unit	$ 50
Selling Price per Unit	$ 90
Contribution Margin Ratio	55.55%
Break-Even (in dollars)	$169,643

Figure 3.12 Manteo Machine's Margin of Safety. (attribution: Copyright Rice University, OpenStax, under CC BY-NC-SA 4.0 license)

As shown in Figure 3.12, the margin of safety of 1,900 units is found from (FC + Margin of Safety)/CM per unit = $95,000/$50. Thus, 1,900 units must be sold in order to meet fixed cost and have a $10,000 margin of safety. Another way to see this is to realize the $10,000 margin of safety will be met in $50 increments based on the current contribution margin. This means the company will need to sell an additional 200 units, which is an additional $18,000 in sales to have the desired margin of safety. The true break-even, where only fixed costs were met, was 1,700 units, or $153,000 in sales. The point at which the company would have a $10,000 margin of safety is 1,900 units, or $171,000 in sales. Note that the new level of units is the break-even units of 1,700 plus the 200 units for the margin of safety. The same can be seen for the sales dollar. The new level of desired sales dollars is the break-even sales of $153,000 plus the additional $18,000 in sales for the margin of safety.

The margin of safety can also be determined when a company knows its sales volume. For example, Manteo Machine sold 2,500 units in March and wants to know its margin of safety at that sales volume:

Sales (at the current volume of 2,500 units)	$225,000
Break-Even Sales (1,900 units)	153,000
Margin of Safety (in dollars)	72,000

From this analysis, Manteo Machine knows that sales will have to decrease by $72,000 from their current level before they revert to break-even operations and are at risk to suffer a loss.

> **ETHICAL CONSIDERATIONS**
>
> **The Importance of Relevant Range Analysis**
>
> Ethical managerial decision-making requires that information be communicated fairly and objectively. The failure to include the demand for individual products in the company's mixture of products may be misleading. Providing misleading or inaccurate managerial accounting information can lead to a company becoming unprofitable. Ignoring relevant range(s) in setting assumptions about cost behavior and ignoring the actual demand for the product in the company's market also distorts the information provided to management and may cause the management of the company to produce products that cannot be sold.

Many companies prefer to consider the margin of safety as a percentage of sales, rather than as a dollar amount. In order to express margin of safety as a percentage, we divide the margin of safety (in dollars) by the total budgeted or actual sales volume. The formula to express margin of safety as a percentage is:

$$\text{Margin of Safety Percentage} = \frac{\text{Margin of Safety (dollars)}}{\text{Total Budget (or Actual) Sales (dollars)}}$$

Previously, we calculated Manteo Machine's margin of safety as $72,000. As a percentage, it would be

$$\frac{\$72,000}{\$225,000} = 0.32 \text{ or } 32\%$$

This tells management that as long as sales do not decrease by more than 32%, they will not be operating at or near the break-even point, where they would run a higher risk of suffering a loss. Often, the margin of safety is determined when sales budgets and forecasts are made at the start of the fiscal year and also are regularly revisited during periods of operational and strategic planning.

Operating Leverage

In much the same way that managers control the risk of incurring a net loss by watching their margin of safety, being aware of the company's operating leverage is critical to the financial well-being of the firm. **Operating leverage** is a measurement of how sensitive net operating income is to a percentage change in sales dollars. Typically, the higher the level of fixed costs, the higher the level of risk. However, as sales volumes increase, the payoff is typically greater with higher fixed costs than with higher variable costs. In other words, the higher the risk the greater the payoff.

First, let's look at this from a general example to understand payoff. Suppose you had $10,000 to invest and you were debating between putting that money in low risk bonds earning 3% or taking a chance and buying stock in a new company that currently is not profitable but has an innovative product that many analysts predict will take off and be the next "big thing." Obviously, there is more risk with buying the stock than with buying the bonds. If the company remains unprofitable, or fails, you stand to lose all or a portion of your investment ,whereas the bonds are less risky and will continue to pay 3% interest. However, the risk associated with the stock investment could result in a much higher payoff if the company is successful.

So how does this relate to fixed costs and companies? Companies have many types of fixed costs including salaries, insurance, and depreciation. These costs are present regardless of our production or sales levels. This makes fixed costs riskier than variable costs, which only occur if we produce and sell items or services. As we sell items, we have learned that the contribution margin first goes to meeting fixed costs and then to profits. Here is an example of how changes in fixed costs affects profitability.

Gray Co. has the following income statement:

Sales (10,000 units x $10 SP)	$100,000
Variable Costs (10,000 units x $4 VC)	$ 40,000
Contribution Margin	$ 60,000
Fixed Costs	$ 25,000
Net Income	$ 35,000

What is the effect of switching $10,000 of fixed costs to variable costs? What is the effect of switching $10,000 of variable costs to fixed costs?

Effect of Changing $10,000 of FC to VC

Sales (10,000 units x $10 SP)	$100,000
Variable Costs	50,000
Contribution Margin	50,000
Fixed Costs	15,000
Net Income	35,000

Effect of Changing $10,000 of VC to FC

Sales (10,000 units x $10 SP)	$100,000
Variable Costs	30,000
Contribution Margin	70,000
Fixed Costs	35,000
Net Income	35,000

Notice that in this instance, the company's net income stayed the same. Now, look at the effect on net income of changing fixed to variable costs or variable costs to fixed costs as sales volume increases. Assume sales volume increase by 10%.

Effect of Changing $10,000 of FC to VC and 10% Increase in Sales

Sales (11,000 units x $10 SP)	$110,000
Variable Costs (also increases 10%)	$ 55,000
Contribution Margin	$ 55,000
Fixed Costs	$ 15,000
Net Income	$ 40,000

Effect of Changing $10,000 of VC to FC and 10% Increase in Sales

Sales (11,000 units x $10 SP)	$110,000
Variable Costs (also increases 10%)	$ 33,000
Contribution Margin	$ 77,000
Fixed Costs	$ 35,000
Net Income	$ 45,000

As you can see from this example, moving variable costs to fixed costs, such as making hourly employees salaried, is riskier in that fixed costs are higher. However, the payoff, or resulting net income, is higher as sales volume increases.

This is why companies are so concerned with managing their fixed and variable costs and will sometimes move costs from one category to another to manage this risk. Some examples include, as previously mentioned, moving hourly employees (variable) to salaried employees (fixed), or replacing an employee (variable) with a machine (fixed). Keep in mind that managing this type of risk not only affects operating leverage but can have an effect on morale and corporate climate as well.

CONCEPTS IN PRACTICE

Fluctuating Operating Leverage: Why Do Stores Add Self-Service Checkout Lanes?

Operating leverage fluctuations result from changes in a company's cost structure. While any change in either variable or fixed costs will change operating leverage, the fluctuations most often result from management's decision to shift costs from one category to another. As the next example shows, the advantage can be great when there is economic growth (increasing sales); however, the disadvantage can be just as great when there is economic decline (decreasing sales). This is the risk that must be managed when deciding how and when to cause operating leverage to fluctuate.

Consider the impact of reducing variable costs (fewer employee staffed checkout lanes) and increasing fixed costs (more self-service checkout lanes). A store with $125,000,000 per year in sales installs some self-service checkout lanes. This increases its fixed costs by 10% but reduces its variable costs by 5%. As Figure 3.13 shows, at the current sales level, this could produce a whopping 35% increase in net operating income. And, if the change results in higher sales, the increase in net operating income would be even more dramatic. Do the math and you will see that each 1% increase in sales would produce a 6% increase in net operating income: well worth the change, indeed.

	Without Self-service Checkout Lanes	With Self-service Checkout Lanes
Sales	$125,000	$125,000
Variable Costs	$ 93,750	$ 89,063
Contribution Margin	$ 31,250	$ 35,937
Fixed costs	$ 25,000	$ 27,500
Net Operating Income	$ 6,250	$ 8,437
% Increase in Income		35%

Figure 3.13 Impact of Self-Service Checkout Lanes. (attribution: Copyright Rice University, OpenStax, under CC BY-NC-SA 4.0 license)

(in 000s) Without Selfservice Checkout Lanes, With Selfservice Checkout Lanes (respectively): Sales $125,000, 125,000; Variable Costs 93,750, 89,063; Contribution Margin 31,250, 35,938; Fixed Costs 25,000, 27,500; Net Operating Income 6,250 8,438; Percent Increase in Income 35 percent.

The company in this example also faces a downside risk, however. If customers disliked the change enough that sales decreased by more than 6%, net operating income would drop below the original level of $6,250 and could even become a loss.

Operating leverage has a multiplier effect. A **multiplier effect** is one in which a change in an input (such as variable cost per unit) by a certain percentage has a greater effect (a higher percentage effect) on the output (such as net income). To explain the concept of a multiplier effect, think of having to open a very large, heavy wooden crate. You could pull and pull with your hands all day and still not exert enough force to get it open. But, what if you used a lever in the form of a pry bar to multiply your effort and strength? For every additional amount of force you apply to the pry bar, a much larger amount of force is applied to the crate. Before you know it, you have the crate open. Operating leverage works much like that pry bar: if operating leverage is high, then a very small increase in sales can result in a large increase in net operating income.

How does a company increase its operating leverage? Operating leverage is a function of cost structure, and companies that have a high proportion of fixed costs in their cost structure have higher operating leverage. There is, however, a cautionary side to operating leverage. Since high operating leverage is the result of high fixed costs, if the market for the company's products, goods, or services shrinks, or if demand for the company's products, goods, or services declines, the company may find itself obligated to pay for fixed costs with little or no sales revenue to spare. Managers who have made the decision to chase large increases in net operating income through the use of operating leverage have found that, when market demand falls, their only recourse is to close their doors. In fact, many large companies are making the decision to shift costs *away* from fixed costs to protect them from this very problem.

LINK TO LEARNING

During periods of sales downturns, there are many examples of companies working to shift costs away from fixed costs. This Yahoo Finance article reports that many airlines are changing their cost structure to move away from fixed costs and toward variable costs (https://openstax.org/l/50AirlineVarCst) such as Delta Airlines. Although they are decreasing their operating leverage, the decreased risk of insolvency more than makes up for it.

In order to calculate the degree of operating leverage at a given level of sales, we will apply the following formula:

$$\text{Degree of Operating Leverage} = \frac{\text{Contribution Margin}}{\text{Net Operating Income}}$$

To explain further the concept of operating leverage, we will look at two companies and their operating leverage positions:

	Company A	Company B
Sales	$250,000	$315,000
Variable Costs	102,000	105,000
Contribution Margin (a)	148,000	210,000
Fixed Costs	63,000	125,000
Net Income (loss) (b)	85,000	85,000
Operating Leverage (a) ÷ (b)	1.74	2.47

Both companies have the same net income of $85,000, but company B has a higher degree of operating leverage because its fixed costs are higher than that of company A. If we want to see how operating leverage impacts net operating income, then we can apply the following formula:

$$\text{Degree of Operating Leverage} \times \text{Percentage Change in Sales} = \text{Percentage Change in Net Operating Income}$$

Let's assume that both company A and company B are anticipating a 10% increase in sales. Based on their respective degrees of operating leverage, what will their percentage change in net operating income be?

$$\text{Company A: } 1.71 \times 10\% = 17.4\%$$
$$\text{Company B: } 2.47 \times 10\% = 24.7\%$$

For company A, for every 10% increase in sales, net operating income will increase 17.4%. But company B has a much higher degree of operating leverage, and a 10% increase in sales will result in a 24.7% increase in net operating income. These examples clearly show why, during periods of growth, companies have been willing to risk incurring higher fixed costs in exchange for large percentage gains in net operating income. But what happens in periods where income declines?

We will return to Company A and Company B, only this time, the data shows that there has been a 20% decrease in sales. Note that the degree of operating leverage changes for each company. The reduced income resulted in a higher operating leverage, meaning a higher level of risk.

	Company A	Company B
Sales (20% decrease)	$200,000	$252,000
Variable Costs (20% decrease)	81,600	84,000
Contribution Margin (a)	118,400	168,000
Fixed Costs	63,000	125,000
Net Income (b)	$ 55,400	$ 43,000
Operating Leverage (a ÷ b)	2.14	3.91
% Change in Net Income (Prior Net Income – Current Net Income)/Prior Net Income	34.8% decrease	49.4% decrease

It is equally important to realize the percentage decrease in income for both companies. The decrease in sales by 20% resulted in a 31.9% decrease in net income for Company A. For Company B, the 20% decrease in sales resulted in a 46.9% decrease in net income. This also could have been found by taking the initial operating leverage times the 20% decrease:

$$\text{Company A: 20\% decreases} \times 1.74 \text{ operating leverage} = 34.8\% \text{ decrease in net income}$$
$$\text{Company B: 20\% decreases} \times 2.47 \text{ operating leverage} = 49.4\% \text{ decrease in net income}$$

This example also shows why, during periods of decline, companies look for ways to reduce their fixed costs to avoid large percentage reductions in net operating income.

THINK IT THROUGH

Moving Costs

You are the managerial accountant for a large manufacturing firm. The company has sales that are well above its break-even point, but they have historically carried most of their costs as fixed costs. The outlook for the industry you are in is not positive. How could you move more costs away from fixed costs to put the company in a better financial position if the industry does, in fact, take a downturn?

CONTINUING APPLICATION AT WORK

Viking Grocery Stores

You might wonder why the grocery industry is not comparable to other big-box retailers such as hardware or large sporting goods stores. Just like other big-box retailers, the grocery industry has a similar product mix, carrying a vast of number of name brands as well as house brands. The main difference, then, is that the profit margin per dollar of sales (i.e., profitability) is smaller than the typical big-box retailer. Also, the inventory turnover and degree of product spoilage is greater for grocery stores. Overall, while the fixed and variable costs are similar to other big-box retailers, a grocery store must sell vast quantities in order to create enough revenue to cover those costs.

This is reflected in the business plan. Unlike a manufacturer, a grocery store will have hundreds of products at one time with various levels of margin, all of which will be taken into account in the development of their break-even analysis. Review a business plan developed by Viking Grocery Stores (https://openstax.org/l/GroceryStore) in consideration of opening a new site in Springfield, Missouri to see how a grocery store develops a business plan and break-even based upon multiple products.

Key Terms

break-even point dollar amount (total sales dollars) or production level (total units produced) at which the company has recovered all variable and fixed costs; it can also be expressed as that point where Total Cost (TC) = Total Revenue (TR)

composite unit selection of discrete products associated together in relation or proportion to their sales mix

contribution margin amount by which a product's selling price exceeds its total variable cost per unit

contribution margin ratio percentage of a unit's selling price that exceeds total unit variable costs

margin of safety difference between current sales and break-even sales

multi-product environment business environment in which a company sells different products, manufactures different products, or offers different types of services

multiplier effect when the change in an input by a certain percentage has a greater effect (a higher percentage effect) on the output

operating leverage measurement of how sensitive net operating income is to a percentage change in sales dollars

relevant range quantitative range of units that can be produced based on the company's current productive assets; for example, if a company has sufficient fixed assets to produce up to 10,000 units of product, the relevant range would be between 0 and 10,000 units

sales mix relative proportions of the products that a company sells

sensitivity analysis what will happen if sales price, units sold, variable cost per unit, or fixed costs change

target pricing process in which a company uses market analysis and production information to determine the maximum price customers are willing to pay for a good or service in addition to the markup percentage

total contribution margin amount by which total sales exceed total variable costs

Summary

3.1 Explain Contribution Margin and Calculate Contribution Margin per Unit, Contribution Margin Ratio, and Total Contribution Margin

- Contribution margin can be used to calculate how much of every dollar in sales is available to cover fixed expenses and contribute to profit.
- Contribution margin can be expressed on a per-unit basis, as a ratio, or in total.
- A specialized income statement, the Contribution Margin Income Statement, can be useful in looking at total sales and total contribution margin at varying levels of activity.

3.2 Calculate a Break-Even Point in Units and Dollars

- Break-even analysis is a tool that almost any business can use for planning and evaluation purposes. It helps identify a level of activity that is necessary before an organization starts to generate a profit.
- A break-even point can be found on a per-unit basis or as a dollar amount, depending upon whether a per-unit contribution margin or a contribution margin ratio is applied.

3.3 Perform Break-Even Sensitivity Analysis for a Single Product Under Changing Business Situations

- Cost-volume-profit analysis can be used to conduct a sensitivity analysis that shows what will happen if there are changes in any of the variables: sales price, units sold, variable cost per unit, or fixed costs.
- The break-even point may or may not be impacted by changes in costs depending on the type of cost affected.

3.4 Perform Break-Even Sensitivity Analysis for a Multi-Product Environment Under Changing Business Situations

- Companies provide multiple products, goods, and services to the consumer and, as result, need to calculate their break-even point based on the mix of the products, goods, and services.
- In a multi-product environment, calculating the break-even point is more complex and is usually calculated using a composite unit, which represents the sales mix of the business.
- If the sales mix of a company changes, then the break-even point changes, regardless of whether total sales dollars change or not.

3.5 Calculate and Interpret a Company's Margin of Safety and Operating Leverage

- Businesses determine a margin of safety (sales dollars beyond the break-even point). The higher the margin of safety is, the lower the risk is of not breaking even and incurring a loss.
- Operating leverage is a measurement of how sensitive net operating income is to a percentage change in sales dollars. A high degree of operating leverage results from a cost structure that is heavily weighted in fixed costs.

Multiple Choice

1. LO 3.1 The amount of a unit's sales price that helps to cover fixed expenses is its _____.
  A. contribution margin
  B. profit
  C. variable cost
  D. stepped cost

2. LO 3.1 A company's product sells for $150 and has variable costs of $60 associated with the product. What is its contribution margin per unit?
  A. $40
  B. $60
  C. $90
  D. $150

3. LO 3.1 A company's product sells for $150 and has variable costs of $60 associated with the product. What is its contribution margin ratio?
  A. 10%
  B. 40%
  C. 60%
  D. 90%

4. LO 3.1 A company's contribution margin per unit is $25. If the company increases its activity level from 200 units to 350 units, how much will its total contribution margin increase?
  A. $1,250
  B. $3,750
  C. $5,000
  D. $8,750

5. LO 3.2 A company sells its products for $80 per unit and has per-unit variable costs of $30. What is the contribution margin per unit?

A. $30
B. $50
C. $80
D. $110

6. LO 3.2 If a company has fixed costs of $6,000 per month and their product that sells for $200 has a contribution margin ratio of 30%, how many units must they sell in order to break even?

A. 100
B. 180
C. 200
D. 2,000

7. LO 3.2 Company A wants to earn $5,000 profit in the month of January. If their fixed costs are $10,000 and their product has a per-unit contribution margin of $250, how many units must they sell to reach their target income?

A. 20
B. 40
C. 60
D. 120

8. LO 3.2 A company has wants to earn an income of $60,000 after-taxes. If the tax rate is 32%, what must be the company's pre-tax income in order to have $60,000 after-taxes?

A. $88,235
B. $19,200
C. $79,200
D. $143,000

9. LO 3.2 A company has pre-tax or operating income of $120,000. If the tax rate is 40%, what is the company's after-tax income?

A. $300,000
B. $240,000
C. $48,000
D. $72,000

10. LO 3.3 When sales price increases and all other variables are held constant, the break-even point will _____.

A. remain unchanged
B. increase
C. decrease
D. produce a lower contribution margin

11. LO 3.3 When sales price decreases and all other variables are held constant, the break-even point will _____.

A. remain unchanged
B. increase
C. decrease
D. produce a higher contribution margin

12. LO 3.3 When variable costs increase and all other variables remain unchanged, the break-even point will _____.

A. remain unchanged
B. increase
C. decrease
D. produce a lower contribution margin

13. LO 3.3 When fixed costs decrease and all other variables remain unchanged, the break-even point will _____.

A. remain unchanged
B. increase
C. decrease
D. produce a lower contribution margin

14. LO 3.3 When fixed costs increase and all other variables remain unchanged, the contribution margin will _____.

A. remain unchanged
B. increase
C. decrease
D. increase variable costs per unit

15. LO 3.4 If the sales mix in a multi-product environment shifts to a higher volume in low contribution margin products, the break-even point will _____.

A. remain unchanged because all products are included in the calculation of break-even
B. increase because the low contribution margin products have little effect on break-even
C. increase because the per composite unit contribution margin will decrease
D. decrease because the per composite unit contribution margin will increase

16. LO 3.4 Break-even for a multiple product firm _____.

A. can be calculated by dividing total fixed costs by the contribution margin of a composite unit
B. can be calculated by multiplying fixed costs by the contribution margin ratio of a composite unit
C. can only be calculated when the proportion of products sold is the same for all products
D. can be calculated by multiplying fixed costs by the contribution margin ratio of the most common product in the sales mix

17. LO 3.4 Waskowski Company sells three products (A, B, and C) with a sales mix of 3:2:1. Unit sales price are shown. What is the sales price per composite unit?

Product A	Product B	Product C
$7	$4	$6

A. $17.00
B. $25.00
C. $35.00
D. $20.00

18. LO 3.4 Beaucheau Farms sells three products (E, F, and G) with a sale mix ratio of 3:1:2. Unit sales price are shown. What is the sales price per composite unit?

Product E	Product F	Product G
$11	$8	$9

A. $28.00
B. $20.00
C. $59.00
D. $41.00

19. LO 3.4 A company sells two products, Model 101 and Model 202. For every one unit of Model 101, they sell they sell two units of Model 202. Sales and cost information for the two products is shown. What is the contribution margin for a composite unit based on the sales mix?

	Sales Price	Variable Cost
Model 101	$25	$11
Model 202	28	7

A. $14
B. $21
C. $35
D. $56

20. LO 3.5 Wallace Industries has total contribution margin of $58,560 and net income of $24,400 for the month of April. Wallace expects sales volume to increase by 5% in May. What are the degree of operating leverage and the expected percent change in income for Wallace Industries?
A. 0.42 and 2.2%
B. 0.42 and 5%
C. 2.4 and 12%
D. 2.5 and 13%

21. LO 3.5 Macom Manufacturing has total contribution margin of $61,250 and net income of $24,500 for the month of June. Marcus expects sales volume to increase by 10% in July. What are the degree of operating leverage and the expected percent change in income for Macom Manufacturing?
A. 0.4 and 10%
B. 2.5 and 10%
C. 2.5 and 25%
D. 5.0 and 50%

22. LO 3.5 If a firm has a contribution margin of $59,690 and a net income of $12,700 for the current month, what is their degree of operating leverage?
A. 0.18
B. 1.18
C. 2.4
D. 4.7

23. LO 3.5 If a firm has a contribution margin of $78,090 and a net income of $13,700 for the current month, what is their degree of operating leverage?
- A. 0.21
- B. 1.21
- C. 2.4
- D. 5.7

Questions

1. LO 3.1 Define and explain contribution margin on a per unit basis.

2. LO 3.1 Define and explain contribution margin ratio.

3. LO 3.1 Explain how a contribution margin income statement can be used to determine profitability.

4. LO 3.2 In a cost-volume-profit analysis, explain what happens at the break-even point and why companies do not want to remain at the break-even point.

5. LO 3.2 What is meant by a product's contribution margin ratio and how is this ratio useful in planning business operations?

6. LO 3.3 Explain how a manager can use CVP analysis to make decisions regarding changes in operations or pricing structure.

7. LO 3.3 After conducting a CVP analysis, most businesses will then recreate a revised or projected income statement incorporating the results of the CVP analysis. What is the benefit of taking this extra step in the analysis?

8. LO 3.3 Explain how it is possible for costs to change without changing the break-even point.

9. LO 3.4 Explain what a sales mix is and how changes in the sales mix affect the break-even point.

10. LO 3.4 Explain how break-even analysis for a multi-product company differs from a company selling a single product.

11. LO 3.5 Explain margin of safety and why it is an important measurement for managers.

12. LO 3.5 Define operating leverage and explain its importance to a company and how it relates to risk.

Exercise Set A

EA1. LO 3.1 Calculate the per-unit contribution margin of a product that has a sale price of $200 if the variable costs per unit are $65.

EA2. LO 3.1 Calculate the per-unit contribution margin of a product that has a sale price of $400 if the variable costs per unit are $165.

EA3. LO 3.1 A product has a sales price of $150 and a per-unit contribution margin of $50. What is the contribution margin ratio?

EA4. LO 3.1 A product has a sales price of $250 and a per-unit contribution margin of $75. What is the contribution margin ratio?

EA5. LO 3.2 Maple Enterprises sells a single product with a selling price of $75 and variable costs per unit of $30. The company's monthly fixed expenses are $22,500.
  A. What is the company's break-even point in units?
  B. What is the company's break-even point in dollars?
  C. Construct a contribution margin income statement for the month of September when they will sell 900 units.
  D. How many units will Maple need to sell in order to reach a target profit of $45,000?
  E. What dollar sales will Maple need in order to reach a target profit of $45,000?
  F. Construct a contribution margin income statement for Maple that reflects $150,000 in sales volume.

EA6. LO 3.2 Marlin Motors sells a single product with a selling price of $400 with variable costs per unit of $160. The company's monthly fixed expenses are $36,000.
  A. What is the company's break-even point in units?
  B. What is the company's break-even point in dollars?
  C. Prepare a contribution margin income statement for the month of November when they will sell 130 units.
  D. How many units will Marlin need to sell in order to realize a target profit of $48,000?
  E. What dollar sales will Marlin need to generate in order to realize a target profit of $48,000?
  F. Construct a contribution margin income statement for the month of February that reflects $200,000 in sales revenue for Marlin Motors.

EA7. LO 3.3 Flanders Manufacturing is considering purchasing a new machine that will reduce variable costs per part produced by $0.15. The machine will increase fixed costs by $18,250 per year. The information they will use to consider these changes is shown here.

	Current
Units sold	216,000
Sales price per unit	$ 2.15
Variable cost per unit	$ 1.75
Contribution margin per unit	$ 0.40
Fixed costs	$ 56,000
Break-even (in units)	140,000
Break-even (in dollars)	$301,000
Sales	$464,400
Variable costs	$378,000
Contribution margin	$ 86,400
Fixed costs	$ 56,000
Net income (loss)	$ 30,400

EA8. LO 3.3 Marchete Company produces a single product. They have recently received the results of a market survey that indicates that they can increase the retail price of their product by 8% without losing customers or market share. All other costs will remain unchanged. Their most recent CVP analysis is shown. If they enact the 8% price increase, what will be their new break-even point in units and dollars?

	Current
Units sold	950
Sales price per unit	$ 125
Variable cost per unit	$ 98
Contribution margin per unit	$ 27
Fixed costs	$ 23,000
Break-even (in units)	852
Break-even (in dollars)	$106,500
Sales	$118,750
Variable costs	$ 93,100
Contribution margin	$ 25,650
Fixed costs	$ 23,000
Net income (loss)	$ 2,650

EA9. LO 3.3 Brahma Industries sells vinyl replacement windows to home improvement retailers nationwide. The national sales manager believes that if they invest an additional $25,000 in advertising, they would increase sales volume by 10,000 units. Prepare a forecasted contribution margin income statement for Brahma if they incur the additional advertising costs, using this information:

Sales (6,500 units at $115)	$747,500
Variable costs (6,500 units at $69)	448,500
Contribution margin	299,000
Fixed costs	19,500
Net income (loss)	279,500

EA10. LO 3.4 Salvador Manufacturing builds and sells snowboards, skis and poles. The sales price and variable cost for each are shown:

Product	Sellings price per unit	Variable cost per unit
Snowboards	$320.00	$170.00
Skis	$400.00	$225.00
Poles	$ 50.00	$ 20.00

Their sales mix is reflected in the ratio 7:3:2. What is the overall unit contribution margin for Salvador with their current product mix?

EA11. LO 3.4 Salvador Manufacturing builds and sells snowboards, skis and poles. The sales price and variable cost for each follows:

Product	Sellings price per unit	Variable cost per unit
Snowboards	$320.00	$170.00
Skis	$400.00	$225.00
Poles	$ 50.00	$ 20.00

Their sales mix is reflected in the ratio 7:3:2. If annual fixed costs shared by the three products are $196,200, how many units of each product will need to be sold in order for Salvador to break even?

EA12. LO 3.4 Use the information from the previous exercises involving Salvador Manufacturing to determine their break-even point in sales dollars.

EA13. LO 3.5 Company A has current sales of $10,000,000 and a 45% contribution margin. Its fixed costs are $3,000,000. Company B is a service firm with current service revenue of $5,000,000 and a 20% contribution margin. Company B's fixed costs are $500,000. Compute the degree of operating leverage for both companies. Which company will benefit most from a 25% increase in sales? Explain why.

EA14. LO 3.5 Marshall & Company produces a single product and recently calculated their break-even point as shown.

	Current
Units sold	400
Sales price per unit	$ 550
Variable cost per unit	$ 375
Contribution margin per unit	$ 175
Fixed costs	$ 3,500
Break-even (in units)	20
Contribution margin ratio	31.82%
Break-even (in dollars)	$11,000

What would Marshall's target margin of safety be in units and dollars if they required a $14,000 margin of safety?

Exercise Set B

EB1. LO 3.1 Calculate the per-unit contribution margin of a product that has a sale price of $150 if the variable costs per unit are $40.

EB2. LO 3.1 Calculate the per-unit contribution margin of a product that has a sale price of $350 if the variable costs per unit are $95.

EB3. LO 3.1 A product has a sales price of $175 and a per-unit contribution margin of $75. What is the contribution margin ratio?

EB4. LO 3.1 A product has a sales price of $90 and a per-unit contribution margin of $30. What is the contribution margin ratio?

EB5. LO 3.2 Cadre, Inc., sells a single product with a selling price of $120 and variable costs per unit of $90. The company's monthly fixed expenses are $180,000.
  A. What is the company's break-even point in units?
  B. What is the company's break-even point in dollars?
  C. Prepare a contribution margin income statement for the month of October when they will sell 10,000 units.
  D. How many units will Cadre need to sell in order to realize a target profit of $300,000?
  E. What dollar sales will Cadre need to generate in order to realize a target profit of $300,000?
  F. Construct a contribution margin income statement for the month of August that reflects $2,400,000 in sales revenue for Cadre, Inc.

EB6. LO 3.2 Kerr Manufacturing sells a single product with a selling price of $600 with variable costs per unit of $360. The company's monthly fixed expenses are $72,000.
   A. What is the company's break-even point in units?
   B. What is the company's break-even point in dollars?
   C. Prepare a contribution margin income statement for the month of January when they will sell 500 units.
   D. How many units will Kerr need to sell in order to realize a target profit of $120,000?
   E. What dollar sales will Kerr need to generate in order to realize a target profit of $120,000?
   F. Construct a contribution margin income statement for the month of June that reflects $600,000 in sales revenue for Kerr Manufacturing.

EB7. LO 3.2 Delta Co. sells a product for $150 per unit. The variable cost per unit is $90 and fixed costs are $15,250. Delta Co.'s tax rate is 36% and the company wants to earn $44,000 after taxes.
   A. What would be Delta's desired pre-tax income?
   B. What would be break-even point in units to reach the income goal of $44,000 after taxes?
   C. What would be break-even point in sales dollars to reach the income goal of $44,000 after taxes?
   D. Create a contribution margin income statement to show that the break-even point calculated in B, generates the desired after-tax income.

EB8. LO 3.3 Shonda & Shonda is a company that does land surveys and engineering consulting. They have an opportunity to purchase new computer equipment that will allow them to render their drawings and surveys much more quickly. The new equipment will cost them an additional $1,200 per month, but they will be able to increase their sales by 10% per year. Their current annual cost and break-even figures are as follows:

	Current
Units sold	1,400
Sales price per unit	$ 225
Variable cost per unit	$ 145
Fixed costs	$ 52,000
Break-even (in units)	650
Contribution margin ratio	$ 0.36
Break-even (in dollars)	$146,250
Sales	$315,000
Variable costs	$203,000
Contribution margin	$112,000
Fixed costs	$ 52,000
Net income (loss)	$ 60,000

   A. What will be the impact on the break-even point if Shonda & Shonda purchases the new computer?
   B. What will be the impact on net operating income if Shonda & Shonda purchases the new computer?
   C. What would be your recommendation to Shonda & Shonda regarding this purchase?

EB9. LO 3.3 Baghdad Company produces a single product. They have recently received the result of a market survey that indicates that they can increase the retail price of their product by 10% without losing customers or market share. All other costs will remain unchanged. If they enact the 10% price increase, what will be their new break-even point in units and dollars? Their most recent CVP analysis is:

	Current
Units sold	1,450
Sales price per unit	$ 90
Variable cost per unit	$ 40
Contribution margin per unit	$ 50
Fixed costs	$ 20,650
Break-even (in units)	413
Break-even (in dollars)	$ 37,170
Sales	$130,500
Variable costs	$ 58,000
Contribution margin	$ 72,500
Fixed costs	$ 20,650
Net income (loss)	$ 51,850

EB10. LO 3.3 Keleher Industries manufactures pet doors and sells them directly to the consumer via their web site. The marketing manager believes that if the company invests in new software, they will increase their sales by 10%. The new software will increase fixed costs by $400 per month. Prepare a forecasted contribution margin income statement for Keleher Industries reflecting the new software cost and associated increase in sales. The previous annual statement is as follows:

Sales (3,100 units at $250)	$775,000
Variable costs (3,100 units at $115)	356,500
Contribution margin	418,500
Fixed costs	19,500
Net income (loss)	399,000

EB11. LO 3.4 JJ Manufacturing builds and sells switch harnesses for glove boxes. The sales price and variable cost for each follows:

Product	Selling price per unit	Variable cost per unit
Trunk switch	$60.00	$28.00
Gas door switch	$75.00	$33.00
Glove box light	$40.00	$22.00

Their sales mix is reflected in the ratio 4:4:1. What is the overall unit contribution margin for JJ Manufacturing with their current product mix?

EB12. LO 3.4 JJ Manufacturing builds and sells switch harnesses for glove boxes. The sales price and variable cost for each follows:

Product	Selling price per unit	Variable cost per unit
Trunk switch	$60.00	$28.00
Gas door switch	$75.00	$33.00
Glove box light	$40.00	$22.00

Their sales mix is reflected in the ratio 4:4:1. If annual fixed costs shared by the three products are $18,840 how many units of each product will need to be sold in order for JJ to break even?

EB13. LO 3.4 Use the information from the previous exercises involving JJ Manufacturing to determine their break-even point in sales dollars.

EB14. LO 3.5 Company A has current sales of $4,000,000 and a 45% contribution margin. Its fixed costs are $600,000. Company B is a service firm with current service revenue of $2,800,000 and a 15% contribution margin. Company B's fixed costs are $375,000. Compute the degree of operating leverage for both companies. Which company will benefit most from a 15% increase in sales? Explain why.

EB15. LO 3.5 Best Wholesale recently calculated their break-even point for their Midwest operations. The national sales manager has asked them to include a $10,500 margin of safety in their calculations. Using the following information, recalculate Best Wholesale's break-even point in units and dollars with the $10,500 margin of safety included.

	Current
Units sold	1,200
Sales price per unit	$ 750
Variable cost per unit	$ 575
Contribution margin per unit	$ 175
Fixed costs	$ 96,250
Break-even (in units)	550
Contribution margin ratio	23.33%
Break-even (in dollars)	$412,500

 Problem Set A

PA1. LO 3.1 A company sells small motors as a component part to automobiles. The Model 101 motor sells for $850 and has per-unit variable costs of $400 associated with its production. The company has fixed expenses of $90,000 per month. In August, the company sold 425 of the Model 101 motors.
  A. Calculate the contribution margin per unit for the Model 101.
  B. Calculate the contribution margin ratio of the Model 101.
  C. Prepare a contribution margin income statement for the month of August.

PA2. LO 3.1 A company manufactures and sells racing bicycles to specialty retailers. The Bomber model sells for $450 and has per-unit variable costs of $200 associated with its production. The company has fixed expenses of $40,000 per month. In May, the company sold 225 of the Bomber model bikes.
  A. Calculate the contribution margin per unit for the Bomber.
  B. Calculate the contribution margin ratio of the Bomber.
  C. Prepare a contribution margin income statement for the month of May.

PA3. LO 3.2 Fill in the missing amounts for the four companies. Each case is independent of the others. Assume that only one product is being sold by each company.

	Company A	Company B	Company C	Company D
Units sold	600	?	?	900
Sales in dollars	$30,000	$70,000	$240,000	?
Total variable expenses	$ 7,200	?	?	$144,000
Per unit C/M	?	$ 80	$ 270	$ 140
Total fixed expenses	$20,000	$50,000	$145,000	?
Net operating income (loss)	?	$ 6,000	$ (10,000)	$ (24,000)

PA4. LO 3.2 Markham Farms reports the following contribution margin income statement for the month of August. The company has the opportunity to purchase new machinery that will reduce its variable cost per unit by $2 but will increase fixed costs by 15%. Prepare a projected contribution margin income statement for Markham Farm assuming it purchases the new equipment. Assume sales level remains unchanged.

MARKHAM FARMS	
Contribution Margin Income Statement	
For Year Ended December 31, 2019	
Sales (1,500 units at $75 per unit)	$112,500
Variable costs (1,500 units at $15 per unit)	22,500
Contribution margin	90,000
Fixed cost	40,000
Net income (loss)	$ 50,000

PA5. LO 3.3 Kylie's Cookies is considering the purchase of a larger oven that will cost $2,200 and will increase her fixed costs by $59. What would happen if she purchased the new oven to realize the variable cost savings of $0.10 per cookie, and what would happen if she raised her price by just $0.20? She feels confident that such a small price increase will decrease the sales by only 25 units and may help her offset the increase in fixed costs. Given the following current prices how would the break-even in units and dollars change if she doesn't increase the selling price and if she does increase the selling price? Complete the monthly contribution margin income statement for each of these cases.

Selling price, variable cost, and fixed cost change analysis			
	With Current Price	With decreased VC and increased FC	With increased SP, decreased VC, and increased FC
Sales price per unit	$1.75		
Variable cost per unit	0.40		
Contribution margin per unit	$1.35		
Fixed costs	$ 405		
Break-even in units	300		
Break-even in dollars	$ 525		
Monthly contribution margin income statement			
Unit sales, expected	800		
Sales			
Variable costs			
Contribution margin			
Fixed costs			
Net income			

PA6. LO 3.4 Morris Industries manufactures and sells three products (AA, BB, and CC). The sales price and unit variable cost for the three products are as follows:

Product	Sales Price per Unit	Variable Cost per Unit
AA	$50	$30
BB	40	15
CC	30	10

Their sales mix is reflected as a ratio of 5:3:2. Annual fixed costs shared by the three products are $258,000 per year.

A. What are total variable costs for Morris with their current product mix?
B. Calculate the number of units of each product that will need to be sold in order for Morris to break even.
C. What is their break-even point in sales dollars?
D. Using an income statement format, prove that this is the break-even point.

PA7. LO 3.4 Manatoah Manufacturing produces 3 models of window air conditioners: model 101, model 201, and model 301. The sales price and variable costs for these three models are as follows:

Product	Sales Price per Unit	Variable Cost per Unit
Model 101	$275	$185
Model 201	350	215
Model 301	400	245

The current product mix is 4:3:2. The three models share total fixed costs of $430,000.

  A. Calculate the sales price per composite unit.
  B. What is the contribution margin per composite unit?
  C. Calculate Manatoah's break-even point in both dollars and units.
  D. Using an income statement format, prove that this is the break-even point.

PA8. LO 3.5 Jakarta Company is a service firm with current service revenue of $400,000 and a 40% contribution margin. Its fixed costs are $80,000. Maldives Company has current sales of $6,610,000 and a 45% contribution margin. Its fixed costs are $1,800,000.
  A. What is the margin of safety for Jakarta and Maldives?
  B. Compare the margin of safety in dollars between the two companies. Which is stronger?
  C. Compare the margin of safety in percentage between the two companies. Now, which one is stronger?
  D. Compute the degree of operating leverage for both companies. Which company will benefit most from a 15% increase in sales? Explain why. Illustrate your findings in an Income Statement that is increased by 15%.

Problem Set B

PB1. LO 3.1 A company sells mulch by the cubic yard. Grade A much sells for $150 per cubic yard and has variable costs of $65 per cubic yard. The company has fixed expenses of $15,000 per month. In August, the company sold 240 cubic yards of Grade A mulch.
  A. Calculate the contribution margin per unit for Grade A mulch.
  B. Calculate the contribution margin ratio of the Grade A mulch.
  C. Prepare a contribution margin income statement for the month of August.

PB2. LO 3.1 A company manufactures and sells blades that are used in riding lawnmowers. The 18-inch blade sells for $15 and has per-unit variable costs of $4 associated with its production. The company has fixed expenses of $85,000 per month. In January, the company sold 12,000 of the 18-inch blades.
  A. Calculate the contribution margin per unit for the 18-inch blade.
  B. Calculate the contribution margin ratio of the 18-inch blade.
  C. Prepare a contribution margin income statement for the month of January.

PB3. LO 3.2 Fill in the missing amounts for the four companies. Each case is independent of the others. Assume that only one product is being sold by each company.

	Company A	Company B	Company C	Company D
Units sold	700	?	?	600
Sales in dollars	$35,000	$40,000	$35,000	?
Total variable expenses	$14,000	?	?	$18,000
Per unit C/M	?	$ 90	$ 100	$ 60
Total fixed expenses	$10,000	$ 9,000	$12,000	?
Net operating income (loss)	?	$27,000	$ 8,000	$16,000

PB4. LO 3.2 West Island distributes a single product. The company's sales and expenses for the month of June are shown.

Sales price per unit	$ 150
Variable costs per unit	80
Fixed expenses	42,000

Using the information presented, answer these questions:

A. What is the break-even point in units sold and dollar sales?
B. What is the total contribution margin at the break-even point?
C. If West Island wants to earn a profit of $21,000, how many units would they have to sell?
D. Prepare a contribution margin income statement that reflects sales necessary to achieve the target profit.

PB5. LO 3.2 Wellington, Inc., reports the following contribution margin income statement for the month of May. The company has the opportunity to purchase new machinery that will reduce its variable cost per unit by $10 but will increase fixed costs by 20%. Prepare a projected contribution margin income statement for Wellington, Inc., assuming it purchases the new equipment. Assume sales level remains unchanged.

WELLINGTON, INC.
Contribution Margin Income Statement
For Year Ended December 31, 2019

Sales (800 units at $225 per unit)	$180,000
Variable costs (800 units at $120 per unit)	96,000
Contribution margin	84,000
Fixed cost	35,000
Net income (loss)	$ 49,000

PB6. LO 3.3 Karen's Quilts is considering the purchase of a new Long-arm Quilt Machine that will cost $17,500 and will increase her fixed costs by $119. What would happen if she purchased the new quilt machine to realize the variable cost savings of $5.00 per quilt, and what would happen if she raised her price by just $5.00? She feels confident that such a small price increase will not decrease the sales in units that will help her offset the increase in fixed costs. Given the following current prices how would the break-even in units and dollars change? Complete the monthly contribution margin income statement for each of these cases.

Selling Price, Variable Cost and Fixed Cost Change Analysis			
	With Current Price	With Decreased VC and Increased FC	With Increased SP, Decreased VC and Increased FC
Sales price per unit	$ 65.00		
Variable cost per unit	15.50		
Contribution margin per unit	$ 49.50		
Fixed costs	$ 99.00		
Break-even in units	2		
Break-even in dollars	$130.00		
Monthly Contribution Margin Income Statement			
Unit sales, expected	10	10	10
Sales			
Variable costs			
Contribution margin			
Fixed costs			
Net income			

PB7. LO 3.4 Abilene Industries manufactures and sells three products (XX, YY, and ZZ). The sales price and unit variable cost for the three products are as follows:

Product	Sales Price per Unit	Variable Cost per Unit
XX	$75	$45
YY	60	25
ZZ	55	15

Their sales mix is reflected as a ratio of 4:2:1. Annual fixed costs shared by the three products are $345,000 per year.

A. What are total variable costs for Abilene with their current product mix?
B. Calculate the number of units of each product that will need to be sold in order for Abilene to break even.
C. What is their break-even point in sales dollars?
D. Using an income statement format, prove that this is the break-even point.

PB8. LO 3.4 Tim-Buck-II rents jet skis at a beach resort. There are three models available to rent: Junior, Adult, and Expert. The rental price and variable costs for these three models are as follows:

Product	Sales Price per Unit	Variable Cost per Unit
Junior	$ 50	$15
Adult	75	25
Expert	110	60

The current product mix is 5:4:1. The three models share total fixed costs of $114,750

- A. Calculate the sales price per composite unit.
- B. What is the contribution margin per composite unit?
- C. Calculate Tim-Buck-II's break-even point in both dollars and units.
- D. Using an income statement format, prove that this is the break-even point.

PB9. LO 3.5 Fire Company is a service firm with current service revenue of $900,000 and a 40% contribution margin. Its fixed costs are $200,000. Ice Company has current sales of $420,000 and a 30% contribution margin. Its fixed costs are $90,000.

- A. What is the margin of safety for Fire and Ice?
- B. Compare the margin of safety in dollars between the two companies. Which is stronger?
- C. Compare the margin of safety in percentage between the two companies. Now which one is stronger?
- D. Compute the degree of operating leverage for both companies. Which company will benefit most from a 10% increase in sales? Explain why. Illustrate your findings in an Income Statement that is increased by 10%.

Thought Provokers

TP1. LO 3.1 Mariana Manufacturing and Bellow Brothers compete in the same industry and in all respects their products are virtually identical. However, most of Mariana's costs are fixed while Bellow's costs are primarily variable. If sales increase for both companies, which will realize the greatest increase in profits? Why?

TP2. LO 3.2 Roald is the sales manager for a small regional manufacturing firm you own. You have asked him to put together a plan for expanding into nearby markets. You know that Roald's previous job had him working closely with many of your competitors in this new market, and you believe he will be able to facilitate the company expansion. He is to prepare a presentation to you and your partners outlining his strategy for taking the company into this expanded market. The day before the presentation, Roald comes to you and explains that he will not be making a presentation on market expansion but instead wants to discuss several ways he believes the company can reduce both fixed and variable costs. Why would Roald want to focus on reducing costs rather than on expanding into a new market?

TP3. LO 3.3 As a manager, you have to choose between two options for new production equipment. Machine A will increase fixed costs by a substantial margin but will produce greater sales volume at the current price. Machine B will only slightly increase fixed costs but will produce considerable savings on variable cost per unit. No additional sales are anticipated if Machine B is selected. What are the relative merits of both machines, and how could you go about analyzing which machine is the better investment for the company in terms of both net operating income and break-even?

TP4. LO 3.5 Couture's Creations is considering offering Joe, an hourly employee, the opportunity to become a salaried employee. Why is this a good idea for Couture's Creations? Is this a good idea for Joe? What if Couture's Creations entices Joe to agree to the change by offering him a salaried position with no risk of layoff during the winter lull? What if Joe agrees and Couture's Creations lays him off anyway six months into the agreement?

4 Job Order Costing

Figure 4.1 Hallie Refinishing Furniture. Companies can generally choose from two systems—job order costing or process costing—to account for the costs involved in making a product. Job order costing is the optimal decision when costs are readily assigned to the individual product. Managers should consider their options to select the best accounting system for their company's production and pricing. (credit: modification of "120425-staining-wood-hand-brush" by r. nial bradshaw/Flickr, CC BY 2.0)

Chapter Outline

4.1 Distinguish between Job Order Costing and Process Costing

4.2 Describe and Identify the Three Major Components of Product Costs under Job Order Costing

4.3 Use the Job Order Costing Method to Trace the Flow of Product Costs through the Inventory Accounts

4.4 Compute a Predetermined Overhead Rate and Apply Overhead to Production

4.5 Compute the Cost of a Job Using Job Order Costing

4.6 Determine and Dispose of Underapplied or Overapplied Overhead

4.7 Prepare Journal Entries for a Job Order Cost System

4.8 Explain How a Job Order Cost System Applies to a Nonmanufacturing Environment

Why It Matters

Hallie graduated from college last year and moved to Tempe, Arizona, to begin her career. Before moving, she purchased a secondhand dresser for $35 and spent $25 on refinishing materials. After two hours of work, she posted a picture of the dresser on social media, and a friend offered her $100 to refinish another dresser exactly the same way.

Fortunately, Hallie understands cost accounting and knew she needed to calculate the cost to refinish another dresser. She found a similar dresser for $65. She knows that the refinishing materials will cost $25, and thus before adding in any cost for labor she is already at a cost of $90, without considering any overhead, such as electricity to run her sander.

Hallie estimated that her labor costs should be $20 per hour. The total cost then would be $130, and accepting less would mean accepting less for her labor. For a business in this situation, agreeing to the $100 offer would be considered a loss. If Hallie accepts the $100 price before checking her costs, she would have received only $10 for her labor (the sales price of $100 less the $90 cost of the dresser and materials).

Hallie didn't know if she would lose a potential customer by raising the price, so she found a different style dresser costing $25. A sales price of $100 would be fair with the two hours to refinish at $20 per hour and a materials cost of $25. She offered her friend the original style dresser for $130 or the alternate style dresser for $100.

As this example illustrates, it was essential for Hallie to know the cost to complete her project. It is also essential for all types and sizes of organizations to know the costs to complete their project. Manufacturing organizations need to know the costs of production, retail organizations need to know the cost to sell their products, and service organizations need to know the cost of providing their services. Management strives to eliminate unnecessary costs and needs to know the costs associated with using large pieces of equipment as well as seemingly insignificant office supplies. Cost accounting involves measuring and reporting the cost of production or service, while also providing data to determine the cost of the individual unit produced.

4.1 Distinguish between Job Order Costing and Process Costing

Pet Smart, H&R Block, Chili's, and Marshalls are popular chains often found at the same shopping center, even though they are very different businesses. Although they have a retail store, the Pet Smart Corporation also manufactures large volumes of its own products, whereas H&R Block prepares taxes for individual customers. Chili's prepares food, and its wait staff provides a service, whereas Marshalls sells a variety of products at retail.

The management of each business relies on knowing each cost when making decisions, such as setting the sales price, planning production and staffing schedules, and ordering materials. Although these companies share a common location, which suggests similar rental costs, all the other costs vary significantly. Because of these cost differences, each company must have a system for gathering its cost data. For example, Pet Smart manufactures Great Choice squeaker balls in large batches and collects cost data through a process costing system. A process costing system is often used to trace and determine production costs when similar products or services are provided. The concept and mechanics of a process costing system are addressed in Process Costing.

Since a typical tax return can vary significantly from one taxpayer to the next, H&R Block provides a service that they customize for each customer. Its cost data are collected via a job order cost system, which is designed to allow for individualized products or services.

Marshalls does not produce a product yet still needs a system to assign overhead costs to the products it sells. (Overhead was addressed in Building Blocks of Managerial Accounting.) And while Chili's has the same nationwide menu, it needs a system to collect the costs for each menu item within each location.

While companies may choose different cost accounting systems, each system must be capable of accumulating the costs incurred and allocating the costs to the product. Each costing system also requires the ability to obtain and analyze the cost data, and the more detailed the information needed, the higher the cost of collecting the data. The choice of cost accumulation system depends on the variety and type of products or services sold, or the type of manufacturing processes employed. The system used should be determined by weighing the cost of collecting the data and the benefit of having that information.

Companies use different costing systems for determining the cost of custom products than they do for determining the cost of mass-produced products. When products are custom ordered, knowing the cost of the materials, labor, and overhead is critical to determining the sales price. As an easy example, think of a tailor who alters, repairs, and makes custom clothes for customers. If a customer orders a custom-made suit, the specific fabric, detail of any special features, and the time involved in sewing are all factors that will determine the total cost and, therefore, the selling price of the garment. Each component of the cost of producing the clothing will be tracked as it occurs, thus improving the accuracy of determining the price. However, in mass production, wherein one batch leads to a second batch, stopping the process to properly identify the materials, labor, and overhead costs used for each batch does not provide enough valuable data to justify determining the individual costing of each product. For example, in the case of a mass-produced clothing item, such as jeans, a company like Levi's will track costs for a batch of jeans rather than for a pair of jeans. Levi's had over $4.9 billion in revenue in 2017 generated from the many different styles and brands of clothing items they produce and sell. It would be difficult, and not cost effective, to track the cost of each individual clothing item; rather, it is more efficient to track the costs in each phase of the clothing-making process. Levi's can then accumulate the costs of the phases of production to determine the total cost of production for a batch and allocate those costs over the number of pairs of jeans made. This process allows them to determine the cost of each item.

Even retail companies need to know the cost of the purchased products before the sales price is set. While it seems simple to think of the sales price as the purchase price plus a markup, determining the markup costs needs to be an accurate process in order to ensure the sale price is higher than the product cost. To properly capture the information necessary for decision-making, there are different costing systems that track costs in order to determine sales prices, and to measure profits and manufacturing efficiency.

As previously mentioned, the two traditional types of costing systems are job order costing and process costing. Each anticipates or determines unit costs of products being manufactured and/or services being provided prior to year-end. Companies may decide to use only one or a combination of methods. This chapter examines job order costing and demonstrates how it differs from process costing. Process Costing and other costing systems (Activity-Based, Variable, and Absorption Costing) are covered in other chapters.

In this chapter, you will also learn the terminology used to track costs within the job order cost system and how to segregate and aggregate these costs to determine the costs of production in a job order costing environment. You will also learn how to record these job costs and where they appear on financial statements.

Job Order Costing versus Process Costing

Job order costing is an accounting system that traces the individual costs directly to a final job or service, instead of to the production department. It is used when goods are made to order or when individual costs are easy to trace to individual jobs, assuming that the additional information provides value. In these circumstances, the individual costs are easy to trace to the individual jobs.

For example, assume that a homeowner wants to have a custom deck added to her home. Also assume that in order to fit her lot's topography and her anticipated uses for the addition, she needs a uniquely designed deck. Her contractor will design the deck, price the necessary components (in this case, the direct materials, direct labor, and overhead), and construct it.

The final cost will be unique to this project. If another homeowner wanted the contractor to construct a deck, the contractor would go through the same design and pricing process, and you would expect that the design and costs would not be the same as those of the deck in the first example, since the decks would differ from one another.

The job order costing method also works well for companies such as movie production companies, print service providers, advertising agencies, building contractors, accounting firms, consulting entities, and repair service providers. For example, *Star Wars: The Last Jedi* is believed to have cost $200 million to produce, whereas *Logan* only cost $97 million. The production processes for both films differed significantly, so that the accumulated costs for each job also differed significantly. Both were made in 2017.[1]

In contrast, process costing is used when the manufacturing process is continuous, so it is difficult to establish how much of each material is used and exactly how much time is invested in each unit of finished product. Therefore, in process costing, costs are accounted for by the production process or production department instead of by the product or by the job. This method works well for manufacturers of products such as Titleist golf balls, Kellogg's cereal, Turkey Hill ice cream, CITGO gasoline, Dow Chemicals, or Sherwin Williams' paints. However, process costing is not limited to basic manufacturing activities: It can also be used in the manufacturing of more complex items, such as small engines. A process costing system assigns costs to each department as the costs are incurred, and the costs to produce one unit are calculated based on the information from the production department. Unit costs are determined after total production costs are determined.

One factor that can complicate the choice between job order costing and process costing is the growth of automation in the production process, which typically is accompanied by a reduction in direct labor. The cost of the increase in equipment (typically reflected as a depreciation expense) is allocated to overhead, while the decreased need for labor usually reduces the direct labor cost. Because of these issues, some companies choose a hybrid system, using process costing to account for mass producing a part and using job order costing to account for assembling some of those individual parts into a custom product. Table 4.1 summarizes the use of these two systems.

Job Order and Process Cost Systems

	Job Order Cost System	**Process Cost System**
Product type	Custom order	Mass production
Examples	Signs, buildings, tax returns	Folding tables, toys, buffet restaurants
Cost accumulation	Job lot	Accumulated per process
Work in process inventory	Individual job cost sheets	Separate work in process inventory department
Record keeping	Individual job cost sheets	Production cost report

Table 4.1 This table shows some of the differences between job order costing and process costing.

---

1 "Production Costs and Global Box Office Revenue of Star Wars Movies from 1977 to 2018 (in million U.S. dollars)." The Statistics Portal. https://www.statista.com/statistics/311356/star-wars-production-costs-box-office-revenue/.

To illustrate how a company can determine whether to use job order costing or process costing, consider the cost accounting options for a local restaurant. Macs & Cheese makes specialty macaroni and cheese, and the company wants to erect a special sign on an already constructed billboard outside a stadium. It wants to use this space to target stadium customers; thus, the company wants a sign built specifically for that site. Dinosaur Vinyl is secured as the sign manufacturer and would use job order costing to account for the associated manufacturing costs because of the unique nature of the sign, including the art work involved. However, if Macs & Cheese was designing a costing system for the specialty food product they market, they typically would use a process costing approach because their product is made and marketed in homogeneous, similar batches.

LINK TO LEARNING

Dynamic Systems provides bar code-traceable software that helps companies track the costs associated with production (https://openstax.org/l/50barcode) . The company explains the difference between job order cost systems and process cost systems to their customers who often ask if their job order cost software is also the process cost software.

Organization of Flow of Goods through Production

Regardless of the costing method used (job order costing, process costing, or another method), manufacturing companies are generally similar in their organizational structure and have a similar flow of goods through production. The diagram in Figure 4.2 shows a partial organizational chart for sign manufacturer Dinosaur Vinyl. The CEO has several direct reporting units—Financing, Production, Information Technology, Marketing, Human Resources, and Maintenance—each with a director responsible for several departments.

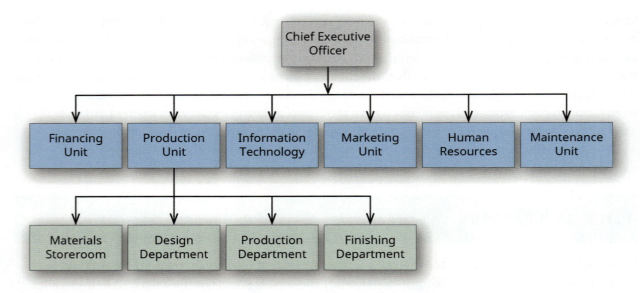

Figure 4.2 Organizational Chart for a Manufacturing Company. The different units within Dinosaur Vinyl illustrate the two main cost categories of a manufacturing company: manufacturing costs (the production unit), and selling and administrative costs. (attribution: Copyright Rice University, OpenStax, under CC BY-NC-SA 4.0 license)

The diagram also shows the departments that report to the production unit director and gives an indication as to the flow of goods through production. The flow of goods through production is more evident in Figure 4.3, which depicts Dinosaur Vinyl as a simple factory with three stages of production.

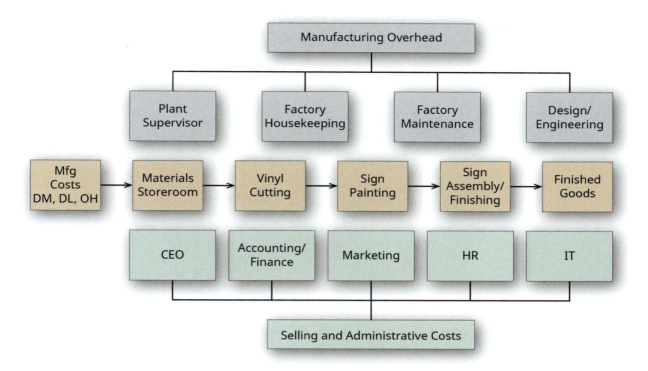

Figure 4.3 Factory Layout for Dinosaur Vinyl. The flow of goods and areas of manufacturing versus administrative costs are more easily seen by looking at the factory layout for Dinosaur Vinyl. The departments across the bottom represent administrative costs, whereas the departments in the middle represent manufacturing costs—although Design/Engineering can sometimes be considered part of administrative costs, depending on how management chooses to categorize those costs. The departments listed across the top represent examples of manufacturing overhead. (attribution: Copyright Rice University, OpenStax, under CC BY-NC-SA 4.0 license)

Raw materials are stored in the materials storeroom and delivered to the appropriate production department—cutting, painting, or assembly/finishing. The design department uses direct labor to create the design specifications, and, when completed, it sends them to the production department. The production department uses the material and design specifications and adds additional labor to create the sign. The sign is transferred to the finishing department for final materials and labor, before the sign is installed or delivered to the customer.

Manufacturing Costs

In a manufacturing environment, the **manufacturing costs** are also called *product costs* and include all expenses used to manufacture the product: direct materials, direct labor, and manufacturing overhead. To review these costs, see Building Blocks of Managerial Accounting. The total of these costs becomes the cost of ending inventory and later becomes the cost of goods sold when the product is sold. Both job order costing and process costing use categorized cost information to make decisions and evaluate the effectiveness of the cost tracking process. Because of the difference in how each of the two costing systems track costs, different terminology is used. Thus, it is important to separate product costs from period costs, and it is sometimes important to separate product costs into **prime costs** and **conversion costs**. Prime costs are costs that include the primary (or direct) product costs: direct materials and direct labor. Conversion costs are costs that include the expenses necessary to convert direct materials into a finished product: direct labor and manufacturing overhead. Their relationship is shown in Figure 4.4.

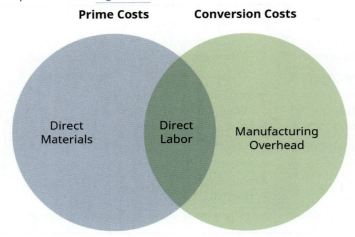

Figure 4.4 Manufacturing Costs. Management sometimes needs additional information to make decisions and needs the costs categorized as prime costs or conversion costs. Prime costs and conversion costs are not included together as direct labor is included in both categories. (attribution: Copyright Rice University, OpenStax, under CC BY-NC-SA 4.0 license)

Job order costing systems assign costs directly to the product by assigning direct materials and direct labor to the work in process (WIP) inventory. As you learned in Building Blocks of Managerial Accounting, direct materials are the components that can be directly traced to the products produced, whereas direct labor is the labor cost that can be directly traced to the products produced.

Material and labor costs that cannot be traced directly to the product produced are included in the overhead costs that are allocated in the production costing process. Overhead is applied to each product based on an activity base, which will be explained in Compute a Predetermined Overhead Rate and Apply Overhead to Production.

The assignment of direct materials and direct labor to each production unit illustrates the job order costing system's focus on prime costs, in contrast to the process costing system, which assigns costs to the department and focuses on direct materials and conversion costs, which are composed of a combination of direct labor and overhead. Process costs will be demonstrated in Process Costing.

Selling and Administrative Costs

Selling and administrative costs (S&A) are period costs, and these costs are expensed as incurred, instead of being included in the product's costs, as they move through the relevant inventory accounts. A **period cost** is a cost tied to a specific time period, such as a month, quarter, or year, instead of being associated with a particular job order. For example, if a company paid an insurance company $12,000 for one year's liability insurance coverage, the first month's expense would be $1,000. This expense would not be related to a particular job order, but instead would be classified as a period cost, and in this case recorded monthly as an administrative expense. Selling costs are the expenses related to the promotion and sale of the company's products, whereas administrative costs are the expenses related to the operations of the company. The S&A

costs are considered period costs because they include costs of departments not directly associated with manufacturing but necessary to operate the business. Some examples include research and development costs, marketing costs, sales commissions, administration building rent, the CEO's salary expense, and accounting, payroll, and IT department expenses.

YOUR TURN

Maria's Market

A grocery store's analysis of a recent customer survey finds an increasing number of customers interested in being able to custom-order meals to go. Maria sees this as an opportunity to enter a niche market for busy families or individuals who want home-cooked meals with a variety of options and combinations, but who have little time. Maria already has an expansive deli, bakery, and prepared foods section in the store and sees this opportunity as a viable option to increase sales and its customer base. With meals to go, customers can choose from an array of options and can indicate the quantity of each item and the time of pickup. The customer simply pulls up in a designated spot at Maria's and the food is brought to their car, packaged, and ready to take home to enjoy.

What type of costing system will work best for the Maria's Market? What sales price information, cost information, and other options are important to this decision?

Solution

A job order cost system will work well for this store. In addition to specific price and cost, these are other important considerations.

- The optimal sales price should be set to encourage customers to purchase the meals.
- The materials, labor, and overhead cost should be considered for each meal option.
    - Direct material costs may include the cost of the protein, grain, and vegetable option, as well as the cost of the packing containers.
    - The direct labor cost is for employees who are directly involved in preparing the meals.
    - Manufacturing overhead includes the cost of gloves used when preparing the meals, the cost of employees who support but are not directly involved in preparing the meals, and the cost to operate the oven.
- The cost of the various meal options should all be less than the sales price.
- The meal options should change to take advantage of seasonal items.
- There may be a need to vary the sales price, depending on the combinations selected.

Recording Costs in Job Order Costing versus Process Costing

Both job order costing and process costing track the costs of materials, labor, and overhead as components of virtually all products. The process of production does not change because of the costing method: The costing method is chosen based on the process of production and is intended to provide the most accurate representation of the costs incurred in the production process.

Maintaining accounting records for each system has its advantages. A job order costing system uses a **job cost sheet** to keep track of individual jobs and the direct materials, direct labor, and overhead associated with each job. The focus of a job order costing system is tracking costs per job, since each job is unique and therefore has different costs relative to other jobs. Maintaining this information is typically more expensive than process costing, and it is often used for the production of smaller, more individualized jobs because the benefit of knowing the cost of each product outweighs the additional cost of maintaining a job order costing system.

In contrast, a process costing system does not need to maintain the cost for individual jobs because the jobs use a continual system of production, and the items are typically not significantly unique but instead are basically equivalent. The accounting emphasis is in keeping records for the individual departments, which is useful for large batches or runs. Process costing is the optimal system to use when the production process is continuous and when it is difficult to trace a particular input cost to an individual product. Process costing systems assign costs to each department as the costs are incurred. The costs to produce one unit are calculated, based on the information from the production department. Therefore, the focus of process costing systems is on measuring and assigning the conversion costs to the proper department in order to best determine the cost of individual units.

Under either costing method, accounting theory explains why it is important to understand when costs become expenses. A primary reason for separating production costs from other company expenses is the **expense recognition principle**, which requires costs to be expensed when they match the revenue being earned and to separate the costs of production from other costs for the proper timing of recognition of expenses. Think about measuring the profit from the sale of an item, say a TV, in a nonmanufacturing environment. It is logical to subtract the costs associated with buying the TV in order to determine the profit, before applying other costs from that sale. Suppose the TV was purchased as inventory by the store in January and sold to a customer in March. This requires that the cost of the TV not be recorded as an expense (cost of goods sold) until March, when the sale from the TV is recorded, thus matching the revenue with the expense. Until that time, the TV and its cost are considered inventory. This same idea applies to the manufacturing process.

Per the expense recognition principle, product costs—the direct materials, direct labor, and manufacturing overhead incurred to produce the job—are expensed on the income statement for the period of the sale as cost of goods sold when the completed job is sold. If the products are not sold, their costs remain in ending inventory.

Prior to the sale of the product, separating production costs and assigning them to the product results in these costs remaining with the inventory. Until they are sold, the costs incurred are reflected in an assortment of inventory accounts, such as raw materials inventory, work in process inventory, and finished goods inventory.

In contrast, period costs are not directly related to the production process and are expensed during the period in which they are incurred. This approach matches administrative and other expenses shown on the income statement in the same period in which the company earns income.

4.2 Describe and Identify the Three Major Components of Product Costs under Job Order Costing

In order to set an appropriate sales price for a product, companies need to know how much it costs to produce an item. Just as a company provides financial statement information to external stakeholders for decision-making, they must provide costing information to internal managerial decision makers. Virtually every tangible product has direct materials, direct labor, and overhead costs that can include indirect materials and indirect labor, along with other costs, such as utilities and depreciation on production equipment. To account for these and inform managers making decisions, the costs are tracked in a cost accounting system.

While the flow of costs is generally the same for all costing systems, the difference is in the details: Product costs have material, labor, and overhead costs, which may be assessed differently. In most production facilities, the raw materials are moved from the raw materials inventory into the work in process inventory. The work in process involves one or more production departments and is where labor and overhead convert the raw materials into finished goods. The movement of these costs through the work in process inventory is shown in Figure 4.5.

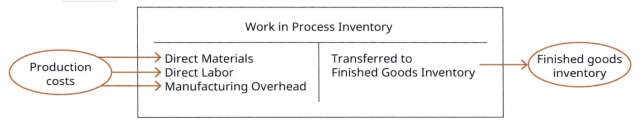

Figure 4.5 Work in Process Inventory. Direct materials, direct labor, and manufacturing overhead enter the work in process inventory as the costs associated with the products that are in production. Once the products are completed, their costs are transferred to the finished goods inventory. (attribution: Copyright Rice University, OpenStax, under CC BY-NC-SA 4.0 license)

At this stage, the completed products are transferred into the finished goods inventory account. When the product is sold, the costs move from the finished goods inventory into the cost of goods sold.

While many types of production processes could be demonstrated, let's consider an example in which a contractor is building a home for a client. The accounting system will track direct materials, such as lumber, and direct labor, such as the wages paid to the carpenters constructing the home. Along with these direct materials and labor, the project will incur manufacturing overhead costs, such as indirect materials, indirect labor, and other miscellaneous overhead costs. Samples of these costs include indirect materials, such as nails, indirect labor, such as the supervisor's salary, assuming that the supervisor is overseeing several projects at the same time, and miscellaneous overhead costs such as depreciation on the equipment used in the construction project.

As direct materials, direct labor, and overhead are introduced into the production process, they become part of the work in process inventory value. When the home is completed, the accumulated costs become part of the finished goods inventory value, and when the home is sold, the finished goods value of the home becomes the cost of goods sold. Figure 4.6 illustrates the flow of these costs through production.

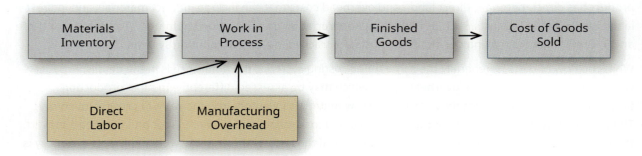

Figure 4.6 Flow of Materials from Raw Materials to Finished Goods. Accounting methods track a product's material, labor, and overhead costs, as it moves through production. (attribution: Copyright Rice University, OpenStax, under CC BY-NC-SA 4.0 license)

The three general categories of costs included in manufacturing processes are direct materials, direct labor, and overhead. Note that there are a few exceptions, since some service industries do not have direct material costs, and some automated manufacturing companies do not have direct labor costs. For example, a tax accountant could use a job order costing system during tax season to trace costs. The one major difference between the home builder example and this one is that the tax accountant will not have direct material costs to track. The few assets used will typically be categorized as overhead.

A benefit of knowing the production costs for each job in a job order costing system is the ability to set appropriate sales prices based on all the production costs, including direct materials, direct labor, and overhead. The unique nature of the products manufactured in a job order costing system makes setting a price even more difficult. For each job, management typically wants to set the price higher than its production cost. Even if management is willing to price the product as a loss leader, they still need to know how much money will be lost on each product. To achieve this, management needs an accounting system that can accurately assign and document the costs for each product.

If you're not familiar with the concept of a loss leader, a simple example might help clarify the concept. A **loss leader** is a product that is sold at a price that is often less than the cost of producing it in order to entice you to buy accessories that are necessary for its use. For example, you might pay $50 or $60 for a printer (for which the producer probably does not make any profit) in order to then sell you extremely expensive printer cartridges that only print a few pages before they have to be replaced. However, even pricing a product as a loss leader requires analysis of the three categories of costs: direct materials, direct labor, and overhead.

Direct Materials

Direct materials are those materials that can be directly traced to the manufacturing of the product. Some examples of direct materials for different industries are shown in Table 4.2. In order to respond quickly to production needs, companies need raw materials inventory on hand. While production volume might change, management does not want to stop production to wait for raw materials to be delivered. Further, a company needs raw materials on hand for future jobs as well as for the current job. The materials are sent to the production department as it is needed for production of the products.

Common Direct Materials by Industry

Industry	Direct Materials
Automotive	Iron, aluminum, glass, rubber
Cell phones	Glass, various metals, plastic
Furniture	Wood, leather, vinyl
Jewelry	Gold, silver, diamonds, rubies
Pharmaceuticals	Natural or synthetic biological ingredients

Table 4.2

Each job begins when raw materials are put into the work in process inventory. When the materials are requested for production, a materials requisition slip is completed and shows the exact items and quantity requested, along with the associated cost. The completed form is signed by the requestor and approved by the manager responsible for the budget.

Returning to the example of Dinosaur Vinyl's order for Macs & Cheese's stadium sign, Figure 4.7 shows the **materials requisition form** for Job MAC001. This form indicates the quantity and specific items to be put into the work in process. It also transfers the cost of those items to the work in process inventory and decreases the raw materials inventory by the same amount. The raw materials inventory department maintains a copy to document the change in inventory levels, and the accounting department maintains a copy to properly assign the costs to the particular job.

```
                    MATERIALS REQUISITION FORM
                         Dinosaur Vinyl, Inc.

Material Requisition No.: 3392
Job No.: MAC001
Date of Request: 4/5/2017
Date Needed: 4/5/2017
```

Description	Quantity	Unit Cost	Total Cost
Raw materials inventory: Vinyl	1	$300	$300
Raw materials inventory: Black ink	2	50	100
Raw materials inventory: Red ink	1	60	60
Raw materials inventory: Gold ink	1	60	60
Raw materials inventory: Grommets	12	10	120
Raw materials inventory: Framing wood	40	1.50	60
			$700

Requested by: _john ming_   Date: 4/5/17
Authorized by: _Tala Clark_   Date: 4/5/17

Figure 4.7 Materials Requisition Form for Job MAC001. The materials requisition form allows different departments to track and account for the direct materials needed to manufacture the product. (attribution: Copyright Rice University, OpenStax, under CC BY-NC-SA 4.0 license)

Dinosaur Vinyl has a beginning inventory of $1,000 in *raw materials: vinyl*, and $300 in each of its ink inventories: *raw materials: black ink*, *raw materials: red ink*, and *raw materials: gold ink*. In order to have enough inventory on hand for all of its jobs, it purchases $10,000 in vinyl and $500 in black ink. The T-accounts in Figure 4.8 show the stated beginning debit balances. An additional $10,000 of vinyl and $500 of black ink were then purchased for anticipated use, providing the demonstrated final account balances. The red ink and gold ink balances did not change, since no additional quantities were purchased.

The beginning balances and purchases in each of these accounts are illustrated in Figure 4.8.

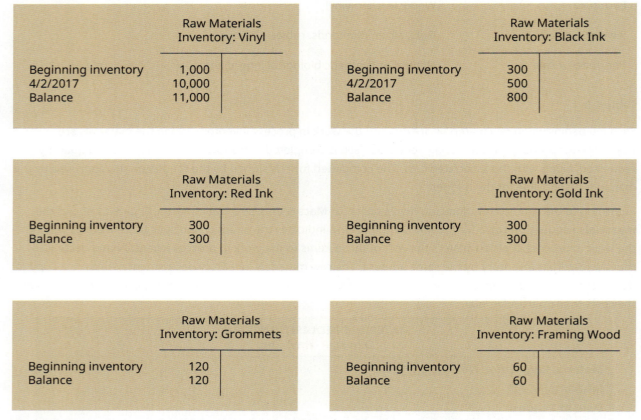

Figure 4.8 Beginning Balances and Purchases. These T-accounts show the balances for the raw materials inventory. (attribution: Copyright Rice University, OpenStax, under CC BY-NC-SA 4.0 license)

Traditional billboards with the design printed on vinyl include direct materials of vinyl and printing ink, plus the framing materials, which consist of wood and grommets. The typical billboard sign is 14 feet high by 48 feet wide, and Dinosaur Vinyl incurs a vinyl cost of $300 per billboard. The price for the ink varies by color. For this job, Dinosaur Vinyl needs two units of black ink at a cost of $50 each, one unit of red ink and one unit of gold ink at a cost of $60 each, twelve grommets at a cost of $10 each, and forty units of wood at a cost of $1.50 per unit. The total cost of direct materials is $700, as shown in Figure 4.9.

Item	Units	Cost per Unit	Item Cost	Total Cost
Production Department				
Vinyl	1	$ 300	$300	
Black ink	2	50	100	
Red ink	1	60	60	
Gold ink	1	60	60	$520
Finishing Department				
Grommets	12	$ 10	$120	
Framing wood	40	1.50	60	180
Total Direct Materials				$700

Figure 4.9 Direct Materials Needed for Job MAC001. The costs for direct materials needed by both the production and finishing departments are shown. (attribution: Copyright Rice University, OpenStax, under CC BY-NC-SA 4.0 license)

Some items are more difficult to measure per unit, such as adhesives and other materials not directly traceable to the final product. Their costs are assigned to the product as part of manufacturing overhead as indirect materials.

When Dinosaur Vinyl requests materials to complete Job MAC001, the materials are moved from raw materials inventory to work in process inventory. We will use the beginning inventory balances in the accounts that were provided earlier in the example. The requisition is recorded on the job cost sheet along with the cost of the materials transferred. The costs assigned to job MAC001 are $300 in vinyl, $100 in black ink, $60 in red ink, and $60 in gold ink. During the finishing stages, $120 in grommets and $60 in wood are requisitioned and put into work in process inventory. The costs are tracked from the materials requisition form to the work in process inventory and noted specifically as part of Job MAC001 on the preceding job order cost sheet. The movement of goods is illustrated in Figure 4.10.

Raw Materials Inventory: Vinyl			Raw Materials Inventory: Grommets		
Beginning inventory 4/2/2017	1,000		Beginning inventory 4/14/2017	300	
4/2/2017	10,000	300	Balance	180	120
Balance	10,700				

Raw Materials Inventory: Black Ink			Raw Materials Inventory: Framing Wood		
Beginning inventory 4/2/2017	300		Beginning inventory 4/14/2017	300	
4/2/2017	500	100	Balance	240	60
Balance	700				

Raw Materials Inventory: Red Ink			Work in Process Inventory		
Beginning inventory 4/2/2017	300		4/2/2017	520	
Balance	240	60	4/14/2017	180	

Raw Materials Inventory: Gold Ink		
Beginning inventory 4/2/2017	300	
Balance	240	60

Figure 4.10 Movement of Goods. These T-accounts illustrate the tracking of costs from raw materials inventory to the work in process inventory as the product moves through the manufacturing process. (attribution: Copyright Rice University, OpenStax, under CC BY-NC-SA 4.0 license)

Each of the T-accounts traces the movement of the raw materials from inventory to work in process. The vinyl and ink were used first to print the billboard, and then the billboard went to the finishing department for the grommets and frame, which were moved to work in process after the vinyl and ink. The final T-account shows the total cost for the raw materials placed into work in process on April 2 (vinyl and ink) and on April 14 (grommets and wood). The journal entries to reflect the flow of costs from raw materials to work in process to finished goods are provided in the section describing how to Prepare Journal Entries for a Job Order Cost System.

Direct Labor

Direct labor is the total cost of wages, payroll taxes, payroll benefits, and similar expenses for the individuals who work directly on manufacturing a particular product. The direct labor costs for Dinosaur Vinyl to complete Job MAC001 occur in the production and finishing departments. In the production department, two individuals each work one hour at a rate of $15 per hour, including taxes and benefits. The finishing department's direct labor involves two individuals working one hour each at a rate of $18 per hour. Figure 4.11 shows the direct labor costs for Job MAC001.

Item	Hours	Rate per Hour	Item Cost	Total Cost
Production Department				
Material Handler	1	$15	$15	
Print Technician	1	15	15	$30
Finishing Department				
Production Assistant	1	$18	$18	
Production Assistant	1	18	18	36
Total Direct Labor				$66

Figure 4.11 Direct Labor for Job MAC001. Labor costs account for individuals working directly on the product. Individuals whose contributions are indirect will be tracked under manufacturing overhead. (attribution: Copyright Rice University, OpenStax, under CC BY-NC-SA 4.0 license)

Job MAC001 is also manufactured with the work of individuals whose contributions cannot be directly traced to the product: These indirect labor costs are assigned to the product as part of manufacturing overhead.

A company can use various methods to trace employee wages to specific jobs. For example, employees may fill out **time tickets** that include job numbers and time per job, or workers may scan bar codes of specific jobs when they begin a job task. Figure 4.12 shows what time tickets might look like on Job MAC001. Please note that in the employee time tickets that are displayed, each employee worked on more than one job. However, we are only going to track the expenses for Job MAC001.

EMPLOYEE TIME TICKET

Employee Name: Renee Chelsea

Department: Material Handler

Employee ID: 12842

Date: 4/5/2017

Job No.	Hours Worked	Hourly Rate	Total Cost
MAC001	1	$15	$ 15
POR143	7	15	105
			$120

Authorized by:

EMPLOYEE TIME TICKET

Employee Name: Raymond Santiago

Department: Print Technician

Employee ID: 23133

Date: 4/5/2017

Job No.	Hours Worked	Hourly Rate	Total Cost
MAC001	1	$15	$ 15
TJR441	4	15	60
POR143	3	15	45
			$120

Authorized by:

EMPLOYEE TIME TICKET

Employee Name: Rani Fina

Department: Finishing/Assembly

Employee ID: 13353

Date: 4/15/2017

Job No.	Hours Worked	Hourly Rate	Total Cost
MAC001	2	$18	$ 36
TJR441	5	18	90
POR143	1	18	18
			$144

Authorized by: _____   Date: _____

Figure 4.12 Employee Time Tickets. Time tickets (or time cards) are one method a company can use to track direct labor costs per individual and per job. (attribution: Copyright Rice University, OpenStax, under CC BY-NC-SA 4.0 license)

When the accounting department processes time tickets, the costs are assigned to the individual jobs, resulting in labor costs being recorded on the work in process inventory, as shown in Figure 4.13.

	Work in Process Inventory
4/2/2017	520
4/5/2017	30
4/14/2017	180
4/15/2017	36

Figure 4.13 Costs Accounted for in the Work in Process Inventory. The direct material costs of $520 and $180, and the direct labor costs of $30 and $36 assigned to Job MAC001 are shown. (attribution: Copyright Rice University, OpenStax, under CC BY-NC-SA 4.0 license)

Manufacturing Overhead

Recall that the costs of a manufactured item are direct materials, direct labor, and manufacturing overhead. Costs that support production but are not direct materials or direct labor are considered overhead. **Manufacturing overhead** has three components: indirect materials, indirect labor, and overhead.

Indirect Materials

Indirect material costs are derived from the goods not directly traced to the finished product, like the sign adhesive in the Dinosaur Vinyl example. Tracking the exact amount of adhesive used would be difficult, time consuming, and expensive, so it makes more sense to classify this cost as an indirect material.

Indirect materials are materials used in production but not traced to specific products because the net informational value from the time and effort to trace the cost to each individual product produced is impossible or inefficient. For example, a furniture factory classifies the cost of glue, stain, and nails as indirect materials. Nails are often used in furniture production; however, one chair may need 15 nails, whereas another may need 18 nails. At a cost of less than one cent per nail, it is not worth keeping track of each nail per product. It is much more practical to track how many pounds of nails were used for the period and allocate this cost (along with other costs) to the overhead costs of the finished products.

Indirect Labor

Indirect labor represents the labor costs of those employees associated with the manufacturing process, but whose contributions are not directly traceable to the final product. These would include the costs of the factory floor supervisor, the factory housekeeping staff, and factory maintenance workers. For Dinosaur Vinyl, for example, labor costs for the technician who maintains the printers would be indirect labor. It would be too time consuming to determine how much of the technician's time is attributable to each sign being produced. It makes much more sense to classify that labor expense as indirect labor.

It is important to understand that the allocation of costs may vary from company to company. What may be a direct labor cost for one company may be an indirect labor cost for another company or even for another department within the same company. Deciding whether the expense is direct or indirect depends on its task. If the employee's work can be directly tied to the product, it is direct labor. If it is tied to the factory but not to the product, it is indirect labor. If it is tied to the marketing department, it is a sales and administrative expense, and not included in the cost of the product. For example, salaries of factory employees assembling parts are direct labor, salaries of factory employees performing maintenance are indirect labor, and salaries of employees in the marketing department are sales and administration expenses.

Overhead

The last category of manufacturing overhead is the overhead itself. These costs are necessary for production but not efficient to assign to individual product production. Examples of typical overhead costs are production facility electricity, warehouse rent, and depreciation of equipment.

But note that while production facility electricity costs are treated as overhead, the organization's administrative facility electrical costs are not included as as overhead costs. Instead, they are treated as period costs, as office rent or insurance would be.

When both administrative and production activities occur in a common building, the production and period costs would be allocated in some predetermined manner. For example, if a 10,000 square foot building were physically allocated at 4,000 square feet for administrative purposes and 6,000 square feet for production, a company might allocate its annual $30,000 property tax expense on a 40%/60% basis, or $12,000 as a period cost for the administrative offices and a production (overhead) cost of $18,000.

LINK TO LEARNING

Do you know of a restaurant that was doing really well until it moved into a larger space? Often this happens because the owners thought their profits could handle the costs of the increased space. Unfortunately, they were not really aware of the production costs. Keeping track of product costs is critical for pricing and cost control. Read advice from restaurant owner John Gutekanst about the importance of understanding food costs (https://openstax.org/l/50pizza) and his approach to account for these in his pizzeria.

Accounting for Manufacturing Overhead

In all costing systems, the expense recognition principle requires costs to be recorded in the period in which they are incurred. The costs are expensed when matched to the revenue with which they are associated; this is commonly referred to as *having the expenses follow the revenues*. This explains why raw material purchases are not assigned to the job until the materials are requested. When companies use an inventory account, the product costs are expensed when the inventory is sold. It is common to have an item produced in one year, such as 2017, and expensed as cost of goods sold in a later year, such as 2018. In addition to the previously mentioned *revenue recognition* treatment, this treatment is justified under GAAP's *matching principle*. If the inventory has not been sold, the company has an inventory asset rather than an expense.

The expense recognition principle also applies to manufacturing overhead costs. The manufacturing overhead is an expense of production, even though the company is unable to trace the costs directly to each specific job. For example, the electricity needed to run production equipment typically is not easily traced to a particular product or job, yet it is still a cost of production. As a cost of production, the electricity—one type of manufacturing overhead—becomes a cost of the product and part of inventory costs until the product or job is sold. Fortunately, the accounting system keeps track of the manufacturing overhead, which is then applied to each individual job in the overhead allocation process.

ETHICAL CONSIDERATIONS

Ethical Job Order Costing

Job order costing requires the assignment of direct materials, direct labor, and overhead to each production unit. The primary focus on costs allows some leeway in recording amounts because the accountant assigns the costs. When jobs are billed on a cost-plus-fee basis, management may be tempted to overcharge the cost of the job. Cost-based contracts may include a guaranteed maximum, time and materials, or cost reimbursable contract. An example is the design and delivery of a corporate training program. The training company may charge for the hours worked by instructors in preparation and delivery of the course, plus a fee for the course materials.

One major issue in all of these contracts is adding too much overhead cost and fraudulent invoicing for unused materials or unperformed work by subcontractors. Management might be tempted to direct the accountant to avoid the appearance of going over the original estimate by manipulating job order costing. It is the accountant's job to ensure that the amounts recorded in the accounting system fairly represent the economic activity of the company, and the fair and proper allocation of costs.

Managers use the information in the manufacturing overhead account to estimate the overhead for the next fiscal period. This estimated overhead needs to be as close to the actual value as possible, so that the allocation of costs to individual products can be accurate and the sales price can be properly determined.

Properly allocating overhead to the individual jobs depends on finding a cost driver that provides a fair basis for the allocation. A **cost driver** is a production factor that causes a company to incur costs. An example would be a bakery that produces a line of apple pies that it markets to local restaurants. To make the pies requires that the bakery incur labor costs, so it is safe to say that pie production is a cost driver. It should also be safe to assume that the more pies made, the greater the number of labor hours experienced (also assuming that direct labor has not been replaced with a greater amount of automation). We assume, in this case, that one of the marketing advantages that the bakery advertises is 100% handmade pastries.

In traditional costing systems, the most common activities used as cost drivers are direct labor in dollars, direct labor in hours, or machine hours. Often in the production process, there is a correlation between an increase in the amount of direct labor used and an increase in the amount of manufacturing overhead incurred. If the company can demonstrate such a relationship, they then often allocate overhead based on a formula that reflects this relationship, such as the upcoming equation. In the case of the earlier bakery, the company could determine an overhead allocation amount based on each hour of direct labor or, in other cases, based on the ratio of anticipated total direct labor costs to total manufacturing overhead costs.

For example, assume that the company estimates total manufacturing overhead for the year to be $400,000 and the direct labor costs for the year to be $200,000. This relationship would lead to $2.00 of applied overhead for each $1.00 of direct labor incurred. The manufacturing overhead cost can be calculated and applied to each specific job, based on the direct labor costs. The formula that represents the overhead allocation relationship is shown, and it is the formula for overhead allocation:

$$\frac{\text{Estimated Annual Overhead Costs (\$)}}{\text{Expected Annual Activity (DL \$)}} = \text{Overhead Allocation Rate}$$

For example, Dinosaur Vinyl determined that the direct labor cost is the appropriate driver to use when establishing an overhead rate. The estimated annual overhead cost for Dinosaur Vinyl is $250,000. The total direct labor cost is estimated to be $100,000, so the allocation rate is computed as shown:

$$\frac{\text{Estimated Annual Overhead Costs (\$250,000)}}{\text{Expected Annual Activity (\$100,000)}} = \$2.50 \text{ per \$1.00 Direct Labor Expense}$$

Since the direct labor expense for MAC001 is $66, the overhead allocated is $66 times the overhead application rate of $2.50 per direct labor dollar, or $165, as shown:

$$\text{Overhead Allocated} = \$66 \text{ (Direct Labor)} \times \$2.50 \text{ (Overhead Application Rate)} = \$165$$

Figure 4.14 shows the journal entry to record the overhead allocation.

	JOURNAL		
Date	Account	Debit	Credit

4/18/17	Work in Process Inventory
	    Manufacturing Overhead
	    To assign overhead to Job MAC001
		165	165

Work in Process Inventory	
4/2/2017	520
4/5/2017	30
4/14/2017	180
4/15/2017	36
4/18/2017	165

Figure 4.14 Overhead Allocation. (attribution: Copyright Rice University, OpenStax, under CC BY-NC-SA 4.0 license)

THINK IT THROUGH

Franchise or Unique Venture?

You are deciding whether to purchase a pizza franchise or open your own restaurant specializing in pizza. List the expenses necessary to sell pizza and identify them as a fixed cost or variable cost; as a manufacturing cost or sales and administrative costs; and as a direct materials, direct labor, or overhead. For each overhead item, state whether it is an indirect material expense, indirect labor expense, or other. For each cost, identify its origination in a job order costing environment.

4.3 Use the Job Order Costing Method to Trace the Flow of Product Costs through the Inventory Accounts

Job order costing can be used for many different industries, and each industry maintains records for one or more inventory accounts. The manufacturing industry keeps track of the costs of each inventory account as the product is moved from raw materials inventory into work in process, through work in process, and into the finished goods inventory.

Conversely, typical companies in the merchandising industry sell products they do not manufacture and purchase their inventory in an already completed state. It is relatively easy to keep track of the inventory cost for a merchandising company through its application of first-in/first-out (FIFO), last-in/last-out (LIFO), weighted average, or specific identification inventory techniques on the unsold items. The primary difference in the four methods is the valuation of the cost of goods sold and the remaining ending inventory valuation, assuming that the company did not sell 100% of the inventory that they had available for sale during a given period. Companies are allowed to choose the method that they feel best represents their cost flows through their cost of goods sold and their ending inventory balances.

Not all service companies have inventory, and those companies do not have direct materials nor do they consider their work in process their inventory, since their final product is often an intangible asset, such as a legal document or tax return. Regardless of whether the service has inventory accounts, service companies all keep track of the direct labor and overhead costs incurred while completing each job in progress.

Inventory is an asset reported on the balance sheet, and each company needs to maintain accurate records for the cost of each type of inventory: raw materials inventory, work in process inventory, and finished goods inventory. All three costs are computed in a similar manner. You can see in Figure 4.15 that the general format is the same for maintaining all accounts, whether the company uses a job order, process, or hybrid cost system.

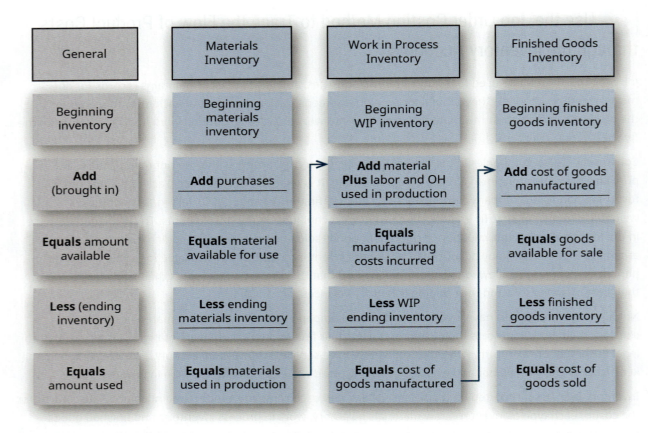

Figure 4.15 Cost of Inventory Accounts. Inventory is accounted for across the flow through production. (attribution: Copyright Rice University, OpenStax, under CC BY-NC-SA 4.0 license)

Each inventory account starts with a beginning balance at the start of an accounting period. During the period, if additional inventory is purchased, the new inventory amount is added to the beginning balance to calculate the total inventory available for use or sale. The ending inventory balance at the end of the accounting period can then be subtracted from the inventory available for use, and the total represents the cost of the inventory used during the period.

For example, if the beginning inventory balance were $400, and the company bought an additional $1,000, it would have $1,400 of inventory available for use. If the ending inventory balance were $500, the amount of inventory used during the period would be $900 ($400 + $1,000 = $1,400 − $500 = $900).

Raw Materials Inventory

Raw materials inventory is the total cost of materials that will be used in the production process. Usually, several accounts make up the raw materials inventory, and these can be actual accounts or accounts subsidiary to the general raw materials inventory account. In our example, Dinosaur Vinyl has several raw materials accounts: vinyl, red ink, black ink, gold ink, grommets, and wood.

Within the raw materials inventory account, purchases increase the inventory, whereas raw materials sent into production reduce it. It is easy to reconcile the amount of ending inventory and the cost of direct materials used in production, since the materials requisition form (Figure 4.7) keeps track of the inventory requested and sent into each specific job. Since the costs are transferred with production, the calculation shows the amount of materials used in production:

Beginning materials inventory
+ Net materials purchased
= Materials available for use
− Ending raw materials inventory
= Materials used in production

Note: this equation can be easily modified with algebra to compute the cost of the ending raw materials inventory.

Materials available for use
− Materials used in production
= Ending raw materials inventory

Work in Process Inventory

In a job order cost system, the balance in the work in process inventory account is continually updated as job costs are recorded and is the total of all unfinished jobs, as shown on the individual job cost sheets.

The production cycle is a continuous cycle that begins with raw materials being transferred to work in process, moving through production, and ending as finished goods inventory. Typically, as goods are being produced, additional jobs are being started and finished, and the work in process inventory includes unit costs of jobs still in production at the end of the accounting period. At the end of the accounting cycle, there will be jobs that remain unfinished in the production cycle, and these represent the work in process inventory. The costs on the job order cost sheet help reconcile the cost of the items transferred to the finished goods inventory and the cost of the work in process inventory.

For example, Dinosaur Vinyl has completed Job MAC001. The total cost of $931 is transferred to the finished goods inventory:

JOURNAL			
Date	Account	Debit	Credit

	Finished Goods Inventory
	    Work in Process Inventory
	    To transfer Job MAC001 to Finished Goods
		931	931

At this point, we need to examine an important component of the costing process. The **cost of goods manufactured** (COGM) is the costs of all of the units that a company completed and transferred to the finished goods inventory during an accounting period. Obviously, the cost of goods manufactured is not just a single number that can be pulled from one location. We have to look at all costs included in the manufacturing process to determine the cost of goods manufactured. The calculation begins with the beginning balance in the work in process inventory, incorporates the new production costs incurred during the current period (typically a year), and then subtracts the ending balance in the work in process inventory since these costs will be included in the subsequent accounting period's cost of goods manufactured, as shown:

```
Beginning work in process inventory
+ Current manufacturing costs
    Direct materials used in production
    Direct labor
    Overhead
= Manufacturing costs incurred
− Ending work in process inventory
= Cost of goods manufactured during
  the period (completed)
```

Note: this equation can be easily modified with algebra to compute the cost of the ending work in process inventory.

```
Manufacturing costs incurred
− Cost of goods manufactured
= Ending work in process inventory
```

Finished Goods Inventory

After each job has been completed and overhead has been applied, the product is transferred to the finished goods inventory where it stays until it is sold. As each job is transferred, the costs are summarized and transferred as well, and the job cost sheet is completed to show the actual production cost of the product and the sales price of the items produced.

A job order cost system continually updates each job cost sheet as materials, labor, and overhead are added. As a result, all inventory accounts are constantly maintained. The materials inventory balance is continually updated, as materials are purchased and requisitioned for individual jobs. The work in process inventory and finished goods inventory are master accounts, and their balances are determined by adding the total of the job cost sheets. The total of the incomplete jobs becomes the total work in process inventory, and the total of the completed and unsold jobs becomes the total of the finished goods inventory.

Similar to the raw materials and work in process inventories, the cost of goods sold can be calculated as shown:

```
Beginning finished goods
+ Cost of goods manufactured
= Goods available for sale
− Ending finished goods inventory
= Cost of goods sold
```

Note: this equation can be easily modified with algebra to compute the cost of the finished goods inventory.

```
Cost of goods available for sale
− Cost of goods sold
= Ending finished goods inventory
```

Cost of Goods Sold

The **cost of goods sold** is the manufacturing cost of the items sold during the period. It is calculated by adding the beginning finished goods inventory and the cost of goods manufactured to arrive at the cost of goods available for sale. The cost of goods available for sale less the ending inventory results in the cost of goods sold.

In our example, when the sale has occurred, the goods are transferred to the buyer, and the product is transferred from the finished goods inventory to the cost of goods sold. A corresponding entry is also made to record the sale. Dinosaur Vinyl's sales price for Job MAC001 was $2,000, and its cost of goods sold was $931:

JOURNAL			
Date	Account	Debit	Credit
	Cost of Goods Sold	931	
	Finished Goods Inventory		931
	To transfer sold Job MAC001		
	Accounts Receivable	2,000	
	Sales		2,000
	To record sale of Job MAC001		

Figure 4.16 shows the flow to cost of goods sold.

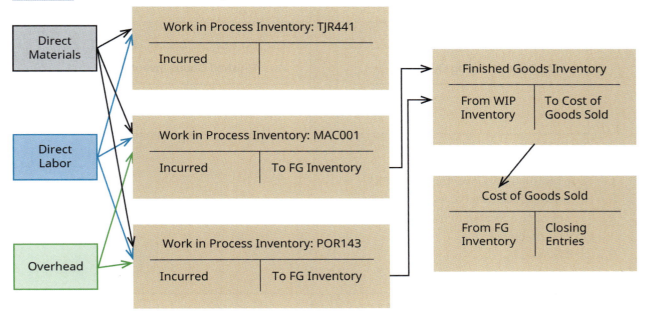

Figure 4.16 Flow of Manufacturing Costs under the Job Order Costing Method. (attribution: Copyright Rice University, OpenStax, under CC BY-NC-SA 4.0 license)

YOUR TURN

Tracking the Flow with Selected T-Accounts

Use the transaction letters to show the flow in and out of the T-accounts. Note: some items may be used more than once. Also, not every possible T-account entry is required in this exercise. For example, for the purchase of raw materials, the credit entry for either cash or accounts payable is not required.

Raw Materials Inventory: Vinyl	Work in Process Inventory

Factory Wage Expense	Cost of Goods Sold

Manufacturing Overhead	Finished Goods Inventory

A. Purchase raw materials inventory
B. Factory wage expense incurred
C. Issue raw materials inventory to Job P33
D. Factory wage allocated to Job P33
E. Factory wage allocated to overhead
F. Job P33 completed
G. Job P33 sold

Solution

Raw Materials Inventory: Vinyl		Work in Process Inventory	
A	C	C E	D

Factory Wage Expense		Cost of Goods Sold	
B	E F	G	

Manufacturing Overhead		Finished Goods Inventory	
F		D	G

4.4 Compute a Predetermined Overhead Rate and Apply Overhead to Production

Job order cost systems maintain the actual direct materials and direct labor for each individual job. Since production consists of overhead—indirect materials, indirect labor, and other overhead—we need a methodology for applying that overhead. Unfortunately, the nature of indirect material, indirect labor, and other overhead expenses makes it impossible to determine the exact amount of overhead for each specific job. For example, how do you know the cost of electricity and heat for manufacturing one job? And, if you did, is it fair to say products manufactured in January are more expensive than the same product manufactured in March because of heat expense?

Fundamental Characteristics of the Overhead Determination Environment

Added to these issues is the nature of establishing an overhead rate, which is often completed months before being applied to specific jobs. Establishing the overhead allocation rate first requires management to identify which expenses they consider manufacturing overhead and then to estimate the manufacturing overhead for the next year. Manufacturing overhead costs include all manufacturing costs except for direct materials and direct labor. Therefore, in order to estimate manufacturing overhead, management must estimate the future purchase prices of dozens, or sometimes hundreds, of individual components, such as utilities, raw materials, contract labor, or diesel fuel. Estimating overhead costs is difficult because many costs fluctuate significantly from when the overhead allocation rate is established to when its actual application occurs during the production process. You can envision the potential problems in creating an overhead allocation rate within these circumstances.

Before demonstrating the calculation of a predetermined overhead allocation rate, let's review the basic principles of revenue recognition and expense. In accounting, there are three ways to recognize expenses:

1. Direct relationship between the expense and the associated revenue. This method is used for many costs, and the expense is recognized when a direct relationship exists. For example, sales commission expenses can be directly traced to product sales, and a commission expense is recorded when a sale is made.
2. Systematic and rational allocation of expenses. This approach is used when costs exist and there is an expected benefit, even though the costs cannot be directly traced to the benefit. The assigning of expenses to a product or time period must be done in an objective and consistent manner. Examples of such expenses would include equipment rental for a factory or property insurance for the factory.
   Both of these expenses (direct relationship and systematic and rational) are also examples of the types of expenses that compose manufacturing overhead. An example of the current revenue recognition principle is a company paying $4,800 a year for property insurance. Since production rates can vary month to month, most producers would allocate $400 each month for property insurance, and this cost would be incorporated into the total overhead costs anticipated when estimating a manufacturing overhead allocation rate.
   The direct benefit is that the product will be sold and the revenue recognized. The overhead is associated but cannot be directly traced to an individual product, so the overhead expenses need to be assigned in a systematic and rational manner.
3. Immediate recognition. This method is used when expenses exist but there is no direct expected benefit. In this case, the expense is recognized immediately. For example, research and development costs are necessary expenses but cannot be traced to a specific product, so they are expensed as incurred.

The allocation of overhead to the cost of the product is also recognized in a systematic and rational manner. The expected overhead is estimated, and an allocation system is determined. The actual costs are accumulated in a manufacturing overhead account. The overhead is then applied to the cost of the product from the manufacturing overhead account. The overhead used in the allocation is an estimate due to the timing considerations already discussed.

The application rate that will be used in a coming period, such as the next year, is often estimated months before the actual overhead costs are experienced. Often, the actual overhead costs experienced in the coming period are higher or lower than those budgeted when the estimated overhead rate or rates were determined. At this point, do not be concerned about the accuracy of the future financial statements that will be created using these estimated overhead allocation rates. You will learn in Determine and Disposed of Underapplied or Overapplied Overhead how to adjust for the difference between the allocated amount and the actual amount.

Despite improvements in technology and information flow, using the actual overhead to calculate the application rate is usually not possible because the actual overhead information is available too late for management to make decisions. Also, as you will learn, the results of the actual overhead costs, if they were available, could be misleading. Therefore, most manufacturing companies use predetermined overhead rates for these reasons:

- Overhead costs are not uniform throughout the year. An example is electricity costs that vary by weather and time of day.
- Some overhead costs are fixed, and the cost per unit varies with production. For example, rent may be $1,000 per month. If 500 units were made during one month, and 2,000 units were made the next month, the cost per unit would vary from $2 per unit to $0.50 per unit.
- The total number of units produced varies and is often known sooner than the cost of overhead. For example, a company may know it will have a contract to produce 100 custom units long before it knows the utility costs for the next year.

As previously described, a predetermined overhead rate is established prior to the beginning of the fiscal year and typically is not changed during the year. The predetermined rate is calculated as shown and is used to apply overhead costs to work in process:

$$\frac{\text{Estimated (budgeted) Overhead Cost}}{\text{Expected (budgeted) Level of Activity}} = \text{Predetermined Overhead Rate}$$

CONCEPTS IN PRACTICE

Overhead in the Movie Industry

The movie industry uses job order costing, and studios need to allocate overhead to each movie. Their amount of allocated overhead is not publicly known because while publications share how much money a movie has produced in ticket sales, it is rare that the actual expenses are released to the public.

It has been speculated that *Star Wars: The Force Awakens* cost $201,000,000, with $30,000,000 considered overhead. Studios have estimated that the higher the movie expenses, the more studio overhead is required, and it has also been estimated that 10% of the total cost is assigned to studio overhead.

Determining Estimated Overhead Cost

The estimated or budgeted overhead is the amount of overhead determined during the budgeting process and consists of manufacturing costs but, as you have learned, excludes direct materials and direct labor. Examples of manufacturing overhead costs include indirect materials, indirect labor, manufacturing utilities, and manufacturing equipment depreciation. Another way to view it is overhead costs are those production costs that are not categorized as direct materials or direct labor.

Selecting an Estimated Activity Base

As you have learned, the overhead needs to be allocated to the manufactured product in a systematic and rational manner. This allocation process depends on the use of a cost driver, which drives the production activity's cost. Examples can include labor hours incurred, labor costs paid, amounts of materials used in production, units produced, or any other activity that has a cause-and-effect relationship with incurred costs.

Direct labor hours, direct labor dollars, or machine hours are often chosen as the allocation base because those costs are associated with each product, and as the activity increases, so does the manufacturing overhead. In other words, the products that involve more direct labor hours, direct labor dollars, or machine hours also increase utility expenses, supervisor time (and thus indirect labor), equipment usage and the related depreciation expense, and so forth.

Traditionally, direct labor hours were used as the activity base, but technology continually decreases the amount of direct labor used in production, and machine hours or units produced have become more common activity bases. Management analyzes the costs and selects the activity as the **estimated activity base** because it drives the overhead costs of the unit.

Computing a Predetermined Overhead Rate

Dinosaur Vinyl uses the expenses from the prior two years to estimate the overhead for the upcoming year to be $250,000, as shown in Figure 4.17.

	Annual Estimate
Indirect labor	$ 5,000
Indirect materials	20,000
Utilities	75,000
Depreciation	90,000
Insurance	35,000
Interest expense	25,000
	$250,000

Figure 4.17 Dinosaur Vinyl's Estimated Overhead. (attribution: Copyright Rice University, OpenStax, under CC BY-NC-SA 4.0 license)

Dinosaur Vinyl also used its payroll records to estimate that it will spend $100,000 on direct labor. Using the predetermined overhead rate calculation, the overhead rate is $2.50 per direct labor dollar:

$$\frac{\text{Estimated (budgeted) Overhead Cost (\$250,000)}}{\text{Expected (budgeted) Level of Activity (\$100,000)}} = \$2.50 \text{ per Direct Labor Dollar}$$

Over the fiscal year, the actual costs are recorded as debits into the account called manufacturing overhead. When the overhead is applied to the jobs, the amount is first calculated using the application rate. If the total labor paid for the job is $66, the overhead applied to the job is $2.50 times that amount, or $165. The entry to record the overhead for Job MAC001 is:

JOURNAL			
Date	Account	Debit	Credit

	Work in Process Inventory
	  Manufacturing Overhead
	  To apply overhead to Job MAC001
		165	165

That amount is added to the cost of the job, and the amount in the manufacturing overhead account is reduced by the same amount. At the end of the year, the amount of overhead estimated and applied should be close, although it is rare for the applied amount to exactly equal the actual overhead. For example, Figure 4.18 shows the monthly costs, the annual actual cost, and the estimated overhead for Dinosaur Vinyl for the year. While the total amounts are close to each other, they are not exact.

	Monthly Actual	Annual Amount	Annual Estimate
Indirect labor	$ 375	$ 4,500	$ 5,000
Indirect materials	1,500	18,000	20,000
Utilities	7,000	84,000	75,000
Depreciation	7,500	90,000	90,000
Insurance	2,917	35,000	35,000
Interest expense	2,083	25,000	25,000
	$21,000	$256,500	$250,000

Figure 4.18 Dinosaur Vinyl's Actual and Estimated Overhead. While the total amounts are close to each other, they are not an exact match. (attribution: Copyright Rice University, OpenStax, under CC BY-NC-SA 4.0 license)

Calculating Manufacturing Overhead Cost for an Individual Job

Figure 4.18 shows the monthly manufacturing actual overhead recorded by Dinosaur Vinyl. As explained previously, the overhead is allocated to the individual jobs at the predetermined overhead rate of $2.50 per direct labor dollar when the jobs are complete. When Job MAC001 is completed, overhead is $165, computed as $2.50 times the $66 of direct labor, with the total job cost of $931, which includes $700 for direct materials, $66 for direct labor, and $165 for manufacturing overhead.

LINK TO LEARNING

Companies need to make certain the sales price is higher than the prime costs and the overhead costs. This can be a difficult task in industries in which overhead costs change. In some industries, the company has no control over the costs it must pay, like tire disposal fees. To ensure that the company is profitable, an additional cost is added and the price is modified as necessary. In this example, the guarantee offered by Discount Tire (https://openstax.org/l/50tireguarantee) does not include the disposal fee in overhead and increases that fee as necessary.

4.5 Compute the Cost of a Job Using Job Order Costing

To summarize the job order cost system, the cost of each job includes direct materials, direct labor, and manufacturing overhead. While the product is in production, the direct materials and direct labor costs are included in the work in process inventory. The direct materials are requested by the production department, and the direct material cost is directly attached to each individual job, as the materials are released from raw materials inventory. The cost of direct labor is recorded by the employees and assigned to each individual job. When the allocation base is known, usually when the product is completed, the overhead is allocated to the product on the basis of the predetermined overhead rate.

LINK TO LEARNING

The construction industry typically uses job order costing and accounts for its costing (https://openstax.org/l/50construction) in a manner similar to the businesses profiled in this chapter.

Determining the Costs of an Individual Job Using Job Order Costing

When a job is completed, the costs of the job—the direct materials, direct labor, and manufacturing overhead—are totaled on the job cost sheet, and the total amount is transferred to finished goods at the same time the product is transferred, either physically or legally, such as in the case of a home built by a contractor. Finally, when the product is sold, the sale is recorded at the sale price, while the cost is transferred from finished goods inventory to the cost of goods sold expense account. Figure 4.19 shows the flow of costs from raw materials inventory to cost of goods sold.

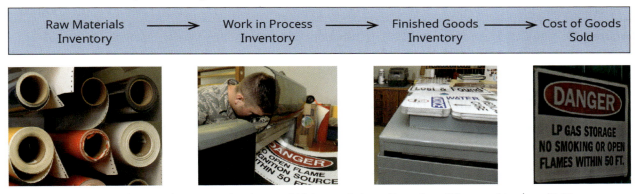

Figure 4.19 Flow of Costs during Production and Ultimate Sale or Transfer of Ownership. (credit "Raw Materials Inventory," "Work in Process Inventory," "Finished Goods Inventory": modifications of "160810-F-UY190-027.JPG," "160810-F-UY190-073.JPG," and "160810-F-UY190-105.JPG" by Jessica Weissman, Minot Air Force Base Public Affairs, Public Domain; credit Cost of Goods Sold": "Rustic Sign" by Grace Byrd/Flickr, CC BY 2.0)

At all points in the process, the work in process should include the cost of direct materials and direct labor. When the job is completed and overhead assigned, the overhead allocation increases the cost of the work in process inventory. The cost of each individual job is maintained on a job cost sheet, and the total of all the work in process job cost sheets equals the work in process inventory and the statement of cost of goods manufactured, as you have learned.

A job cost sheet is a subsidiary ledger that identifies the individual costs for each job. Figure 4.20 shows the job cost sheet for Job MAC001.

JOB COST SHEET
Dinosaur Vinyl, Inc.

Job No.: 5416
Customer: Macs & Cheese
Units Ordered: 1

Customer No.: 2501723
Date Started: Dec. 22, 2018
Date Completed: Feb. 22, 2019

Direct Material	Units	Price	Amount
Vinyl	1	$300	$ 300
Black printing ink	2	50	100
Red printing ink	1	60	60
Gold printing ink	1	60	60
Grommets	12	10	120
Framing wood	40	1.5	60
Total Direct Materials			$ 700

Direct Labor	Hours	Wage Rate	Amount
Material Handler	1	$ 15	$ 15
Print Technician	1	15	15
Production Assistants	2	18	36
Total Direct Labor			$ 66

Manufacturing Overhead	Base Units	Rate	Amount
Direct Labor Cost	66	$ 2.5	$ 165
Total Manufacturing Overhead			$ 165
Total Job Cost			$ 931
Total Revenue			$2,000

Figure 4.20 Job Cost Sheet for Job MAC001. (attribution: Copyright Rice University, OpenStax, under CC BY-NC-SA 4.0 license)

Sample Cost Information for Dinosaur Vinyl

Dinosaur Vinyl worked on three jobs during the month: POR143, MAC001, and TRJ441, and a fourth Job SWM505 had been finished and moved to the finished goods inventory account during the previous month.

At the beginning of the month, the company had a beginning raw materials inventory balance of $2,500, and during the month, it purchased an additional $10,500, giving it a total of $13,000 in raw materials available for use in production.

The following example will examine four different production jobs. Each of the four will be at beginning stages at either the beginning of the current month or the end of the current month.

1. Job POR 143: This job was the only work in process inventory at the beginning of the current month, and it had $1,000 in direct material costs, and $0 of direct labor costs already allocated to the work in process inventory. During the current month, additional direct materials of $200 and direct labor of $150 were added to POR143. An overhead cost of $375 was applied to POR143 at the predetermined overhead rate of $2.50 per direct labor dollar. It was finished during the month and transferred to the finished goods inventory. The sale was not finalized during the month, so it continues to be part of the finished goods inventory.

2. Job MAC 001: This job was started and completed during the month. Since the job began in and was completed in the same month, there was no beginning balance in the work in process inventory. During the month it incurred $700 in direct materials costs, $66 in direct labor, and $165 of overhead applied to the job before it was transferred to the finished goods inventory upon completion. The sale was finalized during the month at a sale price of $2,000, so the costs were transferred from finished goods inventory to cost of goods sold.
3. Job TRJ441: This job was started during the current month. Its costs consist of $500 in direct material cost, $150 in direct labor expenses, and $375 in applied overhead. The job remains in the work in process inventory awaiting assembly.
4. Job SWM505: At the beginning of the month, this job was completed and already in the finished goods inventory at a cost of $1,531. Since it was completed, it did not incur any additional costs in the current month. It was sold during the month for $3,500, and the costs were transferred from the finished goods inventory to cost of goods sold.

The cost of raw materials used is calculated as shown:

Beginning RM inventory	$ 2,500
Purchases	10,500
Materials available for use	13,000
Ending RM inventory	11,600
Materials used in production	$ 1,400

The individual job cost sheets show the $1,400 worth of materials used in production:

POR143	$ 200
MAC001	700
TJR441	500
	$1,400

The cost of goods manufactured is accounted for as shown:

	POR143	MAC001	TJR441	Total
Materials added	$200	$700	$ 500	$1,400
Labor added	150	66	150	366
Overhead applied	375	165	375	915
Total added during month	$725	$931	$1,025	$2,681
	POR143	MAC001	TJR441	Total
Beginning WIP inventory	$1,000	$ 0	$ 0	$1,000
Materials, labor, & OH added	725	931	1,025	2,681
Manufacturing costs incurred	1,725	931	1,025	3,681
Ending WIP inventory	0	0	1,025	1,025
Cost of Goods Manufactured	$1,725	$931	$ 0	$2,656

Notice the costs for Job TJR441 are included in the work in process inventory, whereas the costs for POR143 and MAC001 were transferred to the cost of goods manufactured. The costs of the jobs transferred are shown in the cost of goods sold and the finished goods inventory:

	SWM505	POR143	MAC001	TJR441	Total
Beginning FG inventory	$1,531	$ 0	$ 0	$0	$1,531
Cost of Goods Manufactured	0	1,725	931	0	2,656
Goods Available for Sale	1,531	1,725	931	0	4,187
Ending FG inventory	0	1,725	0	0	1,725
Cost of Goods Sold	$1,531	$ 0	$931	$0	$2,462

Mechanics of Job Order Costing for Dinosaur Vinyl

The amounts in raw materials, work in process, and finished goods inventories compose the total cost for each account, whereas the job cost sheets contain the costs for each individual job. A summary of the jobs for Dinosaur Vinyl is given in Figure 4.21.

	SWM505	POR143	MAC001	TJR441	Total	
Beginning balance	$1,531	$1,000	$ 0	$ 0	$2,531	← Beginning WIP
Direct materials		200	700	500	1,400	
Direct labor		150	66	150	366	
Overhead applied		375	165	375	915	
Total cost	$1,531	$1,725	$931	$1,025	$5,212	← Total for WIP, FG, & COGS
Status	Sold	Finished	Sold	Unfinished		
Final account location	COGS	FG	COGS	WIP		

Figure 4.21 Summary of Dinosaur Vinyl's Jobs during the Year. (attribution: Copyright Rice University, OpenStax, under CC BY-NC-SA 4.0 license)

THINK IT THROUGH

Allocating Costs

A manufacturing company has incurred these costs:

Purchase raw materials inventory	$15,000
Issue raw materials inventory to Job A	3,000
Factory wage expense incurred	23,000
Factory wage allocated to Job A	2,000
Factory wage allocated to overhead	500
Manufacturing overhead incurred	7,500
Manufacturing overhead allocated to Job A	1,000

What is the cost allocated to Job A? For any costs not used, explain why they are not used.

4.6 Determine and Dispose of Underapplied or Overapplied Overhead

As you've learned, the actual overhead incurred during the year is rarely equal to the amount that was applied to the individual jobs. Thus, at year-end, the manufacturing overhead account often has a balance, indicating overhead was either overapplied or underapplied.

If, at the end of the term, there is a debit balance in manufacturing overhead, the overhead is considered **underapplied overhead**. A debit balance in manufacturing overhead shows either that not enough overhead was applied to the individual jobs or overhead was underapplied. If, at the end of the term, there is a credit balance in manufacturing overhead, more overhead was applied to jobs than was actually incurred. This shows the actual amount was **overapplied overhead**.

The actual overhead costs are recorded through a debit to manufacturing overhead. The same account is credited when overhead is applied to the individual jobs in production, as shown:

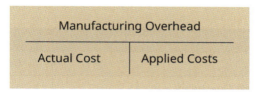

Since the overhead is first recorded in the manufacturing overhead account, then applied to the individual jobs, traced through finished goods inventory, and eventually transferred to cost of goods sold, the year-end balance is eliminated through an adjusting entry, offsetting the cost of goods sold. If manufacturing overhead has a debit balance, the overhead is underapplied, and the resulting amount in cost of goods sold is understated. The adjusting entry is:

	JOURNAL		
Date	Account	Debit	Credit
	Cost of Goods Sold Manufacturing Overhead	$$$	$$$

If manufacturing overhead has a credit balance, the overhead is overapplied, and the resulting amount in cost of goods sold is overstated. The adjusting entry is:

	JOURNAL		
Date	Account	Debit	Credit
	Manufacturing Overhead Cost of Goods Sold *Application of overhead to Cost of Goods Sold*	$$$	$$$

Returning to our example, at the end of the year, Dinosaur Vinyl had actual overhead expenses of $256,500 and applied overhead expenses of $250,000, as shown:

Manufacturing Overhead

Actual Costs	Applied Costs
$256,500	$250,000

Since manufacturing overhead has a debit balance, it is underapplied, as it has not been completely allocated. The adjusting journal entry is:

JOURNAL			
Date	Account	Debit	Credit
	Cost of Goods Sold	6,500	
	Manufacturing Overhead		6,500
	Application of underapplied overhead to Cost of Goods Sold		

If the overhead was overapplied, and the actual overhead was $248,000 and the applied overhead was $250,000, the entry would be:

JOURNAL			
Date	Account	Debit	Credit
	Manufacturing Overhead	2,000	
	Cost of Goods Sold		2,000
	Application of overapplied overhead to Cost of Goods Sold		

To adjust for overapplied or underapplied manufacturing overhead, some companies have a more complicated, three-part allocation to work in process, finished goods, and cost of goods sold. This method is typically used in the event of larger variances in their balances or in bigger companies. (You will learn more about this in future cost or advanced managerial accounting courses.)

YOUR TURN

Kraken Boardsports

Figure 4.22 (credit: modification of images provided courtesy of Kraken Boardsports, CC BY 4.0)

Kraken Boardsports manufactures winches for snow and ski boarders to snow ski without a mountain or water ski without a lake (Figure 4.22). End-of-year data show these overhead expenses:

Indirect materials	$25,000
Indirect labor	31,750
Depreciation of factory equipment	50,000
Factory utility expenses	17,500
Factory supervisor salaries	85,000

Kraken Boardsports had 6,240 direct labor hours for the year and assigns overhead to the various jobs at the rate of $33.50 per direct labor hour.

How much overhead was overapplied or underapplied during the year? What would be the journal entry to adjust manufacturing overhead?

Solution

The total overhead incurred is the total of:

Indirect materials	$ 25,000
Indirect labor	31,750
Depreciation of factory equipment	50,000
Factory utility expenses	17,500
Supervisor salaries	85,000
Actual overhead incurred	$209,250

The total overhead applied is $209,040, which is calculated as:

$33.50/direct labor hours × 6,240 direct labor hours.

The balance in manufacturing overhead is a debit balance of $210:

Manufacturing Overhead	
Actual Costs	Applied Costs
$209,250	$209,040
Balance 210	

The adjusting journal entry is:

JOURNAL			
Date	Account	Debit	Credit
	Cost of Goods Sold	210	
	Manufacturing Overhead		210

LINK TO LEARNING

Job order costing and overhead allocation are not new methods of accounting and apply to governmental units as well. See it applied in this 1992 report on Accounting for Shipyard Costs and Nuclear Waste Disposal Plans (https://openstax.org/l/50shipyard) from the United States General Accounting Office.

4.7 Prepare Journal Entries for a Job Order Cost System

Although you have seen the job order costing system using both T-accounts and job cost sheets, it is necessary to understand how these transactions are recorded in the company's general ledger.

Journal Entries to Move Direct Materials, Direct Labor, and Overhead into Work in Process

Dinosaur Vinyl keeps track of its inventory and orders additional inventory to have on hand when the production department requests it. This inventory is not associated with any particular job, and the purchases stay in raw materials inventory until assigned to a specific job. For example, Dinosaur Vinyl purchased an additional $10,000 of vinyl and $500 of black ink to complete Macs & Cheese's billboard. If the purchase is made on account, the entry is as shown:

JOURNAL			
Date	Account	Debit	Credit
	Raw Materials Inventory: Vinyl Raw Materials Inventory: Black ink Accounts Payable *To record purchase of vinyl and ink inventory*	10,000 500	 10,500

As shown in Figure 4.20, for the production process for job MAC001, the job supervisor submitted a materials requisition form for $300 in vinyl, $100 in black ink, $60 in red ink, and $60 in gold ink. For the finishing process for Job MAC001, $120 in grommets and $60 in finishing wood were requisitioned. The entry to reflect these actions is:

JOURNAL			
Date	Account	Debit	Credit

	Work in Process Inventory
	    Raw Materials Inventory: Vinyl
	    Raw Materials Inventory: Black ink
	    Raw Materials Inventory: Red ink
	    Raw Materials Inventory: Gold ink
	    Raw Materials Inventory: Grommets
	    Raw Materials Inventory: Finishing wood
	To record requisition of vinyl and ink inventory
		700	
			300
			100
			60
			60
			120
			60

The production department employees work on the sign and send it over to the finishing/assembly department when they have completed their portion of the job.

The direct cost of factory labor includes the direct wages paid to the employees and all other payroll costs associated with that labor. Typically, this includes wages and the payroll taxes and fringe benefits directly tied to those wages. The accounting system needs to keep track of the labor and the other related expenses assigned to a particular job. These records are typically kept in a time ticket submitted by employees daily.

On April 10, the labor time sheet totaling $30 is recorded for Job MAC001 through this entry:

JOURNAL			
Date	Account	Debit	Credit
	Work in Process Inventory (MAC001) Factory Wages Payable *To record labor for Job MAC001*	30	 30

The assembly personnel in the finishing/assembly department complete Job MAC001 in two hours. The labor is recorded as shown:

JOURNAL			
Date	Account	Debit	Credit

	Work in Process Inventory
	    Factory Wages Payable
	    To record labor for Job MAC001
		36	36

Indirect materials also have a materials requisition form, but the costs are recorded differently. They are first transferred into manufacturing overhead and then allocated to work in process. The entry to record the indirect material is to debit manufacturing overhead and credit raw materials inventory.

Indirect labor records are also maintained through time tickets, although such work is not directly traceable to a specific job. The difference between direct labor and indirect labor is that the indirect labor records the debit to manufacturing overhead while the credit is to factory wages payable.

Dinosaur Vinyl's time tickets indicate that $4,000 in indirect labor costs were incurred during the period. The entry is:

JOURNAL			
Date	Account	Debit	Credit

	Manufacturing Overhead
	    Factory wages payable
	    To record indirect labor for WIP inventories
		4,000	4,000

Dinosaur Vinyl also records the actual overhead incurred. As shown in Figure 4.18, manufacturing overhead costs of $21,000 were incurred. The entry to record these expenses increases the amount of overhead in the manufacturing overhead account. The entry is:

JOURNAL			
Date	Account	Debit	Credit

	Manufacturing Overhead
	    Supplies Inventory
	    Utilities Payable
	    Accumulated Depreciation
	    Prepaid Insurance
	    Interest Payable
	    To record April's overhead expenses
		21,000	1,500
			7,000
			7,500
			2,917
			2,083

The amount of overhead applied to Job MAC001 is $165. The process of determining the manufacturing overhead calculation rate was explained and demonstrated in Accounting for Manufacturing Overhead. The journal entry to record the manufacturing overhead for Job MAC001 is:

JOURNAL			
Date	Account	Debit	Credit

	Work in Process Inventory
	    Manufacturing Overhead
	    To apply overhead to Job MAC001
		165	165

Journal Entry to Move Work in Process Costs into Finished Goods

When each job and job order cost sheet have been completed, an entry is made to transfer the total cost from the work in process inventory to the finished goods inventory. The total cost of the product for Job MAC001 is $931 and the entry is:

JOURNAL			
Date	Account	Debit	Credit
	Finished Goods Inventory	931	
	Work in Process Inventory		931
	To recognize completion of Job MAC001		

Journal Entries to Move Finished Goods into Cost of Goods Sold

When the sale has occurred, the goods are transferred to the buyer. The product is transferred from the finished goods inventory to cost of goods sold. A corresponding entry is also made to record the sale. The sign for Job MAC001 had a sales price of $2,000 and a cost of $931. These are the entries to record the transfer of goods and sale to the buyer:

JOURNAL			
Date	Account	Debit	Credit
	Cost of Goods Sold	931	
	Finished Goods Inventory		931
	To recognize sale of Job MAC001		
	Accounts Receivable	2,000	
	Sales		2,000
	To recognize sale of Job MAC001		

The resulting accounting is shown on the company's income statement:

DINOSAUR VINYL, INC.
Income Statement

Sales	$2,000
Cost of Goods Sold	931
Gross profit	$1,069

THINK IT THROUGH

Ongoing Overapplied Overhead

At the end of each year, manufacturing overhead is analyzed, and an adjusting entry is made to dispose of the under- or overapplied overhead. How would you advise a company that has had overapplied overhead for each of the last five years?

4.8 Explain How a Job Order Cost System Applies to a Nonmanufacturing Environment

Job order cost systems can be used beyond the manufacturing realm and are often used in the production of services. The same cost tracking and journaling techniques apply, as the outcome still consists of materials, labor, and overhead. However, the terminology changes in a nonmanufacturing environment. For example, a movie production studio and an accounting firm produce movies and financial statement audits, respectively, instead of manufacturing units.

Fundamentals of the Job Order Costing Method for Service Entities

Instead of being dependent on materials, service industries depend on labor. Since their work is labor intensive, it makes sense to use labor as an activity base with billable hours often as the best allocation base. For example, in an audit, there often will be several accountants, with differing levels of experience and expertise involved in the assignment. The accounting firms have more billable hours at the staff level and fewer billable hours at the partner level. And since the firm bills the partner's time at a significantly higher rate than the staff, it makes sense to apply overhead at the billable hours instead of the billable costs.

In service industries, there is no manufacturing overhead because they are not manufacturing a product, but instead are providing a service. Accordingly, overhead is called **operating overhead**.

Another terminology difference is the inventory accounts. The jobs are considered movies or assignments in process, and are transferred to a cost of service sold account instead of to a finished goods inventory.

CONCEPTS IN PRACTICE

Tracking Costs in Healthcare

Healthcare is one of the industries that keeps track of materials, such as medicine. In this industry, direct labor is shown to the patient as the cost of the provider, such as a physician, physician assistant, or nurse practitioner. Indirect labor includes all other personnel from front desk staff to the nurse who gathers vital signs or a technician who performs tests. Patients do not see the overhead cost on their bill, but it is built into the invoice as part of the practitioner or testing fees.

Service Entity Use of a Job Order Costing System

To understand how a service provider uses a job order cost system, let's consider the case of IFixIT. IFixIT Systems is a Sony-authorized repair provider that fixes audiovisual equipment brought in by customers. IFixIT requires customers to pay $50 to diagnose the problem. IFixIt pays its employees $25 per hour and assigns overhead equal to its direct labor cost. The customers' bills do not show overhead and are instead itemized as parts plus labor, where the cost for parts is the original cost plus a markup, and the labor rate is $80 per hour.

A customer brought in his TV and paid the $50 diagnostic fee. IFixIT determined a new power cord was needed. To fix it, IFixIT purchases the part from its suppliers at $42 and pays $75 in direct labor for 3 hours at $25 per hour. Overhead is applied equal to the direct labor cost of $75. The customer is charged $310, consisting of $70 for the part and 3 hours of labor at a rate of $80 per hour. IFixIT records the journal entries shown:

JOURNAL			
Date	Account	Debit	Credit
	Cash	50	
	Diagnosis revenue		50
	Diagnosis of Sony Bravia for Job 4740325		
	Repair in process	42	
	Accounts Payable		42
	Purchase of new power cord for Job 4740325		
	Repair in process	75	
	Salaries Payable		75
	Assigning labor to Job 4740325		
	Repair in process	75	
	Operating overhead		75
	Assigning overhead costs to Job 4740325		
	Cost of completed repair	192	
	Repair in Process		192
	Completion of Job 4740325		
	Cash	310	
	Repair revenue		310
	Completion of Job 4740325		

ETHICAL CONSIDERATIONS

Subcontractor Misrepresentation of Costs of Jobs Used to Overbill Clients

Construction is a typical industry where job order costing and related accounting misstatements can be used to commit fraud. A construction subcontractor might overstate the units of production accomplished, the units of labor, or the equipment actually used.[2] This occurs most commonly with subcontractor fraud, where the subcontractor does not perform the work but bills for it anyway.

Another complicating issue is that many subcontractors are disadvantaged business enterprises that are required by law to be included in governmental construction contracts. In Chicago, for example, McHugh Construction paid $12 million in fines to settle the claims that its disadvantaged business enterprise subcontractor did not perform work.[3] The subcontractor received a prison sentence, and a related party was put on probation. An accountant had to prepare the invoices that allowed this common type of scheme to operate.

---

2   Jim Schmid and Todd F. Taggart, "The Most Common Types of Construction Fraud," *Construction Business Owner*, November 2, 2011, http://www.constructionbusinessowner.com/insurance/risk-management/most-common-types-construction-fraud.
3   Kim Slowey, "Chicago Subcontractor Sentenced to 1-year Prison Term for DBE Fraud Scheme," *Construction Dive*, March 20, 2017, https://www.constructiondive.com/news/chicago-subcontractor-sentenced-to-1-year-prison-term-for-dbe-fraud-scheme/438441/.

Key Terms

conversion costs total of labor and overhead for a product; the costs that "convert" the direct material into the finished product

cost driver activity that is the reason for the increase or decrease of another cost; examples include labor hours incurred, labor costs paid, amounts of materials used in production, units produced, machine hours, or any other activity that has a cause-and-effect relationship with incurred costs

cost of goods manufactured manufacturing costs incurred less the ending work in process inventory

cost of goods sold expense account that houses all costs associated with getting a product ready for sale

direct labor labor directly related to the manufacturing of the product or the production of a service

direct materials materials used in the manufacturing process that can be traced directly to the product

estimated activity base total amount of the activity for the year

expense recognition principle (also, matching principle) matches expenses with associated revenues in the period in which the revenues were generated

indirect labor labor not directly involved in the active conversion of materials into finished products or the provision of services

indirect materials materials used in production but not efficiently traceable to a specific unit of production

job cost sheet document created for each job that includes all material, labor, and overhead costs for that job

job order costing information system that traces the individual costs directly to the final product and not to production departments

loss leader product sold at a price that is often less than the cost of producing it in order to entice customers to buy accessories that are necessary for its use

manufacturing costs total of all costs expended in the manufacturing process; generally consists of direct material, direct labor, and manufacturing overhead

manufacturing overhead costs incurred in the production process that are not economically feasible to measure as direct material or direct labor costs; examples include indirect material, indirect labor, utilities, and depreciation

materials requisition form form showing which specific raw materials and costs are transferred from raw materials inventory to work in process inventory

operating overhead overhead account used for service industries

overapplied overhead situation when the overhead applied to the individual jobs is greater than the actual overhead; when overhead is overapplied, the manufacturing overhead has a credit balance

period costs typically related to a particular time period instead of attached to the production of an asset; treated as an expense in the period incurred (examples include many sales and administrative expenses)

prime costs direct material expenses and direct labor costs

time ticket document used to record the particular job worked on by each employee

underapplied overhead situation when the overhead applied to the individual jobs is less than the actual overhead; when overhead is underapplied, the manufacturing overhead has a debit balance

Summary

4.1 Distinguish between Job Order Costing and Process Costing

- Job order costing (JOC) is the optimal costing method for producing custom goods or when it is easy to identify the cost directly with the product.

- A JOC system assigns costs to each individual job as the costs are incurred, so that at all points in the manufacturing process, the costs assigned to that particular job are known.

4.2 Describe and Identify the Three Major Components of Product Costs under Job Order Costing

- Direct materials are requested on a materials requisition form and recorded on the job cost sheet when transferred from raw materials inventory to the work in process inventory.
- Time tickets are used to accumulate the labor associated with particular jobs and assigned to those jobs on the job cost sheet.
- Manufacturing overhead costs are accumulated in the manufacturing overhead account and assigned to the individual jobs using the predetermined overhead rate.

4.3 Use the Job Order Costing Method to Trace the Flow of Product Costs through the Inventory Accounts

- Materials used in production include the beginning raw materials inventory and purchases, less the ending inventory. This amount is the amount added to the work in process inventory.
- The cost of goods manufactured includes the beginning work in process inventory, the materials used in production, the direct labor assigned to each job, and the manufacturing overhead costs assigned, less the costs remaining in the work in process inventory. This amount is transferred to the finished goods inventory.
- The cost of goods sold include the beginning finished goods inventory and the cost of goods manufactured during the period, less the ending inventory.
- When the job is completed, the costs are transferred from the work in process inventory to the finished goods inventory.
- When the jobs are sold, the costs are transferred from the finished goods inventory to the cost of goods sold.

4.4 Compute a Predetermined Overhead Rate and Apply Overhead to Production

- Expenses are recognized when they have a direct relationship with the associated revenue, when there is a systematic and rational method to allocate them, or immediately when there is no expected benefit.
- The estimated activity base is typically direct labor dollars or direct labor hours, and is based on an allocation base that increases or decreases as overhead increases or decreases.
- The predetermined overhead rate is the estimated overhead divided by the activity base.

4.5 Compute the Cost of a Job Using Job Order Costing

- Costs from the materials requisition sheet and time tickets are recorded on the job cost sheet.
- Overhead is allocated from the manufacturing overhead account to the individual jobs and recorded on the job cost sheet.
- Each job has its own job cost sheet, showing the materials, labor, and overhead for each job.

4.6 Determine and Dispose of Underapplied or Overapplied Overhead

- Overhead is allocated to individual jobs based on the estimated overhead costs for the year and may be overapplied or underapplied for the year.
- Overhead is underapplied when not all of the costs accumulated in the manufacturing overhead account are applied during the year.
- Overhead is overapplied when more overhead is applied to the jobs than was actually incurred.
- The amount of overhead overapplied or underapplied is adjusted into the cost of goods sold account.

4.7 Prepare Journal Entries for a Job Order Cost System

- Job cost sheets record the material, labor, and overhead costs for each job, whereas journal entries actually transfer the costs into the work in process inventory, the finished goods inventory, and cost of goods sold.

4.8 Explain How a Job Order Cost System Applies to a Nonmanufacturing Environment
- Job order costing can be used in nonmanufacturing companies and with the same techniques, even though there are not any inventory accounts.

Multiple Choice

1. LO 4.1 Which of the following product situations is better suited to job order costing than to process costing?
- A. Each product batch is exactly the same as the prior batch.
- B. The costs are easily traced to a specific product.
- C. Costs are accumulated by department.
- D. The value of work in process is based on assigning standard costs.

2. LO 4.1 A job order costing system is most likely used by which of the following?
- A. a pet food manufacturer
- B. a paper manufacturing company
- C. an accounting firm specializing in tax returns
- D. a stereo manufacturing company

3. LO 4.1 Which of the following is a prime cost?
- A. indirect materials
- B. direct labor
- C. administrative expenses
- D. factory depreciation expenses

4. LO 4.1 Which of the following is a conversion cost?
- A. raw materials
- B. direct materials
- C. administrative expenses
- D. factory depreciation expenses

5. LO 4.1 During production, to what are the costs in job order costing applied?
- A. manufacturing overhead
- B. cost of goods sold
- C. each individual product
- D. each individual department

6. LO 4.2 Which document lists the inventory that will be removed from the raw materials inventory?
- A. job cost sheet
- B. purchase order
- C. materials requisition form
- D. receiving document

7. LO 4.2 Which document shows the cost of direct materials, direct labor, and overhead applied for each specific job?
   A. job cost sheet
   B. purchase order
   C. materials requisition form
   D. receiving document

8. LO 4.2 Which document lists the total direct materials used in a specific job?
   A. job cost sheet
   B. purchase order
   C. materials requisition form
   D. receiving document

9. LO 4.2 Which document lists the total direct labor used in a specific job?
   A. job cost sheet
   B. purchase order
   C. employee time ticket
   D. receiving document

10. LO 4.4 Assigning indirect costs to specific jobs is completed by which of the following?
   A. applying the costs to manufacturing overhead
   B. using the predetermined overhead rate
   C. using the manufacturing costs incurred
   D. applying the indirect labor to the work in process inventory

11. LO 4.4 In a job order cost system, which account shows the overhead used by the company?
   A. work in process inventory
   B. finished goods inventory
   C. cost of goods sold
   D. manufacturing overhead

12. LO 4.7 In a job order cost system, raw materials purchased are debited to which account?
   A. raw materials inventory
   B. work in process inventory
   C. finished goods inventory
   D. cost of goods sold

13. LO 4.7 In a job order cost system, overhead applied is debited to which account?
   A. work in process inventory
   B. finished goods inventory
   C. manufacturing overhead
   D. cost of goods sold

14. LO 4.7 In a job order cost system, factory wage expense is debited to which account?
   A. raw materials inventory
   B. work in process inventory
   C. finished goods inventory
   D. cost of goods sold

15. LO 4.7 In a job order cost system, utility expense incurred is debited to which account?
   A. work in process inventory
   B. finished goods inventory
   C. manufacturing overhead
   D. cost of goods sold

16. LO 4.7 In a job order cost system, indirect labor incurred is debited to which account?
   A. work in process inventory
   B. finished goods inventory
   C. manufacturing overhead
   D. cost of goods sold

17. LO 4.8 The activity base for service industries is most likely to be _____.
   A. machine hours
   B. administrative salaries
   C. direct labor cost
   D. direct labor hours

Questions

1. LO 4.1 A printing company manufactures notebooks of various sizes. The company manufactures 3,000 notebooks each day. Should the company use process costing or job order costing?

2. LO 4.1 Burnham Industries incurs these costs for the month:

Direct materials	$2,000
Direct labor	3,000
Factory depreciation expense	3,500
Factory utilities expense	750
CEO's salary	4,000

What is the prime cost?

3. LO 4.1 Choco's Chocolates incurs these costs for the month:

Direct materials	$15,000
Direct labor	25,000
Factory depreciation expense	45,000
Factory utilities expense	2,000
Payroll staff's salary	15,000

What is the conversion cost?

4. LO 4.1 How do job order costing and process costing differ with respect to recording direct materials and direct labor?

5. LO 4.1 Why are product costs assigned to the product and period costs immediately expensed?

6. LO 4.3 Is the cost of goods manufactured the same as the cost of goods sold?

7. LO 4.3 From beginning to end, place these items in the order of the flow of goods.
   A. cost of goods sold
   B. raw materials inventory
   C. finished goods inventory
   D. work in process inventory

8. LO 4.4 How is the predetermined overhead rate determined?

9. LO 4.4 How is the predetermined overhead rate applied?

10. LO 4.5 Why are the overhead costs first accumulated in the manufacturing overhead account instead of in the work in process inventory account?

11. LO 4.6 Why is the manufacturing overhead account debited as expenses are recognized and then credited when overhead is applied?

12. LO 4.7 Match the concept on the left to its correct description.

A. job order costing	i. computes the overhead applied to each job
B. materials requisition sheet	ii. source document indicating the number of hours an employee worked on specific jobs
C. overapplied overhead	iii. source document indicating the raw materials assigned to a specific production job
D. predetermined overhead rate	iv. the cost accounting system used by pet food manufacturers
E. process costing	v. the cost accounting system used by law firms
F. time ticket	vi. the result when the actual overhead is less than the amount assigned to each specific job
G. underapplied overhead	vii. the result when the actual overhead is more than the amount assigned to each specific job

13. LO 4.8 When compared to manufacturing companies, service industries do not generally use _____ as a component of product cost.

Exercise Set A

EA1. **LO** 4.1 Little Things manufactures toys. For each item listed, identify whether it is a product cost, a period cost, or not an expense.
- A. internet provider services
- B. material expense
- C. raw materials inventory
- D. production equipment rental
- E. showroom rental
- F. factory employee salary
- G. Human Resource Director salary

EA2. LO 4.2 Table 4.3 shows a list of expenses involved in the production of custom, professional lacrosse sticks.
  A. For each item listed, state whether the cost should be applied to manufacturing or sales and administration.
  B. If the cost is a manufacturing cost, state whether it is direct materials, direct labor, or manufacturing overhead.
  C. If the cost is a manufacturing overhead cost, state whether it is indirect materials, indirect labor, or another type of manufacturing overhead.

Expenses Involved in Lacrosse Stick Production

Lacrosse Stick Production Costs	Manufacturing or Sales & Administration Cost?	If Manufacturing: Direct Materials, Direct Labor, or Overhead?	If Overhead: Indirect Materials, Indirect Labor, or Other?
Carbon, fiberglass			
Administrative building rent			
Accountant salary			
Factory building depreciation			
Strings for the pocket			
Advertising			
Production supervisor salary			
Paint for sticks			
Research and development costs			
Wages of person who strings the sticks			
Cutting machine depreciation			

Table 4.3

Expenses Involved in Lacrosse Stick Production

Lacrosse Stick Production Costs	Manufacturing or Sales & Administration Cost?	If Manufacturing: Direct Materials, Direct Labor, or Overhead?	If Overhead: Indirect Materials, Indirect Labor, or Other?
Human resources salaries			
Factory maintenance			

Table 4.3

EA3. LO 4.2 Burnham Industries incurs these costs for the month:

Direct materials	$2,000
Direct labor	3,000
Factory depreciation expense	3,500
Factory utilities expense	750
CEO's salary	4,000

A. What is the prime cost?
B. What is the conversion cost?

EA4. LO 4.3 Marzoni's records show raw materials inventory had a beginning balance of $200 and an ending balance of $300. If the cost of materials used during the month was $900, what were the purchases made during the month?

EA5. LO 4.3 Sterling's records show the work in process inventory had a beginning balance of $4,000 and an ending balance of $3,000. How much direct labor was incurred if the records also show:

Materials used	$1,500
Overhead applied	500
Cost of goods manufactured	7,500

EA6. LO 4.3 Logo Gear purchased $2,250 worth of merchandise during the month, and its monthly income statement shows cost of goods sold of $2,000. What was the beginning inventory if the ending inventory was $1,000?

EA7. LO 4.4 A company estimates its manufacturing overhead will be $750,000 for the next year. What is the predetermined overhead rate given the following independent allocation bases?
  A. Budgeted direct labor hours: 60,000
  B. Budgeted direct labor expense: $1,500,000
  C. Estimated machine hours: 100,000

EA8. LO 4.4 Job order cost sheets show the following costs assigned to each job:

	Job 13	Job 14	Job 15
Direct materials	$7,560	$1,525	$3,290
Direct labor	3,760	3,824	3,796

The company assigns overhead at $1.25 for each direct labor dollar spent. What is the total cost for each of the jobs?

EA9. LO 4.4 A new company started production. Job 10 was completed, and Job 20 remains in production. Here is the information from job cost sheets from their first and only jobs so far:

Job 10	Hours	Total Cost
Direct materials		$ 765
Direct labor	75	1,575
Manufacturing overhead		60
Total cost		$2,400

Job 20	Hours	Total Cost
Direct materials		$ 145
Direct labor	113	2,373
Manufacturing overhead		90
Total cost		$2,608

Using the information provided,

A. What is the balance in work in process?
B. What is the balance in the finished goods inventory?
C. If manufacturing overhead is applied on the basis of direct labor hours, what is the predetermined overhead rate?

EA10. LO 4.5 K company production was working on Job 1 and Job 2 during the month. Of the $780 in direct materials, $375 in materials was requested for Job 1. Direct labor cost, including payroll taxes, are $23 per hour, and employees worked 18 hours on Job 1 and 29 hours on Job 2. Overhead is applied at the rate of $20 per direct labor hours. Prepare job order cost sheets for each job.

EA11. LO 4.7 A company has the following transactions during the week.
- Purchase of $1,000 raw materials inventory
- Assignment of $500 of raw materials inventory to Job 5
- Payroll for 20 hours with $1,000 assigned to Job 5
- Factory utility bills of $750
- Overhead applied at the rate of $10 per hour

What is the cost assigned to Job 5 at the end of the week?

EA12. LO 4.7 During the month, Job AB2 used specialized machinery for 450 hours and incurred $500 in utilities on account, $300 in factory depreciation expense, and $100 in property tax on the factory. Prepare journal entries for the following:
A. Record the expenses incurred.
B. Record the allocation of overhead at the predetermined rate of $1.50 per machine hour.

EA13. LO 4.7 Job 113 was completed at a cost of $5,000, and Job 85 was completed at a cost of $3,000 and sold on account for $4,500. Prepare journal entries for the following:
A. Completion of Job 113.
B. Completion and sale of Job 85.

EA14. LO 4.7 A company's individual job sheets show these costs:

	Job 131	Job 132	Job 133
Direct materials	$4,585	$8,723	$1,575
Direct labor	2,385	2,498	2,874

Overhead is applied at 1.25 times the direct labor cost. Use the data on the cost sheets to perform these tasks:

A. Apply overhead to each of the jobs.
B. Prepare an entry to record the assignment of direct materials to work in process.
C. Prepare an entry to record the assignment of direct labor to work in process.
D. Prepare an entry to record the assignment of manufacturing overhead to work in process.

EA15. LO 4.7 A summary of material requisition slips and time tickets, along with the overhead allocation, show these costs:

Job No.	Material Requisition Slips	Factory Labor Time Tickets	Overhead Applied
131	$ 505	$ 200	$ 70
132	251	260	91
133	393	180	63
134	340	300	105
Not job specific	76	145	0
	$1,565	$1,085	$329

A. Prepare an entry to record the assignment of direct material to work in process.
B. Prepare an entry to record the assignment of direct labor to work in process.
C. Prepare an entry to record the assignment of manufacturing overhead to work in process.

Exercise Set B

EB1. LO 4.1 Abuah Goods manufactures clothing. For each item listed, identify whether it is a product cost, a period cost, or not an expense.
A. pins to keep materials together while garment is being manufactured
B. real estate taxes on store
C. advertising expense
D. product inspector wages
E. shirts for sale
F. Chief Financial Officer salary
G. cost of goods sold

EB2. LO 4.2 Choco's Chocolates incurs the following costs for the month:

Direct materials	$15,000
Direct labor	25,000
Factory depreciation expense	45,000
Factory utilities expense	2,000
Payroll staff's salary	15,000

A. What is the prime cost?
B. What is the conversion cost?

EB3. LO 4.2 The table shows a list of expenses involved in the production of custom snowboard bindings.
  A. For each item listed, state if the cost is manufacturing or sales and administration.
  B. If the cost is a manufacturing cost, state if it is direct materials, direct labor, or manufacturing overhead.
  C. If the cost is a manufacturing overhead cost, state if it is indirect materials, indirect labor, or another type of manufacturing overhead.

Snowboard Binding Production Costs

Snowboard Bindings Production Costs	Manufacturing or Sales & Administration Cost?	If Manufacturing: Direct Materials, Direct Labor, or Overhead?	If Overhead: Indirect Materials, Indirect Labor, or Other?
Aluminum			
Factory building rent			
Fiberglass framework for each pair of bindings			
Accountant salary			
Administration building depreciation			
Straps			
Advertising			
Production supervisor salary			
Glue			
Research and development costs			
Inspector wages			
Metal shaping machine depreciation			
Human resources salaries			

Table 4.4

Snowboard Binding Production Costs

Snowboard Bindings Production Costs	Manufacturing or Sales & Administration Cost?	If Manufacturing: Direct Materials, Direct Labor, or Overhead?	If Overhead: Indirect Materials, Indirect Labor, or Other?
Factory repair			

Table 4.4

EB4. LO 4.3 Masonry's records show the raw materials inventory had purchases of $1,000 and an ending raw materials inventory balance of $200. If the cost of materials used during the month was $900, what was the beginning inventory?

EB5. LO 4.3 Steinway's records show their work in process inventory had a beginning balance of $3,000 and an ending balance of $3,500. How much overhead was applied if the records also show the following:

Materials used	$2,500
Direct labor	5,000
Cost of goods manufactured	7,700

EB6. LO 4.3 Langston's purchased $3,100 of merchandise during the month, and its monthly income statement shows a cost of goods sold of $3,000. What was the beginning inventory if the ending inventory was $1,250?

EB7. LO 4.4 A company estimates its manufacturing overhead will be $840,000 for the next year. What is the predetermined overhead rate given each of the following independent allocation bases?
  A. Budgeted direct labor hours: 90,615
  B. Budgeted direct labor expense: $750,000
  C. Estimated machine hours: 150,000

EB8. LO 4.4 Job order cost sheets show the following costs assigned to each job:

	Job 131	Job 132	Job 133	Total
Direct materials	$3,485	$39,853	$2,301	$45,639
Direct labor	2,353	34,245	2,037	38,635

The company assigns overhead at twice the direct labor cost. What is the total cost for each job?

EB9. LO 4.4 A new company started production. Job 1 was completed, and Job 2 remains in production. Here is the information from the job cost sheets from their first and only jobs so far:

Job 1	Hours	Total Cost
Direct materials		$ 375
Direct labor	231	5,313
Manufacturing overhead		4,620
Total cost		$10,308

Job 2	Hours	Total Cost
Direct materials		$ 405
Direct labor	85	1,955
Manufacturing overhead		1,700
Direct materials		$4,060

Using the information provided,

- A. What is the balance in work in process?
- B. What is the balance in finished goods inventory?
- C. If manufacturing overhead is applied on the basis of direct labor hours, what is the predetermined overhead rate?

EB10. LO 4.5 Inez has the following information relating to Job AA5. Direct material cost was $200,000, direct labor was $36,550, and overhead applied on the basis of direct labor hours was $73,100. What was the predetermined overhead rate using the labor rate of $17 per hour?

EB11. LO 4.6 A company has the following information relating to its production costs:

Machine hours	25,000
Direct labor cost	$550,000
Indirect labor	45,000
Plant maintenance	259,300
Plant supervision	90,000
Plant depreciation	150,000
Plant utilities	48,000
Indirect materials	5,000

Compute the actual and applied overhead using the company's predetermined overhead rate of $23.92 per machine hour. Was the overhead overapplied or underapplied, and by how much?

EB12. LO 4.7 A company has the following transactions during the week.
- Purchase of $3,000 raw materials inventory
- Assignment of $700 of raw materials inventory to Job 7
- Payroll for 10 hours and $3,000 is assigned to Job 7
- Factory depreciation of $1,750
- Overhead applied at the rate of $200 per hour

What is the cost assigned to Job 7 at the end of the week?

EB13. LO 4.7 During the month, Job Arch2 used specialized machinery for 350 hours and incurred $700 in utilities on account, $400 in factory depreciation expense, and $200 in property tax on the factory. Prepare journal entries for the following:
- A. Record the expenses incurred.
- B. Record the allocation of overhead at the predetermined rate of $1.50 per machine hour.

EB14. LO 4.7 Job 113 was completed at a cost of $7,500, and Job 85 was completed at a cost of $2,300 and sold on account for $4,500. Prepare journal entries for the following:
- A. Completion of Job 113.
- B. Completion and sale of Job 85.

EB15. LO 4.7 A company's individual job sheets show these costs:

	Job 298	Job 299	Job 300
Direct material	$2,228	$23,945	$ 4,231
Direct labor	2,391	23,492	3,413
Overhead	?	?	?
Total	$8,803	$88,548	$13,617

Overhead is applied at 1.75 times the direct labor cost. Use the data on the cost sheets to perform these tasks:

A. Apply overhead to each of the jobs.
B. Prepare an entry to record the assignment of direct material to work in process.
C. Prepare an entry to record the assignment of direct labor to work in process.
D. Prepare an entry to record the assignment of manufacturing overhead to work in process.

EB16. LO 4.7 A summary of materials requisition slips and time tickets, along with the overhead allocation, show these costs:

Job Number	Material Requisition Slips	Factory Labor Time Tickets	Overhead Applied
AA001	$ 3,423	$ 5,004	$1,750
AA002	4,342	4,530	1,568
AA003	3,431	5,345	1,813
AA004	3,421	2,423	840
Not specific to one job	570	3,353	
	$15,187	$20,655	$5,971

A. Prepare an entry to record the assignment of direct material to work in process.
B. Prepare an entry to record the assignment of direct labor to work in process.
C. Prepare an entry to record the assignment of manufacturing overhead to work in process.

Problem Set A

PA1. LO 4.1 For each item listed, state whether a job order costing system or process costing system would be best.
A. cereal
B. team uniforms
C. houses
D. beach chairs
E. plastic
F. restaurant-specific pizza boxes
G. sneakers customized with number and colors

PA2. LO 4.4 York Company is a machine shop that estimated overhead will be $50,000, consisting of 5,000 hours of direct labor. The cost to make Job 0325 is $70 in aluminum and two hours of labor at $20 per hour. During the month, York incurs $50 in indirect material cost, $150 in administrative labor, $300 in utilities, and $250 in depreciation expense.
A. What is the predetermined overhead rate if direct labor hours are considered the cost driver?
B. What is the cost of Job 0325?
C. What is the overhead incurred during the month?

PA3. LO 4.4 Pocono Cement Forms expects $900,000 in overhead during the next year. It does not know whether it should apply overhead on the basis of its anticipated direct labor hours of 60,000 or its expected machine hours of 30,000. Determine the product cost under each predetermined allocation rate if the last job incurred $1,550 in direct material cost, 90 direct labor hours, and 75 machine hours. Wages are paid at $16 per hour.

PA4. LO 4.5 Job cost sheets show the following information:

Job	January	February	March	Completed	Sold
AA2	$2,500	$1,200		February	Not sold
AA4	4,838			January	February
AA5		3,250		February	March
AA3		3,409	$2,319	April	Not sold
Total	7,338	7,859	2,319		

What are the balances in the work in process inventory, finished goods inventory, and cost of goods sold for January, February, and March?

PA5. LO 4.5 Complete the information in the cost computations shown here:

Raw Materials

Beginning inventory	$ 342
Purchases	1,533
Materials available for use	?
Ending inventory	321
Materials used in production	?

Work in Process Inventory

Beginning inventory	$ 932
Materials used in production	?
Direct labor	1,535
Overhead applied	?
Manufacturing costs incurred	22,441
Ending inventory	935
Cost of Goods Manufactured	?

Finished Goods Inventory

Beginning inventory	?
Cost of Goods Manufactured	?
Goods Available for Sale	$25,002
Ending inventory	?
Cost of Goods Sold	21,788

PA6. LO 4.5 During the year, a company purchased raw materials of $77,321, and incurred direct labor costs of $125,900. Overhead is applied at the rate of 75% of the direct labor cost. These are the inventory balances:

	Beginning	Ending
Raw materials inventory	$ 17,433	$ 16,428
Work in process inventory	241,439	234,423
Finished goods inventory	312,842	342,384

Compute the cost of materials used in production, the cost of goods manufactured, and the cost of goods sold.

PA7. LO 4.5 Freeman Furnishings has summarized its data as shown:

Depreciation of factory building	$100,000
Factory real estate taxes	15,000
Factory utility expenses	85,000
Indirect materials	32,000
Indirect labor	25,000
Direct labor cost	85,000
Direct labor hours incurred	23,500
Estimated direct labor hours	24,000
Raw materials purchased	$350,000
Raw materials, beginning inventory	30,000
Raw materials, ending inventory	28,000
Work in process, beginning inventory	51,000
Work in process, ending inventory	67,000
Estimated overhead	270,000

Compute the cost of goods manufactured, assuming that the overhead is allocated based on direct labor hours.

PA8. LO 4.6 Coop's Stoops estimated its annual overhead to be $85,000 and based its predetermined overhead rate on 24,286 direct labor hours. At the end of the year, actual overhead was $90,000 and the total direct labor hours were 24,100. What is the entry to dispose of the overapplied or underapplied overhead?

PA9. LO 4.6 Mountain Peaks applies overhead on the basis of machine hours and reports the following information:

	Budget	Actual
Overhead	$350,000	$352,000
Machine hours	50,000	49,000
Direct materials		$210,000
Direct labor		$350,000

A. What is the predetermined overhead rate?
B. How much overhead was applied during the year?
C. Was overhead over- or underapplied, and by what amount?
D. What is the journal entry to dispose of the over- or underapplied overhead?

PA10. LO 4.6 The actual overhead for a company is $74,539. Overhead was based on 6,000 direct labor hours and was $2,539 underapplied for the year.

A. What is the overhead application rate per direct labor hour?
B. What is the journal entry to dispose of the underapplied overhead?

PA11. LO 4.6 When setting its predetermined overhead application rate, Tasty Box Meals estimated its overhead would be $100,000 and would require 25,000 machine hours in the next year. At the end of the year, it found that actual overhead was $102,000 and required 26,000 machine hours.

A. Determine the predetermined overhead rate.
B. What is the overhead applied during the year?
C. Prepare the journal entry to eliminate the underapplied or overapplied overhead.

PA12. LO 4.7 The following data summarize the operations during the year. Prepare a journal entry for each transaction.
  A. Purchase of raw materials on account: $3,000
  B. Raw materials used by Job 1: $500
  C. Raw materials used as indirect materials: $100
  D. Direct labor for Job 1: $300
  E. Indirect labor incurred: $50
  F. Factory utilities incurred on account: $700
  G. Adjusting entry for factory depreciation: $250
  H. Manufacturing overhead applied as percent of direct labor: 200%
  I. Job 1 is transferred to finished goods
  J. Job 1 is sold: $3,000
  K. Manufacturing overhead is overapplied: $100

PA13. LO 4.7 The following events occurred during March for Ajax Company. Prepare a journal entry for each transaction.
  A. Materials were purchased on account for $35,429.
  B. Materials were requisitioned to begin work on Job C15 in the amount of $25,259.
  C. Direct labor expense for Job C15 was $24,129.
  D. Actual overhead was incurred on account of $32,852.
  E. Factory overhead was charged to Job C15 at the rate of 200% of direct labor.
  F. Job C15 was transferred to finished goods at $97,646.
  G. Job C15 was sold on account for $401,000.

PA14. LO 4.8 A movie production studio incurred the following costs related to its current movie:
  A. Purchased office supplies on account: $33,000
  B. Issued direct supplies: $22,512
  C. Issued indirect supplies: $7,535
  D. Time tickets showing direct labor: $32,503,230
  E. Time tickets showing indirect labor: $574,326
  F. Utilities expense on account: $957,323
  G. Overhead applied: 10% of direct labor cost

Create journal entries for the listed transactions.

Problem Set B

PB1. LO 4.1 For each item listed, state whether a job order costing system or process costing system would be best.
  A. television repair
  B. cell phone charge cords
  C. glassware with company logo
  D. dog food
  E. golf balls
  F. hotel signs to welcome guests
  G. highlighters and pens

PB2. LO 4.4 Rulers Company is a neon sign company that estimated overhead will be $60,000, consisting of 1,500 machine hours. The cost to make Job 416 is $95 in neon, 15 hours of labor at $13 per hour, and five machine hours. During the month, it incurs $95 in indirect material cost, $130 in administrative labor, $320 in utilities, and $350 in depreciation expense.
  A. What is the predetermined overhead rate if machine hours are considered the cost driver?
  B. What is the cost of Job 416?
  C. What is the overhead incurred during the month?

PB3. LO 4.4 Event Forms expects $120,000 in overhead during the next year. It doesn't know whether it should apply overhead on the basis of its anticipated direct labor hours of 6,000 or its expected machine hours of 5,000. What would be the product cost under each predetermined allocation rate if the last job incurred $3,500 in direct material cost, 55 direct labor hours, and 55 machine hours? Wages are paid at $17 per hour.

PB4. LO 4.5 Summary information from a company's job cost sheets shows the following information:

Job	April	May	June	Completed	Sold
BB3	$3,500	$1,500		May	Not sold
BB4	9,231			April	May
BB5		2,540		May	June
BB6		3,230	$1,434	July	Not sold

What are the balances in the work in process inventory, finished goods inventory, and cost of goods sold for April, May, and June?

PB5. LO 4.5 Complete the information in the cost computations shown here:

Beginning Inventory	$74,323
Purchases	?
Materials available for use	?
Ending inventory	?
Materials used in production	78,413

Work in Process Inventory	
Beginning inventory	$253,210
Materials used in production	?
Direct labor	125,900
Overhead applied	94,425
Manufacturing costs incurred	?
Ending inventory	242,932
Cost of goods manufactured	?

Finished Goods Inventory	
Finished goods inventory	?
Beginning inventory	$333,149
Cost of goods manufactured	309,016
Goods available for sale	?
Ending inventory	354,235
Cost of goods sold	287,930

PB6. LO 4.5 During the year, a company purchased raw materials of $77,321 and incurred direct labor costs of $125,900. Overhead is applied at the rate of 75% of the direct labor cost. These are the inventory balances:

	Beginning	Ending
Raw materials inventory	$ 15,394	$ 17,432
Work in process inventory	57,304	53,721
Finished goods inventory	120,432	132,432

Compute the cost of materials used in production, the cost of goods manufactured, and the cost of goods sold.

PB7. LO 4.5 Freeman Furnishings has summarized its data as shown. Direct labor hours will be used as the activity base to allocate overhead:

Raw materials purchased	$320,000
Raw materials, beginning inventory	15,000
Raw materials, ending inventory	14,000
Work in process, beginning inventory	35,000
Work in process, ending inventory	37,000
Estimated overhead	300,000
Depreciation of factory building	50,000
Factory real estate taxes	7,382
Factory utility expenses	45,000
Indirect materials	20,000
Indirect labor	11,000
Direct labor cost	100,000
Direct labor hours incurred	24,000
Estimated direct labor hours	25,000

Compute the cost of goods manufactured.

PB8. LO 4.6 Queen Bee's Honey, Inc., estimated its annual overhead to be $110,000 and based its predetermined overhead rate on 27,500 direct labor hours. At the end of the year, actual overhead was $106,000 and the total direct labor hours were 29,000. What is the entry to dispose of the overapplied or underapplied overhead?

PB9. LO 4.6 Mountain Tops applies overhead on the basis of direct labor hours and reports the following information:

	Budget	Actual
Overhead	$450,000	$452,000
Direct labor hours	75,000	77,000
Direct materials		$195,000
Direct labor		$333,865

A. What is the predetermined overhead rate?
B. How much overhead was applied during the year?
C. Was overhead overapplied or underapplied, and by what amount?
D. What is the journal entry to dispose of the overapplied or underapplied overhead?

PB10. LO 4.6 The actual overhead for a company is $73,175. Overhead was based on 4,500 machine hours and was $3,325 overapplied for the year.
A. What is the overhead application rate per direct labor hour?
B. What is the journal entry to dispose of the underapplied overhead?

PB11. LO 4.6 When setting its predetermined overhead application rate, Tasty Turtle estimated its overhead would be $75,000 and manufacturing would require 25,000 machine hours in the next year. At the end of the year, it found that actual overhead was $74,000 and manufacturing required 24,000 machine hours.
A. Determine the predetermined overhead rate.
B. What is the overhead applied during the year?
C. Prepare the journal entry to eliminate the under- or overapplied overhead.

PB12. LO 4.7 The following data summarize the operations during the year. Prepare a journal entry for each transaction.
A. Purchase of raw materials on account: $1,500
B. Raw materials used by Job 1: $400
C. Raw materials used as indirect materials: $50
D. Direct labor for Job 1: $200
E. Indirect labor incurred for Job 1: $30
F. Factory utilities incurred on account: $500
G. Adjusting entry for factory depreciation: $200
H. Manufacturing overhead applied as percent of direct labor: 100%
I. Job 1 is transferred to finished goods
J. Job 1 is sold: $1,000
K. Manufacturing overhead is underapplied: $100

PB13. LO 4.7 The following events occurred during March for Ajax Company. Prepare a journal entry for each transaction.
A. Materials were purchased on account for $5,429.
B. Materials were requisitioned to begin work on Job C15 in the amount of $2,500.
C. Direct labor expense for Job C15 was $4,250.
D. Actual overhead was incurred on account for $5,385.
E. Factory overhead was charged to Job C15 at the rate of 200% direct labor.
F. Job C15 was transferred to finished goods at $15,250.
G. Job C15 was sold on account for $28,000.

PB14. LO 4.8 A leather repair shop incurred the following expenses while repairing luggage for a major airline.
  A. Time cards showing direct labor: $750
  B. Time cards showing indirect labor: $100
  C. Purchased repair supplies on account: $1,500
  D. Issued indirect supplies: $350
  E. Utilities expense on account: $24,000
  F. Overhead applied: 100% of direct labor costs

Journalize the listed transactions.

Thought Provokers

TP1. LO 4.1 Can a company use both job order costing and process costing? Why or why not?

TP2. LO 4.4 If a job order cost system tracks the direct materials and direct labor, why doesn't it track the actual overhead used for a specific job?

TP3. LO 4.5 What are the similarities in calculating the cost of materials used in production, the cost of goods manufactured, and the cost of goods sold?

TP4. LO 4.6 If a company bases its predetermined overhead rate on 100,000 machine hours, and it actually has 100,000 machine hours, would there be an underapplied or overapplied overhead?

TP5. LO 4.7 How do the job cost sheets act as a subsidiary ledger for the work in process inventory if journal entries are not made to the job cost sheets?

TP6. LO 4.8 How is a job order cost system used in a service industry?

5 Process Costing

Figure 5.1 David and William's Family Cookie Venture. (credit: modification of "Big Giant cookies" by Sayuri Miss/Flickr, CC BY 2.0)

Chapter Outline

5.1 Compare and Contrast Job Order Costing and Process Costing

5.2 Explain and Identify Conversion Costs

5.3 Explain and Compute Equivalent Units and Total Cost of Production in an Initial Processing Stage

5.4 Explain and Compute Equivalent Units and Total Cost of Production in a Subsequent Processing Stage

5.5 Prepare Journal Entries for a Process Costing System

Why It Matters

David and William's family has used a secret family recipe for generations to make amazing chocolate chip cookies. While in college, they helped their grandmother, who used only locally sourced products, make and sell the cookies to a local restaurant. They helped her become more efficient, discovered how to retain the quality taste while making larger batches, and developed a plate-sized version that could be decorated similar to a birthday cake. After creating an equally successful peanut butter cookie recipe, David and William decided to expand the business and sell to high-end grocers as well as to a second restaurant. They found it was optimal in terms of cost, efficiency, and quality to produce 100 cookies per batch for each regular-sized cookie and 5 cookies per batch for the large cookies. They surveyed restaurants and grocery stores and determined that each flavor should be offered in four different package sizes. They also analyzed the marketability at various sale prices. David and William now know they need to use their information to identify the costs associated with making the cookies. They need to know the cost to produce one unit of their product in order to price their cookies correctly, determine the optimal product mix, manage efficiency and process improvement, and make other management decisions.

5.1 Compare and Contrast Job Order Costing and Process Costing

As you've learned, job order costing is the optimal accounting method when costs and production specifications are not identical for each product or customer but the direct material and direct labor costs can easily be traced to the final product. Job order costing is often a more complex system and is appropriate when the level of detail is necessary, as discussed in Job Order Costing. Examples of products manufactured using the job order costing method include tax returns or audits conducted by a public accounting firm, custom furniture, or, in a comprehensive example, semitrucks. At the Peterbilt factory in Denton, Texas, the company can build over 100,000 unique versions of their semitrucks without making the same truck twice.

Process costing is the optimal costing system when a standardized process is used to manufacture identical products and the direct material, direct labor, and manufacturing overhead cannot be easily or economically traced to a specific unit. Process costing is used most often when manufacturing a product in batches. Each department or production process or batch process tracks its direct material and direct labor costs as well as the number of units in production. The actual cost to produce each unit through a process costing system varies, but the average result is an adequate determination of the cost for each manufactured unit. Examples of items produced and accounted for using a form of the process costing method could be soft drinks, petroleum products, or even furniture such as chairs, assuming that the company makes batches of the same chair, instead of customizing final products for individual customers.

For example, small companies, such as David and William's, and large companies, such as Nabisco, use similar cost-determination processes. In order to understand how much each product costs—for example, Oreo cookies—Nabisco uses process costing to track the direct materials, direct labor, and manufacturing overhead used in the manufacturing of its products. Oreo production has six distinct steps or departments: (1) make the cookie dough, (2) press the cookie dough into a molding machine, (3) bake the cookies, (4) make the filling and apply it to the cookies, (5) put the cookies together into a sandwich, and (6) and place the cookies into plastic trays and packages. Each department keeps track of its direct materials used and direct labor incurred, and manufacturing overhead applied to facilitate determining the cost of a batch of Oreo cookies.

As previously mentioned, process costing is used when similar items are produced in large quantities. As such, many individuals immediately associate process costing with assembly line production. Process costing works best when products cannot be distinguished from each other and, in addition to obvious production line products like ice cream or paint, also works for more complex manufacturing of similar products like small engines. Conversely, products in a job order cost system are manufactured in small quantities and include custom jobs such as custom manufacturing products. They can also be legal or accounting tasks, movie production, or major projects such as construction activities.

The difference between process costing and job order costing relates to how the costs are assigned to the products. In either costing system, the ability to obtain and analyze cost data is needed. This results in the costing system selected being the one that best matches the manufacturing process.

A job order cost system is often more expensive to maintain than a basic process costing system, since there is a cost associated with assigning the individual material and labor to the product. Thus, a job order cost system is used for custom jobs when it is easy to determine the cost of materials and labor used for each job. A process cost system is often less expensive to maintain and works best when items are identical and it is difficult to trace the exact cost of materials and labor to the final product. For example, assume that your company uses three production processes to make jigsaw puzzles. The first process glues the picture on the cardboard backing, the second process cuts the puzzle into pieces, and the final process loads the pieces into the boxes and seals them. Tracing the complete costs for the batch of similar puzzles would likely entail three steps, with three separate costing system components. In this environment, it would be difficult and not economically feasible to trace the exact materials and the exact labor to each individual puzzle; rather, it would be more efficient to trace the costs per batch of puzzles.

The costing system used typically depends on whether the company can most efficiently and economically trace the costs to the job (favoring job order costing system) or to the production department or batch (favoring a process costing system).

While the costing systems are different from each other, management uses the information provided to make similar managerial decisions, such as setting the sales price. For example, in a job order cost system, each job is unique, which allows management to establish individual prices for individual projects. Management also needs to establish a sales price for a product produced with a process costing system, but this system is not designed to stop the production process and individually cost each batch of a product, so management must set a price that will work for many batches of the product.

In addition to setting the sales price, managers need to know the cost of their products in order to determine the value of inventory, plan production, determine labor needs, and make long- and short-term plans. They also need to know the costs to determine when a new product should be added or an old product removed from production.

In this chapter, you will learn when and why process costing is used. You'll also learn the concepts of conversion costs and equivalent units of production and how to use these for calculating the unit and total cost of items produced using a process costing system.

Basic Managerial Accounting Terms Used in Job Order Costing and Process Costing

Regardless of the costing system used, manufacturing costs consist of direct material, direct labor, and manufacturing overhead. Figure 5.2 shows a partial organizational chart for Rock City Percussion, a drumstick manufacturer. In this example, two groups—administrative and manufacturing—report directly to the chief financial officer (CFO). Each group has a vice president responsible for several departments. The organizational chart also shows the departments that report to the production department, illustrating the production arrangement. The material storage unit stores the types of wood used (hickory, maple, and birch), the tips (nylon and felt), and packaging materials.

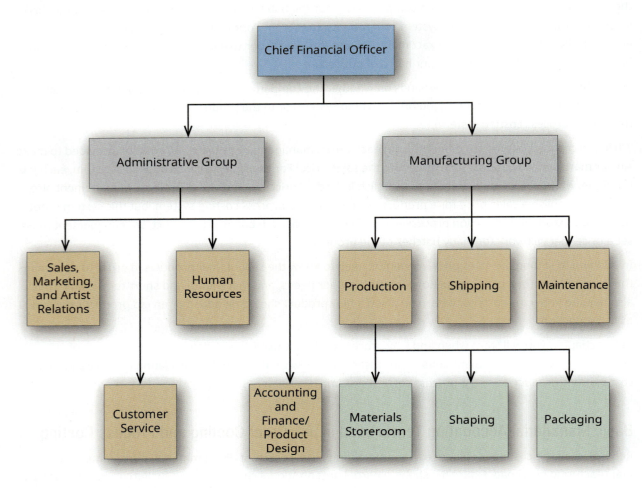

Figure 5.2 The Organizational Chart for Rock City Percussion. (attribution: Copyright Rice University, OpenStax, under CC BY-NC-SA 4.0 license)

Understanding the company's organization is an important first step in any costing system. Next is understanding the production process. The most basic drumstick is made of hickory and has a wooden tip. When the popular size 5A stick is manufactured, the hickory stored in the materials storeroom is delivered to the shaping department where the wood is cut into pieces, shaped into dowels, and shaped into the size 5A shape while under a stream of water. The sticks are dried, and then sent to the packaging department, where the sticks are embossed with the Rock City Percussion logo, inspected, paired, packaged, and shipped to retail outlets such as Guitar Center. The manufacturing process is described in Figure 5.3.

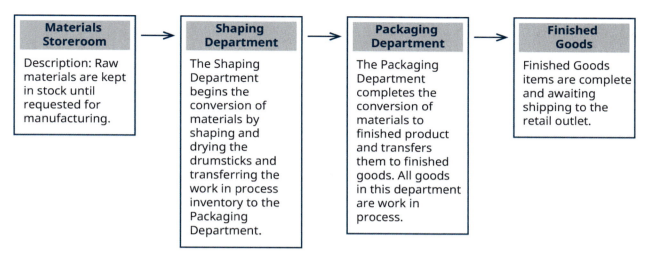

Figure 5.3 Rock City Percussion Manufacturing Process. (attribution: Copyright Rice University, OpenStax, under CC BY-NC-SA 4.0 license)

The different units within Rock City Percussion illustrate the two main cost categories of a manufacturing company: manufacturing costs and administrative costs.

> ### LINK TO LEARNING
>
> Understanding the full manufacturing process for a product helps with tracking costs. This video on how drumsticks are made (https://openstax.org/l/50drumsticks) shows the production process for drumsticks at one company, starting with the raw wood and ending with packaging.

Manufacturing Costs

Manufacturing costs or **product costs** include all expenses required to manufacture the product: direct materials, direct labor, and manufacturing overhead. Since process costing assigns the costs to each department, the inventory at the end of the period includes the finished goods inventory, and the work in process inventory for each manufacturing department. For example, using the departments shown in Figure 5.3, raw materials inventory is the cost paid for the materials that remain in the storeroom until requested.

While still in production, the work in process units are moved from one department to the next until they are completed, so the work in process inventory includes all of the units in the shaping and packaging departments. When the units are completed, they are transferred to finished goods inventory and become costs of goods sold when the product is sold.

When assigning costs to departments, it is important to separate the product costs from the **period costs**, which are those that are typically related with a particular time period, instead of attached to the production of an asset. Management often needs additional information to make decisions and needs the product costs further categorized as prime costs or conversion costs (Figure 5.4). **Prime costs** are costs that include the primary (or direct) product costs: direct material and direct labor. **Conversion costs** are the costs necessary to convert direct materials into a finished product: direct labor and manufacturing overhead, which includes other costs that are not classified as direct materials or direct labor, such as plant insurance, utilities, or property taxes. Also, note that direct labor is considered to be a component of both prime costs and conversion costs.

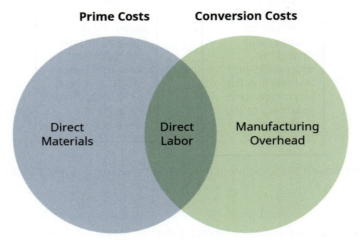

Figure 5.4 Prime Costs and Conversion Costs. Product costs can be categorized as prime costs (direct product costs) or conversion costs (costs incurred while converting the materials into a finished product). Direct labor is accounted for in both categories. (attribution: Copyright Rice University, OpenStax, under CC BY-NC-SA 4.0 license)

Job order costing tracks prime costs to assign direct material and direct labor to individual products (jobs). Process costing also tracks prime costs to assign direct material and direct labor to each production department (batch). Manufacturing overhead is another cost of production, and it is applied to products (job order) or departments (process) based on an appropriate activity base.

ETHICAL CONSIDERATIONS

The Unethical Bakery Accountant[1],[2]

According to the Federal Bureau of Investigation (FBI), "Sandy Jenkins was a shy, daydreaming accountant at the Collin Street Bakery, the world's most famous fruitcake company. He was tired of feeling invisible, so he started stealing—and got a little carried away." Being unethical netted the accountant ten years in federal prison, and his wife Kay was sentenced to five years' probation and 100 hours of community service, and she was required to write a formal apology to the bakery. According to the FBI, "Jenkins spent over $11 million on a Black American Express card alone—roughly $98,000 per month over the course of the scheme—for a couple that had a legitimate income, through the Bakery, of approximately $50,000 per year."

How did this happen? *Texas Monthly* reports that Sandy found a way to write unapproved checks in the accounting system. He implemented his accounting system and created checks that were "signed" by the owner of the company, Bob McNutt. McNutt was perplexed as to why his bakery was not more

> profitable year after year. The accountant was stealing the money while making the stolen checks appear to be paying for material costs or operating costs. According to *Texas Monthly*, "Once Sandy was sure that nobody had noticed the first fraudulent check, he tried it again. And again and again. Each time, Sandy would repeat the scheme, pairing his fraudulent check with one that appeared legitimate. Someone would have to closely examine the checks to see any discrepancies, and that seemed unlikely." The multimillion dollar fraud was exposed when another accountant looked closely at the checks and noticed discrepancies.

Selling and Administrative Expenses

Selling and administrative (S&A) expenses are period costs, which means that they are recorded in the period in which they were incurred. Selling and administrative expenses typically are not directly assigned to the items produced or services provided and include costs of departments not directly associated with manufacturing but necessary to operate the business. The selling costs component of S&A expenses is related to the promotion and sale of the company's products, while administrative expenses are related to the administration of the company. Some examples of S&A expenses include marketing costs; administration building rent; the chief executive officer's salary expense; and the accounting, payroll, and data processing department expenses.

These general rules for S&A expenses, however, have their exceptions. For example, some items that are classified as overhead, such as plant insurance, are period costs but are classified as overhead and are attached to the items produced as product costs.

The **expense recognition principle** is the primary reason to separate the costs of production from the other expenses of the company. This principle requires costs to be recorded in the period in which they are incurred. The costs are expensed when matched to the revenue with which they are associated; this is commonly referred to as *having the expenses follow the revenues*.

Period costs are expensed during the period in which they are incurred; this allows a company to apply the administrative and other expenses shown on the income statement to the same period in which the company earns income. Under generally accepted accounting principles (GAAP), separating the production costs and assigning them to the department results in the costs of the product staying with the work in process inventory for each department. This follows the expense recognition principle because the cost of the product is expensed when revenue from the sale is recognized.

Equivalent Units

In a process cost system, costs are maintained by each department, and the method for determining the cost per individual unit is different than in a job order costing system. Rock City Percussion uses a process cost system because the drumsticks are produced in batches, and it is not economically feasible to trace the direct labor or direct material, like hickory, to a specific drumstick. Therefore, the costs are maintained by each

---

1 Katy Vine. "Just Desserts." *Texas Monthly*. October 2010. https://features.texasmonthly.com/editorial/just-desserts/
2 Federal Bureau of Investigation (FBI). "Former Collin Street Bakery Executive and Wife Sentenced." September 16, 2015. https://www.fbi.gov/contact-us/field-offices/dallas/news/press-releases/former-collin-street-bakery-executive-and-wife-sentenced

department, rather than by job, as they are in job order costing.

How does an organization determine the cost of each unit in a process costing environment? The costs in each department are allocated to the number of units produced in a given period. This requires determination of the number of units produced, but this is not always an easy process. At the end of the accounting period, there typically are always units still in production, and these units are only partially complete. Think of it this way: At midnight on the last day of the month, all accounting numbers need to be determined in order to process the financial statements for that month, but the production process does not stop at the end of each accounting period. However, the number of units produced must be calculated at the end of the accounting period to determine the number of **equivalent units**, or the number of units that would have been produced if the units were produced sequentially and in their entirety in a particular time period. The number of equivalent units is different from the number of actual units and represents the number of full or whole units that could have been produced given the amount of effort applied. To illustrate, consider this analogy. You have five large pizzas that each contained eight slices. Your friends served themselves, and when they were finished eating, there were several partial pizzas left. In equivalent units, determine how many whole pizzas are left if the remaining slices are divided as shown in Figure 5.5.

- Pie 1 had one slice
- Pie 2 had two slices
- Pie 3 had two slices
- Pie 4 had three slices
- Pie 5 had eight slices

Together, there are sixteen slices left. Since there are eight slices per pizza, the leftover pizza would be considered two full equivalent units of pizzas. The equivalent unit is determined separately for direct materials and for conversion costs as part of the computation of the per-unit cost for both material and conversion costs.

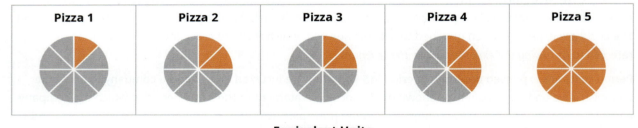

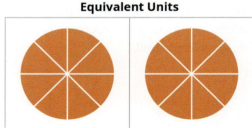

Figure 5.5 Equivalent Units. (attribution: Copyright Rice University, OpenStax, under CC BY-NC-SA 4.0 license)

Major Characteristics of Process Costing

Process costing is the optimal system for a company to use when the production process results in many similar units. It is used when production is continuous or occurs in large batches and it is difficult to trace a particular input cost to a specific individual product.

For example, before David and William found ways to make five large cookies per batch, their family always made one large cookie per batch. In order to make five cookies at a time, they had to gather the ingredients and baking materials, including five bowls and five cookie sheets. The exact amount of ingredients for one large cookie was mixed in each separate bowl and then placed on the cookie sheet. When this method was used, it was easy to establish that exactly one egg, two cups of flour, three-quarter cup of chocolate chips, three-quarter cup of sugar, one-quarter teaspoon salt, and so forth, were in each cookie. This made it easy to determine the exact cost of each cookie. But if David and William used one bowl instead of five bowls, measured the ingredients into it and then divided the dough into five large cookies, they could not know for certain that each cookie has exactly two cups of flour. One cookie may have 1 7/8 cups and another may have 1 15/16 cups, and one cookie may have a few more chocolate chips than another. It is also impossible to trace the chocolate chips from each bag to each cookie because the chips were mixed together. These variations do not affect the taste and are not important in this type of accounting. Process costing is optimal when the products are relatively homogenous or indistinguishable from one another, such as bottles of vegetable oil or boxes of cereal.

Often, process costing makes sense if the individual costs or values of each unit are not significant. For example, it would not be cost effective for a restaurant to make each cup of iced tea separately or to track the direct material and direct labor used to make each eight-ounce glass of iced tea served to a customer. In this scenario, job order costing is a less efficient accounting method because it costs more to track the costs per eight ounces of iced tea than the cost of a batch of tea. Overall, when it is difficult or not economically feasible to track the costs of a product individually, process costing is typically the best cost system to use.

Process costing can also accommodate increasingly complex business scenarios. While making drumsticks may sound simple, an immense amount of technology is involved. Rock City Percussion makes 8,000 hickory sticks per day, four days each week. The sticks made of maple and birch are manufactured on the fifth day of the week. It is difficult to tell the first drumstick made on Monday from the 32,000th one made on Thursday, so a computer matches the sticks in pairs based on the tone produced.

Process costing measures and assigns the costs to the associated department. The basic 5A hickory stick consists only of hickory as direct material. The rest of the manufacturing process involves direct labor and manufacturing overhead, so the focus is on properly assigning those costs. Thus, process costing works well for simple production processes such as cereal, rubber, and steel, and for more complicated production processes such as the manufacturing of electronics and watches, if there is a degree of similarity in the production process.

In a process cost system, each department accumulates its costs to compute the value of work in process inventory, so there will be a work in process inventory for each manufacturing or production department as well as an inventory cost for finished goods inventory. Manufacturing departments are often organized by the various stages of the production process. For example, blending, baking, and packaging could each be categorized as manufacturing or production departments for the cookie producer, while cutting, assembly, and finishing could be manufacturing or production departments with accompanying costs for a furniture manufacturer. Each department, or process, will have its own work in process inventory account, but there will only be one finished goods inventory account.

There are two methods used to compute the values in the work in process and finished goods inventories. The first method is the weighted-average method, which includes all costs (costs incurred during the current period and costs incurred during the prior period and carried over to the current period). This method is often favored, because in the process cost production method there often is little product left at the end of the period and most has been transferred out. The second method is the first-in, first-out (FIFO) method, which calculates the unit costs based on the assumption that the first units sold come from the prior period's work in process that was carried over into the current period and completed. After these units are sold, the newer completed units can then be sold. The theory is similar to the FIFO inventory valuation process that you learned about in Inventory (http://cnx.org/content/m67888/latest/) . (Since the FIFO process costing method is more complicated than the weighted-average method, the FIFO method is typically covered in more advanced accounting courses.)

With processing, it is difficult to establish how much of each material, and exactly how much time is in each unit of finished product. This will require the use of the equivalent unit computation, and management selects the method (weighted average or FIFO) that best fits their information system.

Process costing can also be used by service organizations that provide homogeneous services and often do not have inventory to value, such as a hotel reservation system. Although they have no inventory, the hotel might want to know its costs per reservation for a period. They could allocate the total costs incurred by the reservation system based on the number of inquiries they served. For example, assume that in a year they incurred costs of $200,000 and served 50,000 potential guests. They could determine an average cost by dividing costs by number of inquiries, or $200,000/50,000 = $4.00 per potential guest.

In the case of a not-for-profit company, the same process could be used to determine the average costs incurred by a department that performs interviews. The department's costs would be allocated based on the number of cases processed. For example, assume a not-for-profit pet adoption organization has an annual budget of $180,000 and typically matches 900 shelter animals with new owners each year. The average cost would be $200 per match.

Similarities between Process Costing and Job Order Costing

Both process costing and job order costing maintain the costs of direct material, direct labor, and manufacturing overhead. The process of production does not change because of the costing method. The costing method is chosen based on the production process.

In job order cost production, the costs can be directly traced to the job, and the job cost sheet contains the total expenses for that job. Process costing is optimal when the costs cannot be traced directly to the job. For example, it would be impossible for David and William to trace the exact amount of eggs in each chocolate chip cookie. It is also impossible to trace the exact amount of hickory in a drumstick. Even two sticks made sequentially may have different weights because the wood varies in density. These types of manufacturing are optimal for the process cost system.

The similarities between job order cost systems and process cost systems are the product costs of materials, labor, and overhead, which are used determine the cost per unit, and the inventory values. The differences between the two systems are shown in Table 5.1.

Differences between Job Order Costing and Process Costing

Job Order Costing	Process Costing
Product costs are traced to the product and recorded on each job's individual job cost sheet.	Product costs are traced to departments or processes.
Each department tracks its expenses and adds them to the job cost sheet. As jobs move from one department to another, the job cost sheet moves to the next department as well.	Each department tracks its expenses, the number of units started or transferred in, and the number of units transferred to the next department.
Unit costs are computed using the job cost sheet.	Unit costs are computed using the departmental costs and the equivalent units produced.
Finished goods inventory includes the products completed but not sold, and all incomplete jobs are work in process inventory.	Finished goods inventory is the number of units completed at the per unit cost. Work in process inventory is the cost per unit and the equivalent units remaining to be completed.

Table 5.1

CONCEPTS IN PRACTICE

Choosing Between Process Costing and Job Order Costing

Process costing and job order costing are both acceptable methods for tracking costs and production levels. Some companies use a single method, while some companies use both, which creates a hybrid costing system. The system a company uses depends on the nature of the product the company manufactures.

Companies that mass produce a product allocate the costs to each department and use process costing. For example, General Mills uses process costing for its cereal, pasta, baking products, and pet foods. Job order systems are custom orders because the cost of the direct material and direct labor are traced directly to the job being produced. For example, Boeing uses job order costing to manufacture planes.

When a company mass produces parts but allows customization on the final product, both systems are used; this is common in auto manufacturing. Each part of the vehicle is mass produced, and its cost is calculated with process costing. However, specific cars have custom options, so each individual car costs the sum of the specific parts used.

THINK IT THROUGH

Direct or Indirect Material

Around Again is a wooden frame manufacturer. Wood and fastener metals are typically added at the beginning of the process and are easily tracked as direct material. Sometimes, after inspection, the product needs to be reworked and additional pieces are added. Because the frames have already been through each department, the additional work is typically minor and often entails simply adding an additional fastener to keep the back of the frame intact. Other times, all the frame needs is additional glue for a corner piece.

How does a company differentiate between direct and indirect material? Many direct material costs, as the wood in the frame, are easy to identify as direct costs because the material is identifiable in the final product. But not all readily identifiable material is a direct material cost.

Technology makes it easy to track costs as small as one fastener or ounce of glue. However, if each fastener had to be requisitioned and each ounce of glue recorded, the product would take longer to make and the direct labor cost would be higher. So, while it is possible to track the cost of each individual product, the additional information may not be worth the additional expense. Managerial accountants work with management to decide which products should be accounted for as direct material and tracked individually, versus which should be considered indirect material and allocated to the departments through overhead application.

Should Around Again consider the fasteners or glue added after inspection as direct material or indirect material?

5.2 Explain and Identify Conversion Costs

In a processing environment, there are two concepts important to determining the cost of products produced. These are the concepts of equivalent units and conversion costs. As you have learned, equivalent units are the number of units that would have been produced if one unit was completed before starting a second unit. For example, four units that are one-fourth finished would equal one equivalent unit. Conversion costs are the labor and overhead expenses that "convert" raw materials into a completed unit. Each department tracks its conversion costs in order to determine the quantity and cost per unit (see TBD; we discuss this concept in more detail later). Management often uses the cost information generated to set the sales price; to set standard usage data and price for material, labor, and overhead; and to allow management to evaluate the efficiency of production and plan for the future.

Definition of Conversion Costs

Conversion costs are the total of direct labor and factory overhead costs. They are combined because it is the labor and overhead together that convert the raw material into the finished product. Remember that factory, manufacturing, or organizational overhead (you might see all three terms in practice) is composed of three sources: indirect materials, indirect labor, and all other overhead costs that are not indirect materials or indirect labor. Materials are often added in stages at discrete points of production, such as at the beginning, middle, or end of a process, but conversion is usually applied equally throughout the process. For example, in the opening example, David and William do not add direct material (ingredients) evenly throughout the cookie-making process. They are all added at the beginning of the production process, so they begin with the direct materials but add labor and overhead throughout the rest of the process.

Conversion costs can be explained through the process of making Just Born's Peeps. Just Born makes 5.5 million Peeps per day using three ingredients and the following process:[3]

1. Use machines to add and mix the sugar, corn syrup, and gelatin into a mixture called a slurry. Send slurry through a whipper to give the marshmallow its fluffy texture.
2. Color the sugar.
3. Deposit marshmallows on sugar-coated belts in the Peep shape. Send Peeps on belts through a wind tunnel that stirs up the sugar to coat the entire shape.
4. Add eyes, and inspect.
5. Move the Peeps via belt into their appropriate tray, and wrap with cellophane.

In the Peep-making process, the direct materials of sugar, corn syrup, gelatin, color, and packaging materials are added at the beginning of steps 1, 2, and 5. While the fully automated production does not need direct labor, it does need indirect labor in each step to ensure the machines are operating properly and to perform inspections (step 4).

Mechanics of Applying Conversion Costs

Let's return to our drumstick example to learn how to work with conversion costs. Rock City Percussion has two departments critical to manufacturing drumsticks: the shaping and packaging departments.

The shaping department uses only wood as its direct material and water as its indirect material. In the shaping department, the material is added first. Then, machines cut the wood underwater into dowels, separate them, and move them to machines that shape the dowels into drumsticks. These machines need electricity to operate and personnel to monitor and adjust the processes and to maintain the equipment. When the shaping is finished, a conveyer belt transfers the sticks to the finishing department.

Since the drumsticks are made by performing one process on one batch at a time, instead of producing one stick at a time from start to finish, it is difficult to determine the exact materials, labor, and overhead for a single pair of drumsticks. It is easier to track the materials and conversion costs for one batch and have those costs follow the batch to the next process.

Therefore, once the batch of sticks gets to the second process—the packaging department—it already has

---

3 Just Born. "Marshmallow Peeps Factory Tour." n.d. http://www.justborn.com/resource/corporate/popups/virtualTour.cfm

costs attached to it. In other words, the packaging department receives both the drumsticks and their related costs from the shaping department. For the basic size 5A stick, the packaging department adds material at the beginning of the process. The 5A uses only packaging sleeves as its direct material, while other types may also include nylon, felt, and/or the ingredients for the proprietary handgrip. Direct labor and manufacturing overhead are used to test, weigh, and sound-match the drumsticks into pairs.

Thus, at the end of the accounting period, there are two work in process inventories: one in the shaping department and one in the packaging department.

Direct materials are added at the beginning of shaping and packaging departments, so the work in process inventory for those departments is 100% complete with regard to materials, but it is not complete with regard to conversion costs. If they were 100% complete with regard to conversion costs, then they would have been transferred to the next department.

LINK TO LEARNING

Management needs to understand its costs in order to set prices, budget for the upcoming year, and evaluate performance. Sometimes individuals become managers due to their knowledge of the production process but not necessarily the costs. Managers can view this information on the importance of identifying prime and conversion costs (https://openstax.org/l/50PrimeConvCost) from Investopedia, a resource for managers.

5.3 Explain and Compute Equivalent Units and Total Cost of Production in an Initial Processing Stage

As described previously, process costing can have more than one work in process account. Determining the value of the work in process inventory accounts is challenging because each product is at varying stages of completion and the computation needs to be done for each department. Trying to determine the value of those partial stages of completion requires application of the equivalent unit computation. The equivalent unit computation determines the number of units if each is manufactured in its entirety before manufacturing the next unit. For example, forty units that are 25% complete would be ten (40 × 25%) units that are totally complete.

Direct material is added in stages, such as the beginning, middle, or end of the process, while conversion costs are expensed evenly over the process. Often there is a different percentage of completion for materials than there is for labor. For example, if material is added at the beginning of the process, the forty units that are 100% complete with respect to material and 25% complete with respect to conversion costs would be the same as forty units of material and ten units (40 × 25%) completed with conversion costs.

For example, during the month of July, Rock City Percussion purchased raw material inventory of $25,000 for the shaping department. Although each department tracks the direct material it uses in its own department, all material is held in the material storeroom. The inventory will be requisitioned for each department as needed.

During the month, Rock City Percussion's shaping department requested $10,179 in direct material and started into production 8,700 hickory drumsticks of size 5A. There was no beginning inventory in the shaping department, and 7,500 drumsticks were completed in that department and transferred to the finishing department. Wood is the only direct material in the shaping department, and it is added at the beginning of the process, so the work in process (WIP) is considered to be 100% complete with respect to direct materials. At the end of the month, the drumsticks still in the shaping department were estimated to be 35% complete with respect to conversion costs. All materials are added at the beginning of the shaping process. While beginning the size 5A drumsticks, the shaping department incurred these costs in July:

Direct materials	$10,179
Direct labor	15,176
Applied overhead	7,000
Total cost	$32,355

These costs are then used to calculate the equivalent units and total production costs in a four-step process.

Step One: Determining the Units to Which Costs Will Be Assigned

In addition to the equivalent units, it is necessary to track the units completed as well as the units remaining in ending inventory. A similar process is used to account for the costs completed and transferred. Reconciling the number of units and the costs is part of the process costing system. The reconciliation involves the total of beginning inventory and units started into production. This total is called "units to account for," while the total of beginning inventory costs and costs added to production is called "costs to be accounted for." Knowing the total units or costs to account for is helpful since it also equals the units or costs transferred out plus the amount remaining in ending inventory.

When the new batch of hickory sticks was started on July 1, Rock City Percussion did not have any beginning inventory and started 8,700 units, so the total number of units to account for in the reconciliation is 8,700:

Units to Account For	Units
Beginning work in process	0
Units started into production	8,700
Total units to account for	8,700

The shaping department completed 7,500 units and transferred them to the testing and sorting department. No units were lost to **spoilage**, which consists of any units that are not fit for sale due to breakage or other imperfections. Since the maximum number of units that could possibly be completed is 8,700, the number of units in the shaping department's ending inventory must be 1,200. The total of the 7,500 units completed and transferred out and the 1,200 units in ending inventory equal the 8,700 possible units in the shaping department.

Units Accounted For	Units
Completed and transferred out	7,500
Ending work in process	1,200
Total units to account for	8,700

Step Two: Computing the Equivalent Units of Production

All of the materials have been added to the shaping department, but all of the conversion elements have not; the numbers of equivalent units for material costs and for conversion costs remaining in ending inventory are different. All of the units transferred to the next department must be 100% complete with regard to that department's cost or they would not be transferred. So the number of units transferred is the same for material units and for conversion units. The process cost system must calculate the equivalent units of production for units completed (with respect to materials and conversion) and for ending work in process with respect to materials and conversion.

For the shaping department, the materials are 100% complete with regard to materials costs and 35% complete with regard to conversion costs. The 7,500 units completed and transferred out to the finishing department must be 100% complete with regard to materials and conversion, so they make up 7,500 (7,500 × 100%) units. The 1,200 ending work in process units are 100% complete with regard to material and have 1,200 (1,200 × 100%) equivalent units for material. The 1,200 ending work in process units are only 35% complete with regard to conversion costs and represent 420 (1,200 × 35%) equivalent units.

Work in Process Completion %		100%	35%
Units accounted for	Total Units	Material Units	Conversion Units
Completed and transferred out	7,500	7,500	7,500
Ending work in process	1,200	1,200	420
Total equivalent units for shaping	8,700	8,700	7,920

Step Three: Determining the Cost per Equivalent Unit

Once the equivalent units for materials and conversion are known, the cost per equivalent unit is computed in a similar manner as the units accounted for. The costs for material and conversion need to reconcile with the total beginning inventory and the costs incurred for the department during that month.

Costs to Account For	Materials	Conversion	Total
Beginning work in process	$ 0	$ 0	$ 0
Incurred during the period	$10,179	$22,176	$32,355
Total costs to account for	$10,179	$22,176	$32,355
Equivalent units	8,700	7,920	
Cost per equivalent unit	$ 1.17	$ 2.80	$ 3.97

The total materials costs for the period (including any beginning inventory costs) is computed and divided by the equivalent units for materials. The same process is then completed for the total conversion costs. The total of the cost per unit for material ($1.17) and for conversion costs ($2.80) is the total cost of each unit transferred to the finishing department ($3.97).

Step Four: Allocating the Costs to the Units Transferred Out and Partially Completed in the Shaping Department

Now you can determine the cost of the units transferred out and the cost of the units still in process in the shaping department. To calculate the goods transferred out, simply take the units transferred out times the sum of the two equivalent unit costs (materials and conversion) because all items transferred to the next department are complete with respect to materials and conversion, so each unit brings all its costs. But the ending WIP value is determined by taking the product of the work in process material units and the cost per equivalent unit for materials plus the product of the work in process conversion units and the cost per equivalent unit for conversion.

Transferred out costs	(7,500 units × $1.17) + (7,500 units × $2.80) = $29,775
Ending work in process: materials	(1,200 × $1.17) = $1,404
Ending work in process: conversion	(420 × $2.80) = $1,176
Ending work in process: total	$1,404 + $1,176 = $2,580

This information is accumulated in a **production cost report**. This report shows the costs used in the preparation of a product, including the cost per unit for materials and conversion costs, and the amount of work in process and finished goods inventory. A complete production cost report for the shaping department is illustrated in Figure 5.6.

Units to account for	Units		
Beginning work in process	—		
Units started into production	8,700		
Total units to account for	8,700		
Work in process completion %	100%	35%	
Units accounted for	**Materials Units**	**Conversion Units**	**Total**
Completed and transferred out	7,500	7,500	7,500
Ending work in process	1,200	420	1,200
Total units to account for	8,700	7,920	8,700
Costs to account for	**Materials**	**Conversion**	**Total**
Beginning work in process	$ 0	$ 0	$ 0
Incurred during the period	$10,179	$22,176	$32,355
Total costs to account for	$10,179	$22,176	$32,355
Equivalent units	8,700	7,920	
Cost per equivalent unit	$ 1.17	$ 2.80	$ 3.97
	Materials	**Conversion**	**Total**
Value of ending work in process	$ 1,404	$ 1,176	$ 2,580
Completed and transferred	8,775	21,000	29,775
Total costs	$10,179	$22,176	$32,355

Figure 5.6 Production Cost Report for the Shaping Department. (attribution: Copyright Rice University, OpenStax, under CC BY-NC-SA 4.0 license)

YOUR TURN

Calculating Inventory Transferred and Work in Process Costs

Kyler Industries started a new batch of paint on October 1. The new batch consists of 8,700 cans of paint, of which 7,500 was completed and transferred to finished goods. During October, the manufacturing process recorded the following expenses: direct materials of $10,353; direct labor of $17,970; and applied overhead of $9,000. The inventory still in process is 100% complete with respect to materials and 30% complete with respect to conversion. What is the cost of inventory transferred out and work in process? Assume that there is no beginning work in process inventory.

Solution

	Units		
Units to account for			
Beginning work in process	0		
Units started into production	8,700		
Total units to be account for	8,700		

	Materials	Conversion	Total
Work in process completion %	100%	30%	
Units accounted for			
Completed and transferred out	7,500	7,500	7,500
Ending work in process	1,200	360	1,200
Total units to account for	8,700	7,860	8,700
Costs to account for	Materials	Conversion	Total
Beginning work in process	0	0	0
Incurred during the period	$10,353	$26,970	$37,323
Total costs to account for	$10,353	$26,970	$37,323
Equivalent units	8,700	7,860	
Cost per equivalent unit	$ 1.19	$ 3.43	$ 4.62

5.4 Explain and Compute Equivalent Units and Total Cost of Production in a Subsequent Processing Stage

In many production departments, units are typically transferred from the initial stage to the next stage in the process. When the units are transferred, the accumulated cost per unit is transferred along with them. Since the unit being produced includes work from all of the prior departments, the transferred-in cost is the cost of the work performed in all earlier departments.

When the hickory size 5A drumsticks have completed the shaping process, they are transferred to the packaging department along with the inventory costs of $29,775. The inventory costs of $29,775 were $8,775 for materials and $21,000 for conversion costs and were calculated in Figure 5.6. During the month of July, Rock City Percussion purchased raw material inventory of $2,000 for the packaging department. As with the shaping department, the packaging department tracks its costs and requisitions the raw material from the material storeroom. The packaging department has computed direct material costs of $2,000, direct labor costs of $13,000, and applied overhead of $9,100, for a total of $22,100 in conversion costs. Equivalent units are computed for this department, and a new cost per unit is computed.

	Materials	Conversion	Total
Beginning work in process	$ 1,600	$ 6,580	$ 8,180
Transferred in	8,775	21,000	29,775
Added this month	2,000	22,100	24,100
Total	$12,375	$49,680	$62,055

As with calculating the equivalent units and total cost of production in the initial processing stage, there are four steps for calculating these costs in a subsequent processing stage.

Step One: Determining the Stage 2 Units to Which Costs Will Be Assigned

In the initial manufacturing department, there is beginning inventory, and units are started in production. In subsequent stages, instead of starting new units, units are transferred in from the prior department, but the accounting process is the same. Returning to the example, Rock City Percussion had a beginning inventory of 750 units in the packaging department. When the 7,500 sticks are transferred into the packaging department from the shaping department, the total number of units to account for in the reconciliation is 8,250, which is the total of the beginning WIP and the units transferred in:

Units to Account For	Units
Beginning work in process	750
Units transferred in	7,500
Total units to account for	8,250

The reconciliation of units to account for are the same for each department. The units that were completed and transferred out plus the ending inventory equal the total units to account for. The packaging department for Rock City Percussion completed 6,500 units and transferred them into finished goods inventory. Since the maximum number of units to possibly be completed is 8,250 and no units were lost to spoilage, the number of units in the packaging department's ending inventory must be 1,750. The total of the 6,500 units completed and transferred out and the 1,750 units in ending inventory equal the 8,250 possible units in the packaging department.

Units Accounted For	Units
Completed and transferred out	6,500
Ending work in process	1,750
Total units to account for	8,250

Step Two: Computing the Stage 2 Equivalent Units of Production

The only direct material added in the packaging department for the 5A sticks is packaging. The packaging materials are added at the beginning of the process, so all the materials have been added before the units are transferred out, but all of the conversion elements have not. As a result, the number of equivalent units for material costs and for conversion costs remaining in ending inventory is different for the testing and sorting department. As you've learned, all of the units transferred to the next department must be 100% complete with regard to that department's cost, or they would not be transferred. The process cost system must calculate the equivalent units of production for units completed (with respect to materials and conversion) and for ending WIP with respect to materials and conversion.

For the packaging department, the materials are 100% complete with regard to materials costs and 40% complete with regard to conversion costs. The 6,500 units completed and transferred out to the finishing department must be 100% complete with regard to materials and conversion, so they make up 6,500 (6,500 × 100%) units. The 1,750 ending WIP units are 100% complete with regard to material and have 1,750 (1,750 × 100%) equivalent units for material. The 1,750 ending WIP units are only 40% complete with regard to conversion costs and represent 700 (1,750 × 40%) equivalent units.

Work in process completion %		100%	40%
Units accounted for	Total Units	Material Units	Conversion Units
Completed and transferred out	6,500	6,500	6,500
Ending work in process	1,750	1,750	700
Total equivalent units for packaging	8,250	8,250	7,200

Step Three: Determining the Stage 2 Cost per Equivalent Unit

Once the equivalent units for materials and conversion are known for the packaging department, the cost per equivalent unit is computed in a manner similar to the calculation for the units accounted for. The costs for material and conversion need to reconcile with the department's beginning inventory and the costs incurred for the department during that month.

Costs to account for	Materials	Conversion	Total
Beginning work in process	$ 1,600	$ 6,580	$ 8,180
Incurred during the period	$10,775	$43,100	$53,875
Total costs to account for	$12,375	$49,680	$62,055
Equivalent units	8,250	7,200	15,450
Cost per equivalent unit	$ 1.50	$ 6.90	$ 8.40

The total materials costs for the period (including any beginning inventory costs) are computed and divided by the equivalent units for materials. The same process is then completed for the total conversion costs. The total of the cost per unit for materials ($1.50) and for conversion costs ($6.90) is the total cost of each unit transferred to the testing and sorting department.

Step Four: Allocating the Costs to the Units in the Finishing Department

Now you can determine the cost of the units transferred out and the cost of the units still in process in the finishing department. For the goods transferred out, simply take the units transferred out times the sum of the two equivalent unit costs (materials and conversion) because all items transferred to the next department are complete with respect to materials and conversion, so each unit brings all its costs. But the ending WIP value is determined by taking the product of the work in process materials units and the cost per equivalent unit for materials plus the product of the work in process conversion units and the cost per equivalent unit for conversion.

Transferred out costs	(6,500 units × $1.50) + (6,500 units × $6.90) = $54,600
Ending work in process: materials	(1,750 × $1.50) = $2,625
Ending work in process: conversion	(700 × $6.90) = $4,830
Ending work in process: total	$2,625 + $4,830 = $7,455

LINK TO LEARNING

Knowing the cost to produce a unit is critical to management's decisions. Sometimes that knowledge leads to management's decision to stop production, but sometimes that decision isn't as simple as it seems. The cost to produce a penny is more than one cent, and yet, the United States still makes

> pennies. See this article from Forbes that explains the difference among cost, worth, and value (https://openstax.org/l/50CostValWorth) to learn more.

5.5 Prepare Journal Entries for a Process Costing System

Calculating the costs associated with the various processes within a process costing system is only a part of the accounting process. Journal entries are used to record and report the financial information relating to the transactions. The example that follows illustrates how the journal entries reflect the process costing system by recording the flow of goods and costs through the process costing environment.

Purchased Materials for Multiple Departments

Each department within Rock City Percussion has a separate work in process inventory account. Raw materials totaling $33,500 were ordered prior to being requisitioned by each department: $25,000 for the shaping department and $8,500 for the packaging department. The July 1 journal entry to record the purchases on account is:

JOURNAL			
Date	Account	Debit	Credit
July 1	Raw Materials Inventory	33,500	
	Accounts Payable		33,500
	To record purchase of raw materials		

Direct Materials Requisitioned by the Shaping and Packaging Departments and Indirect Material Used

During July, the shaping department requisitioned $10,179 in direct material. Similar to job order costing, indirect material costs are accumulated in the manufacturing overhead account. The overhead costs are applied to each department based on a predetermined overhead rate. In the example, assume that there was an indirect material cost for water of $400 in July that will be recorded as manufacturing overhead. The journal entry to record the requisition and usage of direct materials and overhead is:

JOURNAL			
Date	Account	Debit	Credit
July 1	Work in Process Inventory: Shaping Department	10,179	
	Manufacturing Overhead	400	
	Materials Inventory		10,579
	To record direct and indirect material cost for July in the Shaping Department		

During July, the packaging department requisitioned $2,000 in direct material and overhead costs for indirect material totaled $300 for the month of July. The journal entry to record the requisition and usage of materials is:

JOURNAL			
Date	Account	Debit	Credit
July 1	Work in Process Inventory: Packaging Department Manufacturing Overhead Materials Inventory *To record direct and indirect material cost for July in the Packaging Department*	2,000 300	 2,300

Direct Labor Paid by All Production Departments

During July, the shaping department incurred $15,000 in direct labor costs and $600 in indirect labor. The journal entry to record the labor costs is:

JOURNAL			
Date	Account	Debit	Credit
July 1	Work in Process Inventory: Shaping Department Manufacturing Overhead Wages Payable *To record direct and indirect labor for July in the Shaping Department*	15,000 600	 15,600

During July, the packaging department incurred $13,000 of direct labor costs and indirect labor of $1,000. The journal entry to record the labor costs is:

JOURNAL			
Date	Account	Debit	Credit
July 1	Work in Process Inventory: Packaging Department Manufacturing Overhead Wages Payable *To record direct and indirect labor for July in the Packaging Department*	13,000 1,000	 14,000

Applied Manufacturing Overhead to All Production Departments

Manufacturing overhead includes indirect material, indirect labor, and other types of manufacturing overhead. It is difficult, if not impossible, to trace manufacturing overhead to a specific product, and yet, the total cost per unit needs to include overhead in order to make management decisions.

Overhead costs are accumulated in a manufacturing overhead account and applied to each department on the basis of a predetermined overhead rate. Properly allocating overhead to each department depends on finding an activity that provides a fair basis for the allocation. It needs to be an activity common to each department and influential in driving the cost of manufacturing overhead. In traditional costing systems, the most common activities used are machine hours, direct labor in dollars, or direct labor in hours. If the number of machine hours can be related to the manufacturing overhead, the overhead can be applied to each department based on the machine hours. The formula for overhead allocation is:

$$\text{Overhead Allocation} = \frac{\text{Estimated Overhead Costs (\$)}}{\text{Expected Annual Activity (machine hours)}}$$

Rock City Percussion determined that machine hours is the appropriate base to use when allocating overhead.

The estimated annual overhead cost is $340,000 per year. It was also estimated that the total machine hours will be 34,000 hours, so the allocation rate is computed as:

$$\frac{\text{Estimated Overhead Costs (\$340,000)}}{\text{Expected Annual Activity (34,000)}} = \$10 \text{ per machine hour}$$

The shaping department used 700 machine hours, and with an overhead application rate of $10 per direct labor hour, the journal entry to record the overhead allocation is:

JOURNAL			
Date	Account	Debit	Credit
July 1	Work in Process Inventory: Shaping Department Manufacturing Overhead *To record overhead applied to the Shaping Department*	7,000	7,000

The finishing department used 910 machine hours, and with an overhead application rate of $10 per direct labor hour, the journal entry to record the overhead allocation is:

JOURNAL			
Date	Account	Debit	Credit
July 1	Work in Process Inventory: Finishing Department Manufacturing Overhead *To record overhead applied to the Finishing Department*	9,100	9,100

Transferred Costs of Finished Goods from the Shaping Department to the Packaging Department

When the units are transferred from the shaping department to the packaging department, they are transferred at $3.97 per unit, as calculated previously. The amount transferred from the shaping department is the same amount listed on the production cost report in Figure 5.6. The journal entry is:

JOURNAL			
Date	Account	Debit	Credit
July 1	Work in Process Inventory: Finishing Department Work in Process Inventory: Shaping Department *To record the weighted-average method of the cost of goods transferred from the Shaping Department to the Packaging Department*	29,775	29,775

Transferred Goods from the Packaging Department to Finished Goods

The computation of inventory for the packaging department is shown in Figure 5.7.

Costs to Account For		Units to Account For	
Beginning work in process	$ 8,180	Beginning WIP	750
Direct material	2,000	Units started into production	7,500
Direct labor	13,000	Total units to account for:	8,250
Applied overhead	9,100		
Transferred in	29,775		
Total costs to account for	$62,055		

Step 1: Units to Assign Costs

Completed and transferred out	6,500
Ending work in process	1,750
Total units to account for	8,250

Step 2: Computing Equivalent Units of Production

Work in process completion % 40%

	Material Units	Conversion Units	Total
Completed and transferred out	6,500	6,500	6,500
Ending work in process	1,750	700	1,750
Total units to account for	8,250	7,200	8,250

Step 3: Determining Cost per Equivalent Unit

Costs to account for	Materials	Conversion	Total
Beginning work in process	$ 1,600	$ 6,580	$ 8,180
Incurred during the period	$10,775	$43,100	$53,875
Total costs to account for	$12,375	$49,680	$62,055
Equivalent units	8,250	7,200	
Cost per equivalent unit for department	$ 1.50	$ 6.90	$ 8.40

Step 4: Allocating the Costs to Units Transferred to Finished Goods and Partially Completed Units

Transferred-out costs	(6,500 units × $1.50) + (6,500 units × $8.40) =	$54,600
End work in process: materials	(1,750 × $1.50) = $2,625	
End work in process: conversion	(700 × $6.90) = $4,830	
End work in process: total	$2,625 + $4,830 =	7,455
Total Costs Accounted For		$62,055

Figure 5.7 Inventory Computation for Packaging Department. (attribution: Copyright Rice University, OpenStax, under CC BY-NC-SA 4.0 license)

The value of the inventory transferred to finished goods in the production cost report is the same as in the journal entry:

	JOURNAL		
Date	Account	Debit	Credit
July 1	Finished Goods Inventory	54,600	
	Work in Process Inventory: Packaging Department		54,600
	To transfer completed goods into Finished Goods		

Recording the Cost of Goods Sold Out of the Finished Goods Inventory

Each unit is a package of two drumsticks that cost $8.40 to make and sells for $24.99. There are two transactions when recording a sale. One entry is to transfer the inventory from finished goods inventory to cost of goods sold and is at the cost of the product. The second transaction is to record the sale at the sales price. The compound entry to record both transactions for the sale of 500 units on account is:

	JOURNAL		
Date	Account	Debit	Credit

July 1	Cost of Goods Sold
	    Finished Goods Inventory
	    To record the manufacturing costs of items sold
		4,200	4,200

July 1	Accounts Receivable
	    Sales
	    To record the sale of 500 units
		12,495	12,495

LINK TO LEARNING

The importance of properly recording the production process is illustrated in this report on work in process inventory (https://openstax.org/l/50WorkInProcess) from InventoryOps.com.

Key Terms

conversion cost total of labor and overhead for a product; the costs that "convert" the direct material into the finished product

equivalent units number of units that would have been produced if the units were produced sequentially and in their entirety in a particular time period

expense recognition principle (also, matching principle) matches expenses with associated revenues in the period in which the revenues were generated

manufacturing costs (also, product costs) total of all costs expended in the manufacturing process; generally consists of direct material, direct labor, and manufacturing overhead

period costs typically related to a particular time period instead of attached to the production of an asset; treated as an expense in the period incurred (examples include many sales and administrative expenses)

prime costs direct material expenses and direct labor costs

process costing costing system used when a standardized process is used to manufacture identical products and the direct material, direct labor, and manufacturing overhead cannot be traced to a specific unit

product costs all expenses required to manufacture the product: direct materials, direct labor, and manufacturing overhead

production cost report shows the costs used in the preparation of a product, including the cost per unit for materials and conversion costs and the amount of work in process and finished goods inventory

selling and administrative (S&A) expenses period costs not directly assigned to the items produced or services provided; include costs of departments not directly associated with manufacturing but necessary to operate the business

spoilage any units that are not fit for sale due to breakage or other imperfections

Summary

5.1 Compare and Contrast Job Order Costing and Process Costing

- The three categories of costs incurred in producing an item are direct material, direct labor, and manufacturing overhead.
- Process costing is the system of accumulating costs within each department for large-volume, mass-produced units.
- Process costing often groups direct labor and manufacturing overhead as conversion costs.
- Costs under GAAP are categorized as period costs when they are not related to production and instead cover a time period.
- Selling and administrative costs are period costs related to the sales of products and management of the company and are not directly tied to a specific product.
- Process costing determines the cost per unit through the use of equivalent units, or the number of units that would have been produced if production was sequential instead of in batches.

5.2 Explain and Identify Conversion Costs

- Conversion costs are the costs of direct labor and manufacturing overhead used to convert raw materials into a finished product.
- Materials are added during various stages of the manufacturing process, such as the beginning or end, while conversion of the product from raw material into finished goods is considered to occur uniformly through the process. Thus, it is possible for a product to have all of its materials and not be complete.

- Equivalent units for direct materials can be different than the equivalent units for conversion costs because materials are added in steps through the manufacturing process, while conversion costs are incurred evenly throughout the process.

5.3 Explain and Compute Equivalent Units and Total Cost of Production in an Initial Processing Stage
- Process costing has a work in process inventory account for each department.
- Equivalent units of production for materials may differ from the equivalent units for conversion costs.
- The total units to account for is the number of units in the beginning work in process inventory plus the number of units started into production; this total also represents the sum of the number of units completed and the number of units in the ending work in process inventory.
- The cost per equivalent unit for materials is the total of the material costs for the beginning work in process inventory and the total of material costs incurred during the period.
- The cost per equivalent unit for conversion costs is the total of the conversion costs for the beginning work in process inventory and the total of conversion costs incurred during the period.
- The cost of units transferred to the next department is the number of units transferred times the total of the cost per equivalent unit of material plus the cost per equivalent unit for conversion costs.

5.4 Explain and Compute Equivalent Units and Total Cost of Production in a Subsequent Processing Stage
- The total units to account for is the number of units in the beginning work in process inventory plus the number of units transferred from the prior department; this total also represents the number of units completed plus the number of units in the ending work in process inventory.
- The cost per equivalent units for materials is the total of the material costs for the beginning work in process inventory plus the cost of material transferred in to the department plus the total of material costs incurred during the period.
- The cost per equivalent unit for conversion costs is the total of the conversion costs for the beginning work in process inventory plus the conversion costs transferred in plus the total of conversion costs incurred during the period.

5.5 Prepare Journal Entries for a Process Costing System
- Traditional journal entries show the purchase of material and the incurring of overhead costs.
- Each department records the transfer of material from the storeroom into production, its direct labor costs, the application of overhead, and the transfer of goods to the next department or finished goods.
- The value of the inventory transferred to the next department or to finished goods equals the amount listed as transferred on the production cost report.

Multiple Choice

1. LO 5.1 Which of the following production characteristics is better suited for process costing and *not* job order costing?
  A. Each product batch is distinguishable from the prior batch.
  B. The costs are easily traced to a specific product.
  C. Costs are accumulated by department.
  D. The value of work in process is the direct material used, the direct labor incurred, and the overhead applied to the job in process.

2. LO 5.1 A process costing system is most likely used by which of the following?
   A. airplane manufacturing
   B. a paper manufacturing company
   C. an accounting firm specializing in tax returns
   D. a hospital

3. LO 5.1 Which of the following is a prime cost?
   A. direct labor
   B. work in process inventory
   C. administrative labor
   D. factory maintenance expenses

4. LO 5.1 Which of the following is a conversion cost?
   A. raw materials
   B. direct labor
   C. sales commissions
   D. direct material used

5. LO 5.1 During production, how are the costs in process costing accumulated?
   A. to cost of goods sold
   B. to each individual product
   C. to manufacturing overhead
   D. to each individual department

6. LO 5.2 Which is *not* needed to compute equivalent units of production?
   A. the percentage of completion for inventory still in process
   B. the number of units transferred out
   C. the number of units started and completed
   D. the material cost per unit

7. LO 5.2 What is the cost of direct labor if the conversion costs are $330,000 and manufacturing overhead is $275,000?
   A. $55,000
   B. $275,000
   C. $330,000
   D. $605,000

8. LO 5.2 What is the conversion cost to manufacture insulated travel cups if the costs are: direct materials, $17,000; direct labor, $33,000; and manufacturing overhead, $70,000?
   A. $16,000
   B. $50,000
   C. $103,000
   D. $120,000

9. LO 5.2 Which of the following lists contains only conversion costs for an inflatable raft manufacturing corporation?
   A. vinyl for raft, machine operator, electricity, insurance
   B. machine operator, electricity, depreciation, plastic for air valves
   C. machine operator, electricity, depreciation, insurance
   D. vinyl for raft, electricity, insurance, plastic for air valves

10. LO 5.3 Direct material costs $3 per unit, direct labor costs $5 per unit, and overhead is applied at the rate of 100% of the direct labor cost. What is the value of the inventory transferred to the next department if beginning inventory was 2,000 units; 9,000 units were started; and 1,000 units were in ending inventory?
   A. $1,000
   B. $13,000
   C. $130,000
   D. $20,000

11. LO 5.3 Beginning inventory and direct material cost added during the month total $55,000. What is the value of the ending work in process inventory if beginning inventory was 2,000 units; 9,000 units were started; and 1,000 units were in ending inventory?
   A. $1,000
   B. $5,000
   C. $50,000
   D. $55,000

12. LO 5.3 The initial processing department had a beginning inventory of 750 units and an ending inventory of 1,350 units, and it started 9,500 units into production. How many were transferred out to the next department?
   A. 750
   B. 1,350
   C. 8,900
   D. 10,250

13. LO 5.3 There were 1,000 units in ending inventory after transferring 16,000 units to finished goods inventory. If the beginning inventory was 2,000 units, how many units were started in process?
   A. 1,000
   B. 2,000
   C. 15,000
   D. 17,000

14. LO 5.4 The costs to be accounted for consist of which of the following?
   A. costs added during the period
   B. costs of the units in ending inventory
   C. costs started and transferred during the period
   D. costs in the beginning inventory and costs added during the period

15. LO 5.4 Which of the following is the step in which materials, labor, and overhead are detailed?
   A. determining the units to which costs are assigned
   B. determining the equivalent units of production
   C. determining the cost per equivalent units
   D. allocating the costs to the units transferred out and the units partially completed

16. LO 5.5 The journal entry to record the $500 of work in process ending inventory that consists of $300 of direct materials, $50 of manufacturing overhead, and $150 od direct labor is which of the following?

A.

Work in Process Inventory	500	
Accounts Payable		500

(When added to the process)

B.

Work in Process Inventory	500	
Materials Inventory		300
Wages Payable		150
Manufacturing Overhead		50

(As incurred or applied)

C.

Cost of Goods Sold	500	
Work in Process Inventory		500

(When transferred)

D.

Accounts Payable	500	
Work in Process Inventory		500

(When added to the process)

17. LO 5.5 Assigning indirect costs to departments is completed by _____.
  A. applying the predetermined overhead rate
  B. debiting the manufacturing costs incurred
  C. applying the costs to manufacturing overhead
  D. applying the costs to work in process inventory

18. LO 5.5 In a process costing system, which account shows the overhead assigned to the department?
  A. cost of goods sold
  B. finished goods inventory
  C. raw material inventory
  D. work in process inventory

19. LO 5.5 In a process cost system, factory depreciation expense incurred is debited to _____.
  A. finished goods inventory
  B. work in process inventory
  C. manufacturing overhead
  D. cost of goods sold

Questions

1. LO 5.1 Explain how process costing differs from job order costing.

2. LO 5.1 Would a pharmaceutical manufacturer use process or job order costing? Why?

3. **LO 5.1** Which costs are assigned using the weighted-average method?

4. **LO 5.1** What is the primary purpose of process costing?

5. **LO 5.2** What is the difference between prime costs and conversion costs?

6. **LO 5.2** Explain conversion costs using an example.

7. **LO 5.2** Why are there conversion costs in both job order costing and process costing?

8. **LO 5.2** What are equivalent units of production, and how are they used in process costing?

9. **LO 5.2** How can there be a different number of equivalent units for materials as compared to conversion costs?

10. **LO 5.2** Why is the number of equivalent units for materials only sometimes equal to the equivalent units for conversion?

11. **LO 5.3** What are the four steps involved in determining the cost of inventory transferred from one department to the next and the cost of work in process inventory?

12. **LO 5.3** What is the weighted-average method for computing the equivalent units of production?

13. **LO 5.4** How does process costing treat the costs transferred in from another department?

14. **LO 5.4** Why does each department have its own work in process inventory?

15. **LO 5.5** Match each term with its description.

A. conversion costs	i. total of direct material costs and direct labor costs
B. cost of goods sold	ii. manufacturing costs of the items sold
C. cost of production report	iii. number of units produced if each unit was produced sequentially
D. cost per equivalent unit	iv. total of direct labor costs, indirect labor costs, indirect material costs, and manufacturing overhead
E. equivalent units of production	v. where costs in a process cost system are reported before being applied to the product
F. manufacturing department	vi. detailed listing of the total costs of the product including the value of work in process
G. prime costs	vii. cost of materials or conversion for a specific department during production
H. transferred out costs	viii. product of the total cost per unit and the number of units completed and transferred during the time period

16. **LO 5.5** How is manufacturing overhead handled in a process cost system?

17. **LO 5.5** How are predetermined overhead rates used in process costing?

Exercise Set A

EA1. LO 5.1 How many units were started into production in a period if there were zero units of beginning work in process inventory, 1,100 units in ending work in process inventory, and 21,500 completed and transferred out units?

EA2. LO 5.1 A company started a new product, and in the first month started 100,000 units. The ending work in process inventory was 20,000 units that were 100% complete with materials and 75% complete with conversion costs. There were 100,000 units to account for, and the equivalent units for materials was $6 per unit while the equivalent units for conversion was $8 per unit. What is the value of the inventory transferred out, using the weighted-average inventory method?

EA3. LO 5.3 Given the following information, determine the equivalent units of ending work in process for materials and conversion under the weighted-average method:
- beginning inventory of 2,500 units is 100% complete with regard to materials and 60% complete with regard to conversion
- 18,000 units were started during the period
- 17,500 units were completed and transferred
- ending inventory is 100% complete with materials and 65% complete with conversion

EA4. LO 5.3 There were 1,700 units in beginning inventory that were 40% complete with regard to conversion. During the month, 8,550 units were started and 9,000 were transferred to finished goods. The ending work in process was 60% complete with regard to conversion costs, and materials are added at the beginning of the process. What is the total amount of equivalent units for materials and conversion at the end of the month using the weighted-average method?

EA5. LO 5.3 A company has 1,500 units in ending work in process that are 30% complete after transferring out 10,000 units. All materials are added at the beginning of the process. If the cost per unit is $4 for materials and $7 for conversion, what is the cost of units transferred out and in ending work in process inventory using the weighted-average method?

EA6. LO 5.3 There were 2,400 units in ending work in process inventory that were 100% complete with regard to material and 25% complete with regard to conversion costs. Ending work in process inventory had a cost of $9,000 and a per-unit material cost of $2. What was the conversion cost per unit using the weighted-average method?

EA7. LO 5.3 How many units must be in ending inventory if beginning inventory was 15,000 units, 55,000 units were started, and 57,000 units were completed and transferred out?

EA8. LO 5.3 How many units must have been completed and transferred if beginning inventory was 75,000 units, ending inventory was 72,000 units, and 290,000 units were started?

EA9. LO 5.3 Using the weighted-average method, compute the equivalent units of production if the beginning inventory consisted of 20,000 units; 55,000 units were started in production; and 57,000 units were completed and transferred to finished goods inventory. For this process, materials are added at the beginning of the process, and the units are 35% complete with respect to conversion.

EA10. LO 5.3 Using the weighted-average method, compute the equivalent units of production for a new company that started 85,000 units into production and transferred 67,000 to the second department. Assume that beginning inventory was 0. Conversion is considered to occur evenly throughout the process, while materials are added at the beginning of the process. The ending inventory for Equivalent Units: Conversion is 9,000 units.

EA11. LO 5.3 Mazomanie Farm completed 20,000 units during the quarter and has 2,500 units still in process. The units are 100% complete with regard to materials and 55% complete with regard to conversion costs. What are the equivalent units for materials and conversion?

EA12. LO 5.3 What are the total costs to account for if a company's beginning inventory had $231,432 in materials, $186,450 in conversion costs, and added direct material costs ($4,231,392), direct labor ($2,313,392), and manufacturing overhead ($1,156,696)?

EA13. LO 5.3 A company started the month with 8,329 units in work in process inventory. It started 23,142 units and had an ending inventory of 9,321. The units were 100% complete to materials and 67% complete with conversion. How many units were transferred out during the period?

EA14. LO 5.4 A production department within a company received materials of $10,000 and conversion costs of $10,000 from the prior department. It added material of $27,200 and conversion costs of $53,000. The equivalent units are 20,000 for material and 18,000 for conversion. What is the unit cost for materials and conversion?

EA15. LO 5.4 Production data show 35,920 units were transferred out of a stage of production and 6,150 units remained in ending WIP inventory that was 100% complete to material and 35% complete to conversion. The unit material cost is $5 for material and $8 for conversion. What is the amount of inventory transferred out and remaining in ending work in process inventory?

EA16. LO 5.5 Overhead is assigned to the manufacturing department at the rate of $10 per machine hour. There were 3,500 machine hours during October in the shaping department and 2,500 in the packaging department. Prepare the journal entry to apply overhead to the manufacturing departments.

EA17. LO 5.5 Prepare the journal entry to record the factory wages of $28,000 incurred for a single production department assuming payment will be made in the next pay period.

EA18. LO 5.5 Prepare the journal entry to record the transfer of 3,000 units from the packaging department to finished goods if the material cost per unit is $4 and the conversion cost per unit is $5.50.

EA19. LO 5.5 Prepare the journal entry to record the sale of 2,000 units that cost $8 per unit and sold for $15 per unit.

Exercise Set B

EB1. LO 5.3 Given the following information, determine the equivalent units of ending work in process for materials and conversion using the weighted-average method:
- Beginning inventory of 750 units is 100% complete with regard to materials and 30% complete with regard to conversion.
- 9,500 units were started during the period.
- 8,900 units were completed and transferred.
- Ending inventory is 100% complete with regard to materials and 68% complete with regard to conversion.

EB2. LO 5.3 There were 2,000 units in beginning inventory that were 70% complete with regard to conversion. During the month, 15,000 units were started, and 16,000 were transferred to finished goods. The ending work in process was 55% complete with regard to conversion costs, and materials are added at the beginning of the process. What is the total amount of equivalent units for materials and conversion at the end of the month using the weighted-average method?

EB3. LO 5.3 A company has 100 units in ending work in process that are 40% complete after transferring out 750 units. If the cost per unit is $5 for materials and $2.50 for conversion, what is the cost of units transferred out and in ending work in process inventory using the weighted-average method?

EB4. LO 5.3 There were 1,500 units in ending work in process inventory that were 100% complete with regard to material and 60% complete with regard to conversion costs. Ending work in process inventory had a cost of $7,200 and a per-unit material cost of $3. What was the conversion cost per unit using the weighted-average method?

EB5. LO 5.3 Using the weighted-average method, compute the equivalent units of production if the beginning inventory consisted of 20,000 units, 55,000 units were started in production, and 57,000 units were completed and transferred to finished goods inventory. For this process, materials are 70% complete and the units are 30% complete with respect to conversion.

EB6. LO 5.3 What are the total costs to account for if a company's beginning inventory had $23,432 in materials and $18,450 in conversion costs, and added direct material costs ($41,392), direct labor ($23,192), and manufacturing overhead ($62,500)?

EB7. LO 5.3 A company started the month with 4,519 units in work in process inventory. It started 15,295 units and had an ending inventory of 4,936. The units were 100% complete to materials and 30% complete with conversion. How many units were transferred out during the period?

EB8. LO 5.4 A production department within a company received materials of $7,000 and conversion costs of $5,000 from the prior department. It added material of $78,400 and conversion costs of $47,000. The equivalent units are 5,000 for material and 4,000 for conversion. What is the unit cost for materials and conversion?

EB9. LO 5.4 Production data show 15,200 units were transferred out of a stage of production and 3,500 units remained in ending WIP inventory that was 100% complete to material and 60% complete to conversion. The unit material cost is $9 for material and $4 for conversion. What is the amount of inventory transferred out and remaining in ending work in process inventory?

EB10. LO 5.5 Overhead is assigned to the manufacturing department at the rate of $5 per machine hour. There were 3,000 machine hours used in the molding department. Prepare the journal entry to apply overhead to the manufacturing department.

EB11. LO 5.5 Prepare the journal entry to record the factory wages of $25,000 incurred in the processing department and $15,000 incurred in the production department assuming payment will be made in the next pay period.

EB12. LO 5.5 Prepare the journal entry to record the transfer of 3,500 units from the separation department to the mash department if the material cost per unit is $2 and the conversion cost per unit is $5.

EB13. LO 5.5 Prepare the journal entry to record the sale of 700 units that cost $5 per unit and sold for $15 per unit.

Problem Set A

PA1. LO 5.1 The following product costs are available for Haworth Company on the production of chairs: direct materials, $15,500; direct labor, $22,000; manufacturing overhead, $16,500; selling expenses, $6,900; and administrative expenses, $15,200.
- A. What are the prime costs?
- B. What are the conversion costs?
- C. What is the total product cost?
- D. What is the total period cost?
- E. If 7,750 equivalent units are produced, what is the equivalent material cost per unit?
- F. If 22,000 equivalent units are produced, what is the equivalent conversion cost per unit?

PA2. LO 5.1 The following product costs are available for Arrez Company on the production of DVD cases: direct materials, $1,450; direct labor, $15.50; manufacturing overhead, applied at 150% of direct labor cost; selling expenses, $1,550; and administrative expenses, $950. The direct labor hours worked for the month are 90 hours.
- A. What are the prime costs?
- B. What are the conversion costs?
- C. What is the total product cost?
- D. What is the total period cost?
- E. If 1,450 equivalent units are produced, what is the equivalent material cost per unit?
- F. What is the equivalent conversion cost per unit?

PA3. LO 5.3 Pant Risers manufactures bands for self-dressing assistive devices for mobility-impaired individuals. Manufacturing is a one-step process where the bands are cut and sewn. This is the information related to this year's production:

Units to Account For	Units	Materials	Conversion
Beginning WIP inventory	500	500	250
Started	20,500		
To account for	21,000		

Ending inventory was 100% complete as to materials and 70% complete as to conversion, and the total materials cost is $57,540 and the total conversion cost is $36,036. Using the weighted-average method, what are the unit costs if the company transferred out 17,000 units? What is the value of the inventory transferred out and the value of the ending WIP inventory?

PA4. LO 5.3 During March, the following costs were charged to the manufacturing department: $14,886 for materials; $14,656 for labor; and $13,820 for manufacturing overhead. The records show that 30,680 units were completed and transferred, while 2,400 remained in ending inventory. There were 33,080 equivalent units of material and 31,640 of conversion costs. Using the weighted-average method, what is the cost of inventory transferred and the balance in work in process inventory?

PA5. LO 5.3 Materials are added at the beginning of a production process, and ending work in process inventory is 30% complete with respect to conversion costs. Use the information provided to complete a production cost report using the weighted-average method.

Costs to Account For	
Beginning inventory: materials	$ 10,000
Beginning inventory: conversion	19,000
Direct material	50,000
Direct labor	75,000
Applied overhead	37,248
Total costs to account for	$191,248

Units to Account For	
Beginning work in process	5,000
Units started into production	20,000
Transferred out	19,000

PA6. LO 5.3 Narwhal Swimwear has a beginning work in process inventory of 13,500 units and transferred in 130,000 units before ending the month with 14,000 units that were 100% complete with regard to materials and 30% complete with regard to conversion costs. The cost per unit of material is $5.80 and the cost per unit for conversion is $8.20 per unit. Using the weighted-average method, what is the amount of material and conversion costs assigned to the department for the month?

PA7. LO 5.3 The following data show the units in beginning work in process inventory, the number of units started, the number of units transferred, and the percent completion of the ending work in process for conversion. Given that materials are added at the beginning of the process, what are the equivalent units for material and conversion costs for each quarter using the weighted-average method? Assume that the quarters are independent.

Quarter	Beginning Work in Process	Started	Transferred Out	Conversion (%)
1	—	134,250	133,250	25
2	523	132,593	132,541	24
3	338	133,245	133,443	20
4	489	134,843	134,232	23

PA8. LO 5.4 The finishing department started the month with 700 units in WIP inventory. It received 2,200 units from the molding department and transferred out 2,150 units. How many units were in process at the end of the month?

PA9. LO 5.4 The packaging department began the month with 500 units that were 100% complete with regard to material and 85% complete with regard to conversion. It received 9,500 units from the processing department and ended the month with 750 units that were 100% complete with regard to materials and 30% complete with regard to conversion. With a $5 per unit cost for conversion and a $5 per unit cost for materials, what is the cost of the units transferred out and remaining in ending inventory?

PA10. LO 5.4 Production information shows these costs and units for the smoothing department in August.

	Cost		Units
Work in process			
Beginning balance: materials	$ 1,550	Beginning units	650
Beginning balance: conversion	2,500	Transferred in	1,780
Materials	7,441	Transferred out	1,810
Labor	14,520		
Overhead	7,930		

All materials are added at the beginning of the period. The ending work in process is 30% complete as to conversion. What is the value of the inventory transferred to finished goods and the value of the WIP inventory at the end of the month?

PA11. LO 5.4 Given the following information, prepare a production report with materials added at the beginning and ending work in process inventory being 25% complete with regard to conversion costs.

Costs to Account For	
Beginning inventory: materials	$ 5,000
Beginning inventory: conversion	1,000
Direct material	24,170
Direct labor	44,500
Applied overhead	12,400
Transferred-in materials	8,000
Transferred-in conversion	10,200
Total costs to account for	$105,270

Units to Account For	
Beginning work in process	3,500
Units started into production	85,000
Transferred out	84,000

PA12. LO 5.4 Complete this production cost report:

Beginning inventory	20,000		
Started during the month	75,000		
Total units to account for	?		
Completed and transferred out	70,000		
Ending work in process	?		
Total units accounted for	?		
Work in process completion %	100%	25%	
	Material Units	**Conversion Units**	**Total**
Completed and transferred out	70,000	70,000	70,000
Ending work in process	?	?	?
Total units accounted for	?	?	?
Costs to account for	**Materials**	**Conversion**	**Total**
Beginning work in process	$ 3,500	$16,000	$19,500
Transferred in	0	0	0
Incurred during the period	$25,000	$45,000	$70,000
Total costs to account for	?	?	?
Equivalent units	?	?	
Cost per equivalent unit for department	?	?	
Transferred-out costs			?
End work in process: materials	?		
End work in process: conversion	?		
End work in process: total		?	
Costs to account for		?	

PA13. LO 5.5 Selected information from Skylar Studios shows the following:

Raw materials purchased	$ 5,000
Direct materials	$ 1,500
Direct labor	$11,000
Factory depreciation	$ 2,000
Total manufacturing overhead incurred	$15,000
Machine hours per month	28,000
Unit cost for material	$ 2
Unit cost of conversion	$ 8
Number units transferred	15,000

Prepare journal entries to record the following:

A. raw material purchased
B. direct labor incurred
C. depreciation expense (hint: this is part of manufacturing overhead)
D. raw materials used
E. overhead applied on the basis of $0.50 per machine hour
F. the transfer from department 1 to department 2

PA14. LO 5.5 Loanstar had 100 units in beginning inventory before starting 950 units and completing 800 units. The beginning work in process inventory consisted of $2,000 in materials and $5,000 in conversion costs before $8,500 of materials and $11,200 of conversion costs were added during the month. The ending WIP inventory was 100% complete with regard to materials and 40% complete with regard to conversion costs. Prepare the journal entry to record the transfer of inventory from the manufacturing department to the finished goods department.

Problem Set B

PB1. LO 5.3 The following product costs are available for Stellis Company on the production of erasers: direct materials, $22,000; direct labor, $35,000; manufacturing overhead, $17,500; selling expenses, $17,600; and administrative expenses; $13,400.

A. What are the prime costs?
B. What are the conversion costs?
C. What is the total product cost?
D. What is the total period cost?
E. If 13,750 equivalent units are produced, what is the equivalent material cost per unit?
F. If 17,500 equivalent units are produced, what is the equivalent conversion cost per unit?

PB2. LO 5.3 The following product costs are available for Kellee Company on the production of eyeglass frames: direct materials, $32,125; direct labor, $23.50; manufacturing overhead, applied at 225% of direct labor cost; selling expenses, $22,225; and administrative expenses, $31,125. The direct labor hours worked for the month are 3,200 hours.
  A. What are the prime costs?
  B. What are the conversion costs?
  C. What is the total product cost?
  D. What is the total period cost?
  E. If 6,425 equivalent units are produced, what is the equivalent material cost per unit?
  F. What is the equivalent conversion cost per unit?

PB3. LO 5.3 Vexar manufactures nails. Manufacturing is a one-step process where the nails are forged. This is the information related to this year's production:

Cost to Account For	
Beginning inventory: conversion	$ 14,300
Direct material	34,950
Direct labor	55,000
Applied overhead	23,940
Total costs to account for	$148,190

Units to Account For	
Units started into production	25,000
Transferred out	26,000

Ending inventory was 100% complete as to materials and 70% complete as to conversion, and the total materials cost is $115,080 and the total conversion cost is $72,072. Using the weighted-average method, what are the unit costs if the company transferred out 34,000 units? Using the weighted-average method, prepare the company's process cost summary for the month.

PB4. LO 5.3 During March, the following costs were charged to the manufacturing department: $22,500 for materials; $45,625 for labor; and $50,000 for manufacturing overhead. The records show that 40,000 units were completed and transferred, while 10,000 remained in ending inventory. There were 45,000 equivalent units of material and 42,500 units of conversion costs. Using the weighted-average method, prepare the company's process cost summary for the month.

PB5. LO 5.3 Ardt-Barger has a beginning work in process inventory of 5,500 units and transferred in 25,000 units before ending the month with 3,000 units that were 100% complete with regard to materials and 80% complete with regard to conversion costs. The cost per unit of material is $5.45, and the cost per unit for conversion is $6.20 per unit. Using the weighted-average method, prepare the company's process cost summary for the month.

PB6. LO 5.3 The following data show the units in beginning work in process inventory, the number of units started, the number of units transferred, and the percent completion of the ending work in process for conversion. Given that materials are added at the beginning of the process, what are the equivalent units for material and conversion costs for each quarter using the weighted-average method? Assume that the quarters are independent.

Quarter	Beginning Work in Process	Started	Transferred Out	Conversion (%)
1	—	134,250	133,250	25
2	523	132,593	132,541	24
3	338	133,245	133,443	20
4	489	134,843	134,232	23

PB7. LO 5.3 The following data show the units in beginning work in process inventory, the number of units started, the number of units transferred, and the percent completion of the ending work in process for conversion. Given that materials are added 50% at the beginning of the process and 50% at the end of the process, what are the equivalent units for material and conversion costs for each quarter using the weighted-average method? Assume that the quarters are independent.

Quarter	Beginning Work in Process	Started	Transferred Out	Conversion (%)
1	—	255,000	235,000	50
2	2,500	275,000	250,000	40
3	3,600	290,000	275,000	45
4	6,500	300,000	280,000	60

PB8. LO 5.3 The following data show the units in beginning work in process inventory, the number of units started, the number of units transferred, and the percent completion of the ending work in process for conversion. Given that materials are added 50% at the beginning of the process and 50% at the end of the process, what are the equivalent units for material and conversion costs for each quarter using the weighted-average method? Assume that the quarters are independent.

Quarter	Beginning Work in Process	Started	Transferred Out	Conversion (%)
1	—	255,000	235,000	50
2	2,500	275,000	250,000	40
3	3,600	290,000	275,000	45
4	6,500	300,000	280,000	60

PB9. LO 5.4 The finishing department started the month with 600 units in WIP inventory. It received 1,500 units from the molding department and ended the month with 550 units still in process. How many units were transferred out?

PB10. LO 5.4 The packaging department began the month with 750 units that were 100% complete with regard to material and 25% complete with regard to conversion. It received 9,500 units from the processing department and ended the month with 500 units that were 100% complete with regard to materials and 75% complete with regard to conversion. With a $7 per unit material cost and a $4 per unit cost for conversion, what is the cost of the units transferred out and remaining in ending inventory?

PB11. LO 5.4 Production information shows these costs and units for the smoothing department in August.

	Cost		Units
Work in process			
Beginning balance: materials	$ 5,213	Beginning units	1,100
Beginning balance: conversion	8,321	Transferred in	24,500
Materials	10,403	Transferred out	1,300
Labor	16,000		
Overhead	$13,475		

What is the value of the inventory transferred out to finished goods and the value of the WIP inventory at the end of the month, assuming conversion costs are 30% complete?

PB12. LO 5.4 Given the following information, prepare a production report with materials added at the beginning and ending work in process inventory being 80% complete with regard to conversion costs.

Costs to Account For	
Beginning inventory: materials	$ 25,000
Beginning inventory: conversion	30,500
Direct material	2,000
Direct labor	45,000
Applied overhead	11,840
Transferred-in materials	12,015
Transferred-in conversion	33,500
Total costs to account for	$159,855

Units to Account For	
Beginning work in process	4,000
Units started into production	9,500
Transferred out	9,600

PB13. LO 5.5 Selected information from Hernandez Corporation shows the following:

Raw materials purchased	$11,000
Direct materials	$25,000
Direct labor	$75,000
Factory depreciation	$13,000
Total manufacturing overhead incurred	$20,000
Machine hours per month	12,000
Predetermined OH rate	$ 1.20
Unit cost for material	$ 9
Units conversion	5
Number units transferred	15,000

Prepare journal entries to record the following:

A. raw material purchased
B. direct labor incurred
C. depreciation expense (hint: this is part of manufacturing overhead)
D. raw materials used
E. overhead applied on the basis of $0.50 per machine hour
F. the transfer from department 1 to department 2

PB14. LO 5.5 Rexar had 1,000 units in beginning inventory before starting 9,500 units and completing 8,000 units. The beginning work in process inventory consisted of $5,000 in materials and $8,500 in conversion costs before $16,000 of materials and $18,500 of conversion costs were added during the month. The ending WIP inventory was 100% complete with regard to materials and 40% complete with regard to conversion costs. Prepare the journal entry to record the transfer of inventory from the manufacturing department to the finished goods department.

 Thought Provokers

TP1. LO 5.1 How would process costing exist in a service industry?

TP2. LO 5.2 Why are labor and manufacturing overhead grouped together as conversion costs?

TP3. LO 5.4 How is process costing for a single manufacturing department different from a manufacturing company with multiple departments?

TP4. LO 5.5 What is different between the journal entries for process costing and that of job order costing?

6 Activity-Based, Variable, and Absorption Costing

Figure 6.1 Allocating Time. The number of activities is one way to determine how resources, such as time, are allocated. (credit: modification of work by West Point – The U.S. Military Academy/Flickr, CC BY 2.0; modification of work by United States Government/Flickr, Public Domain; modification of "training" by Cory Zanker/Flickr, CC BY 4.0)

Chapter Outline

LO 6.1 Calculate Predetermined Overhead and Total Cost under the Traditional Allocation Method

LO 6.2 Describe and Identify Cost Drivers

LO 6.3 Calculate Activity-Based Product Costs

LO 6.4 Compare and Contrast Traditional and Activity-Based Costing Systems

LO 6.5 Compare and Contrast Variable and Absorption Costing

Why It Matters

Barry thinks of his education as a job and spends forty hours a week in class or studying. Barry estimates he has about eighty hours per week to allocate between school and other activities and believes everyone should follow his fifty-fifty rule of time allocation. His roommate, Kamil, disagrees with Barry and argues that allocating 50 percent of one's time to class and studying is not a great formula because everyone has different activities and responsibilities. Kamil points out, for example, that he has a job tutoring other students, is involved with student activities, and plays in a band, while Barry spends some of his nonstudy time doing volunteer work and working out.

Kamil plans each week based on how many hours he will need for each activity: classes, studying and coursework, tutoring, and practicing and performing with his band. In essence, he considers the details of each week's needs to budget his time. Kamil explains to Barry that being aware of the activities that consume his limited resources (time, in this example) helps him to better plan his week. He adds that individuals who have activities with lots of time commitments (class, work, study, exercise, family, friends, and so on) must be efficient with their time or they risk doing poorly in one or more areas. Kamil argues these individuals cannot simply assign a percentage of their time to each activity but should use each specific activity as the basis for allocating their time. Barry insists that assigning a set percentage to everything is easy and the better method. Who is correct?

6.1 Calculate Predetermined Overhead and Total Cost under the Traditional Allocation Method

Both roommates make valid points about allocating limited resources. Ultimately, each must decide which method to use to allocate time, and they can make that decision based on their own analyses. Similarly, businesses and other organizations must create an allocation system for assigning limited resources, such as overhead. Whereas Kamil and Barry are discussing the allocation of hours, the issue of allocating costs raises similar questions. For example, for a manufacturer allocating maintenance costs, which are an overhead cost, is it better to allocate to each production department equally by the number of machines that need to be maintained or by the square footage of space that needs to be maintained?

In the past, overhead costs were typically allocated based on factors such as total direct labor hours, total direct labor costs, or total machine hours. This allocation process, often called the traditional allocation method, works most effectively when direct labor is a dominant component in production. However, many industries have evolved, primarily due to changes in technology, and their production processes have become more complicated, with more steps or components. Many of these industries have significantly reduced their use of direct labor and replaced it with technology, such as robotics or other machinery. For example, a mobile phone production facility in China replaced 90 percent of its workforce with robots.[1]

In these situations, a direct cost (labor) has been replaced by an overhead cost (e.g., depreciation on equipment). Because of this decrease in reliance on labor and/or changes in the types of production complexity and methods, the traditional method of overhead allocation becomes less effective in certain production environments. To account for these changes in technology and production, many organizations today have adopted an overhead allocation method known as activity-based costing (ABC). This chapter will explain the transition to ABC and provide a foundation in its mechanics.

Activity-based costing is an accounting method that recognizes the relationship between product costs and a production activity, such as the number of hours of engineering or design activity, the costs of the set up or preparation for the production of different products, or the costs of packaging different products after the production process is completed. Overhead costs are then allocated to production according to the use of that activity, such as the number of machine setups needed. In contrast, the traditional allocation method commonly uses cost drivers, such as direct labor or machine hours, as the single activity.

Because of the use of multiple activities as cost drivers, ABC costing has advantages over the traditional allocation method, which assigns overhead using a single predetermined overhead rate. Those advantages come at a cost, both in resources and time, since additional information needs to be collected and analyzed. Chrysler, for instance, shifted its overhead allocation to ABC in 1991 and estimates that the benefits of cost savings, product improvement, and elimination of inefficiencies have been ten to twenty times greater than the investment in the program at some sites. It believes other sites experienced savings of fifty to one hundred times the cost to implement the system.[2]

---

1 June Javelosa and Kristin Houser. "This Company Replaced 90% of Its Workforce with Machines. Here's What Happened." *Futurism / World Economic Forum*. https://www.weforum.org/agenda/2017/02/after-replacing-90-of-employees-with-robots-this-companys-productivity-soared

2 Joseph H. Ness and Thomas G. Cucuzza. "Tapping the Full Potential of ABC." *Harvard Business Review*. July-Aug. 1995. https://hbr.org/1995/07/tapping-the-full-potential-of-abc

As you've learned, understanding the cost needed to manufacture a product is critical to making many management decisions (Figure 6.2). Knowing the total and component costs of the product is necessary for price setting and for measuring the efficiency and effectiveness of the organization. Remember that product costs consist of direct materials, direct labor, and manufacturing overhead. It is relatively simple to understand each product's direct material and direct labor cost, but it is more complicated to determine the overhead component of each product's costs because there are a number of indirect and other costs to consider. A company's **manufacturing overhead costs** are all costs other than direct material, direct labor, or selling and administrative costs. Once a company has determined the overhead, it must establish how to allocate the cost. This allocation can come in the form of the traditional overhead allocation method or activity-based costing..

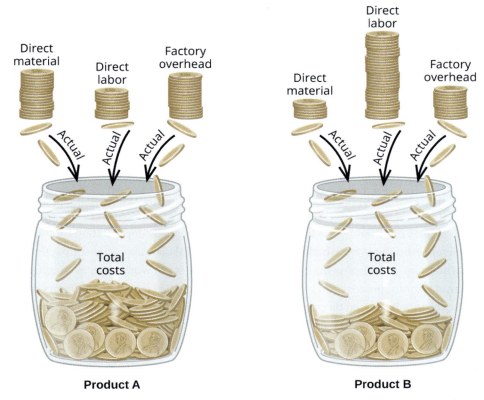

Figure 6.2 Allocating Costs among Products. The total cost of a product is based on direct labor, direct material, and factory overhead costs. (attribution: Copyright Rice University, OpenStax, under CC BY-NC-SA 4.0 license)

Component Categories under Traditional Allocation

Traditional allocation involves the allocation of factory overhead to products based on the volume of production resources consumed, such as the amount of direct labor hours consumed, direct labor cost, or machine hours used. In order to perform the traditional method, it is also important to understand each of the involved cost components: direct materials, direct labor, and manufacturing overhead. Direct materials and direct labor are cost categories that are relatively easy to trace to a product. **Direct material** comprises the supplies used in manufacturing that can be traced directly to the product. **Direct labor** is the work used in manufacturing that can be directly traced to the product. Although the processes for tracing the costs differ, both job order costing and process costing trace the material and labor through materials requisition requests and time cards or electronic mechanisms for measuring labor input. Job order costing traces the costs directly to the product, and process costing traces the costs to the manufacturing department.

> ### ETHICAL CONSIDERATIONS
>
> #### Ethical Cost Modeling
>
> The proper use of management accounting skills to model financial and non-financial data optimizes the organization's evaluation and use of resources and assists in the proper evaluation of costs and revenues in an organization. The IFAC provides guidance on the use of cost models and how to ethically design proper cost models: "Cost models should be designed and maintained to reflect the cause-and-effect interrelationships and the behavioral dynamics of the way the organization functions. The information needs of decision makers at all levels of an organization should be taken into account, by incorporating an organization's business and operational models, strategy, structure, and competitive environment."[3]

Estimated Total Manufacturing Overhead Costs

The more challenging product component to track is manufacturing overhead. Overhead consists of indirect materials, indirect labor, and other costs closely associated with the manufacturing process but not tied to a specific product. Examples of other overhead costs include such items as depreciation on the factory machinery and insurance on the factory building. **Indirect material** comprises the supplies used in production that cannot be traced to an individual product, and **indirect labor** is the work done by employees not directly involved in the manufacturing process, such as the supervisors' salaries or the maintenance staff's wages. Because these costs cannot be traced directly to the product like direct costs are, they have to be allocated among all of the products produced and added, or applied, to the production and product cost.

For example, the recipe for shea butter has easily identifiable quantities of shea nuts and other ingredients. Based on the manufacturing process, it is also easy to determine the direct labor cost. But determining the exact overhead costs is not easy, as the cost of electricity needed to dry, crush, and roast the nuts changes depending on the moisture content of the nuts upon arrival.

Until now, you have learned to apply overhead to production based on a predetermined overhead rate typically using an activity base. An **activity base** is considered to be a primary driver of overhead costs, and traditionally, direct labor hours or machine hours were used for it. For example, a production facility that is fairly labor intensive would likely determine that the more labor hours worked, the higher the overhead will be. As a result, management would likely view labor hours as the activity base when applying overhead costs.

A predetermined overhead rate is calculated at the start of the accounting period by dividing the estimated manufacturing overhead by the estimated activity base. The predetermined overhead rate is then applied to production to facilitate determining a standard cost for a product. This estimated overhead rate will allow a company to determine a cost for the product without having to wait, possibly several months, until all of the actual overhead costs are determined, and to help with issues such as seasonal production or variable overhead costs, such as utilities.

---

3   International Federation of Accountings (IFAC) PAIB Committee. "Evaluating and Improving Costing in Organizations." *International Good Practice Guidance*. June 30, 2009. https://www.ifac.org/system/files/publications/files/IGPG-Evaluating-and-Improving-Costing-July-2009.pdf

Calculation of Predetermined Overhead and Total Cost under Traditional Allocation

The predetermined overhead rate is set at the beginning of the year and is calculated as the estimated (budgeted) overhead costs for the year divided by the estimated (budgeted) level of activity for the year. This activity base is often direct labor hours, direct labor costs, or machine hours. Once a company determines the overhead rate, it determines the overhead rate per unit and adds the overhead per unit cost to the direct material and direct labor costs for the product to find the total cost.

$$\text{Predetermined Overhead Rate} = \frac{\text{Estimated Overhead Cost (\$)}}{\text{Estimated Activity Base (units or \$)}}$$

To put this method into context, consider this example. Musicality Manufacturing developed a recording device similar to a microphone that allows musicians and music aficionados to record their playing or singing along with any song publicly available. There are three products that vary in features and ability: Solo, Band, and Orchestra. Musicality was started by musicians who majored in math and software engineering while in college. Their main concern was building a quality manufacturing plant, so they used the simpler traditional allocation method. They started by determining their direct costs, which are shown in Figure 6.3.

	Solo	Band	Orchestra
Direct Materials per Unit	$ 3.50	$6.00	$11.70
Direct Labor Cost per Unit	10.00	2.75	4.30

Figure 6.3 Material and Labor Costs for Musicality. (attribution: Copyright Rice University, OpenStax, under CC BY-NC-SA 4.0 license)

Musicality determines the overhead rate based on direct labor hours. At the beginning of the year, the company estimates total overhead costs to be $2,500,000 and total direct labor hours to be 1,250,000. The predetermined overhead rate is

$$\frac{\$2{,}500{,}000 \text{ overhead}}{1{,}250{,}000 \text{ labor hours}} = \$2.00 \text{ per labor hour}$$

Musicality uses this information to determine the cost of each product. For example, the total direct labor hours estimated for the solo product is 350,000 direct labor hours. With $2.00 of overhead per direct hour, the Solo product is estimated to have $700,000 of overhead applied. When the $700,000 of overhead applied is divided by the estimated production of 140,000 units of the Solo product, the estimated overhead per product for the Solo product is $5.00 per unit. The computation of the overhead cost per unit for all of the products is shown in Figure 6.4.

	Solo	Band	Orchestra	Total
Direct Labor Hours per Product	350,000	400,000	500,000	1,250,000
Overhead Rate per Direct Labor Hour	× $2	× $2	× $2	× $2
Overhead Assign per Product	$700,000	$800,000	$1,000,000	$2,500,000
Number Units	140,000	100,000	250,000	490,000
Overhead per Unit	$ 5	$ 8	$ 4	

Figure 6.4 Musicality's Overhead per Unit Using Traditional Allocation. (attribution: Copyright Rice University, OpenStax, under CC BY-NC-SA 4.0 license)

The overhead cost per unit from Figure 6.4 is combined with the direct material and direct labor costs as shown in Figure 6.3 to compute the total cost per unit as shown in Figure 6.5.

	Solo	Band	Orchestra
Direct Materials per Unit	$ 3.50	$ 6.00	$11.70
Direct Labor per Unit	10.00	2.75	4.30
Overhead per Unit	$ 5.00	$ 8.00	$ 4.00
Cost per Unit	$18.50	$16.75	$20.00

Figure 6.5 Musicality's Product Costs Using Traditional Allocation. (attribution: Copyright Rice University, OpenStax, under CC BY-NC-SA 4.0 license)

After reviewing the product cost and consulting with the marketing department, the sales prices were set. The sales price, cost of each product, and resulting gross profit are shown in Figure 6.6.

	Solo	Band	Orchestra
Sales Price	$20.00	$25.00	$30.00
Cost per Unit (traditional)	18.50	16.75	20.00
Gross Profit per Unit	$ 1.50	$ 8.25	$10.00

Figure 6.6 Musicality's Gross Profit per Unit Using Traditional Allocation. (attribution: Copyright Rice University, OpenStax, under CC BY-NC-SA 4.0 license)

Sales of each product have been strong, and the total gross profit for each product is shown in Figure 6.7. Using the Solo product as an example, 150,000 units are sold at a price of $20 per unit resulting in sales of $3,000,000. The cost of goods sold consists of direct materials of $3.50 per unit, direct labor of $10 per unit, and manufacturing overhead of $5.00 per unit. With 150,000 units, the direct material cost is $525,000; the direct labor cost is $1,500,000; and the manufacturing overhead applied is $750,000 for a total Cost of Goods Sold of $2,775,000. The resulting Gross Profit is $225,000 or $1.50 per unit.

Traditional Costing	Solo	Band	Orchestra	Total
Number of Units Sold	150,000	110,000	200,000	460,000
Sales	$3,000,000	$2,750,000	$6,000,000	$11,750,000
Less Cost of Goods Sold				
Direct Material	525,000	660,000	2,340,000	3,525,000
Direct Labor	1,500,000	302,500	860,000	2,662,500
Manufacturing Overhead	750,000	880,000	800,000	2,430,000
Cost of Goods Sold	2,775,000	1,842,500	4,000,000	8,617,500
Gross Profit	$ 225,000	$ 907,500	$2,000,000	$ 3,132,500

Figure 6.7 Musicality's Gross Profit by Product Line Using Traditional Allocation. (attribution: Copyright Rice University, OpenStax, under CC BY-NC-SA 4.0 license)

THINK IT THROUGH

Computing Actual Overhead Costs

As manufacturing technology becomes less expensive and more efficient, the mix between overhead and labor changes so that tasks are more computerized tasks and involve less direct labor; the traditional use of direct labor hours or direct labor dollars changes accordingly. If the predetermined overhead rate is based on direct labor hours and set at the beginning of the year but manufacturing technology leads to a reduction in direct labor during the year, the number of direct labor hours may be less than estimated. This reduces the amount of overhead applied so that the overhead is more likely to be underapplied at the end of the year. Why do companies not wait until the end of the period and compute an actual overhead rate based on actual manufacturing costs and actual units?

6.2 Describe and Identify Cost Drivers

As you've learned, the most common bases for predetermined overhead are direct labor hours, direct labor dollars, or machine hours. Each of these costs is considered a **cost driver** because of the causal relationship between the base and the related costs: As the cost driver's usage increases, the cost of overhead increases as well. Table 6.1 shows various costs and potential cost drivers.

Common Manufacturing Expenses and Potential Cost Drivers

Common Expenses	Potential Cost Drivers
• Customer Service	• Number of product returns from customers
• Cleaning Equipment Costs	• Number of square feet
• Marketing Expenses	• Number of customer contacts
• Office Supplies	• Number of employees
• Green Floral Tape (indirect material)	• Number of customer orders
• Website Maintenance Expense	• Number of customer online orders

Table 6.1

The more accurately a company can determine the cost drivers for its products, the more accurate the costing information will be, which in turn allows management to make better use of the cost data in making decisions. As technology changes, however, the mix between materials, labor, and overhead changes. Often, improved technology means less waste of material and fewer direct labor hours, but possibly more overhead. For example, technology has changed the way pharmaceuticals are manufactured. Advancing technology allows for the now smaller labor force to be more productive than a larger labor force from earlier years. While the labor cost has changed, this decrease may only be temporary as a labor force with higher costs and different skills is often needed. Additionally, an increase in technology often raises overhead costs. How accurate, then, is the company's product cost information if it has become more efficient in its production process? Should the company still be using a predetermined overhead application rate based on direct labor hours or machine hours? A detailed analysis of the cost drivers will answer these questions.

Another benefit of looking at cost drivers is that doing so allows a company to analyze all costs. A company can differentiate among costs that drive overhead and have value, those that do not drive overhead but still add value, and those that may or may not drive the overhead but do not add any value. For example, a furniture manufacturer produces and sells wooden tables in various colors. The painting process involves a white base coat, a color coat, and a clear protective top coat. The three coats are applied in a sealed room using a spraying process followed by an ultraviolet drying process. The depreciation on the spraying machines and the ultraviolet bulbs used in the painting process are overhead costs. These costs drive or increase overhead, and they add value to the product by increasing the quality. Costs associated with repainting or fixing any blemishes are overhead costs that are necessary to sell the product but would not be considered value-added costs. The goal is to eliminate as many of the non-value-added costs as possible and subsequently reduce overhead costs.

Cost Drivers and Overhead

In today's production environment, there are many activities within the production process that can contribute to the cost of the product, but determining the cost drivers may be complicated because some of those activities may change over time. Additionally, the appropriate level of assigning cost drivers needs to be determined. In some cases, overhead costs such as inspection increase with each unit inspected, and the costs need to be allocated on a per-unit level. In other cases, the overhead costs, such as machine setup costs, are incurred each time a batch of products is manufactured and need to be allocated at the batch level.

For example, the labor hours for the staff taking, fulfilling, and inspecting orders may increase as the number of orders increases, driving up the overhead. Furthermore, the costs of taking orders or of quality inspections can vary per product and may not be captured properly. Technology improvements, including switching to automated processes for production, may decrease the labor hours of the production staff, driving the labor-related overhead downward but potentially increasing other overhead expenses. These activities—order taking, fulfillment, and quality inspections—are potential cost drivers associated with production, and they each drive the overhead at varying rates.

THINK IT THROUGH

Identifying Cost Drivers

Cost drivers vary widely among companies.

1. After costs are accumulated into cost pools, what information would help management select the appropriate cost driver?
2. Name an appropriate cost driver for each of the following cost pools:
    A. Plant cleaning and maintenance
    B. Factory supervision
    C. Machine maintenance
    D. Machine setups

Identify Cost Drivers

How does a company determine its cost drivers for indirect materials, indirect labor, and other overhead costs? To begin the determination of appropriate cost drivers, an accountant analyzes the activities in the product production process that contribute to the cost of that product. An activity is any action that consumes company resources, such as taking orders for a product, setting up machines to produce the product, inspecting the product, and providing customer support before and through the order process. For example, Musicality's direct costs can be traced to the products, but there are indirect costs associated with using various types of material for each product. While the Orchestra product has more intricate materials and labor, it has fewer costs associated with requisitioning and conveying materials to the production line than the other products have. Additionally, examining the inspection costs indicates the Orchestra product is a simple product to inspect, so random quality inspections are sufficient. But individual inspections for both the Solo and Band products are critical, and the overhead related to inspection costs should be based on the number of inspections.

As you can imagine, the unique aspects of the production process for each product affect the overhead cost of each product. However, these costs may not be allocated to the products appropriately when overhead is applied using a predetermined rate based on one activity. While Solo, Band, and Orchestra might appear to be different only in quality, they are actually very different from each other when it comes to manufacturing overhead costs.

Whether the products produced require significantly different overhead resources or not, the company benefits from understanding what its cost drivers are. The more efficiently each product's activities are tracked, the more actual cost drivers are discovered, and the more accurately overhead can be assigned to each product.

CONCEPTS IN PRACTICE

Cost Drivers for Small Businesses

The value of analyzing cost drivers can be used in budgeting beyond allocating overhead to products. American Express has forums designed to help small businesses be successful. Knowing the cost drivers for your business can help with budgeting. American Express states that all business activities are related to five main cost drivers:[4]

- Employee head count is often the driver for office supply expense.
- Salesperson head count is often the driver for auto and other employee travel expense.
- The number of leads required to reach the target sales goal is often the driver for advertising, public relations, social media, search engine optimization expense, and other expenses associated with generating leads.
- Sales and all related variable expenses are often the driver for commissions, bad debt, insurance expense, and so on.
- Fixed costs, such as postage, web hosting fees, business licenses, and banking fees, are often overlooked as cost drivers.

---

4 American Express. "5 Cost Drivers to Help You Make Accurate Expense Projections." June 23, 2011. https://www.americanexpress.com/us/small-business/openforum/articles/5-cost-drivers-to-help-you-make-accurate-expense-projections/

6.3 Calculate Activity-Based Product Costs

As technology changes the ratio between direct labor and overhead, more overhead costs are linked to drivers other than direct labor and machine hours. This shift in costs gives companies the opportunity to stop using the traditional single predetermined overhead rate applied to all units of production and instead use an overhead allocation approach based on the actual activities that drive overhead. Making this change allows management to obtain more accurate product cost information, which leads to more informed decisions. **Activity-based costing** (ABC) is the process that assigns overhead to products based on the various activities that drive overhead costs.

Historical Perspective on Determination of Manufacturing Overhead Allocation

All products consist of material, labor, and overhead, and the major cost components have historically been materials and labor. Manufacturing overhead was not a large cost of the product, so an overhead allocation method based on labor or machine hours was logical. For example, as shown in Figure 6.3, Musicality determined the direct costs and direct labor for their three products: Solo, Band, and Orchestra. Under the traditional method of costing, the predetermined overhead rate of $2 per direct labor hour was computed by dividing the estimated overhead by the estimated direct labor hours. Based on the number of direct labor hours and the number of units produced for each product, the overhead per product is shown in Figure 6.4.

As technology costs decreased and production methods became more efficient, overhead costs changed and became a much larger component of product costs. For many companies, and in many cases, overhead costs are now significantly larger than labor costs. For example, in the last few years, many industries have increased technology, and the amount of overhead has doubled.[5] Technology has changed the manufacturing labor force, and therefore, the type and cost of labor associated with those jobs have changed. In addition, technology has made it easier to track the various activities and their related overhead costs.

> *Many manufacturing companies use MRP (material requirements planning) or ERP (enterprise resource planning) systems. MRP helps management organize the planning, scheduling, and tracking of materials while ERP systems help plan, organize, and track the materials as well as the accounting, marketing, supply chain, and other management functions.*

Costs can be gathered on a unit level, batch level, product level, or factory level. The idea behind these various levels is that at each level, there are additional costs that are encountered, so a company must decide at which level or levels it is best for the company to accumulate costs. A **unit-level cost** is incurred each time a unit of product is produced and includes costs such as materials and labor. A **batch-level cost** is incurred every time a batch of items is manufactured, for example, costs associated with purchasing and receiving materials. A **product-level cost** is incurred each time a product is produced and includes costs such as engineering costs, testing costs, or quality control costs. A **factory-level cost** is incurred because products are being produced and includes costs such as the plant supervisor's salary and rent on the factory building. By definition, indirect labor is not traced to individual products. However, it is possible to track some indirect labor to several jobs or batches. A similar amount of information can be derived for indirect material. An example of an indirect material in some manufacturing processes is cleaning solution. For example, one type of cleaning solution is used in the manufacturing of pop sockets. It is not practical to measure every ounce of cleaning solution used in the manufacture of an individual pop socket; rather, it makes sense to allocate to a particular batch of pop

---

5   Mary Ellen Biery. "A Sure-Fire Way to Boost the Bottom Line." *Forbes*. January 12, 2014. https://www.forbes.com/sites/sageworks/2014/01/12/control-overhead-compare-industry-data/#47a9ea69d068

sockets the cost of the cleaning solution needed to make that batch. Likewise, a manufacturer of frozen french fries uses a different type of solution to clean potatoes prior to making the french fries and would allocate the cost of the solution based on how much is used to make each batch of fries.

Establishing an Activity-Based Costing System

ABC is a five-stage process that allocates overhead more precisely than traditional allocation does by applying it to the products that use those activities. ABC works best in complex processes where the expenses are not driven by a single cost driver. Instead, several cost drivers are used as the overhead costs are analyzed and grouped into activities, and each activity is allocated based on each group's cost driver. The five stages of the ABC process are:

1. Identify the activities performed in the organization
2. Determine activity cost pools
3. Calculate activity rates for each cost pool
4. Allocate activity rates to products (or services)
5. Calculate unit product costs

The first step is to identify activities needed for production. An activity is an action or process involved in the production of inventory. There can be many activities that consume resources, and management will need to narrow down the activities to those that have the biggest impact on overhead costs. Examples of these activities include:

- Taking orders
- Setting up machines
- Purchasing material
- Assembling products
- Inspecting products
- Providing customer service

The second step is assigning overhead costs to the identified activities. In this step, overhead costs are assigned to each of the activities to become a cost pool. A **cost pool** is a list of costs incurred when related activities are performed. Table 6.2 illustrates the various cost pools along with their activities and related costs.

Cost Pools and Their Activities and Related Costs

Cost Pool	Activities and Related Costs
Production	• Indirect labor setting up machines • Indirect labor cost of accepting and verifying orders • Machine maintenance costs • Costs to operate the machine: utilities, insurance, etc.
Purchasing material	• Preparing purchase requisitions for the material • Cost to move material from receiving department into production • Depreciation of equipment used to move material
Inspect products	• Inspection supervisor costs • Cost to move product to and from the inspection area

Table 6.2

Cost Pools and Their Activities and Related Costs

Cost Pool	Activities and Related Costs
Assemble products	• Cost of assembly machine • Cost of label machine • Cost of labels
Technological production	• Website maintenance • Depreciation of computers

Table 6.2

For example, the production cost pool consists of costs such as indirect labor for those accepting the order, verifying the customer has credit to pay for the order, maintenance and depreciation on the machines used to produce the orders, and utilities and rent for operating the machines. Figure 6.8 illustrates how the costs in each pool are allocated to each product in a different proportion.

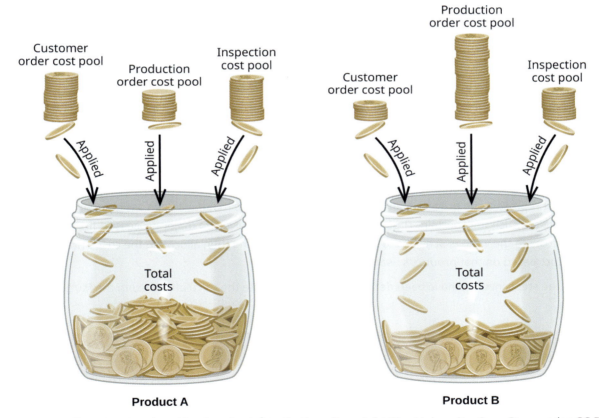

Figure 6.8 Allocating Overhead by Cost Pool. (attribution: Copyright Rice University, OpenStax, under CC BY-NC-SA 4.0 license)

Once the costs are grouped into similar cost pools, the activities in each pool are analyzed to determine which activity "drives" the costs in that pool, leading to the third step of ABC: identify the cost driver for each cost pool and estimate an annual level of activity for each cost driver. As you've learned, the cost driver is the specific activity that drives the costs in the cost pools. Table 6.3 shows some activities and cost drivers for those activities.

Activities and Their Common Cost Drivers

Cost Pool	Cost Driver
Customer order	Number of orders
Production	Machine setups
Purchasing materials	Purchase requisitions
Assembling products	Direct labor hours
Inspecting products	Inspection hours
Customer service	Number of contacts with customer

Table 6.3

The fourth step is to compute the predetermined overhead rate for each of the cost drivers. This portion of the process is similar to finding the traditional predetermined overhead rate, where the overhead rate is divided by direct labor dollars, direct labor hours, or machine hours. Each cost driver will have its own overhead rate, which is why ABC is a more accurate method of allocating overhead.

Finally, step five is to allocate the overhead costs to each product. The predetermined overhead rate found in step four is applied to the actual level of the cost driver used by each product. As with the traditional overhead allocation method, the actual overhead costs are accumulated in an account called manufacturing overhead and then applied to each of the products in this step.

Notice that steps one through three represent the process of allocating overhead costs to activities, and steps four and five represent the process of allocating the overhead costs that have been assigned to activities to the products to which they pertain. Thus, the five steps of ABC involve two major processes: first, allocating overhead costs to the various activities to get a cost per activity, and then allocating the cost per activity to each product based on that product's usage of the activities.

Now that the steps involved have been detailed, let's demonstrate the calculations using the Musicality example.

YOUR TURN

Comparing Estimates to Actual Costs

A company has determined that its estimated 500,000 machine hours is the optimal driver for its estimated $1,000,000 machine overhead cost pool. The $750,000 in the material overhead cost pool should be allocated using the estimated 15,000 material requisition requests. How much is over- or underapplied if there were actually 490,000 machine hours and 15,500 material requisitions that resulted in $950,000 in the machine overhead cost pool, and $780,000 in the material cost pool? What does this difference indicate?

Solution

The predetermined overhead rate is $2 per machine hour ($1,000,000/500,000 machine hours) and $50 per material requisition ($750,000/15,000 requisitions). The actual and applied overhead can then be calculated to determine whether it is over- or underapplied:

	Rate	Actual	Applied	Difference	Overapplied or Underapplied?
Machine Overhead	$ 2*	490,000*	$980,000	$30,000	Overapplied
Material Overhead	$50**	15,500**	$775,000	$(5,000)	Underapplied

* machine hours
**requisitions

The difference is a combination of factors. There were fewer machine hours than estimated, but there was also less overhead than estimated. There were more requisitions than estimated, and there was also more overhead.

The Calculation of Product Costs Using the Activity-Based Costing Allocation Method

Musicality is considering switching to an activity-based costing approach for determining overhead and has collected data to help them decide which overhead allocation method they should use. Performing the analysis requires these steps:

1. Identify cost pools necessary to complete the product. Musicality determined its cost pools are:
   - Setting up machines
   - Purchasing material
   - Inspecting products
   - Assembling products
   - Technological production

2. Assign overhead cost to the cost pools. Musicality has estimated the overhead for each cost pool to be:

Activity	Estimated Overhead Costs
Setting Up Machines	$ 200,000
Purchasing Material	500,000
Inspecting Products	300,000
Assembling Products	600,000
Technological Production	900,000
Total	$2,500,000

3. Identify the cost driver for each activity, and estimate an annual activity for each driver. Musicality determined the driver and estimated activity for each product to be the following:

	Expected Cost Driver Activities			
Cost Driver	Solo	Band	Orchestra	Total
Machine Setups	2,000	1,500	1,500	5,000
Number of Purchase Requisitions	5,000	4,000	1,000	10,000
Inspection Hours	10,000	9,000	1,000	20,000
Number of Parts Requiring Labor	15,000	3,000	12,000	30,000
Machine Hours	80,000	60,000	10,000	150,000

4. Compute the predetermined overhead for each cost driver. Musicality determined this predetermined overhead rate for each driver:

Activity	Cost Driver	Estimated Overhead Costs	Total Activity	ABC Rate per Activity
Setting Up Machines	Machine setups	$ 200,000	5,000	$40
Purchasing Material	Number of purchase requisitions	500,000	10,000	50
Inspecting Products	Inspection hours	300,000	20,000	15
Assembling Products	Number of parts requiring labor	600,000	30,000	20
Technological Production	Machine hours	900,000	150,000	6
Total		$ 2,500,000		

5. Allocate overhead costs to products. Assuming Musicality's activities were as estimated, the amount allocated to each product is:

	Expected Cost Driver Activities			
Activity	Solo	Band	Orchestra	Total
Machine Setups	$ 80,000	$ 60,000	$ 60,000	$ 200,000
Number of Purchase Requisitions	250,000	200,000	50,000	500,000
Inspection Hours	150,000	135,000	15,000	300,000
Number of Parts Requiring Labor	300,000	60,000	240,000	600,000
Machine Hours	480,000	360,000	60,000	900,000
Total Overhead	$1,260,000	$815,000	$425,000	$2,500,000

Now that Musicality has applied overhead to each product, they can calculate the cost per unit. Management can review its sales price and make necessary decisions regarding its products. The overhead cost per unit is the overhead for each product divided by the number of units of each product:

Activity	Solo	Band	Orchestra	Total
Total Overhead	$1,260,000	$815,000	$425,000	$2,500,000
Number Units	140,000	100,000	250,000	490,000
Overhead per Unit	$ 9.00	$ 8.15	$ 1.70	

The overhead per unit can be added to the unit cost for direct material and direct labor to compute the total product cost per unit:

	Solo	Band	Orchestra
Direct Materials per Unit	$ 3.50	$ 6.00	$11.70
Direct Labor per Unit	10.00	2.75	4.30
Overhead per Unit	9.00	8.15	1.70
Cost per Unit via ABC	$22.50	$16.90	$17.70

The sales price was set after management reviewed the product cost with traditional allocation along with other factors such as competition and product demand. The current sales price, cost of each product using ABC, and the resulting gross profit are shown in Figure 6.9.

	Solo	Band	Orchestra
Sales Price	$20.00	$25.00	$30.00
Cost per Unit (ABC)	22.50	16.90	17.70
Gross Profit (loss) per Unit	$(2.50)	$ 8.10	$12.30

Figure 6.9 Solo's Sales Price, ABC Costing, and Gross Profit. (attribution: Copyright Rice University, OpenStax, under CC BY-NC-SA 4.0 license)

The loss on each sale of the Solo product was not discovered until the company did the calculations for the ABC method, because the sales of the other products were strong enough for the company to retain a total gross profit.

Additionally, the more accurate gross profit for each product calculated using ABC is shown in Figure 6.10:

	Solo	Band	Orchestra	Total
Number of Units Sold	150,000	110,000	200,000	460,000
ABC Costing				
Sales	$3,000,000	$2,750,000	$6,000,000	$11,750,000
Cost of Goods Sold	3,375,000	1,859,000	3,540,000	8,774,000
Gross Profit (loss)	$ (375,000)	$ 891,000	$2,460,000	$ 2,976,000

Figure 6.10 Solo's Gross Profit by Product. (attribution: Copyright Rice University, OpenStax, under CC BY-NC-SA 4.0 license)

The calculations Musicality did in order to switch to ABC revealed that the Solo product was generating a loss for every unit sold. Knowing this information will allow Musicality to consider whether they should make changes to generate a profit from the Solo product, such as increase the selling price or carefully analyze the costs to identify potential cost reductions. Musicality could also decide to continue selling Solo at a loss, because the other products are generating enough profit for the company to absorb the Solo product loss and still be profitable. Why would a company continue to sell a product that is generating a loss? Sometimes these products are ones for which the company is well known or that draw customers into the store. For example, companies will sometimes offer extreme sales, such as on Black Friday, to attract customers in the hope that the customers will purchase other products. This information shows how valuable ABC can be in many situations for providing a more accurate picture than traditional allocation.

The Service Industries and Their Use of the Activity-Based Costing Allocation Method

ABC costing was developed to help management understand manufacturing costs and how they can be better managed. However, the service industry can apply the same principles to improve its cost management. Direct material and direct labor costs range from nonexistent to minimal in the service industry, which makes the overhead application even more important. The number and types of cost pools may be completely different in the service industry as compared to the manufacturing industry. For example, the health-care industry may have different overhead costs and cost drivers for the treatment of illnesses than they have for injuries. Some of the overhead related to monitoring a patient's health status may overlap, but most of the overhead related to diagnosis and treatment differ from each other.

LINK TO LEARNING

Activity-based costing is not restricted to manufacturing. Service industries also have cost drivers and can benefit from analyzing what drives their costs. See this report on activity-based costing at UPS (https://openstax.org/l/50ABC) for an example.

6.4 Compare and Contrast Traditional and Activity-Based Costing Systems

Calculating an accurate manufacturing cost for each product is a vital piece of information for a company's decision-making. For example, knowing the cost to produce a unit of product affects not only how a business budgets to manufacture that product, but it is often the starting point in determining the sales price.

An important component in determining the total production costs of a product or job is the proper allocation of overhead. For some companies, the often less-complicated traditional method does an excellent job of allocating overhead. However, for many products, the allocation of overhead is a more complex issue, and an activity-based costing (ABC) system is more appropriate.

Another factor to consider in determining which of the two major overhead allocation methods to use is the cost associated with collecting and analyzing information. When making their decision regarding which method to use, the company must consider these costs, both in time and money. Table 6.4 compares overhead in the two systems. In many cases, the ABC method is more expensive in terms of time and other costs.

The difference between the traditional method (using one cost driver) and the ABC method (using multiple cost drivers) is more complex than simply the number of cost drivers. When direct labor is a large portion of the product cost, the overhead costs tend to be consistently driven by one cost driver, which is typically direct labor or machine hours; the traditional method appropriately allocates those costs. When technology is a large portion of the product cost, the overhead costs tend to be driven by multiple drivers, so using multiple cost drivers in the ABC method allows for a more precise allocation of overhead.

Overhead in Traditional versus ABC Costing

	Traditional	ABC
Overhead assigned	Single cost driver	Multiple cost drivers
Optimal usage	When direct labor is a large portion of the product cost	When technology is a large portion of the product cost
Orientation	Cost driven	Process driven

Table 6.4

As shown with Musicality's products, not only are there different costs for each product when comparing traditional allocation with an activity-based costing, but ABC showed that the Solo product creates a loss for the company. Activity-based costing is a more accurate method, because it assigns overhead based on the activities that drive the overhead costs. It can be concluded, then, that the cost and subsequent gross loss for each unit's sales provide a more accurate picture than the overall cost and gross profit under the traditional method. image compares the cost per unit using the different cost systems and shows how different the costs can be depending on the method used.

	Solo	Band	Orchestra
Cost per Unit via ABC	$22.50	$16.90	$17.70
Cost per Unit via Traditional	18.50	16.75	20.00
Difference	$ 4.00	$ 0.15	$(2.30)

Advantages and Disadvantages of the Traditional Method of Calculating Overhead

The traditional allocation system assigns manufacturing overhead based on a single cost driver, such as direct labor hours, direct labor dollars, or machine hours, and is optimal when there is a relationship between the activity base and overhead. This most often occurs when direct labor is a large part of the product cost. The theory supporting the single cost driver is that the cost driver selected increases as overhead increases, and further analysis is more costly than it is valuable. Each method has its advantages and disadvantages. These are advantages of the traditional method:

- All manufacturing costs are classified as material, labor, or overhead and assigned to products regardless of whether they drive or are driven by production.
- All manufacturing costs are considered to be part of the product cost, whereas nonmanufacturing costs are not considered to be production costs and are not assigned to products, regardless of whether the costs are based on the products. For example, the machines used to receive and process customer orders are necessary because product orders must be taken, but their costs are not allocated to particular products.
- There is only one overhead cost pool and a single measure of activity, such as direct labor hours, which makes the traditional method simple and less costly to maintain. The predetermined overhead rate is based on estimated costs at the budgeted level of activity. Therefore, the overhead rate is consistent across products, but overhead may be over- or underapplied.

Disadvantages of the traditional method include:

- The use of the single cost driver does not allocate overhead as accurately as using multiple cost drivers.
- The use of the single cost driver may overallocate overhead to one product and underallocate overhead to another product, resulting in erroneous total costs and potentially setting an incorrect sales price.
- Traditional allocation assigns costs as period or product costs, and all product costs are included in the cost of inventory, which makes this method acceptable for generally accepted accounting principles (GAAP).

> **THINK IT THROUGH**
>
> **ABC Method and Financial Statements**
>
> There are pros and cons to both the traditional and the ABC system. One advantage of the ABC system is that it provides more accurate information on the costs to manufacture products, but it does not show up on the financial statements. Explain how this costing information has value if it does not appear on the financial statements.

Advantages and Disadvantages of Creating an Activity-Based Costing System for Allocating Overhead

While ABC systems more accurately allocate the costs based on the various resources used to make the product, they cost more to use and, therefore, are not always the best method. Management needs to consider each system and how it will work within its own organization. Some advantages of activity-based costing include:

- There are multiple overhead cost pools, and each has its own unique measure of activity. This provides more accurate rates for applying overhead, but it takes more time to implement and results in a higher cost.
- The allocation bases (i.e., measures of activity) often differ from those used in traditional allocation. Multiple cost pools allow management to group costs being influenced by similar drivers and to consider cost drivers beyond the typical labor or machine hour. This results in a more accurate overhead application rate.
- The activity rates may consider the level of activity at capacity instead of the budgeted level of activity.
- Both nonmanufacturing costs and manufacturing costs may be assigned to products. The main rationale in assigning costs is the relationship between the cost and the product. If the cost increases as the volume of the product increases, it is considered part of overhead.

There are disadvantages to using ABC costing that management needs to consider when determining which method to use. Those disadvantages include:

- Some manufacturing costs may be excluded from product costs. For example, the cost to heat the factory may be excluded as a product cost because, while it is necessary for production, it does not fit into one of the activity-driven cost pools.
- It is more expensive, as there is a cost to collect and analyze cost driver information as well as to allocate overhead on the basis of multiple cost drivers.
- An ABC system takes much more to implement and operate, as information on cost drivers must be

collected in an objective manner.

The advantages and disadvantages of both methods are as previously listed, but what is the practical impact on the product cost? There are several items to consider at the product costs level:

- Adopting an ABC overhead allocation system can allow a company to shift manufacturing overhead costs between products based on their volume.
- Using an ABC method to better assign unit-level, batch-level, product-level, and factory-level costs can increase the per-unit costs of the low-volume products and decrease the per-unit costs of the high-volume products.
- The effects are not symmetrical; there is usually a larger change in the per-unit costs of the low-volume products.
- The cost of the products may include some period costs but not some of the product costs, so it is not considered GAAP compliant. The information is supplemental and very helpful to management, but the company still needs to compute the product's cost under the traditional method for financial reporting.

LINK TO LEARNING

Changing from the traditional allocation method to ABC costing is not as simple as having management dictate that employees follow the new system. There are often challenges that begin with convincing employees that it will provide benefits and that they should buy into the new system. See this 1995 article, Tapping the Full Potential of ABC, illustrating some of Chrysler's challenges (https://openstax.org/l/50Chrysler) to learn more.

6.5 Compare and Contrast Variable and Absorption Costing

ABC costing assigns a proportion of overhead costs on the basis of the activities under the presumption that the activities drive the overhead costs. As such, ABC costing converts the indirect costs into product costs. There are also cost systems with a different approach. Instead of focusing on the overhead costs incurred by the product unit, these methods focus on assigning the fixed overhead costs to inventory.

There are two major methods in manufacturing firms for valuing work in process and finished goods inventory for financial accounting purposes: variable costing and absorption costing. **Variable costing**, also called *direct costing* or *marginal costing*, is a method in which all variable costs (direct material, direct labor, and variable overhead) are assigned to a product and fixed overhead costs are expensed in the period incurred. Under variable costing, fixed overhead is not included in the value of inventory. In contrast, **absorption costing**, also called *full costing*, is a method that applies all direct costs, fixed overhead, and variable manufacturing overhead to the cost of the product. The value of inventory under absorption costing includes direct material, direct labor, and all overhead.

The difference in the methods is that management will prefer one method over the other for internal decision-making purposes. The other main difference is that only the absorption method is in accordance with GAAP.

Variable Costing Versus Absorption Costing Methods

The difference between the absorption and variable costing methods centers on the treatment of fixed manufacturing overhead costs. Absorption costing "absorbs" all of the costs used in manufacturing and includes fixed manufacturing overhead as product costs. Absorption costing is in accordance with GAAP, because the product cost includes fixed overhead. Variable costing considers the variable overhead costs and does not consider fixed overhead as part of a product's cost. It is not in accordance with GAAP, because fixed overhead is treated as a period cost and is not included in the cost of the product.

CONCEPTS IN PRACTICE

Absorbing Costs through Overproduction

While companies use absorption costing for their financial statements, many also use variable costing for decision-making. The Big Three auto companies made decisions based on absorption costing, and the result was the manufacturing of more vehicles than the market demanded. Why? With absorption costing, the fixed overhead costs, such as marketing, were allocated to inventory, and the larger the inventory, the lower was the unit cost of that overhead. For example, if a fixed cost of $1,000 is allocated to 500 units, the cost is $2 per unit. But if there are 2,000 units, the per-unit cost is $0.50. While this was not the only reason for manufacturing too many cars, it kept the period costs hidden among the manufacturing costs. Using variable costing would have kept the costs separate and led to different decisions.

Deferred Costs

Absorption costing considers all fixed overhead as part of a product's cost and assigns it to the product. This treatment means that as inventories increase and are possibly carried over from the year of production to actual sales of the units in the next year, the company allocates a portion of the fixed manufacturing overhead costs from the current period to future periods.

Carrying over inventories and overhead costs is reflected in the ending inventory balances at the end of the production period, which become the beginning inventory balances at the start of the next period. It is anticipated that the units that were carried over will be sold in the next period. If the units are not sold, the costs will continue to be included in the costs of producing the units until they are sold. Finally, at the point of sale, whenever it happens, these deferred production costs, such as fixed overhead, become part of the costs of goods sold and flow through to the income statement in the period of the sale. This treatment is based on the **expense recognition principle**, which is one of the cornerstones of accrual accounting and is why the absorption method follows GAAP. The principle states that expenses should be recognized in the period in which revenues are incurred. Including fixed overhead as a cost of the product ensures the fixed overhead is expensed (as part of cost of goods sold) when the sale is reported.

For example, assume a new company has fixed overhead of $12,000 and manufactures 10,000 units. Direct materials cost is $3 per unit, direct labor is $15 per unit, and the variable manufacturing overhead is $7 per unit. Under absorption costing, the amount of fixed overhead in each unit is $1.20 ($12,000/10,000 units); variable costing does not include any fixed overhead as part of the cost of the product. Figure 6.11 shows the cost to produce the 10,000 units using absorption and variable costing.

	Absorption	Variable
Materials ($3 per unit)	$ 30,000	$ 30,000
Labor ($15 per unit)	150,000	150,000
Variable Overhead ($7 per unit)	70,000	70,000
Fixed Overhead ($1.20 per unit)	12,000	
Total Finished Goods Inventory	$262,000	$250,000

Figure 6.11 Finished Goods Inventory under Absorption and Variable Costing. (attribution: Copyright Rice University, OpenStax, under CC BY-NC-SA 4.0 license)

Assume each unit is sold for $33 each, so sales are $330,000 for the year. If the entire finished goods inventory is sold, the income is the same for both the absorption and variable cost methods. The difference is that the absorption cost method includes fixed overhead as part of the cost of goods sold, while the variable cost method includes it as an administrative cost, as shown in Figure 6.12. When the entire inventory is sold, the total fixed cost is expensed as the cost of goods sold under the absorption method or it is expensed as an administrative cost under the variable method; net income is the same under both methods.

	Absorption	Variable
Sales	$330,000	$330,000
Cost of Goods Sold	262,000	250,000
Gross Profit	68,000	80,000
– Fixed Overhead	0	12,000
Net Income	$162,400	$160,000

Figure 6.12 Income Statement When the Entire Inventory Is Sold. (attribution: Copyright Rice University, OpenStax, under CC BY-NC-SA 4.0 license)

Now assume that 8,000 units are sold and 2,000 are still in finished goods inventory at the end of the year. The cost of the fixed overhead expensed on the income statement as cost of goods sold is $9,600 ($1.20/unit × 8,000 units), and the fixed overhead cost remaining in finished goods inventory is $2,400 ($1.20/unit × 2,000 units). The amount of the fixed overhead paid by the company is not totally expensed, because the number of units in ending inventory has increased. Eventually, the fixed overhead cost will be expensed when the inventory is sold in the next period. Figure 6.13 shows the cost to produce the 8,000 units of inventory that became cost of goods sold and the 2,000 units that remain in ending inventory.

	Absorption	Variable
Cost of Goods Sold		
Materials	$ 24,000	$ 24,000
Labor	120,000	120,000
Variable Overhead	56,000	14,000
Fixed Overhead	9,600	
Cost of Goods Sold	$209,600	$200,000
Ending Inventory		
Materials	$ 6,000	$ 6,000
Labor	30,000	30,000
Variable Overhead	14,000	14,000
Fixed Overhead	2,400	
Ending Inventory	$ 52,400	$ 50,000

Figure 6.13 Cost of Goods Sold and Ending Inventory with the Absorption and Variable Costing Methods. (attribution: Copyright Rice University, OpenStax, under CC BY-NC-SA 4.0 license)

If the 8,000 units are sold for $33 each, the difference between absorption costing and variable costing is a timing difference. Under absorption costing, the 2,000 units in ending inventory include the $1.20 per unit share, or $2,400 of fixed cost. That cost will be expensed when the inventory is sold and accounts for the difference in net income under absorption and variable costing, as shown in Figure 6.14.

	Absorption	Variable
Sales	$264,000	$264,000
Cost of Goods Sold	209,600	200,000
Gross Profit	54,400	64,000
− Fixed Overhead	0	12,000
Net Income	$ 54,400	$ 52,000

Figure 6.14 Net Income under Absorption and Variable Costing When Ending Inventory Remains. (attribution: Copyright Rice University, OpenStax, under CC BY-NC-SA 4.0 license)

Under variable costing, the fixed overhead is not considered a product cost and would not be assigned to ending inventory. The fixed overhead would have been expensed on the income statement as a period cost.

Inventory Differences

Because absorption costing defers costs, the ending inventory figure differs from that calculated using the variable costing method. As shown in Figure 6.13, the inventory figure under absorption costing considers both variable and fixed manufacturing costs, whereas under variable costing, it only includes the variable manufacturing costs.

Suitability for Cost-Volume-Profit Analysis

Using the absorption costing method on the income statement does not easily provide data for cost-volume-profit (CVP) computations. In the previous example, the fixed overhead cost per unit is $1.20 based on an activity of 10,000 units. If the company estimated 12,000 units, the fixed overhead cost per unit would decrease to $1 per unit. This calculation is possible, but it must be done multiple times each time the volume of activity changes in order to provide accurate data, as CVP analysis makes no distinction between variable costing and absorption costing income statements.

> **YOUR TURN**
>
> ### Comparing Variable and Absorption Methods
>
> A company expects to manufacture 7,000 units. Its direct material costs are $10 per unit, direct labor is $9 per unit, and variable overhead is $3 per unit. The fixed overhead is estimated at $49,000. How much would each unit cost under both the variable method and the absorption method?
>
> **Solution**
>
> The variable cost per unit is $22 (the total of direct material, direct labor, and variable overhead). The absorption cost per unit is the variable cost ($22) plus the per-unit cost of $7 ($49,000/7,000 units) for the fixed overhead, for a total of $29.

Advantages and Disadvantages of the Variable Costing Method

Variable costing only includes the product costs that vary with output, which typically include direct material, direct labor, and variable manufacturing overhead. Fixed overhead is not considered a product cost under variable costing. Fixed manufacturing overhead is still expensed on the income statement, but it is treated as a period cost charged against revenue for each period. It does not include a portion of fixed overhead costs that remains in inventory and is not expensed, as in absorption costing.

If absorption costing is the method acceptable for financial reporting under GAAP, why would management prefer variable costing? Advocates of variable costing argue that the definition of fixed costs holds, and fixed manufacturing overhead costs will be incurred regardless of whether anything is actually produced. They also argue that fixed manufacturing overhead costs are true period expenses and have no future service potential, since incurring them now has no effect on whether these costs will have to be incurred again in the future.

Advantages of the variable approach are:

- **More useful for CVP analysis**. Variable costing statements provide data that are immediately useful for CVP analysis because fixed and variable overhead are separate items. Computations from financial statements prepared with absorption costing need computations to break out the fixed and variable costs from the product costs.
- **Income is not affected by changes in production volume**. Fixed overhead is treated as a period cost and does not vary as the volume of inventory changes. This results in income increasing in proportion to sales, which may not happen under absorption costing. Under absorption costing, the fixed overhead assigned to a cost changes as the volume changes. Therefore, the reported net income changes with production, since fixed costs are spread across the changing number of units. This can distort the income picture and may even result in income moving in an opposite direction from sales.
- **Understandability**. Managers may find it easier to understand variable costing reports because overhead changes with the cost driver.

- **Fixed costs are more visible.** Variable costing emphasizes the impact fixed costs have on income. The total amount of fixed costs for the period is reported after gross profit. This emphasizes the direct impact fixed costs have on net income, whereas in absorption costing, fixed costs are included as product costs and thus are part of cost of goods sold, which is a determinant of gross profit.
- **Margins are less distorted.** Gross margins are not distorted by the allocation of common fixed costs. This facilitates appraisal of the profitability of products, customers, and business segments. **Common fixed costs**, sometimes called allocated fixed costs, are costs of the organization that are shared by the various revenue-generating components of the business, such as divisions. Examples of these costs include the chief executive officer (CEO) salary and corporate headquarter costs, such as rent and insurance. These overhead costs are typically allocated to various components of the organization, such as divisions or production facilities. This is necessary, because these costs are needed for doing business but are generated by a part of the company that does not directly generate revenues to offset these costs. The company's revenues are generated by the goods that are produced and sold by the various divisions of the company.
- **Control is facilitated.** Variable costing considers only variable production costs and facilitates the use of control mechanisms such as flexible budgets that are based on differing levels of production and therefore designed around variable costs, since fixed costs do not change within a relevant range of production.
- **Incremental analysis is more straightforward.** Variable cost corresponds closely with the current out-of-pocket expenditure necessary to manufacture goods and can therefore be used more readily in incremental analysis.

While the variable cost method helps management make decisions, especially when the number of units in ending inventory fluctuates, there are some disadvantages:

- **Financial reporting.** The variable cost method is not acceptable for financial reporting under GAAP. GAAP requires expenses to be recognized in the same period as the related revenue, and the variable method expenses fixed overhead as a period cost regardless of how much inventory remains.
- **Tax reporting.** Tax laws in the United States and many other countries do not allow variable costing and require absorption costing.

Advantages and Disadvantages of the Absorption Costing Method

Under the absorption costing method, all costs of production, whether fixed or variable, are considered product costs. This means that absorption costing allocates a portion of fixed manufacturing overhead to each product.

Advocates of absorption costing argue that fixed manufacturing overhead costs are essential to the production process and are an actual cost of the product. They further argue that costs should be categorized by function rather than by behavior, and these costs must be included as a product cost regardless of whether the cost is fixed or variable.

The advantages of absorption costing include:

- **Product cost.** Absorption costing includes fixed overhead as part of the inventory cost, and it is expensed as cost of goods sold when inventory is sold. This represents a more complete list of costs involved in producing a product.
- **Financial reporting.** Absorption costing is the acceptable reporting method under GAAP.
- **Tax reporting.** Absorption costing is the method required for tax preparation in the United States and

many other countries.

While financial and tax reporting are the main advantages of absorption costing, there is one distinct disadvantage:

- **Difficulty in understanding.** The absorption costing method does not list the incremental fixed overhead costs and is more difficult to understand and analyze as compared to variable costing.

ETHICAL CONSIDERATIONS

Cost Accounting for Ethical Business Managers

An ethical and evenhanded approach to providing clear and informative financial information regarding costing is the goal of the ethical accountant. Ethical business managers understand the benefits of using the appropriate costing systems and methods. The accountant's entire business organization needs to understand that the costing system is created to provide efficiency in assisting in making business decisions. Determining the appropriate costing system and the type of information to be provided to management goes beyond providing just accounting information. The costing system should provide the organization's management with factual and true financial information regarding the organization's operations and the performance of the organization. Unethical business managers can game the costing system by unfairly or unscrupulously influencing the outcome of the costing system's reports.

Comparing the Operating Income Statements for Both Methods Assuming No Ending Inventory in the First Year, and the Existence of Ending Inventory in the Second Year

In order to understand how to prepare income statements using both methods, consider a scenario in which a company has no ending inventory in the first year but does have ending inventory in the second year. Outdoor Nation, a manufacturer of residential, tabletop propane heaters, wants to determine whether absorption costing or variable costing is better for internal decision-making. It manufactures 5,000 units annually and sells them for $15 per unit. The total of direct material, direct labor, and variable overhead is $5 per unit with an additional $1 in variable sales cost paid when the units are sold. Additionally, fixed overhead is $15,000 per year, and fixed sales and administrative expenses are $21,000 per year.

Production is estimated to hold steady at 5,000 units per year, while sales estimates are projected to be 5,000 units in year 1; 4,000 units in year 2; and 6,000 in year 3.

Under absorption costing, the ending inventory costs include all manufacturing costs, including overhead. If fixed overhead is $15,000 per year and 5,000 units are manufactured each year, the fixed overhead per unit is $3:

$$\frac{\$15{,}000}{5{,}000 \text{ units}} = \$3 \text{ per unit}$$

The projected income statement using absorption costing is shown in Figure 6.15:

	Year 1	Year 2	Year 3
Sales	$75,000	$60,000	$90,000
Cost of Goods Sold			
Beginning Inventory	0	0	8,000
+ Cost of Goods Manufactured			
Direct Material, Labor, and Overhead			
(5,000 units × $5 per unit)	25,000	25,000	25,000
Fixed Manufacturing Overhead	15,000	15,000	15,000
Cost of Goods Available for Sale	40,000	40,000	48,000
– Ending Inventory	0	8,000	0
Cost of Goods Sold	40,000	32,000	48,000
Gross Margin	35,000	28,000	42,000
– Sales and Administrative Expenses			
Fixed Sales and Administration Expenses	21,000	21,000	21,000
Variable Sales and Administration Expenses	5,000	4,000	6,000
Net Income	$ 9,000	$ 3,000	$15,000

Figure 6.15 Outdoor Nation's Income Statement Using Absorption Costing. (attribution: Copyright Rice University, OpenStax, under CC BY-NC-SA 4.0 license)

In variable costing, the fixed overhead is not included in the cost of goods sold even if it relates to manufacturing. As a result, the net income under variable costing differs from absorption costing by the same amount as inventory differential. The projected income under variable costing is shown in Figure 6.16:

	Year 1	Year 2	Year 3
Sales	$75,000	$60,000	$90,000
– Variable Expenses			
Beginning Inventory	0	0	5,000
+ Variable Manufacturing Overhead	25,000	25,000	25,000
Cost of Goods Available for Sale	25,000	25,000	30,000
– Ending Inventory	0	5,000	0
Variable Cost to Manufacturing	25,000	20,000	30,000
Variable Selling and Administrative Expenses	5,000	4,000	6,000
Cost of Goods Sold	30,000	24,000	36,000
Contribution Margin	45,000	36,000	54,000
– Fixed Expenses			
Fixed Overhead Expenses	15,000	15,000	15,000
Fixed Sales and Administration Expenses	21,000	21,000	21,000
Net Income	$ 9,000	$ 0	$18,000

Figure 6.16 Outdoor Nation's Income Statement Using Variable Costing. (attribution: Copyright Rice University, OpenStax, under CC BY-NC-SA 4.0 license)

The difference between the methods is attributable to the fixed overhead. Therefore, the methods can be reconciled with each other, as shown in Figure 6.17.

Reconciliation	Year 1	Year 2	Year 3
Income under Variable Costing	$9,000	$ 0	$18,000
+ Fixed Manufacturing Overhead in Ending Inventory	0	3,000	0
− Fixed Manufacturing Overhead in Beginning Inventory	0	0	3,000
Income under Absorption	$9,000	$3,000	$15,000

Figure 6.17 Outdoor Nation's Reconciliation of Net Incomes. (attribution: Copyright Rice University, OpenStax, under CC BY-NC-SA 4.0 license)

Each method results in different amounts for net income when the inventory amounts change. More specifically, the effects on income are:

- **Sales and Production equal.** When a company sells the same quantity of products produced during the period, the resulting net income will be identical whether absorption costing or variable costing is used. When sales equals production, all manufacturing costs are accounted for in net income, and none of the costs are waiting in finished goods inventory to be recognized in a future period. Remember, with absorption costing, all manufacturing costs are added to the cost of the product during the work in process phase; thus, as the goods are sold, all costs have been accounted for. With variable costing, only the variable costs or production are added to the cost of the product during the work in process phase, and the fixed costs are expensed in the period in which they are incurred. Thus, in the example where sales and production are equal, all costs have been accounted for since all of the produced inventory has moved through cost of goods sold. This means that net income under absorption costing would be the same as net income under variable costing.
- **Sales less than Production.** When a company produces more than it sells, net income will be less under variable costing than under absorption costing. In this scenario, there will be a buildup, or an increase, in inventory from the beginning of the period to the end of the period. Under variable costing, fixed manufacturing costs are still in the finished goods inventory account. But under absorption costing, those fixed costs have been expensed during the current production period and thus have reduced net income.
- **Sales greater than Production.** When a company sells more than it produces during the current period, this indicates it is selling goods produced in a prior period. This will result in net income under variable costing being greater than under absorption costing. With absorption costing, all manufacturing costs are captured in the finished goods inventory account, and as those goods are sold, those costs become expenses. Selling items that were produced in a prior period defers the recognition of the costs of those products until the future period in which they are sold. Variable costing results in all of the variable costs associated with the sold products being in the current period net income, but only the current period fixed expenses would be included in the current period net income. The fixed expenses associated with the items produced in a prior period were recognized in the period in which they were incurred, not the period in which the products are sold. This results in fewer expenses and therefore greater income with the variable cost method.
- **Effect of differences in Sales and Production Long Term.** The differences between net income generated under absorption costing and variable costing will be almost zero over the long run, as all costs associated with the production of goods will eventually be recognized in net income. The use of absorption versus variable costing creates more of a timing issue for the recognition of fixed expenses, and this is why net income would vary from period to period under the two methods but in the long run would not. In addition, absorption costing does allow for manipulation of income by managers through

overproduction. Increasing production at year-end results in a higher net income than if the additional goods had not been produced, since increasing the number of units decreases the fixed cost per unit. Under absorption costing, these fixed costs follow the units produced and do not become a part of cost of goods sold until they are sold. Instead, a portion of the fixed costs is in the inventory accounts. Why would a manager want to manipulate income by overproducing? If the manager's annual bonus or other compensation is linked to net income, then the manager may be motivated to overproduce in order to increase the potential for or the amount of a bonus. If the level of sales remain constant while manipulating the production level, such an action would increase the company's expenses (including the amount of bonus) while not increasing its revenue. Barring any other justification for the increase in production, such an action by the manager would typically be considered an ethical violation, since the manager's actions would be in the manager's best interests, but contrary to the best interests of the company.

LINK TO LEARNING

Absorption costing is not as well understood as variable costing because of its financial statement limitations. But understanding how it can help management make decisions is very important. See the Strategic CFO forum on Absorption Cost Accounting that helps managers understand its uses (https://openstax.org/l/50Absorption) to learn more.

Key Terms

absorption costing (also, full costing) system of accounting where all costs are treated as product costs regardless of whether they are variable or fixed

activity base activity that has been considered to be a primary driver of overhead costs and for which, traditionally, direct labor hours or machine hours were used

activity-based costing process of assigning overhead to products based on the cost driver for each activity cost pool

batch-level cost one that is incurred when a group (or batch) of items is produced

common fixed costs expenses that are shared among all divisions or production units and include such costs as the CEO salary and corporate headquarter costs

cost driver activity that is the reason for the increase or decrease of another cost; examples include labor hours incurred, labor costs paid, amounts of materials used in production, units produced, or any other activity that has a cause-and-effect relationship with incurred costs

cost pool accumulation of costs that are incurred during the production of the activities included in the activity cost pool

direct labor labor directly related to the manufacturing of the product or the production of a service

direct materials materials used in the manufacturing process that can be traced directly to the product

expense recognition principle (also, matching principle) matches expenses with associated revenues in the period in which the revenues were generated

factory-level cost one that is incurred when production occurs, such as production supervisor salary

indirect labor labor not directly involved in the active conversion of materials into finished products or the provision of services

indirect materials materials used in production but not efficiently traceable to a specific unit of production

manufacturing overhead costs all manufacturing costs excluding direct material and direct labor

product-level cost one that occurs as support of the product, such as engineering

traditional allocation allocation of factory overhead to products based on the volume of production resources consumed

unit-level cost one that is incurred for each unit produced

variable costing (also, *direct costing* or *marginal costing*) system of accounting where only variable costs are treated as product costs

Summary

6.1 Calculate Predetermined Overhead and Total Cost under the Traditional Allocation Method
- Manufacturing overhead is estimated for the upcoming period.
- An activity base is selected to allocate overhead. This is traditionally direct labor hours, direct labor cost, or machine hours.
- A predetermined overhead rate is calculated by dividing the estimated overhead by the allocation base.
- Overhead is allocated to each product based on the estimated predetermined overhead rate and the number of units in the selected activity base.

6.2 Describe and Identify Cost Drivers
- Overhead costs are analyzed and grouped based on similar activity bases. A cost driver, such as inspections, machine setups, or order taking, is selected for each cost grouping.

- Analysis of cost drivers allows for better selection of true overhead cost drivers and more appropriate allocation of overhead.

6.3 Calculate Activity-Based Product Costs
- Costs can be traced to the unit level or batch level.
- There are five steps in the ABC process:
  - identify activities needed for production
  - assign overhead expenses
  - assign a cost driver for each expense
  - determine a predetermined overhead rate
  - allocate overhead to each product

6.4 Compare and Contrast Traditional and Activity-Based Costing Systems
- Traditional allocation assigns overhead based on a single overhead rate, while ABC assigns overhead based on several cost pools and the activities that drive costs.
- Traditional allocation is optimal when the manufacturing process is labor driven and overhead increases based on traditional activity bases, such as direct labor hours, direct labor dollars, or machine hours.
- ABC costing is optimal when the manufacturing process is technology driven and overhead increases based on various activities that differ for each product.

6.5 Compare and Contrast Variable and Absorption Costing
- Absorption costing assigns all manufacturing costs to products, whereas variable costing only assigns variable costs to the products.
- Income statements from both methods can be reconciled by starting with the net income or loss using variable costing and adding the amount of fixed costs included in ending inventory and subtracting the fixed costs included in beginning inventory.
- Variable costing is not considered GAAP compliant but lends itself to cost-volume-profit analysis.

Multiple Choice

1. LO 6.1 Active Frame, Inc., manufactures clear and tinted sport glasses. The manufacturing of clear glasses takes 45,000 direct labor hours and involves 1,700 parts and 115 inspections. The manufacturing of tinted glasses takes 115,000 direct labor hours and involves 1,400 parts and 450 inspections. The traditional method applies $560,000 of overhead on the basis of direct labor hours. What is the amount of overhead per direct labor hour applied to the clear glass products?
   A. $933.33
   B. $157,500
   C. $322.500
   D. $402,500

2. **LO 6.1** TyeDye Lights makes two products: Party and Holiday. It takes 80,900 direct labor hours to manufacture the Party Line and 93,500 direct labor hours to manufacture the Holiday Line. Overhead consists of $225,000 in the machine setup cost pool and $149,960 in the packaging cost pool. The machine setup pool has 52,000 setups for the Party product and 98,000 setups for the Holiday product. The packaging cost pool has 26,000 parts in the Party product and 39,200 parts for the Holiday product. Using the traditional cost method of direct labor hours, what is the predetermined overhead rate?
   A. $1.50 per direct labor hour
   B. $2.15 per direct labor hour
   C. $2.30 per direct labor hour
   D. $3.80 per direct labor hour

3. **LO 6.2** Which is *not* a step in analyzing the cost driver for manufacturing overhead?
   A. identify the cost
   B. identify non-value-added costs
   C. analyze the effect on manufacturing overhead
   D. identify the correlation between the potential driver and manufacturing overhead

4. **LO 6.2** Overhead costs are assigned to each product based on _____.
   A. the proportion of that product's use of the cost driver
   B. a predetermined overhead rate for a single cost driver
   C. price of the product
   D. machine hours per product

5. **LO 6.3** Which of the following is a reason a company would implement activity-based costing?
   A. The cost of record keeping is high.
   B. The additional data obtained through traditional allocation are not worth the cost.
   C. They want to improve the data on which decisions are made.
   D. A company only has one cost driver.

6. **LO 6.3** Which is the correct formula for computing the overhead rate?
   A. estimated use of the cost driver for production/estimated overhead for the activity
   B. estimated overhead for the product/estimated use of the cost driver for the activity
   C. estimated use of the cost driver for production/estimated overhead for the activity
   D. estimated overhead for the activity/estimated use of the cost driver for the activity

7. **LO 6.3** A company anticipates the cost to heat the building will be $21,000. Product A takes up 500 square feet of space, while Product B takes up 200 square feet. The activity rate per product using activity-based costing would be which of the following?
   A. $30/square foot
   B. $4.20/square foot
   C. $11/square foot
   D. $15.20/square foot

8. **LO 6.3** A company calculated the predetermined overhead based on an estimated overhead of $70,000, and the activity for the cost driver was estimated as 2,500 hours. If product A utilized 1,350 hours and product B utilized 1,100 hours, what was the total amount of overhead assigned to the products?
   A. $35,000
   B. $30,800
   C. $37,800
   D. $68,600

9. LO 6.3 Which is *not* a step in activity-based costing?
   A. identify the activities performed by the organization
   B. identify the cost driver(s) associated with each activity
   C. compute a cost rate per production
   D. assign costs to products by multiplying the cost driver rate by the volume of the cost driver units consumed by the product

10. LO 6.3 What is the proper order of tasks in an ABC system?
   A. identify the cost drivers, assign the costs to the products, calculate the overhead application rate for each cost pool, identify the cost pools
   B. assign the costs to the products, identify the cost drivers, calculate the overhead application rate for each cost pool, identify the cost pools
   C. identify the cost drivers, identify the cost pools, calculate the overhead application rate for each cost pool, assign the costs to the products
   D. identify the cost pools, identify the cost drivers, calculate the overhead application rate for each cost pool, assign the costs to the products

11. LO 6.3 Which is not a task typically associated with ABC systems?
   A. calculating the overhead application rate for each cost pool
   B. applying a single cost rate
   C. identifying a cost driver
   D. more correctly allocating overhead costs

12. LO 6.4 Which statement is correct?
   A. Activity-based cost systems are less costly than traditional cost systems.
   B. Activity-based cost systems are easier to implement than traditional cost systems.
   C. Activity-based cost systems are more accurate than traditional cost systems.
   D. Activity-based cost systems provide the same data as traditional cost systems.

13. LO 6.4 Activity-based costing systems:
   A. use a single predetermined overhead rate based on machine hours instead of on direct labor
   B. frequently increase the overhead allocation to at least one product while decreasing the overhead allocation to at least one other product
   C. limit the number of cost pools
   D. always result in an increase of at least one product's selling price

14. LO 6.4 Activity-based costing is preferable in a system:
   A. when multiple products have similar product volumes and costs
   B. with a large direct labor cost as a percentage of the total product cost
   C. with multiple, diverse products
   D. where management needs to support an increase in sales price

15. LO 6.5 Absorption costing is also referred to as:
   A. direct costing
   B. marginal costing
   C. full costing
   D. variable costing

16. LO 6.5 Under variable costing, a unit of product includes which costs?
   A. direct material, direct labor, and manufacturing overhead
   B. direct material, direct labor, and variable manufacturing overhead
   C. direct material, direct labor, and fixed manufacturing overhead
   D. direct material, direct labor, and all variable manufacturing overhead

17. LO 6.5 Under absorption costing, a unit of product includes which costs?
   A. direct material, direct labor, and manufacturing overhead
   B. direct material, direct labor, and variable manufacturing overhead
   C. direct material, direct labor, and fixed manufacturing overhead
   D. direct material, direct labor, and all variable manufacturing overhead

18. LO 6.5 A downside to absorption costing is:
   A. not including fixed manufacturing overhead in the cost of the product
   B. that it is not really useful for managerial decisions
   C. that it is not allowable under GAAP
   D. that it is not well designed for cost-volume-profit analysis

19. LO 6.5 When the number of units in ending inventory increases through the year, which of the following is true?
   A. Net income is the same for variable and absorption costing.
   B. Net income is higher for variable costing than for absorption costing.
   C. Net income is higher for absorption costing than for variable costing.
   D. There is no relationship between net income and the costing method.

20. LO 6.5 Product costs under variable costing are typically:
   A. higher than under absorption costing
   B. lower than under absorption costing
   C. the same as with absorption costing
   D. higher than absorption costing when inventory increases

Questions

1. LO 6.1 What is the predetermined overhead rate, and when is it typically estimated?

2. LO 6.1 LO 6.3 When is an activity-based costing system better than a traditional allocation system?

3. LO 6.2 What is the advantage of labeling activities as value added or nonvalue added?

4. LO 6.2 What conditions are necessary to designate an activity as a cost driver?

5. LO 6.2 For each cost pool, identify an appropriate cost driver.
   A. order department
   B. accounts receivable processing
   C. catering
   D. raw material inventory

6. LO 6.3 How is the primary focus of activity-based costing different from that of traditional allocation?

7. LO 6.3 What are the primary differences between traditional and activity-based costing?

8. LO 6.3 How are service companies similar or different from manufacturing companies in using ABC costing?

9. LO 6.3 How are costs allocated in an ABC system?

10. LO 6.4 In production, what has changed to allow ABC costing to become valuable?

11. LO 6.4 Why is it important to know the true cost for a product or service?

12. LO 6.5 What is the primary difference between variable costing and absorption costing?

13. LO 6.5 Why would managers prefer variable costing over absorption costing?

14. LO 6.5 Why is absorption costing the method allowable for GAAP?

15. LO 6.5 Can a company gather information for both variable and absorption costing systems?

Exercise Set A

EA1. LO 6.1 Steeler Towel Company estimates its overhead to be $250,000. It expects to have 100,000 direct labor hours costing $2,500,000 in labor and utilizing 12,500 machine hours. Calculate the predetermined overhead rate using:
  A. Direct labor hours
  B. Direct labor dollars
  C. Machine hours

EA2. LO 6.1 Crystal Pools estimates overhead will utilize 250,000 machine hours and cost $750,000. It takes 2 machine hours per unit, direct material cost of $14 per unit, and direct labor of $20 per unit. What is the cost of each unit produced?

EA3. LO 6.1 A company estimated 100,000 direct labor hours and $800,000 in overhead. The actual overhead was $805,100, and there were 99,900 direct labor hours. What is the predetermined overhead rate, and how much was applied during the year?

EA4. LO 6.1 Cozy, Inc., manufactures small and large blankets. It estimates $350,000 in overhead during the manufacturing of 75,000 small blankets and 25,000 large blankets. What is the predetermined overhead rate if a small blanket takes 1 machine hour and a large blanket takes 2 machine hours?

EA5. LO 6.2 Identify appropriate cost drivers for these cost pools:
  A. setup cost pools
  B. assembly cost pool
  C. supervising cost pool
  D. testing cost pool

EA6. LO 6.2 Match the activity with the most appropriate cost driver.

Activities and Cost Drivers

Activity	Cost Driver
Fringe benefits	Square feet
Electricity	Direct labor hours
Depreciation	Machine hours
Machine maintenance	
Heat and air conditioning	

Table 6.5

EA7. LO 6.3 Rex Industries has two products. They manufactured 12,539 units of product A and 8,254 units of product B. The data are:

Activity in Cost Pool	Estimated Overhead	Product A	Product B
1	$45,900	1,000	500
2	67,300	200	800
3	25,200	600	5,400

What is the activity rate for each cost pool?

EA8. LO 6.3 Rex Industries has identified three different activities as cost drivers: machine setups, machine hours, and inspections. The overhead and estimated usage are:

Activity	Overhead per Activity	Annual Usage
Machine setups	$155,000	4,000
Machine hours	352,800	14,112
Inspections	120,750	3,500

Compute the overhead rate for each activity.

EA9. LO 6.3 Custom's makes two types of hats: polyester (poly) and silk. There are two cost pools: setup, with an estimated $100,000 in overhead, and inspection, with $25,000 in overhead. Poly is estimated to have 750,000 setups and 170,000 inspections, while silk has 250,000 setups and 80,000 inspections. How much overhead is applied to each product?

EA10. LO 6.3 Custom's has three cost pools and an associated cost driver to allocate the costs to the product. The cost pools, cost driver, estimated overhead, and estimated activity for the cost pool are:

Cost Pool	Cost Driver	Estimated Activity per Driver	Estimated Overhead
Material	Material requisitions	14,000	$ 52,500
Machining	Machine hours	186,400	363,500
Inspection	Number of inspections	10,000	75,000

What is the predetermined overhead rate for each activity?

EA11. LO 6.3 Potterii sells its products to large box stores and recently added a retail line of products to sell directly to consumers. These estimates are to be used in determining the overhead allocation rate for ABC:

Cost Pool	Cost Driver	Estimated Overhead	Wholesale	Retail
Ordering	Number of orders	$120,000	180,000	60,000
Machine setups	Number of setups	85,000	200,000	140,000
Inspection	Number of inspections	75,000	60,000	15,000

What would be the predetermined rate for each cost pool?

EA12. LO 6.3 Assign each of the following expenses to either the machine setup cost pool or the factory cost pool:
  A. indirect materials
  B. inspections
  C. factory insurance
  D. machine depreciation
  E. machine setup (indirect labor)
  F. machine setup (indirect material)

EA13. LO 6.4 Tri-bikes manufactures two different levels of bicycles: the Standard and the Extreme. The total overhead of $300,000 has traditionally been allocated by direct labor hours, with 150,000 hours for the Standard and 50,000 hours for the Extreme. After analyzing and assigning costs to two cost pools, it was determined that machine hours is estimated to have $200,000 of overhead, with 4,000 hours used on the Standard product and 1,000 hours used on the Extreme product. It was also estimated that the setup cost pool would have $100,000 of overhead, with 1,000 hours for the Standard and 1,500 hours for the Extreme. What is the overhead rate per product, under traditional and under ABC costing?

EA14. LO 6.5 Cool Pool has these costs associated with production of 20,000 units of accessory products: direct materials, $70; direct labor, $110; variable manufacturing overhead, $45; total fixed manufacturing overhead, $800,000. What is the cost per unit under both the variable and absorption methods?

EA15. LO 6.5 Using this information from Planters, Inc., what is the cost per unit under both variable and absorption costing?

Production	10,000
Direct materials	$ 240
Direct labor	280
Variable manufacturing overhead	100
Fixed manufacturing overhead	1,200,000

Exercise Set B

EB1. LO 6.1 Green Bay Cheese Company estimates its overhead to be $375,000. It expects to have 125,000 direct labor hours costing $1,500,000 in labor and utilizing 15,000 machine hours. Calculate the predetermined overhead rate using:
  A. Direct labor hours
  B. Direct labor dollars
  C. Machine hours

EB2. LO 6.1 Boarders estimates overhead will utilize 160,000 machine hours and cost $80,000. It takes 4 machine hours per unit, direct material cost of $5 per unit, and direct labor of $5 per unit. What is the cost of each unit produced?

EB3. LO 6.1 A company estimated 50,000 direct labor hours and $450,000 in overhead. The actual overhead was $445,000, and there were 50,500 direct labor hours. What is the predetermined overhead rate, and how much was applied during the year?

EB4. LO 6.1 Cozy, Inc., manufactures small and large blankets. It estimates $950,000 in overhead during the manufacturing of 360,000 small blankets and 120,000 large blankets. What is the predetermined overhead rate if a small blanket takes 2 hours of direct labor and a large blanket takes 3 hours of direct labor?

EB5. LO 6.2 Identify appropriate cost drivers for these cost pools:
  A. material cost pool
  B. machine cost pool
  C. painting cost pool
  D. maintenance cost pool

EB6. LO 6.2 Match the activity with the most appropriate cost driver.

Activities and Cost Drivers

Activity	Cost Driver
Factory maintenance	Number of setups
Payroll tax	Number of employees
Rent	Square feet
Machine setups	Direct labor hours
Factory supervision	

Table 6.6

EB7. LO 6.3 Rocks Industries has two products. They manufactured 12,539 units of product A and 8,254 units of product B. The data are:

Cost Pool	Estimated Overhead	Product A	Product B
1	$32,400	1,500	3,000
2	54,900	1,700	1,300
3	51,385	1,390	1,000

What is the activity rate for each cost pool?

EB8. LO 6.3 Rocks Industries has identified three different activities as cost drivers: machine setups, machine hours, and inspections. The overhead and estimated usage are:

Activity	Overhead per Activity	Annual Usage
Machine setups	$75,000	6,000
Machine hours	$85,002	5,484
Inspections	70,000	20,000

Compute the overhead rate for each activity.

EB9. LO 6.3 Frenchy's makes two types of scarves: polyester (poly) and silk. There are two cost pools: setup, with an estimated $120,000 in overhead, and inspection, with $30,000 in overhead. Poly is estimated to have 800,000 setups and 450,000 inspections, while silk has 400,000 setups and 150,000 inspections. How much overhead is applied to each product?

EB10. LO 6.3 Frenchy's has three cost pools and an associated cost driver to allocate the costs to the product. The cost pools, cost driver, estimated overhead, and estimated activity for the cost pool are:

Cost Pool	Cost Driver	Estimated Activity per Driver	Estimated Overhead
Material	Material requisitions	250,000	$105,000
Machining	Machine hours	360,750	432,900
Inspection	Number of inspections	25,000	15,750

What is the predetermined overhead rate for each activity?

EB11. LO 6.3 Carboni recently added a carbon line in addition to its aluminum line. The following are estimates to be used in determining the overhead allocation rate for ABC.

Cost Pool	Cost Driver	Estimated Overhead	Carbon	Aluminum
Material handling	Material requisitions	$45,000	120,000	60,000
Machine setups	Number of setups	55,000	80,000	30,000
Assembly	Number of parts	25,000	35,000	15,000

What would be the predetermined rate for each cost pool?

EB12. LO 6.3 Assign each of the following expenses to either the machine cost pool or the factory cost pool:
A. property taxes
B. heat and air-conditioning
C. electricity, machines
D. plant depreciation
E. electricity, plant
F. machine maintenance wages

EB13. LO 6.4 Stacks manufactures two different levels of hockey sticks: the Standard and the Slap Shot. The total overhead of $600,000 has traditionally been allocated by direct labor hours, with 400,000 hours for the Standard and 200,000 hours for the Slap Shot. After analyzing and assigning costs to two cost pools, it was determined that machine hours is estimated to have $450,000 of overhead, with 30,000 hours used on the Standard product and 15,000 hours used on the Slap Shot product. It was also estimated that the inspection cost pool would have $150,000 of overhead, with 25,000 hours for the Standard and 5,000 hours for the Slap Shot. What is the overhead rate per product, under traditional and under ABC costing?

EB14. LO 6.5 Crafts 4 All has these costs associated with production of 12,000 units of accessory products: direct materials, $19; direct labor, $30; variable manufacturing overhead, $15; total fixed manufacturing overhead, $450,000. What is the cost per unit under both the variable and absorption methods?

EB15. LO 6.5 Using this information from Outdoor Grills, what is the cost per unit under both variable and absorption costing?

Production	90,000
Direct materials	$ 110
Direct labor	150
Variable manufacturing overhead	75
Fixed manufacturing overhead	2,700,000

Problem Set A

PA1. LO 6.1 Colonels uses a traditional cost system and estimates next year's overhead will be $480,000, with the estimated cost driver of 240,000 direct labor hours. It manufactures three products and estimates these costs:

	Small	Medium	Large
Units	32,000	12,000	4,000
Direct Material Cost	$ 5	$ 8	$ 9
Direct Labor Hours per Unit	4	6	10

If the labor rate is $25 per hour, what is the per-unit cost of each product?

PA2. LO 6.1 Five Card Draw manufactures and sells 24,000 units of Diamonds, which retails for $180, and 27,000 units of Clubs, which retails for $190. The direct materials cost is $25 per unit of Diamonds and $30 per unit of Clubs. The labor rate is $25 per hour, and Five Card Draw estimated 180,000 direct labor hours. It takes 3 direct labor hours to manufacture Diamonds and 4 hours for Clubs. The total estimated overhead is $720,000. Five Card Draw uses the traditional allocation method based on direct labor hours.
  A. What is the gross profit per unit for Diamonds and Clubs?
  B. What is the total gross profit for the year?

PA3. LO 6.2 A local picnic table manufacturer has budgeted these overhead costs:

Purchasing	$70,000
Handling materials	33,333
Machine setups	70,500
Inspections	25,500
Utilities	45,000

They are considering adapting ABC costing and have estimated the cost drivers for each pool as shown:

Cost Driver	Activity
Orders	700
Material moves	1,334
Machine setups	15,000
Number of inspections	5,000
Square feet	180,000

Recent success has yielded an order for 1,000 tables. Assume direct labor costs per hour of $20. Determine how much the job would cost given the following activities:

	Activity
Order (units)	1,000
Direct materials	112,700
Machine hours	15,200
Direct labor hours	5,300
Number of purchase orders	60
Number of material moves	800
Number of machine setups	100
Number of inspections	450
Number of square feet occupied	8,000

PA4. LO 6.2 Explain how each activity in this list can be associated with the corresponding unit or batch level provided.

A. Assembling products: unit level
B. Issuing raw materials: batch level
C. Machine setup: batch level
D. Inspection: unit level
E. Loading the labeling machine: batch level
F. Equipment maintenance: batch level
G. Printing a banner: unit level
H. Moving material: batch level
I. Ordering a part: batch level

PA5. LO 6.3 Medical Tape makes two products: Generic and Label. It estimates it will produce 423,694 units of Generic and 652,200 of Label, and the overhead for each of its cost pools is as follows:

Cost pool	Estimated Overhead
Material receipts	$ 133,000
Machine setups	300,000
Assembly	700,000
Inspection	250,000
Total	$1,383,000

It has also estimated the activities for each cost driver as follows:

Driver	Generic	Label
Inspections	400	600
Requisitions	450	950
Parts	300	400
Setups	250	350

How much is the overhead allocated to each unit of Generic and Label?

PA6. LO 6.3 Box Springs, Inc., makes two sizes of box springs: twin and double. The direct material for the twin is $25 per unit and $40 is used in direct labor, while the direct material for the double is $40 per unit, and the labor cost is $50 per unit. Box Springs estimates it will make 5,000 twins and 9,000 doubles in the next year. It estimates the overhead for each cost pool and cost driver activities as follows:

Activity Cost Pools	Driver	Estimated Overhead	Use per Twin	Use per Double
Framing	Square feet of pine	210,000	5,000	2,000
Padding	Square feet of quilting	220,000	120,000	100,000
Filling	Square feet of filling	320,000	500,000	300,000
Labeling	Number of boxes	240,000	800,000	400,000
Inspection	Number of inspections	170,000	12,000	5,000

How much does each unit cost to manufacture?

PA7. LO 6.3 Please use the information from this problem for these calculations. After grouping cost pools and estimating overhead and activities, Box Springs determined these rates:

Purchasing (per order)	$55
Utilities (per square foot)	3
Machine setups (per machine hour)	8
Supervision (per direct labor hour)	5

It estimates there will be five orders in the next year, and those jobs will involve:

Orders	5
Square feet	200
Machine hours	50
Direct labor hours	35
Direct materials	1,500
Direct labor rate	$ 25

What is the total cost of the jobs?

PA8. LO 6.4 A company has traditionally allocated its overhead based on machine hours but had collected this information to change to activity-based costing:

	Estimated Activity		
Activity Center	Product 1	Product 2	Estimated Cost
Machine setups	15	45	$ 10,800
Assembly parts	3,000	3,000	144,600
Packaging pieces	500	400	55,350
Machine hour per unit	4	3	
Production volume	750	1,500	

A. How much overhead would be allocated to each unit under the traditional allocation method?
B. How much overhead would be allocated to each unit under activity-based costing?

PA9. LO 6.4 Carlton's Kitchens makes two types of pasta makers: Strands and Shapes. The company expects to manufacture 70,000 units of Strands, which has a per-unit direct material cost of $10 and a per-unit direct labor cost of $60. It also expects to manufacture 30,000 units of Shapes, which has a per-unit material cost of $15 and a per-unit direct labor cost of $40. It is estimated that Strands will use 140,000 machine hours and Shapes will require 60,000 machine hours. Historically, the company has used the traditional allocation method and applied overhead at a rate of $21 per machine hour. It was determined that there were three cost pools, and the overhead for each cost pool is shown:

Machine setups	$ 900,000
Machine processing	4,000,000
Material requisitions	100,000
Total overhead	$4,190,000

The cost driver for each cost pool and its expected activity is shown:

	Strands	Shapes	Total
Machine setups	100	200	300
Machine hours	140,000	60,000	200,000
Parts requisitions	80	120	200

A. What is the per-unit cost for each product under the traditional allocation method?
B. What is the per-unit cost for each product under ABC costing?

PA10. LO 6.4 Carlton's Kitchen's three cost pools and overhead estimates are as follows:

Activity Cost Pool	Cost Driver	Estimated Overhead	Use per Product A	Use per Product B
Machine setups	Setups	$128,000	5,000	3,000
Assembly	Number of parts	105,000	25,000	45,000
Machine maintenance	Machine hours	150,000	12,500	37,500

Compare the overhead allocation using:

A. The traditional allocation method
B. The activity-based costing method

(Hint: the traditional method uses machine hours as the allocation base.)

PA11. LO 6.4 Lampierre makes brass and gold frames. The company computed this information to decide whether to switch from the traditional allocation method to ABC:

	Brass	Gold
Units planned	750	125
Material moves	400	100
Machine setups	400	600
Direct labor hours	700	1,200

The estimated overhead for the material cost pool is estimated as $12,500, and the estimate for the machine setup pool is $35,000. Calculate the allocation rate per unit of brass and per unit of gold using:

A. The traditional allocation method
B. The activity-based costing method

PA12. LO 6.4 Portable Seats makes two chairs: folding and wooden. This information was obtained to review the decision to consider ABC:

	Folding Chairs	Wooden Chairs	Total Cost
Material requisitions	500*	200*	$55,000
Inspections	150	50	25,000
Labor hours	2,600	2,400	

*lbs

Compute the overhead assigned to each product under:

A. The traditional allocation method
B. The activity-based costing method

PA13. LO 6.5 Grainger Company produces only one product and sells that product for $100 per unit. Cost information for the product is:

Direct Material	$15 per Unit
Direct Labor	$25 per Unit
Variable Overhead	$5 per Unit
Fixed Overhead	$34,000

Selling expenses are $4 per unit and are all variable. Administrative expenses of $20,000 are all fixed. Grainger produced 5,000 units; sold 4,000; and had no beginning inventory.

A. Compute net income under
   i. absorption costing
   ii. variable costing
B. Reconcile the difference between the income under absorption and variable costing.

PA14. LO 6.5 Summarized data for Walrus Co. for its first year of operations are:

Sales (100,000 units)	$5,000,000
Production costs (120,000 units)	
Direct material	1,800,000
Direct labor	1,500,000
Manufacturing overhead	
Variable	900,000
Fixed	300,000
Selling and administrative expenses	
Variable	260,000
Fixed	440,000

A. Prepare an income statement under absorption costing
B. Prepare an income statement under variable costing

PA15. LO 6.5 Happy Trails has this information for its manufacturing:

Direct Materials	$15
Direct labor	$15
Variable manufacturing overhead	$ 3
Fixed manufacturing overhead	$25
Units produced	27,000
Units sold	19,000

Its income statement under absorption costing is:

Sales	$1,900,500
Beginning Inventory	0
Cost of Goods Manufactured	1,566,000
Cost of Goods Available for Sale	1,566,000
− Ending Inventory	464,000
Cost of Goods Sold	1,102,000
Gross Profit	798,500
− Sales and Administration Expenses	
Variable	133,000
Fixed	300,000
Total Sales and Administration Expenses	433,000
Net Operating Income	$ 365,500

Prepare an income statement with variable costing and a reconciliation statement between both methods.

PA16. LO 6.5 Appliance Apps has the following costs associated with its production and sale of devices that allow appliances to receive commands from cell phones.

Beginning inventory	0
Units produced	25,000
Units sold	20,000
Selling price per unit	$ 145
Variable sales and administration expenses	$ 5
Fixed sales and administration expenses	$975,000
Direct material cost per unit	$ 25
Direct labor cost per unit	$ 11
Variable manufacturing overhead cost per unit	$ 3
Fixed manufacturing overhead cost per month	$980,000

Prepare an income statement under both the absorption and variable costing methods along with a reconciliation between the two statements.

PA17. LO 6.5 This information was collected for the first year of manufacturing for Appliance Apps:

Direct materials per unit	$ 2.50
Direct labor per unit	$ 1.50
Variable manufacturing overhead per unit	$ 0.25
Variable selling and administration expenses	$ 1.75
Units produced	40,000
Units sold	35,000
Sales price	$ 12
Fixed manufacturing expenses	$140,000
Fixed selling and administration expenses	$ 20,000

Prepare an income statement under variable costing, and prepare a reconciliation to the income under the absorption method.

Problem Set B

PB1. LO 6.1 Bobcat uses a traditional cost system and estimates next year's overhead will be $800,000, as driven by the estimated 25,000 direct labor hours. It manufactures three products and estimates the following costs:

	Bobcat	Jaguar	Tiger
Units	250,000	80,000	12,000
Direct Material Cost	$ 13	$ 22	$ 37
Direct Labor Hours per Unit	2	3	5

If the labor rate is $30 per hour, what is the per-unit cost of each product?

PB2. LO 6.1 Five Card Draw manufactures and sells 10,000 units of Aces, which retails for $200, and 8,000 units of Kings, which retails for $170. The direct materials cost is $20 per unit of Aces and $15 per unit of Kings. The labor rate is $30 per hour, and Five Card Draw estimated 64,000 direct labor hours. It takes 4 direct labor hours to manufacture Aces and 3 hours for Kings. The total estimated overhead is $128,000. Five Card Draw uses the traditional allocation method based on direct labor hours.
  A. How much is the gross profit per unit for Aces and Kings?
  B. What is the total gross profit for the year?

PB3. LO 6.2 A local picnic table manufacturer has budgeted the following overhead costs:

	Estimated Overhead
Purchasing	$80,000
Handling materials	45,000
Machine setups	55,000
Assembly	60,000
Utilities	90,000

They are considering adapting ABC costing and have estimated the cost drivers for each pool as shown:

Cost Driver	Activity
Orders	10,000
Material moves	1,500
Machine setups	5,000
Number of parts	5,000
Square feet	60,000

Recent success has yielded an order for 1,500 tables. Determine how much the job would cost given the following activities, and assuming an hourly rate for direct labor of $25 per hour:

	Activity
Order (units)	1,500
Direct materials	75,900
Machine hours	3,310
Direct labor hours	4,590
Number of purchase orders	70
Number of material moves	750
Number of machine setups	85
Number of parts	290
Number of square feet occupied	3,000

PB4. LO 6.2 Explain how each activity in this list can be associated with the corresponding unit or batch level provided.
- A. Assembling products: batch level
- B. Issuing raw materials: unit level
- C. Machine setup: unit level
- D. Inspection: batch level
- E. Loading the labeling machine: unit level
- F. Equipment maintenance: unit level
- G. Printing a banner: batch level
- H. Moving material: unit level
- I. Ordering a part: unit level

PB5. LO 6.3 Wrappers Tape makes two products: Simple and Removable. It estimates it will produce 369,991 units of Simple and 146,100 of Removable, and the overhead for each of its cost pools is as follows:

Cost Pool	Estimated Overhead
Material receipts	$ 249,975
Machine setups	150,000
Assembly	450,000
Machine maintenance	175,000
	$1,024,975

It has also estimated the activities for each cost driver as follows:

Driver	Simple	Removable
Machine hours	2,000	1,500
Requisitions	300	450
Parts	100	200
Setups	150	50

How much is the overhead allocated to each unit of Simple and Removable?

PB6. LO 6.3 Box Springs, Inc., makes two sizes of box springs: queen and king. The direct material for the queen is $35 per unit and $55 is used in direct labor, while the direct material for the king is $55 per unit, and the labor cost is $70 per unit. Box Springs estimates it will make 4,300 queens and 3,000 kings in the next year. It estimates the overhead for each cost pool and cost driver activities as follows:

Activity Cost Pools	Driver	Estimated Overhead	Use per Queen	Use per King
Framing	Square feet of pine	$150,000	4,500	3,000
Padding	Square feet of quilting	156,000	80,000	40,000
Filling	Square feet of filling	210,000	150,000	60,000
Labeling	Number of boxes	190,000	38,000	38,000
Inspection	Number of inspections	180,000	120,000	60,000

How much does each unit cost to manufacture?

PB7. LO 6.3 Please use the information from this problem for these calculations. After grouping cost pools and estimating overhead and activities, Box Springs determined these rates:

	ABC Rate
Purchasing	$21
Utilities	15
Machine setups	10
Supervision	3

Box Springs estimates there will be four orders in the next year, and those jobs will involve:

Order	4
Square feet	150
Machine hours	60
Direct labor hours	25
Direct materials	900
Direct labor rate	35

What is the total cost of the jobs?

PB8. LO 6.4 A company has traditionally allocated its overhead based on machine hours but collected this information to change to activity-based costing:

Activity Center	Estimated Activity Product 1	Product 2	Estimated Cost
Machine setups	10	15	$50,000
Assembly parts	1,000	1,500	75,000
Packaging units	500	300	80,000
Machine hours per unit	1	1.5	
Production volume	2,000	2,000	

A. How much overhead would be assigned to each unit under the traditional allocation method?
B. How much overhead would be assigned to each unit under activity-based costing?

PB9. LO 6.4 Casey's Kitchens makes two types of food smokers: Gas and Electric. The company expects to manufacture 20,000 units of Gas smokers, which have a per-unit direct material cost of $15 and a per-unit direct labor cost of $25. It also expects to manufacture 50,000 units of Electric smokers, which have a per-unit material cost of $20 and a per-unit direct labor cost of $45. Historically, it has used the traditional allocation method and applied overhead at a rate of $125 per machine hour. It was determined that there were three cost pools, and the overhead for each cost pool is as follows:

Machine setups	$ 5,000
Machine processing	6,000,000
Material requisitions	25,000
Total overhead	$6,030,000

The cost driver for each cost pool and its expected activity is as follows:

	Gas	Electric	Total
Machine setups	100	150	250
Machine hours	45,000	105,000	150,000
Parts requisitions	360	140	500

A. What is the per-unit cost for each product under the traditional allocation method?
B. What is the per-unit cost for each product under ABC costing?
C. Compared to ABC costing, was each product's overhead under- or overapplied?
D. How much was overhead under- or overapplied for each product?

PB10. LO 6.4 Casey's Kitchens' three cost pools and overhead estimates are as follows:

Activity Cost Pool	Cost Driver	Estimated Overhead	Use per Product A	Use per Product B
Machine setups	Setups	$250,000	7,000	3,000
Assembly	Number of parts	300,000	25,000	35,000
Machine maintenance	Machine hours	500,000	10,000	40,000

Compare the overhead allocation using:

A. The traditional allocation method
B. The activity-based costing method

(Hint: the traditional method uses machine hours as the allocation base.)

PB11. LO 6.4 Lampierre makes silver and gold candlesticks. The company computed this information to decide whether to switch from the traditional allocation method to ABC.

	Silver	Gold
Units planned	500	250
Material moves	250	750
Machine setups	5,600	4,400
Direct labor hours	500	1,500

The estimated overhead for the material cost pool is estimated as $45,000, and the estimate for the machine setup pool is $55,000. Calculate the allocation rate per unit of silver and per unit of gold using:

A. The traditional allocation method
B. The activity-based costing method

PB12. LO 6.4 Portable Seats makes two chairs: folding and wooden. This information was obtained to review the decision to consider ABC:

	Folding Chairs	Wooden Chairs	Total Cost
Material requisitions	450*	250*	$105,000
Inspections	250	150	30,000
Labor hours	1,300	1,700	

*lbs

Compute the overhead assigned to each product under:

A. The traditional allocation method
B. The activity-based costing method

PB13. LO 6.5 Submarine Company produces only one product and sells that product for $150 per unit. Cost information for the product is as follows:

Direct material	$40 per unit
Direct labor	$50 per unit
Variable overhead	$10 per unit
Fixed overhead	$ 40,000

Selling expenses are $2 per unit and are all variable. Administrative expenses of $15,000 are all fixed, Submarine produced 2,000 units and sold 1,800. Grainger had no beginning inventory.

A. Compute net income under
   i. absorption costing
   ii. variable costing
B. Reconcile the difference between the income under absorption and variable costing.

PB14. LO 6.5 Summarized data for Backdraft Co. for its first year of operations are as follows:

Sales (90,000 units)	$3,500,000
Production costs (100,000 units)	
Direct material	1,100,000
Direct labor	400,000
Manufacturing overhead	
Variable	200,000
Fixed	100,000
Selling and administrative expenses	
Variable	80,000
Fixed	50,000

A. Prepare an income statement under absorption costing
B. Prepare an income statement under variable costing

PB15. LO 6.5 Trail Outfitters has this information for its manufacturing:

Direct materials	$ 15
Direct labor	$ 15
Variable manufacturing overhead	$ 3
Fixed manufacturing overhead	$ 25
Units produced	30,000
Units sold	38,000

Its income statement under absorption costing is as follows:

Sales	$3,200,000
Beginning inventory	464,000
Cost of goods manufactured	1,740,000
Cost of goods available for sale	2,204,000
– Ending inventory	0
Cost of goods sold	2,204,000
Gross profit	996,000
– Sales and administration expenses	
Variable	266,000
Fixed	300,000
Total sales and administration expenses	566,000
Net operating income	$ 430,000

Prepare an income statement with variable costing and a reconciliation statement between both methods.

PB16. LO 6.5 Wifi Apps has these costs associated with its production and sale of devices that allow visual communications between cell phones:

Beginning inventory	$ 0
Units produced	33,000
Units sold	23,000
Selling price per unit	$ 170
Variable sales and administration expenses	$ 4
Fixed sales and administration expenses	$895,000
Direct material cost per unit	$ 23
Direct labor cost per unit	$ 15
Variable manufacturing overhead Cost per unit	$ 4
Fixed manufacturing overhead Cost per month	$858,000

Prepare an income statement under both the absorption and variable costing methods along with a reconciliation between the two statements.

PB17. LO 6.5 This information was collected for the first year of manufacturing for Wifi Apps:

Direct materials per unit	$ 1.75
Direct labor per unit	$ 3.50
Variable manufacturing overhead per unit	$ 0.55
Variable selling and administration expenses	$ 1.25
Units produced	50,000
Units sold	40,000
Sales price	$ 13
Fixed manufacturing expenses	$120,000
Fixed selling and administration expenses	$ 35,000

Prepare an income statement under variable costing and prepare a reconciliation to the income under the absorption method.

 Thought Provokers

TP1. LO 6.1 What conditions are optimal for using traditional allocation? Is the allocation more effective when there is high-volume production?

TP2. LO 6.2 College Cases sells cases for electronic devices such as phones, computers, and tablets. These cases have college logos or mascots on them and can be customized by adding such things as the customer's name, initials, sport, or fraternity letters. The company buys the cases in various colors and then uses laser technology to do the customization of the letters and to add school names, logos, mascots, and so on. What are potential activity-based costing pools for College Cases, and what would be appropriate cost drivers?

TP3. LO 6.3 How would a service industry apply activity-based costing?

TP4. LO 6.4 Cape Cod Adventures makes foam noodles with sales of 3,000,000 units per year and retractable boat oars with sales of 50,000 pairs per year. What information would Cape Cod Adventures need in order to change from traditional to ABC costing? What are the limitations to activity-based costing?

TP5. LO 6.5 In designing a bonus structure to reward your production managers, one of the options is to reward the managers based on reaching annual income targets. What are the differences between a reward system for a company that uses absorption costing and one for a company that uses variable costing?

Figure 7.1 Budget. Chris and Nikki needed to budget effectively in order to take advantage of sightseeing opportunities while studying abroad. (credit: modification of "Tourists: Here or there?" by "morebyless"/Flickr, CC BY 2.0)

Chapter Outline

LO 7.1 Describe How and Why Managers Use Budgets

LO 7.2 Prepare Operating Budgets

LO 7.3 Prepare Financial Budgets

LO 7.4 Prepare Flexible Budgets

LO 7.5 Explain How Budgets Are Used to Evaluate Goals

Why It Matters

Chris and Nikki are studying abroad next semester. Chris wants to spend her weekends sightseeing, but she does not have a lot of extra money. She creates a budget so she can save money to sightsee. She can reliably predict costs such as tuition, books, travel, and much of the sightseeing costs. She can also predict the amount of resources she will have to meet those costs, including scholarships, some savings, and earnings from her job.

Chris developed a budget from this information and planned for emergencies by including extra working hours and listing expenses that could be eliminated. On her trip, Chris was very careful with expenses and visited all the places she budgeted to visit.

Chris's roommate, Nikki, on the other hand, did not plan ahead before going abroad. She did not have any travel funds for the last several weeks and lamented that she should not have purchased so many souvenirs.

Chris and Nikki are clear illustrations of why people and companies prepare budgets. Preparing a budget for future anticipated activities requires a company to look critically at its revenue and expenses. A good budget gives management the ability to evaluate results at the end of the budget cycle. Even well-planned budgets can have emergencies or unplanned financial disruptions, but having a budget provides a company with the information to develop an alternative budget. A good budget can be adjusted to work with changes in income and still produce similar results.

In this chapter, you will learn the basic process companies use to create budgets and the general composition of basic budgets that are summed up in a master budget. You will also learn the importance of the flexible budget and be introduced to the idea of how budgets are used to evaluate company and management performance.

7.1 Describe How and Why Managers Use Budgets

Implementation of a company's strategic plan often begins by determining management's basic expectations about future economic, competitive, and technological conditions, and their effects on anticipated goals, both long-term and short-term. Many firms at this stage conduct a situational analysis that involves examining their *strengths* and *weaknesses* and the external *opportunities* available and the *threats* that they might face from competitors. This common analysis is often labeled as SWOT.

After performing the situational analysis, the organization identifies potential strategies that could enable achievement of its goals. Finally, the company will create, initiate, and monitor both long-term and short-term plans.

An important step in the initiation of the company's strategic plan is the creation of a budget. A good budgeting system will help a company reach its strategic goals by allowing management to plan and to control major categories of activity, such as revenue, expenses, and financing options. As detailed in Accounting as a Tool for Managers, planning involves developing future objectives, whereas controlling involves monitoring the planning objectives that have been put into place.

There are many advantages to budgeting, including:

- Communication
  - Budgeting is a formal method to communicate a company's plans to its internal stakeholders, such as executives, department managers, and others who have an interest in—or responsibility for—monitoring the company's performance.
  - Budgeting requires managers to plan for both revenues and expenses.
- Planning
  - Preparing a budget requires managers to consider and evaluate
    - The assumptions used to prepare the budget.
    - Long-term financial goals.
    - Short-term financial goals.
    - The company's position in the market.
    - How each department supports the strategic plan.
  - Preparing a budget requires departments to work together to
    - Determine realizable sales goals.
    - Compute the manufacturing or other requirements necessary to meet the sales goals.
    - Solve bottlenecks that are predicted by the budget.
    - Allocate resources so they can be used effectively to meet the sales and manufacturing goals.
    - Compare forecasted or flexible budgets with actual results.

- Evaluation
    - When compared to actual results, budgets are early alerts and they forecast:
        - Cash flows for various levels of production.
        - When loans may be required or when loans may be reduced.
    - Budgets show which areas, departments, units, and so forth, are profitable or meet their appropriate goals. Similarly, they also show which components are unprofitable or do not reach their anticipated goals.
    - Budgets set defined benchmarks that may be used for evaluating company and management performance, including raises and bonuses, as well as negative consequences, such as firing.

To understand the benefits of budgeting, consider Big Bad Bikes, a company that manufactures high-end mountain bikes. The company will begin producing and selling trainers this year. Trainers are stands that allow a rider to ride their bike indoors similar to the way bikes are used in spinning classes. Big Bad Bikes has a 5-year plan and has always been successful in managing its budget. Managers participate in developing the budget and are aware that all expenses must be related to the company's strategic plan. They know that managing their departments is much easier when the budget is developed to support the strategic plan.

The plan for Big Bad Bikes is to introduce itself to the trainer market with a sales price of $70 for the first two quarters of the year and then raise the price to $75 per unit. The marketing department estimates that sales will be 1,000 units for the first two quarters, 1,500 for the third quarter, and 2,500 per quarter through the second year. Management will work with each department to communicate goals and build a budget based on the sales plan. The resulting budget can be evaluated by all departments involved.

ETHICAL CONSIDERATIONS

Break-Even Analysis and Profitability

In the long run, proper budget reporting assists management in making good decisions. Management uses budgets to evaluate the performance of employees and their department. They can also use budgets to evaluate and benchmark the performance of a business unit in a large business organization or of the entire performance of a small company. They can also use budgets to evaluate separate projects. In budgeting situations, employees may feel a tension between reporting actual results and reporting results that reach the predetermined goals created by the budget. This creates a situation where managers may choose to act unethically and pressure accountants to report favorable financial results not supported by the operations.

Accountants need to be aware of this circumstance and use ethical standards when assisting the development and creation of budgets. After a proper budget has been created, the reporting of the actual results will assist in creating a realistic and honest picture of the actual operations for the managers reviewing the budget. The budget accountant needs to take steps to ensure that employees are not trying to misreport the budget results; for example, managers might be tempted to set artificially low standards to ensure that targets are hit and significantly exceeded. Such results could lead to what might be considered as excessive bonuses paid to managers.

The Basics of Budgeting

All companies—large and small—have limits on the amount of money or resources they can receive and pay out. How these resources are used to reach their goals and objectives must be planned. The quantitative plan estimating when and how much cash or other resources will be received and when and how the cash or other resources will be used is the **budget**. As you've learned, some of the benefits of budgeting include improved communication, planning, coordination, and evaluation.

All budgets are quantitative plans for the future and will be constructed based on the needs of the organization for which the budget is being created. Depending on the complexity, some budgets can take months or even years to develop. The most common time period covered by a budget is one year, although the time period may vary from strategic, long-term budgets to very detailed, short-term budgets. Generally, the closer the company is to the start of the budget's time period, the more detailed the budget becomes.

Management begins with a vision of the future. The long-term vision sets the direction of the company. The vision develops into goals and strategies that are built into the budget and are directly or indirectly reflected on the master budget.

The master budget has two major categories: the financial budget and the operating budget. The financial budget plans the use of assets and liabilities and results in a projected balance sheet. The operating budget helps plan future revenue and expenses and results in a projected income statement. The operating budget has several subsidiary budgets that all begin with projected sales. For example, management estimates sales for the upcoming few years. It then breaks down estimated sales into quarters, months, and weeks and prepares the sales budget. The sales budget is the foundation for other operating budgets. Management uses the number of units from the sales budget and the company's inventory policy to determine how many units need to be produced. This information in units and in dollars becomes the production budget.

The production budget is then broken up into budgets for materials, labor, and overhead, which use the standard quantity and standard price for raw materials that need to be purchased, the standard direct labor rate and the standard direct labor hours that need to be scheduled, and the standard costs for all other direct and indirect operating expenses. Companies use the historic quantities of the amount of material per unit and the hours of direct labor per unit to compute a standard used to estimate the quantity of materials and labor hours needed for the expected level of production. Current costs are used to develop standard costs for the price of materials, the direct labor rate, as well as an estimate of overhead costs.

The budget development process results in various budgets for various purposes, such as revenue, expenses, or units produced, but they all begin with a plan. To save time and eliminate unnecessary repetition, management often starts with the current year's budget and adjusts it to meet future needs.

There are various strategies companies use in adjusting the budget amounts and planning for the future. For example, budgets can be derived from a top-down approach or from a bottom-up approach. Figure 7.2 shows the general difference between the top-down approach and the bottom-up approach. The top-down approach typically begins with senior management. The goals, assumptions, and predicted revenue and expenses information are passed from the senior manager to middle managers, who further pass the information downward. Each department must then determine how it can allocate its expenses efficiently while still meeting the company goals. The benefit of this approach is that it ties in to the strategic plan and company goals. Another benefit of passing the amount of allowed expenses downward is that the final anticipated costs are reduced by the *vetting* (fact checking and information gathering) process.

In the top-down approach, management must devote attention to efficiently allocating resources to ensure that expenses are not padded to create budgetary slack. The drawback to this approach to budgeting is that the budget is prepared by individuals who are not familiar with specific operations and expenses to understand each department's nuances.

Figure 7.2 Top-Down versus Bottom-Up Approach to Budgeting. The top-down approach to budgeting starts with upper level management, while the bottom-up approach starts with input from lower-level management. (attribution: Copyright Rice University, OpenStax, under CC BY-NC-SA 4.0 license)

The bottom-up approach (sometimes also named a self-imposed or participative budget) begins at the lowest level of the company. After senior management has communicated the expected departmental goals, the departments then plans and predicts their sales and estimates the amount of resources needed to reach these goals. This information is communicated to the supervisor, who then passes it on to upper levels of management. The advantages of this approach are that managers feel their work is valued and that knowledgeable individuals develop the budget with realistic numbers. Therefore, the budget is more likely to be attainable. The drawback is that managers may not fully understand or may misunderstand the strategic plan.

Other approaches in addition to the top-down and bottom-up approaches are a combination approach and the zero-based budgeting approach. In the combination approach, guidelines and targets are set at the top while the managers work to develop a budget within the targeted parameters.

Zero-based budgeting begins with zero dollars and then adds to the budget only revenues and expenses that can be supported or justified. Figure 7.3 illustrates the difference between traditional budget preparation and zero-based budgeting in a bottom-up budgeting scenario. The advantage to zero-based budgeting is that unnecessary expenses are eliminated because managers cannot justify them. The drawback is that every expense needs to be justified, including obvious ones, so it takes a lot of time to complete. A compromise tactic is to use a zero-based budgeting approach for certain expenses, like travel, that can be easily justified and linked to the company goals.

Figure 7.3 Comparison of Traditional Budgeting Process and Zero-Based Budgeting Process. In a bottom-up budgeting environment, the budget process begins with lower level or operational management. Under a traditional budgeting, last year's budget would be the starting point for creating the current budget. Under a zero-based budgeting approach, all budget numbers are derived newly each year or budget cycle. (attribution: Copyright Rice University, OpenStax, under CC BY-NC-SA 4.0 license)

Often budgets are developed so they can adjust for changes in the volume or activity and help management make decisions. Changes and challenges can affect the budget and have an impact on a company's plans. A flexible budget adjusts the cost of goods produced for varying levels of production and is more useful than a static budget, which remains at one amount regardless of the production level. A flexible budget is created at the end of the accounting period, whereas the static budget is created before the fiscal year begins.

Additionally Figure 7.4 shows a comparison of a static budget and a flexible budget for Bingo's Bags, a company that produces purses and backpacks. In the flexible budget, the budgeted costs are calculated with actual sales, whereas in the static budget, budgeted costs are calculated with budgeted sales. The flexible budget allows management to see what they would expect the budget to look like based on the actual sales and budgeted costs. Flexible budgets are addressed in greater detail in Prepare Flexible Budgets.

	Flexible budget			Static budget			Sales Volume Variance
	Budgeted Cost (A)	Actual Sales Volume (B)	Flexible Budget (A × B)	Budgeted Cost (C)	Budgeted Sales Volume (D)	Static Budget (C × D)	Flexible Budget – Static Budget (A × B) – (C × D)
Direct Materials							
Backpacks	$5.720	71,600	$409,552	$5.720	72,000	$411,840	$ (2,288) F
Purses	7.460	37,000	276,020	7.460	35,000	261,100	14,920 U
Total direct materials cost			$685,572			$672,940	$12,632 U
Direct labor							
Backpacks	$3.450	71,600	$247,020	$3.450	72,000	$248,400	$ (1,380) F
Purses	2.220	37,000	82,140	2.220	35,000	77,700	4,440 U
Total direct labor cost			$329,160			$326,100	$ 3,060 U
Variable Overhead (60% x Direct labor cost)							
Backpacks	$2.130	71,600	$152,508	$2.130	72,000	$153,360	$ (852) F
Purses	1.820	37,000	67,340	1.820	35,000	63,700	3,640 U
Total variable overhead cost			$219,848			$217,060	$ 2,788 U

Figure 7.4 Comparison of a Flexible Budget and a Static Budget. (attribution: Copyright Rice University, OpenStax, under CC BY-NC-SA 4.0 license)

In order to handle changes that occur in the future, companies can also use a **rolling budget**, which is one that is continuously updated. While the company's goals may be multi-year, the rolling budget is adjusted monthly, and a new month is added as each month passes. Rolling budgets allow management to respond to changes in estimates or actual occurrences, but it also takes management away from other duties as it requires continual updating. Figure 7.5 shows an example of how a rolling quarterly budget would work. Notice that as one month rolls off (is completed) another month is added to the budget so that four quarters of a year are always presented.

	A	B	C	D	E	F	G	H	I
1		QUARTERLY ROLLING BUDGET							
2			Year 1				Year 2		
3			Q1	Q2	Q3	Q4	Q1	Q2	Q3	Q4
4	INITIAL ANNUAL BUDGET								
5	ROLLING BUDGET Year 1/Q2								
6	ROLLING BUDGET Year 1/Q3								
7	ROLLING BUDGET Year 1/Q4								
8	ROLLING BUDGET Year 2/Q1								

Figure 7.5 Rolling Budget. In a quarterly operating budget, the budget always projects forward for four months, or one quarter. (attribution: Copyright Rice University, OpenStax, under CC BY-NC-SA 4.0 license)

Because budgets are used to evaluate a manager's performance as well as the company's, managers are responsible for specific expenses within their own budget. Each manager's performance is evaluated by how well he or she manages the revenues and expenses under his or her control. Each individual who exercises control over spending should have a budget specifying limits on that spending.

The Role of the Master Budget

Most organizations will create a master budget—whether that organization is large or small, public or private, or a merchandising, manufacturing, or service company. A **master budget** is one that includes two areas, operational and financial, each of which has its own sub-budgets. The **operating budget** spans several areas that help plan and manage day-to-day business. The **financial budget** depicts the expectations for cash inflows and outflows, including cash payments for planned operations, the purchase or sale of assets, the payment or financing of loans, and changes in equity. Each of the sub-budgets is made up of separate but interrelated budgets, and the number and type of separate budgets will differ depending on the type and size of the organization. For example, the sales budget predicts the sales expected for each quarter. The direct materials budget uses information from the sales budget to compute the number of units necessary for production. This information is used in other budgets, such as the direct materials budget, which plans when materials will be purchased, how much will be purchased, and how much that material should cost. You will review some specific examples of budgeting for direct materials in Prepare Operating Budgets.

Figure 7.6 shows how operating budgets and financial budgets are related within a master budget.

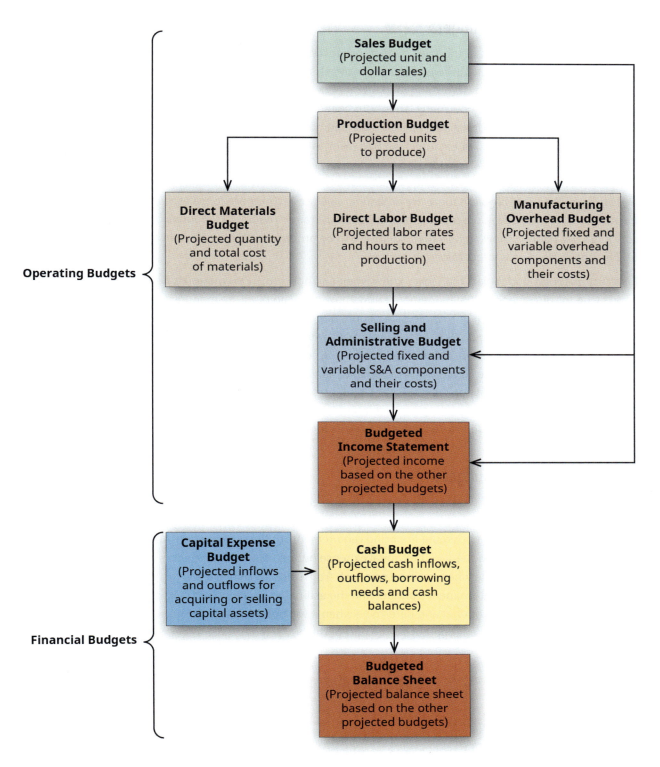

Figure 7.6 Operating Budgets, Financial Budgets, and the Relationship between Budgets. (attribution: Copyright Rice University, OpenStax, under CC BY-NC-SA 4.0 license)

The Role of Operating Budgets

An operating budget consists of the sales budget, production budget, direct material budget, direct labor budget, and overhead budget. These budgets serve to assist in planning and monitoring the day-to-day activities of the organization by informing management of how many units need to be produced, how much material needs to be ordered, how many labor hours need to be scheduled, and the amount of overhead expected to be incurred. The individual pieces of the operating budget collectively lead to the creation of the budgeted income statement. For example, Big Bad Bikes estimates it will sell 1,000 trainers for $70 each in the first quarter and prepares a sales budget to show the sales by quarter. Management understands that it needs to have on hand the 1,000 trainers that it estimates will be sold. It also understands that additional inventory needs to be on hand in the event there are additional sales and to prepare for sales in the second quarter. This information is used to develop a production budget. Each trainer requires 3.2 pounds of material that usually costs $1.25 per pound. Knowing how many units are to be produced and how much inventory needs to be on hand is used to develop a direct materials budget.

The direct materials budget lets managers know when and how much raw materials need to be ordered. The same is true for direct labor, as management knows how many units will be manufactured and how many hours of direct labor are needed. The necessary hours of direct labor and the estimated labor rate are used to develop the direct labor budget. While the materials and labor are determined from the production budget, only the variable overhead can be determined from the production budget. Existing information regarding fixed manufacturing costs are combined with variable manufacturing costs to determine the manufacturing overhead budget. The information from the sales budget is used to determine the sales and administrative budget. Finally, the sales, direct materials, direct labor, fixed manufacturing overhead budget, and sales and administrative budgets are used to develop a pro-forma income statement.

The Role of Financial Budgets

A financial budget consists of the cash budget, the budgeted balance sheet, and the budget for capital expenses. Similar to the individual budgets that make up the operating budgets, the financial budgets serve to assist with planning and monitoring the financing requirements of the organization. Management plans its capital asset needs and states them in the capital expense budget. Management addresses its collection and payment policies to determine when it will receive cash from sales and when it will pay the material, labor, and overhead expenses. The capital expense budget and the estimated payment and collection of cash allow management to build a cash budget and determine when it will need financing or have additional funds to pay back loans. These budgets taken together will be part of the budgeted balance sheet. Figure 7.6 shows how these budgets relate.

YOUR TURN

Maintaining a Cash Balance

DaQuan recently began work as a senior accountant at Mad Coffee Company. He learned he would be responsible for monitoring the cash balance because there is a bank loan requirement that a minimum balance of $10,000 be maintained with the bank at all times. DaQuan asked to see the cash budget so he could anticipate when the balance was most likely to go below $10,000. How can DaQuan determine potential cash balance issues by looking at the budget?

Solution

Budgeting helps plan for those times when cash is in short supply and bills need to be paid. Proper budgeting shows when and for how long a cash shortage may exist. DaQuan can see the months when the cash payments exceed the cash receipts and when the company is in danger of having a cash balance below the minimum requirement of $10,000. Knowing the inflow and outflow of cash will help him plan and manage the shortage through a line of credit, delay in purchasing, delay in hiring, or delay in payment of non-essential items.

LINK TO LEARNING

Budgeting is a task that should be completed by all organizations, not only those limited to manufacturing. Unfortunately, there are many individuals who want to operate a business and know nothing about budgeting. Often, professional organizations or industry trade groups offer information to help their members succeed in business. For example, the real estate profession provides information and suggestions such as this article on preparing a marketing budget (https://openstax.org/l/50RealtorMag) to help professionals.

7.2 Prepare Operating Budgets

Operating budgets are a primary component of the master budget and involve examining the expectations for the primary operations of the business. Assumptions such as sales in units, sales price, manufacturing costs per unit, and direct material needed per unit involve a significant amount of time and input from various parts of the organization. It is important to obtain all of the information, however, because the more accurate the information, the more accurate the resulting budget, and the more likely management is to effectively monitor and achieve its budget goals.

Individual Operating Budgets

In order for an organization to align the budget with the strategic plan, it must budget for the day-to-day operations of the business. This means the company must understand when and how many sales will occur, as well as what expenses are required to generate those sales. In short, each component—sales, production, and other expenses—must be properly budgeted to generate the operating budget components and the resulting pro-forma budgeted income statement.

The budgeting process begins with the estimate of sales. When management has a solid estimate of sales for each quarter, month, week, or other relevant time period, they can determine how many units must be produced. From there, they determine the expenditures, such as direct materials necessary to produce the units. It is critical for the sales estimate to be accurate so that management knows how many units to produce. If the estimate is understated, the company will not have enough inventory to satisfy customers, and they will not have ordered enough material or scheduled enough direct labor to manufacture more units. Customers may then shop somewhere else to meet their needs. Likewise, if sales are overestimated, management will have purchased more material than necessary and have a larger labor force than needed. This overestimate will cause management to have spent more cash than was necessary.

Sales Budget

The **sales budget** details the expected sales in units and the sales price for the budget period. The information from the sales budget is carried to several places in the master budget. It is used to determine how many units must be produced as well as when and how much cash will be collected from those sales.

For example, Big Bad Bikes used information from competitor sales, its marketing department, and industry trends to estimate the number of units that will be sold in each quarter of the coming year. The number of units is multiplied by the sales price to determine the sales by quarter as shown in Figure 7.7.

BIG BAD BIKES Sales Budget For the Year Ended December 31, 2019					
	Quarter 1	Quarter 2	Quarter 3	Quarter 4	Total
Expected Sales (Units)	1,000	1,000	1,500	2,500	6,000
Sales Price per Unit	$ 70	$ 70	$ 75	$ 75	
Total Sales Revenue	$70,000	$70,000	$112,500	$187,500	$440,000

Figure 7.7 Sales Budget for Big Bad Bikes. (attribution: Copyright Rice University, OpenStax, under CC BY-NC-SA 4.0 license)

The sales budget leads into the production budget to determine how many units must be produced each week, month, quarter, or year. It also leads into the cash receipts budget, which will be discussed in Prepare Financial Budgets.

Production Budget

Estimating sales leads to identifying the desired quantity of inventory to meet the demand. Management wants to have enough inventory to meet production, but they do not want too much in the ending inventory to avoid paying for unnecessary storage. Management often uses a formula to estimate how much should remain in ending inventory. Management wants to be flexible with its budgeting, wants to create budgets that can grow or shrink as needed, and needs to have inventory on hand. So the amount of ending inventory often is a percentage of the next week's, month's, or quarter's sales.

In creating the production budget, a major issue is how much inventory should be on hand. Having inventory on hand helps the company avoid losing a customer because the product isn't available. However, there are storage costs associated with holding inventory as well as having a lag time between paying to manufacture a product and receiving cash from selling that product. Management must balance the two issues and determine the amount of inventory that should be available.

When determining the number of units needed to be produced, start with the estimated sales plus the desired ending inventory to derive the maximum number of units that must be available during the period. Since the number of units in beginning inventory are already produced, subtracting the beginning inventory from the

Chapter 7 Budgeting

goods available results in the number of units that need to be produced.

After management has estimated how many units will sell and how many units need to be in ending inventory, it develops the **production budget** to compute the number of units that need to be produced during each quarter. The formula is the reverse of the formula for the cost of goods sold.

Cost of Goods Sold	Number of Units Produced
Beginning Inventory	Goods Sold
+ Purchases (or produced)	+ Ending Inventory
Goods available for sale	Goods available for sale
− Ending Inventory	− Beginning Inventory

The number of units expected to be sold plus the desired ending inventory equals the number of units that are available. When the beginning inventory is subtracted from the number of units available, management knows how many units must be produced during that quarter to meet sales.

In a merchandising firm, retailers do not produce their inventory but purchase it. Therefore, stores such as Walmart do not have raw materials and instead substitute the number of units to be purchased in place of the number of units to be produced; the result is the merchandise inventory to be purchased.

To illustrate the steps in developing a production budget, recall that Big Bad Bikes is introducing a new product that the marketing department thinks will have strong sales. For new products, Big Bad Bikes requires a target ending inventory of 30% of the next quarter's sales. Unfortunately, they were unable to manufacture any units before the end of the current year, so the first quarter's beginning inventory is 0 units. As shown in Figure 7.7, sales in quarter 2 are estimated at 1,000 units; since 30% is required to be in ending inventory, the ending inventory for quarter 1 needs to be 300 units. With expected sales of 1,000 units for quarter 2 and a required ending inventory of 30%, or 300 units, Big Bad Bikes needs to have 1,300 units available during the quarter. Since 1,300 units needed to be available and there are zero units in beginning inventory, Big Bad Bikes needs to manufacture 1,300 units, as shown in Figure 7.8.

BIG BAD BIKES
Production Budget
For the Year Ended December 31, 2019

	Quarter 1	Quarter 2	Quarter 3	Quarter 4
Expected Sales	1,000	1,000	1,500	2,500
Desired Ending Inventory	300	450	750	1,050
Total Required Units	1,300	1,450	2,250	3,550
− Beginning Inventory	0	300	450	750
Required Production	1,300	1,150	1,800	2,800

Figure 7.8 Production Budget for Big Bad Bikes. (attribution: Copyright Rice University, OpenStax, under CC BY-NC-SA 4.0 license)

The ending inventory from one quarter is the beginning inventory for the next quarter and the calculations are all the same. In order to determine the ending inventory in quarter 4, Big Bad Bikes must estimate the sales for the first quarter of the next year. Big Bad Bikes's marketing department believes sales will increase in each of the next several quarters, and they estimate sales as 3,500 for the first quarter of the next year and 4,500 for the second quarter of the next year. Thirty percent of 3,500 is 1,050, so the number of units required in the ending inventory for quarter 4 is 1,050.

The number of units needed in production for the first quarter of the next year provides information needed for other budgets such as the direct materials budget, so Big Bad Bikes must also determine the number of units needed in production for that first quarter. The estimated sales of 3,500 and the desired ending inventory of 1,350 (30% of the next quarter's estimated sales of 4,500) determines that 4,850 units are required during the quarter. The beginning inventory is estimated to be 1,050, which means the number of units that need to be produced during the first quarter of year 2 is 3,800.

The number of units needed to be produced each quarter was computed from the estimated sales and is used to determine the quantity of direct or raw material to purchase, to schedule enough direct labor to manufacture the units, and to approximate the overhead required for production. It is also necessary to estimate the sales for the first quarter of the next year. The ending inventory for the current year is based on the sales estimates for the first quarter of the following year. From this amount, the production budget and direct materials budget are calculated and flow to the operating and cash budget.

Direct Materials Budget

From the production budget, management knows how many units need to be produced in each budget period. Management is already aware of how much material it needs to produce each unit and can combine the direct material per unit with the production budget to compute the **direct materials budget**. This information is used to ensure the correct quantity of materials is ordered and the correct amount is budgeted for those materials.

Similar to the production budget, management wants to have an ending inventory available to ensure there are enough materials on hand. The direct materials budget illustrates how much material needs to be ordered and how much that material costs. The calculation is similar to that used in the production budget, with the addition of the cost per unit.

If Big Bad Bikes uses 3.2 pounds of material for each trainer it manufactures and each pound of material costs $1.25, we can create a direct materials budget. Management's goal is to have 20% of the next quarter's material needs on hand as the desired ending materials inventory. Therefore, the determination of each quarter's material needs is partially dependent on the following quarter's production requirements. The desired ending inventory of material is readily determined for quarters 1 through 3 as those needs are based on the production requirements for quarters 2 through 4. To compute the desired ending materials inventory for quarter 4, we need the production requirements for quarter 1 of year 2. Recall that the number of units to be produced during the first quarter of year 2 is 3,800. Thus, quarter 4 materials ending inventory requirement is 20% of 3,800. That information is used to compute the direct materials budget shown in Figure 7.9.

BIG BAD BIKES Direct Materials Budget For the Year Ended December 31, 2019					
	Quarter 1	Quarter 2	Quarter 3	Quarter 4	Total
Units to be Produced	1,300	1,150	1,800	2,800	7,050
Direct Material per Unit	3.20	3.20	3.20	3.20	3.20
Total Pounds Needed for Production	4,160	3,680	5,760	8,960	22,560
+ Desired Ending Inventory	736	1,152	1,792	2,432	2,432
Total Material Required	4,896	4832	7,552	11,392	24,992
− Beginning Inventory	0	736	1,152	1,792	0
Pounds of Direct Material Required	4,896	4,096	6,400	9,600	24,992
Cost per Pound	$ 1.25	$ 1.25	$ 1.25	$ 1.25	$ 1.25
Total Cost of Direct Material Purchase	$6,120	$5,120	$8,000	$12,000	$31,240

Figure 7.9 Direct Materials Budget for Big Bad Bikes. (attribution: Copyright Rice University, OpenStax, under CC BY-NC-SA 4.0 license)

Management knows how much the materials will cost and integrates this information into the schedule of expected cash disbursements, which will be shown in Prepare Financial Budgets. This information will also be used in the budgeted income statement and on the budgeted balance sheet. With 6,000 units estimated for sale, 3.2 pounds of material per unit, and $1.25 per pound, the direct materials used represent $24,000 of the cost of goods sold. The remaining $7,240 is included in ending inventory as units completed and raw material.

Direct Labor Budget

Management uses the same information in the production budget to develop the **direct labor budget**. This information is used to ensure that the proper amount of staff is available for production and that there is money available to pay for the labor, including potential overtime. Typically, the number of hours is computed and then multiplied by an hourly rate, so the total direct labor cost is known.

If Big Bad Bikes knows that they need 45 minutes or 0.75 hours of direct labor for each unit produced, and the labor rate for this type of manufacturing is $20 per hour, the computation for direct labor simply begins with the number of units in the production budget. As shown in Figure 7.10, the number of units produced each quarter multiplied by the number of hours per unit equals the required direct labor hours needed to be scheduled in order to meet production needs. The total number of hours is next multiplied by the direct labor rate per hour, and the labor cost can be budgeted and used in the cash disbursement budget and operating budget illustrated in Prepare Financial Budgets.

BIG BAD BIKES Direct Labor Budget For the Year Ended December 31, 2019					
	Quarter 1	Quarter 2	Quarter 3	Quarter 4	Total
Units to be Produced	1,300	1,150	1,800	2,800	7,050
Direct Labor Hours per Unit	00.75	00.75	00.75	00.75	00.75
Total Required Direct Labor Hours	975	862.50	1,350	2,100	5,287.50
Labor Cost per Hour	$ 20	$ 20	$ 20	$ 20	$ 20
Total Direct Labor Cost	$19,500	$17,250	$27,000	$42,000	$ 105,750

Figure 7.10 Direct Labor Budget for Big Bad Bikes. (attribution: Copyright Rice University, OpenStax, under CC BY-NC-SA 4.0 license)

The direct labor of $105,750 will be apportioned to the budgeted income statement and budgeted balance sheet. With 0.75 hours of direct labor per unit and $20 per direct labor hour, each unit will cost $15 in direct labor. Of the 7,050 units produced, 6,000 units will be sold, so $90,000 represents the labor portion of the cost of goods sold and will be shown on the income statement, while the remaining $15,750 will be the labor portion of ending inventory and will be shown on the balance sheet.

Manufacturing Overhead Budget

The **manufacturing overhead budget** includes the remainder of the production costs not covered by the direct materials and direct labor budgets. In the manufacturing overhead budgeting process, producers will typically allocate overhead costs depending upon their cost behavior production characteristics, which are generally classified as either variable or fixed. Based on this allocation process, the variable component will be treated as occurring proportionately in relation to budgeted activity, while the fixed component will be treated as remaining constant. This process is similar to the overhead allocation process you learned in studying product, process, or activity-based costing.

For Big Bad Bikes to create their manufacturing overhead budget, they first determine that the appropriate driver for assigning overhead costs to products is direct labor hours. The overhead allocation rates for the variable overhead costs are: indirect material of $1.00 per hour, indirect labor of $1.25 per hour, maintenance of $0.25 per hour, and utilities of $0.50 per hour. The fixed overhead costs per quarter are: supervisor salaries of $15,000, fixed maintenance salaries of $4,000, insurance of $7,000, and depreciation expenses of $3,000.

Given the direct labor hours for each quarter from the direct labor budget, the variable costs are the number of hours multiplied by the variable overhead application rate. The fixed costs are the same for each quarter, as shown in the manufacturing overhead budget in Figure 7.11.

BIG BAD BIKES					
Manufacturing Overhead Budget					
For the Year Ended December 31, 2019					
	Quarter 1	Quarter 2	Quarter 3	Quarter 4	Total
Variable Costs					
Indirect Material	$ 975	$ 863	$ 1,350	$ 2,100	$ 5,288
Indirect Labor	1,219	1,078	1,688	2,625	6,609
Maintenance	244	216	338	525	1,322
Utilities	488	431	675	1,050	2,644
Total Variable Manufacturing Costs	$ 2,926	$ 2,588	$ 4,051	$ 6,300	$ 15,863
Fixed Costs					
Supervisory Salaries	$15,000	$15,000	$15,000	$15,000	$ 60,000
Maintenance Salaries	4,000	4,000	4,000	4,000	16,000
Insurance	7,000	7,000	7,000	7,000	28,000
Depreciation	3,000	3,000	3,000	3,000	12,000
Total Fixed Manufacturing Costs	$29,000	$29,000	$29,000	$29,000	$116,000
Total Manufacturing Overhead	$31,925	$31,588	$33,050	$35,300	$131,863

Figure 7.11 Manufacturing Overhead Budget for Big Bad Bikes. (attribution: Copyright Rice University, OpenStax, under CC BY-NC-SA 4.0 license)

The total manufacturing overhead cost was $131,863 for 7,050 units, or $18.70 per unit (rounded). Since 6,000 units are sold, $112,200 (6,000 units × $18.70 /unit) will be expensed as cost of goods sold, while the remaining $19,663 will be part of finished goods ending inventory.

Sales and Administrative Expenses Budget

The direct materials budget, the direct labor budget, and the manufacturing overhead budget plan for all costs related to production, while the **selling and administrative expense budget** contains a listing of variable and fixed expenses estimated to be incurred in all areas other than production costs. While this one budget contains all nonmanufacturing expenses, in practice, it actually comprises several small budgets created by managers in sales and administrative positions. All managers must follow the budget, but setting an appropriate budget for selling and administrative functions is complicated and is not always thoroughly understood by managers without a background in managerial accounting.

If Big Bad Bikes pays a sales commission of $2 per unit sold and a transportation cost of $0.50 per unit, they can use these costs to put together their sales and administrative budget. All other costs are fixed costs per quarter: sales salaries of $5,000; administrative salaries of $5,000; marketing expenses of $5,000; insurance of $1,000; and depreciation of $2,000. The sales and administrative budget is shown in Figure 7.12, along with the budgeted sales used in the computation of variable sales and administrative expenses.

BIG BAD BIKES Sales and Administrative Expense Budget For the Year Ended December 31, 2019					
	Quarter 1	Quarter 2	Quarter 3	Quarter 4	Total
Budgeted Sales in Units	1,000	1,000	1,500	2,500	6,000
Variable Expenses					
Sales Commissions	2,000	2,000	3,000	5,000	12,000
Transportation	500	500	750	1,250	3,000
Total Variable Expenses	$ 2,500	$ 2,500	$ 3,750	$ 6,250	$15,000
Fixed Expenses					
Sales Salaries	$ 5,000	$ 5,000	$ 5,000	$ 5,000	$20,000
Administrative Salaries	5,000	5,000	5,000	5,000	20,000
Marketing Expenses	5,000	5,000	5,000	5,000	20,000
Insurance Expenses	1,000	1,000	1,000	1,000	4,000
Depreciation Expenses	2,000	2,000	2,000	2,000	8,000
Total Fixed Expenses	$18,000	$18,000	$18,000	$18,000	$72,000
Total Selling and Administrative expenses	$20,500	$20,500	$21,750	$24,250	$87,000

Figure 7.12 Sales and Administrative Expense Budget for Big Bad Bikes. (attribution: Copyright Rice University, OpenStax, under CC BY-NC-SA 4.0 license)

Only manufacturing costs are treated as a product cost and included in ending inventory, so all of the expenses in the sales and administrative budget are period expenses and included in the budgeted income statement.

Budgeted Income Statement

A **budgeted income statement** is formatted similarly to a traditional income statement except that it contains budgeted data. Once all of the operating budgets have been created, these costs are used to prepare a budgeted income statement and budgeted balance sheet. The manufacturing costs are allocated to the cost of goods sold and the ending inventory.

Big Bad Bikes uses the information on direct materials (Figure 7.9), direct labor (Figure 7.10), and manufacturing overhead (Figure 7.11) to allocate the manufacturing costs between the cost of goods sold and the ending work in process inventory, as shown in (Figure 7.13).

	Cost of Goods Sold	Ending Inventory	Total
Direct Materials	$ 24,000*	$ 7,240	$ 31,240
Direct Labor	90,000**	15,750	105,750
Manufacturing Overhead	112,200	19,639	131,863
Total	$226,224	$42,629	$268,853

*6,000 units × 3.2 lbs/unit × $1.25/lb
**6,000 units × 0.75 hr/unit × $20/hr

Figure 7.13 Allocating Costs to Cost of Goods Sold and Ending Work in Process Inventory for Big Bad Bikes. (attribution: Copyright Rice University, OpenStax, under CC BY-NC-SA 4.0 license)

Once they perform this allocation, the budgeted income statement can be prepared. Big Bad Bikes estimates an interest of $954. It also estimates that $22,000 of its income will not be collected and will be reported as uncollectible expense. The budgeted income statement is shown in Figure 7.14.

BIG BAD BIKES Budgeted Income Statement For the Year Ended December 31, 2019	
Sales	$440,000
Cost of Goods Sold	226,200
Gross Profit	213,800
Sales and Administrative Expenses	87,000
Uncollectible Expense	22,000
Income before Interest	104,800
Interest Expense	954
Income Tax	4,000
Net Income	$ 99,846

Figure 7.14 Budgeted Income Statement for Big Bad Bikes. (attribution: Copyright Rice University, OpenStax, under CC BY-NC-SA 4.0 license)

THINK IT THROUGH

Errors in a Budgeted Balance Sheet

Which error has the potential to cause more problems with the budgeted balance sheet: overstating sales or understating the cash collected?

7.3 Prepare Financial Budgets

Now that you have developed an understanding of operating budgets, let's turn to the other primary component of the master budget: financial budgets. Preparing financial budgets involves examining the expectations for financing the operations of the business and planning for the cash needs of the organization. The budget helps estimate the source, amount, and timing of cash collection and cash payments as well as determine if and when additional financing is needed or debt can be paid.

Individual Financial Budgets

Preparing a financial budget first requires preparing the capital asset budget, the cash budgets, and the budgeted balance sheet. The capital asset budget represents a significant investment in cash, and the amount is carried to the cash budget. Therefore, it needs to be prepared before the cash budget. If the cash will not be available, the capital asset budget can be adjusted and, again, carried to the cash budget.

When the budgets are complete, the beginning and ending balance from the cash budget, changes in financing, and changes in equity are shown on the budgeted balance sheet.

Capital Asset Budget

The **capital asset budget**, also called the capital expenditure budget, shows the company's plans to invest in long-term assets. Some assets, such as computers, must be replaced every few years, while other assets, such as manufacturing equipment, are purchased very infrequently. Some assets can be purchased with cash, whereas others may require a loan. Budgeting for these types of expenditures requires long-range planning because the purchases affect cash flows in current and future periods and affect the income statement due to depreciation and interest expenses.

Cash Budget

The **cash budget** is the combined budget of all inflows and outflows of cash. It should be divided into the shortest time period possible, so management can be quickly made aware of potential problems resulting from fluctuations in cash flow. One goal of this budget is to anticipate the timing of cash inflows and outflows, which allows a company to try to avoid a decrease in the cash balance due to paying out more cash than it receives. In order to provide timely feedback and alert management to short-term cash needs, the cash flow budget is commonly geared toward monthly or quarterly figures. Figure 7.15 shows how the other budgets tie into the cash budget.

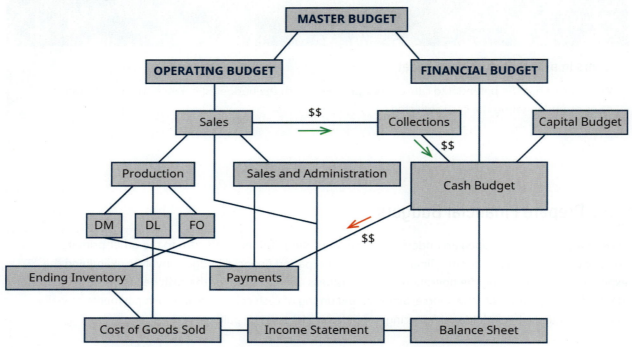

Figure 7.15 Relationship between Budgets. (attribution: Copyright Rice University, OpenStax, under CC BY-NC-SA 4.0 license)

Cash is so important to the operations of a company that, often, companies will arrange to have an emergency cash source, such as a *line of credit*, to avoid defaulting on current payables due and also to protect against other unanticipated expenses, such as major repair costs on equipment. This line of credit would be similar in function to the *overdraft protection* offered on many checking accounts.

Because the cash budget accounts for every inflow and outflow of cash, it is broken down into smaller components. The **cash collections schedule** includes all of the cash inflow expected to be received from customer sales, whether those customers pay at the same rate or even if they pay at all. The cash collections schedule includes all the cash expected to be received and does not include the amount of the receivables estimated as uncollectible. The **cash payments schedule** plans the outflow or payments of all accounts payable, showing when cash will be used to pay for direct material purchases. Both the cash collections schedule and the cash payments schedule are included along with other cash transactions in a cash budget. The cash budget, then, combines the cash collection schedule, the cash payment schedule, and all other budgets that plan for the inflow or outflow of cash. When everything is combined into one budget, that budget shows if financing arrangements are needed to maintain balances or if excess cash is available to pay for additional liabilities or assets.

The operating budgets all begin with the sales budget. The cash collections schedule does as well. Since purchases are made at varying times during the period and cash is received from customers at varying rates, data are needed to estimate how much will be collected in the month of sale, the month after the sale, two months after the sale, and so forth. Bad debts also need to be estimated, since that is cash that will not be collected.

To illustrate, let's return to Big Bad Bikes. They believe cash collections for the trainer sales will be similar to the collections from their bicycle sales, so they will use that pattern to budget cash collections for the trainers. In the quarter of sales, 65% of that quarter's sales will be collected. In the quarter after the sale, 30% will be collected. This leaves 5% of the sales considered uncollectible. Figure 7.16 illustrates when each quarter's sales will be collected. An estimate of the net realizable balance of Accounts Receivable can be reconciled by using information from the cash collections schedule:

Quarter 4: Beginning balance of Accounts Receivable (Quarter 3 Sales of $112,500 × 30%)	$ 33,750
+ Quarter 4: Sales	187,500
− Quarter 4: Cash Receipts (65% of Quarter 4 Sales)	121,875
= Quarter 4: Ending Balance in Gross Accounts Receivable	$ 99,375

Note the Ending Balance is gross accounts receivable which includes the 5% estimated uncollectible, but that amount would be excluded from net realizable accounts receivable.

	Percentage of Sales Collected			
	Quarter 1	Quarter 2	Quarter 3	Quarter 4
Prior year, Quarter 4 Sales	30%			
Quarter 1 Sales	65%	30%		
Quarter 2 Sales		65%	30%	
Quarter 3 Sales			65%	30%
Quarter 4 Sales				65%

Figure 7.16 Illustration of a Cash Collections Schedule. (attribution: Copyright Rice University, OpenStax, under CC BY-NC-SA 4.0 license)

For example, in quarter 1 of year 2, 65% of the quarter 1 sales will be collected in cash, as well as 30% of the sales from quarter 4 of the prior year. There were no sales in quarter 4 of the prior year so 30% of zero sales shows the collections are $0. Using information from Big Bad Bikes sales budget, the cash collections from the sales are shown in Figure 7.17.

BIG BAD BIKES Cash Collections Schedule For the Year Ended December 31, 2019						
	Sales	Quarter 1	Quarter 2	Quarter 3	Quarter 4	Total
Collections from						
prior year Quarter 4	0	0				
Quarter 1	$ 70,000	$45,500	$21,000			$ 66,500
Quarter 2	70,000		45,500	$21,000		66,500
Quarter 3	112,500			73,125	$ 33,750	106,875
Quarter 4	187,500				121,875	121,875
Total Collections	$440,000	$45,500	$66,500	$94,125	$155,625	$361,750
Accounts Receivable	$ 78,250					

Figure 7.17 Cash Collections Schedule for Big Bad Bikes. (attribution: Copyright Rice University, OpenStax, under CC BY-NC-SA 4.0 license)

When the cash collections schedule is made for sales, management must account for other potential cash collections such as cash received from the sale of equipment or the issuance of stock. These are listed individually in the cash inflows portion of the cash budget.

The cash payments schedule, on the other hand, shows when cash will be used to pay for Accounts Payable. One such example are direct material purchases, which originates from the direct materials budget. When the production budget is determined from the sales, management prepares the direct materials budget to determine when and how much material needs to be ordered. Orders for materials take place throughout the quarter, and payments for the purchases are made at different intervals from the orders. A schedule of cash payments is similar to the cash collections schedule, except that it accounts for the company's purchases instead of the company's sales. The information from the cash payments schedule feeds into the cash budget.

Big Bad Bikes typically pays half of its purchases in the quarter of purchase. The remaining half is paid in the following quarter, so payments in the first quarter include payments for purchases made during the first quarter as well as half of the purchases for the preceding quarter. Figure 7.18 shows when each quarter's purchases will be paid. Additionally, the balance of purchases in Accounts Payable can be reconciled by using information from the cash payment schedule as follows:

Quarter 4: Beginning balance of Accounts Payable	$ 4,000*
+ Quarter 4: purchase of direct material	12,000
− Quarter 4: Cash Payments	10,000
= Quarter 4: Ending balance in Accounts Payable	$ 6,000*

* Big Bad Bikes has a policy of paying 50% of purchases in the quarter of purchases, and the remaining 50% the month after the purchase. The beginning balance of accounts payable should be 50% of the prior quarter's purchases.

	Percentage of Cash Payments for Purchases			
	Quarter 1	Quarter 2	Quarter 3	Quarter 4
Prior year, Quarter 4 Purchases	50%			
Quarter 1 Purchases	50%	50%		
Quarter 2 Purchases		50%	50%	
Quarter 3 Purchases			50%	50%
Quarter 4 Purchases				50%

Figure 7.18 Cash Payment Schedule. (attribution: Copyright Rice University, OpenStax, under CC BY-NC-SA 4.0 license)

The first quarter of the year plans cash payments from the prior quarter as well as the current quarter. Again, since the trainers are a new product, in this example, there are no purchases in the preceding quarter, and the payments are $0. Figure 7.19.

BIG BAD BIKES
Cash Payments Schedule
For the Year Ended December 31, 2019

Payments	Purchases	Quarter 1	Quarter 2	Quarter 3	Quarter 4	Total
Quarter 4, prior year	$ 0	$ 0				
Quarter 1	6,120	3,060	$3,060			$ 6,120
Quarter 2	5,120		2,560	$2,560		5,120
Quarter 3	8,000			4,000	$ 4,000	8,000
Quarter 4	12,000				6,000	6,000
Total payments	$31,240	$3,060	$5,620	$6,560	$10,000	$25,240
Accounts Payable	$ 6,000					

Figure 7.19 Cash Payments Schedule for Big Bad Bikes. (attribution: Copyright Rice University, OpenStax, under CC BY-NC-SA 4.0 license)

While the cash payments schedule is made for purchases of material on account, there are other outflows of cash for the company, and management must estimate all other cash payments for the year. Typically, this includes the manufacturing overhead budget, the sales and administrative budget, the capital asset budget, and any other potential payments of cash. Since depreciation is an expense not requiring cash, the cash budget includes the amount from the budgets less depreciation. Cash payments are listed on the cash budget following cash receipts. Figure 7.20 shows the major components of the cash budget.

> **JOB COST SHEET**
> **General Overview of Cash Budget Components***
>
> Cash Receipts from Sales
> + Other cash receipts (issuance of stock, borrowing money, receiving interest or dividends, from selling assets such as equipment, etc.)
> − Cash Payments for Purchases or Production of Inventory
> − Cash Payments for manufacturing expenses**
> − Cash Payments for selling and administrative expenses**
> − Cash payments for capital asset purchases
> − Other cash payments (paying interest, paying loan payments, etc.)
> = Net Cash
>
> *This is a general overview of the types of cash transactions that might appear in a cash budget and is representative of the components but not of a typical presentation of those components
> **Note that depreciation, a non-cash expense, would be excluded from these expenses

Figure 7.20 General Overview of Cash Budget Components. A cash budget will contain all the budgeted cash inflows and out flows from the sub-budgets as well as any cash items that might not appear on one of the sub-budgets. (attribution: Copyright Rice University, OpenStax, under CC BY-NC-SA 4.0 license)

The cash budget totals the cash receipts and adds it to the beginning cash balance to determine the available cash. From the available cash, the cash payments are subtracted to compute the net cash excess or deficiency of cash for the quarter. This amount is the potential ending cash balance. Organizations typically require a minimum cash balance. If the potential ending cash balance does not meet the minimum amount, management must plan to acquire financing to reach that amount. If the potential ending cash balance exceeds the minimum cash balance, the excess amount may be used to pay any financing loans and interest.

Big Bad Bikes has a minimum cash balance requirement of $10,000 and has a line of credit available for an interest rate of 19%. They also plan to issue additional capital stock for $5,000 in the first quarter, to pay taxes of $1,000 during each quarter, and to purchase a copier for $8,500 cash in the third quarter. The beginning cash balance for Big Bad Bikes is $13,000, which can be used to create the cash budget shown in Figure 7.21.

BIG BAD BIKES					
Cash Budget					
For the Year Ended December 31, 2019					
	Quarter 1	Quarter 2	Quarter 3	Quarter 4	Total
Beginning Cash Balance	$13,000	$10,000	$ 10,000	$ 10,000	$ 13,000
Collections from Customers					
(Cash Collections Schedule)	45,500	66,500	94,125	155,625	361,750
Issuing of Stock	5,000				5,000
Total Cash Collected during the Period	$50,500	$66,500	$ 94,125	$155,625	$366,750
Total Available Cash	$63,500	$76,500	$104,125	$165,625	$379,750
– Disbursements					
Direct Materials (Cash Payments Schedule)	3,060	5,620	6,560	10,000	25,240
Direct Labor (Direct Labor Budget)	19,500	17,250	27,000	42,000	105,750
Manufacturing Overhead Less Depreciation					
(MFG OH Budget)	28,925	28,588	30,050	32,300	119,863
Selling and Administrative Expenses Less					
Depreciation (Sales and Administrative					
Expense Budget)	18,500	18,500	19,750	22,250	79,000
Income Tax Expense	1,000	1,000	1,000	1,000	4,000
Purchase of Copier (Capital Asset Budget)			8,500		8,500
Total Disbursements	$70,985	$70,958	$ 92,860	$107,550	$342,353
Excess (deficiency) of Available Cash	($ 7,485)	$ 5,542	$ 11,265	$ 58,075	$ 37,397
Financing					
+ Borrowings	17,485	4,458			21,943
– Repayments Including Interest			(1,265)	(21,632)	(22,897)
Ending Cash Balance	$10,000	$10,000	$ 10,000	$ 36,443	$ 36,443

Figure 7.21 Cash Budget for Big Bad Bikes. (attribution: Copyright Rice University, OpenStax, under CC BY-NC-SA 4.0 license)

Budgeted Balance Sheet

The cash budget shows how cash changes from the beginning of the year to the end of the year, and the ending cash balance is the amount shown on the budgeted balance sheet. The **budgeted balance sheet** is the estimated assets, liabilities, and equities that the company would have at the end of the year if their performance were to meet its expectations. Table 7.1 shows a list of the most common changes to the balance sheet and where the information is derived.

Common Changes in the Budgeted Balance Sheet

Information Source	Balance Sheet Change
Cash balance	ending cash balance from the cash budget
Accounts Receivable balance	uncollected receivables from the cash collections schedule

Table 7.1

Common Changes in the Budgeted Balance Sheet

Information Source	Balance Sheet Change
Inventory	ending balance in inventory as shown from calculations to create the income statement
Machinery & Equipment	ending balance in the capital asset budget
Accounts Payable	unpaid purchases from the cash payments schedule

Table 7.1

Other balance sheet changes throughout the year are reflected in the income statement and statement of cash flows. For example, the beginning cash balance of Accounts Receivable plus the sales, less the cash collected results in the ending balance of Accounts Receivable. A similar formula is used to compute the ending balance in Accounts Payable. Other budgets and information such as the capital asset budget, depreciation, and financing loans are used as well.

To explain how to use a budgeted balance sheet, let's return to Big Bad Bikes. For simplicity, assume that they did not have accounts receivable or payable at the beginning of the year. They also incurred and paid back their financing during the year, so there is no ending debt. However, the cash budget shows cash inflows and outflows not related to sales or the purchase of materials. The company's capital assets increased by $8,500 from the copier purchase, and their common stock increased by $5,000 from the additional issue as shown in Figure 7.22.

BIG BAD BIKES
Budgeted Balance Sheet
December 31, 2019

	Jan. 1	Dec. 31
Cash	$13,000	$ 36,443
Accounts Receivable	0	78,250
– Allowance for Doubtful Accounts		(22,000)
Inventory	0	42,629
Machinery and Equipment	15,000	23,500
Accumulated Depreciation	(2,000)	(22,000)
Total Assets	$26,000	$136,822
Accounts Payable	$ 0	$ 6,000
Line of Credit		
Common Stock	15,000	20,000
Retained Earnings	11,000	110,822
Total Liability and Owner's Equity	$26,000	$136,822

Figure 7.22 Budgeted Balance Sheet for Big Bad Bikes. (attribution: Copyright Rice University, OpenStax, under CC BY-NC-SA 4.0 license)

Though there seem to be many budgets, they all fit together like a puzzle to create an overall picture of how a company expects the upcoming business year to look. Figure 7.15 detailed the components of the master budget, and can be used to summarize the budget process. All budgets begin with the sales budget. This budget estimates the number of units that need to be manufactured and precedes the production budget. The production budget (refer to Figure 7.6) provides the necessary information for the budgets needed to plan how many units will be produced. Knowing how many units need to be produced from the production budget, the direct materials budget, direct labor budget, and the manufacturing overhead budget are all prepared. The sales and administrative budget is a nonmanufacturing budget that relies on the sales estimates to pay commissions and other variable expenses. The sales and expenses estimated in all of these budgets are used to develop a budgeted income statement.

The estimated sales information is used to prepare the cash collections schedule, and the direct materials budget is used to prepare the cash payment schedule. The cash receipts and cash payments budget are combined with the direct labor budget, the manufacturing overhead budget, the sales and administrative budget, and the capital assets budget to develop the cash budget. Finally, all the information is used to flow to the budgeted balance sheet.

YOUR TURN

Creating a Master Budget

Molly Malone is starting her own company in which she will produce and sell Molly's Macaroons. Molly is trying to learn about the budget process as she puts her business plan together. Help Molly by explaining the optimal order for preparing the following budgets and schedules and why this is the optimal order.

- budgeted balance sheet
- budgeted income statement
- capital asset budget
- cash budget
- cash collections schedule
- cash payments schedule
- direct materials budget
- direct labor budget
- master budget
- manufacturing overhead
- production budget
- sales budget
- selling and administrative budget

Solution

A master budget always begins with the sales budget must be prepared first as this determines the number of units that will need to be produced. The next step would be to create the production budget, which helps determine the number of units that will need to be produced each period to meet sales goals. Once Molly knows how many units she will need to produce, she will need to budget the costs associated with those units, which will require her to create the direct materials budget, the direct labor budget and the manufacturing overhead budget. But Molly will have costs other than manufacturing costs so she will need to create a selling and administrative expenses budget. Molly will need to determine what are her capital asset needs and budget for those. Now that Molly has all her revenues budgeted and her costs budgeted, she can determine her budgeted cash inflows and outflows by putting together the cash schedules that lead to the cash budget. Molly will then need to create a cash collections schedule and a cash payments schedule and that information, along with the cash inflow and outflow information from her other budgets, will allow her to create her cash budget. Once Molly has completed her cash budget she will be able to put together her budgeted income statement and budgeted balance sheet.

7.4 Prepare Flexible Budgets

A company makes a budget for the smallest time period possible so that management can find and adjust problems to minimize their impact on the business. Everything starts with the estimated sales, but what happens if the sales are more or less than expected? How does this affect the budget? What adjustments does a company have to make in order to compare the actual numbers to budgeted numbers when evaluating results? If production is higher than planned and has been increased to meet the increased sales, expenses will be over budget. But is this bad? To account for actual sales and expenses differing from budgeted sales and expenses, companies will often create flexible budgets to allow budgets to fluctuate with future demand.

Flexible Budgets

A **flexible budget** is one based on different volumes of sales. A flexible budget flexes the static budget for each anticipated level of production. This flexibility allows management to estimate what the budgeted numbers would look like at various levels of sales. Flexible budgets are prepared at each analysis period (usually monthly), rather than in advance, since the idea is to compare the operating income to the expenses deemed appropriate at the actual production level.

Big Bad Bikes is planning to use a flexible budget when they begin making trainers. The company knows its variable costs per unit and knows it is introducing its new product to the marketplace. Its estimations of sales and sales price will likely change as the product takes hold and customers purchase it. Big Bad Bikes developed a flexible budget that shows the change in income and expenses as the number of units changes. It also looked at the effect a change in price would have if the number of units remained the same. The expenses that do not change are the fixed expenses, as shown in Figure 7.23.

BIG BAD BIKES				
Flexible Budget				
For Year Ended December 31, 2019				
Units Sold		1,000	1,500	1,500
Sales Price		$ 70	$ 70	$ 75
Sales		$70,000	$105,000	$112,500
	Per-unit cost			
Cost of Goods Sold				
Direct Material	$ 4	$ 4,000	$ 6,000	$ 6,000
Direct Labor	15	15,000	22,500	22,500
Variable Manufacturing Overhead	3	3,000	4,500	4,500
Fixed Manufacturing Overhead		29,000	29,000	29,000
Total Cost of Goods Sold		51,000	62,000	62,000
Gross Profit		19,000	43,000	50,500
Variable Sales and Admin	2.50	2,500	3,750	3,750
Fixed Sales and Admin		18,000	18,000	18,000
Income Taxes		1,000	1,000	1,000
Total Other Expenses		21,500	22,750	22,750
Net Income (Loss)		(2,500)	20,250	27,750

Figure 7.23 Flexible Budget for Big Bad Bikes. (attribution: Copyright Rice University, OpenStax, under CC BY-NC-SA 4.0 license)

Static versus Flexible Budgets

A **static budget** is one that is prepared based on a single level of output for a given period. The master budget, and all the budgets included in the master budget, are examples of static budgets. Actual results are compared to the static budget numbers as one means to evaluate company performance. However, this comparison may be like comparing apples to oranges because variable costs should follow production, which should follow sales. Thus, if sales differ from what is budgeted, then comparing actual costs to budgeted costs may not provide a clear indicator of how well the company is meeting its targets. A flexible budget created each period allows for a comparison of apples to apples because it will calculate budgeted costs based on the actual sales activity.

For example, Figure 7.24 shows a static quarterly budget for 1,500 trainers sold by Big Bad Bikes. The budget will change if there are more or fewer units sold.

BIG BAD BIKES Static Quarterly Budget For Each Quarter	
Units Sold	1,500
Sales Price	$ 70
Sales	105,000
Cost of Goods Sold	
Direct Material	6,000
Direct Labor	22,500
Variable Manufacturing Overhead	4,500
Fixed Manufacturing Overhead	29,000
Total Cost of Goods Sold	$ 62,000
Gross Profit	$ 43,000
Variable Sales and Admin	3,750
Fixed Sales and Admin	18,000
Interest Expense	0
Income Taxes	1,000
Total Other Expenses	$ 22,750
Net Income (Loss)	$ 20,250

Figure 7.24 Static Budget for Big Bad Bikes. (attribution: Copyright Rice University, OpenStax, under CC BY-NC-SA 4.0 license)

Budget with Varying Levels of Production

Companies develop a budget based on their expectations for their most likely level of sales and expenses. Often, a company can expect that their production and sales volume will vary from budget period to budget period. They can use their various expected levels of production to create a flexible budget that includes these different levels of production. Then, they can modify the flexible budget when they have their actual production volume and compare it to the flexible budget for the same production volume. A flexible budget is more complicated, requires a solid understanding of a company's fixed and variable expenses, and allows for greater control over changes that occur throughout the year. For example, suppose a proposed sale of items does not occur because the expected client opted to go with another supplier. In a static budget situation, this would result in large variances in many accounts due to the static budget being set based on sales that included the potential large client. A flexible budget on the other hand would allow management to adjust their expectations in the budget for both changes in costs and revenue that would occur from the loss of the potential client. The changes made in the flexible budget would then be compared to what actually occurs to result in more realistic and representative variance. This ability to change the budget also makes it easier to pinpoint who is responsible if a revenue or cost target is missed.

Big Bad Bikes used the flexible budget concept to develop a budget based on its expectation that production levels will vary by quarter. By the fourth quarter, sales are expected to be strong enough to pay back the financing from earlier in the year. The budget shown in Figure 7.25 illustrates the payment of interest and contains information helpful to management when determining which items should be produced if production capacity is limited.

BIG BAD BIKES Varying Production Budget Flexible Budget					
		Quarter 1	Quarter 2	Quarter 3	Quarter 4
Units Sold		1,000	1,000	1,500	2,500
Sales Price		$ 70	$ 70	$ 75	$ 75
Sales		70,000	70,000	112,500	187,500
	Per-unit cost				
Cost of Goods Sold					
Direct Material	$ 4	$ 4,000	$ 4,000	$ 6,000	$ 10,000
Direct Labor	15	15,000	15,000	22,500	37,500
Variable Manufacturing Overhead	3	3,000	3,000	4,500	7,500
Fixed Manufacturing Overhead		29,000	29,000	29,000	29,000
Total Cost of Goods Sold		51,000	51,000	62,000	84,000
Gross Profit		19,000	19,000	50,500	103,500
Variable Sales and Admin	2.50	2,500	2,500	3,750	6,250
Fixed Sales and Admin		18,000	18,000	18,000	18,000
Interest Expense					1,653
Income Taxes		1000	1000	1000	1000
Total Other Expenses		21,500	21,500	22,750	26,903
Net Income (Loss)		(2,500)	(2,500)	27,750	76,597

Figure 7.25 Varying Production Levels for Big Bad Bikes. (attribution: Copyright Rice University, OpenStax, under CC BY-NC-SA 4.0 license)

CONCEPTS IN PRACTICE

Flexible Budgets and Sustainability

The ability to provide flexible budgets can be critical in new or changing businesses where the accuracy of estimating sales or usage my not be strong. For example, organizations are often reporting their sustainability efforts and may have some products that require more electricity than other products. The reporting of the energy per unit of output has sometimes been in error and can mislead management into making changes that may or may not help the company. For example, based on the energy per unit reported, management may decide to change the product mix, the amount that is outsourced, and/or the amount that is produced.[1] If the energy output isn't correct, the decisions may be wrong and create an adverse impact on the budget.

LINK TO LEARNING

In theory, a flexible budget is not difficult to develop since the variable costs change with production and

---

1 Jon Bartley, et al. "Using Flexible Budgeting to Improve Sustainability Measures.: *American Institute of CPAs*. Jan. 23, 2017. https://www.aicpa.org/interestareas/businessindustryandgovernment/resources/sustainability/improvesustainabilitymeasures.html

the fixed costs remain the same. However, planning to meet an organization's goals can be very difficult if there are not many variable costs, if the cash inflows are relatively fixed, and if the fixed costs are high. For example, this article shows some large U.S. cities are faced with complicated budgets (https://openstax.org/l/50HighFixedCost) because of high fixed costs.

7.5 Explain How Budgets Are Used to Evaluate Goals

As you've learned, an advantage of budgeting is evaluating performance. Having a strong understanding of their budgets helps managers keep track of expenses and work toward the company's goals. Companies need to understand their revenue and expense details to develop budgets as a tool for planning operations and cash flow. Part of understanding revenue and expenses is evaluating the prior year. Did the company earn the expected profit? Could it have earned a higher profit? What expenses or revenues were not on the budget? Critically evaluating the actual results versus the estimated budgetary results can help management plan for the future. Variance analysis helps the manager analyze its results. It does not necessarily find a problem, but it does indicate where a problem may exist. The same is true for favorable variances as well as unfavorable variances. A favorable variance occurs when revenue is higher than budgeted or expenses are lower than budgeted. An unfavorable variance is when revenue is lower than budgeted or expenses are higher than budgeted.

Comparing Favorable to Unfavorable Variances

Favorable	Unfavorable
Actual Sales > Budgeted Sales	Actual Sales < Budgeted Sales
Actual Expenses < Budgeted Expenses	Actual Expenses > Budgeted expenses

Table 7.2

It is easy to understand that an unfavorable variance may be a problem. But that is not always true, as a higher labor rate may mean the company has a higher quality employee who is able to waste less material. Likewise, having a favorable variance indicates that more revenue was earned or less expenses were incurred but further analysis can indicate if costs were cut too far and better materials should have been purchased.

If a company has only a static budget, meaningful comparisons are difficult. Analyzing the sales for Bid Bad Bikes will illustrate whether there was a profit and how net income impacts the company. In the third quarter, Big Bad Bikes sold 1,400 trainers and had third quarter net income of $15,915 as shown in Figure 7.26.

BIG BAD BIKES	
Income Statement	
For the Quarter Ended September 30, 2019	
Units Sold	1,400
Sales Price	$ 75
Sales	$98,000
Cost of Goods Sold	
Direct Material	$ 5,550
Direct Labor per Unit	21,500
Variable Manufacturing Overhead	4,100
Fixed Manufacturing Overhead	28,900
Total Cost of Goods Sold	60,050
Gross Profit	37,950
Variable Sales and Administration	3,550
Fixed Sales and Administration	17,500
Interest Expense	0
Income Taxes	985
Total Other Expenses	22,035
Net Income (Loss)	22,915

Figure 7.26 Actual Quarter 3 Income Statement for Big Bad Bikes. (attribution: Copyright Rice University, OpenStax, under CC BY-NC-SA 4.0 license)

The company earned a profit during the third quarter, but what does that mean to the company? Simply having net income instead of a net loss does not help plan for the future. The third quarter static budget was for the sale of 1,500 units. Comparing that budget to the actual results shows whether there is a favorable variance or an unfavorable variance. A comparison of the actual costs with the budget for the third quarter, as shown in Figure 7.27, has a favorable variance for all of the expenses and an unfavorable variance for everything associated with revenues.

BIG BAD BIKES				
Actual Versus Static Budget Variance				
Quarter Ended September 30, 2019				
	Actual	Budget	Variance	
Units Sold	1,400	1,500	(100)	Unfavorable
Sales Price	$ 75	$ 75	$ 75	
Sales	$105,000	$112,500	($7,500)	Unfavorable
Cost of Goods Sold				
Direct Material	$ 5,550	$ 6,000	$ 450	Favorable
Direct Labor	21,500	22,500	1,000	Favorable
Variable Manufacturing Overhead	4,100	4,500	400	Favorable
Fixed Manufacturing Overhead	28,900	29,000	100	Favorable
Total Cost of Goods Sold	60,050	62,000	1,950	Favorable
Gross Profit	44,950	50,500	(5,550)	Unfavorable
Variable Sales and Administration	3,550	3,750	200	Favorable
Fixed Sales and Administration	17,500	18,000	500	Favorable
Income Taxes	985	1,000	15	Favorable
Total Other Expenses	22,035	22,750	715	Favorable
Net Income (Loss)	22,915	27,750	(4,835)	Unfavorable

Figure 7.27 Actual versus Static Budget for Big Bad Bikes. (attribution: Copyright Rice University, OpenStax, under CC BY-NC-SA 4.0 license)

How do those results advise management when evaluating the company's performance? It is difficult to look at one variance and make a conclusion about the company or its management. However, the variances can help narrow down the areas that need addressing because they differ from the budgeted amount. For example, looking at the variance when using a static budget does not indicate the amount of the variance results because they sold 100 fewer units than budgeted. The variance for the cost of goods sold is favorable, but it should be if production was less than the budget. A static budget does not evaluate whether costs for 1,400 were appropriate for production of those 1,400 units.

Using a static budget to evaluate performance affects the bottom line as well as the individual expenses. The net income for the sale of 1,400 units is less than the budgeted net income for 1,500 units, but it does not indicate whether expenses were appropriate for 1,400 units. If there had been 1,600 units sold, the expenses would be more than the budgeted amount, but sales would be higher. Would it be fair to evaluate a manager's control over their expenses using a static budget?

ETHICAL CONSIDERATIONS

Budget Manipulation and Ethics Training

Why is ethics training important? An organization that bases a manager's evaluation and pay on how close to the budget the division performs may inadvertently encourage that manager to act unethically in order to get a pay raise. Many employees manipulate the budget process to enhance their earnings by garnering bonuses based upon questionably ethical behavior and improper financial reporting. Generally, this unethical behavior involves either manipulating the numbers in the budget or modifying the timing of reports to apply income to a different budget period. Kenton Walker and Gary Fleischman studied ethics in budgeting and determined that certain ethics-related structures in a business created a better operational environment.

The study found that the existence of formal ethical codes, ethics training, good management role models, and social pressure to be disclosing within an organization can be a deterrent to budget manipulation by employees. The authors recommended: "Therefore, organizations should carefully cultivate an ethical atmosphere that is sensitive to the pressures employees may feel to game the budget through actions that involve cheating and/or manipulating earnings targets to maximize bonuses." [2] The study concluded that requiring organizational ethics training that includes role playing helps teach ethical behavior in budgeting and other areas of business. Ethics training never goes out so style.

Evaluating the expenses on a flexible budget computed for the number of units sold would provide an indication of management's ability to control expenses. As shown in Figure 7.28, some expenses have a favorable variance, while others have an unfavorable variance. This type of variance analysis provides more information to evaluate management and help prepare the next year's budget. For example, the direct labor in the flexible budget comparison shows an unfavorable variance, meaning the direct labor expense was more than budgeted for the production of 1,400 units. When comparing direct labor expense, the direct labor in the static budget mentioned earlier was even larger because it computed direct labor required to manufacture 1,500 units. It is not surprising that the static budget variance is favorable because 100 fewer units were actually produced. However, that information is not as useful as the unfavorable variance when comparing 1,400 units produced versus the budgeted direct labor for 1,400 units used.

BIG BAD BIKES Actual Versus Flexible Budget Variance Quarter Ended September 30, 2019				
	Actual	Budget	Variance	
Units Sold	1,400	1,400	None	
Sales Price	$ 75	$ 75		
Sales	$105,000	$105,000	None	
Cost of Goods Sold				
Direct Material	$ 5,550	$ 5,600	$ 50	Favorable
Direct Labor	21,500	21,000	(500)	Unfavorable
Variable Manufacturing Overhead	4,100	4,200	100	Favorable
Fixed Manufacturing Overhead	28,900	29,000	100	Favorable
Total Cost of Goods Sold	60,050	59,800	(250)	Unfavorable
Gross Profit	44,950	45,200	(250)	Unfavorable
Variable Sales and Administration	3,550	3,500	(50)	Unfavorable
Fixed Sales and Administration	17,500	18,000	500	Favorable
Interest Expense	0	0	0	
Income Taxes	985	1,000	15	Favorable
Total Other Expenses	22,035	22,500	465	Favorable
Net Income (Loss)	22,915	22,700	215	Favorable

Figure 7.28 Actual versus Flexible Budget for Big Bad Bikes. (attribution: Copyright Rice University, OpenStax, under CC BY-NC-SA 4.0 license)

---

2   Kenton B. Walker, et al. "Toeing the Line: The Ethics of Manipulating Budgets and Earnings." *Management Accounting Quarterly* 14, no. 3 (Spring 2013). https://www.imanet.org/-/media/f4869589d9d444de8c211d245a0192ff.ashx

THINK IT THROUGH

A Budget for a New Business

You are beginning your own business and developed a budget based on modest sales and expense assumptions. The actual results are very close to the budget at the end of the first and second months. During the third month, both cash collected and paid differ significantly from the budget. What could be the cause and what should you do?

LINK TO LEARNING

Budgeting is only the beginning of the process. Evaluating the results to determine if the financial goals are being met can make the difference in whether an organization or individual meets its goals or not. Forbes recognizes that budgeting is an important personal task that should start early in one's professional career. This [article provides some custom budgeting guidelines for young adults (https://openstax.org/l/50BudgetGuide)](https://openstax.org/l/50BudgetGuide) to help.

 **Key Terms**

budget quantitative plan estimating when and how much cash or other resources will be received and how the cash or other resources will be used

budgeted balance sheet estimated assets, liabilities, and equities that the company would have at the end of the year if their performance were to meet its expectations

budgeted income statement statement similar to a traditional income statement except it contains budgeted data

capital asset budget budget showing the organization's plans to invest in long-term assets

cash budget combined budget of all cash inflows and outflows of the organization

cash collections schedule schedule showing when cash will be received from customers

cash payments schedule schedule showing when cash will be used to pay for direct material purchases

direct labor budget budget based on the production budget used to ensure the proper amount of staff is available for production and that there is money available to pay for the labor

direct materials budget budget combining the production budget with the direct material per unit to ensure the proper quantity of direct materials is available when needed for production

financial budget category of budgeting that details estimates for cash inflows and outflows through planned operations and changes capital investments of assets, liabilities, and equities

flexible budget budget based on different levels of activity

manufacturing overhead budget budget including the remainder of the production costs not covered by the direct materials and direct labor budgets

master budget overall budget that includes the operating and financial budgets

operating budget category of budgeting that helps managers plan and manage production, order materials, schedule direct labor, and monitor overhead expenses

production budget budget showing the number of units that need to be produced for each period based on sales estimates and required inventory levels

rolling budget budget that is continuously updated by adding an additional budget period at the end of the current budget period

sales budget budget showing the expected sales in units and the sales price for the budget period

selling and administrative expense budget budget showing the variable and fixed expenses estimated to be incurred in all areas other than production

static budget budget prepared for a single level of activity for a given period

zero-based budgeting budget that begins with zero dollars and then includes in the budget only revenue and expenses that can be supported or justified

 **Summary**

7.1 Describe How and Why Managers Use Budgets
- A good budgeting system assists management in reaching their goals through the planning and control of cash inflows through revenue and financing and outflows through payment and expenses.
- There are various budgeting strategies including bottom-up, top-down, and zero-based budgeting.
- A static budget is prepared at one level of activity, while a flexible budget allows the variable expenses to be adjusted for various levels of activity.
- A master budget includes the subcategories of operating budgets and financial budgets.
- A master budget is developed at the estimated level of activity.

7.2 Prepare Operating Budgets
- The sales budget is the first budget developed, and the estimated sales in turn guide the production budget.
- The production budget shows the quantity of goods produced for each time period and leads to computing when and how much direct material needs to be ordered, when and how much labor needs to be scheduled, and when and how much manufacturing overhead needs to be planned.
- The sales and administrative budget plans for the nonmanufacturing expenses.
- All operating budgets combine to develop the budgeted income statement.

7.3 Prepare Financial Budgets
- The financial budgets include the capital asset budget and the cash budget. The cash collections schedule and cash payments schedule are computed and combined with the other budgets to develop the cash budget.
- Information from the other budgets and the budgeted income statement are used to develop the budgeted balance sheet.

7.4 Prepare Flexible Budgets
- A master budget and related budgets are prepared as static budgets for the estimated level of activity.
- A flexible budget adjusts the budgets for various levels of activity and allows for the actual results to be evaluated at the actual volume of activity.

7.5 Explain How Budgets Are Used to Evaluate Goals
- Management's evaluations of the actual results versus the estimated budgetary results help plan for the future.
- Favorable variances occur when sales are higher or expenses are lower than budgeted.
- Unfavorable variances occur when sales are lower or expenses are higher than budgeted.

Multiple Choice

1. **LO 7.1** Which of the following is *not* a part of budgeting?
   A. planning
   B. finding bottlenecks
   C. providing performance evaluations
   D. preventing net operating losses

2. **LO 7.1** Which of the following is an operating budget?
   A. cash budget
   B. production budget
   C. tax budget
   D. capital budget

3. **LO 7.1** Which of the following is a finance budget?
   A. cash budget
   B. production budget
   C. direct materials purchasing budget
   D. tax budget

4. **LO 7.1** Which approach is most likely to result in employee buy-in to the budget?
   A. top-down approach
   B. bottom-up approach
   C. total participation approach
   D. basing the budget on the prior year

5. **LO 7.1** Which approach requires management to justify all its expenditures?
   A. bottom-up approach
   B. zero-based budgeting
   C. master budgeting
   D. capital allocation budgeting

6. **LO 7.1** Which of the following is true in a bottom-up budgeting approach?
   A. Every expense needs to be justified.
   B. Supervisors tell departments their budget amount and the departments are free to work within those amounts.
   C. Departments budget their needs however they see fit.
   D. Departments determine their needs and relate them to the overall goals.

7. **LO 7.1** The most common budget is prepared for a _____.
   A. week
   B. month
   C. quarter
   D. year

8. **LO 7.2** Which of the operating budgets is prepared first?
   A. production budget
   B. sales budget
   C. cash received budget
   D. cash payments budget

9. **LO 7.2** The direct materials budget is prepared using which budget's information?
   A. cash payments budget
   B. cash receipts budget
   C. production budget
   D. raw materials budget

10. **LO 7.2** Which of the following is *not* an operating budget?
    A. sales budget
    B. production budget
    C. direct labor budget
    D. cash budget

11. **LO 7.2** Which of the following statements is *not* correct?
    A. The sales budget is computed by multiplying estimated sales by the sales price.
    B. The production budget begins with the sales estimated for each period.
    C. The direct materials budget begins with the sales estimated for each period.
    D. The sales budget is typically the first budget prepared.

12. LO 7.2 The units required in production each period are computed by which of the following methods?
    A. adding budgeted sales to the desired ending inventory and subtracting beginning inventory
    B. adding beginning inventory, budgeted sales, and desired ending inventory
    C. adding beginning inventory to budgeted sales and subtracting desired ending inventory
    D. adding budgeted sales to the beginning inventory and subtracting the desired ending inventory.

13. LO 7.3 The cash budget is part of which category of budgets?
    A. sales budget
    B. cash payments budget
    C. finance budget
    D. operating budget

14. LO 7.3 Which is *not* a section of the cash budget?
    A. cash receipts
    B. cash disbursements
    C. allowance for uncollectible accounts
    D. financing needs

15. LO 7.3 Which budget is the starting point in preparing financial budgets?
    A. the budgeted income statement
    B. the budgeted balance sheet
    C. the capital expense budget
    D. the cash receipts budget

16. LO 7.3 Which of the following includes only financial budgets?
    A. capital asset budget, budgeted income statement, sales budget
    B. production budget, capital asset budget, budgeted balance sheet
    C. cash budget, budgeted balance sheet, capital asset budget
    D. budgeted income statement, direct material purchases budget, cash budget

17. LO 7.4 Which budget evaluates the results of operations at the actual level of activity?
    A. capital budget
    B. cash budget
    C. flexible budget
    D. static budget

18. LO 7.4 What is the main difference between static and flexible budgets?
    A. The fixed manufacturing overhead is adjusted for units sold in the flexible budget.
    B. The variable manufacturing overhead is adjusted in the static budget.
    C. There is no difference between the budgets.
    D. The variable costs are adjusted in a flexible budget.

Questions

1. LO 7.1 What is a budget and what are the different types of budgets?

2. LO 7.1 What is the difference between budgeting and long-range planning?

3. LO 7.1 What are the advantages and disadvantages of the bottom-up budgeting approach?

4. **LO 7.1** Why might a rolling budget require more management participation than an annual budget?

5. **LO 7.2** What information is necessary for the operating budgets?

6. **LO 7.2** What operating budget exists for manufacturing but not for a retail company?

7. **LO 7.3** What is the process for developing a budgeted balance sheet?

8. **LO 7.3** Which of the financial budgets is the most important? Why?

9. **LO 7.4** A company has prepared the operating budget and the cash budget. It is now preparing the budgeted balance sheet. Identify the document that contains each of these balances.
    A. cash
    B. accounts receivable
    C. finished goods inventory
    D. accounts payable
    E. equipment purchases

10. **LO 7.4** Fill in the blanks: A flexible budget summarizes _____ and _____ for various volume levels by adjusting the _____ costs for the various levels of activities. The _____ costs remain the same for all levels of activities.

11. **LO 7.4** What information is included in the capital asset budget?

12. **LO 7.5** Why does budget planning typically begin with the sales forecast?

13. **LO 7.5** What steps should be considered if a budget is to be set and later have its results evaluated?

Exercise Set A

EA1. LO 7.2 Blue Book printing is budgeting sales of 25,000 units and already has 5,000 in beginning inventory. How many units must be produced to also meet the 7,000 units required in ending inventory?

EA2. LO 7.2 How many units are in beginning inventory if 32,000 units are budgeted for sales, 35,000 units are produced, and the desired ending inventory is 9,000 units?

EA3. LO 7.2 Navigator sells GPS trackers for $50 each. It expects sales of 5,000 units in quarter 1 and a 5% increase each subsequent quarter for the next 8 quarters. Prepare a sales budget by quarter for the first year.

EA4. LO 7.2 One Device makes universal remote controls and expects to sell 500 units in January, 800 in February, 450 in March, 550 in April, and 600 in May. The required ending inventory is 20% of the next month's sales. Prepare a production budget for the first four months of the year.

EA5. LO 7.2 Sunrise Poles manufactures hiking poles and is planning on producing 4,000 units in March and 3,700 in April. Each pole requires a half pound of material, which costs $1.20 per pound. The company's policy is to have enough material on hand to equal 10% of the next month's production needs and to maintain a finished goods inventory equal to 25% of the next month's production needs. What is the budgeted cost of purchases for March?

EA6. LO 7.2 Given the following information from Rowdy Enterprises' direct materials budget, how much direct materials needs to be purchased?

Beginning materials inventory	$ 75,800
Ending materials inventory	79,200
Materials needed for production	500,000

EA7. LO 7.2 Each unit requires direct labor of 2.2 hours. The labor rate is $11.50 per hour and next year's direct labor budget totals $834,900. How many units are included in the production budget for next year?

EA8. LO 7.2 How many units are estimated to be sold if Skyline, Inc., has a planned production of 900,000 units, a desired beginning inventory of 160,000 units, and a desired ending inventory of 100,000 units?

EA9. LO 7.3 Cash collections for Wax On Candles found that 60% of sales were collected in the month of the sale, 30% was collected the month after the sale, and 10% was collected the second month after the sale. Given the sales shown, how much cash will be collected in January and February?

Nov.	Dec.	Jan.	Feb.
$25,000	$35,000	$20,000	$25,000

EA10. LO 7.3 Nonna's Re-Appliance Store collects 55% of its accounts receivable in the month of sale and 40% in the month after the sale. Given the following sales, how much cash will be collected in February?

Dec. 2017	Jan. 2018	Feb. 2018
$20,000	$60,000	$70,000

EA11. LO 7.3 Dream Big Pillow Co. pays 65% of its purchases in the month of purchase, 30% the month after the purchase, and 5% in the second month following the purchase. It made the following purchases at the end of 2017 and the beginning of 2018:

Nov. 2017	Dec. 2017	Jan. 2018	Feb. 2018	Mar. 2018
$60,000	$50,000	$35,000	$40,000	$45,000

EA12. LO 7.3 Desiccate purchases direct materials each month. Its payment history shows that 70% is paid in the month of purchase with the remaining balance paid the month after purchase. Prepare a cash payment schedule for March if in January through March, it purchased $35,000, $37,000, and $39,000, respectively.

EA13. LO 7.3 What is the amount of budgeted cash payments if purchases are budgeted for $420,000 and the beginning and ending balances of accounts payable are $95,000 and $92,000, respectively?

EA14. LO 7.3 Halifax Shoes has 30% of its sales in cash and the remainder on credit. Of the credit sales, 65% is collected in the month of sale, 25% is collected the month after the sale, and 5% is collected the second month after the sale. How much cash will be collected in August if sales are estimated as $75,000 in June, $65,000 in July, and $90,000 in August?

EA15. LO 7.4 Cold X, Inc. uses this information when preparing their flexible budget: direct materials of $2 per unit, direct labor of $3 per unit, and manufacturing overhead of $1 per unit. Fixed costs are $35,000. What would be the budgeted amounts for 20,000 and 25,000 units?

EA16. LO 7.4 Using the provided budgeted information for production of 10,000 and 15,000 units, prepare a flexible budget for 17,000 units.

Production	10,000 units	15,000 units
Expense A	$15,000	$22,500
Expense B	21,000	21,000
Expense C	43,000	43,000

EA17. LO 7.5 The production cost for a waterproof phone case is $7 per unit and fixed costs are $23,000 per month. How much is the favorable or unfavorable variance if 5,500 units were produced for a total of $61,000?

Exercise Set B

EB1. LO 7.2 Lovely Wedding printing is budgeting sales of 32,000 units and already has 4,000 in beginning inventory. How many units must be produced to also meet the 6,000 units required in ending inventory?

EB2. LO 7.2 How many units are in beginning inventory if 32,000 units are budgeted for sales, 35,000 units are produced, and the desired ending inventory is 9,000 units?

EB3. LO 7.2 Barnstormer sells airplane accessories for $20 each. It expects sales of 120,000 units in quarter 1 and a 7% increase each subsequent quarter for the next 8 quarters. Prepare a sales budget by quarter for the first year.

EB4. LO 7.2 Rehydrator makes a nutrition additive and expects to sell 3,000 units in January, 2,000 in February, 2,500 in March, 2,700 in April, and 2,900 in May. The required ending inventory is 20% of the next month's sales, and the beginning inventory on January 1 was 600 units. Prepare a production budget for the first four months of the year.

EB5. LO 7.2 Cloud Shoes manufactures recovery sandals and is planning on producing 12,000 units in March and 11,500 in April. Each sandal requires 1.2 yards if material, which costs $3.00 per yard. The company's policy is to have enough material on hand to equal 15% of next month's production needs and to maintain a finished goods inventory equal to 20% of the next month's production needs. What is the budgeted cost of purchases for March?

EB6. LO 7.2 Given the following information from Power Enterprises' direct materials budget, how much direct materials needs to be purchased?

Beginning materials inventory	$101,200
Ending materials inventory	105,300
Materials needed for production	890,250

EB7. LO 7.2 Each unit requires direct labor of 4.1 hours. The labor rate is $13.75 per hour and next year's production is estimated at 75,000 units. What is the amount to be included in next year's direct labor budget?

EB8. LO 7.2 How many units are estimated to be sold if Kino, Inc., has planned production of 750,000 units, a desired beginning inventory of 30,000 units, and a desired ending inventory of 45,000 units?

EB9. LO 7.3 Cash collections for Renew Lights found that 65% of sales were collected in the month of sale, 25% was collected the month after the sale, and 10% was collected the second month after the sale. Given the sales shown, how much cash will be collected in March and April?

Jan.	Feb.	Mar.	Apr.
$90,000	$120,000	$75,000	$85,000

EB10. LO 7.3 My Aunt's Closet Store collects 60% of its accounts receivable in the month of sale and 35% in the month after the sale. Given the following sales, how much cash will be collected in March?

Feb. 2018	Mar. 2018	Apr. 2018
$20,000	$60,000	$70,000

EB11. LO 7.3 Gear Up Co. pays 65% of its purchases in the month of purchase, 30% in the month after the purchase, and 5% in the second month following the purchase. What are the cash payments if it made the following purchases in 2018?

Feb. 2018	Mar. 2018	Apr. 2018	May 2018	June 2018
$90,000	$92,000	$101,000	$98,000	$99,500

EB12. LO 7.3 Drainee purchases direct materials each month. Its payment history shows that 65% is paid in the month of purchase with the remaining balance paid the month after purchase. Prepare a cash payment schedule for January using this data: in December through February, it purchased $22,000, $25,000, and $23,000 respectively.

EB13. LO 7.3 What is the amount of budgeted cash payments if purchases are budgeted for $190,500 and the beginning and ending balances of accounts payable are $21,000 and $25,000, respectively?

EB14. LO 7.3 Earthie's Shoes has 55% of its sales in cash and the remainder on credit. Of the credit sales, 70% is collected in the month of sale, 15% is collected the month after the sale, and 10% is collected the second month after the sale. How much cash will be collected in June if sales are estimated as $75,000 in April, $65,000 in May, and $90,000 in June?

EB15. LO 7.4 Judge's Gavel uses this information when preparing their flexible budget: direct materials of $3 per unit, direct labor of $2.50 per unit, and manufacturing overhead of $1.25 per unit. Fixed costs are $49,000. What would be the budgeted amounts for 33,000 and 35,000 units?

EB16. LO 7.4 Using the following budgeted information for production of 5,000 and 12,000 units, prepare a flexible budget for 9,000 units.

Production	5,000 units	12,000 units
Expense A	$17,500	$42,000
Expense B	19,000	19,000
Expense C	21,000	21,000

EB17. LO 7.5 The production cost for UV protective sunglasses is $5.50 per unit and fixed costs are $19,400 per month. How much is the favorable or unfavorable variance if 14,000 units were produced for a total of $97,000?

Problem Set A

PA1. LO 7.2 Lens Junction sells lenses for $45 each and is estimating sales of 15,000 units in January and 18,000 in February. Each lens consists of 2 pounds of silicon costing $2.50 per pound, 3 oz of solution costing $3 per ounce, and 30 minutes of direct labor at a labor rate of $18 per hour. Desired inventory levels are:

	Jan. 31	Feb. 28	Mar. 31
Beginning inventory			
Finished goods	4,500	4,900	5,000
Direct materials: silicon	8,500	9,100	9,200
Direct materials: solution	11,200	12,000	13,000

Prepare a sales budget, production budget, direct materials budget for silicon and solution, and a direct labor budget.

PA2. LO 7.2 The data shown were obtained from the financial records of Italian Exports, Inc., for March:

Estimated sales	$560,000
Sales	567,923
Purchases	294,823
Ending inventory	10%*
Administrative salaries	50,320
Marketing expense	5%**
Sales commissions	2%**
Rent expense	7,500
Depreciation expense	1,100
Utilities	2,500
Taxes	15%***

*of next month's sales
**of sales
***of income before taxes

Sales are expected to increase each month by 10%. Prepare a budgeted income statement.

PA3. LO 7.2 Echo Amplifiers prepared the following sales budget for the first quarter of 2018:

	Jan.	Feb.	Mar.
Units	1,000	1,200	1,500
Sales price	$ 100	$ 100	$ 100
Budgeted sales	$10,000	$12,000	$15,000

It also has this additional information related to its expenses:

Direct material per unit	$ 1.50
Direct labor per unit	2
Variable manufacturing overhead per hour	0.50
Fixed manufacturing overhead per month	3,000
Sales commissions per unit	15
Sales salaries per month	5,000
Delivery expense per unit	0.50
Factory utilities per month	5,000
Administrative salaries per month	20,000
Marketing expenses per month	8,000
Insurance expense per month	11,000
Depreciation expense per month	9,000

Prepare a sales and administrative expense budget for each month in the quarter ending March 31, 2018.

PA4. LO 7.2 Prepare a budgeted income statement using the information shown.

Sales (units)	15,000
Sales price per unit	$ 40
Uncollectible expense	1%*
Direct material per unit	$ 2
Direct labor per unit (hours)	0.5
Direct labor rate per hour	$ 20
Manufacturing overhead	$15,000
Variable sales and administration expenses per unit	$ 2
Fixed sales and administration expenses	$20,000
Taxes	15%**

*of sales
**of income before taxes

PA5. LO 7.2 Spree Party Lights overhead expenses are:

Indirect material, pounds per unit	0.25
Indirect material, cost per pound	$ 2
Indirect labor hours	1
Indirect labor rate per hour	$ 16.50
Variable maintenance per unit	$ 0.75
Variable utilities per unit	$ 0.20
Supervisor salaries	$10,000
Maintenance salaries	$ 9,000
Insurance	$ 3,000
Depreciation	$ 1,500

Prepare a manufacturing overhead budget if the number of units to produce for January, February, and March are 2,500, 3,000, and 2,700, respectively.

PA6. LO 7.3 Relevant data from the Poster Company's operating budgets are:

	Quarter 1	Quarter 2
Sales	$208,470	$211,539
Direct material purchases	115,295	120,832
Direct labor	75,205	73,299
Manufacturing overhead	25,300	25,300
Selling and administration expenses	33,500	33,500
Depreciation included in selling and administration	1,500	1,000
Collections from customers	215,392	240,155
Cash payments for purchases	114,295	119,253

Additional data: Capital assets were sold in January for $10,000 and $4,500 in May. Dividends of $4,500 were paid in February. The beginning cash balance was $60,359 and a required minimum cash balance is $59,000. Use this information to prepare a cash budget for the first two quarters of the year

PA7. LO 7.3 Fill in the missing information from the following schedules:

Sales Budget
For the Year Ended December 31, 2018

	Quarter 1	Quarter 2	Quarter 3	Quarter 4	Total
Expected sales (units)	7,500	8,250	8,750	9,000	?
Sales price per unit	$ 45	$ 50	$ 50	$ 55	
Total sales revenue	$337,500	$412,500	$437,500	?	?

Production Budget
For the Year Ended December 31, 2018

	Quarter 1	Quarter 2	Quarter 3	Quarter 4	Q1, Year 2
Expected sales	7,500	8,250	8,750	9,000	8,000
Desired ending inventory	1,650	1,750	1,800	?	900
Total required units	9,150	10,000	10,550	10,600	8,900
– beginning inventory	1,500	1,650	1,750	1,800	1,600
Required production Total	7,650	8,350	8,800	?	7,300

Direct Materials Budget
For the Year Ended December 31, 2018

	Quarter 1	Quarter 2	Quarter 3	Quarter 4	Total
Units to be produced	7,650	8,350	8,800	8,800	33,600
Direct material per unit	2	2	2	2	2
Total pounds needed for production	15,300	16,700	17,600	17,600	67,200
+ desired ending inventory	4,175	4,400	4,400	3,650	3,650
Total material required	19,475	21,100	22,000	21,250	70,850
– beginning inventory	0	4,175	4,400	4,400	0
Pounds of direct material purchase requirements	19,475	16,925	17,600	16,850	70,850
Cost per pound	$ 1.50	$ 1.50	$ 1.50	$ 1.50	$ 1.50
Total cost of direct material purchase Total	$29,213	$25,388	$26,400	$25,275 ?	$106,275 $106,275

Direct Labor Budget
For the Year Ended December 31, 2018

	Quarter 1	Quarter 2	Quarter 3	Quarter 4	Total
Units to be produced	7,650	8,350	8,800	?	?
Direct labor hours per unit	0.75	0.75	0.75	0.75	0.75
Total required direct labor hours	5,738	6,263	6,600	6,600	?
Labor cost per hour	$ 25	$ 25	$ 25	$ 25	$ 25
Total direct labor cost	$143,438	$156,563	$165,000	?	$630,000

PA8. LO 7.3 Direct labor hours are estimated as 2,000 in Quarter 1; 2,100 in Quarter 2; 1,900 in Quarter 3; and 2,300 in Quarter 4. Prepare a manufacturing overhead budget using the information provided.

Indirect material per hour	$1.00	Supervisory salaries	$17,000
Indirect labor per hour	1.25	Maintenance	5,000
Maintenance per hour	0.25	Property taxes and insurance	6,000
Utilities per hour	0.50	Depreciation	3,500

PA9. LO 7.3 Fitbands' estimated sales are:

October	$131,982
November	195,723
December	249,283
January	124,298
February	124,284
March	124,373

What are the balances in accounts receivable for January, February, and March if 65% of sales is collected in the month of sale, 25% is collected the month after the sale, and 10% is second month after the sale?

PA10. LO 7.3 Sports Socks has a policy of always paying within the discount period and each of its suppliers provides a discount of 2% if paid within 10 days of purchase. Because of the purchase policy, 85% of its payments are made in the month of purchase and 15% are made the following month. The direct materials budget provides for purchases of $129,582 in November, $294,872 in December, $239,582 in January, and $234,837 in February. What is the balance in accounts payable for January 31, and February 28?

PA11. LO 7.4 Prepare a flexible budgeted income for 120,000 units using the following information from a static budget for 100,000 units:

Sales price	$ 90
Direct material per unit	30
Direct labor per unit	15
Variable manufacturing overhead per unit	13
Fixed manufacturing overhead	75,000
Variable sales and administration expenses per unit	3
Fixed sales and administration expenses	25,000
Taxes	30%*

*of income before taxes

PA12. LO 7.4 Before the year began, the following static budget was developed for the estimated sales of 100,000. Sales are sluggish and management needs to revise its budget. Use this information to prepare a flexible budget for 80,000 and 90,000 units of sales.

Sales	$3,500,000
Cost of goods sold	
Direct material	900,000
Direct labor	1,000,000
Variable manufacturing overhead	250,000
Fixed manufacturing overhead	80,000
Cost of goods sold	2,230,000
Gross profit	1,270,000
Variable sales and administration expenses	100,000
Fixed sales and administration expenses	950,000
Income before taxes	220,000
Taxes	66,000
Net income	$ 154,000

PA13. LO 7.4 Caribbean Hammocks currently sells 75,000 units at $50 per unit. Its expenses are:

Direct materials per unit	$ 9
Direct labor per unit	10
Variable manufacturing overhead per unit	7
Variable sales and administration expenses per unit	2
Fixed manufacturing overhead	75,000
Fixed sales and administration expenses	850,000
Taxes	30%*

*of income before taxes

Management believes it can increase sales by 5,000 units for every $5 decrease in sales price. It also believes the additional sales will allow a decrease in direct material of $1 for each additional 5,000 units. Prepare a flexible budgeted income statement for 75,000-, 80,000-, and 85,000-unit sales.

PA14. LO 7.4 Total Pop's data show the following information:

	Jan.	Feb.	Mar.	Apr.	May
Estimated sales units	15,000	14,500	16,000	15,500	15,800
Sales price per unit	$ 45	$ 45	$ 45	$ 45	$ 45
Direct labor per unit	3	3	2.25	2	2
Labor rate per hour	$ 18	$ 18	$ 21	$ 21	$ 21

New machinery will be added in April. This machine will reduce the labor required per unit and increase the labor rate for those employees qualified to operate the machinery. Finished goods inventory is required to be 20% of the next month's requirements. Direct material requires 2 pounds per unit at a cost of $3 per pound. The ending inventory required for direct materials is 15% of the next month's needs. In January, the beginning inventory is 3,000 units of finished goods and 4,470 pounds of material. Prepare a production budget, direct materials budget, and direct labor budget for the first quarter of the year.

PA15. LO 7.4 Identify the document that contains the information listed in these lines from the budgeted balance sheet shown.
- A. Cash
- B. Accounts receivable
- C. Raw materials inventory
- D. Computers
- E. Accounts payable

Cash	$ 2,500,000
Accounts receivable	5,381,239
Raw materials inventory	3,149,183
Finished goods inventory	6,239,138
Total current assets	$17,269,560
Property, plant, and equipment	
Computers	$ 150,000
Machinery	9,745,231
Accumulated depreciation	(5,385,733)
Net property, plant, and equipment	$ 4,509,498
Total assets	$21,779,058
Liabilities	
Accounts payable	$ 3,242,938
Notes payable	8,289,722
Total liabilities	$11,532,660
Stockholders' equity	
Common stock	$ 5,000,000
Retained earnings	5,246,398
Total stockholders' equity	$ 10,246,398
Total liabilities and stockholders' equity	$ 21,779,058

PA16. LO 7.5 Titanium Blades refines titanium for use in all brands of razor blades. It prepared a static budget for the sales of 5,000 units. These variances were observed:

	Actual Results	Variances	
Sales	$150,000	$25,000	Favorable
Variable expenses	77,800	12,800	Unfavorable
Fixed expenses	70,300	300	Unfavorable
Net income (loss)	1,900	11,900	Unfavorable

Determine the static budget and use the information to prepare a flexible budget and analysis for the 6,000 units actually sold.

Problem Set B

PB1. LO 7.2 Lens & Shades sells sunglasses for $37 each and is estimating sales of 21,000 units in January and 19,000 in February. Each lens consists of 2.00 mm of plastic costing $2.50 per mm, 1.7 oz of dye costing $2.80 per ounce, and 0.50 hours direct labor at a labor rate of $18 per unit. Desired inventory levels are:

	Jan.	Feb.	Mar.
Beginning inventory			
Finished goods	3,500	3,800	4,500
Direct materials: plastic	4,100	4,500	4,600
Direct materials: dye	10,100	11,300	12,200

Prepare a sales budget, production budget, direct materials budget for silicon and solution, and a direct labor budget.

PB2. LO 7.2 The following data were obtained from the financial records of Sonicbrush, Inc., for March:

Estimated sales	$330,000
Purchases	$179,431
Ending inventory	15%*
Administrative salaries per month	$ 70,200
Marketing expense	3%**
Sales commissions	4%**
Rent expense per month	$ 8,400
Depreciation expense per month	$ 1,200
Utilities per month	$ 2,800
Taxes	15%***

*of next month's sales
**of sales
***of income before taxes

Sales are expected to increase each month by 15%. Prepare a budgeted income statement.

PB3. LO 7.2 TIB makes custom guitars and prepared the following sales budget for the second quarter

	April	May	June
Units	80	86	84
Sales price	$ 1,200	$ 1,200	$ 1,200
Budgeted sales	$96,000	$103,200	$100,800

It also has this additional information related to its expenses:

Direct material per unit $55, Direct labor per hour 20, Variable manufacturing overhead per hour 3.50, Fixed manufacturing overhead per month 3,000, Sales commissions per unit 20, Sales salaries per month 5,000, Delivery expense per unit 0.50, Utilities per month 4,000, Administrative salaries per month 20,000, Marketing expenses per month 8,000, Insurance expense per month 11,000, Depreciation expense per month 9,000.

Prepare a sales and administrative expense budget for each month in the quarter ended June 30, 2018.

PB4. LO 7.2 Prepare a budgeted income statement using the information shown.

Sales units	84,000
Sales price per unit	$ 22
Uncollectible expense	1%
Direct material per unit	$ 1.50
Direct labor hours per unit	0.8
Direct labor rate per hour	$ 19
Manufacturing overhead	$14,000
Variable sales and administration expenses per unit sold	$ 2.10
Fixed sales and administration expenses	$23,000
Taxes	15%*

*of income before taxes

PB5. LO 7.2 Sunshine Gardens overhead expenses are:

Indirect material pounds per unit	0.50
Indirect material cost per pound	$ 1.00
Indirect labor hours	1.00
Indirect labor rate per hour	$ 16.50
Variable maintenance per unit	$ 0.75
Variable utilities per unit	$ 0.20
Supervisor salaries	$10,000
Maintenance salaries	$ 9,000
Insurance	$ 3,000
Depreciation	$ 1,500

Given production of 10,200; 11,300; 12,900; and 13,200 for each quarter of the next year, prepare a manufacturing overhead budget for each quarter.

PB6. LO 7.3 Relevant data from the operating budget of The Framers are:

	Quarter 1	Quarter 2
Sales	$33,948	$76,482
Direct material purchases	25,312	26,423
Direct labor	29,948	24,328
Manufacturing overhead	9,322	10,299
Selling and administration	19,283	19,238
Depreciation included in selling and administration	950	800
Collections	34,324	76,938
Cash payments	29,349	20,937
Cash received: other	8,000	500
Dividend	0	500

Other data:
- Capital assets were sold in quarter 1 and $8,000 was collected in quarter 1 and $500 collected in quarter 2.
- Dividends of $500 will be paid in May
- The beginning cash balance was $50,000 and a required minimum cash balance is $10,000.
- Prepare a cash budget for the first two quarters of the year.

PB7. LO 7.3 Fill in the missing information from the following schedules:

Sales Budget
For the Year Ended December 31, 2018

	Quarter 1	Quarter 2	Quarter 3	Quarter 4	Total
Expected sales (units)	21,000	26,250	8,750	9,000	65,000
Sales price per unit	?	?	?	?	
Total sales revenue	$315,000	?	?	?	$975,000

Production Budget
For the Year Ended December 31, 2018

	Quarter 1	Quarter 2	Quarter 3	Quarter 4	Q1, Year 2
Expected sales	21,000	26,250	8,750	9,000	8,000
Desired ending inventory	5,250	?	?	1,600	0
Total required units	26,250	28,000	10,550	10,600	8,000
− beginning inventory	5,250	5,250	1,750	1,800	1,600
Required production	?	?	?	?	6,400
Total				61,350	

Direct Materials Budget
For the Year Ended December 31, 2018

	Quarter 1	Quarter 2	Quarter 3	Quarter 4	Total
Units to be produced	?	?	?	?	61,350
Direct material per unit	2	2	2	2	2
Total pounds needed for production	42,000	45,500	17,600	17,600	122,700
+ desired ending inventory	11,375	?	?	3,200	3,200
Total material required	53,375	49,900	22,000	20,800	125,900
− beginning inventory	0	11,375	4,400	4,400	0
Pounds of direct material purchase requirements	53,375	38,525	17,600	16,400	125,900
Cost per pound	$ 1.5	$ 1.5	$ 1.5	$ 1.5	$ 1.5
Total cost of direct material purchase	$80,063	$57,788	$26,400	$ 24,600	$188,850
Total				$188,850	$188,850

Direct Labor Budget
For the Year Ended December 31, 2018

	Quarter 1	Quarter 2	Quarter 3	Quarter 4	Total
Units to be produced	?	?	?	?	?
Direct labor hours per unit	0.75	0.75	0.75	0.75	0.75
Total required direct labor hours	15,750	17,063	6,600	6,600	46,013
Labor cost per hour	$ 25	?	?	?	?
Total direct labor cost	$393,750	$426,563	$165,000	$165,000	$1,150,313

PB8. LO 7.3 Mesa Aquatics, Inc. estimated direct labor hours as 1,900 in quarter 1, 2,000 in quarter 2, 2,200 in quarter 3, and 1,800 in quarter 4. a sales and administration budget using the information provided.

Indirect material per hour	$1.00	Supervisory salaries	$17,000
Indirect labor per hour	1.25	Maintenance	5,000
Maintenance per hour	0.25	Property taxes and insurance	6,000
Utilities per hour	0.50	Depreciation	3,500

PB9. LO 7.3 Amusement tickets estimated sales are:

January	$231,837
February	231,937
March	381,274
April	212,947
May	282,172
June	281,836

What are the balances in accounts receivable for April, May, and June if 60% of sales are collected in the month of sale, 30% are collected the month after the sale, and 10% are collected the second month after the sale?

PB10. LO 7.3 All Temps has a policy of always paying within the discount period, and each of its suppliers provides a discount of 2% if paid within 10 days of purchase. Because of the purchase policy, 80% of its payments are made in the month of purchase and 20% are made the following month. The direct materials budget provides for purchases of $23,812 in February, $23,127 in March, $21,836 in April, and $28,173 in May. What is the balance in accounts payable for April 30, and May 31?

PB11. LO 7.4 Prepare a flexible budgeted income statement for 47,000 units using the following information from a static budget for 45,000 units:

Sales price per unit	$ 50
Direct material per unit	12
Direct labor per unit	5
Variable manufacturing overhead per unit	3
Fixed manufacturing overhead	25,000
Variable sales and administration expenses per unit	3
Fixed sales and administration expenses	9,000
Taxes	15%*

*of income before taxes

PB12. LO 7.4 Before the year began, the following static budget was developed for the estimated sales of 50,000. Sales are higher than expected and management needs to revise its budget. Prepare a flexible budget for 100,000 and 110,000 units of sales.

Sales	50,000 units
Cost of goods sold	$1,250,000
Direct material	450,000
Direct labor	500,000
Variable manufacturing overhead	125,000
Fixed manufacturing overhead	32,000
Cost of goods sold	$1,107,000
Gross profit	$ 143,000
Variable sales and administration expenses	50,000
Fixed sales and administration expenses	105,000
Income before taxes	(12,000)
Taxes	(1,800)
Net income	($ 10,200)

PB13. LO 7.4 Artic Camping Gear's currently sells 35,000 units at $73 per unit. Its expenses are as follows:

Direct materials per unit	$ 4
Direct labor per unit	7
Variable manufacturing overhead per unit	3
Variable sales and administration expenses per unit	1.50
Fixed manufacturing overhead	21,000
Fixed sales and administration expenses	89,000
Taxes	15%*

*of income before taxes

Management believes it can increase sales by 2,000 units for every $5 decrease in sales price. It also believes the additional sales will allow a decrease in direct material of $1 for each additional 2,000 units. Prepare a flexible budgeted income statement for 35,000-, 37,000-, and 39,000-unit sales.

PB14. LO 7.4 Fruit Tea's data show the following information:

	Aug.	Sept.	Oct.	Nov.	Dec.
Estimated sales (units)	25,000	25,000	27,000	27,500	28,000
Sales price per unit	$ 31	$ 31	$ 31	$ 31	$ 31
Direct labor per unit	$ 1.75	$ 1.75	$ 1.50	$ 1.50	$ 1.50
Labor rate per hour	$ 21	$ 21	$ 24	$ 24	$ 24

New machinery will be added in October. This machine will reduce the labor required per unit and increase the labor rate for those employees qualified to operate the machinery. Finished goods inventory is required to be 20% of the next month's requirements. Direct material requires 2.5 pounds per unit at a cost of $5 per pound. The ending inventory required for direct materials is 20% of the next month's needs. In August, the beginning inventory is 3,750 units of finished goods and 13,125 pounds of materials. Prepare a production budget, direct materials budget, and direct labor budget for the first quarter of the year.

PB15. LO 7.4 Identify the document that contains the information listed in these lines from the budgeted balance sheet shown.

A. Accounts receivable
B. Finished goods inventory
C. Machinery
D. Accumulated depreciation
E. Notes payable
F. Common stock

Assets	
Cash	$ 2,500,000
Accounts receivable	5,381,239
Raw materials inventory	3,149,183
Finished goods inventory	6,239,138
Total current assets	$17,269,560
Property, plant, and equipment	
Computers	$ 150,000
Machinery	9,745,231
Accumulated depreciation	(5,385,733)
Net property, plant, and equipment	$ 4,509,498
Total assets	$21,779,058
Liabilities	
Accounts payable	$ 3,242,938
Notes payable	8,289,722
Total liabilities	$11,532,660
Stockholders' equity	
Common stock	$ 5,000,000
Retained earnings	5,246,398
Total stockholders' equity	$10,246,398
Total liabilities and stockholders' equity	$21,779,058

PB16. LO 7.5 Replenish sells shampoo that removes chlorine from hair. It prepared a static budget for the sales of 10,000 units. These variances were observed:

	Actual Results	Variances	
Sales	$264,000	$66,000	Unfavorable
Variable expenses	70,500	19,500	Favorable
Fixed expenses	70,270	270	Unfavorable
Net income (loss)	123,230	46,770	Unfavorable

Determine the static budget and use the information to prepare a flexible budget and analysis for the 8,000 units actually sold.

Thought Provokers

TP1. LO 7.1 Why is a clear understanding of management's goals and objectives necessary for effective budgets?

TP2. LO 7.1 It is proper budgeting procedure to begin with estimated revenues, but why might some nonprofit entities begin planning their expenditures instead of their revenues?

TP3. LO 7.2 How would a human resources department use information in the operating budgets?

TP4. LO 7.2 How would maintenance departments use information in the budget?

TP5. LO 7.2 How might service industries predict revenue?

TP6. LO 7.4 The management of Hess, Inc., is developing a flexible budget for the upcoming year. It was not pleased with the small amount of net income the budget showed at all sales levels and is contemplating using a less expensive material. This action reduces direct material cost by $1 per unit. What would be the effects on financial statements and a flexible budget if management takes this approach? Are there other factors that need to be considered?

TP7. LO 7.4 When would a static budget be effective in evaluating a manager's performance?

TP8. LO 7.5 If management is being evaluated on their ability to manage a budget, what can they do to increase cash flow?

TP9. LO 7.5 If management is being evaluated on their ability to manage a budget, what can they do to decrease cash outflow?

8 Standard Costs and Variances

Figure 8.1 Coffee Shop. How do they know what each cup of coffee, muffin, or bagel costs so they can determine what price to charge? (credit: modification of "Bakery Coffee" by "veerasantinithi"/Pixabay, CC0)

Chapter Outline

LO 8.1 Explain How and Why a Standard Cost Is Developed

LO 8.2 Compute and Evaluate Materials Variances

LO 8.3 Compute and Evaluate Labor Variances

LO 8.4 Compute and Evaluate Overhead Variances

LO 8.5 Describe How Companies Use Variance Analysis

Why It Matters

Sam saw how much coffee his fellow students were drinking and decided to open a student-run coffee shop on campus. Sam knew that developing a plan for the coffee shop would help make the shop successful. He researched what types of coffee to offer, the hours the shop would be open, and the number of employees needed, by researching other coffee shops near campus. He brewed coffee to determine the cost of the coffee and the time it took to brew. He also served several friends to determine how long it would take to serve customers. He observed, in other coffee shops, how much cream and other additives are used by customers. He talked to several coffee suppliers for prices of his various materials. He looked at empty stores near campus to determine what his rent would be. Now that he has this information, he is not sure how to make it useful to him. How could he use this information to plan and control the operations of the shop? One calculation he can do is determine his standard costs.

What is the difference between a *budget* and a *standard*? A budget usually refers to a company's projections for costs, revenues, and cash flows associated with the overall operations of the organization, or a subsection of the corporation such as a division. A standard usually refers to a company's projected costs for a single unit of a product or service and includes the expected, or standard, cost for the various cost components of each unit, such as materials, labor, and overhead.

8.1 Explain How and Why a Standard Cost Is Developed

A syllabus is one way an instructor can communicate expectations to students. Students can use the syllabus to plan their studying to maximize their grade and to coordinate the amount and timing of studying for each course. Knowing what is expected, and when it is expected, allows for better plans and performance. When your performance does not match your expectations, a **variance** arises—a difference between the standard and the actual performance. You then need to determine why the difference occurred. You want to know why you did not receive the grade you expected so you can make adjustments for the next assignment to earn a better grade.

Companies operate in a similar manner. They have an expectation, or **standard**, for production. For example, if a company is producing tables, it might establish standards for such components as the amount of board feet of lumber expected to be used in producing each table or the number of hours of direct labor hours it expected to use in the table's production. These standards can then be used in establishing standard costs that can be used in creating an assortment of different types of budgets.

When a variance occurs in its standards, the company investigates to determine the causes, so they can perform better in the future. For example, General Motors has standards for each item on a vehicle. It can determine the cost and selling price of a power antenna by knowing the standard material cost for the antenna and the standard labor cost of adding the antenna to the vehicle. General Motors also can add up all of the standard times for all vehicles it makes to determine if too much or too little labor was used in production.

LINK TO LEARNING

Developing standards is a complicated and costly process. Review this article on how to develop a standard cost system (https://openstax.org/l/50StandardCost) for more details.

Fundamentals of Standard Costs

It is important to establish standards for cost at the beginning of a period to prepare the budget; manage material, labor, and overhead costs; and create a reasonable sales price for a good. A **standard cost** is an expected cost that a company usually establishes at the beginning of a fiscal year for prices paid and amounts used. The standard cost is an expected amount paid for materials costs or labor rates. The standard quantity is the expected usage amount of materials or labor. A standard cost may be determined by past history or industry norms. The company can then compare the standard costs against its actual results to measure its efficiency. Sometimes when comparing standard costs against actual results, there is a difference.

This difference can be attributed to many reasons. For example, the coffee company mentioned in the opening vignette may expect to pay $0.50 per ounce for coffee grounds. After the company purchased the coffee grounds, it discovered it paid $0.60 per ounce. This variance would need to be accounted for, and possible operational changes would occur as a result. Cost accounting systems become more useful to management when they include budgeted amounts to serve as a point of comparison with actual results.

Many departments help determine standard cost. Product design, in conjunction with production, purchasing, and sales, determines what the product will look like and what materials will be used. Production works with purchasing to determine what material will work best in production and will be the most cost efficient. Sales will also help decide the material in terms of customer demand. Production will work with personnel to determine labor costs for the product, which is based on how long it will take to make the product, which departments will be involved, and what type and number of employees it will take.

Consider how many different materials can go into a product. For example, there are approximately 14,000 parts that comprise the average automobile. The manufacturer will set a standard price and a quantity used per automobile for each part, and it will determine the labor required to install the part. At Fiat Chrysler Automobiles' Belvidere Assembly Plant, for example, there are approximately 5,000 employees assembling automobiles.[1] In addition to having standard costs associated with each part, each employee has standards for the job he or she performs.

Standard costs are typically established for reasonably attainable levels of efficiency (production). They serve as a target and are useful in motivating standard performance. An **ideal standard** level is set assuming that everything is perfect, machines do not break down, employees show up on time, there are no defects, there is no scrap, and materials are perfect. This level of standard is not the best motivator, because employees may see this level as unattainable. For example, consider whether you would take a course if the letter grades were as follows: an A is 99–100%, a B is 98–99%, a C is 97–98%, a D is 96–97%, and below 96% is an F. These standards are unreasonable and unrealistic, and they would not motivate students to do well in the course.

At the other end of the spectrum, if the standards are too easy, there is little motivation to do better, and products may not be properly built, may be built with inferior materials, or both. For example, consider how you would handle the following grading scale for your course: an A is 50–100%, a B is 35–50%, a C is 10–35%, a D is 2–10%, and below 2% is an F. Would you learn anything? Would you try very hard? The same considerations come into play for employees with standards that are too easy.

Instead of these two extremes, a company would set an **attainable standard**, which is one that employees can reach with reasonable effort. The standards are not so high that employees will not try to reach them and not so low that they do not give any incentive for employees to achieve profitability.

In order for a company to establish its attainable standard cost for each product, it must consider the standard costs for materials, labor, and overhead. The material standard cost consists of a standard price per unit of material and a standard amount of material per unit. Returning to the opening vignette, let us say the coffee shop is trying to establish the standard materials cost for one cup of regular coffee. To keep the example simple, we are not incorporating the cost of water or the ceramic cup cost (since they are reused). Two components for the cup of coffee will need to be considered:

1. Price per ounce of coffee grounds
2. Amount of coffee grounds (materials) used per cup of coffee

To determine the standards for labor, the coffee shop would need to consider two additional components:

1. Labor rate per minute
2. Amount of time to make one cup of regular coffee

To determine the standard for overhead, the coffee shop would first need to consider the fact that it has two types of overhead as shown in Figure 8.2. Greater detail about the calculation of the variable and fixed overhead is provided in Compute and Evaluate Overhead Variances.

---

1 "Belvidere Assembly Plant and Belvidere Satellite Stamping Plant." Fiat Chrysler Automobiles. June 2018. http://media.fcanorthamerica.com/newsrelease.do?id=323&mid=1

1. Fixed overhead (does not change in total with production)
2. Variable overhead (does change in total with production)

All of this information is entered on a standard cost card.

STANDARD COST CARD
Product: 1 Cup of Coffee

Manufacturing Cost Information	Standard Quantity	×	Standard Cost per Unit	=	Cost Summary
Direct Materials					
Material (coffee grounds)	0.5 ounces		$.50 per ounce		$0.25
Direct Labor					
Barista	1 minute		$0.20 per minute		$0.20
Manufacturing Overhead					
Variable overhead	1 minute		$0.05 per direct labor minute		$0.05
Fixed overhead	1 minute		$0.10 per direct labor minute		$0.10
Standard Cost per cup of coffee					**$0.60**

Figure 8.2 Standard Cost Card for a Coffee Shop. (attribution: Copyright Rice University, OpenStax, under CC BY-NC-SA 4.0 license)

Once a company determines a standard cost, they can then evaluate any variances. A variance is the difference between a standard cost and actual performance. There are favorable and unfavorable variances. A **favorable variance** involves spending less, or using less, than the anticipated or estimated standard. An **unfavorable variance** involves spending more, or using more, than the anticipated or estimated standard. Before determining whether the variance is favorable or unfavorable, it is often helpful for the company to determine why the variance exists.

YOUR TURN

Developing a Standard Cost Card

Use the information provided to create a standard cost card for production of one deluxe bicycle from Bicycles Unlimited.

To make one bicycle it takes four pounds of material. The material can usually be purchased for $5.25 per pound. The labor necessary to build a bicycle consists of two types. The first type of labor is assembly, which takes 2.75 hours. These workers are paid $11.00 per hour. The second type of labor is finishing, which takes 4 hours. These workers are paid $15.00 per hour. Overhead is applied using labor hours. The variable overhead rate is $5.00 per labor hour. The fixed overhead rate is $3.00 per hour.

Solution

Manufacturing Cost Information	Standard Quantity	×	Standard Cost per Unit	=	Cost Summary
Direct Materials					
Grade A material	4 pounds		$5.25 per pound		$21.00
Direct Labor					
Assembly	2.75 hours		$11.00 per hour		$30.25
Finish	4 hours		$15.00 per hour		$60.00
Manufacturing Overhead					
Variable overhead	6.75 hours		$5.00 per direct labor hour		$33.75
Fixed overhead	6.75 hours		$3.00 per direct labor hour		$20.25
Standard Cost					$165.25

ETHICAL CONSIDERATIONS

Ethical Variance Analysis

Variance analysis allows managers to see whether costs are different than planned. Once a difference between expected and actual costs is identified, variance analysis should delve into why the costs differ and what the magnitude of the difference means. To determine why a cost differs, it should be established if the additional cost provides a benefit or detriment to an organization's stakeholders, the people or entities that are affected by the organization's actions or inactions. Not all stakeholders are equal in the analysis, but an organization should recognize each stakeholder's interest in the organization's business and operational decisions, while ranking the importance of the stakeholder in relation to any decision made.

Ranking should look to how stakeholders are affected by costs and any decisions related to cost variance, or why the variance occurred. For example, if a cost variance is due to an additional cost to make a product eco-friendly, then an organization may determine that incurring the cost is a benefit to its stakeholders. However, if the additional cost creates an unfavorable situation for a stakeholder, the process incurring the cost should be investigated. Remember that the owners of a company, including shareholders, are also stakeholders. To determine the best course of action for an organization, cost analysis should help inform stakeholder analysis—the process of systematically gathering and analyzing all of the information related to a business decision.

Different factors may produce a variance. The company could have paid too much or too little for production. It may have purchased the wrong grade of material or hired employees with more or less experience than required. Sometimes the variances are interrelated. For example, purchasing substandard materials may lead to using more time to make the product and may produce more scrap. The substandard material may have been more difficult to work with or had more defects than the proper grade material. In such a situation, a favorable material price variance could cause an unfavorable labor efficiency variance and an unfavorable material quantity variance. Employees who do not have the expected experience level may save money in the wage rate but may require more hours to be worked and more material to be used because of their inexperience.

Another situation in which a variance may occur is when the cost of labor and/or material changes after the standard was established. Toward the end of the fiscal year, standards often become less reliable because time has passed and the environment has changed. It is not reasonable to expect the price of all materials and labor to remain constant for 12 months. For example, the grade of material used to establish the standard may no longer be available.

Manufacturing Cost Variances

As you've learned, the standard price and standard quantity are anticipated amounts. Any change from these budgeted amounts will produce a variance. There can be variances for materials, labor, and overhead. Direct materials may have a variance in price of materials or quantity of materials used. Direct labor may have a variance in the rate paid to workers or the amount of time used to make a product. Overhead may produce a variance in expected fixed or variable costs, leading to possible differences in production capacity and management's ability to control overhead. More specifics on the formulas, processes, and interpretations of the direct materials, direct labor, and overhead variances are discussed in each of this chapter's following sections.

CONCEPTS IN PRACTICE

Qualcomm[2]

Qualcomm Inc. is a large producer of telecommunications equipment focusing mainly on wireless products and services. As with any company, Qualcomm sets labor standards and must address any variances in labor costs to stay on budget, and control overall manufacturing costs.

In 2018, Qualcomm announced a reduction to its labor force, affecting many of its full-time and temporary workers. The reduction in labor was necessary to suppress rising expenses that could not be controlled through overhead or materials cost-cutting measures. The variances between standard labor rates and actual labor rates, and diminishing profit margins will have contributed to this decision. It is important for Qualcomm management to keep labor variances minimal in the future so that large workforce reductions are not required to control costs.

THINK IT THROUGH

Chocolate Cow Ice Cream Company

The Chocolate Cow Ice Cream Company has grown substantially recently, and management now feels the need to develop standards and compute variances. A consulting firm was hired to develop the standards and the format for the variance computation. One standard in particular that the consulting firm developed seemed too excessive to plant management. The consulting firm's standard was production of 100 gallons of ice cream every 45 minutes. The plant's middle level of management thought the standard should be 100 gallons every 55 minutes, while the top management of the

---

2 Munsif Vengattil. "Qualcomm Begins Layoffs as Part of Cost Cuts." *Reuters*. April 18, 2018. https://www.reuters.com/article/us-qualcomm-layoffs/qualcomm-begins-layoffs-as-part-of-cost-cuts-idUSKBN1HP33L

company thought that the consulting firm's standard would provide more motivation to the employees.

1. Why is the company establishing a standard for production?
2. What are some factors the company may need to consider before selecting one of the proposed standards?

8.2 Compute and Evaluate Materials Variances

As you've learned, direct materials are those materials used in the production of goods that are easily traceable and are a major component of the product. The amount of materials used and the price paid for those materials may differ from the standard costs determined at the beginning of a period. A company can compute these materials variances and, from these calculations, can interpret the results and decide how to address these differences.

CONCEPTS IN PRACTICE

Buttering Popcorn

In a movie theater, management uses standards to determine if the proper amount of butter is being used on the popcorn. They train the employees to put two tablespoons of butter on each bag of popcorn, so total butter usage is based on the number of bags of popcorn sold. Therefore, if the theater sells 300 bags of popcorn with two tablespoons of butter on each, the total amount of butter that should be used is 600 tablespoons. Management can then compare the predicted use of 600 tablespoons of butter to the actual amount used. If the actual usage of butter was less than 600, customers may not be happy, because they may feel that they did not get enough butter. If more than 600 tablespoons of butter were used, management would investigate to determine why. Some reasons why more butter was used than expected (unfavorable outcome) would be because of inexperienced workers pouring too much, or the standard was set too low, producing unrealistic expectations that do not satisfy customers.

Fundamentals of Direct Materials Variances

The direct materials variances measure how efficient the company is at using materials as well as how effective it is at using materials. There are two components to a **direct materials variance**, the direct materials price variance and the direct materials quantity variance, which both compare the actual price or amount used to the standard amount.

Direct Materials Price Variance

The **direct materials price variance** compares the actual price per unit (pound or yard, for example) of the direct materials to the standard price per unit of direct materials. The formula for direct materials price variance is calculated as:

$$\text{Direct Materials Price Variance} = \begin{pmatrix} \text{Actual Quantity Used} \\ \times \\ \text{Actual Price Paid} \end{pmatrix} - \begin{pmatrix} \text{Actual Quantity Used} \\ \times \\ \text{Standard Price} \end{pmatrix}$$

Factoring out actual quantity used from both components of the formula, it can be rewritten as:

$$\text{Direct Materials Price Variance} = \begin{pmatrix} \text{Actual Price per Unit of Materials} - \text{Standard Price per Unit of Materials} \end{pmatrix} \times \text{Actual Quantity of Materials Used}$$

With either of these formulas, the actual quantity used refers to the actual amount of materials used to create one unit of product. The standard price is the expected price paid for materials per unit. The actual price paid is the actual amount paid for materials per unit. If there is no difference between the standard price and the actual price paid, the outcome will be zero, and no price variance exists.

If the actual price paid per unit of material is lower than the standard price per unit, the variance will be a favorable variance. A favorable outcome means you spent less on the purchase of materials than you anticipated. If, however, the actual price paid per unit of material is greater than the standard price per unit, the variance will be unfavorable. An unfavorable outcome means you spent more on the purchase of materials than you anticipated.

The actual price can differ from the standard or expected price because of such factors as supply and demand of the material, increased labor costs to the supplier that are passed along to the customer, or improvements in technology that make the material cheaper. The producer must be aware that the difference between what it expects to happen and what actually happens will affect all of the goods produced using these particular materials. Therefore, the sooner management is aware of a problem, the sooner they can fix it. For that reason, the material price variance is computed at the time of purchase and not when the material is used in production.

Let us consider an example. Connie's Candy Company produces various types of candies that they sell to retailers. Connie's Candy establishes a standard price for candy-making materials of $7.00 per pound. Each box of candy is expected to use 0.25 pounds of candy-making materials. Connie's Candy found that the actual price of materials was $6.00 per pound. They still actually use 0.25 pounds of materials to make each box. The direct materials price variance computes as:

$$\text{Direct Materials Price Variance} = (\$6.00 - \$7.00) \times 0.25 \text{ lb.} = \$0.25 \text{ or } \$0.25 \text{ (Favorable)}$$

In this case, the actual price per unit of materials is $6.00, the standard price per unit of materials is $7.00, and the actual quantity used is 0.25 pounds. This computes as a favorable outcome. This is a favorable outcome because the actual price for materials was less than the standard price. As a result of this favorable outcome information, the company may consider continuing operations as they exist, or could change future budget projections to reflect higher profit margins, among other things.

Let us take the same example except now the actual price for candy-making materials is $9.00 per pound. The direct materials price variance computes as:

$$\text{Direct Materials Price Variance} = (\$9.00 - \$7.00) \times 0.25 \text{ lbs.} = \$0.50 \text{ or } \$0.50 \text{ (Unfavorable)}$$

In this case, the actual price per unit of materials is $9.00, the standard price per unit of materials is $7.00, and the actual quantity used is 0.25 pounds. This computes as an unfavorable outcome. This is an unfavorable outcome because the actual price for materials was more than the standard price. As a result of this unfavorable outcome information, the company may consider using cheaper materials, changing suppliers, or increasing prices to cover costs.

Another element this company and others must consider is a direct materials quantity variance.

> ### THINK IT THROUGH
>
> #### Don't "Skirt" the Issue
>
> You run a fabric store and order materials through a supplier. At the end of the month, you review your materials cost and discover that your direct materials price and quantity variances produced unfavorable results. What could be attributed to these unfavorable outcomes? How would these unfavorable outcomes impact the total direct materials variance?

Direct Materials Quantity Variance

The **direct materials quantity variance** compares the actual quantity of materials used to the standard materials that were expected to be used to make the actual units produced. The variance is calculated using this formula:

$$\text{Direct Materials Quantity Variance} = (\text{Actual Quantity Used} \times \text{Standard Price}) - (\text{Standard Quantity} \times \text{Standard Price})$$

Factoring out standard price from both components of the formula, it can be rewritten as:

$$\text{Direct Materials Quantity Variance} = (\text{Actual Quantity of Materials Used for Units Produced} - \text{Standard Quantity of Materials Expected for the Units Produced}) \times \text{Standard Price}$$

With either of these formulas, the actual quantity used refers to the actual amount of materials used at the actual production output. The standard price is the expected price paid for materials per unit. The standard quantity is the expected amount of materials used at the actual production output. If there is no difference between the actual quantity used and the standard quantity, the outcome will be zero, and no variance exists.

If the actual quantity of materials used is less than the standard quantity used at the actual production output level, the variance will be a favorable variance. A favorable outcome means you used fewer materials than anticipated, to make the actual number of production units. If, however, the actual quantity of materials used is greater than the standard quantity used at the actual production output level, the variance will be unfavorable. An unfavorable outcome means you used more materials than anticipated to make the actual number of production units.

The actual quantity used can differ from the standard quantity because of improved efficiencies in production, carelessness or inefficiencies in production, or poor estimation when creating the standard usage.

Consider the previous example with Connie's Candy Company. Connie's Candy established a standard price for candy-making materials of $7.00 per pound. Each box of candy is expected to use 0.25 pounds of candy-making materials. Connie's Candy found that the actual quantity of candy-making materials used to produce one box of candy was 0.20 per pound. The direct materials quantity variance computes as:

$$\text{Direct Materials Quantity Variance} = (0.20 \text{ lb.} - 0.25 \text{ lb.}) \times \$7.00 = -\$0.35 \text{ or } \$0.35 \text{ (Favorable)}$$

In this case, the actual quantity of materials used is 0.20 pounds, the standard price per unit of materials is $7.00, and the standard quantity used is 0.25 pounds. This computes as a favorable outcome. This is a favorable outcome because the actual quantity of materials used was less than the standard quantity expected at the actual production output level. As a result of this favorable outcome information, the company may consider continuing operations as they exist, or could change future budget projections to reflect higher profit margins, among other things.

Let us take the same example except now the actual quantity of candy-making materials used to produce one box of candy was 0.50 per pound. The direct materials quantity variance computes as:

$$\text{Direct Materials Quantity Variance} = (0.50 \text{ lb.} - 0.25 \text{ lb.}) \times \$7.00 = \$1.75 \text{ or } \$1.75 \text{ (Unfavorable)}$$

In this case, the actual quantity of materials used is 0.50 pounds, the standard price per unit of materials is $7.00, and the standard quantity used is 0.25 pounds. This computes as an unfavorable outcome. This is an unfavorable outcome because the actual quantity of materials used was more than the standard quantity expected at the actual production output level. As a result of this unfavorable outcome information, the company may consider retraining workers to reduce waste or change their production process to decrease materials needs per box.

The combination of the two variances can produce one overall total direct materials cost variance.

LINK TO LEARNING

Watch this video featuring a professor of accounting walking through the steps involved in calculating a material price variance and a material quantity variance (https://openstax.org/l/50Variances) to learn more.

Total Direct Materials Cost Variance

When a company makes a product and compares the actual materials cost to the standard materials cost, the result is the **total direct materials cost variance**.

$$\text{Total Direct Materials Variance} = \begin{pmatrix} \text{Actual Quantity} \\ \times \\ \text{Actual Price} \end{pmatrix} - \begin{pmatrix} \text{Standard Quantity} \\ \times \\ \text{Standard Price} \end{pmatrix}$$

An unfavorable outcome means the actual costs related to materials were more than the expected (standard) costs. If the outcome is a favorable outcome, this means the actual costs related to materials are less than the expected (standard) costs.

The total direct materials cost variance is also found by combining the direct materials price variance and the direct materials quantity variance. By showing the total materials variance as the sum of the two components, management can better analyze the two variances and enhance decision-making.

Figure 8.3 shows the connection between the direct materials price variance and direct materials quantity variance to total direct materials cost variance.

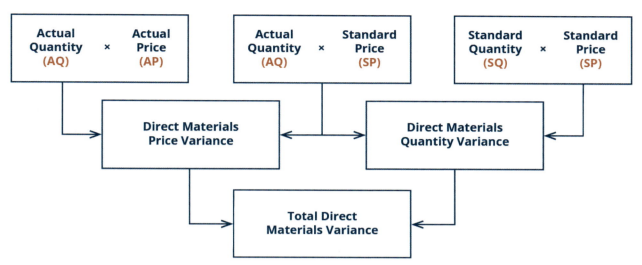

Figure 8.3 Direct Materials Variance.

For example, Connie's Candy Company expects to pay $7.00 per pound for candy-making materials but actually pays $9.00 per pound. The company expected to use 0.25 pounds of materials per box but actually used 0.50 per box. The total direct materials variance is computed as:

Total Direct Materials Variance = (0.50 lbs. × $9.00) − (0.25 lbs. × $7.00) = $4.50 − $1.75 = $2.75 (Unfavorable)

In this case, two elements contribute to the unfavorable outcome. Connie's Candy paid $2.00 per pound more for materials than expected and used 0.25 pounds more of materials than expected to make one box of candy.

The same calculation is shown using the outcomes of the direct materials price and quantity variances.

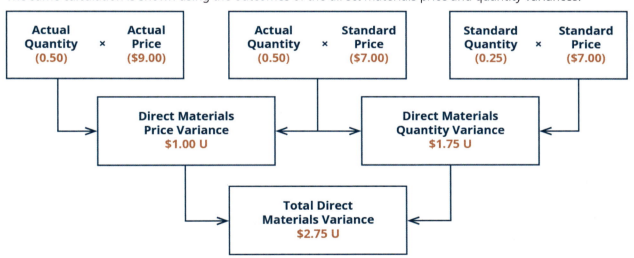

As with the interpretations for the materials price and quantity variances, the company would review the individual components contributing to the overall unfavorable outcome for the total direct materials variance, and possibly make changes to production elements as a result.

> ## YOUR TURN
>
> ### Sweet and Fresh Shampoo Materials
>
> Biglow Company makes a hair shampoo called Sweet and Fresh. Each bottle has a standard material cost of 8 ounces at $0.85 per ounce. During May, Biglow manufactured 11,000 bottles. They bought 89,000 ounces of material at a cost of $74,760. All 89,000 ounces were used to make the 11,000 bottles. Calculate the material price variance and the material quantity variance.
>
> **Solution**
>
> Actual price per pound: 74,760/89,000 = $0.84
>
> Material price variance: 89,000 × (0.84 − 0.85) = $890 favorable
>
> Material quantity variance: 0.85 × (89,000 − 88,000) = $850 unfavorable
>
>

8.3 Compute and Evaluate Labor Variances

In addition to evaluating materials usage, companies must assess how efficiently and effectively they are using labor in the production of their products. Direct labor is a cost associated with workers working directly in the production process. The company must look at both the quantity of hours used and the rate of the labor and compare outcomes to standard costs. Determining efficiency and effectiveness of labor leads to individual labor variances. A company can compute these labor variances and make informed decisions about labor operations based on these differences.

Fundamentals of Direct Labor Variances

The **direct labor variance** measures how efficiently the company uses labor as well as how effective it is at pricing labor. There are two components to a labor variance, the direct labor rate variance and the direct labor time variance.

Direct Labor Rate Variance

The **direct labor rate variance** compares the actual rate per hour of direct labor to the standard rate per hour of labor for the hours worked. The direct labor rate variance is calculated using this formula:

$$\text{Direct Labor Rate Variance} = \left(\begin{array}{c}\text{Actual Hours Worked} \\ \times \\ \text{Actual Rate per Hour}\end{array}\right) - \left(\begin{array}{c}\text{Actual Hours Worked} \\ \times \\ \text{Standard Rate per Hour}\end{array}\right)$$

Factoring out the actual hours worked from both components of the formula, it can be rewritten as

$$\text{Direct Labor Rate Variance} = \left(\text{Actual Rate per Hour} - \text{Standard Rate per Hour}\right) \times \text{Actual Hours Worked}$$

With either of these formulas, the actual rate per hour refers to the actual rate of pay for workers to create one unit of product. The standard rate per hour is the expected rate of pay for workers to create one unit of product. The actual hours worked are the actual number of hours worked to create one unit of product. If there is no difference between the standard rate and the actual rate, the outcome will be zero, and no variance exists.

If the actual rate of pay per hour is less than the standard rate of pay per hour, the variance will be a favorable variance. A favorable outcome means you paid workers less than anticipated. If, however, the actual rate of pay per hour is greater than the standard rate of pay per hour, the variance will be unfavorable. An unfavorable outcome means you paid workers more than anticipated.

The actual rate can differ from the standard or expected rate because of supply and demand of the workers, increased labor costs due to economic changes or union contracts, or the ability to hire employees at a different skill level. Once the manufacturer makes the products, the labor costs will follow the goods through production, so the company should evaluate how the difference between what it expected to happen and what actually happened will affect all the goods produced using these particular labor rates.

Let us again consider Connie's Candy Company with respect to labor. Connie's Candy establishes a standard rate per hour for labor of $8.00. Each box of candy is expected to require 0.10 hours of labor (6 minutes). Connie's Candy found that the actual rate of pay per hour for labor was $7.50. They still actually required 0.10 hours of labor to make each box. The direct labor rate variance computes as:

$$\text{Direct Labor Rate Variance} = (\$7.50 - \$8.00) \times 0.10 \text{ hours} = -\$0.05 \text{ or } \$0.05 \text{ (Favorable)}$$

In this case, the actual rate per hour is $7.50, the standard rate per hour is $8.00, and the actual hour worked is 0.10 hours per box. This computes as a favorable outcome. This is a favorable outcome because the actual rate of pay was less than the standard rate of pay. As a result of this favorable outcome information, the company may consider continuing operations as they exist, or could change future budget projections to reflect higher profit margins, among other things.

Let us take the same example except now the actual rate of pay per hour is $9.50. The direct labor rate variance computes as:

$$\text{Direct Labor Rate Variance} = (\$9.50 - \$8.00) \times 0.10 \text{ hours} = \$0.15 \text{ or } \$0.15 \text{ (Unfavorable)}$$

In this case, the actual rate per hour is $9.50, the standard rate per hour is $8.00, and the actual hours worked per box are 0.10 hours. This computes as an unfavorable outcome. This is an unfavorable outcome because the actual rate per hour was more than the standard rate per hour. As a result of this unfavorable outcome information, the company may consider using cheaper labor, changing the production process to be more efficient, or increasing prices to cover labor costs.

Another element this company and others must consider is a direct labor time variance.

Direct Labor Time Variance

The **direct labor time variance** compares the actual labor hours used to the standard labor hours that were expected to be used to make the actual units produced. The variance is calculated using this formula:

$$\text{Direct Labor Time Variance} = \left(\begin{array}{c}\text{Actual Hours Worked} \\ \times \\ \text{Standard Rate per Hour}\end{array}\right) - \left(\begin{array}{c}\text{Standard Hours} \\ \times \\ \text{Standard Rate per Hour}\end{array}\right)$$

Factoring out the standard rate per hour from both components of the formula, it can be rewritten as:

$$\text{Direct Labor Time Variance} = \left(\begin{array}{c}\text{Actual Hours} \\ \text{Worked}\end{array} - \begin{array}{c}\text{Standard Hours Expected} \\ \text{for the Units Produced}\end{array}\right) \times \begin{array}{c}\text{Standard Rate} \\ \text{per Hour}\end{array}$$

With either of these formulas, the actual hours worked refers to the actual number of hours used at the actual production output. The standard rate per hour is the expected hourly rate paid to workers. The standard hours are the expected number of hours used at the actual production output. If there is no difference between the actual hours worked and the standard hours, the outcome will be zero, and no variance exists.

If the actual hours worked are less than the standard hours at the actual production output level, the variance will be a favorable variance. A favorable outcome means you used fewer hours than anticipated to make the actual number of production units. If, however, the actual hours worked are greater than the standard hours at the actual production output level, the variance will be unfavorable. An unfavorable outcome means you used more hours than anticipated to make the actual number of production units.

The actual hours used can differ from the standard hours because of improved efficiencies in production, carelessness or inefficiencies in production, or poor estimation when creating the standard usage.

Consider the previous example with Connie's Candy Company. Connie's Candy establishes a standard rate per hour for labor of $8.00. Each box of candy is expected to require 0.10 hours of labor (6 minutes). Connie's Candy found that the actual hours worked per box were 0.05 hours (3 minutes). The actual rate per hour for labor remained at $8.00 to make each box. The direct labor time variance computes as:

$$\text{Direct Labor Time Variance} = (0.05 - 0.10) \times \$8.00 \text{ per hour} = -\$0.40 \text{ or } \$0.40 \text{ (Favorable)}$$

In this case, the actual hours worked are 0.05 per box, the standard hours are 0.10 per box, and the standard rate per hour is $8.00. This computes as a favorable outcome. This is a favorable outcome because the actual hours worked were less than the standard hours expected. As a result of this favorable outcome information, the company may consider continuing operations as they exist, or could change future budget projections to reflect higher profit margins, among other things.

Let us take the same example except now the actual hours worked are 0.20 hours per box. The direct labor time variance computes as:

$$\text{Direct Labor Time Variance} = (\$0.20 - \$0.10) \times \$8.00 \text{ per hour} = \$0.80 \text{ or } \$0.80 \text{ (Unfavorable)}$$

In this case, the actual hours worked per box are 0.20, the standard hours per box are 0.10, and the standard rate per hour is $8.00. This computes as an unfavorable outcome. This is an unfavorable outcome because the actual hours worked were more than the standard hours expected per box. As a result of this unfavorable outcome information, the company may consider retraining its workers, changing the production process to be more efficient, or increasing prices to cover labor costs.

The combination of the two variances can produce one overall total direct labor cost variance.

THINK IT THROUGH

Package Deliveries

UPS drivers are evaluated on how many miles they drive and how quickly they deliver packages. The drivers are given the route and time they are expected to take, so they are expected to complete their route in a timely and efficient manner. They also work until all packages are delivered. A GPS tracking system tracks the trucks throughout the day. The system keeps track of how much they back up and if they take any left turns because right turns are much more time efficient.[3] Tracking drivers like this does not leave them very much time to deal with customers. Customer service is a major part of the driver's job. Can the driver service the customer and drive the route in the time and distance allotted? Which is more important: customer service or driving the route in a timely and efficient manner?

LINK TO LEARNING

Watch this video presenting an instructor walking through the steps involved in calculating direct labor variances (https://openstax.org/l/50DirLaborVar) to learn more.

Total Direct Labor Variance

When a company makes a product and compares the actual labor cost to the standard labor cost, the result is the **total direct labor variance**.

$$\text{Total Direct Labor Variance} = (\text{Actual Hours} \times \text{Actual Rate}) - (\text{Standard Hours} \times \text{Standard Rate})$$

If the outcome is unfavorable, the actual costs related to labor were more than the expected (standard) costs. If the outcome is favorable, the actual costs related to labor are less than the expected (standard) costs.

The total direct labor variance is also found by combining the direct labor rate variance and the direct labor time variance. By showing the total direct labor variance as the sum of the two components, management can better analyze the two variances and enhance decision-making.

Figure 8.4 shows the connection between the direct labor rate variance and direct labor time variance to total

---

3 Graham Kendall. "Why UPS Drivers Don't Turn Left and Why You Shouldn't Either." *The Conversation*. January 20, 2017. http://theconversation.com/why-ups-drivers-dont-turn-left-and-you-probably-shouldnt-either-71432

direct labor variance.

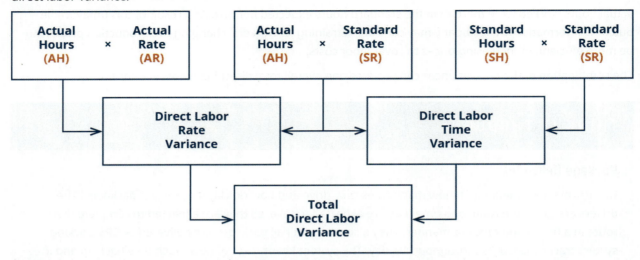

Figure 8.4 Direct Labor Variance. (attribution: Copyright Rice University, OpenStax, under CC BY-NC-SA 4.0 license)

For example, Connie's Candy Company expects to pay a rate of $8.00 per hour for labor but actually pays $9.50 per hour. The company expected to use 0.10 hours of labor per box but actually used 0.20 hours per box. The total direct labor variance is computed as:

Total Direct Labor Time Variance $= (0.20 \text{ hours} \times \$9.50) - (0.10 \text{ hours} \times \$8.00) = \$1.90 - \$0.80 = \$1.10 \,(\text{Unfavorable})$

In this case, two elements are contributing to the unfavorable outcome. Connie's Candy paid $1.50 per hour more for labor than expected and used 0.10 hours more than expected to make one box of candy. The same calculation is shown as follows using the outcomes of the direct labor rate and time variances.

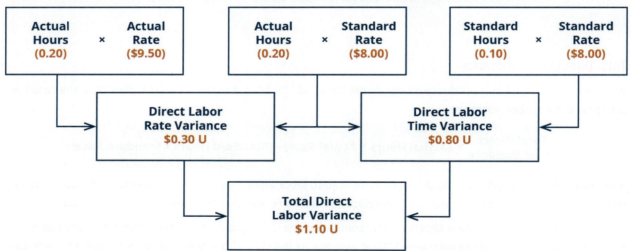

As with the interpretations for the labor rate and time variances, the company would review the individual components contributing to the overall unfavorable outcome for the total direct labor variance, and possibly make changes to production elements as a result.

YOUR TURN

Sweet and Fresh Shampoo Labor

Biglow Company makes a hair shampoo called Sweet and Fresh. Each bottle has a standard labor cost of 1.5 hours at $35.00 per hour. During May, Biglow manufactured 11,000 bottles. They used 16,000 hours at a cost of $565,600. Calculate the labor rate variance, labor time variance, and total labor variance.

Solution

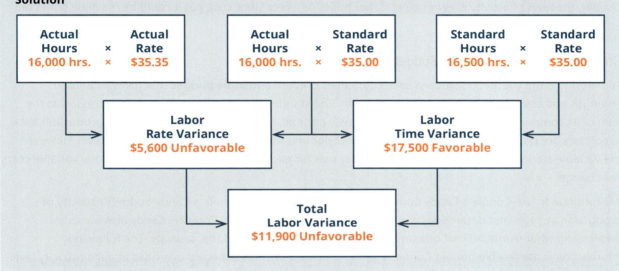

CONCEPTS IN PRACTICE

Labor Costs in Service Industries

In the service industry, labor is the main cost. Doctors, for example, have a time allotment for a physical exam and base their fee on the expected time. Insurance companies pay doctors according to a set schedule, so they set the labor standard. They pay a set rate for a physical exam, no matter how long it takes. If the exam takes longer than expected, the doctor is not compensated for that extra time. This would produce an unfavorable labor variance for the doctor. Doctors know the standard and try to schedule accordingly so a variance does not exist. If anything, they try to produce a favorable variance by seeing more patients in a quicker time frame to maximize their compensation potential.

8.4 Compute and Evaluate Overhead Variances

Recall that the standard cost of a product includes not only materials and labor but also variable and fixed overhead. It is likely that the amounts determined for standard overhead costs will differ from what actually occurs. This will lead to overhead variances.

Determination and Evaluation of Overhead Variance

In a standard cost system, overhead is applied to the goods based on a standard overhead rate. This is similar to the predetermined overhead rate used previously. The standard overhead rate is calculated by dividing budgeted overhead at a given level of production (known as normal capacity) by the level of activity required for that particular level of production.

$$\text{Standard Overhead Rate} = \frac{\text{Budgeted Overhead Rate}}{\text{Level of Activity}}$$

Usually, the level of activity is either direct labor hours or direct labor cost, but it could be machine hours or units of production.

Creation of Flexible Overhead Budget

To determine the overhead standard cost, companies prepare a **flexible budget** that gives estimated revenues and costs at varying levels of production. The standard overhead cost is usually expressed as the sum of its component parts, fixed and variable costs per unit. Note that at different levels of production, total fixed costs are the same, so the standard fixed cost per unit will change for each production level. However, the variable standard cost per unit is the same per unit for each level of production, but the total variable costs will change.

We continue to use Connie's Candy Company to illustrate. Suppose Connie's Candy budgets capacity of production at 100% and determines expected overhead at this capacity. Connie's Candy also wants to understand what overhead cost outcomes will be at 90% capacity and 110% capacity. The following information is the flexible budget Connie's Candy prepared to show expected overhead at each capacity level.

Percent of capacity	90%	100%	110%
Direct labor hours	1,800	2,000	2,200
Units of output	900	1,000	1,100
Variable overhead	$3,600	$ 4,000	$ 4,400
Fixed overhead	$6,000	$ 6,000	$ 6,000
Total overhead	$9,600	$10,000	$10,400

Normal capacity = 100% and overhead is applied based on direct labor hours
Standard Overhead Rate = $10,000/2,000 = $5 per direct labor hour

Units of output at 100% is 1,000 candy boxes (units). The standard overhead rate is the total budgeted overhead of $10,000 divided by the level of activity (direct labor hours) of 2,000 hours. Notice that fixed overhead remains constant at each of the production levels, but variable overhead changes based on unit output. If Connie's Candy only produced at 90% capacity, for example, they should expect total overhead to be $9,600 and a standard overhead rate of $5.33 (rounded). If Connie's Candy produced 2,200 units, they should expect total overhead to be $10,400 and a standard overhead rate of $4.73 (rounded). In addition to the total standard overhead rate, Connie's Candy will want to know the variable overhead rates at each activity level.

Using the flexible budget, we can determine the standard variable cost per unit at each level of production by taking the total expected variable overhead divided by the level of activity, which can still be direct labor hours or machine hours.

$$\text{Variable Overhead Rate} = \frac{\text{Budgeted Variable Overhead}}{\text{Level of Activity}}$$

Looking at Connie's Candies, the following table shows the variable overhead rate at each of the production capacity levels.

Production Capacity	Variable/Unit
90%	$3,600/1,800 = $2
100%	$4,000/2,000 = $2
110%	$4,400/2,200 = $2

Sometimes these flexible budget figures and overhead rates differ from the actual results, which produces a variance.

Determination of Variable Overhead Variances

There are two components to variable overhead rates: the overhead application rate and the activity level against which that rate was applied. If we compare the actual variable overhead to the standard variable overhead, by analyzing the difference between actual overhead costs and the standard overhead for current production, it is difficult to determine if the variance is due to application rate differences or activity level differences. Thus, there are two variable overhead variances that will better provide these answers: the variable overhead rate variance and the variable overhead efficiency variance.

Determination of Variable Overhead Rate Variance

The **variable overhead rate variance**, also known as the spending variance, is the difference between the actual variable manufacturing overhead and the variable overhead that was expected given the number of hours worked. The variable overhead rate variance is calculated using this formula:

$$\text{Variable Overhead Rate Variance} = \left(\begin{array}{c}\text{Actual Hours Worked} \\ \times \\ \text{Actual Variable} \\ \text{Overhead Rate per Hour}\end{array}\right) - \left(\begin{array}{c}\text{Actual Hours Worked} \\ \times \\ \text{Standard Variable} \\ \text{Overhead Rate per Hour}\end{array}\right)$$

Factoring out actual hours worked, we can rewrite the formula as

$$\text{Variable Overhead Rate Variance} = \left(\text{Actual Variable Overhead Rate} - \text{Standard Variable Overhead Rate}\right) \times \text{Actual Hours Worked}$$

If the outcome is favorable (a negative outcome occurs in the calculation), this means the company spent less than what it had anticipated for variable overhead. If the outcome is unfavorable (a positive outcome occurs in the calculation), this means the company spent more than what it had anticipated for variable overhead.

Connie's Candy Company wants to determine if its variable overhead spending was more or less than anticipated. Connie's Candy had this data available in the flexible budget:

Percent of capacity	100%
Direct labor hours	2,000
Units of output	1,000
Variable overhead	$ 4,000
Fixed overhead	$ 6,000
Total overhead	$10,000

Connie's Candy also had this actual output information:

Percent of capacity	100%
Direct labor hours	2,500
Units of output	1,000
Variable overhead	$ 7,000
Fixed overhead	$ 6,000
Total overhead	$13,000

To determine the variable overhead rate variance, the standard variable overhead rate per hour and the actual variable overhead rate per hour must be determined. The standard variable overhead rate per hour is $2.00 ($4,000/2,000 hours), taken from the flexible budget at 100% capacity. The actual variable overhead rate is $2.80 ($7,000/2,500), taken from the actual results at 100% capacity. Therefore,

$$\text{Variable Overhead Rate Variance} = (\$2.80 - \$2.00) \times 2,500 = \$2,000 \, (\text{Unfavorable})$$

This produces an unfavorable outcome. This could be for many reasons, and the production supervisor would need to determine where the variable cost difference is occurring to make production changes.

Let us look at another example producing a favorable outcome. Connie's Candy had this data available in the flexible budget:

Percent of capacity	100%
Direct labor hours	2,000
Units of output	1,000
Variable overhead	$ 4,000
Fixed overhead	$ 6,000
Total overhead	$10,000

Connie's Candy also had this actual output information:

Percent of capacity	100%
Direct labor hours	2,000
Units of output	1,000
Variable overhead	$3,500
Fixed overhead	$6,000
Total overhead	$9,500

To determine the variable overhead rate variance, the standard variable overhead rate per hour and the actual variable overhead rate per hour must be determined. The standard variable overhead rate per hour is $2.00 ($4,000/2,000 hours), taken from the flexible budget at 100% capacity. The actual variable overhead rate is $1.75 ($3,500/2,000), taken from the actual results at 100% capacity. Therefore,

$$\text{Variable Overhead Rate Variance} = (\$1.75 - \$2.00) \times \$2,000 = -\$500 \text{ or } \$500 \, (\text{Favorable})$$

This produces a favorable outcome. This could be for many reasons, and the production supervisor would need to determine where the variable cost difference is occurring to better understand the variable overhead reduction.

Interpretation of the variable overhead rate variance is often difficult because the cost of one overhead item, such as indirect labor, could go up, but another overhead cost, such as indirect materials, could go down. Often, explanation of this variance will need clarification from the production supervisor. Another variable overhead variance to consider is the variable overhead efficiency variance.

Determination of Variable Overhead Efficiency Variance

The **variable overhead efficiency variance**, also known as the controllable variance, is driven by the difference between the actual hours worked and the standard hours expected for the units produced. This variance measures whether the allocation base was efficiently used. The variable overhead efficiency variance is calculated using this formula:

$$\text{Variable Overhead Efficiency Variance} = \left(\text{Actual Hours Worked} \times \text{Standard Variable Overhead Rate per Hour}\right) - \left(\text{Standard Hours} \times \text{Standard Variable Overhead Rate per Hour}\right)$$

Factoring out standard overhead rate, the formula can be written as

$$\text{Variable Overhead Efficiency Variance} = \left(\text{Actual Labor Hours} - \text{Standard Labor Hours}\right) \times \text{Standard Overhead Rate}$$

If the outcome is favorable (a negative outcome occurs in the calculation), this means the company was more efficient than what it had anticipated for variable overhead. If the outcome is unfavorable (a positive outcome occurs in the calculation), this means the company was less efficient than what it had anticipated for variable overhead.

Connie's Candy Company wants to determine if its variable overhead efficiency was more or less than anticipated. Connie's Candy had the following data available in the flexible budget:

Percent of capacity	100%
Direct labor hours	2,000
Units of output	1,000
Variable overhead	$ 4,000
Fixed overhead	$ 6,000
Total overhead	$10,000

Connie's Candy also had the following actual output information:

Percent of capacity	100%
Direct labor hours	2,500
Units of output	1,000
Variable overhead	$ 7,000
Fixed overhead	$ 6,000
Total overhead	$13,000

To determine the variable overhead efficiency variance, the actual hours worked and the standard hours worked at the production capacity of 100% must be determined. Actual hours worked are 2,500, and standard hours are 2,000. The standard variable overhead rate per hour is $2.00 ($4,000/2,000 hours), taken from the flexible budget at 100% capacity. Therefore,

$$\text{Variable Overhead Efficiency Variance} = (2{,}500 - 2{,}000) \times \$2.00 = \$1{,}000 \, (\text{Unfavorable})$$

This produces an unfavorable outcome. This could be for many reasons, and the production supervisor would need to determine where the variable cost difference is occurring to make production changes.

Let us look at another example producing a favorable outcome. Connie's Candy had the following data available in the flexible budget:

Percent of capacity	100%
Direct labor hours	2,000
Units of output	1,000
Variable overhead	$ 4,000
Fixed overhead	$ 6,000
Total overhead	$10,000

Connie's Candy also had the following actual output information:

Percent of capacity	100%
Direct labor hours	1,800
Units of output	1,000
Variable overhead	$3,500
Fixed overhead	$6,000
Total overhead	$9,500

To determine the variable overhead efficiency variance, the actual hours worked and the standard hours worked at the production capacity of 100% must be determined. Actual hours worked are 1,800, and standard hours are 2,000. The standard variable overhead rate per hour is $2.00 ($4,000/2,000 hours), taken from the flexible budget at 100% capacity. Therefore,

$$\text{Variable Overhead Efficiency Variance} = (1{,}800 - 2{,}000) \times \$2.00 = -\$400 \text{ or } \$400 \, (\text{Favorable})$$

This produces a favorable outcome. This could be for many reasons, and the production supervisor would need to determine where the variable cost difference is occurring to better understand the variable overhead efficiency reduction.

The **total variable overhead cost variance** is also found by combining the variable overhead rate variance and the variable overhead efficiency variance. By showing the total variable overhead cost variance as the sum of the two components, management can better analyze the two variances and enhance decision-making.

Figure 8.5 shows the connection between the variable overhead rate variance and variable overhead efficiency variance to total variable overhead cost variance.

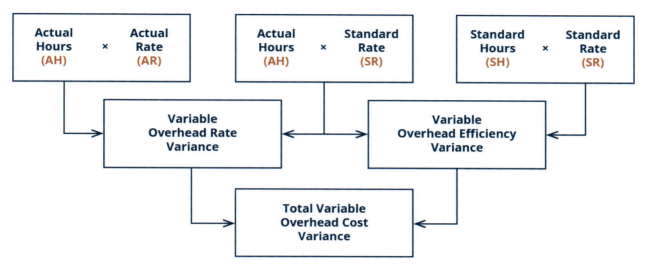

Figure 8.5 Variable Overheard Cost Variance. (attribution: Copyright Rice University, OpenStax, under CC BY-NC-SA 4.0 license)

For example, Connie's Candy Company had the following data available in the flexible budget:

Percent of capacity	100%
Direct labor hours	2,000
Units of output	1,000
Variable overhead	$ 4,000
Fixed overhead	$ 6,000
Total overhead	$10,000

Connie's Candy also had the following actual output information:

Percent of capacity	100%
Direct labor hours	1,800
Units of output	1,000
Variable overhead	$3,500
Fixed overhead	$6,000
Total overhead	$9,500

The variable overhead rate variance is calculated as (1,800 × $1.94) – (1,800 × $2.00) = –$108, or $108 (favorable). The variable overhead efficiency variance is calculated as (1,800 × $2.00) – (2,000 × $2.00) = –$400, or $400 (favorable).

The total variable overhead cost variance is computed as:

$$\text{Total Variable Overhead Cost Variance} = (-\$108) + (-\$400) = -\$508 \text{ or } \$508 \text{ (Favorable)}$$

In this case, two elements are contributing to the favorable outcome. Connie's Candy used fewer direct labor hours and less variable overhead to produce 1,000 candy boxes (units).

The same calculation is shown as follows in diagram format.

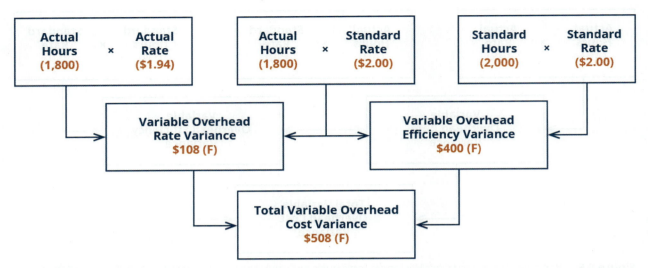

As with the interpretations for the variable overhead rate and efficiency variances, the company would review the individual components contributing to the overall favorable outcome for the total variable overhead cost variance, before making any decisions about production in the future. Other variances companies consider are fixed factory overhead variances.

Fundamentals of Fixed Factory Overhead Variances

The **fixed factory overhead variance** represents the difference between the actual fixed overhead and the applied fixed overhead. There are two fixed overhead variances. One variance determines if too much or too little was spent on fixed overhead. The other variance computes whether or not actual production was above or below the expected production level.

YOUR TURN

Sweet and Fresh Shampoo Overhead

Biglow Company makes a hair shampoo called Sweet and Fresh. They have the following flexible budget data:

	90%	100%	110%
Direct labor hours	14,000	16,000	18,000
Units of output	10,000	10,000	10,000
Direct labor	$525,000	$ 346,500	$ 378,000
Variable overhead	$315,000	$ 346,000	$ 378,000
Fixed overhead	$ 45,500	$ 45,500	$ 45,500
Total	$953,500	$1,044,300	$1,135,100

What is the standard variable overhead rate at 90%, 100%, and 110% capacity levels?

Solution

90% = $315,000/14,000 = $22.50, 100% = $346,000/16,000 = $21.63 (rounded), 110% = $378,000/18,000 =

$21.00.

> ### THINK IT THROUGH
>
> **Purchasing Planes**
>
> The XYZ Firm is bidding on a contract for a new plane for the military. As the management team is going over the bid, they come to the conclusion it is too high on a per-plane basis, but they cannot find any costs they feel can be reduced. The information from the military states they will purchase between 50 and 100 planes, but will more likely purchase 50 planes rather than 100 planes. XYZ's bid is based on 50 planes. The controller suggests that they base their bid on 100 planes. This would spread the fixed costs over more planes and reduce the bid price. The lower bid price will increase substantially the chances of XYZ winning the bid. Should XYZ Firm keep the bid at 50 planes or increase its bid to 100 planes? What are the pros and cons to keeping the bid at 50 or increasing to 100 planes?

8.5 Describe How Companies Use Variance Analysis

Companies use variance analysis in different ways. The starting point is the determination of standards against which to compare actual results. Many companies produce variance reports, and the management responsible for the variances must explain any variances outside of a certain range. Some companies only require that unfavorable variances be explained, while many companies require both favorable and unfavorable variances to be explained.

Requiring managers to determine what caused unfavorable variances forces them to identify potential problem areas or consider if the variance was a one-time occurrence. Requiring managers to explain favorable variances allows them to assess whether the favorable variance is sustainable. Knowing what caused the favorable variance allows management to plan for it in the future, depending on whether it was a one-time variance or it will be ongoing.

Another possibility is that management may have built the favorable variance into the standards. Management may overestimate the material price, labor rate, material quantity, or labor hours per unit, for example. This method of overestimation, sometimes called *budget slack*, is built into the standards so management can still look good even if costs are higher than planned. In either case, managers potentially can help other managers and the company overall by noticing particular problem areas or by sharing knowledge that can improve variances.

Often, management will manage "to the variances," meaning they will make decisions that may not be advantageous to the company's best interests over the long run, in order to meet the variance report threshold limits. This can occur when the standards are improperly established, causing significant differences between actual and standard numbers.

ETHICAL CONSIDERATIONS

Ethical Long-Term Decisions in Variance Analysis

The proper use of variance analysis is a significant tool for an organization to reach its long-term goals. When its accounting system recognizes a variance, an organization needs to understand the significant influence of accounting not only in recording its financial results, but also in how reacting to that variance can shape management's behavior toward reaching its goals.[4] Many managers use variance analysis only to determine a short-term reaction, and do not analyze why the variance occurred from a long-term perspective. A more long-term analysis of variances allows an approach that "is responsibility accounting in which authority and accountability for tasks is delegated downward to those managers with the most influence and control over them."[5] It is important for managers to analyze the reported variances with more than just a short-term perspective.

Managers sometimes focus only on making numbers for the current period. For example, a manager might decide to make a manufacturing division's results look profitable in the short term at the expense of reaching the organization's long-term goals. A recognizable cost variance could be an increase in repair costs as a percentage of sales on an increasing basis. This variance could indicate that equipment is not operating efficiently and is increasing overall cost. However, the expense of implementing new, more efficient equipment might be higher than repairing the current equipment. In the short term, it might be more economical to repair the outdated equipment, but in the long term, purchasing more efficient equipment would help the organization reach its goal of eco-friendly manufacturing. If the system use for controlling costs is not aligned to reinforce management of the organization with a long-term perspective, "the manager has no organizational incentive to be concerned with important issues unrelated to anything but the immediate costs"[6] related to the variance. A manager needs to be cognizant of his or her organization's goals when making decisions based on variance analysis.

Management can use standard costs to prepare the budget for the upcoming period, using the past information to possibly make changes to production elements. Standard costs are a measurement tool and can thus be used to evaluate performance. As you've learned, management may manage "to the variances" and can manipulate results to meet expectations. To reduce this possibility, performance should be measured on multiple outcomes, not simply on standard cost variances.

As shown in Table 8.1, standard costs have pros and cons to consider when using them in the decision-making and evaluation processes.

---

4 Jeffrey R. Cohen and Laurie W. Pant. "The Only Thing That Counts Is That Which Is Counted: A Discussion of Behavioral and Ethical Issues in Cost Accounting That Are Relevant for the OB Professor." September 18, 2018. http://citeseerx.ist.psu.edu/viewdoc/download?doi=10.1.1.1026.5569&rep=rep1&type=pdf

5 Jeffrey R. Cohen and Laurie W. Pant. "The Only Thing That Counts Is That Which Is Counted: A Discussion of Behavioral and Ethical Issues in Cost Accounting That Are Relevant for the OB Professor." September 18, 2018. http://citeseerx.ist.psu.edu/viewdoc/download?doi=10.1.1.1026.5569&rep=rep1&type=pdf

6 Jeffrey R. Cohen and Laurie W. Pant. "The Only Thing That Counts Is That Which Is Counted: A Discussion of Behavioral and Ethical Issues in Cost Accounting That Are Relevant for the OB Professor." September 18, 2018. http://citeseerx.ist.psu.edu/viewdoc/download?doi=10.1.1.1026.5569&rep=rep1&type=pdf

Standard Costs

Pros	Cons
• Useful when developing a future budget • Can be used as a benchmark for performance and quality expectations • Can individually identify areas of success and areas for improvement	• Might ignore customer and employee satisfaction rates • Information could be historical data and not useful in real-time decision-making needs • The system to manage and develop standard costs requires a lot of resources, which could be costly and time consuming

Table 8.1

Standard costing provides many benefits and challenges, and a thorough analysis of each variance and the possible unfavorable or favorable outcomes is required to set future expectations and adjust current production goals.

The following is a summary of all direct materials variances (Figure 8.6), direct labor variances (Figure 8.7), and overhead variances (Figure 8.8) presented as both formulas and tree diagrams. Note that for some of the formulas, there are two presentations of the same formula, for example, there are two presentations of the direct materials price variance. While both arrive at the same answer, students usually prefer one formula structure over the other.

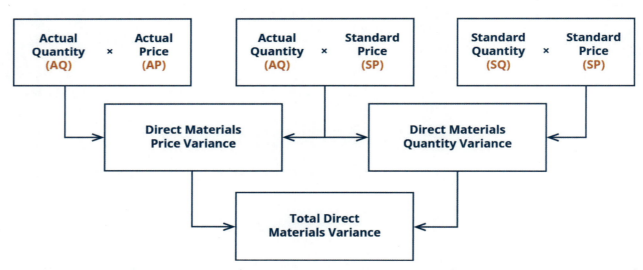

Figure 8.6 Direct Materials Variances. (attribution: Copyright Rice University, OpenStax, under CC BY-NC-SA 4.0 license)

Chapter 8 Standard Costs and Variances

$$\text{Direct Labor Rate Variance} = \begin{pmatrix} \text{Actual Hours Worked} \\ \times \\ \text{Actual Rate per Hour} \end{pmatrix} - \begin{pmatrix} \text{Actual Hours Worked} \\ \times \\ \text{Standard Rate per Hour} \end{pmatrix}$$

$$\text{Direct Labor Rate Variance} = \begin{pmatrix} \text{Actual Rate per Hour} - \text{Standard Rate per Hour} \end{pmatrix} \times \text{Actual Hours Worked}$$

$$\text{Direct Labor Time Variance} = \begin{pmatrix} \text{Actual Hours Worked} \\ \times \\ \text{Standard Rate per Hour} \end{pmatrix} - \begin{pmatrix} \text{Standard Hours} \\ \times \\ \text{Standard Rate per Hour} \end{pmatrix}$$

$$\text{Direct Labor Time Variance} = \begin{pmatrix} \text{Actual Hours Worked} - \text{Standard Hours Expected for the Units Produced} \end{pmatrix} \times \text{Standard Rate per Hour}$$

$$\text{Total Direct Labor Variance} = (\text{Actual Hours} \times \text{Actual Rate}) - (\text{Standard Hours} \times \text{Standard Rate})$$

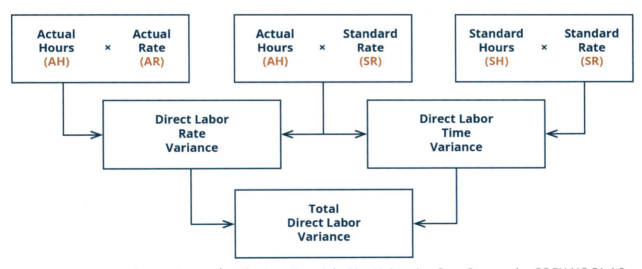

Figure 8.7 Direct Labor Variances. (attribution: Copyright Rice University, OpenStax, under CC BY-NC-SA 4.0 license)

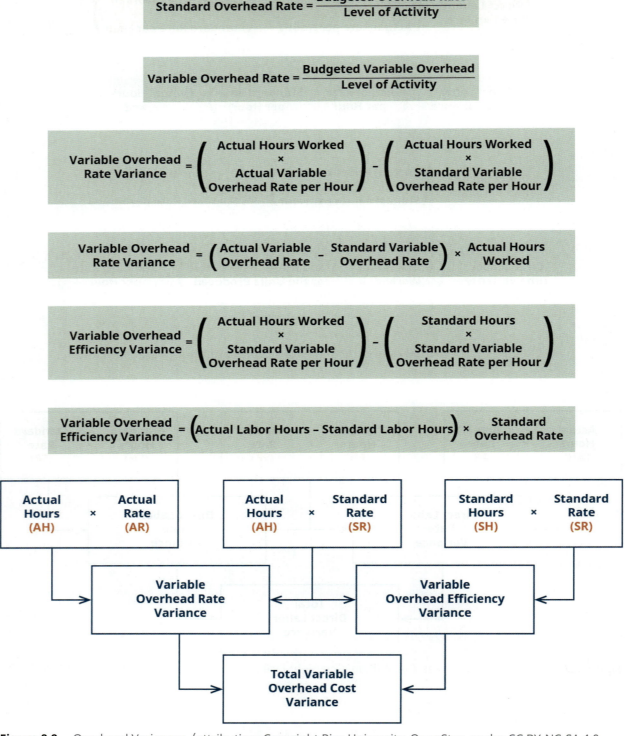

Figure 8.8 Overhead Variances. (attribution: Copyright Rice University, OpenStax, under CC BY-NC-SA 4.0 license)

YOUR TURN

Barley, Inc. Production

Barley, Inc., produces a product and has the following as standard costs per unit for materials and labor:

Materials	4 pounds @ $15 per pound
Labor	2 hours @ $20 per hour

For the month of October, the following information was gathered related to production:

Beginning inventory	0
Units completed	10,000
Budgeted output units	12,000
Materials used (50,000 pounds)	$800,000
Labor (25,000 hours)	$450,000

Compute:

A. The materials price and quantity variances
B. The labor rate and efficiency variances

Provide possible explanations for each variance.

Solution

A.

Materials price variance:

$50,000 unfavorable = ($16* − $15) × 50,000 lb.

*$800,000/50,000

An unfavorable materials price variance occurred because the actual cost of materials was greater than the expected or standard cost. This could occur if a higher-quality material was purchased or the suppliers raised their prices.

Materials quantity variance:

$150,000 unfavorable = (50,000 lb. − 40,000* lb.) × $15 per lb.

*4 lb. × 10,000 units

An unfavorable materials quantity variance occurred because the pounds of materials used were greater than the pounds expected to be used. This could occur if there were inefficiencies in production or the quality of the materials was such that more needed to be used to meet safety or other standards.

Materials inputs:

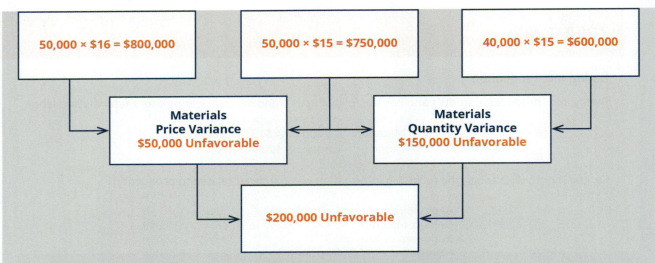

B.

Labor rate variance:

$50,000 favorable = ($18* per hour − $20 per hour) × 25,000 hours

*$450,000/25,000

A favorable labor rate variance occurred because the rate paid per hour was less than the rate expected to be paid (standard) per hour. This could occur because the company was able to hire workers at a lower rate, because of negotiated union contracts, or because of a poor labor rate estimate used in creating the standard.

Labor quantity variance:

$100,000 unfavorable = (25,000 hours − 20,000* hours) × $20 per hour

*2 hours × 10,000 units

An unfavorable labor quantity variance occurred because the actual hours worked to make the 10,000 units were greater than the expected hours to make that many units. This could occur because of inefficiencies of the workers, defects and errors that caused additional time reworking items, or the use of new workers who were less efficient.

Labor inputs:

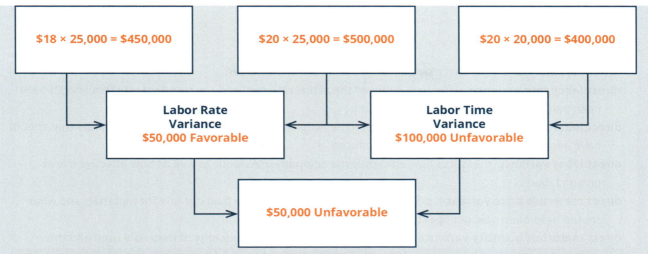

Figure 8.9 Labor variance for Barley, Inc. (attribution: Copyright Rice University, OpenStax, under CC BY-NC-SA 4.0 license)

THINK IT THROUGH

Explaining Differences in Expected and Actual Operational Outcomes

The manager of a plant has called operations, purchasing, and personnel into her office to discuss the results of the last month. She notes that there was more than normal scrap, and employees worked more hours than expected. She is looking for an explanation for these results. What system might she have used to determine these material and labor issues? Why might these variances have occurred? What should she do about it for future periods?

LINK TO LEARNING

Standard Costing Advantages Explained

See this article on the four major advantages of standard costing (https://openstax.org/l/50StandCosting) to learn more.

Key Terms

attainable standard level that may be reached with reasonable effort

direct labor rate variance difference between the actual rate paid and the standard rate that should have been paid based on the actual hours worked

direct labor time variance difference between the actual hours worked and the standard hours that should have been worked for the actual units produced

direct labor variance measures how efficiently the company uses labor as well as how effective it is at pricing labor

direct materials price variance difference between the actual price paid per unit for materials and what should have been paid per the standards

direct materials quantity variance difference between the actual quantity of materials used and the standard materials that were expected to be used to make the actual units produced

direct materials variance difference between the actual price or amount used and the standard amount

favorable variance difference involving spending less, or using less, than the standard amount

fixed factory overhead variance difference between the actual fixed overhead and applied fixed overhead

flexible budget measurement and prediction of estimated revenues and costs at varying levels of production

ideal standard level that could be achieved if everything ran perfectly

standard expectation for a component used in production

standard cost cost expectation for price paid and amount (quantities) used

total direct labor variance actual labor costs compared to standard labor costs

total direct materials cost variance difference between actual materials cost and standard materials cost

total variable overhead cost variance total cost variance found by combining variable overhead rate variance and variable overhead efficiency variance

unfavorable variance difference involving spending more or using more than the standard amount

variable overhead efficiency variance difference between the actual hours worked and the standard hours expected for the units produced

variable overhead rate variance difference between the actual variable manufacturing overhead and the variable overhead that was expected given the number of hours worked

variance difference between standard and actual performance

Summary

8.1 Explain How and Why a Standard Cost Is Developed
- Standards are budgeted unit amounts for price paid and amount used.
- Variances are the difference between actual and standard amounts.
- A favorable variance is when the actual price or quantity is less than the standard amount.
- An unfavorable variance is when the actual price or amount is greater than the standard amount.

8.2 Compute and Evaluate Materials Variances
- There are two components to material variances: the direct materials price variance and the direct materials quantity variance.
- The direct materials price variance is caused by paying too much or too little for material.
- The direct materials quantity variance is caused by using too much or too little material.

8.3 Compute and Evaluate Labor Variances
- There are two labor variances: the direct labor rate variance and the direct labor time variance.
- The direct labor rate variance determines if the rate paid is greater than or less than the standard rate.
- The direct labor time variance determines if the actual hours used are greater than or less than the standards that should have been used.

8.4 Compute and Evaluate Overhead Variances
- There are two sets of overhead variances: variable and fixed.
- The variable variances are caused by the overhead application rate and the activity level against which the rate was applied.
- The variable overhead rate variance is the difference between the actual variable manufacturing overhead and the variable overhead that was expected given the number of hours worked.
- The variable overhead efficiency variance is driven by the difference between the actual hours worked and the standard hours expected for the units produced.
- There are two fixed overhead variances. One is caused by spending too much or too little on fixed overhead. The other is caused by actual production being above or below the expected production level.

8.5 Describe How Companies Use Variance Analysis
- The key to analyzing variances is to determine why the variance occurred.
- If a company cannot determine why there is a variance, it will not know if the variance is indicative of a problem or not.
- All firms—manufacturing, retail, and service—use standards and variances.

Multiple Choice

1. LO 8.1 Why does a company use a standard costing system?
   A. to identify variances from actual cost that assist them in maintaining profits
   B. to identify nonperformers in the workplace
   C. to identify what vendors are unreliable
   D. to identify defective materials

2. LO 8.1 This standard is set at a level that may be reached with reasonable effort.
   A. ideal standard
   B. attainable standard
   C. unattainable standard
   D. variance from standard

3. LO 8.1 This standard is set at a level that could be achieved if everything ran perfectly.
   A. ideal standard
   B. attainable standard
   C. unattainable standard
   D. variance from standard

4. **LO** 8.1 This variance is the difference involving spending more or using more than the standard amount.
   A. favorable variance
   B. unfavorable variance
   C. no variance
   D. variance

5. **LO** 8.1 This variance is the difference involving spending less, or using less than the standard amount.
   A. favorable variance
   B. unfavorable variance
   C. no variance
   D. variance

6. **LO** 8.2 What are some possible reasons for a material price variance?
   A. substandard material
   B. labor rate increases
   C. labor rate decreases
   D. labor efficiency

7. **LO** 8.2 When is the material price variance unfavorable?
   A. when the actual quantity used is greater than the standard quantity
   B. when the actual quantity used is less than the standard quantity
   C. when the actual price paid is greater than the standard price
   D. when the actual price is less than the standard price

8. **LO** 8.2 When is the material price variance favorable?
   A. when the actual quantity used is greater than the standard quantity
   B. when the actual quantity used is less than the standard quantity
   C. when the actual price paid is greater than the standard price
   D. when the actual price is less than the standard price

9. **LO** 8.2 What are some reasons for a material quantity variance?
   A. building rental charges increase
   B. labor rate decreases
   C. more qualified workers
   D. labor efficiency increases

10. **LO** 8.2 When is the material quantity variance favorable?
    A. when the actual quantity used is greater than the standard quantity
    B. when the actual quantity used is less than the standard quantity
    C. when the actual price paid is greater than the standard price
    D. when the actual price is less than the standard price

11. **LO** 8.2 When is the material quantity unfavorable?
    A. when the actual quantity used is greater than the standard quantity
    B. when the actual quantity used is less than the standard quantity
    C. when the actual price paid is greater than the standard price
    D. when the actual price is less than the standard price

12. LO 8.3 What are some possible reasons for a labor rate variance?
    A. hiring of less qualified workers
    B. an excess of material usage
    C. material price increase
    D. utilities usage change

13. LO 8.3 When is the labor rate variance unfavorable?
    A. when the actual quantity used is greater than the standard quantity
    B. when the actual quantity used is less than the standard quantity
    C. when the actual price paid is greater than the standard price
    D. when the actual price is less than the standard price

14. LO 8.3 When is the labor rate variance favorable?
    A. when the actual quantity used is greater than the standard quantity
    B. when the actual quantity used is less than the standard quantity
    C. when the actual price paid is greater than the standard price
    D. when the actual price is less than the standard price

15. LO 8.3 What are some possible reasons for a direct labor time variance?
    A. utility usage decrease
    B. less qualified workers
    C. office supplies spending
    D. sales decline

16. LO 8.3 When is the direct labor time variance favorable?
    A. when the actual quantity used is greater than the standard quantity
    B. when the actual quantity used is less than the standard quantity
    C. when the actual price paid is greater than the standard price
    D. when the actual price is less than the standard price

17. LO 8.3 When is the direct labor time variance unfavorable?
    A. when the actual quantity used is greater than the standard quantity
    B. when the actual quantity used is less than the standard quantity
    C. when the actual price paid is greater than the standard price
    D. when the actual price is less than the standard price

18. LO 8.4 A flexible budget _____.
    A. predicts estimated revenues and costs at varying levels of production
    B. gives actual figures for selling price
    C. gives actual figures for variable and fixed overhead
    D. is not used in overhead variance calculations

19. LO 8.4 The variable overhead rate variance is caused by the sum between which of the following?
    A. actual and standard allocation base
    B. actual and standard overhead rates
    C. actual and budgeted units
    D. actual units and actual overhead rates

20. LO 8.4 The variable overhead efficiency variance is caused by the difference between which of the following?
   A. actual and budgeted units
   B. actual and standard allocation base
   C. actual and standard overhead rates
   D. actual units and actual overhead rates

21. LO 8.4 The fixed factory overhead variance is caused by the difference between which of the following?
   A. actual and standard allocation base
   B. actual and budgeted units
   C. actual fixed overhead and applied fixed overhead
   D. actual and standard overhead rates

22. LO 8.5 Which of the following is a possible cause of an unfavorable material price variance?
   A. purchasing too much material
   B. purchasing higher-quality material
   C. hiring substandard workers
   D. buying substandard material

23. LO 8.5 Which of the following is a possible cause of an unfavorable material quantity variance?
   A. purchasing substandard material
   B. hiring higher-quality workers
   C. paying more than should have for workers
   D. purchasing too much material

24. LO 8.5 Which of the following is a possible cause of an unfavorable labor efficiency variance?
   A. hiring substandard workers
   B. making too many units
   C. buying higher-quality material
   D. paying too much for workers

25. LO 8.5 Which of the following is a possible cause of an unfavorable labor rate variance?
   A. hiring too many workers
   B. hiring higher-quality workers at a higher wage
   C. making too many units
   D. purchasing too much material

Questions

1. LO 8.1 What two components are needed to determine a standard for materials?

2. LO 8.1 What two components are needed to determine a standard for labor?

3. LO 8.1 What elements require consideration before establishing an overhead standard?

4. LO 8.1 What is a variance?

5. LO 8.2 What causes the material price variance?

6. LO 8.2 What causes the material quantity variance?

7. LO 8.2 What are some possible causes of a material price variance?

8. LO 8.2 What are some possible causes of a material quantity variance?

9. LO 8.3 What is the direct labor rate variance?

10. LO 8.3 What is the direct labor time variance?

11. LO 8.3 What are some possible causes of a direct labor rate variance?

12. LO 8.3 What are some possible causes of a direct labor time variance?

13. LO 8.3 How is the total direct labor variance calculated?

14. LO 8.4 What causes the variable overhead rate variance?

15. LO 8.4 What causes the variable overhead efficiency variance?

16. LO 8.4 What is the main difference between a flexible budget and a master budget?

17. LO 8.5 What causes a favorable variance?

18. LO 8.5 What causes an unfavorable variance?

19. LO 8.5 When might a favorable variance not be a good outcome?

20. LO 8.5 When might an unfavorable variance be a good outcome?

21. LO 8.5 Identify several causes of a favorable material price variance.

22. LO 8.5 Identify several causes of an unfavorable material price variance.

23. LO 8.5 Identify several causes of a favorable material quantity variance.

24. LO 8.5 Identify several causes of an unfavorable material quantity.

25. LO 8.5 Identify several causes of a favorable labor rate variance.

26. LO 8.5 Identify several causes of an unfavorable labor rate variance.

27. LO 8.5 Identify several causes of a favorable labor efficiency variance.

28. LO 8.5 Identify several causes of an unfavorable labor efficiency variance.

Exercise Set A

EA1. LO 8.1 Moisha is developing material standards for her company. The operations manager wants grade A widgets because they are the easiest to work with and are the quality the customers want. Grade B will not work because customers do not want the lower grade, and it takes more time to assemble the product than with grade A materials. Moisha calls several suppliers to get prices for the widget. All are within $0.05 of each other. Since they will use millions of widgets, she decides that the $0.05 difference is important. The supplier who has the lowest price is known for delivering late and low-quality materials. Moisha decides to use the supplier who is $0.02 more but delivers on time and at the right quality. This supplier charges $0.48 per widget. Each unit of product requires four widgets. What is the standard cost per unit for widgets?

EA2. LO 8.1 Rene is working with the operations manager to determine what the standard labor cost is for a spice chest. He has watched the process from start to finish and taken detailed notes on what each employee does. The first employee selects and mills the wood, so it is smooth on all four sides. This takes the employee 1 hour for each chest. The next employee takes the wood and cuts it to the proper size. This takes 30 minutes. The next employee assembles and sands the chest. Assembly takes 2 hours. The chest then goes to the finishing department. It takes 1.5 hours to finish the chest. All employees are cross-trained so they are all paid the same amount per hour, $17.50.

    A. What are the standard hours per chest?
    B. What is the standard cost per chest for labor?

EA3. LO 8.1 Fiona cleans offices. She is allowed 5 seconds per square foot. She cleans building A, which is 3,000 square feet, and building B, which is 2,460 square feet. Will she finish these two buildings in an 8-hour shift? Will she have time for a break?

EA4. LO 8.1 Use the information provided to create a standard cost card for production of one glove box switch. To make one switch it takes 16 feet of plastic-coated copper wire and 0.5 pounds of plastic material. The plastic material can usually be purchased for $20.00 per pound, and the wire costs $2.50 per foot. The labor necessary to assemble a switch consists of two types. The first type of labor is assembly, which takes 3.5 hours. These workers are paid $27.00 per hour. The second type of labor is finishing, which takes 2 hours. These workers are paid $29.00 per hour. Overhead is applied using labor hours. The variable overhead rate is $14.90 per labor hour. The fixed overhead rate is $15.60 per hour.

EA5. LO 8.2 Sitka Industries uses a cost system that carries direct materials inventory at a standard cost. The controller has established these standards for one ladder (unit):

	Standard Quantity	×	Standard Price	=	Standard Cost
Direct materials	3 pounds		$4.50 per pound		$13.50
Direct labor	2.00 hours		$12.00 per hour		$24.00
Total cost					$37.50

Sitka Industries made 3,000 ladders in July and used 8,800 pounds of material to make these units. Smith Industries bought 15,500 pounds of material in the current period. There was a $250 unfavorable direct materials price variance.

    A. How much in total did Sitka pay for the 15,500 pounds?
    B. What is the direct materials quantity variance?
    C. What is the total direct material cost variance?
    D. What if 9,500 pounds were used to make these ladders, what would be the direct materials quantity variance?
    E. If there was a $340 favorable direct materials price variance, how much did Sitka pay for the 15,500 pounds of material?

EA6. LO 8.2 Use the information provided to answer the questions.

Actual price paid per pound of material	$ 14.50
Total standard pounds for units produced this period	12,500
Pounds of material used	13,250
Direct materials price variance favorable	$4,637.50

All material purchased was used in production.

- A. What is the standard price paid for materials?
- B. What is the direct materials quantity variance?
- C. What is the total direct materials cost variance?
- D. If the direct materials price variance was unfavorable, what would be the standard price?

EA7. LO 8.2 Dog Bone Bakery, which bakes dog treats, makes a special biscuit for dogs. Each biscuit uses 0.75 cup of pure semolina flour. They buy 4,000 cups of flour at $0.55 per cup. They use 3,550 cups of flour to make 4,750 biscuits. The standard cost per cup of flour is $0.53.

- A. What are the direct materials price variance, the direct materials quantity variances, and the total direct materials cost variance?
- B. What is the standard cost per biscuit for the semolina flour?

EA8. LO 8.3 Queen Industries uses a standard costing system in the manufacturing of its single product. It requires 2 hours of labor to produce 1 unit of final product. In February, Queen Industries produced 12,000 units. The standard cost for labor allowed for the output was $90,000, and there was an unfavorable direct labor time variance of $5,520.

- A. What was the standard cost per hour?
- B. How many actual hours were worked?
- C. If the workers were paid $3.90 per hour, what was the direct labor rate variance?

EA9. LO 8.3 Penny Company manufactures only one product and uses a standard cost system. The following information is from Penny's records for May:

Direct labor rate variance	$15,000 favorable
Direct labor time variance	$25,000 unfavorable
Standard hours per unit produced	2.5
Standard rate per hour	$25

During May, the company used 12.5% more hours than the standard allowed.

- A. What were the total standard hours allowed for the units manufactured during the month?
- B. What were the actual hours worked?
- C. How many actual units were produced during May?

EA10. LO 8.4 ThingOne Company has the following information available for the past year. They use machine hours to allocate overhead.

Actual total overhead	$75,000
Actual fixed overhead	$32,500
Actual machine hours	10,000
Standard hours for the units produced	9,500
Standard variable overhead rate	$ 4.50

What is the variable overhead efficiency variance?

EA11. LO 8.4 A manufacturer planned to use $78 of variable overhead per unit produced, but in the most recent period, it actually used $76 of variable overhead per unit produced. During this same period, the company planned to produce 500 units but actually produced 540 units. What is the variable overhead spending variance?

EA12. LO 8.5 Acme Inc. has the following information available:

Actual price paid for material	$1.00
Standard price for material	$1.20
Actual quantity purchased and used in production	100
Standard quantity for units produced	110
Actual labor rate per hour	$ 15
Standard labor rate per hour	$ 16
Actual hours	200
Standard hours for units produced	220

A. Compute the material price and quantity, and the labor rate and efficiency variances.
B. Describe the possible causes for this combination of favorable and unfavorable variances.

EA13. LO 8.5 Acme Inc. has the following information available:

Actual price paid for material	$1.00
Standard price for material	$0.90
Actual quantity purchased and used in production	100
Standard quantity for units produced	110
Actual labor rate per hour	$ 15
Standard labor rate per hour	$ 16
Actual hours	200
Standard hours for units produced	220

A. Compute the material price and quantity, and the labor rate and efficiency variances.
B. Describe the possible causes for this combination of favorable and unfavorable variances.

EA14. LO 8.5 Acme Inc. has the following information available:

Actual price paid for material	$1.00
Standard price for material	$0.90
Actual quantity purchased and used in production	100
Standard quantity for units produced	110
Actual labor rate per hour	$ 15
Standard labor rate per hour	$ 14
Actual hours	200
Standard hours for units produced	220

A. Compute the material price and quantity, and the labor rate and efficiency variances.
B. Describe the possible causes for this combination of favorable and unfavorable variances.

Exercise Set B

EB1. LO 8.1 Bristol is developing material standards for her company. The operations manager wants grade A plastic tops because they are the easiest to work with and are the quality the customers want. Grade B will not work because customers do not want the lower grade, and it takes more time to assemble the product than with grade A materials. Bristol calls several suppliers to get prices for the plastic top. All are within $0.10 of each other. Since the company will use millions of the plastic tops, she decides that the $0.10 difference is important. The supplier who has the lowest price is known for delivering late and low-quality materials. Bristol decides to use the supplier who is $0.04 more but delivers on time and at the right quality. This supplier charges $0.52 per plastic top. Each unit of product requires six plastic tops. What is the standard cost per unit for plastic tops?

EB2. LO 8.1 Salley is developing material and labor standards for her company. She finds that it costs $0.55 per pound of material per widget. Each widget requires 6 pounds of material per widget. Salley is also working with the operations manager to determine what the standard labor cost is for a widget. Upon observation, Salley notes that it takes 3 hours in the assembly department and 1 hour in the finishing department to complete one widget. All employees are paid $10.50 per hour.
  A. What is the standard materials cost per unit for a widget?
  B. What is the standard labor cost per unit for a widget?

EB3. LO 8.1 Use the following information to create a standard cost card for production of one photography drone from Drone Experts.

To make one drone it takes 2 pounds of plastic material. The material can usually be purchased for $25.00 per pound. The labor necessary to build a drone consists of two types. The first type of labor is assembly, which takes 10.5 hours. These workers are paid $21.00 per hour. The second type of labor is finishing, which takes 7 hours. These workers are paid $25.00 per hour. Overhead is applied using labor hours. The variable overhead rate is $14.00 per labor hour. The fixed overhead rate is $16.00 per hour.

EB4. LO 8.1 Mateo makes gizmos. He would like to set up a system to help him manage his business. The gizmos are made in a standard process. There is a certain amount of material and labor that goes into each gizmo. The only difference between the gizmo is the color of the material. What information should Mateo collect, how should he format it, and what kind of reports should he prepare to help him run his business?

EB5. LO 8.2 Smith Industries uses a cost system that carries direct materials inventory at a standard cost. The controller has established these standards for the cost of one basket (unit):

	Standard Quantity	×	Standard Price	=	Standard Cost
Direct materials	5 pounds		$2.60 per pound		$18.00
Direct labor	1.25 hours		$12.00 per hour		$15.00
Total prime cost					$33.00

Smith Industries made 3,000 baskets in July and used 15,500 pounds of material to make these units. Smith Industries paid $39,370 for the 15,500 pounds of material.

A. What was the direct materials price variance for July?
B. What was the direct materials quantity variance for July?
C. What is the total direct materials cost variance?
D. If Smith Industries used 15,750 pounds to make the baskets, what would be the direct materials quantity variance?

EB6. LO 8.2 Lizbeth, Inc., makes ice cream. The toffee coffee ice cream takes 4 quarts of cream, 3 cups of sugar, 2 tablespoons of toffee flavoring, and 1.5 tablespoons of coffee flavoring per gallon. The standard prices are $2.00 per quart of cream, $0.40 per cup of sugar, $0.50 per tablespoon of toffee flavoring, and $0.75 per tablespoon of coffee flavoring.

A. What is the standard material cost for a gallon of toffee coffee ice cream?
B. If Lizbeth makes 35 gallons of toffee coffee ice cream, how much of each of the ingredients should she use?
C. If Lizbeth uses 105 quarts of cream to make 25 gallons of ice cream, what would be the cream (direct materials) quantity variance?
D. If Lizbeth uses 45 tablespoons of toffee flavoring to make 25 gallons of ice cream, what would be the toffee flavoring (direct materials) quantity variance?

EB7. LO 8.2 Woodpecker manufactures sawmill equipment. They use a standard costing system and recognize material price variance at the time of material purchases. They use carbide to make the teeth on their band-saw blades. They received an order for 250 band-saw blades, but they did not have any carbide in stock. They purchased 3,500 pounds of carbide for $14,875 but should have spent $16,275. Each saw blade has a standard carbide direct materials quantity of 7.8 pounds.

A. If they used 8 pounds per blade, what would be the direct materials quantity variance?
B. If they used 7.5 pounds per blade, what would be the direct materials quantity variance?
C. Compute the direct materials price variance based on 7.5 pounds of carbide per blade actually used.

EB8. LO 8.3 Case made 24,500 units during June, using 32,000 direct labor hours. They expected to use 31,450 hours per the standard cost card. Their employees were paid $15.75 per hour for the month of June. The standard cost card uses $15.50 as the standard hourly rate.

A. Compute the direct labor rate and time variances for the month of June, and also calculate the total direct labor variance.
B. If the standard rate per hour was $16.00, what would change?

EB9. LO 8.3 Eagle Inc. uses a standard cost system. During the most recent period, the company manufactured 115,000 units. The standard cost sheet indicates that the standard direct labor cost per unit is $1.50. The performance report for the period includes an unfavorable direct labor rate variance of $3,700 and a favorable direct labor time variance of $10,275.
What was the total actual cost of direct labor incurred during the period?

EB10. LO 8.4 A manufacturer planned to use $45 of variable overhead per unit produced, but in the most recent period, it actually used $47 of variable overhead per unit produced. During this same period, the company planned to produce 200 units but actually produced 220 units. What is the variable overhead spending variance?

EB11. LO 8.4 Fitzgerald Company manufactures sewing machines, and they produced 2,500 this past month. The standard variable manufacturing overhead (MOH) rate used by the company is $6.75 per machine hour. Each sewing machine requires 13.5 machine hours. Actual machine hours used last month were 33,500, and the actual variable MOH rate last month was $7.00.
Calculate the variable overhead rate variance and the variable overhead efficiency variance.

EB12. LO 8.5 Acme Inc. has the following information available:

Actual price paid for material	$1.00
Standard price for material	$0.90
Actual quantity purchased and used in production	100
Standard quantity for units produced	90
Actual labor rate per hour	$ 15
Standard labor rate per hour	$ 14
Actual hours	200
Standard hours for units produced	190

A. Compute the material price and quantity, and the labor rate and efficiency variances.
B. Describe the possible causes for this combination of favorable and unfavorable variances.

EB13. LO 8.5 Acme Inc. has the following information available:

Actual price paid for material	$1.00
Standard price for material	$1.10
Actual quantity purchased and used in production	100
Standard quantity for units produced	110
Actual labor rate per hour	$ 15
Standard labor rate per hour	$ 14
Actual hours	200
Standard hours for units produced	190

A. Compute the material price and quantity, and the labor rate and efficiency variances.
B. Describe the possible causes for this combination of favorable and unfavorable variances.

EB14. LO 8.5 Acme Inc. has the following information available:

Actual price paid for material	$1.00
Standard price for material	$0.90
Actual quantity purchased and used in production	100
Standard quantity for units produced	90
Actual labor rate per hour	$ 15
Standard labor rate per hour	$ 16
Actual hours	200
Standard hours for units produced	220

A. Compute the material price and quantity, and the labor rate and efficiency variances.
B. Describe the possible causes for this combination of favorable and unfavorable variances.

Problem Set A

PA1. LO 8.1 The comptroller wants to set the standards according to a study done by a consulting firm for a company. The consulting firm used the following assumptions: The machines never break down. Workers never take a break. The material used is perfect. The material arrives on time. No one takes a day off. Workers are well trained. Workers do not make defective units. What kinds of standards are these? Will the workers be motivated to achieve these standards?

PA2. LO 8.1 Stan is opening a coffee shop next to Big State University. He knows that controlling his costs will be important to the success of the shop. He will not be able to work all the hours the shop is open, so the employees will need some guidelines to perform their jobs correctly. After talking to an accounting professor, he decides he needs a standard cost system for his shop. Describe the process Stan should follow in setting his standards for materials and labor.

PA3. LO 8.1 What makes a variance favorable? Give an example of a favorable variance involving materials. What makes a variance unfavorable? Give an example of an unfavorable variance involving labor.

PA4. LO 8.2 April Industries employs a standard costing system in the manufacturing of its sole product, a park bench. They purchased 60,000 feet of raw material for $300,000, and it takes 5 feet of raw materials to produce one park bench. In August, the company produced 10,000 park benches. The standard cost for material output was $100,000, and there was an unfavorable direct materials quantity variance of $6,000.
A. What is April Industries' standard price for one unit of material?
B. What was the total number of units of material used to produce the August output?
C. What was the direct materials price variance for August?

PA5. LO 8.2 Ed Co. manufactures two types of O rings, large and small. Both rings use the same material but require different amounts. Standard materials for both are shown.

	Large	Small
Rubber	3 feet at $0.25 per foot	1.25 feet at $0.25 per foot
Connector	1 at $0.03	1 at $0.03

At the beginning of the month, Edve Co. bought 25,000 feet of rubber for $6,875. The company made 3,000 large O rings and 4,000 small O rings. The company used 14,500 feet of rubber.

   A. What are the direct materials price variance, the direct materials quantity variance, and the total direct materials cost variance?
   B. If they bought 10,000 connectors costing $310, what would the direct materials price variance be for the connectors?
   C. If there was an unfavorable direct materials price variance of $125, how much did they pay per foot for the rubber?

PA6. LO 8.2 The Whizbang Company makes a special type of toy. Each top takes 6 ounces of a special material that costs $3 per ounce. Whizbang bought 4,000 ounces of the material at a cost of $11,300. They used 3,400 ounces to make 534 toys. Compute the direct materials price variance, the direct materials quantity variance, and the total direct materials cost variance.

PA7. LO 8.3 Ellis Company's labor information for September is as follows:

Direct labor hourly rate paid	$ 32.00
Total standard direct labor hours for units produced	11,000
Direct labor hours worked	10,850
Direct labor rate variance	$8,137.50 (favorable)

   A. Compute the standard direct labor rate per hour.
   B. Compute the direct labor time variance.
   C. Compute the standard direct labor rate if the direct labor rate variance was $2,712.50 (unfavorable).

PA8. LO 8.3 Breakaway Company's labor information for May is as follows:

Actual direct labor hours worked	48,000
Standard direct labor hours allowed	47,400
Total payroll for direct labor	$1,128,000
Direct labor time variance	$ 13,800 (unfavorable)

   A. What is the actual direct labor rate per hour?
   B. What is the standard direct labor rate per hour?
   C. What was the total standard direct labor cost for May?
   D. What was the direct labor rate variance for May?

PA9. LO 8.3 Power Co.'s labor information for June is as follows:

Direct labor hours worked	67,200
Standard labor hours for units manufactured	70,000
Unfavorable direct labor rate variance	$ 23,520
Total payroll for labor	$823,200

A. What was the actual labor rate per hour?
B. What was the standard labor rate per hour?
C. What was the total standard labor cost for units produced in June?
D. What was the direct labor time variance for June?

PA10. LO 8.4 Prepare a flexible budget for overhead based on the following data:

Percent of capacity	90%	100%	110%
Direct labor hours	3,600	4,000	4,400
Units of output	900	1,000	1,100
Variable overhead	$3,600	$ 4,000	$ 4,400
Fixed overhead	$6,000	$ 6,000	$ 6,000
Total overhead	$9,600	$10,000	$10,400

Normal capacity = 100% and overhead is applied based on direct labor hours
Standard overhead rate = $10,000/4,000 = $2.50 per direct labor hour
Direct materials are $67.50 per unit.
Direct labor is $23.50 per hour.

PA11. LO 8.4 Reddy Corporation has collected the following data for the month of June:

Actual total factory overhead incurred	$61,250
Budgeted fixed factory overhead costs	$42,000
Activity level, in direct labor hours	15,000
Actual direct labor hours	18,000
Standard hours for output this period	17,000
Total factory overhead rate	$ 4.35

What is the variable overhead efficiency variance?

PA12. LO 8.4 ABC Inc. spent a total of $48,000 on factory overhead. Of this, $28,000 was fixed overhead. ABC Inc. had budgeted $27,000 for fixed overhead. Actual machine hours were 5,000. Standard hours for units made were 4,800. The standard variable overhead rate was $4.10. What is the variable overhead rate variance?

PA13. LO 8.5 Recompute the variances from the second Acme Inc. exercise using $0.0725 as the standard cost of the material and $14 as the standard labor cost per hour. How has your explanation of the variances changed?

Problem Set B

PB1. LO 8.1 Sameerah is trying to determine the standard hours to make one unit. She has studied the manufacturing process and is trying to determine what portion of the employees' time should be included in the standard time to make the product. She knows that the actual time the worker is assembling, cutting, and painting should be part of the standard hours. She is questioning whether setup, down time, rest periods, and cleanup should be part of the standard hours. Explain why you would or would not include these times.

PB2. LO 8.1 Carl cleans offices. He has the following buildings to clean every day: building A, which is 12,500 square feet; building B, which is 24,500 square feet; building C, which is 10,500 square feet; and building D, which is 6,700 square feet. He is allowed 5 seconds per square foot. Each employee is allowed one 30-minute lunch per shift. How many employees will he need to hire?

PB3. LO 8.1 Freidrich is working with the operations manager to determine what the standard material cost is for a spice chest. He has watched the process from start to finish and taken detailed notes on what material is used. The easiest material to measure is the wood. Each chest uses 5 board feet and produces 1.5 feet of scrap. He is not sure what to do with the scrap that is produced; the company cannot buy the boards in any other dimensions. What amount of materials should be included in the standard for material costs?

PB4. LO 8.2 A company bought 45,000 pounds of plastic pellets to make DVDs at a cost of $9,900. The standard cost per pound for the pellets is 20.5 cents. Some of these pellets were used in three jobs. The first job called for 7,500 pounds but used 7,250 pounds. The second job called for 8,800 pounds but used 9,000 pounds. The third job called for 2,300 pounds but used 2,250 pounds. Compute the direct materials price variance and the direct materials quantity variance for each job and in total. Why would you want to calculate the direct materials quantity variance for each job?

PB5. LO 8.2 Illinois Company is a medium-sized company that makes dresses. During the month of June, 8,575 dresses were made. All material purchases were used to make the dresses. The company had this information: standard per dress of 6 yards of material at $6.20 per yard. The actual quantity was 52,000 yards at a cost of $325,520. Compute the direct materials price variance, the direct materials quantity variance, and the total direct materials cost variance.

PB6. LO 8.2 Corolla Manufacturing has a standard cost for steel of $20 per pound for a product that uses 4 pounds of steel. During September, Corolla purchased and used 4,200 pounds of steel to make 1,040 units. They paid $20.75 per pound for the steel. Compute the direct materials price variance, the direct materials quantity variance, and the total direct materials cost variance for the month of September. What would change if Corolla had made 2,200 units?

PB7. LO 8.3 Marymount Company makes one product. In the month of April, it made 3,500 units. Workers were paid $32 per hour for labor, for a total of $718,848. The standard hours per unit are 6.4, and the standard labor wage rate is $38.40 per hour.
   A. What are the actual hours worked?
   B. What are the standard hours for the units made?
   C. What is the direct labor rate variance for April?
   D. What is the direct labor time variance for April?
   E. What is the total direct labor variance for April?

PB8. LO 8.3 Adam Inc.'s records for May include the following information:

Actual payroll	$40,000
Actual hours worked	3,200
Labor rate variance	$ 8,000 (favorable)
Labor time variance	$ 4,800 (unfavorable)

   A. What are Adam's standard labor hours for the units made?
   B. What is Adam's total standard labor cost for the units made?

PB9. LO 8.3 Ribco's labor cost information for making its only product for March is as follows:

Standard hours per unit	1.25
Budgeted units for the period	12,000
Finished units for the period	10,000
Standard rate per hour	$ 40
Actual labor costs incurred	$414,000
Actual rate paid per hour	$ 36

A. What is the direct labor rate variance?
B. What is the direct labor time variance?
C. What is the total direct labor variance?

PB10. LO 8.5 Use the following standard cost card for 1 gallon of ice cream to answer the questions.

STANDARD COST CARD
Product: Gallon of Ice Cream

Manufacturing Cost Information	Standard Quantity	×	Standard Cost per Unit	=	Cost Summary
Direct Materials					
Cream	5 quarts		$1.15 per quart		$5.75
Sugar	16 ounces		$0.08 per ounce		$1.28
Direct Labor	3 minutes		$36.00 per hour		$1.80
Total Direct Costs					$8.83

Actual direct costs incurred to make 50 gallons of ice cream:

- 275 quarts of cream at $1.05 per quart
- 832 ounces of sugar at $0.075 per ounce
- 165 minutes of labor at $37 per hour

All material used was bought during the current period.

A. Compute the material and labor variances.
B. Comment on the results and possible causes of the variances.

PB11. LO 8.5 Use the following standard cost card for 1 gallon of ice cream to answer the questions.

STANDARD COST CARD						
Product: Gallon of Ice Cream						
Manufacturing Cost Information	Standard Quantity	×	Standard Cost per Unit	=	Cost Summary	
Direct Materials						
Cream	6 quarts		$1.00 per quart		$6.00	
Sugar	15 ounces		$0.07 per ounce		$1.05	
Direct Labor	3 minutes		$38.00 per hour		$1.90	
Total Direct Costs					$8.95	

Actual direct costs incurred to make 50 gallons of ice cream:

- 275 quarts of cream at $1.05 per quart
- 832 ounces of sugar at $0.075 per ounce
- 165 minutes of labor at $37 per hour

All materials used were bought during the current period.

A. Compute the material and labor variances.
B. Comment on the results and possible causes of the variances.

Thought Provokers

TP1. LO 8.1 How do you balance a firm's need to succeed and the need for not asking the workers for perfection?

TP2. LO 8.1 What type of firm would use standard costing? What type of firm would not use standard costing?

TP3. LO 8.2 You started your own construction business and need to determine the cost of materials used to build one house, and how many materials you will need to do so.
- Where would you begin to determine the standard price and quantity needs to build one house?
- What would produce a difference between the standard cost to build a house and the actual cost? What would cause a favorable outcome? What would cause an unfavorable outcome?
- What action might your company take if you had an unfavorable total direct materials cost variance?

TP4. LO 8.3 Is labor a true variable cost?

TP5. LO 8.4 Why would managers use a flexible budget? What information does it provide that a regular budget does not?

TP6. LO 8.4 Fill in the blanks in the following flexible budget:

Percent of Capacity			100%	
Direct labor hours	3,600			
Units of output	1,800		2,000	2,200
Variable overhead			$ 8,000	
Fixed overhead			$10,000	
Total overhead			$18,000	

TP7. LO 8.4 Before automation became more prevalent, overhead was often calculated and allocated as a function of direct labor costs or direct labor hours. Why was this the case, and has this pattern changed?

TP8. LO 8.5 In your opinion, is it important that an organization set standards and measure them monthly? Why or why not?

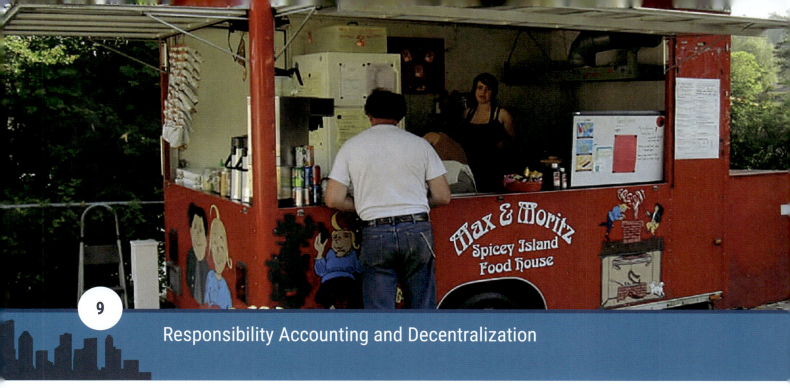

9 Responsibility Accounting and Decentralization

Figure 9.1 Food Trucks. Food trucks have grown significantly in popularity. They allow customers to try a variety of foods that are served quickly, and they often set up in locations that are convenient for customers. The mobility of food trucks adds another dimension that has broad appeal. (credit: modification of "Food Truck" by David Stanley/Wikimedia Commons, CC BY 2.0)

Chapter Outline

LO 9.1 Differentiate between Centralized and Decentralized Management

LO 9.2 Describe How Decision-Making Differs between Centralized and Decentralized Environments

LO 9.3 Describe the Types of Responsibility Centers

LO 9.4 Describe the Effects of Various Decisions on Performance Evaluation of Responsibility Centers

Why It Matters

Lauren is a good cook who can make delicious meals quickly, and she enjoys cooking tremendously. Several friends have suggested she consider opening a food truck. She is intrigued by this idea and decides to further explore the possibility.

After several years of research and planning, Lauren opens her food truck and finds instant success. She is so busy that she decides to recruit several others to join her in her food truck business. While this is an exciting next step, she has some questions about expanding the food truck concept. In particular, she wants to know if she can grow the business while maintaining the level of quality in her food that has led to her success.

Since the concept of multiple food trucks is similar to the franchising concept, Lauren reaches out to a good friend who is the founder of a franchise that now has 10 regional locations. Her friend shares with her the concepts of a decentralized business and responsibility accounting. Under this approach, her friend tells her, she will be able to allow the individual food truck owners to have autonomy over their food truck while achieving the broader goals of financial success and serving quality food.

9.1 Differentiate between Centralized and Decentralized Management

All businesses start with an idea. After putting the idea into action and forming the business, measuring the performance of the business is a crucial next step for the business owners. As the business begins operations, it is fairly easy for the entrepreneur to measure the performance because the owner is heavily involved in the daily activities and decisions of the business. As the business grows through increased sales volume, additional products and locations, and more employees, however, it becomes more complicated to measure the performance of the organization. Owners and managers must design organizational systems that allow for operational efficiency, performance measurement, and the achievement of organizational goals.

In this chapter, you will learn the difference between centralized and decentralized management and how that relates to decision-making. You will learn about responsibility accounting and the type of decision-making authority that may be granted through different responsibility centers. Finally, you will learn how certain types of decisions have differing effects, depending on the type of responsibility center.

Management Control System

It is important for those studying business (and accounting, in particular) to understand the concept of a management control system. A **management control system** is a structure within an organization that allows managers to establish, implement, and monitor progress toward the strategic goals of the organization.

Establishing strategic goals within any organization is important. Strategic goals relate to all facets of the business, including which markets to operate in, what products and services to offer to customers, and how to recruit and retain a talented workforce. It is the responsibility of the organization's management to establish strategic goals and to ensure that all activities of the business help meet goals.

Once an organization establishes its strategic goals, it must implement them. Implementing the strategic goals of the organization requires communication and providing plans that guide the work of those in the organization.

The final factor in creating a management control system is to design mechanisms to monitor the activities of the organization to assess how well they are meeting the strategic goals. This aspect of the management control system includes the accounting system (both financial and managerial). Monitoring the performance of the organization allows management to repeat the activities that lead to good performance and to adjust activities that are not supporting the strategic goals. In addition, monitoring the activities of the organization provides feedback to management as to whether adjustments to the organization's strategy are necessary.

Establishing a management control system is very important to an organization. Organizations must continually evaluate ways to improve and remain competitive in an ever-changing market. This requires the organization to be both forward-looking (via strategic planning) and backward-looking (by evaluating what has occurred), constantly monitoring performance and making necessary adjustments.

CONCEPTS IN PRACTICE

Double Loop Learning

In the fall of 1977, Harvard professor Chris Argyris wrote an article entitled "Double Loop Learning in

Organizations." The article describes how organizations "learn," defined by Argyris as "a process of detecting and correcting error."[1] Argyris suggests there are two types of learning—single loop and double loop.

Single loop learning is characterized as a system that evaluates the organization from the perspective of the organization's present policies. The result of single loop learning is binary: the organization is either meeting or not meeting the company's objectives. There is no further evaluation or additional information fed back into the management control system.

Double loop learning, on the other hand, allows for a more comprehensive evaluation. In addition to evaluating whether or not the organization is meeting the current goals, double loop learning takes into consideration whether or not the current goals of the organization are relevant or should be adjusted in any way. That is, double loop learning requires organizations to evaluate the underlying assumptions that serves as the basis for establishing the current goals.

Argyris's introduction of double loop learning has had a significant impact on the study of management and organizations. The concept of double loop learning also highlights how accounting systems, both financial and managerial, play a vital role in helping the organization attain its strategic goals.

Establishing effective management control systems is important for organizations of all sizes. It is important for businesses to determine how they should structure the organization to ease decision-making and subsequent evaluation. First, levels of management within an organization help the organization form a structure that establishes levels of authority and roles within the organization. **Lower-level management** provides basic supervision and oversight for the operations of the organization. **Mid-level management** supervises and provides direction to lower-level management. Mid-level management often directs the various departments or divisions within the organization. Mid-level managers receive direction and are responsible for achieving the goals established by upper management. **Upper management** consists of the board of directors and chief executives charged with providing strategic guidance for the organization. Upper management has the ultimate authority within the organization and is accountable to the owners of the organization.

Once a company establishes its management levels, it must determine whether the business is set up as centralized or decentralized—opposite ends of a spectrum. Many businesses fall somewhere between the two ends. Understanding the structures of both centralized and decentralized organizations provides a foundation for understanding the variations in management accounting the organizations use.

ETHICAL CONSIDERATIONS

The Ethical Bakery Accountant

Bakery accountant Keith Roberts worked at Archway & The Mother's Cookie Company as the director of finance. According to the *New York Times*, Roberts found himself perplexed by some numbers: "he knew

---

1 Chris Argyris "Double Loop Learning in Organizations." *Harvard Business Review* 55, no. 5 (1977): 115–116.

things had been bad—daily reports he had been monitoring for six months showed that cookie sales at the company had been dismal. But the financial data he was looking at showed much more robust sales." He could not figure out where the sales were coming from, and after researching the accounting records, he determined that the company was booking nonexistent sales.

Why? Roberts reasoned that sham transactions allowed Archway, which was owned by a private-equity firm, Catterton Partners, to maintain access to badly needed money from its lender, Wachovia. Roberts played a major role in alerting Archway's auditing firm of the possibility of accounting fraud. When challenged with the deceptive accounting, Roberts's supervisor invoked a crucial period in the business as a rationale for the unorthodox accounting for sales. Roberts finally quit his job and the accounting misstatements were brought to the attention of the bank and the auditors.

Centralized Organizations

Centralization is a business structure in which one individual makes the important decisions (such as resource allocation) and provides the primary strategic direction for the company. Most small businesses are centralized in that the owner makes all decisions regarding products, services, strategic direction, and most other significant areas. However, a business does not have to be small to be centralized. Apple is an example of a business with a centralized management structure. Within Apple, much of the decision-making responsibility lies with the Chief Executive Officer (CEO) Tim Cook, who assumed the leadership role within Apple following the death of Steve Jobs. Apple has long been viewed as an organization that maintains a high level of centralized control over the company's strategic initiatives such as new product development, markets to operate in, and company acquisitions. Many businesses in rapidly changing technological environments have a centralized form of management structure. The decisions made by the lower level management are limited in a centralized environment.

The advantages of centralized organizations include clarity in decision-making, streamlined implementation of policies and initiatives, and control over the strategic direction of the organization. The primary disadvantages of centralized organizations can include limited opportunities for employees to provide feedback and a higher risk of inflexibility.

Decentralized Organizations

Decentralization is a business structure in which the decision-making is made at various levels of the organization. Typically, decentralized businesses are divided into smaller segments or groups in order to make it easier to measure the performance of the company and the individuals within each of the sub-groups.

Advantages of Decentralized Management

Many businesses operate in markets and industries that are highly competitive. In order to be successful, a company must work hard to develop strategic competitive advantages that distinguish the company from its peers. To accomplish this, the organizational structure must allow the organization to quickly adapt and take advantage of opportunities. Therefore, many organizations adopt a decentralized management structure in

Chapter 9 Responsibility Accounting and Decentralization

order to maintain a competitive advantage.

There are numerous advantages of a decentralized management, such as:

- Quick decision and response times—it is important for decisions to be made and implemented in a timely manner. In order to remain competitive, it is important for organizations to take advantage of opportunities that fit within the organization's strategy.
- Better ability to expand company—it is important for organizations to constantly explore new opportunities to provide goods and services to its customers.
- Skilled and/or specialized management—organizations must invest in developing highly skilled employees who are able to make sound decisions that help the organization achieve its goals.
- Increased morale of employees—the success of an organization depends on its ability to obtain, develop, and retain highly motivated employees. Empowering employees to make decisions is one way to help increase employee morale.
- Link between compensation and responsibility—promotional opportunities are often linked with a corresponding increase in compensation. In a decentralized organization, a compensation increase often corresponds to a commensurate increase in the responsibilities associated with learning new skills, increased decision-making authority, and supervision of other employees.
- Better use of lower and middle management—many tasks must be performed in order to achieve success in an organization. Decentralized organizations often rely on lower and middle management to perform many of these tasks. This allows managers to gain valuable experience and expertise in different areas.

Disadvantages of Decentralized Management

While a decentralized organizational structure can be an advantage for many organizations, there are also disadvantages to this type of structure, including:

- Coordination problems—it is important for an organization to be working toward a common goal. Because decision-making is delegated in a decentralized organization, it is often difficult to ensure that all segments of the company are working in a consistent manner to achieve the strategic goals of the organization.
- Increased administrative costs due to duplication of efforts—because similar decisions need to be made and activities undertaken across all divisions of an organization, decentralized organizations are susceptible to duplicating efforts, which results in inefficiency and increased costs.
- Incongruity in operations—when autonomy is dispersed throughout the organization, as is the case in decentralized organizations, division managers may be tempted to customize/alter the operations of the division in an effort to maximize efficiency and suit the best interest of the division. In this structure, it is important to ensure the shortcuts taken by one division of the organization do not conflict with or disrupt the operations of another division within the organization.
- Each department/division is often self-centered (its own fiefdom)—it is not uncommon for separate divisions within an organization to be measured on the performance of the division rather than of the entire company. In a decentralized organization, it is possible for division managers to prioritize divisional goal over organizational goals. Leaders of decentralized organizations should ensure the organization's goals remain the priority for all divisions to attain.
- Significant, if not almost total, reliance on the divisional or department managers—because divisions within decentralized organizations have a high level of autonomy, the division may become operationally isolated from other divisions within the organization, focusing solely on the priorities of the division. If

divisional or departmental managers do not have a wide breadth of experience or skills, the division may be at a disadvantage due to limited access to other expertise.

> ### CONCEPTS IN PRACTICE
>
> **Johnson & Johnson**
>
> Johnson & Johnson was founded in 1886. The first factory had 14 employees: eight women and six men.[2] Today, Johnson & Johnson, employs over 125,000 associates and operates in over 60 countries. You may recognize some of Johnson & Johnson's products, which include Johnson's Baby Shampoo, Neutrogena, Band-Aid, Tylenol, Listerine, and Neosporin.
>
> William Weldon was Chief Executive Officer (CEO) of Johnson & Johnson from 2002 to 2012. Under Weldon's leadership, Johnson & Johnson operated under a decentralized structure. This interview on successfully operating a decentralized organization (https://openstax.org/l/50decentralized) shows it is clear that the key is the people within the organization. Weldon notes that to be successful, a decentralized organization must empower employees to innovate, develop expertise, and collaborate to achieve organizational goals.

Daily and Strategic Decision-Making

An underlying assumption is that businesses possess a single structure (either centralized or decentralized) at any given point. That is not necessarily the case. For example, businesses often add employees who specialize in the various needs of the organization. Over the life of an organization, it is not uncommon for businesses to demonstrate aspects of both centralization and decentralization.

New businesses, for example, are often centralized. When a business first opens, it is common for the owner(s) to be highly involved in the day-to-day operations. In addition, the small size of a new business allows the owner to have a high level of involvement in both the daily and the strategic decisions of the business. Daily decisions are ongoing, immediate decisions that must be made in order to effectively and efficiently meet the needs of the organization's customers. Strategic decisions, on the other hand, are made fairly infrequently and involve long-term goals of the organization. Being actively involved in the business allows new business owners to gain experience in all aspects of the business so that they can get a sense of the patterns of the daily operations and the decisions that need to be made. For example, the owner can be involved in determining the number of workers needed to meet the day's production goal. Having too many workers would be inefficient and require the company to incur unnecessary expenses. Having too few workers, on the other hand, may result in inferior quality of products, missed shipments, or lost sales.

Additionally, an owner involved in daily operations has the opportunity to evaluate and, if necessary, alter any strategic goals that may impact the daily operations. Strategic goals relate to all facets of the business, including in which markets to operate, what products and services to offer to customers, how to recruit and retain a talented workforce, and many other aspects of the business.

If an owner is involved in daily operations, an example of a potential strategic goal could be tha he or she can

---

2 "Our Story." Johnson & Johnson. https://ourstory.jnj.com/timeline

determine whether to pursue a cost leadership perspective. When pursuing a cost leadership perspective, companies undertake activities to eliminate costs in order to produce a product or provide a service that has a cost advantage compared to competing products or services. While providing a high-quality goods or service is important to a company pursuing a cost leadership perspective, the competitive advantage of the company is eliminating wasteful activities that add unnecessary costs, entering into strategic partnerships with suppliers and other companies, and focusing on activities that allow the organization to offer the good or service at a lower price than its competitors. Being highly involved in both the daily and strategic decisions can be very beneficial as the business is established, but it is demanding on the business owner and, without adjustments, often cannot be sustained.

As the business grows, management of a centralized organization faces a choice. Remaining highly involved in the daily decisions of the business results in a low level of involvement in the strategic decisions of the organization. While this may be effective in the short-term, the risks associated with not establishing and adjusting long-term strategic goals increase. On the other hand, remaining highly involved in the strategic decisions of the business results in a low level of involvement in the daily decisions of the business. This, too, is risky because ineffectively managing daily business decisions may have long-term, negative consequences.

ETHICAL CONSIDERATIONS

Ethically Directed Strategic Management

Managers in some organizations follow legal and regulatory requirements to operate their business at the lowest level of acceptable behavior in their business environment in order to keep costs low; however, some stakeholders may expect more than the minimum level of ethics. Stakeholders of business organizations are now insisting on higher ethical standards from their organizations. Stakeholders are any group or individual who may be affected by the organization's business decisions. Organizations providing high-quality goods and services need to consider all of their stakeholders when developing a strategic decision-making process to direct the organization's strategic decisions.

Another alternative for growing businesses is to move toward a decentralized operating structure. The management of growing businesses with a decentralized structure has a low level of involvement in the daily decisions of the business. Instead, management in these businesses focuses on strategic decisions that impact the long-term success of the organization. The daily decisions are delegated to others, thereby allowing management to focus on developing, implementing, and monitoring the firm's performance with respect to the strategic goals of the business.

THINK IT THROUGH

Centralized Structure at Procter & Gamble

The organizational chart shows the 10 product categories of Procter & Gamble.[3]

---

3 "Company Strategy." Procter & Gamble. http://www.pginvestor.com/Company-Strategy/Index?KeyGenPage=208821

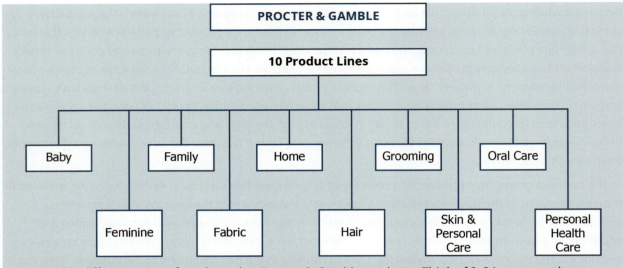

Review the different types of products that Procter & Gamble produces. Think of 2–3 instances where Procter & Gamble would adopt a centralized perspective in its operations. Why would this perspective be beneficial for Procter & Gamble? Don't forget to consider the ingredients used to make these products and how these products are sold to consumers.

9.2 Describe How Decision-Making Differs between Centralized and Decentralized Environments

Businesses are organized with the intention of creating efficiency and effectiveness in achieving organizational goals. To aid in this, larger businesses use **segments**, uniquely identifiable components of the business. A company often creates them because of the specific activities undertaken within a particular portion of the business.[4] Segments are often categorized within the organization based on the services provided (i.e., departments), products produced, or even by geographic region. The purpose of identifying distinguishable segments within an organization is to provide efficiency in decision-making and effectiveness in operational performance.

Organizational Charts

Many organizations use an **organizational chart** to graphically represent the authority for decision-making and oversight. Organizational charts are similar in appearance to flowcharts. An organizational chart for a centralized organization is shown in Figure 9.2. The middle tier represents position held by individuals or departments within the company. The lowest tier represents geographic locations in which the company operates. The lines connecting the boxes indicate the relationship among the segments and branch from the ultimate and decision-making authority. Organizational charts are typically arranged with the highest-ranking person (or group) listed at the top.

---

4 In Building Blocks of Managerial Accounting, you learned that generally accepted accounting principles (GAAP)—also called accounting standards—provide official guidance to the accounting profession. Under the oversight of the Securities and Exchange Commission (SEC), GAAP are created by the Financial Accounting Standards Board (FASB). The official definition of segments as provided by FASB can be reviewed in ASC 280-10-50.

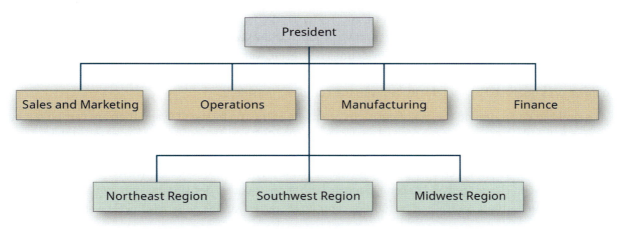

Figure 9.2 An Organizational Chart for a Centralized Organization. Centralized organizations have units that report directly to one person. (attribution: Copyright Rice University, OpenStax, under CC BY-NC-SA 4.0 license)

Notice the organization depicted in Figure 9.2 has segments based on departments as well as geographic regions. In addition, all lines connect directly to the president of the organization. This indicates that the president is responsible for the oversight and decision-making for the production and sales departments as well as the district (Northeast, Southwest, and Midwest) managers; essentially, the president has seven direct reports. In this centralized organizational structure, all decision-making responsibility resides with the president.

Figure 9.3 shows the same organization structured as a decentralized organization.

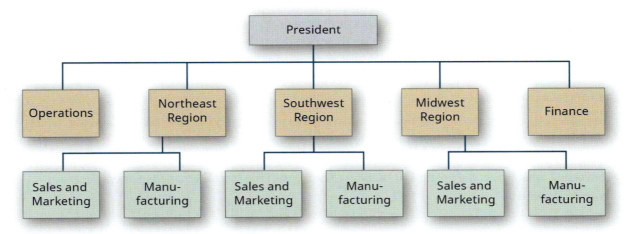

Figure 9.3 An Organizational Chart for a Decentralized Organization. Decentralized organizations have units that report through intermediate management layers. (attribution: Copyright Rice University, OpenStax, under CC BY-NC-SA 4.0 license)

Notice that the organization depicted in Figure 9.3 has the same segments, which represent departments and geographic regions. There are, however, noticeable differences between the centralized and decentralized structure. Instead of seven direct reports, the president now oversees five direct reports, three of which are based on geography—the Western, Southern, and Eastern regional managers. Notice, too, each regional district manager is responsible for their respective production and sales departments. In this decentralized organization, all decision-making responsibility does not reside with the president; regional decisions are delegated to the three regional managers. Understand, however, that responsibility for achieving the organization's goals still ultimately resides with the company president.

In a centralized environment, the major decisions are made at the top by the CEO and then are carried out by everyone below the CEO. In a decentralized environment, the CEO sets the tone for the running of the organization and provides some decision-making guidelines, but the actual decisions for the day-to-day operations are made by the managers at the various levels of the organization. In other words, the essential difference between centralized and decentralized organizations involves decision-making. While no organization can be 100% centralized or 100% decentralized, organizations generally have a well-established structure that outlines the decision-making authority within the organization.

CONTINUING APPLICATION AT WORK

Centralized vs. Decentralized Management

Gearhead Outfitters was founded by Ted Herget in 1997 in a friend's living room in Jonesboro, AR. By 2003, the business moved to its downtown location. In 2006, a second Jonesboro location was opened. Over the next several years, the company's growth allowed for expansion to several different cities, miles and hours away. Eventually Little Rock, AR, Fayetteville, AR, Shreveport, LA, Springfield, MO, and Tulsa, OK became home to Gearhead branches.

With such growth, the company faced many management challenges. Would it be best for management to remain centralized with decision-making coming from a single location, or should the process be decentralized, allowing local management the flexibility and autonomy to run individual locations? If local management is given autonomy to make their own decisions, will those decisions be in line with company, or perhaps, individual goals? How will management be evaluated? Will inventory management be a uniform process, or will people and the process have to adapt to accommodate differences in demand at each location?

These are just some of the hurdles that Gearhead needed to address. What are some other issues which Gearhead might have considered? Think in terms of inventory management, personnel, efficiencies, and leadership development. How could Gearhead have use decentralized management to grow and thrive? Conversely, what would the benefits of keeping all or some of the company's management decisions more centralized be?

How Does Decision-Making Differ in a Centralized versus a Decentralized Environment?

The CEO of a centralized organization will determine the direction of the company and determine how to get the company to its goals. The steps necessary to reach these goals are then passed along to the lower-level managers who carry out these steps and report back to the CEO. The CEO would then evaluate the results and incorporate any necessary operational changes. On the other hand, the CEO of a decentralized organization will determine the goals of the company and either pass along the goals to the divisional managers for them to determine how to reach these goals or work with the managers to determine the strategic plans and how to meet the goals laid out by those plans. The divisional managers will then meet with the managers below them to determine the best way to reach these goals. The lower-level managers are responsible for carrying out the plan and reporting their results to the manager above them. The higher-level managers will combine the results of several managers and evaluate those results before sending them to the divisional manager.

> ## THINK IT THROUGH
>
> ### Determining the Best Structure
>
> Here are some examples of decisions that every business must make:
>
> - Facility and equipment purchases and upgrades
> - Personnel decisions such as hiring and compensation
> - Products and services to offer, prices to charge customers, markets in which to operate
>
> For each decision listed, identify and explain the best structure (centralized, decentralized, or both) for each of the following types of businesses:
>
> - Auto manufacturer with multiple production departments
> - Florist shop (with three part-time employees) owned by a local couple
> - Law firm with four attorneys

9.3 Describe the Types of Responsibility Centers

You've learned how segments are established within a business to increase decision-making and operational effectiveness and efficiency. In other words, segments allow management to establish a structure of operational accountability.

The terminology changes slightly when we think about accountability relating to the financial performance of the segment. In a decentralized organization, the system of financial accountability for the various segments is administered through what is called responsibility accounting.

Responsibility accounting is a basic component of accounting systems for many companies as their performance measurement process becomes more complex. The process involves assigning the responsibility of accounting for particular segments of the company to a specific individual or group. These segments are often structured as **responsibility centers** in which designated supervisors or managers will have both the responsibility for the performance of the center and the authority to make decisions that affect the center.

Often, businesses will use the segment structure to establish the responsibility accounting framework. You might think of segments and responsibility centers as two sides of the same coin: segments establish the structure for operational accountability whereas responsibility centers establish the structure for financial accountability. Both segments and responsibility centers (which will likely be the same) attempt to accomplish the same goal: ensure all sectors of the business achieve the organization's strategic goals.

Before learning about the five types of responsibility centers in detail, it is important to understand the essence of responsibility accounting and responsibility centers.

Fundamentals of Responsibility Accounting and Responsibility Centers

Recall the discussion of management control systems. These systems allow management to establish, implement, monitor, and adjust the activities of the organization toward attainment of strategic goals. Responsibility accounting and the responsibility centers framework focuses on monitoring and adjusting activities, based on financial performance. This framework allows management to gain valuable feedback relating to the financial performance of the organization and to identify any segment activity where adjustments are necessary.

Types of Responsibility Centers

Organizations must exercise care when establishing responsibility centers. In a responsibility accounting framework, decision-making authority is delegated to a specific manager or director of each segment. The manager or director will, in turn, be evaluated based on the financial performance of that segment or responsibility center. It is important, therefore, to establish a responsibility accounting framework that allows for an adequate and equitable evaluation of the financial performance of the responsibility center (and, by default, the manager of the responsibility center) as well as the attainment of the organization's strategic goals.

This is not an easy task. There are several factors that organizations must consider when developing and using a responsibility accounting framework. Before discussing those factors, let's explore the five types of responsibility centers: cost centers, discretionary cost centers, revenue centers, profit centers, and investment centers.

Cost Centers

A **cost center** is an organizational segment in which a manager is held responsible only for costs. In these types of responsibility centers, there is a direct link between the costs incurred and the product or services produced. This link must be recognized by managers and properly structured within the responsibility accounting framework.

An example of a cost center is the custodial department of a department store called Apparel World. On one hand, since the custodial department is structured as a cost center, the goal of the custodial department manager is to keep costs as low as possible, since this is the basis by which the manager will be evaluated by upper-level management. On the other hand, the custodial department manager, who is responsible for cleaning the store entrances, also wants to keep the store as clean as possible for the store's customers. If the store appears unclean and disorganized, customers will not continue to shop at the store. Therefore, the custodial department manager and upper-level management must work together to establish goals of the cost center (the custodial department, in this example) that satisfy the strategic goals of the business—maintaining a clean and organized store while minimizing the costs of managing the custodial department.

Figure 9.4 shows an example of what the cost center report might look like for the Apparel World custodial department.

APPAREL WORLD DEPARTMENT STORE Custodial Department Cost Center For the Month of December 2018				
Account Title	**Actual Expense**	**Budgeted Expense**	**Difference ($)**	**Difference (%)**
Custodian wages	$15,500	$15,000	$500	3.3%
Department manager wages	3,500	3,500	0	0.0%
Cleaning equipment	450	125	325	260.0%
Cleaning supplies	275	120	155	129.2%
Total costs	$19,725	$18,745	$980	5.2%

Figure 9.4 Cost Center Report for the Custodial Department. (attribution: Copyright Rice University, OpenStax, under CC BY-NC-SA 4.0 license)

Let's use this report to explore how the department manager and upper-level management might review and use this information. In total, in December, the custodial department incurred $980 more of actual expenses than budgeted (or expected) expenses. This represents a 5.2% increase in expenses than was expected.

Notice the terminology used to describe the financial information of the custodial department: the department "*incurred* $980 more of actual expenses," rather than the department "*spent* $980 more of actual expenses." Recall from Introduction to Financial Statements (http://cnx.org/content/m67837/latest/) that financial statements are typically prepared using *accrual* accounting rather than *cash* accounting. Under accrual accounting, certain transactions are recorded regardless of when the cash is exchanged. Therefore, to say the custodial department "*spent* $19,725" or "*spent* $980 more for expenses" would technically be incorrect, since the cash may not have been spent.

The managers would then review each line item to determine what caused the $980 increase in expenses over what was expected. Keep in mind, the $980 represents the *total* overage from the budget, so it is possible that some expense accounts could have actually been *below* expectations. Unfortunately, that is not the case in the month of December because every line item, with the exception of department manager wages, exceeded the budgeted amount. It was no surprise to management that the department manager's wages were exactly as expected. Even though the custodial department manager worked more hours in the month of December, the manager is a salaried employee, so the wages are the same regardless of the number of hours worked.

Upon further investigation, it was determined that in December, the town where the Apparel World store is located received an unusually high amount of snow. This had an impact on each of the expense amounts in the custodial department. Because of the need to shovel snow more often, some of the custodial staff had to work overtime to ensure customers could easily and safely enter the store. This led to an increase in custodial wages of $500 compared to the budgeted or expected amount, which was established based on the previous year, when snowfall in the area was closer to average.

The research conducted by management also identified that additional cleaning equipment (mop buckets, mops, and "wet floor" signs) were purchased. The increased snowfall also led to the purchase of more salt than usual for the sidewalks outside the store. Because it was important to promptly clean the snow as well as the salt that was brought into the store on customers' shoes, additional equipment was purchased so that each entrance would have a mop and bucket. The custodial department manager decided this was the best course of action. Normally, the store uses a single mop and bucket to clean all entrances. This would have taken more time and increased the risk of an accident.

The increased application of salt partially explains the 129.2% (or $155) overage in the cleaning supplies expense account. Management has learned that the overage in this account was also caused by an increase in purchases of mop head replacements, floor cleaner, and paper towels.

After reviewing the December information and learning the causes of the increased expenses, the company determined that no corrective action was necessary going forward. The area received an unusually high level of snowfall that year, which was not something the custodial department manager could control. In fact, the upper-level managers praised the custodial department manager for taking action that was in the best interest of the store and its customers. The managers commented that they had received numerous compliments from customers regarding how easy and safe it was to enter the store compared to other local stores. The manager noted that, despite the increased snowfall, store sales were higher than expected and attributed much of the success to the work of the custodial department.

Discretionary Cost Centers

A discretionary cost center is similar to a cost center, with one distinguishing factor. A **discretionary cost center** is an organizational segment in which a manager is held responsible for controllable costs when there is not a well-defined relationship between the center's costs and its services or products. Examples include human resources and accounting departments. Human resources departments often establish policies that affect the entire organization. For instance, while a policy requiring all workers to have annual safety training for fires, injuries, and tornadoes is beneficial to the entire company, it is difficult to evaluate the human resources department manager's performance in relation to impacting the products or services the company provides. As you might expect, reviewing the financial performance of a discretionary cost center is similar to that of the review of a cost center.

Revenue Centers

A **revenue center** is an organizational segment in which a manager is held accountable only for revenues. As the name implies, the goal of a revenue center is to generate revenues for the business. In order to accomplish the goal of increasing revenues, the manager of a revenue center would focus on developing specific skillsets of the revenue center's employees. The reservations group of Southwest Airlines is an example of a segment that may be structured as a revenue center. The employees should be well-trained in providing excellent customer service, handling customer complaints, and converting customer interactions into actual sales. As the financial performance of cost centers and discretionary cost centers is similar, so is the financial performance of a revenue center and a cost center.

Profit Centers

A **profit center** is an organizational segment in which a manager is responsible for both revenues and costs (such as a Starbucks store location). Of the responsibility centers explored so far, a profit center structure is the most complex because a manager must be well-versed in techniques to increase revenues, decrease expenses, and thereby increase profits while also meeting the strategic goals of the organization.

Let's return to the Apparel World department store. Figure 9.5 shows an example of what the profit center report might look like for the Apparel World children's clothing department.

APPAREL WORLD DEPARTMENT STORE				
Children's Clothing Department Profit Center				
For the Month of December 2018				
Revenues	Actual	Budgeted	Difference ($)	Difference (%)
Clothing revenue	$175,000	$145,000	$30,000	20.7%
Clothing accessories revenue	1,400	2,200	(800)	−36.4%
Total revenue	$176,400	$147,200	$29,200	19.8%
Expenses				
Associates wages	$ 22,500	$ 21,750	$ 750	3.4%
Department manager wages	7,200	7,200	0	0.0%
Cost of clothing sold	111,125	87,000	24,125	27.7%
Cost of accessories sold	1,008	1,584	(576)	−36.4%
Equipment/fixture repairs	1,025	290	735	253.4%
Utilities	895	620	275	44.4%
Total expenses	$143,753	$118,444	$25,309	21.4%
Department profit (loss)	$ 32,647	$ 28,756	$ 3,891	13.5%

Figure 9.5 Profit Center Report for the Children's Clothing Department. (attribution: Copyright Rice University, OpenStax, under CC BY-NC-SA 4.0 license)

Just as with the cost center, let's walk through an analysis of the December children's clothing department profit center report. Overall, the department's actual profit exceeded budgeted profit by $3,891, or 13.5%, compared to budgeted (or expected) profit. This increase was driven by a total revenue increase over budget by $29,200 or 19.8%. Recall from Building Blocks of Managerial Accounting that variable costs, unlike fixed costs, change in proportion to the level of activity in a business. Therefore, it should be no surprise that the expenses in the children's clothing department also increased. In fact, the expenses increased $25,309 (or 21.4%) versus the budgeted amount. The revenues of the department increased $29,200, while expenses increased $25,309, yielding an increase in profit of $3,891 over expectations.

The increase in revenue could be further analyzed. Because the store also sells accessories such as belts and socks, the children's clothing department tracks two revenue sources (also called *streams*)—clothing and accessories. Management was pleased to learn that clothing revenue exceeded expectations by $30,000, or 20.7%. Given the higher-than-usual level of snowfall in the area, this is an impressive increase, and the company can attribute a portion of the successful month to the employees of the custodial department, who worked extra hard to ensure customers could easily and safely enter the store.

The overall revenue of the department increased by $29,200. Since the clothing department revenue increased by $30,000, the clothing accessories revenue stream must have experienced a decline in revenue. In fact, the accessories revenue dropped by 36.4%. While this is a large percentage, consider the fact that the actual value of revenue decline was relatively minor—only $800 lower (as indicated by the negative amount) than expected. This indicates the employees may not have encouraged customers to also get belts or socks with their clothing purchase. This is an opportunity for the department manager to remind employees to encourage customers to purchase accessories to complement the clothing purchases. Overall, the increase in revenue attained by the children's clothing department is a highlight for the store.

A review of the department's expenses shows increases in all expenses, except department manager wages and cost of accessories sold. When reviewing the profit center report, pay special attention to how the differences between the actual and budgeted expenses are calculated in this analysis. In the revenue section, a positive number indicates the revenue exceeded the budgeted amount, which means a favorable financial performance. In the expense section, a positive number indicates the expense exceeded the budgeted amount, which means an unfavorable financial performance.

As with the custodial department manager, the manager of the children's clothing department is also a salaried employee, so the wages do not change each month—the wages are a fixed cost for the department. Since the clothing accessories revenue declined, the cost of accessories also declined. The accessories expenses were $576 lower than expected. While this appears to be good news for the department, recall that clothing accessories revenue dropped by $800. Therefore, the department profit margin decreased by a net amount of $224 versus expectations ($800 revenue decline and a corresponding expense decrease of $576).

All other actual expenses were over budget, as indicated by the positive numbers. Remember, these are expenses, and in this analysis, they indicate unfavorable financial performance. It probably comes as no surprise that all of the expense overages are a result of the increased sales. Because of the increased sales, more associates were needed to cover each shift, and they worked more hours to cover the longer store hours, which caused wages to go over budget. The substantial increase in clothing revenue also caused the cost of clothing sold to increase proportionately. Similarly, the increased sales drove an increase in equipment/fixture repairs of $735 (or 253.4%) over budget due to repairs to cash registers and clothing racks. Because the store was open longer hours during the holiday season, the utilities expenses also exceeded budget by $275, or 44.4%.

Overall, the Apparel World department store management was pleased with the December financial performance of the children's clothing department. The department exceeded budgeted sales, which resulted in an increase in department profitability. The review also highlighted an area for improvement in the department—increasing accessory sales—which is easily corrected through additional training.

Notice that the review of the children's clothing department profit center report discussed differences measured in both dollars and percentages. When analyzing financial information, looking only at dollar values can be misleading. Displaying information as percentages—percentage of an entire amount or percentage change—standardizes the information and facilitates an easier and more accurate comparison, especially when dealing with segments (or companies) with vastly different sizes.

Let's look at another scenario using Apparel World. The example so far has explored the financial performance review processes for a cost center and a profit center. Now assume that store management wants to compare two different profit centers—children's clothing and women's clothing. Figure 9.6 shows the December financial information for the children's clothing department, and Figure 9.7 shows the financial information for the women's clothing department.

APAREL WORLD DEPARTMENT STORE Children's Clothing Department Profit Center For the Month of December 2018				
Revenues	Actual	Budgeted	Difference ($)	Difference (%)
Clothing revenue	$175,000	$145,000	$30,000	20.7%
Clothing accessories revenue	1,400	2,200	(800)	−36.4%
Total revenue	$176,400	$147,200	$29,200	19.8%
Expenses				
Associates wages	$ 22,500	$ 21,750	$ 750	3.4%
Department manager wages	7,200	7,200	0	0.0%
Cost of clothing sold	111,125	87,000	24,125	27.7%
Cost of accessories sold	1,008	1,584	(576)	−36.4%
Equipment/fixture repairs	1,025	290	735	253.4%
Utilities	895	620	275	44.4%
Total expenses	$143,753	$118,444	$25,309	21.4%
Department profit (loss)	$ 32,647	$ 28,756	$ 3,891	13.5%

Figure 9.6 Profit Center Report for the Children's Clothing Department, without Percentages. (attribution: Copyright Rice University, OpenStax, under CC BY-NC-SA 4.0 license)

APAREL WORLD DEPARTMENT STORE Women's Clothing Department Profit Center For the Month of December 2018			
Revenues	Actual	Budgeted	Difference ($)
Clothing revenue	$400,000	$308,000	$92,000
Clothing accessories revenue	17,280	14,300	2,980
Total revenue	$417,280	$322,300	$94,980
Expenses			
Associates wages	$ 42,000	$ 38,500	$ 3,500
Department manager wages	12,400	12,400	0
Cost of clothing sold	288,000	201,124	86,876
Cost of accessories sold	12,442	10,296	2,146
Equipment/fixture repairs	275	400	(125)
Utilities	1,050	1,000	50
Total expenses	$356,167	$263,720	$92,447
Department profit (loss)	$ 61,113	$ 58,580	$ 2,533

Figure 9.7 Profit Center Report for the Women's Clothing Department, without Percentages. (attribution: Copyright Rice University, OpenStax, under CC BY-NC-SA 4.0 license)

Comparing the dollar differences in the two departments, notice that the children's clothing department is a smaller department, as measured by total revenue, than the women's clothing department.

Now, let's compare the differences in the two departments by looking at the percentages. The children's clothing department financial information is shown in Figure 9.8, and the women's clothing department financial information is shown in Figure 9.9.

APPAREL WORLD DEPARTMENT STORE
Children's Clothing Department Profit Center
For the Month of December 2018

Revenues	Actual	Budgeted	Difference ($)	Difference (%)
Clothing revenue	$175,000	$145,000	$30,000	20.7%
Clothing accessories revenue	1,400	2,200	(800)	−36.4%
Total revenue	$176,400	$147,200	$29,200	19.8%
Expenses				
Associates wages	$ 22,500	$ 21,750	$ 750	3.4%
Department manager wages	7,200	7,200	0	0.0%
Cost of clothing sold	111,125	87,000	24,125	27.7%
Cost of accessories sold	1,008	1,584	(576)	−36.4%
Equipment/fixture repairs	1,025	290	735	253.4%
Utilities	895	620	275	44.4%
Total expenses	$143,753	$118,444	$25,309	21.4%
Department profit/(loss)	$ 32,647	$ 28,756	$ 3,891	13.5%

Figure 9.8 Profit Center Report for the Children's Clothing Department. (attribution: Copyright Rice University, OpenStax, under CC BY-NC-SA 4.0 license)

APPAREL WORLD DEPARTMENT STORE
Women's Clothing Department Profit Center
For the Month of December 2018

Revenues	Actual	Budgeted	Difference ($)	Difference (%)
Clothing revenue	$400,000	$308,000	$92,000	29.9%
Clothing accessories revenue	$17,280	$14,300	$2,980	20.8%
Total revenue	$417,280	$322,300	$94,980	29.5%
Expenses				
Associates wages	$42,000	$38,500	$3,500	9.1%
Department manager wages	$12,400	$12,400	$0	0.0%
Cost of clothing sold	$288,000	$201,124	$86,876	43.2%
Cost of accessories sold	$12,442	$10,296	$2,146	20.8%
Equipment/fixture repairs	$275	$400	($125)	−31.3%
Utilities	$1,050	$1,000	$50	5.0%
Total expenses	$356,167	$263,720	$92,447	35.1%
Department profit (loss)	$61,113	$58,580	$2,533	4.3%

Figure 9.9 Profit Center Report for the Women's Clothing Department. (attribution: Copyright Rice University, OpenStax, under CC BY-NC-SA 4.0 license)

Does the comparison change when the dollar differences are shown as percentages? Which department was more effective at strengthening the store's financial position? Which department was more efficient with the December revenue? What other factors might the Apparel World management consider?

Adding the percentages to the financial analysis allows managers to more directly make comparisons, to separate departments in this case. Simply reviewing the dollar differences can be misleading because of size differences between the departments being compared. The Women's Department added more value ($61,113) to the store's financial position, while the Children's Department was more efficient, converting 13.5% (or $0.135) of every dollar of revenue to profit.

Investment Centers

It is important for managers to continually invest in the business. Managers must choose investments that improve the value of the business by improving the customer experience, increasing customer loyalty, and, ultimately, increasing the value of the organization. A limitation of the centers explored so far—cost center, discretionary cost center, revenue center, and profit center—is that these structures do not account for the investments made by the various responsibility center managers. The final responsibility center—investment centers—takes into account and evaluates the investments made by the responsibility center managers. The goal of the investment center structure is to ensure that segment managers choose investments that add value and help the organization achieve its strategic goals.

An **investment center** is an organizational segment (such as the northern region of Best Buy or the food trucks used in the Why It Matters opening case) in which a manager is accountable for profits (revenues minus expenses) *and* the invested capital used by the segment.

CONCEPTS IN PRACTICE

Research and Development at Hershey's

As you know by now, financial statements tell users what has occurred in the past—the statements provide feedback value. Responsibility accounting is no exception—it is a system that measures the financial performance of what has already occurred and provides management with a measure of past events.

Have you ever considered how companies measure the outcome of activities that have not yet occurred? As you've learned, many companies invest in research and development activities to determine how to improve existing products and to create entirely new products or processes.

The Hershey Chocolate Company is one company that invests heavily in research and development. Hershey's has created an Advanced Technology & Foresight Lab, which looks for innovative ways to bring chocolate to the market.

Here are some of the innovative things that Hershey's has developed:

- Sourcemap—an interactive, web-based tool to show consumers where the ingredients in their favorite Hershey's snack, such as Hershey's Milk Chocolate with Almonds Bar (https://openstax.org/l/50HersheyMap) comes from. There is also a video and short story for each point on the interactive map (https://openstax.org/l/50HersheyVideo) for more information.
- SmartLabel—a scanable label on each Hershey's product that gives the user up-to-date ingredient, allergen, and other information.
- Chocolate made inside the package—Hershey's developed this process to form a piece of chocolate (https://openstax.org/l/50HersheyChoco) inside the package.
- 3D Chocolate Printing—using a 3D printer, Hershey's has developed an innovative way to create customized chocolate candies.[5]

> Measuring the financial success of innovations such as these is nearly impossible in the short-run. However, in the long-run, investments in product development help companies like Hershey's increase sales, reduce costs, gain market share, and remain competitive in the marketplace.

There are numerous methods used to evaluate the financial performance of investment centers. When discussing profit centers, we used the segment's profit/loss stated in dollars. Another method to evaluate segment financial performance involves using the profit margin percentage.

The profit margin percentage is calculated by taking the net profit (or loss) divided by the net sales. This is a useful calculation to measure the organization's (or segment's) efficiency at converting revenue into profit (net income). While the dollar value of a segment's profit/loss is important, the advantage of using a percentage is that percentages allow for more direct comparisons of different-sized segments.

Let's return to the Apparel World example and look at the profit margin percentage for the children's and women's clothing departments. Figure 9.10 shows the December financial information for the children's clothing department, including the profit margin percentage.

APPAREL WORLD DEPARTMENT STORE
Children's Clothing Department Profit Center
For the Month of December 2018

Revenues	Actual	Budgeted
Clothing revenue	$175,000	$145,000
Clothing accessories revenue	1,400	2,200
Total revenue	$176,400	$147,200
Expenses		
Associates wages	$ 22,500	$ 21,750
Department manager wages	7,200	7,200
Cost of clothing sold	111,125	87,000
Cost of accessories sold	1,008	1,584
Equipment/fixture repairs	1,025	290
Utilities	895	620
Total expenses	$143,753	$118,444
Department profit (loss)	$ 32,647	$ 28,756
Profit margin %	18.5%	19.5%

Figure 9.10 Profit Center Report for the Children's Clothing Department, Including Profit Margin Percentage. (attribution: Copyright Rice University, OpenStax, under CC BY-NC-SA 4.0 license)

The actual profit margin percentage achieved by the children's clothing department was 18.5%, calculated by taking the department profit of $32,647 divided by the total revenue of $176,400 ($32,647 / $176,400). The actual profit margin percentage was slightly lower than the expected percentage of 19.5% ($28,756 / $147,200). To determine why the profit margin percentage slipped slightly compared to expectations, management could compare the actual revenue and expenses with the budgeted revenue and expenses using a vertical analysis, as shown in Financial Statement Analysis. Doing so would highlight the fact that the cost of clothing sold as a

---

5 Sue Gleiter. "Hershey Company Goes Futuristic with 3-D Printed Chocolates." PennLive. https://www.pennlive.com/food/index.ssf/2014/12/hersheys_3-d_chocolate.html

percentage of clothing revenue increased significantly compared to what was expected. Management would want to explore this further, looking at factors influencing both clothing revenue (sales prices and quantity) and the cost of the clothing (which may have increased).

Figure 9.11 shows the December financial information for the women's clothing department, including the profit margin percentage.

APPAREL WORLD DEPARTMENT STORE Women's Clothing Department Profit Center For the Month of December 2018		
Revenues	**Actual**	**Budgeted**
Clothing revenue	$400,000	$308,000
Clothing accessories revenue	17,280	14,300
Total revenue	$417,280	$322,300
Expenses		
Associates wages	$ 42,000	$ 38,500
Department manager wages	12,400	12,400
Cost of clothing sold	288,000	201,124
Cost of accessories sold	12,442	10,296
Equipment/fixture repairs	275	400
Utilities	1,050	1,000
Total expenses	$356,167	$263,720
Department profit (loss)	$ 61,113	$ 58,580
Profit margin %	14.6%	18.2%

Figure 9.11 Profit Center Report for the Women's Clothing Department, Including Profit Margin Percentage. (attribution: Copyright Rice University, OpenStax, under CC BY-NC-SA 4.0 license)

The actual profit margin percentage of the women's clothing department was 14.6%, calculated by taking the department profit of $61,113 divided by the total revenue of $417,280 ($61,113 / $417,280). The actual profit margin percentage was significantly lower than the expected percentage of 18.2% ($58,580 / $322,300). As with the children's clothing department, a vertical analysis indicates the significant decrease from budgeted profit margin percentage was a result of the cost of clothing sold. This would lead management to investigate possible causes that would have influenced the clothing revenue (sales prices and quantity), the cost of the clothing, or both.

Another method used to evaluate investment centers is called return on investment. **Return on investment** (ROI) is the department or segment's profit (or loss) divided by the investment base (Net Income / Base). It is a measure of how effective the segment was at generating profit with a given level of investment. Another way to think about ROI is its use as a measure of leverage. That is, the return on investment calculation measures how much profit the segment can realize per dollar invested.

Several points are in order regarding the definition of return on investment. In practice, the numerator (segment profit or loss) may have different names, depending upon the terms used by the organization. Some organizations may call this value *net income* (or loss) or *operating income* (or loss). These terms relate to the financial performance of the segment, and each organization decides how best to identify and quantify financial performance.

Another significant point in the definition of return on investment relates to the denominator (investment base). There is no uniform definition of "investment base" within the accounting/finance profession. Some organizations define investment base as operating assets, while others define the investment base as average operating assets. Other organizations use the book value of assets, and still others use the historical or even replacement cost of assets. There are valid arguments for all of these definitions for investment base. It is important not to be confused by these variations but instead to know the definition in a particular context and to use it consistently. For our purposes, the denominator in the return on investment formula will be "investment base," and the value will be provided.

Finally, you may recall from Long-Term Assets (http://cnx.org/content/m67894/latest/) that accountants carefully consider where to place certain costs (either on the balance sheet as assets or on the income statement as expenses). While ROI typically deals with long-lived assets such as buildings and equipment that are charged to the balance sheet, the ROI approach also applies to certain "investments" that are expensed. For instance, advertising costs are expensed. If a segment is considering an advertising campaign, management would assess the effectiveness of the advertising campaign in a similar manner as the traditional ROI analysis using large, capitalized investments. That is, management would want to assess the additional revenue (or profit) derived from the advertising campaign (which would be the numerator in the ROI calculation) compared to the investment or cost of the advertising campaign (which would be the denominator in the ROI calculation). To illustrate, let's say management was able to identify that an advertising campaign costing $2,500 brought in an additional $500 of profit. This would be a 20% return on investment ($500 / $2,500).

A return on investment analysis of an investment center begins with the same information as an analysis of a profit center. To explore return on investment, let's return to the December Apparel World profit center information analyzing the children's and women's clothing departments. Assume that a smaller store in another location had the following profit for December:

- Children's clothing department: $3,891
- Women's clothing department: $2,533

Now assume that each department had an investment base of the following amounts:

- Children's clothing department: $15,000
- Women's clothing department: $65,000

To calculate the return on investment (ROI) for each department, divide the segment profit by the segment investment base. The ROI for each department is:

- Children's clothing department: 25.9% ($3,891 / $15,000)
- Women's clothing department: 3.9% ($2,533 / $65,000)

The children's clothing department contributed the most to the financial position of this Apparel World location ($3,891 vs. $2,533). In addition, the children's clothing department was able to better leverage every dollar invested into profit. Stated differently, for every dollar invested, the children's clothing department was able to realize $0.259 of profit while the women's clothing department realized only $0.039 of profit for every dollar invested.

It is also significant that the children's clothing department requires a smaller dollar value of investment. This conserves store resources (financial capital) and helps store management prioritize and efficiently allocate future resources. By investing in the children's clothing department, store management is able to invest a smaller dollar amount while achieving a higher rate of return (profitability) on that investment.

One of the criticisms of the ROI approach is that each segment evaluates potential investments *only* in relation to the individual segment's ROI. This may cause the individual segment manager to select only projects or activities that improve the individual segment's ROI and decline projects that improve the financial position of the overall company. Most often, segment managers are primarily evaluated based on the performance of the segment they manage with only a small portion, if any, of their evaluation based on overall corporate performance. This means that the bonuses of a segment manager are largely dependent on how the segment performs, or in other words, based on the decisions made by that segment manager. A manager may choose to forgo a project or activity because it will lower the segment's ROI even though the project would benefit the entire company. ROI and the many implications of its use are explained further and demonstrated in Balanced Scorecard and Other Performance Measures.

The final investment center evaluation method, residual income (RI), structures the investment selection process to incentivize segment managers to select projects that benefit the entire company, rather than only the specific segment.

> **YOUR TURN**
>
> ### Analyzing Historical Success
>
> Companies want to be sure the investments they make are generating an acceptable return. Additonally, individual investors want to ensure they are receiving the highest financial return for the money they are investing.
>
> This article published in the New York Times on best investments (https://openstax.org/l/50Microsoft) listed Microsoft as having one of the best investments since 1926 (based on a study by Hendrik Bessembinder). Based on stock market returns to investors, Microsoft ranked third, behind ExxonMobil and Apple. According to the article, "since 1986, it has had an annualized return of 25 percent."
>
> Other companies in the ranking included familiar company names such as General Electric (ranked #4), Walmart (ranked #10), McDonald's (#31), and Coca-Cola (#15).
>
> But does historical success ensure future success? General Electric is listed in the article as the 4th highest-ranking company for creating wealth for investors. Conduct internet research to find out the condition of General Electric today. What do you think the future holds for General Electric?
>
> As the world-wide economy changes, General Electric seems to be struggling to evolve, and this issue potentially leaves them with an uncertain future.

Residual income (RI) establishes a minimum level that *all* investments must attain in order to be accepted by management. This minimum acceptable level is defined as a dollar value and is applicable to all departments or segments of the business. Residual income is calculated by taking the segment income less the product of the investment value and cost of capital percentage. The formula is:

$$\text{Residual Income} = \text{Income} - (\text{Investment} \times \text{Cost of Capital Percentage})$$

As with the return on investment calculation, income can be defined as segment operating income (or loss) or segment profit (or loss). Some organizations may use different terms. In RI scenarios, the investment refers to a *specific* project the segment is considering. Investment, in RI calculations, should not be confused with the *total* investment base, which was used in the ROI calculation. Finally, the cost of capital, which is covered in [Short-Term Decision-Making](), refers to the rate at which the company raises (or earns) capital. Essentially, the cost of capital can be considered the same as the interest rate at which the company can borrow funds through a bank loan. By establishing a standard cost of capital rate used by all segments of the company, the company is establishing a minimum investment level that all investment opportunities must achieve. For example, assume a company can borrow funds from a local bank at an interest rate of 10%. The company, then, does not want a segment accepting an investment opportunity that earns anything less than 10%. Therefore, the company will establish a threshold—the cost of capital percentage—that will be used to screen potential investments. At the same time, under the residual income structure, managers of the individual segments (also called responsibility centers) will be incentivized to undertake investments that benefit not only the segment but also the entire company. Recall that the ROI of the children's clothing department was 25.9% ($3,891 profit / $15,000 investment). Under an ROI analysis, the manager of the children's clothing department would not accept an investment that earns less than 25.9% because the rate of return would be negatively impacted, even though the company may benefit. Under a residual income structure, managers would accept all investments with a positive value because the investment would exceeded the investment threshold established by the company.

Let's look at an example. Recall that the children's clothing department of Apparel World had an investment base of $15,000. Assuming the cost of capital (understood as the rate of a bank loan) to Apparel World is 10%. This is the rate that Apparel World will also set as the rate it expects all responsibility centers to earn. Therefore, in the example, the expected amount of residual value—the profit goal, in a sense—for the children's clothing department is $1,500 ($15,000 investment base × 10% cost of capital). Management is pleased with the December performance of the children's clothing department because it earned a profit of $3,891, well in excess of the $1,500 goal.

Now let's examine how the manager of the children's clothing department would evaluate a potential investment opportunity. Assume in December the manager had an opportunity to invest to upgrade the store by adding a supervised children's play area for children to use while parents shopped. The manager believes this enhancement might increase sales because parents could take their time shopping, while knowing their children are safe and having fun. The upgrade would make the customer shopping experience more enjoyable for everyone.

The children's play area requires an investment of $50,000 and the expected increase in income as a result of the children's play area is $5,001. Because the Apparel World store has a cost of capital requirement of 10%, the manager would invest in the children's play area because the residual income on this investment would be positive. To be precise, the residual income is $1. Using the residual income formula, the residual income is $5,001 − ($50,000 × 10%) = $1.

While this is an exaggerated and oversimplified example, it is intended to highlight the fact that, as long as resources (funds) are available to invest, a responsibility manager will (or should) accept projects that have a positive residual value. In this example, the children's clothing department would be in a better financial position by undertaking this project than if they rejected this project. The department earned $3,891 of profit in December but would have earned, based on the estimates, $3,892 if the department added the children's play area.

The benefit of a residual income approach is that all investments in all segments of the organization are evaluated using the same approach. Instead of having each segment select only investments that benefit only the segment, the residual income approach guides managers to select investments that benefit the entire organization.

9.4 Describe the Effects of Various Decisions on Performance Evaluation of Responsibility Centers

Organizations incur various types of costs using decentralization and responsibility accounting, and they need to determine how the costs relate to particular segments of the organization within the responsibility accounting framework. One way to categorize costs is based on the level of autonomy the organization (or responsibility center manager) has over the costs. **Controllable costs** are costs that a company or manager can influence. Examples of controllable costs include the wages paid to employees of the company, the cost of training provided to employees, and the cost of maintaining buildings and equipment. As it relates to controllable costs, managers have a fair amount of discretion. While managers may choose to reduce controllable costs like the examples listed, the long-term implications of reducing certain controllable costs must be considered. For example, suppose a manager chooses to reduce the costs of maintaining buildings and equipment. While the manager would achieve the short-term goal of reducing expenses, it is important to also consider the long-term implications of those decisions. Often, deferring routine maintenance costs leads to a greater expense in the long-term because once the building or equipment ultimately needs repairs, the repairs will likely be more extensive, expensive, and time-consuming compared to investments in routine maintenance.

> ### THINK IT THROUGH
>
> #### The Frequency of Maintenance
>
> If you own your own vehicle, you may have been advised (maybe all too often) to have your vehicle maintained through routine oil changes, inspections, and other safety-related checks. With advancements in technology in both car manufacturing and motor oil technology, the recommended mileage intervals between oil changes has increased significantly. If you ask some of your family members how often to change the oil in your vehicle, you might get a wide range of answers—including both time-based and mileage-based recommendations. It is not uncommon to hear that oil should be changed every three months or 3,000 miles. An article from the Edmunds.com website devoted to automobiles (https://openstax.org/l/50YourOil) suggests automobile manufacturers are extending the recommended intervals between oil changes to up to 15,000 miles.
>
> Do you know what the recommendation is for changing the oil in the vehicle you drive? Why do you think the recommendations have increased from the traditonal 3,000 miles to longer intervals? How might a business apply these concepts to the concept of maintaining and upgrading equipment? If you were the accountant for a business, what factors would you recommend management consider when making the decisions on how frequently to maintain equipment and how big of a priority should equipment maintenace be?

The goal of responsibility center accounting is to evaluate managers only on the decisions over which they have control. While many of the costs that managers will encounter are controllable, other costs are uncontrollable and originate from within the organization. **Uncontrollable costs** are those costs that the organization or manager has little or no ability to influence (in the short-term, at least) and therefore should not be incorporated into the analysis of either the manager or the segment's performance. Examples of uncontrollable costs include the cost of electricity the company uses, the cost per gallon of fuel for a company's delivery trucks, and the amount of real estate taxes charged by the municipalities in which the company operates. While there are some long-term ways that companies can influence these costs, the examples listed are generally considered uncontrollable.

One category of uncontrollable costs is **allocated costs**. These are costs that are often allocated (or charged) to the segments within the organization based on some allocation formula or process, such as the costs of receiving support from corporate headquarters. These costs cannot be controlled by the responsibility center manager and thus should not be considered when that manager is being evaluated. Costs relevant to decision-making and financial performance evaluation will be further explored in Short-Term Decision-Making.

Effects of Decisions on Performance Evaluation of Responsibility Centers

Suppose, as the manager of the maintenance department of a major airline, you become aware of a training session that is available to your mechanics. The disadvantages are that the training will require the mechanics to miss an entire week of work and the associated costs (travel, lodging, training session) are high. The advantage is that, as a result of the training, the time during which the planes are grounded for repairs will significantly decrease. What factors would influence your decision regarding whether or not to send mechanics to school? Considering the fact that each mechanic would miss an entire week of work, what factors would you consider in determining how many mechanics to send? Do these factors align with or conflict with what is best for the company or you as the department manager? Is there a way to quantify the investment in the training compared to the benefit of quicker repairs for the airplanes?

Scenarios such as this are common for managers of the various responsibility centers—cost, discretionary cost, revenue, profit, and investment centers. Managers must be well-versed at using both financial and nonfinancial information to make decisions such as these in order to do what is best for the organization.

ETHICAL CONSIDERATIONS

Pro-Stakeholder Culture Opens Business Opportunities

The use of pro-stakeholder decision-making by managers in their responsibility centers allows managers to determine alternatives that are both profitable and follow stakeholders' ethics-related demands. In an essay in *Business Horizons*, Michael Hitt and Jamie Collins explain that companies with a pro-stakeholder culture should better understand the multiple ethical demands of those stakeholders. They also argue that this understanding should "provide these firms with an advantage in recognizing economic opportunities associated with such concerns."[6] The identification of these opportunities can make a manager's decisions more profitable in the long run.

Hitt and Collins go on to argue that "as products and services may be developed in response to consumers' desires, stakeholders' ethical expectations can, in fact, represent latent signals on emerging economic opportunities."[7] Providing managers the ability to identify alternatives based upon stakeholders' desires and demands gives them a broader decision-making platform that allows for decisions that are in the best interest of the organization.

Often one of the most challenging decisions a manager must make relates to **transfer pricing**, which is the pricing process put into place when one segment of a business "sells" goods to another segment of the same business. In order to understand the significance of transfer pricing, recall that the primary goal of a responsibility center manager is to manage costs and make decisions that contribute to the success of the company. In addition, often the financial performance of the segment impacts the manager's compensation, through bonuses and raises, which are likely tied to the financial performance of the segment. Therefore, the decisions made by the manager will affect both the manager and the company.

Application of Transfer Pricing

Transfer pricing can affect **goal congruence**—alignment between the goals of the segment or responsibility center, or even an individual manager, with the strategic goals of the organization. Recall what you've learned regarding segments of the business. Often, segments will be arranged by the type of product produced or service offered. Segments often sell products to external customers. For example, assume a soft drink company has a segment—called the blending department—dedicated to producing various types of soft drinks. The company may have an external customer to which it sells unique soft drink flavors that the customer will bottle under a different brand name (perhaps a store brand like Kroger or Meijer). The segment may also produce soft drinks for another segment within its own company—the bottling department, for example—for further processing and ultimate sale to external customers. When the internal transfer occurs between the blending segment and the bottling segment, the transaction will be structured as a sale for the blending segment and as a purchase for the bottling department. To facilitate the transaction, the company will establish a transfer price, even though the transaction is internal because each segment is responsible for its own profits and costs.

Figure 9.12 shows a graphical representation of the transfer pricing structure for the soft drink company used in the example.

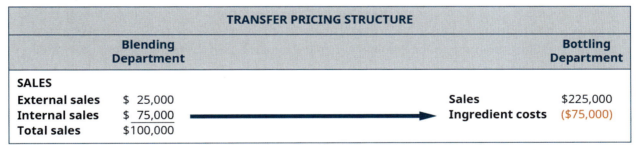

Figure 9.12 Transfer Pricing. The sale for the Blending Department is the purchase for the Bottling Department. (attribution: Copyright Rice University, OpenStax, under CC BY-NC-SA 4.0 license)

---

6   Michael Hitt and Jamie Collins "Business Ethics, Strategic Decision Making, and Firm Performance." *Business Horizons* 50, no. 5 (February 2007): 353–357.

7   Michael Hitt and Jamie Collins "Business Ethics, Strategic Decision Making, and Firm Performance." *Business Horizons* 50, no. 5 (February 2007): 353–357.

Notice that the blending department has two categories of customers—external and internal. External customers purchase the soft drink mixtures and bottle the drinks under a different label, such as a store brand. Internally, the blending department "sells" the soft drink mixtures to the bottling department. Notice the "sale" by the blending department (a positive amount) and the "purchase" by the bottling department (a negative amount) net out to zero. This transaction does not impact the overall financial performance of the organization and allows the responsibility center managers to analyze the financial performance of the segment just as if these were transactions involving outside entities.

What issues might this scenario cause as it relates to goal congruence—that is, meeting the goals of the corporation as a whole as well as meeting the goals of the individual managers?

In situations where the selling division, in this case the blending division, has excess capacity—meaning they can produce more than they currently sell—and ignoring goal congruence issues, the selling division would sell its products internally for variable cost. If there is no excess capacity, though, the opportunity cost of the contribution margin given up by taking internal sales instead of external sales would need to be considered. Let's look at each of these general situations individually.

In the case of excess capacity, the selling division has the ability to produce the goods to sell internally with only variable costs increasing. Thus, it seems logical to make transfer price the same as the variable costs—but is it? Reflecting back on the concept of responsibility centers, the idea is to allow management to have decision-making authority and to evaluate and reward management based on how well they make decisions that lead to increased profitability for their segment. These managers are often rewarded with bonuses or other forms of compensation based on how well they reach certain profitability measures. Does selling goods at variable cost increase the profitability for the selling division? The answer, of course, is no. Thus, why would a manager, who is rewarded based on profitability, sell goods at variable cost? Obviously, the manager would prefer not to sell at variable cost and would rather sell the goods at some amount above variable cost and thus contribute to the segment's profitability. What should the transfer price be? There are various options for choosing a transfer price.

CONCEPTS IN PRACTICE

Transfer Pricing with Overseas Segments

An inherent assumption in transfer pricing is that the divisions of a company are located in the same country. While implementing a transfer pricing framework can be complex for a business located entirely in the United States, transfer pricing becomes even more complex when any of the divisions are located outside of the United States.

Companies with overseas transactions involving transfer pricing must pay particular attention to ensure compliance with the tax, foreign currency exchange rate fluctuations, and other regulations in the countries in which they operate.

This can be expensive and difficult for companies to manage. While many firms use their own employees to manage the process, the Big Four accounting firms, for example, offer expertise in transfer pricing setup and regulatory compliance. This short video from Deloitte on transfer pricing (https://openstax.org/l/50TranferPrice) provides more information about this valuable service that accountants provide.

Available Transfer Pricing Approaches

There are three primary transfer pricing approaches: market-based prices, cost-based prices, or negotiated prices.

Market Price Approach

With the **market price approach**, the transfer price paid by the purchaser is the price the seller would use for an outside customer. Market-based prices are consistent with the responsibility accounting concepts of profit and investment centers, as managers of these units are evaluated based on purchasing and selling goods and services at market prices. Market-based transfer pricing is very common in a situation in which the seller is operating at full capacity.

The benefit of using a market price approach is that the company will need to stay familiar with market prices. This will likely occur naturally because the company will also have outside sales. A potential disadvantage of this approach is that conflicts might arise when there are discrepancies between the current market price and the market price the company sets for transfer prices. Firms should decide at what point and how frequently to update the transfer prices used in a market approach.

For example, assume a company adopts a market approach for transfer prices. As time goes by, the market price will likely change—it will either increase or decrease. When this occurs, the firm must decide if and when to update transfer prices. If current market prices are higher than the market price the company uses, the selling division will be happy because the price earned for intersegment (transfer) sales will increase while inputs (costs) to provide the goods or services remain the same. An increase in the transfer price will, in turn, increase the profit margins of the selling division. The opposite is true for the purchasing division. If the market transfer price increases to match the current market price, the costs (cost of goods sold, in particular) will increase. Without a corresponding increase in the prices charged to its customers or an offset through cost reductions, the profit margins of the purchasing division will decrease. This situation could cause conflict between divisions within same company, an unenviable situation for management as one manager is pleased with the transfer price situation and the other is not. Both managers desire to improve the profits of their respective divisions, but in this situation, the purchasing division may feel they are giving up profits that are then being realized by the selling division due the increase in the market price of the goods and the use of a market-based transfer price.

Cost Approach

When the transfer price uses a **cost approach**, the price may be based on either total variable cost, full cost, or a cost-plus scenario. In the variable cost scenario, as mentioned previously, the transfer of the goods would take place at the total of all variable costs incurred to produce the product. In a full-cost scenario, the goods would be transferred at the variable cost plus the fixed cost per unit associated with making that product. With a cost-plus transfer price, the goods would be transferred at either the variable cost or the full-cost plus a predetermined markup percentage. For example, assume the variable cost to produce a product is $10 and the full cost is $12. If the company uses a cost-plus methodology to calculate the transfer price with a 30% mark-up, the transfer price would be $13 ($10 × 130%) based on just the variable cost or $15.60 ($12 × 130%) based on the full cost. When using the full cost as a basis for applying markup, it is important to understand that the cost structure may include costs that are irrelevant to establishing a transfer price (for example, costs unrelated to producing the actual product to be transferred, such as the fixed cost of the plant supervisor's salary, which will exist whether the product is transferred internally or externally), which may unnecessarily influence decisions.

The benefit of using a cost approach is that the company will invest effort into determining the actual costs involved in making a product or providing another service. The selling division should be able to justify to the purchasing division the cost that will be charged, which likely includes a profit margin, based on what the division would earn on a sale to an outside customer. At the same time, a deeper understanding of what drives the costs within a division provides an opportunity to identify activities that add unnecessary costs. Companies can, in turn, work to increase efficiency and eliminate unnecessary activity and bring down the cost. In essence, the selling division has to justify the costs it is charging the purchasing division.

Negotiated Price Approach

Somewhere in between a transfer price based on cost and one based on market is a **negotiated price approach** in which the company allows the buying segment and the selling segment to negotiate the transfer price. This is common in situations in which there is no external market. When an external price exists and is used as a starting point for establishing the transfer price, the organization must be aware of differences in specific costs between the source of the external price and its own organization. For example, a price from an external source may include a higher profit margin than the profit margin targeted by a company pursuing a cost leadership strategy. In this case, the external price should be reduced to account for such differences.

However, one disadvantage of using a negotiated price system is the possibility of creating a situation in which competition exists between a department and an outside vendor (as occurs when it is cheaper for a department to purchase from an outside vendor rather than another department in the organization) or, worse yet, between departments of the same organization. It is paramount that, when selecting a transfer pricing methodology, the goals of the particular departments involved align with the overall strategic goals of the organization. A transfer pricing structure is not intended to facilitate competition between departments within the same company. Rather, a transfer pricing system should be viewed as a tool to help the company remain competitive in the marketplace and improve a company's overall profit margin.

Other Transfer Pricing Issues

The three approaches to transfer pricing assume that the selling department has excess capacity to produce additional products to sell internally. What happens if the selling department does not have excess capacity—in other words, if the selling department can sell all that it produces to external customers? If an internal department wants to purchase goods from the selling department, what would be an appropriate selling price? In this case, the transfer price must take into consideration the opportunity cost of the contribution margin that would be lost from having to forego external sales in order to meet internal sales.

Suppose in the previous example that the blending department is at full capacity but the bottling department wants to purchase some of its soft drink blends internally. Assume the variable cost to produce one unit of soft drink is $10, the fixed cost per unit is $2, and the market price for selling one unit is $18. What would be an appropriate transfer price in this situation? Since the blending department does not have the capacity to meet external sales plus internal sales, in order to accept the internal sales order, the blending department would have to lose sales to external customers. The contribution margin per unit is $8 ($18 – $10). Thus, $8 per unit would be given up for each external unit that is sold internally.

Looking only at costs, the blending department would be indifferent between an external sale of $18 and an internal sale of $18 ($10 variable cost + $8 contribution margin). Obviously, there are other issues that need to be considered in these situations, such as the effect on external customers if demand cannot be met. Overall, if there is no excess capacity, the transfer price should take into consideration the opportunity cost lost from taking internal sales over external sales.

In addition to the possibility of losing opportunity costs, there are additional transfer pricing issues. Recall that decentralized organizations delegate decision-making authority throughout the organization. A well-designed transfer pricing policy can contribute not only to the segment manager's profits but to overall corporate profits in situations where the transfer price is lower than the external price. However, when a transfer pricing system is used to facilitate transactions between departments, an ill-designed policy is likely to lead to disputes between departments. It is possible the departments view each other as competition rather than strategic partners. When this occurs, it is important for upper-level management to establish a process that allows managers to resolve disagreements in a way that aligns with organizational, rather than departmental, goals.

Transfer pricing systems become even more complicated when departments are located in different countries. The transfer price in an international setting must also account for differences in currencies and fluctuating exchange rate as well as differences in regulations such as tariffs and duties, taxes, and other regulations.

Transfer Pricing Example

Regal Paper has two divisions. The Paper Division produces copy paper, wrapping paper, and paper used on the outside of cardboard displays placed in grocery, office, and department stores. The Box Division produces cardboard boxes sold at Christmas, cardboard boxes purchased by manufacturers for packaging their goods, and cardboard displays for stores, particularly seasonal displays. Both divisions are profit centers, and each manager is evaluated and rewarded based on his division's profitability. The Box Division has approached the Paper Division to buy paper needed to cover cardboard displays that have been ordered by several major snack food manufacturers for the upcoming Superbowl game. The Box Division has been buying the display coverings from an external seller for $12.50 per unit. Currently, the Paper Division has excess capacity and can fill the order for the 500,000 display coverings that the Box Division is requesting.

The cost to the Paper Division to produce one display covering is as follows:

Variable cost per unit	$ 8.00
Fixed cost per unit	1.00
Selling price to external customers	12.00
Price at which Box Division can buy externally	12.50

What would be the transfer price per unit under each of the following scenarios?

1. Market-based transfer price. This transfer price is the same as the selling price to external customers, which is $12.
2. Cost-based transfer price. This transfer price is the same as the variable costs per unit, which is $8.
3. Full-cost–based transfer price. This transfer price is the same as the variable costs plus the fixed cost per unit, which is $9.
4. Cost plus assuming 20% mark-up. This marks up the cost-based transfer price by 20%, which is $8 × 120%, or $9.60.
5. Full-cost plus assuming 20% mark-up. This marks up the full-cost–based transfer price by 20%, which is $9 × 120%, or $10.80.
6. Range of negotiated transfer price. The negotiated transfer price should be between the lowest and highest possible prices: $8–12

7. **What if Paper had no excess capacity?** If the Paper Division had no excess capacity, the transfer price would be the cost plus the contribution margin, which is $8 + $4, or $12.
8. **Which transfer price is best?** If there is excess capacity, then typically a negotiated transfer price is best, as it allows the managers who are evaluated on that decision to have input into the decision and does not take away their autonomy. Table 9.1 shows the per-unit effect on income of each of the transfer pricing options on each division. Remember, the effects provided here cannot necessarily be generalized, as there are two critical factors: whether or not the selling department is at capacity and the price at which the purchasing department could buy the goods externally, which in this case is $0.50 more per unit than the market price of the paper being sold by the Paper Division.

Per-Unit Effect on Division Income of Various Transfer Pricing Methodologies

Transfer Pricing Method	Paper Division	Box Division
Market	$4 per unit increase in income ($12 SP − $8 VC)	$0.50 per unit increase in income ($12.50 − $12 SP)
Cost	$0 per unit increase in income ($8 SP − $8 VC)	$4.50 per unit increase in income ($12.50 − $8)
Full-cost	$1 per unit increase in income ($9 SP − $8 VC)	$3.50 per unit increase in income ($12.50 − $9)
Cost-Plus (20%)	$1.60 per unit increase in income ($9.60 SP − $8 VC)	$2.90 per unit increase in income ($12.50 − $9.60)
Full-cost Plus (20%)	$2.80 per unit increase in income ($10.80 SP − $8VC)	$1.70 per unit increase in income ($12.50 − $10.80)
Negotiated ($0 − $12)	Increase to income between $0 and $4 per unit	Increase to income between $0.50 and $4.50
No Excess Capacity	$4 per unit increase in income ($12 SP − $8 VC)	$0.50 per unit increase in income ($12.50 − $12 SP)
SP = selling price; VC = variable cost		

Table 9.1

As you can see, the transfer price can significantly affect the profitability of the division. It is easy to see which transfer prices most benefit the seller and which most benefit the buyer. Thus, as previously mentioned, a negotiated transfer price is often the best resolution to determining a transfer price.

THINK IT THROUGH

Comparing Transfer Pricing and Outsourcing

Assume you are the President of a manufacturing firm that has a division that transfers products to other divisions within the company. The other divisions have recently complained that the transfer price charged to the departments has increased significantly over the past several quarters. They are frustrated because performance evaluations and bonuses are linked to the profitability of their respective departments.

During a recent management meeting, a cost accountant suggests the company can solve this issue by transferring production to another supplier that has a lower cost of production due to lower labor costs. In addition to solving the conflict between departments, the company's overall profitability will increase because of the substantial cost savings.

Evaluate this scenario and explain how you would respond as the company's President. Consider the perspectives of various stakeholders in this situation.

🔑 Key Terms

allocated costs costs that are generated by non-revenue generating portions of the business, such as corporate headquarters, that are assigned based on some formula to the revenue generating portions of the business

centralization business structure in which one individual makes the important decisions and provides the primary strategic direction for the company

controllable costs those that a company or manager can influence

cost approach transfer pricing structure in which the transfer price may be based on total variable cost, full cost, or a cost-plus scenario, calculated by adding a markup to either variable cost or full cost

cost center organizational segment in which a manager is held responsible only for costs

decentralization business structure in which the decision-making is made at various levels of the organization

discretionary cost center organizational segment in which a manager is held responsible only for controllable costs when there is not a well-defined relationship between the center's costs and its services or products

goal congruence integration of multiple goals, either within an organization or across multiple components or entities; congruence is achieved by aligning goals to achieve an anticipated mission

investment center organizational segment in which a manager is accountable for profits (revenues minus expenses) and the invested capital used by the segment

lower-level management level of management that provides basic supervision and oversight for the operations of the organization

management control system structure within an organization that allows managers to establish, implement, and monitor progress toward the strategic goals of the organization

market price approach transfer pricing structure in which the transfer price is based on the price the seller would use for an outside customer

mid-level management level of management that receives direction from upper management and supervises and provides direction to lower-level management

negotiated price approach transfer pricing structure in which the transfer price is based on negotiations between the buying segment and the selling segment

organizational chart graphical representations illustrating the authority for decision-making and oversight throughout an organization

profit center organizational segment in which a manager is responsible for and evaluted on both revenues and costs

residual income (RI) amount of income a given division (or project) is expected to earn in excess of a firm's minimum return goal

responsibility accounting method of encouraging goal congruence by setting and communicating the financial performance measures by which managers will be evaluated

responsibility centers segments in which supervisors or managers have responsibility for the performance of the center and the authority to make decisions that affect the center

return on investment (ROI) measure of the percentage of income generated by profits that were invested in capital assets

revenue center part of an organization in which management is evaluated based on the ability to generate revenues; the manager's primary control is only revenues

segment portion of the business that management believes has sufficient similarities in product lines, geographic locations, or customers to warrant reporting that portion of the company as a distinct part of the entire company

transfer pricing pricing structure used when one segment of a business "sells" goods to another segment of the same business

uncontrollable costs those that an organization or manager has little or no ability to influence

upper management level of management that consists of the board of directors and chief executives charged with providing strategic guidance for the organization

Summary

9.1 Differentiate between Centralized and Decentralized Management

- Management control systems allow managers to develop a reporting structure to help the organization meet its strategic goals.
- In centralized organizations, primary decisions are made by the person or persons at the top of the organization.
- Decentralized organizations delegate decision-making authority throughout the organization.
- Daily decision-making involves frequent and immediate decisions.
- Strategic decision-making involves infrequent and long-term decisions.

9.2 Describe How Decision-Making Differs between Centralized and Decentralized Environments

- Segments are uniquely identifiable components of the business that facilitate the effective and efficient operation of the business.
- Organizational charts are used to graphically represent the authority structure of an organization.
- The CEO of a centralized organization will establish the strategy and make decisions that will be implemented throughout the organization.
- The CEO of a decentralized organization will establish strategic goals and empower managers to achieve the goals.

9.3 Describe the Types of Responsibility Centers

- A responsibility accounting structure helps management evaluate the financial performance of the segments in the organization.
- Responsibility centers are segments within a responsibility accounting structure.
- Five types of responsibility centers include cost centers, discretionary cost centers, revenue centers, profit centers, and investment centers.
- Cost centers are responsibility centers that focus only on expenses.
- Discretionary cost centers are responsibility centers that focus only on controllable expenses.
- Revenue centers are responsibility centers that focus on revenues.
- Profit centers are responsibility centers that focus on revenues and expenses.
- Investment centers are responsibility centers that consider the investments made by the responsibility center.
- Return on investment is a particular type of investment center structure that calculates a responsibility center's profit percentage relative to the center's investment.
- Residual income is a particular type of investment center structure that evaluates investments using a common cost of capital rate amongst all responsibility centers.

9.4 Describe the Effects of Various Decisions on Performance Evaluation of Responsibility Centers

- Uncontrollable costs are costs that management or an organization has little or no ability to influence.

- Controllable costs are costs that managers or an organization can influence.
- Managers in a responsibility accounting structure should only be evaluated based on controllable costs.
- Businesses with segments that provide goods to other segments within the business often use a transfer pricing structure to record the transaction.
- The general transfer pricing model considers the opportunity costs involved in selling to internal rather than external customers. This method is difficult to implement and businesses often choose other methods.
- The market price model uses market prices that would be used for external customers as the basis for internal transfers.
- The cost approach uses the company's cost to make the product as the basis for establishing the transfer price.
- The negotiated model allows the selling and buying segments within the business to determine the transfer price.
- Transfer price arrangements are more difficult in international businesses because of complexities related to taxes, duties, and currency fluctuations.

Multiple Choice

1. **LO** 9.1 Which of the following is *not* a common goal of an organization?
   A. operational efficiency
   B. being acquired by another business
   C. achieving strategic goals
   D. measuring financial performance

2. **LO** 9.1 Which of the following does *not* describe a management control system?
   A. establishes a company's strategic goals
   B. implements a company's strategic goals
   C. monitors a company's strategic goals
   D. a system that only measures profitability

3. **LO** 9.1 In centralized organizations, primary decisions are made by _____.
   A. an individual at the top of the organization
   B. various managers throughout the organization
   C. outside consultants
   D. low-level management

4. **LO** 9.1 A key advantage of a decentralized organization is _____.
   A. increased administrative costs
   B. quicker decisions and response time
   C. the ease of aligning segment and company goals
   D. duplication of efforts

5. **LO** 9.1 Strategic decisions occur _____.
   A. frequently and involve immediate decisions
   B. frequently and involve long-term decisions
   C. infrequently and involve long-term decisions
   D. infrequently and involve immediate decisions

6. LO 9.2 Segments are uniquely identifiable components of the business and can be categorized by all of the following *except* _____.
   A. products produced
   B. services provided
   C. geographical location
   D. number of employees

7. LO 9.2 Organizational charts _____.
   A. list the salaries of all employees
   B. outline the strategic goals of the organization
   C. show the structure of an organization
   D. help management measure financial performance

8. LO 9.2 In a centralized organization, where are goals established?
   A. at the lower level of the organization and promoted upward
   B. outside the organization based on best practices in the industry
   C. by each segment of the organization
   D. at the highest level of the organization and promoted downward

9. LO 9.2 Managers in decentralized organizations make decisions relating to all of the following *except* _____.
   A. the company's stock price
   B. equipment purchases
   C. personnel
   D. prices to charge customers

10. LO 9.3 Which of the following is *not* a type of responsibility center?
   A. concentrated cost center
   B. investment center
   C. profit center
   D. cost center

11. LO 9.3 A system that establishes financial accountability for operating segments within an organization is called _____.
   A. a financial statement
   B. an internal control system
   C. responsibility accounting
   D. centralization

12. LO 9.3 A responsibility center in which managers are held accountable for both revenues and expenses is called a _____.
   A. discretionary cost center
   B. revenue center
   C. cost center
   D. profit center

13. LO 9.3 A responsibility center structure that considers investments made by the operating segments by using a common cost of capital percentage is called _____.
  A. return on investment
  B. residual income
  C. a profit center
  D. a discretionary cost center

14. LO 9.3 An important goal of a responsibility accounting framework is to help ensure which of the following?
  A. decision-making is made by the top executives.
  B. investments made by each segment are minimized.
  C. identification of operating segments that should be closed.
  D. segment and company financial goals are congruent.

15. LO 9.4 Costs that a company or manager can influence are called _____.
  A. discretionary costs
  B. fixed costs
  C. variable costs
  D. controllable costs

16. LO 9.4 An example of an uncontrollable cost would include all of the following *except* _____.
  A. real estate taxes charged by the county in which the business operates
  B. per-gallon cost of fuel for the company's delivery trucks
  C. hourly rate of pay for the company's purchasing manager
  D. federal income tax rate paid by the company

17. LO 9.4 Internal costs that are charged to the segments of a business are called _____.
  A. controllable costs
  B. variable costs
  C. fixed costs
  D. allocated costs

18. LO 9.4 A transfer pricing arrangement that uses the price that would be charged to an external customer is a _____.
  A. market-based approach
  B. negotiated approach
  C. cost approach
  D. decentralized approach

19. LO 9.4 A transfer pricing structure that considers the opportunity costs of selling to internal rather than external customers uses _____.
  A. the cost approach
  B. the general transfer pricing approach
  C. the market-based approach
  D. the opportunity cost approach

Questions

1. **LO** 9.1 What is a management control system? What are its components and how does the system help the business?

2. **LO** 9.1 Identify and describe the levels of management, including the various types of decisions managers at each level make.

3. **LO** 9.1 Discuss the difference between centralized and decentralized organizations. Does the size of the organization influence whether the organization has a centralized or decentralized structure? Explain.

4. **LO** 9.1 Identify a company where you recently shopped. Assume the company operates with a decentralized structure. Describe how customers might benefit from the decentralized structure.

5. **LO** 9.1 Discuss the difference between daily and strategic decisions. Think of a business and provide an example of a daily and strategic decision.

6. **LO** 9.1 Access PepsiCo's 2017 annual report (https://openstax.org/l/50Pepsi2017) . Starting at the top of the document, use the find (Ctrl + F) or search feature in the browser to search the annual report for the word "segments" to determine how many operating segments PepsiCo has. What are the segments? How are the segments categorized?

7. **LO** 9.1 Another search of PepsiCo's 2017 annual report (https://openstax.org/l/50 Pepsi2017) reveals the company maintains a centralized management perspective on aspects of these items:
- Commodities (items such as sugar and high fructose corn syrup that go into many of the beverages)
- Research and development
- Insurance and benefit program
- Foreign currency transactions
- Debt, investments, and other financing activities

Explain why these activities would be centralized functions within PepsiCo as opposed to decentralized like many other activities.

8. **LO** 9.2 Define segments and describe how identifying segments within a business might help manage the business.

9. **LO** 9.2 Choose a company and describe how a specific issue, policy, or procedure (for example, granting merchandise returns, establishing sales prices) might look if the business is structured as a centralized business.

10. **LO** 9.2 Choose a company and explain how a specific issue, policy, or procedure (for example, granting merchandise returns, establishing sales prices) might look if the business is structured as a decentralized business.

11. **LO** 9.2 Assume you are the manager of a local Starbucks. What factors do you feel would be relevant to hiring workers (including pay), assuming Starbucks is a decentralized organization?

12. **LO** 9.2 Assume you are the manager of a local Starbucks. What factors do you feel would be relevant to hiring workers (including pay), assuming Starbucks is a centralized organization?

13. **LO** 9.2 Use Netflix's 2017 annual report (https://openstax.org/l/50Netflix2017) to answer the following questions. How many segments does Netflix have? What are the segments? The annual report also shows selected nonfinancial and financial information for each segment. Prepare a brief presentation listing the "Paid memberships at end of period," "Revenues," and "Contribution profit" (also called *operating profit*) for the three most recent years (2017, 2016, and 2015). In the presentation, include any observations you notice about the trends of each segment.

14. **LO** 9.2 Reference the Kellogg Company's 2017 annual report (https://openstax.org/l/50Kellogg2017) to answer the following question. In "Note 18: Reportable Segments," you will find selected financial information for segments within Kellogg Company. Prepare a brief presentation listing each segment, along with the "Net Sales," "Operating Profit," and "Total Assets." For Total Assets, you should ignore Corporate and Elimination entries, and you will need to combine the U.S. divisions into a North American total. Report this information for the three most recent years (2017, 2016, and 2015). In the presentation, include any observations you notice about the trends of each segment. You may want to use Microsoft Excel or another spreadsheet application for the numerical data. This information will be used in a subsequent question.

15. **LO** 9.2 Lavell started out mowing lawns in the neighborhood when he was 13 years old. He did such good work that, without advertising, his business grew steadily each year. After college, Lavell decided to continue the business as a full-time career. One of his concerns, however, is the number of hours he is putting in. Once school lets out, he finds himself working long hours nearly every day of the week. Although he has added workers, his business now handles mowing, trimming, and landscaping for residential, corporate, and nonprofit clients. He is considering adding managers but is not quite sure how to structure the organization. Lavell wants to focus on building the business rather than doing the daily work, so he knows a decentralized structure will be best. He has asked you to develop a potential organizational chart to help him envision the best way to organize the business. Describe the advantages to this approach as well as any concerns he should have.

16. **LO** 9.3 Describe the concept of responsibility accounting.

17. **LO** 9.3 Describe the concept of a cost center and, using a specific organization, give an example of how this might be used to achieve the strategic goals of the organization.

18. **LO** 9.3 Describe the concept of a profit center and, using a specific organization, give an example of how this might be used to achieve the strategic goals of the organization.

19. **LO** 9.3 Explain the benefits of a return on investment structure within an investment center framework. It may help to think of an example using an existing company.

20. **LO** 9.3 Explain the benefits of a residual income structure within an investment center framework. It may help to think of an example using an existing company.

21. **LO** 9.4 Discuss the concept of controllable and uncontrollable costs and how they affect the evaluation of the responsibility center's financial performance.

22. **LO** 9.4 Discuss the concept of transfer pricing.

23. **LO** 9.4 Discuss the advantages and disadvantages of a market-based transfer pricing approach.

24. **LO** 9.4 Discuss the advantages and disadvantages of a cost-based transfer pricing approach.

25. **LO** 9.4 Discuss the advantages and disadvantages of a negotiated transfer pricing approach.

Exercise Set A

EA1. LO 9.3 Assume you have been hired by Hilton Hotels and Resorts. As part of your new role in the accounting department, you have been tasked to set up a responsibility accounting structure for the company. As your first task, your supervisor has asked you to give an example of a cost center, profit center, and an investment center within the Hilton organization. Your supervisor is a little unsure of the difference between a profit center and investment center and would like you to explain the difference.

EA2. LO 9.3 Consider the national nonprofit organization the American Red Cross. Assume you are the regional director of the organization, and you just received the quarterly financial reports. Even though the organization is a nonprofit, assume it is set up as a profit center because it is helpful for the financial reports to show both donations and expenses by each region/location. One particular report shows there is one location in your region that is extremely over budget on nearly every expense item. From a management perspective, can you think of a reason(s) when going over budget might actually be a good thing? As the regional manager, how might you respond to the overages to help the particular location in the future?

EA3. LO 9.3 The following information is from Bluff Run Golf Courses. The company runs three courses and the July income statement for each course is shown.

BLUFF RUN GOLF COURSES
Income Statement
Month Ending July 31, 2018

Revenues	Blue Course	Black Course	Gold Course
Greens fees revenue	$62,500	$89,000	$42,800
Outings revenue	?	6,000	28,000
Total revenue	$73,500	$95,000	$70,800
Expenses			
Landscaping	$ 7,800	$14,200	$ 6,400
Wages	43,900	?	32,600
Repairs and maintenance	5,600	2,600	4,400
Fuel	3,100	3,000	1,980
Utilities	1,800	3,000	1,650
Total expenses	$62,200	$79,100	$47,030
Operating income	$11,300	$15,900	?

A. Find the missing value for outings revenue, wages, and operating income.
B. Comment on the financial performance of each course.
C. Identify a limitation of analyzing the information provided.

You may want to consider using Microsoft Excel or another spreadsheet application for the numerical data. This information will be used in a subsequent question.

EA4. LO 9.3 The following information is from Dave's Sporting Goods. Dave's is a Midwest sporting goods store with three regional stores. The August income statement for all stores is shown.

DAVE'S SPORTING GOODS
Income Statement
Month Ending August 31, 2018

	Nebraska	Iowa	Illinois
Sales	$22,000	$51,000	$36,000
Cost of goods sold	10,000	25,000	19,000
Gross profit	$12,000	$26,000	$17,000
Expenses			
Selling expenses	1,000	3,200	2,100
Wages expense	6,000	9,000	8,000
Costs allocated from corporate	3,000	15,000	5,500
Total expenses	$10,000	$27,200	$15,600
Operating income (loss)	$ 2,000	($ 1,200)	$ 1,400

A. Comment on the operating income results for each store.
B. Now assume the costs allocated from corporate is an uncontrollable cost for each store. How does this change your assessment of each store?

EA5. LO 9.4 Assume you are the department B manager for Marley's Manufacturing. Marley's operates under a cost-based transfer structure. Assume you receive the majority of your raw materials from department A, which sells only to department B (they have no outside sales). After calculating the operating income in dollars and operating income in percentage, analyze the following financial information to determine costs that may need further investigation. (Hint: It may be helpful to perform a vertical analysis.)

MARLEY'S MANUFACTURING
Income Statement
Month Ending August 31, 2018

	Dept A	Dept B
Sales	$22,000	$51,000
Cost of goods sold	10,560	26,520
Gross profit	$11,440	$24,480
Utility expenses	1,000	3,200
Wages expense	5,500	10,200
Costs allocated from corporate	2,200	15,000
Total expenses	$ 8,700	$28,400
Operating income/(loss) $	?	?
Operating income/(loss) %	?	?

EA6. LO 9.4 As manager of department B in Marley's Manufacturing, based on the costs you identified in the previous exercise for further research, how does this impact the financial performance of your department, and what might be some questions you want to ask or solutions you might propose to Marley's management?

EA7. LO 9.4 Based on your research of the market in the previous exercises, you have determined the market price for the items your department purchase is 15% below what you are being charged by department A of Marley's Manufacturing. How would you view this as a manager? What steps could you take to solve this discrepancy? What alternatives would you consider, assuming you had control over purchasing decisions?

EA8. LO 9.4 Using the information in the previous exercises about Marley's Manufacturing, determine the operating income for department B, assuming department A "sold" department B 1,000 units during the month and department A reduces the selling price to the market price.

Exercise Set B

EB1. LO 9.3 Assume you have been hired by Cabela's Sporting Goods. As part of your new role in the accounting department, you have been tasked to set up a responsibility accounting structure for the company. As your first task, your supervisor has asked you to give an example of a cost center, profit center, and an investment center within the Cabela's organization. Your supervisor is a little unsure of the difference between a profit center and investment center and would like you to explain the difference.

EB2. LO 9.3 Assume you are the regional manager for a hotel chain. You receive the quarterly financial reports and notice one particular hotel had drastically lower revenue and a corresponding high occupancy rate. Upon further investigation, you discover the manager for the hotel provided lodging for a neighboring town that was hit by a tornado. As the manager, how do you respond to this?

EB3. LO 9.3 The following information is from Dessert Dynasty. The company runs three stores and the December Income Statement for all stores is shown.

	Store X	Store Y	Store Z
DESSERT DYNASTY			
Income Statement			
Month Ending December 31, 2018			
Retail revenue	$17,976	?	$37,380
Events revenue	11,760	4,620	2,520
Total revenue	$29,736	$30,870	$39,900
Ingredients	3,528	3,276	?
Wages	15,792	18,438	$23,646
Baking supplies	1,848	2,352	1,092
Fuel	832	1,302	1,260
Utilities	693	756	1,260
Total expenses	$22,693	$26,124	$33,222
Operating income	?	$ 4,746	$ 6,678

A. Find the missing values for retail revenue, ingredients, and operating income.
B. Comment on the financial performance of each store.
C. Identify a limitation of analyzing the information provided.

You may want to consider using Microsoft Excel or another spreadsheet application for the numerical data. This information will be used in a subsequent question.

EB4. LO 9.3 The following information is from Good Read Books. Good Read is a regional book store with three regional stores. The May income statement for all stores is shown.

GOOD READS BOOKS
Income Statement
Month Ending May 31, 2018

	Store 1	Store 2	Store 3
Sales	$52,920	$32,340	$74,970
Cost of goods sold	27,930	14,700	36,750
Gross profit	$24,990	$17,640	$38,220
Expenses			
Selling expenses	3,087	1,470	4,704
Wages expense	11,760	8,820	13,230
Costs allocated from corporate	8,085	4,410	22,050
Total expenses	$22,932	$14,700	$39,984
Operating income (loss)	$ 2,058	$ 2,940	($ 1,764)

A. Comment on the operating income results for each store.
B. Now assume the costs allocated from corporate is an uncontrollable cost for each store. How does this change your assessment of each store?

EB5. LO 9.4 Assume you are the warehouse manager for Vinnie's Vinyls, a multi-location business specializing in vinyl records. Vinnies's operates under a cost-based transfer structure and the warehouse supplies all stores with the records. The stores can purchase records only from the warehouse, and the warehouse can only sell to Vinnie's stores. The manager of the West store has some concerns relating to the store's financial performance and has asked for your help analyzing transfer costs. After calculating the operating income in dollars and the operating income percent, analyze the following financial information to determine costs that may need further investigation. (Hint: it may be helpful to perform a vertical analysis.)

VINNIE'S VINYLS
Income Statement
Month Ending March 31, 2018

	Warehouse	West Store
Sales	$18,920	$43,860
Cost of goods sold	9,082	21,053
Gross profit	$ 9,838	$22,807
Selling expenses	860	2,752
Wages expense	4,730	15,351
Costs allocated from corporate	2,838	4,386
Total expenses	$ 8,428	$22,489
Operating income/(loss) $	?	?
Operating income/(loss) %	?	?

EB6. LO 9.4 As manager of the warehouse for Vinnie's Vinyls, based on this analysis and the items you identified for further research, what is your advice to the manager of the West store? What might be some questions you want to ask or solutions you might propose to Vinnie's management?

EB7. LO 9.4 Discuss how, as warehouse manager for Vinnie's Vinyls, you view the different rate of allocated costs the warehouse is being charged compared to the West store. Describe the implications of this. What steps could you take to solve this discrepancy? What alternatives would you consider, assuming management is willing to consider making changes in the rate?

EB8. LO 9.4 Determine the operating income for Vinnie's Vinyls' West store, assuming the warehouse allocation is reduced to 10% of sales for the warehouse and the difference will be charged to the West store. Management has determined that the warehouse takes fewer corporate resources and the allocation to the West store was lower than it should have been.

Problem Set A

PA1. LO 9.3 Use the following information to answer the questions that follow.

	BLUFF RUN GOLF COURSES Income Statement Month Ending July 31, 2018		
	Course A	**Course B**	**Course C**
Greens fees revenue	$62,500	$89,000	$42,800
Outings revenue	?	6,000	28,000
Total revenue	$73,500	$95,000	$70,800
Landscaping	$ 7,800	$14,200	$ 6,400
Wages	43,900	?	32,600
Repairs and maintenance	5,600	2,600	4,400
Fuel	3,100	3,000	1,980
Utilities	1,800	3,000	1,650
Total expenses	$62,200	$79,100	$47,030
Operating income	$11,300	$15,900	?
Operating income %	?	?	?

A. Calculate the operating income percentage for each of the courses. Comment on how your analysis has changed for each course.
B. Perform a vertical analysis for each course. Based on your analysis, what accounts would you want to investigate further? How might management utilize this information?
C. Which method of analysis (using a dollar value or percentage) is most relevant and/or useful? Explain.

PA2. LO 9.3 Use Netflix's 2017 annual report (https://openstax.org/l/50Netflix2017) to answer the following questions.

A. Using the revenue and contribution profit information, calculate the contribution profit (loss) percentage for each of the divisions. Comment on how your analysis has changed compared to your analysis of the dollar amounts for each division.

B. Since companies typically do not publicly provide more than macro levels of asset values, let's assume the following level of assets (investment):

Assets (fictitious)	2017	2016	2015
Domestic streaming	$15,000,000	$14,000,000	$10,000,000
International streaming	6,000,000	4,000,000	2,000,000
Domestic DVD	1,500,000	2,000,000	3,000,000

Calculate the return on investment (ROI) for each division. Comment on the results.

C. Assume that Netflix uses a cost of capital of 7%. Calculate the residual income (RI) for each of the divisions. Comment on the results.

PA3. LO 9.3 The income statement comparison for Forklift Material Handling shows the income statement for the current and prior year.

FORKLIFT MATERIAL HANDLING
Income Statement Comparison

	Current Year	Prior Year
(Amounts in thousands)		
Sales	$33,750	$24,750
Cost of goods sold	21,938	16,830
Gross profit	$11,812	$ 7,920
Wages	$ 8,775	$ 6,188
Utilities	675	250
Repairs	169	325
Selling	506	200
Total expenses	$10,125	$ 6,963
Operating income	?	?
Operating income %	?	?
Total assets (investment base)	$ 4,500	$ 1,500
Return on investment	?	?
Residual income (8% cost of capital)	?	?

A. Determine the operating income (loss) (dollars) for each year.
B. Determine the operating income (percentage) for each year.
C. The company made a strategic decision to invest in additional assets in the current year. These amounts are provided. Using the total assets amounts as the investment base, calculate the return on investment. Was the decision to invest additional assets in the company successful? Explain.
D. Assuming an 8% cost of capital, calculate the residual income for each year. Explain how this compares to your findings in part C.

PA4. LO 9.3 Assume you are the leather department manager at the Famous Football Factory. The leather department is a cost center and you are reviewing the scrap costs for the previous year, shown here:

	FAMOUS FOOTBALL FACTORY Cost Center Data-Leather Division					
	Jan.	Feb.	Mar.	Apr.	May	June
Leather Scrap Expense	$10,000	$10,100	$10,302	$10,405	$11,029	$11,801
	July	Aug.	Sep.	Oct.	Nov.	Dec.
Leather Scrap Expense	$13,100	$14,278	$15,135	$11,351	$11,351	$11,465

A. Using Microsoft Excel or another spreadsheet application, create a line chart with markers showing the leather scrap expense. Describe your observations.

B. Knowing that leather is susceptible to indoor temperature, you decide to talk with the maintenance manager and obtain the following information:

	Jan.	Feb.	Mar.	Apr.	May	June
Average indoor temperature (°F)	70	71	70	70	71	73
Air conditioning spare parts inventory	$3,500	$3,150	$2,898	$2,695	$2,426	$2,207
Number of air conditioning breakdowns	0	0	0	1	2	4
	July	Aug.	Sep.	Oct.	Nov.	Dec.
Average indoor temperature (°F)	74	76	74	72	71	70
Air conditioning spare parts inventory	$2,031	$2,010	$2,010	$2,010	$2,010	$1,990
Number of air conditioning breakdowns	4	6	5	1	0	0

Using Microsoft Excel or another spreadsheet application, create individual line charts with markers showing the indoor temperature, spare parts inventory, and breakdowns. Describe your observations and actions you might consider.

PA5. LO 9.4 Financial information for BDS Enterprises for the year-ended December 31, 20xx, was gathered from an accounting intern, who has asked for your guidance on how to prepare an income statement format that will be distributed to management. Subtotals and totals are included in the information, but you will need to calculate the values.

A. In the correct format, prepare the income statement using the following information:
B. Calculate the profit margin, return on investment, and residual income. Assume an investment base of $100,000 and 6% cost of capital.
C. Prepare a short response to accompany the income statement that explains why uncontrollable costs are included in the income statement.

Pretax income	?
Gross profit	?
Allocated costs (uncontrollable)	$2,035
Labor expense	41,580
Sales	189,000
Research and development (uncontrollable)	315
Depreciation expense	17,000
Net income/(loss)	?
Cost of goods sold	119,070
Selling expense	1,250
Total expenses	?
Marketing costs (uncontrollable)	790
Administrative expense	690
Income tax expense (21% of pretax income)	?
Other expenses	320

PA6. LO 9.4 Using the information from BDS Enterprises, prepare the income statement to include all costs, but separate out uncontrollable costs. Insert subtotals where appropriate (include one for operating income) before the uncontrollable costs. Income tax expense should be based on all expenses (that is, it will be the same amount as in question 1). Calculate net income, profit margin, ROI, and RI, excluding uncontrollable expenses. Prepare a short response to accompany the income statement that explains why uncontrollable costs are separated in the income statement.

PA7. LO 9.4 Management of Great Springs Bottled Water Company has asked you, the controller, to develop a transfer pricing system for the company. The Transportation Department of the company sells all of its product to the Bottling Department of the company. Thus the Transportation Department's sales become the Bottling Department's cost of goods sold. In order to determine an optimal transfer pricing system, management would like you to demonstrate what an income statement would look like under a cost, market, and negotiated transfer pricing structure. These various transfer prices are listed as follows. Prepare an income statement for each of the transfer prices by filling in the missing numbers in the provided income statement based on each transfer price (thus four different income statements) and calculate the operating income/loss percentage. Prepare a brief summary of the results.

Cost-based	$ 0.62
Market-based	$ 0.74
Negotiated	$ 0.70
Gallons transferred	278,000

GREAT SPRINGS BOTTLED WATER
Income Statement
Month Ending August 31, 2018

	Transportation	Bottling
Sales	?	$286,000
Cost of goods sold	$89,627	?
Gross profit	?	?
Fuel/utility expense	$15,000	$3,200
Wages expense	43,090	57,200
Costs allocated from corporate	17,236	15,000
Total expenses	$75,326	$75,400
Operating income/(loss) $	?	?
Operating income/(loss) %	?	?

PA8. LO 9.4 The following revenue data were taken from the December 31, 2017, Coca-Cola annual report (10-K):

2017 (in millions)	Europe, Middle East, Africa	Latin America	North America	Asia Pacific	Bottle Investments
Outside sales	$7,332	$3,956	$ 8,651	$4,767	$10,524
Intersegment sales	42	73	1,986	409	81
Total sales	$7,374	$4,029	$10,637	$5,176	$10,605
2016 (in millions)	Europe, Middle East, Africa	Latin America	North America	Asia Pacific	Bottle Investments
Outside sales	$7,014	$3,746	$ 6,437	$4,788	$19,751
Intersegment sales	264	73	3,773	506	134
Total sales	$7,278	$3,819	$10,210	$5,294	$19,885

For each segment and each year, calculate intersegment sales (another name for transfer sales) as a percentage of total sales. Using Microsoft Excel or another spreadsheet application, create a clustered column graph to show the 2016 and 2017 percentages for each division. Comment on your observations of this data. How might a division sales manager use this data?

Problem Set B

PB1. **LO 9.3** Use the following information to answer the questions that follow.

DESSERT DYNASTY Income Statement Month Ending December 31, 2018			
	Store X	Store Y	Store Z
Retail revenue	$17,976	?	$37,380
Events revenue	11,760	4,620	2,520
Total revenue	$29,736	$30,870	$39,900
Ingredients	$3,528	$3,276	?
Wages	15,792	18,438	23,646
Baking supplies	1,848	2,352	1,092
Fuel	832	1,302	1,260
Utilities	693	756	1,260
Total expenses	$22,693	$26,124	$33,222
Operating income	?	$4,746	$6,678
Operating income %	?	?	?

A. Calculate the operating income percentage for each of the stores. Comment on how your analysis has changed for each store.
B. Perform a vertical analysis for each store. Based on your analysis, what accounts would you want to investigate further? How might management utilize this information?
C. Which method of analysis (using a dollar value or percentage) is most relevant and/or useful? Explain.

PB2. **LO 9.3** Use Kellogg's 2017 annual report (https://openstax.org/l/50Kellogg2017) to answer the following questions.

A. Using the information for Kellogg, calculate the operating profit percentage for each of the divisions. Comment on how your analysis has changed compared to your analysis of the dollar amounts for each division.
B. Using total assets as the investment, calculate the ROI for each division. In the total assets information you compile, you should ignore corporate and elimination entries amounts and you will also need to combine the U.S. divisions into a North American total. Comment on the results.
C. Assume that Kellogg uses a cost of capital of 10%. Calculate the RI for each of the divisions (you will need to condense the U.S. divisions into a North American total). Comment on the results.

PB3. LO 9.3 The income statement comparison for Rush Delivery Company shows the income statement for the current and prior year.

RUSH DELIVERY COMPANY Income Statement Comparison		
(Amounts in thousands)	**Current Year**	**Prior Year**
Sales	$15,000	$11,000
Cost of goods sold	9,750	7,480
Gross profit	$5,250	$3,520
Wages	$3,900	$3,080
Utilities	300	250
Repairs	75	325
Selling	225	200
Total expenses	$4,500	$3,855
Operating income/(loss)	?	?
Operating income/(loss) %	?	?
Total assets (investment base)	$4,500	$1,500
Return on investment	?	?
Residual income (8% cost of capital)	?	?

A. Determine the operating income (loss) (dollars) for each year.
B. Determine the operating income (percentage) for each year.
C. The company made a strategic decision to invest in additional assets in the current year. These amounts are provided. Using the total assets amounts as the investment base, calculate the ROI. Was the decision to invest additional assets in the company successful? Explain.
D. Assuming an 8% cost of capital, calculate the RI for each year. Explain how this compares to your findings in part C.

PB4. LO 9.3 Assume you are the manager for the semi-trucks division at the Speedy Delivery Company. The semi-truck division is a cost center and you are reviewing the driver overtime costs for the previous year, shown here:

SPEEDY DELIVERY COMPANY						
Cost Center Data-Semi-Truck Division						
	Jan.	Feb.	Mar.	Apr.	May	June
Driver overtime	$150,000	$172,500	$103,500	$104,535	$106,626	$95,963
	July	Aug.	Sep.	Oct.	Nov.	Dec.
Driver overtime	$91,165	$82,048	$69,741	$87,177	$135,124	$243,222

A. Microsoft Excel or another spreadsheet application, create a line chart with markers showing the driver overtime expense. Describe your observations.
B. Knowing that safety is important in your industry and weather plays a significant role in the safety of drivers, you decide to talk with the safety manager and obtained the following information:

	Jan.	Feb.	Mar.	Apr.	May	June
Average snowfall (inches)	15	12	2	0	0	0
Non-company highway accidents	128	70	42	38	35	56
	July	Aug.	Sep.	Oct.	Nov.	Dec.
Average snowfall (inches)	0	0	0	2	35	62
Non-company highway accidents	78	83	53	35	208	423

Using Microsoft Excel or another spreadsheet application, create individual line charts with markers showing the average snowfall and non-company highway accidents. Describe your observations and actions you might consider.

PB5. LO 9.4 Financial information for Lighthizer Trading Company for the fiscal year-ended September 30, 20xx, was collected. As part of a management training session, you have been asked to prepare an income statement format that will be used to distribute to management. Subtotals and totals are included in the information, but you will need to calculate the values.

A. In the correct format, prepare the income statement using this information:
B. Calculate the profit margin, return on investment, and residual income. Assume an investment base of $42,000 and 8% cost of capital.
C. Prepare a short response to accompany the income statement that explains why uncontrollable costs are included in the income statement.

Pretax income	?
Gross profit	?
Allocated costs (uncontrollable)	$ 855
Labor expense	$17,464
Sales	$79,380
Research and development (uncontrollable)	$ 132
Depreciation expense	$ 7,140
Net income/(loss)	?
Cost of goods sold	$50,009
Selling expense	$ 525
Total expenses	?
Marketing costs (uncontrollable)	$ 332
Administrative expense	$ 290
Income tax expense (21% of pretax income)	?
Other expenses	$ 134

PB6. LO 9.4 Using the information for Lighthizer Trading Company, prepare the income statement to include all costs, but separate out uncontrollable costs. Insert subtotals where appropriate (include one for operating income) before the uncontrollable costs. Income tax expense should be based on all expenses (that is, it will be the same amount as in the previous exercise). Calculate net income, profit margin, ROI, and RI excluding uncontrollable expenses. Prepare a short response to accompany the income statement that explains why uncontrollable costs are separated in the income statement.

PB7. LO 9.4 Management of Green Peak Tea Company has asked you, the controller, to develop a transfer pricing system for the company. The Brewing Department of the company sells all of its product to the Bottling Department of the company. Thus the Brewing Department's sales become the Bottling Department's cost of goods sold. In order to determine an optimal transfer pricing system, management would like you to demonstrate what an income statement would look like under a cost, market, and negotiated transfer pricing structure. These various transfer prices are listed as follows. Prepare an income statement for each of the transfer prices by filling in the missing numbers in the provided income statement based on each transfer price (thus four different income statements) and calculate the operating income/loss percentage. Prepare a brief summary of the results.

Cost-based	$ 1.32
Market-based	$ 1.15
Negotiated	$ 1.24
Gallons transferred	89,000

GREEN PEAK TEA COMPANY
Income Statement
Month Ended November 31, 2018

	Brewing	Bottling
Sales	?	$207,000
Cost of goods sold	$61,090	?
Gross profit	?	?
Fuel/utilities expense	6,000	$ 5,400
Wages expense	22,180	41,400
Costs allocated from corporate	$39,938	28,000
Total expenses	$39,928	$ 74,800
Operating income/(loss) $	?	?
Operating income/(loss) %	?	?

PB8. LO 9.4 The following revenue data were taken from the December 31, 2017, General Electric annual report (10-K):

2017 (in millions)	Power	Renewable Energy	Oil & Gas	Aviation	Health-care	Transport-ation	Lighting
Outside sales	$34,598	$10,211	$16,584	$26,790	$19,098	$4,168	$1,956
Intersegment sales	1,392	69	646	585	18	10	31
Total sales	$35,990	$10,280	$17,230	$27,375	$19,116	$4,178	$1,987
2016 (in millions)	Power	Renewable Energy	Oil & Gas	Aviation	Health-care	Transport-ation	Lighting
Outside sales	$35,465	$9,022	$12,515	$25,530	$18,276	$4,713	$4,795
Intersegment sales	1,330	11	383	730	15	1	28
Total sales	$36,795	$9,033	$12,898	$26,260	$18,291	$4,714	$4,823

For each segment and each year, calculate intersegment sales (another name for transfer sales) as a percentage of total sales. Using Microsoft Excel or another spreadsheet application, create a clustered column graph to show the 2016 and 2017 percentages for each division. Comment on your observations of this data. How might a division sales manager use this data?

Thought Provokers

TP1. LO 9.1 You have just been elected president of a brand-new service club on campus. The club is part of a national organization, but the organization charter gives the local organization a fair amount of flexibility in setting up the management of the club. As president, you can choose to make most of the decisions for the club and pass along your direction to the officers and members below you, or you can create specific committees, such as membership or academic, and allow each of the committees to make its own decisions and rules within the overall guidelines set out by the national charter. Consider the need to manage and evaluate the club and describe which form of organization would you set up for your club and why.

TP2. LO 9.3 Consider these two companies: Apple and ExxonMobil. Write a summary of your perception of each company's financial position. Consider the levels of revenue, profitability, and any other financial measures you feel are relevant. After completing your summary, download Apple's September 30, 2017 annual report (10-K) (https://openstax.org/l/50Apple2017) and download Exxon Mobil's December 31, 2016 annual report (10-K) (https://openstax.org/l/50Exxon2017) for more information.

Gather the following information for each company:

Apple Data

Apple	9/30/2017	9/24/2016	9/26/2015
Net sales			
Income before provision for income taxes			
Net income			

Table 9.2

Exxon Mobile Data

Exxon	2017	2016	2015
Total revenues and other income			
Income before income taxes			
Net income attributable to ExxonMobil			

Table 9.3

What observations do you have about the financial performance of each company? Calculate the net income % (also called profit margin %) of each company. What observations do you have? How do these results compare to your perception of these companies before reviewing the annual reports?

10   Short-Term Decision Making

Figure 10.1 Value Add. Used coffee grounds can add value to a business. (credit left: modification of "Old coffee grounds to sprinkle on your garden" by Tristan Ferne/Flickr; credit right: modification of "Reusing coffee grounds" by Montgomery Cty Division of Solid Waste Services's photostream/Flickr)

Chapter Outline

- **10.1** Identify Relevant Information for Decision-Making
- **10.2** Evaluate and Determine Whether to Accept or Reject a Special Order
- **10.3** Evaluate and Determine Whether to Make or Buy a Component
- **10.4** Evaluate and Determine Whether to Keep or Discontinue a Segment or Product
- **10.5** Evaluate and Determine Whether to Sell or Process Further
- **10.6** Evaluate and Determine How to Make Decisions When Resources Are Constrained

Why It Matters

One day, at your part-time job in a local coffee shop, you realize that the employees throw many pounds of used coffee grounds in the trash each day. From an environmental perspective, you are concerned because of the volume of trash being transferred to the landfill. From a business perspective, you wonder if discarding the used grounds is the only option. Could those coffee grounds be used in a profitable manner? After a bit of research, you discover that, if prepared in certain ways, used coffee grounds are good as fertilizer, can kill insects on some plants, can be used as a body scrub, among other options. A recent radio talk show discussed the possibility that coffee grounds could be used as an alternative fuel source, and you learned that coffee grounds are actually being used to help fuel buses in London.

You consider the options for the used coffee grounds and come up with three possibilities for your coffee shop: (1) throw away the used grounds; (2) sell the used grounds to a company that will process them into fertilizer, bio-fuel, or some other product; or (3) process and package the used grounds for resale in the coffee shop as fertilizer and bug repellant. What information would you need for your analysis? Which decision would you choose and why? Are the revenue and cost components the only components of the decision that you should consider? These and similar issues are the types of questions that the accounting analysis process can help management address when evaluating short-term decisions.

10.1 Identify Relevant Information for Decision-Making

Almost everything we do in life results from choosing between alternatives, and the choices we make result in different consequences. For example, when choosing whether or not to eat breakfast before going to class, you face two alternatives and two sets of consequences. Eating breakfast means you must get up a little earlier, have food available, and be willing to prepare the food. Not eating means sleeping in longer, not having to plan food, and being hungry during class. Just as our lives are fraught with decisions large and small, the same is true for businesses. Almost every aspect of being in business involves choosing between alternatives, and each alternative typically has one or more consequences. Understanding how businesses make decisions paves the way not only to better decision-making processes but potentially to better outcomes.

Decisions made by businesses can have short-term effects or long-term impacts, or in some situations, both. Short-term decisions often address a temporary circumstance or an immediate need while long-term decisions align more with permanent problem solving and meeting strategic goals. Because these two types of decisions require different types of analyses, we will consider short-term decision-making here and long-term decision-making in Capital Budgeting Decision. Accounting distinguishes between short-term and long-term decisions not only because of the difference in the general nature of these decisions but also because the types of analyses differ significantly between short-term and long-term decision categories. As the time horizon over which the decision will have an impact expands, more costs become relevant to the decision-making process. In addition, when a time element is considered, there will be additional factors such as interest (paid or received) that will have a greater influence on decisions. Table 10.1 provides examples of short-term and long-term business decisions.

Examples of Short-Term and Long-Term Business Decisions

Short-Term Business Decisions	Long-Term Business Decisions
• Accepting a special production order • Determining the best product mix from current products • Outsourcing a part or service • Further processing or refining a current product	• Buying new equipment versus remodeling old equipment • Choosing which products to manufacture • Expanding into a new area or country • Diversifying by buying another business

Table 10.1 Short-term and long-term business decisions should be analyzed using different frameworks.

> ### CONTINUING APPLICATION AT WORK
>
> #### Short-Term Decision-Making
>
> Considering the business challenges facing Gearhead Outfitters, what short-term decisions might the company encounter? Remember that the retailer sells men's, women's and children's outdoor clothing, footwear, and accessories. Gearhead must carry a certain level and variety of inventory to meet the demands of its customers. The company will have to maintain appropriate accounting records to make proper business decisions to promote sustainability and growth.
>
> How might Gearhead be able to compete with larger chains and remain profitable? Will every sale result in the anticipated profit to the company? Consider what specialized short-term decision-making processes the company may use to meet its goals. Should more of an item than normal be purchased for resale to receive a larger discount from the supplier? What information about cost, volume, and profit is needed to make a sound business decision in this case? Some items may be sold at a loss (or lesser profit) to attract customers to the store. What type of information and accounting system is needed to help in this situation? The company requires relevant, consistent, and reliable data to determine the proper course of action.
>
> Short-term decision-making is vital in any business. Consider this concept in relation to Centralized vs. Decentralized Management and how a company's approach may affect the decision-making process. Discuss possible short-term issues and decisions, management focuses, and whether or not the centralized versus decentralized style will aid in company flexibility and success. Also, think in terms of how the decision-making process will be evaluated.

Relevant Information for Short-Term Decision-Making

Business decision-making can be outlined as a process that is applied by management with each decision that is made. The process of decision-making in a managerial business environment can be summed up in these steps.

1. Identify the objective or goal. For a business, typically the goal is to maximize revenues or minimize costs.
2. Identify alternative courses of action that can achieve the goal or address an obstacle that is hindering goal achievement.
3. Perform a comprehensive analysis of potential solutions. This includes identifying revenues, costs, benefits, and other financial and qualitative variables.
4. Decide, based upon the analysis, the best course of action.
5. Review, analyze, and evaluate the results of the decision.

The first step of the decision-making process is to identify the goal. In the decisions discussed in this course, the quantitative goal will either be to maximize revenues or to minimize costs. The second step is to identify the alternative courses of action to achieve the goal. (In the real world, steps one and two may require more thought and research that you will learn about in advanced cost accounting and management courses.). This chapter focuses on steps three and four, which involve **short-term decision analysis**: determining the appropriate information necessary for making a decision that will impact the company in the short term, usually 12 months or fewer, and using that information in a proper analysis in order to reach an informed decision among alternatives. Step five, which involves reviewing and evaluating the decision, is briefly addressed with each type of decision analyzed.

Though these same general steps could be used in long-term decision analyses, the nature of long-term decisions is different. Short-term decisions are typically operational in nature: making versus buying a component of a product, using scarce resources, selling a product as-is or processing it further into a different product. It is relatively easy to change a short-term decision with minimal impact on the company. Long-term decisions are strategic in nature and typically involve large sums of money. The effects of a long-term decision can have significant financial impact on a company for years. Examples of long-term decisions include replacing manufacturing equipment, building a new factory, or deciding to eliminate a product line. While you've learned how managerial accounting classifies, tracks, monitors, and controls costs, managerial accountants also closely analyze revenues, which are less controllable than costs, but are important in these decisions. As stated in the first step of the decision-making process, maximizing revenues is usually one of the goals of an organization. Therefore, making some short-term decisions requires analysis of both costs and revenues.

In carrying out step three of the managerial decision-making process, a differential analysis compares the relevant costs and revenues of potential solutions. What does this involve? First, it is important to understand that there are many types of short-term decisions that a business may face, but these decisions always involve choosing between alternatives. Examples of these types of decisions include determining whether to accept a special order; making a product or component versus buying the product or component; performing additional processing on a product; keeping versus eliminating a product or segment; or determining whether to take on a new project. In each of these situations, the business should compare the relevant costs and the relevant revenues of one alternative to the relevant costs and relevant revenues of the other alternative(s). Therefore, an important step in the differential analysis of potential solutions is to identify the relevant costs and relevant revenues of the decision.

What does it mean for something to be relevant? In the context of decision-making, something is relevant if it will influence the decision being made. For example, suppose you have two options for a summer job—either flagging traffic for a road crew or working for a landscaping company doing lawn care. For either job, you will be required to have industrial grade sound protectors (plugs or headphones) for your ears. This cost would not be relevant because it is the same under either alternative, so it will not influence your decision between the two jobs; it would be considered an **irrelevant cost**. You also believe your transportation costs will be the same for either job; thus this would also be an irrelevant cost.

However, if you are required to have steel-toed boots for the road work job but can wear any type of work boot for the landscaping job, you would need to consider the difference between the costs, or the **differential cost**, of these two types of boots. This difference in cost between the two pairs of boots would be designated as a **relevant cost** because it influences your decision.

The two jobs also may have differences in revenues, called a **differential revenue**. Because the differential revenue influences the decision, it is also a **relevant revenue**. If both jobs pay the same hourly wage, it would have an **irrelevant revenue**, but if the road crew job offers overtime for any time worked over 40 hours, then this overtime wage has the potential to be a relevant revenue if overtime is a likely occurrence. Looking only at these differences—of both costs and revenues—between the alternatives, is known as **differential analysis**.

In conducting these types of analyses between alternatives, the initial focus will be on each **quantitative factor** of the analysis—in other words, the component that can be measured numerically. Examples of quantitative factors in business include sales growth, number of defective parts produced, or number of labor hours worked. However, in decision-making, it is important also to consider each **qualitative factor**, which is one that cannot be measured numerically. For example, using the same summer job scenario, qualitative factors may include the environment in which you would be working (road dust and tar odors versus pollen and mower exhaust fumes), the amount of time exposed to the sun, the people with whom you will be working (working with friends versus making new friends), and weather-related issues (both jobs are outdoors, but could one job send you home for the day due to weather?). Examples of qualitative factors in business include employee morale, customer satisfaction, and company or brand image. In making short-term decisions, a business will want to analyze both qualitative and quantitative factors.

In short-term decision-making, revenues are often easier to evaluate than costs. In addition, each alternative typically only has one possible one revenue outcome even though there are many costs to consider for each alternative. How do we know if a cost will have an impact on the decision? The starting point is to understand the various labels that are attached to costs in these decision-making environments.

Avoidable versus Unavoidable Costs

Management must determine if a cost is avoidable or unavoidable because in the short run, only avoidable costs are relevant for decision-making purposes. An **avoidable cost** is one that can be eliminated (in whole or in part) by choosing one alternative over another. For example, assume that a bike shop offers their customers custom paint jobs for bikes that the customers already own. If they eliminate the service, the cost of the bike paint could be eliminated. Also assume that they had been employing a part-time painter to do the work. The painter's compensation would also be an avoidable cost.

An **unavoidable cost** is one that does not change or go away in the short-run by choosing one alternative over another. For example, a company might sign a long-term lease on equipment or a production facility. These types of leases typically don't allow for cancellation, so if this one does not, then their required payments are unavoidable costs for the duration of the lease.

Variable costs are avoidable costs, since variable costs do not exist if the product is no longer made, or if the portion of the business (such as a segment or division) that generated the variable costs ceases to operate. Fixed costs, on the other hand, may be unavoidable, partially unavoidable, or avoidable only in certain circumstances. Remember that fixed costs tend to remain constant for a period of time and within a relevant range of production and are not easily eliminated in the short-run. Therefore, most fixed costs also are unavoidable. If a fixed cost is specific only to one of the alternatives, then that fixed cost also may be avoidable. Avoidable costs are future costs that are relevant to decision-making. Past costs are never an avoidable cost.

Recall that we are using a short-term viewpoint to determine whether or not costs are avoidable. In the long run, virtually all costs are avoidable. For example, assume that a company has a long-term, ten-year lease on a production facility that cannot be cancelled. For the first ten years it would be noncancelable and thus unavoidable. But after ten years it would become avoidable.

YOUR TURN

AlexCo's Wagons

AlexCo produces collapsible wagons that are popular with beachgoers, shoppers, gardeners, parents, and tailgaters. Annual sales have been 100,000 wagons per year. The retail selling price of each wagon is

$67.00. To date, AlexCo has produced each of the components used in making the wagons but has been approached by DAL, Inc. with an offer to provide the axle and wheel assembly for $18.75 per assembly. AlexCo's costs to produce the axle and wheel assembly are $9.00 in direct materials, $6.50 in direct labor, $3.57 in variable overhead, and $2.50 in fixed overhead. Twenty-five percent of the fixed overhead is avoidable if the assembly is produced by DAL. Should AlexCo continue to make the axle and wheel assembly or should it buy the assembly from DAL, Inc.?

Solution

	Relevant Costs	
	Make Internally	Buy from DAL, Inc.
Direct materials	$ 9.00	
Direct labor	6.50	
Variable overhead	3.57	
Avoidable fixed costs	0.63	
Total unit relevant cost	19.70	$ 18.75
Units required	100,000	100,000
Total relevant costs	$1,970,000	$1,875,000

Ignoring qualitative factors, it would be more cost effective for AlexCo to buy the axle and wheel assembly from DAL, Inc. However, AlexCo should be certain of any qualitative issues and not solely base their decision on the quantitative analysis.

Sunk Costs

A **sunk cost** is one that cannot be avoided because it has already occurred. A sunk cost will not change regardless of the alternative that management chooses; therefore, sunk costs have no bearing on future events and are not relevant in decision-making. The basic premise sounds simple enough, but sunk costs are difficult to ignore due to human nature and are sometimes incorrectly included in the decision-making process. For example, suppose you have an old car, a hand-me-down from your grandmother, and last year you spent $1,600 on repairs and new tires and were just told by your mechanic that the car needs $1,200 in repairs to operate safely. Your goal is to have a safe and reliable car. Your alternatives are to get the repairs completed or trade in the car for a newer used car.

From a quantitative perspective, you have gathered the following information to help with your decision. The trade-in value of your old car will be the minimum given by the dealer, or $200. The newer used car will require you to make monthly payments of $150 for two years. In analyzing your two alternatives, what costs do you consider? Remember, the $1,600 you have already spent (note the past tense) is a sunk cost; it is a consequence of a past decision. In this example, the relevant costs for each alternative are the following: $1,200 in current repair costs to keep your current car or $3,400 (from the 24 payments of $150 minus $200 for the trade in) to buy a newer used car. Obviously, you also would consider qualitative factors, such as the sentimental value of your grandmother's car or the excitement of having a newer car.

Sunk costs are most problematic for business decisions when they pertain to existing equipment. The book value of an asset (historical cost – accumulated depreciation) is a sunk cost regardless of whether a business keeps the asset or disposes of it in some manner. The cost of the asset occurred in the past and therefore is sunk and irrelevant to the decision at hand. Mangers may be reluctant to ignore sunk costs when making decisions, especially if the prior decision to purchase the asset was an unwise one. Often, when management takes a path of action that is not achieving the desired results, managers may continue the same path in the hope that the effect of prior decisions will improve the results. The use of the word *prior* is a key indicator that information is nonrelevant to a current decision. Holding on to old decisions or old commitments is common because letting them go forces management to admit they made a bad decision.

Future Costs That Do Not Differ

Any future cost that does not differ between the alternatives is not a relevant cost for the decision. For example, if a company is considering baking either bagels or doughnuts and both baked goods require $0.30 worth of flour, then the cost of flour would not be a relevant cost in determining which of the two had the highest production cost. As relevant information for short-term decision-making, the cost of sound protectors for your summer job would not be relevant to your decision because that cost exists in both scenarios. Another irrelevant cost would be your transportation cost, since that cost is also the same regardless of the job you choose. In another example, if a company is planning to produce either red widgets or blue wingdings and will need to hire 10 additional employees to produce either of the goods, the cost of those 10 employees is irrelevant because it does not differ between the alternatives.

ETHICAL CONSIDERATIONS

Johnson & Johnson's 1982 Recall and Replacement of All Tylenol in the World

In 1982, Johnson & Johnson was faced with a large-scale business and ethical dilemma. During the course of several days beginning on September 29, 1982, seven deaths occurred in the Chicago area that were attributed to consuming capsules of Extra-Strength Tylenol. The painkiller was, at the time, Johnson & Johnson's best-selling product. The company had to decide if the short-term cost of replacing the Tylenol was worth the future cost to their reputation and their customer's health and safety. At tremendous expense, Johnson & Johnson "placed consumers first by recalling 31 million bottles of Tylenol capsules from store shelves and offering replacement product in the safer tablet form free of charge."[1]

As it was later discovered, someone was lacing Tylenol capsules with cyanide and returning the pills in the original packages to store shelves. However, Johnson & Johnson's decision to incur short-term costs by recalling all of their pills ultimately paid off, as in the long run, the company's stock value increased and Tylenol sales recovered. One could look at the decision as an opportunity cost: Johnson & Johnson had to choose between two alternatives. The company could have chosen a short-term solution with reduced short-term losses, but by making an ethical business decision, the long-term rewards were greater than the short-term savings.

Opportunity Costs

When choosing between two alternatives, usually only one of the two choices can be selected. When this is the

---

1 Judith Rehak. "Tylenol Made a Hero of Johnson & Johnson: The Recall That Started Them All." *New York Times*. Mar. 23, 2002. https://www.nytimes.com/2002/03/23/your-money/IHT-tylenol-made-a-hero-of-johnson-johnson-the-recall-that-started.html

case, you may be faced with **opportunity costs**, which are the costs associated with not choosing the other alternative. For example, if you are trying to choose between going to work immediately after completing your undergraduate degree or continuing to graduate school, you will have an opportunity cost. If you choose to go to work immediately, your opportunity cost is forgoing a graduate degree and any potential job limitations or advancements that result from that decision. If you choose instead to go directly into graduate school, your opportunity cost is the income that you could have been earning by going to work immediately upon graduation.

YOUR TURN

Costs and Revenue at Carolina Clusters

Carolina Clusters, Inc., a candy manufacturer in a resort town, just bought a new taffy pulling machine for $27,000 and is planning to increase the production of salt-water taffy. Due to the increased production, Carolina is deciding between hiring two part-time college students or one full-time employee. Each college student would work half days totaling 20 hours per week, and would earn $12 per hour. The full-time employee would work full days 40 hours per week and would earn $12 per hour plus the equivalent of $2 per hour in benefits. Each employee is given two t-shirts to wear as their uniform. The t-shirts cost Carolina $8 each. In addition, Carolina provides disposable hair coverings and gloves for the employees. Each employee uses, on average, six sets of gloves per eight-hour shift or four sets per four-hour shift. One hair covering per shift per person is typical. The cost of the hair covering is $0.05 per covering and the cost of a pair of gloves is $0.02 per pair. Identify any relevant costs, relevant revenues, sunk costs, and opportunity costs that Carolina Clusters needs to consider in making the decision whether to hire two part-time employees or one full-time employee.

Solution

Relevant costs:

- $2 per hour for benefits
- $16 for two t-shirts: Hiring one full-time person will result in a $16 expenditure for t-shirts. Hiring two college students would result in $32 in t-shirt expenditures, thus the relevant t-shirts costs is the $16 difference.
- $0.05 for a hair covering: Hiring one full-time person will result in $0.05 per day in hair covering costs but hiring two college students would result in $0.10 per day in hair covering costs thus the relevant hair covering cost is the $0.05 difference.
- $0.04 for a pair of gloves: Hiring one full-time person will result in $0.12 (6 × $0.02) per day in glove costs, but hiring two college students would result in $0.16 (8 × $0.02) per day in glove costs. Thus, the relevant glove cost is the $0.04 difference.

Relevant revenues: None

Sunk costs: $27,000 for the taffy machine

Opportunity costs: None

10.2 Evaluate and Determine Whether to Accept or Reject a Special Order

Both manufacturing and service companies often receive requests to fill special orders. These **special orders** are typically for goods or services at a reduced price and are usually a one-time order that, in the short-run, does not affect normal sales. When deciding whether to accept a special order, management must consider several factors:

- The capacity required to fulfill the special order
- Whether the price offered by the buyer will cover the cost of producing the products
- The role of fixed costs in the analysis
- Qualitative factors
- Whether the order will violate the Robinson-Patman Act and other fair pricing legislation

Fundamentals of the Decision to Accept or Reject a Special Order

The starting point for making this decision is to assess the company's normal production capacity. The **normal capacity** is the production level a company can achieve without adding additional production resources, such as additional equipment or labor. For example, if the company can produce 10,000 towels a month based on its current production capacity, and it is currently contracted to produce 9,000 a month, it could not take on a special one-time order for 3,000 towels without adding additional equipment or workers. Most companies do not work at maximum capacity; rather, they function at normal capacity, which is a concept related to a company's relevant range. The **relevant range** is the quantitative range of units that can be produced based on the company's current productive assets. These assets can include equipment capacity or its labor capacity. Labor capacity is typically easier to increase on a short-term basis than equipment capacity. The following example assumes that labor capacity is available, so only equipment capacity is considered in the example.

Assume that based on a company's present equipment, it can produce 20,000 units a month. Its relevant range of production would be zero to 20,000 units a month. As long as the units of production fall within this range, it does not need additional equipment. However, if it wanted to increase production from 20,000 units to 24,000 units, it would need to buy or lease additional equipment. If production is fewer than 20,000 units, the company would have unused capacity that could be used to produce additional units for its current customers or for new clients.

If the company does not have the capacity to produce a special order, it will have to reduce production of another good or service in order to fulfill the special order or provide another means of producing the goods, such as hiring temporary workers, running an additional shift, or securing additional equipment. As you will learn, not having the capacity to fill the special order will create a different analysis than it would if there is sufficient capacity.

Next, management must determine if the price offered by the buyer will result in enough revenue to cover the differential costs of producing the items. For example, if price does not meet the variable costs of production, then accepting the special order would be an unprofitable decision.

Additionally, fixed costs may be relevant if the company is already operating at capacity, as there may be additional fixed costs, such as the need to run an extra shift, hire an additional supervisor, or buy or lease additional equipment. If the company is not operating at capacity—in other words, the company has *unused* capacity—then the fixed costs are irrelevant to the decision if the special order can be met with this unused capacity.

Special orders create several qualitative issues. A logical issue is the concern for how existing customers will feel if they discover a lower price was offered to the special-order customer. A special order that might be profitable could be rejected if the company determined that accepting the special order could damage relations with current customers. If the goods in the special order are modified so that they are cheaper to manufacture, current customers may prefer the modified, cheaper version of the product. Would this hurt the profitability of the company? Would it affect the reputation?

In addition to these considerations, sometimes companies will take on a special order that will not cover costs based on qualitative assessments. For example, the business requesting the special order might be a potential client with whom the manufacturer has been trying to establish a business relationship and the producer is willing to take a one-time loss. However, our coverage of special orders concentrates on decisions based on quantitative factors.

Companies considering special orders must also be aware of the anti–price discrimination rules established in the Robinson-Patman Act. The Robinson-Patman Act is a federal law that was passed in 1936. Its primary intent is to prevent some forms of price discrimination in sales transactions between smaller and larger businesses.

LINK TO LEARNING

The Robinson-Patman Act prevents large retailers from purchasing goods in bulk at a greater discount than smaller retailers are able to obtain them. It helps keep competition fair between large and small businesses and is sometimes called the "Anti-Chain Store Act." Read the LegalDictionary.net full definition and example of the Robinson-Patman Act (https://openstax.org/l/50RobPatAct) to learn more.

Sample Data

Franco, Inc., produces dental office examination chairs. Franco has the capacity to produce 5,000 chairs per year and currently is producing 4,000. Each chair retails for $2,800, and the costs to produce a single chair consist of direct materials of $750, direct labor of $600, and variable overhead of $300. Fixed overhead costs of $1,350,000 are met by selling the first 3,000 chairs. Franco has received a special order from Ghanem, Inc., to buy 800 chairs for $1,800. Should Franco accept the special order?

Calculations Using Sample Data

Franco is not operating at capacity and the special order does not take them over capacity. Additionally, all the fixed costs have already been met. Therefore, when evaluating the special order, Franco must determine if the special offer price will meet and exceed the costs to produce the chairs. Figure 10.2 details the analysis.

	Current Cost to Produce	Special Order Price Offer	Difference in Favor of Accepting Special Order
Direct materials	$ 750		
Direct labor	600		
Variable overhead	300		
Variable costs to produce	1,650		
Special offer price		$1,800	$150 per chair

Figure 10.2 Special Order: Supplier Has Excess Capacity. (attribution: Copyright Rice University, OpenStax, under CC BY-NC-SA 4.0 license)

Since Franco has already met his fixed costs with current production and since he has the capacity to produce the additional 800 units, Franco only needs to consider his variable costs for this order. Franco's variable cost to produce one chair is $1,650. Ghanem is offering to buy the chairs for $1,800 apiece. By accepting the special order, Franco would meet his variable costs and make $150 per chair. Considering only quantitative factors, Franco should accept the special offer.

How would Franco's decision change if the factory was already producing at capacity at the time of the special offer? In other words, assume the corporation is already producing the most it can produce without working more hours or adding more equipment. Accepting the order would likely mean that Franco would incur additional fixed costs. Assume that, to fill the order from Ghanem, Franco would have to run an extra shift, and this would require him to hire a temporary production manager at a cost of $90,000. Assume no other fixed costs would be incurred. Also assume Franco will incur additional costs related to maintenance and utilities for this extra shift and estimates those costs will be $70,000. As shown in Figure 10.3, in this scenario, Franco would have to charge Ghanem at least $1,850 in order to meet his cost.

	Current Production	Special Order Current Offer
Selling price	$2,800	$1,800
Variable cost to produce	1,650	1,650
Additional costs to recover*		200
Contribution margin	$1,150	$ (50)

*$90,000 supervisor salary + $70,000 additional costs = $160,000 in costs to recover ÷ 800 chairs in special order = $200 per chair additional costs due to capacity issue.

Figure 10.3 Special Order: Supplier Does Not Have Excess Capacity. (attribution: Copyright Rice University, OpenStax, under CC BY-NC-SA 4.0 license)

Final Analysis of the Decision

The analysis of Franco's options did not consider any qualitative factors, such as the impact on morale if the company is already at capacity and opts to implement overtime or hire temporary workers to fill the special order. The analysis also does not consider the effect on regular customers if management elects to meet the special order by not fulfilling some of the regular orders. Another consideration is the impact on existing customers if the price offered for the special order is lower than the regular price. These effects may create a bad dynamic between the company and its customers, or they may cause customers to seek products from competitors. As in the example, Franco would need to consider the impact of displacing other customers and the risk of losing business from regular customers, such as dental supply companies, if he is unable to meet their orders. The next step is to do an overall cost/benefit analysis in which Franco would consider not only the quantitative but the qualitative factors before making his final decision on whether or not to accept the special order.

> ### THINK IT THROUGH
>
> **Athletic Jersey Special Orders**
>
> Jake's Jerseys has been asked to produce athletic jerseys for a local school district. The special order is for 1,000 jerseys of varying sizes, and the price offered by the school district is $10 less per jersey than the normal $50 market price. The school district interested in the jerseys is one of the largest in the area. What quantitative and qualitative factors should Jake consider in making the decision to accept or reject the special order?

10.3 Evaluate and Determine Whether to Make or Buy a Component

One of the most common outsourcing scenarios is one in which a company must decide whether it is going to make a component that it needs in manufacturing a product or buy that component already made. For example, all of the components of the iPhone are made by companies other than Apple. Ford buys truck and automobile seats, as well as many other components and individual parts, from various suppliers and then assembles them at Ford factories. With each component, Ford must decide if it is more cost effective to make that component internally or to buy that component from an external supplier.

This type of analysis is also relevant to the service industry; for example, ADP provides payroll and data processing services to over 650,000 companies worldwide. Or a law firm may decide to hire certain research activities to be completed by outside experts rather than hire the necessary staff to keep that function in-house. These are all examples of outsourcing. **Outsourcing** is the act of using another company to provide goods or services that your company requires.

Many companies outsource some of their work, but why? Consider this scenario: Today, while driving home from class, one of your car's engine warning lights goes on. You will most likely take your car to an auto repair specialist to have it analyzed and repaired, whereas your grandfather might have popped the hood, grabbed his toolbox, and attempted to diagnose and fix the problem himself. Why? It is often a matter of expertise and sometimes simply a matter of cost benefit. In your grandfather's time, car engines were more mechanical and less electronic, which made learning to repair cars a simpler process that required less expertise and only basic tools. Today, your car has many electronic components and often requires sophisticated monitors to assess the problem and may involve the replacement of computer chips or electronic sensors. Thus, you opt to outsource the repair of your car to someone who has the knowledge and facilities to provide the repair more cost effectively than you could if you did it yourself. Your grandfather likely could have made the repair to his car several decades ago as cheaply as the mechanic with only a sacrifice of his time. To your grandfather, the cost of his time was worth the benefit of completing the repair himself.

Companies outsource for the same reasons. Many companies have found that it is more cost effective to outsource certain activities, such as payroll, data storage, and web design and hosting. It is more efficient to pay an outside expert than to hire the appropriate staff to keep a particular task inside the company.

Fundamentals of the Decision to Make or to Buy

As with other decisions, the make-versus-buy decision involves both quantitative and qualitative analysis. The quantitative component requires cost analysis to determine which alternative is more cost effective. This cost analysis can be performed by looking at the cost to buy the component versus the cost to produce the component, which allows us to make a decision based on an analysis of unavoidable costs. For example, the costs to produce will include direct materials, direct labor, variable overhead, and fixed overhead. If the business chooses to buy the component instead, the avoidable costs will go away but unavoidable costs will remain and would need to be considered as part of the cost to buy the component.

Sample Data

Thermal Mugs, Inc., manufactures various types of leak-proof personal drink carriers. Thermal's T6 container, its most insulated carrier, maintains the temperature of the liquid inside for 6 hours. Thermal has designed a new lid for the T6 carrier that allows for easier drinking and pouring. The cost to produce the new lid is $2.19:

Direct materials	$0.87
Direct labor	0.45
Fixed overhead	0.51
Variable overhead	0.36
Total unit cost	$2.19

Plato Plastics has approached Thermal and offered to produce the 120,000 lids Thermal will require for current production levels of the T6 carrier, at a unit price of $1.75 each. Is this a good deal? Should Thermal buy the lids from Plato rather than produce them themselves? Initially, the $1.75 presented by Plato seems like a much better price than the $2.19 that it would cost Thermal to produce the lids. However, more information about the relevant costs is necessary to determine whether the offer by Plato is the better offer. Remember that all the variable costs of producing the lid will only exist if the lid is produced by Thermal, thus the variable costs (direct materials, direct labor, and variable overhead) are all relevant costs that will differ between the alternatives.

What about the fixed costs? Assume all the fixed costs are not tied directly to the production of the lid and therefore will still exist even if the lid is purchased externally from Plato. This means the fixed costs of $0.51 per unit are unavoidable and therefore are not relevant.

Calculations Using Sample Data

Calculations show that when the relevant costs are compared between the two alternatives, it is more cost effective for Thermal to produce the 120,000 units of the T6 lid internally than to purchase it from Plato.

	Relevant Costs	
	Make Internally	Buy from Plato
Direct materials	$ 0.87	
Direct labor	0.45	
Variable overhead	0.36	
Total unit relevant cost	1.68	$ 1.75
Units required	120,000	120,000
Total relevant costs	$201,600	$210,000

By producing the T6 lid internally, Thermal can save $8,400 ($210,000 − $201,600). How would the analysis change if a portion of the fixed costs were avoidable? Suppose that, of the $0.51 in fixed costs per unit of the T6 lid, $0.12 of those fixed costs are associated with interest costs and insurance expenses and thus would be avoidable if the T6 lid is purchased externally rather than produced internally. How does that change the analysis?

	Relevant Costs	
	Make Internally	Buy from Plato
Direct materials	$ 0.87	
Direct labor	0.45	
Variable overhead	0.36	
Avoidable fixed costs	0.12	
Total unit relevant cost	1.80	$ 1.75
Units required	120,000	120,000
Total relevant costs	$216,000	$210,000

In this scenario, it is more cost effective for Thermal to buy the T6 lid from Plato, as Thermal would save $6,000 ($216,000 − $210,000).

Final Analysis of the Decision

The difference in these two presentations of the data emphasizes the importance of defining which costs are relevant, as improper cost identification can lead to bad decisions.

These analyses only considered the quantitative factors in a make-versus-buy decision, but there are qualitative factors to consider as well, including:

- Will the T6 lid made by Plato meet the quality requirements of Thermal?
- Will Plato continue to produce the T6 lid at the $1.75 price, or is this a teaser rate to obtain the business, with the plan for the rate to go up in the future?
- Can Plato continue to produce the quantity of the lids desired? If more or fewer are needed from Plato, is the adjusted production level obtainable, and does it affect the cost?
- Does using Plato to produce the lids displace Thermal workers or hamper morale?
- Does using Plato to produce the lids affect the reputation of Thermal?

In addition, if the decision is to buy the lid, Thermal is dependent on Plato for quality, timely delivery, and cost control. If Plato fails to deliver the lids on time, this can negatively affect Thermal's production and sales. If the lids are of poor quality, returns, replacements, and the damage to Thermal's reputation can be significant. Without long-term agreements on price increases, Plato can increase the price they charge Thermal, thus making the entire drink container more expensive and less profitable. However, buying the lid likely means that Thermal has excess production capacity that can now be applied to making other products. If Thermal chooses to make the lid, this consumes some of the productive capacity and may affect the relationship Thermal has with the outside supplier if that supplier is already working with Thermal on other products.

Make versus buy, one of many outsourcing decisions, should involve assessing all relevant costs in conjunction with the qualitative issues that affect the decision or arise because of the choice. Although it may appear that these types of outsourcing decisions are difficult to resolve, companies throughout the world make these decisions daily as part of the company's strategic plan, and therefore, each company must weigh the advantages and disadvantages of outsourcing production of goods and services. Some examples are shown in Table 10.2.

Advantages and Disadvantages of Outsourcing

Advantages of Outsourcing	Disadvantages of Outsourcing
• Utilizes external expertise, removes the need for in-house expertise • Frees up capacity for other uses • Frees up capital for other uses • Allows management to focus on competitive strengths • Transfers some production and technological risks to supplier	• Takes away control over quality and timing of production • May limit ability to upsize or downsize production • May have hidden costs and/or a lack of stability of price • May diminish innovation • Often makes it difficult to bring the production back in-house once it has been removed

Table 10.2

In an outsourcing decision, the relevant costs and qualitative issues should be analyzed thoroughly. If there are no qualitative issues that affect the decision and the leasing or purchasing price is less than the relevant (avoidable) costs of producing the good or service in house, the company should outsource the product or service. The following example demonstrates this issue for a service entity.

Lake Law has ten lawyers on staff who handle workers' compensation and workplace discrimination lawsuits. Lake has an excellent success rate and frequently wins large settlements for their clients. Because of the size of their settlements, many clients are interested in establishing trusts to manage the investing and distribution of the funds. Lake Law does not have a trust or estate lawyer on staff and is debating between hiring one or using an attorney at a nearby law firm that specializes in wills, trusts, and estates to handle the trusts of Lake's clients. Hiring a new attorney would require $120,000 in salary for the attorney, an additional 20% in benefits, a legal assistant for the new attorney for 20 hours per week at a cost of $20 per hour, and conversion of a storage room into an office. Lake spent $100,000 on redecorating the offices last year and has sufficient furniture for a new office. The attorney at the nearby firm would charge a retainer of $50,000 plus $200 per hour worked on each trust. The retainer is in addition to the $200 per hour charge for work on trusts. The average trust takes 10 hours to complete and Lake estimates approximately 50 trusts per year. In addition, an external attorney would charge $500 for each trust to cover office expenses and filing fees. Which option should Lake choose?

To determine the solution, first, find the relevant costs for hiring internally and for using an external attorney.

	Hire Internally	Use External Attorney
Salary	$120,000	
Benefits (20%)	24,000	
Legal assistant		
(20 hrs × $20 × 52 weeks)	20,800	
Retainer		$ 50,000
Cost per trust × number of trusts		
($200 × 10 × 50)		$100,000
Additional fees		25,000
Total relevant costs	$164,800	$175,000

Based on the quantitative analysis, Lake should hire an estate attorney to have on staff. For the year, the firm would save $10,200 ($164,800 for internal versus $175,000 with the external attorney) by going with the internal hire. Other potential advantages would be that an in-house attorney could complete more than the estimated 50 trusts without incurring additional costs, and by keeping the work in-house, it helps to build the relationship between the firm and the clients. A disadvantage would be if there is not sufficient work to keep the in-house attorney busy, the company would still have to pay the $120,000 salary plus the additional costs of $44,800 for benefits and the legal assistant's salary, even if the attorney is working at less than full capacity.

LINK TO LEARNING

The iPhone is the ultimate example of outsourcing. Though created in the United States, it is produced all around the globe, with thousands of parts supplied by over 200 suppliers—none of which is Apple. Read this article from The New York Times on where parts for the iPhone are made (https://openstax.org/l/50iPhoneParts) to learn how an iPhone gets from the design phase in the United States to production of components around the world, to assembly in China, and then back to the United States for sale in a retail store.

10.4 Evaluate and Determine Whether to Keep or Discontinue a Segment or Product

Companies tend to divide their organization along product lines, geographic locations, or other management needs for decision-making and reporting. A **segment** is a portion of the business that management believes has sufficient similarities in product lines, geographic locations, or customers to warrant reporting that portion of the company as a distinct part of the entire company. For example, General Electric, Inc., has eight segments and the Walt Disney Company has four segments. Table 10.3 shows these segments.

Examples of Company Segments

General Electric Segments	Disney Segments
• Additive • Aviation • Capital • Digital • Healthcare • Lighting • Power • Renewable Energy • Transportation	• Media Networks • Parks, Experiences, and Consumer Products • Studio Entertainment • Direct to Consumer and International

Table 10.3 Examples of Company Segments[2]

As part of the normal operations of a business, managers make decisions such as whether to keep producing a product, whether to continue operating in certain areas, or whether to close entire segments of their operations. These are historically some of the most difficult decisions that managers make. Examples of these types of decisions include Macy's decision to close 100 stores in 2016 due to increased competition from online retailers such as Amazon.com[3] and Delta Airline's decision to eliminate 16 routes to save costs.[4] What information does management use in making these types of decisions?

As with other decisions, management must consider both the quantitative and qualitative aspects. In choosing between alternatives—that is, in choosing between keeping and eliminating the product, segment, or service—the relevant revenues and costs should be analyzed. Remember that relevant revenues and costs are those that differ between alternatives. Often, the keep-versus-eliminate decision arises because the product or segment appears to be generating less of a profit than in prior periods or is unprofitable. In these situations, the product or segment may produce a positive contribution margin but may appear to have a lower or negative profit because of the allocation of common fixed costs.

Fundamentals of the Decision to Keep or Discontinue a Segment or Product

Two basic approaches can be used to analyze data in this type of decision. One approach is to compare contribution margins and fixed costs. In this method, the contribution margins with and without the segment (or division or product line) are determined. The two contribution margins are compared and the alternative with the greatest contribution margin would be the chosen alternative because it provides the biggest contribution toward meeting fixed costs.

The second approach involves calculating the total net income for retaining the segment and comparing it to the total net income for dropping the segment. The company would then proceed with the alternative that has the highest net income. In order to perform these net income calculations, the company would need more information than they would need in order to follow the contribution margin approach, which does not

---

2   GE Businesses. n.d. https://www.ge.com/; Disney. "Our Businesses." n.d. https://www.thewaltdisneycompany.com/about/#our-businesses
3   Hayley Peterson. "Macy's May Shut Down Even More Stores." *Business Insider*. May 12, 2017. http://www.businessinsider.com/macys-might-shut-down-more-stores-2017-5
4   Jason Williams. "Delta Downsizing Flights to 14 More Cities." Cincinnati.com. Mar. 11, 2015. http://www.cincinnati.com/story/news/2015/03/10/delta-cincinnati-airline-cuts-kentucky/24701445/

consider the costs and revenues that are the same between the alternatives.

> ## THINK IT THROUGH
>
> ### Allocating Common Fixed Costs
>
> Acme, Co., has three retail divisions: Small, Medium, and Large. Sales, variable costs, and fixed costs for each of the divisions are:
>
> | | Sales | Variable Costs | Fixed Costs |
> |---|---|---|---|
> | Small | $ 5,000,000 | $ 2,875,000 | $2,450,000 |
> | Medium | 10,000,000 | 7,235,000 | 5,125,000 |
> | Large | 25,000,000 | 18,960,000 | 8,230,000 |
>
> Included in the fixed costs are $5,400,000 in allocated common costs, which are split evenly among the three divisions. Is an even split the best way to allocate those costs? Why or why not? What other ways might Acme consider using to allocate the common fixed costs?

Sample Data

Suppose SnowBucks, Inc., has three product lines: snow boots, snow sporting equipment, and a clothing line for winter sports. It has been brought to senior management's attention that the snow boot product line is unprofitable. Figure 10.4 shows the data presented to senior management:

	Snow Boots	Snow Sporting Equipment	Clothing Line	Total
Sales	$1,150,000	$1,540,000	$1,354,000	$4,044,000
Cost of goods sold				
Variable manufacturing expenses	423,000	507,000	378,000	1,308,000
Fixed manufacturing expenses	392,000	413,000	353,000	1,158,000
Gross margin	335,000	620,000	623,000	1,578,000
Selling and administrative expenses				
Variable selling and administrative expenses	195,000	130,000	147,000	472,000
Fixed selling and administrative expenses	216,000	216,000	216,000	648,000
Operating income	$ (76,000)	$ 274,000	$ 260,000	$ 458,000

Figure 10.4 Operating Income Report for SnowBucks, by Segment. (attribution: Copyright Rice University, OpenStax, under CC BY-NC-SA 4.0 license)

Upon initial review, it appears that the snow boot product line is unprofitable. Should this product line be eliminated? To adequately analyze this situation, a proper analysis of the relevant revenues and costs must be made. The functional income statement in Figure 10.4 does not separate relevant from non-relevant costs.

In conducting the analysis, the accounting team discovers that each product line is allocated certain costs over which the product line managers have no control. These **allocated costs** are typically associated with areas of the company that do not generate revenue but are necessary for the running of the organization, such as salaries for executives, human resources, and accounting at headquarters.

The cost of these parts of the organization must somehow be shared with the revenue-generating portions of the business. Companies often allocate these costs to other parts of the organization based on some formula, such as dividing the total costs by the number of divisions or segments, as percentage of total revenue, or as percentage of total square footage.

SnowBucks currently allocates these costs equally to the three product lines, and all the fixed selling and administrative expenses are considered allocated costs. In addition, the fixed manufacturing expenses represent factory rent, depreciation, and insurance, and all these costs will continue to exist regardless of whether the snow boot division continues. However, included in the fixed manufacturing expenses is the $75,000 salary of a sales supervisor for each division. This is an avoidable fixed cost as this cost would no longer exist if any division ceased operating.

Calculations Using Sample Data

Based on the new information, a new analysis using a product line margin indicates the following:

	Snow Boots	Snow Sporting Equipment	Clothing Line	Total
Sales	$1,150,000	$1,540,000	$1,354,000	$4,044,000
Variable expenses				
Variable manufacturing expenses	423,000	507,000	378,000	1,308,000
Variable selling and administrative expenses	195,000	130,000	147,000	472,000
Contribution margin	532,000	903,000	829,000	2,264,000
Direct fixed manufacturing expenses	75,000	75,000	75,000	225,000
Product margin	457,000	828,000	754,000	2,039,000
Allocated fixed expenses				
Fixed selling and administrative expenses				648,000
Fixed manufacturing expenses				933,000
Operating income				$ 458,000

Final Analysis of the Decision

This new analysis shows that when the relevant costs and revenues are considered, it is apparent the snow boot product line is contributing toward meeting the fixed costs of the organization and therefore to overall corporate profitability. The reason the snow boot product line was showing an operating loss was due to the allocation of common costs. Consideration should be given to the way allocated costs are assigned to the various products to determine if the allocation is logical or if another allocation method, such as one based on each product line's percentage of the total corporate sales, would provide a better matching of costs and services provided by corporate headquarters. Management should also consider qualitative factors, such as the impact of removing one product line on the overall sales of the other products. If customers commonly buy snow boots and skis together, then discontinuing the snow boot line could impact the sales of snow skis.

> **YOUR TURN**
>
> View Walt Disney Company's 2018 full year earnings report (https://openstax.org/l/50DisneyEarn) on their website. Scroll to the section on Segment Results and answer these questions:
>
> A. How many segments does Disney have?
> B. Which segment had the highest revenue in 2018?
> C. Which segment had the highest operating income in 2018?
> D. Which segment has shown the most revenue growth between 2017 and 2018?
> E. How many segments showed growth in operating income between 2017 and 2018 and how many segments showed a decline in operating income between 2017 and 2018?
> F. Which segment has shown the least operating income growth between 2017 and 2018?
>
> **Solution**
>
> A. Four: Media Networks, Parks & Resorts, Studio Entertainment, and Consumer Products & Interactive Media
> B. Media Networks
> C. Media Networks
> D. Studio Entertainment
> E. Two segments (Parks & Resorts and Studio Entertainment) showed operating income growth, while two segments (Media Networks and Consumer Products & Interactive Media) showed a decline in operating income between 2017 and 2018.
> F. Consumer Products & Interactive Media

10.5 Evaluate and Determine Whether to Sell or Process Further

One major decision a company has to make is to determine the point at which to sell their product—in other words, when it is no longer cost effective to continue processing the product before sale. For example, in refining oil, the refined oil can be sold at various stages of the refining process. The point at which some products are removed from production and sold while others receive additional processing is known as the **split-off point**. As you have learned, the relevant revenues and costs must be evaluated in order to make the best decision for the company.

In making the decision, a company must consider the **joint costs**, or those costs that have been shared by products up to the split-off point. In some manufacturing processes, several end products are produced from a single raw material input. For example, once milk has been processed it can be sold as milk or it can be processed further into cheese, yogurt, cream, or ice cream. The costs of processing the milk to the stage at which it can be sold or processed further are the joint costs. These costs are allocated among all the products that are sold at the split off point as well as those products that are processed further. Ice cream has the basic costs of the milk plus the costs of processing it further into ice cream.

As another example, suppose a company that makes leather jackets realizes it has a reasonable amount of unused leather from the cutting of the patterns for the jackets. Typically, this scrap leather is sold, but the company is beginning to consider using the scrap to make leather belts. How would the company allocate the costs incurred from processing and preparing the leather before cutting it if they decide to make both the jackets and the belts? Would it be financially beneficial to process the scrap leather further into belts?

Fundamentals of the Decision to Sell or Process Further

When facing the choice of selling or processing further, the company must determine the revenues that would be received if the product is sold at the split-off point versus the net revenues that would be received if the product is processed further. This requires knowing the additional costs of further processing. In general, if the differential revenue from further processing is greater than the differential costs, then it will be profitable to process a joint product after the split-off point. Any costs incurred prior to the split-off point are irrelevant to the decision to process further as those are sunk costs; only future costs are relevant costs.

Even though joint product costs are common costs, they are routinely allocated to the joint products. A potential reason for this treatment is the GAAP (generally accepted accounting principles) requirement that all production costs must be inventoried.

Be aware that some complexities can arise when allocating joint product costs. The first issue is that joint production costs can be allocated based on varying production and sales characteristics or assumptions. For example, a physical measurement method, a relative sales value method at the point of split-off, and a net realizable value method based on additional processing after the split-off point can all be used to allocate joint production costs.

A second complexity is that eliminating the production of one or more joint products will not always enable the company to reduce joint production costs. Because of the mechanics of the common cost allocation process, such an action will only work if reductions are made in all of the joint products collectively. If only some of the joint products are eliminated, the remaining joint product or products would absorb all of the joint product costs.

An example of this last issue might help clarify the point. Assume that you have a lumber production company that cuts trees, prepares board lumber for housing and furniture, and also prepares sawdust and wood scraps that is used in the production of particle board. Assume that in a given year the company experienced $1,100,000 in joint costs. Using one of the three previously mentioned cost allocation methods, the company allocated $1,000,000 in joint costs to the production of board lumber and $100,000 to the production of wood scraps and sawdust.

Assume that in the next year it also experienced $1,100,000 in joint costs. However, in that year, the company lost its buyer of wood scraps and sawdust, so it had to give both of them away, without generating any revenue. In this case, the company would still realize $1,100,000 in joint costs. However, the entire amount would be allocated to the production of the board lumber. The only way to reduce the joint costs is to realize joint costs of less than $1,000,000.

YOUR TURN

Luxury Leathers

Luxury Leathers, Inc., produces various leather accessories, such as belts and wallets. In the process of cutting out the leather pieces for each product, 400,000 pounds of scrap leather is produced. Luxury has been selling this leather scrap to Sammy's Scrap Procurement for $2.25 per pound. Luxury has an employee suggestion box and one of the suggestions was to use most of the scrap to make leather watch bands. The management of Luxury is interested in this idea as the machines necessary to produce the watch bands are the same as the ones used in making belts and would merely need reprogramming for the cutting and stitching processes on the watch bands. The process to attach the buckle would be the same for the watch bands as it was for the belts, thus this would require no additional worker training. Luxury would have additional costs for new packaging and for the supply and insertion of the pins that connect the band to the watch. The total variable cost to produce the watch band would be $2.85. Fixed costs would increase by $85,000 per year for the lease of the packaging equipment, and Luxury estimates it could produce and sell 100,000 watch bands per year. Finished watch bands could be sold for $15.00 each. Should Luxury continue to sell the scrap leather or should Luxury process the scrap into watch bands to sell?

Solution

	Sell at Split-Off	Process Further
Selling price per lb of scrap	$ 2.25	
Selling price per watch band		$ 15.00
Variable costs to sell	0	2.85
Contribution margin	2.25	12.15
Units sold	400,000*	100,000**
Total contribution margin	900,000	1,215,000
Additional fixed costs	0	85,000
Effect on operating income	$900,000	$1,130,000

*lbs of scrap
**watch bands

Luxury should process the leather scrap further into watch bands. Not only does the act of processing the scrap further result in an increase in operating income, it offers Luxury another product line that may draw customers to its other products.

Sample Data

Ainsley's Apples grows organic apples and sells them to national grocery chains, local grocers, and markets. Ainsley purchased a machine for $450,000 that sorts the apples by size. The largest apples are sold as loose apples to the various stores, the medium sized apples are bagged and sold to the grocers in their bagged state, and the smallest apples are sold to deep discounters or to a local manufacturing plant that processes the apples into applesauce. Ainsley is considering keeping the small apples and processing them into apple juice that would be sold under Ainsley's own label to local grocers. The small apples currently sell to the deep discounters and local manufacturers for $1.10 per dozen. The variable cost to prepare the small apples for sale, including transporting the apples, is $0.30 per dozen. Ainsley can sell each gallon of organic apple juice for $3.50 per gallon. It takes two dozen small apples to make one gallon of apple juice. The cost to produce the organic apple juice will be $0.60 variable cost per gallon plus $200,000 fixed costs for the one-year lease of the equipment needed to make and bottle the juice. Ainsley normally harvests and sells 2,400,000 small apples per year. Should Ainsley continue to sell the small apples to local grocers and the applesauce manufacturer or should Ainsley process the apples further into organic apple juice?

Calculations of Sample Data

In order to decide whether or not to process the small apples or to process them further into applesauce, Ainsley conducts an analysis of the relevant revenues and costs for the two alternatives: sell at split-off or process further into applesauce.

	Sell at Split-Off	Process Further
Selling price per dozen	$ 1.10	
Selling price per gallon		$ 3.50
Variable costs to sell	0.30	0.60
Contribution margin	0.80	2.90
Units sold	200,000*	100,000**
Total contribution margin	160,000	290,000
Additional fixed costs	0	200,000
Effect on operating income	$160,000	$ 90,000

*2,400,000 ÷ 12 = 200,000 dozen
**200,000 dozen ÷ 2 dozen per gallon = 100,000 gallons

Ainsley should continue to sell the apples at split-off rather than process them further, as selling them generates a $160,000 increase in operating income compared to only $90,000 if she processes the apples further.

Final Analysis of the Decision

When making the decision to sell or process further, the company also must consider that processing a product further may create a new successful market or it may undercut sales of already existing products. For example, a furniture manufacturer that sells unfinished furniture may lose sales of the unfinished pieces if it decides to stain some pieces and sell them as finished products.

THINK IT THROUGH

Disposing of Coffee Grounds

Return to Why It Matters in this chapter. With the knowledge you have gained thus far, answer these questions:

1. From your perspective, what are the alternatives for the used coffee grounds?
2. For the alternatives listed in question 1, what information do you need to evaluate between the alternatives?
3. What type of analysis would you do to choose between alternatives?
4. What qualitative factors might influence your decision regarding which alternative to select?
5. Do you think the quantitative and qualitative components both will lead you to the same decision? Why or why not?

10.6 Evaluate and Determine How to Make Decisions When Resources Are Constrained

Companies use various resources to be productive. These resources, which include time, labor, space, and machines, are limited, thus constraining the ability of a company to have unlimited productive capacity. For example, a retail store is constrained by the amount of floor space available to display its goods, while a law office may be constrained by the number of hours the paralegal team can feasibly work. These constraints require companies to make decisions on the best ways to allocate their resources in a way that maximizes the benefit to the firm. This situation is especially true when a company is operating at capacity or makes multiple products or provides multiple services.

The question as to which products and how many should be made is a common constraint problem. For example, consider a business that runs at capacity, making four products by running two eight-hour shifts per day, seven days a week for 50 weeks per year. This business is limited to 5,600 working hours per year (8 hr. shifts × 2 shifts × 7 days per week × 50 weeks) unless a third shift is added. Adding a third shift may be prohibitive for any number of reasons, including local ordinances that prevent operating twenty-four hours a day, Environmental Protection Agency constraints, or the down-time of the machines that is required several hours a day for maintenance and calibration. What is the best way for this company to use these work hours? Which products should it produce first and how many of each should it produce?

These types of situations constrain, or limit, management's ability to use their facilities and workforce. Having limited availability of a resource, such as time, labor, or machine hours means that item becomes a scarce resource. A **constraint** is a scarce resource that limits the output or productive capacity of the organization.

Ordinarily, there are very few actual constraints in any process. Sometimes, there is only one. However, the existence of a constraint can have a major effect on the productivity of an organization. This fact applies to all types of entities, such as production facilities or service providers. One way to view this issue is to consider the old cliché that *a chain is only as strong as its weakest link.* In the example, when trying to measure or estimate an organization's maximum efficiency, its results will often be reduced by the overall negative effects of the constraints. When the constraint slows production, it is called a **bottleneck**. Managers are often faced with the problem of deciding how to best use a scarce resource to prevent bottlenecks. Under the constraint of limited resources, how do managers make decisions when they are working within these conditions?

Fundamentals of How to Make Decisions When Resources are Constrained

As with other short-term decisions, a company must consider the relevant costs and revenues when making decisions when resources are constrained. Whether the organization facing a constraint is a merchandising, manufacturing, or service organization, the initial step in allocating scarce or constrained resources is to determine the **unit contribution margin**, which is the selling price per unit minus the variable cost per unit, for each product or service. The company should produce or provide the products or services that generate the highest contribution margin first, followed by those with the second highest, and so forth. The total contribution margin will be maximized by promoting those products or accepting those orders with the highest contribution margin in relation to the scarce resource. In other words, products or services should be ranked based on their **unit contribution margin per production restraint**, which is the unit contribution margin divided by the production restraint.

If constraints are not managed, a bottleneck usually results, meaning that production slows and a back-up occurs at stages prior to the bottleneck. For example, in producing boxes of cereal, if the cereal is produced at a rate of 1,000 ounces per minute but the bagging machines can only bag 800 ounces per minute, this will create a bottleneck. Similarly, if on a Saturday morning before a home football game, the local grocery store has ten checkout lines but only opens four of them, long lines will result from the constraint of too few checkout lanes available. Management must decide how many scarce resources (employees, in this example) to pull from stocking the shelves to running cash registers. It may be difficult to see how bottlenecks affect profitability, and they appear to be more of a timing or throughput issue. But bottlenecks can affect profitability in a number of ways. Bottlenecks at the grocery story can result in customers leaving to store shop elsewhere or can negatively affect the reputation of the store, which can impact future sales. In the cereal example, bottlenecks in the packaging area can slow the delivery of boxes of cereal to distributors and individual stores. Poor or inconsistent delivery may drive customers to purchase from other cereal manufacturers, which would have a definite impact on profitability.

A common problem relating to constraints occurs in multi-product production environments. Management will need to evaluate the constraints to determine the best mix of products that will minimize the effects of the constraints. In addition to making sure that the best product mix is chosen, managers should seek ways to increase the effective capacity of the constraint. Conceptually, there are two ways a company can do this: increase the rate of output at the bottleneck, or increase the time available at the bottleneck. Increasing the capacity of the constraint or bottleneck is also called *relaxing the constraint* or *elevating the constraint*. Some specific examples of ways to relax the constraint include:

- Keep the production facilities open longer hours. This may allow the work-flow through the bottleneck area to be slowed and thus prevent the bottleneck from occurring. However, this may require paying workers overtime pay.
- If working extra hours is not a viable option, then moving additional workers to the bottleneck area may be beneficial as long as the areas from which they were moved are adequately covered and additional problem areas do not result.
- Instead of using current workers, additional staff may be hired to smooth the work flow through the bottleneck area.
- Outsource some or all of the work in the area of the bottleneck. It may be cheaper and more cost effective to buy parts of components than to slow production due to the bottleneck.
- Redesign the production process to prevent the bottleneck by adding more resources to eliminate the bottleneck, reorganizing the process to distribute the bottleneck-causing activities to different parts of the production process, or managing processing times at other stages prior to the bottleneck to help prevent the bottleneck form occurring.
- Insuring a minimal number of defects and rework, since they typically slow the production process and thus add to the bottleneck.

Preventing and minimizing bottlenecks can have significant benefits to the bottom line of the company. The reduction of bottlenecks allows the company to move more products through the production phase and thus be ready to sell.

> ### ETHICAL CONSIDERATIONS
>
> **When to Include a Lifesaving Option: The Case of the Ford Pinto**
>
> The case of the fiery Ford Pinto demonstrates that more than cost and revenue should be considered when making an ethical business decision. In the early 1970s, the Ford Motor Company set out to build a Pinto for less than $2,000. Cars were much less expensive then, and Ford had to determine whether or not to include a component part that cost around $10. Given the high cost, Ford decided not to include the component, a rubber bladder for the gas tank. However, in rear-end collisions at over 21 miles per hour, the rubber bladder component functions to prevent the gas tank from flooding the interior of the car with gasoline and gas fumes. Because of the decision not to include the component, a number of Pintos involved in collisions exploded into flames, injuring and sometimes killing the occupants.
>
> Although Ford was aware of the defect, the company's cost/benefit analysis indicated it was less expensive to build Pintos without the rubber bladder, even when including expected reimbursement costs for anyone injured or killed. However, the decision to allow a defective product to be built in order to reduce overall costs caused a significant hit to Ford's reputation. Ultimately, the litigation costs for knowingly constructing a defective car were higher than the original cost of including the rubber bladder component. While Ford's decision seemed profitable in the short-term, their financial analysis could have been improved if it also took into account long-term impacts.

Sample Data

Wood World, Inc., produces wooden desks, chairs, and bookcases. These items are produced using the same machines, and there is a maximum of 80,000 machine-hours available during the year. The information about the production time and costs for these three items is:

	Desks	Chair	Bookcase
Hours to produce	1	0.50	0.25
Selling price	$350	$200	$175
Direct materials	$ 40	$ 30	$ 35
Direct labor	$ 70	$ 65	$ 50
Variable overhead	$ 55	$ 50	$ 45
Fixed overhead	$ 28	$ 32	$ 24

Wood World is limited in producing its products by the number of possible machine-hours. Orders have been received for 60,000 desks, 48,000 chairs, and 40,000 bookcases, which will require 94,000 machine-hours to produce. Since there are not enough machine-hours available to fill all of the orders, which orders should Wood World fill first?

Calculations Using Sample Data

To address this question, Wood World must find the contribution margin per machine-hour since machine-hours are the constraining factor for production.

	Desks	Chair	Bookcase
Selling price	$ 350	$ 200	$ 175
Direct materials	$ 40	$ 30	$ 35
Direct labor	$ 70	$ 65	$ 50
Variable overhead	$ 55	$ 50	$ 42
Contribution margin	$ 185	$ 55	$ 48
Hours to produce	1	0.50	0.25
Contribution margin per machine-hour	$ 185	$ 110	$ 192

Final Analysis of the Decisions

Wood World should fulfill the orders for bookcases first, desks second, and chairs last. The bookcases provide the highest contribution margin per machine-hour, followed by desks and then chairs. Maximizing the contribution margin per constraint, in this case per machine-hour, is the best way for Wood World to manage the constraint. How many of each item will be produced?

Available machine hours	80,000
Hours to fill bookcase orders (40,000 × 0.25)	10,000
Remaining hours	70,000
Hours to fill desk orders (60,000 × 1)	60,000
Remaining hours	10,000
Hours needed to produce chairs	÷ 0.50
Chair orders that would be filled	20,000

Therefore, based on contribution margin and the constraint of machine hours, Wood World should fill all 40,000 of the bookcase orders first, then fill the 60,000 desk orders and, and fill 20,000 of the chair orders last.

Are there any qualitative issues that Wood World should consider? One concern may be that customers who typically buy a desk and chair together may not be able to do so if the chair production is affected by a bottleneck. Another qualitative issue in keeping with the furniture example is that a company might find producing dining room tables to be significantly more profitable than matching chairs or matching cupboards. However, they will still be required to produce the less profitable chairs and cupboards, because many consumers will want to buy all three items as a set.

The benefits of effectively managing constraints can be enormous. Managers need to understand the positive impact effective management of constrained resources can have on the company's bottom line. The contribution margin per unit of the scarce resource can be used to assess the value of relaxing the constraint. When there is unsatisfied demand for a single product because of a constraint, the value of additional time on the constraint is simply the contribution margin per unit of the scarce resource for that product. When there are two or more products with unsatisfied demand, the value of additional time on the bottleneck would be the largest contribution margin per unit of the scarce resource for any product whose demand is unsatisfied. In many situations, when dealing with conflicting time constraints an evaluation of multiple bottlenecks might identify a viable solution. While many bottleneck issues and their solutions could be somewhat complex, others might be addressed more simply. For example, in some cases the problem might be solved by the addition of an additional work shift.

CONCEPTS IN PRACTICE

Distributing Caseloads at a Law Firm

As a new business school graduate, you landed you first job in the human resources department of large national law firm in New York City. Your position is providing you with many opportunities to learn about the company and the various tasks for which the human resources department is responsible. Your most recent assignment is to determine the best way to distribute caseloads to the junior level attorneys based on their areas of expertise and to assign paralegal hours to assist the junior level attorneys. What are the constraints with which you are dealing? What information do you need to properly complete this assignment? What type of analysis would be required to effectively allocate caseload hours?

Key Terms

allocated costs costs that are generated by non–revenue generating portions of the business, such as corporate headquarters, that are assigned based on some formula to the revenue generating portions of the business

avoidable cost cost that can be eliminated (in whole or in part) by choosing one alternative over another

bottleneck point at which a constraint slows production

constraint scarce resource that limits output or productive capacity of an organization

differential analysis type of analysis that considers only the differences between variables that are important to the analysis

differential cost difference between costs for alternatives

differential revenue difference between revenues for alternatives

irrelevant cost cost that has no effect on the decision being made because it is the same under either alternative

irrelevant revenue revenue that has no effect on the decision being made

joint costs costs that have been shared by products up to the split-off point

normal capacity company's maximum production level, without adding additional production resources, or within the company's relevant range

opportunity costs costs associated with not choosing the other alternative

outsourcing act of using another company to provide goods or services that your company requires

qualitative factor component of a decision-making process that cannot be measured numerically

quantitative factor component of a decision-making process that can be measured numerically

relevant cost cost that influences the decision being made

relevant range quantitative range of units that can be produced based on the company's current productive assets; for example, if a company has sufficient fixed assets to produce up to 10,000 units of product, the relevant range would be between 0 and 10,000 units

relevant revenue revenue that influences the decision being made

segment portion of the business that management believes has sufficient similarities in product lines, geographic locations, or customers to warrant reporting that portion of the company as a distinct part of the entire company

short-term decision analysis determining the appropriate elements of information necessary for making a decision that will impact the company in the short term, usually 12 months or fewer, and using that information in a proper analysis in order to reach an informed decision among alternatives

special order one-time order that does not typically affect current sales

split-off point point at which some products are removed from production and sold while others receive additional processing

sunk cost cost that cannot be avoided because it has already occurred

unavoidable cost cost that does not go away in the short-run by choosing one alternative over another

unit contribution margin selling price per unit minus variable cost per unit

unit contribution margin per production restraint unit contribution margin divided by the production restrain

Summary

10.1 Identify Relevant Information for Decision-Making

- Decision-making involves choosing between alternatives.
- A critical step in the decision-making process is identification of all the relevant information for each alternative. Relevant information is any information that would have an impact on the decision.
- Relevant information can come in the form of costs or revenues, or be nonfinancial in form. For information regarding costs, this means determining which costs are avoidable and which are unavoidable.

10.2 Evaluate and Determine Whether to Accept or Reject a Special Order
- Deciding to accept or reject a special order is a choice between alternatives.
- Accepting or rejecting a special order involves comparing the purchase price associated with the special order to the cost to produce the items.
- This decision is highly influenced by whether the firm being offered the special order is operating below or at capacity.
- Qualitative factors would include consequences such as potential loss of current customers or displacement of jobs.

10.3 Evaluate and Determine Whether to Make or Buy a Component
- Deciding to outsource a component of the operations or manufacturing of a business is a choice between alternatives.
- Choosing whether to make or to buy a product, or choosing to have services performed by an outside company, are outsourcing decisions.
- Outsourcing decisions involve comparing the cost to keep the product or service in-house to the cost of buying the product or service from an outside party.
- An important consideration in these types of decisions is unavoidable costs.

10.4 Evaluate and Determine Whether to Keep or Discontinue a Segment or Product
- Deciding to keep or discontinue a product line or a segment of a business is a choice between alternatives.
- The choice to keep or eliminate involves comparing the business's total operating income generated from keeping the product or segment and comparing this to the business's total operating income generated if the product or segment is eliminated.
- An important consideration in these types of decisions is allocated costs.

10.5 Evaluate and Determine Whether to Sell or Process Further
- Deciding to do more work on a product to develop it into a new product is a choice between alternatives.
- Choosing whether to sell a product as is or to process it further involves comparing the selling price without further processing (at split-off) to the net price (selling price less additional processing costs) that would be obtained if the product were processed further.
- An important consideration in these types of decisions is the realization that the costs incurred up to the split-off point are irrelevant to the decision.

10.6 Evaluate and Determine How to Make Decisions When Resources Are Constrained
- Deciding to how to use scare resources is a choice between alternatives.
- Scarce resources can include anything that limits productive capacity, such as machine-hours or labor hours.
- Choosing how to use the scarce resource involves determining the contribution margin for each product or service that uses the constrained resource. The products or services with the highest contribution margin have the largest impact on income.

- Choosing how to manage the scarce resource will help reduce bottlenecks.

Multiple Choice

1. LO 10.1 _____ are the costs associated with *not* choosing the other alternative.
   A. Sunk costs
   B. Opportunity costs
   C. Differential costs
   D. Avoidable costs

2. LO 10.1 Which type of incurred costs are *not* relevant in decision-making (i.e., they have no bearing on future events) and should be excluded in decision-making?
   A. avoidable costs
   B. unavoidable costs
   C. sunk costs
   D. differential costs

3. LO 10.1 The managerial decision-making process has which of the following as its third step?
   A. Review, analyze and evaluate the results of the decision.
   B. Decide, based upon the analysis, the best course of action.
   C. Identify alternative courses of action to achieve a goal or solve a problem.
   D. Perform a comprehensive differential (differential) analysis of potential solutions.

4. LO 10.1 Which of the following is *not* one of the five steps in decision-making process?
   A. identify alternatives
   B. review, analyze, and evaluate decision
   C. decide best action
   D. consult with CFO concerning variable costs

5. LO 10.2 Which of the following is sometimes referred to as the "Anti Chain Store Act"?
   A. Sarbanes-Oxley Act
   B. Robinson-Patman Act
   C. Wright-Patman Act
   D. Securities Act of 1939

6. LO 10.2 Jansen Crafters has the capacity to produce 50,000 oak shelves per year and is currently selling 44,000 shelves for $32 each. Cutrate Furniture approached Jansen about buying 1,200 shelves for bookcases it is building and is willing to pay $26 for each shelf. No packaging will be required for the bulk order. Jansen usually packages shelves for Home Depot at a price of $1.50 per shelf. The $1.50 per-shelf cost is included in the unit variable cost of $27, with annual fixed costs of $320,000. However, the $1.50 packaging cost will not apply in this case. The fixed costs will be unaffected by the special order and the company has the capacity to accept the order. Based on this information, what would be the profit if Jansen accepts the special order?
   A. Profits will decrease by $1,200.
   B. Profits will increase by $31,200.
   C. Profits will increase by $600.
   D. Profits will increase by $7,200.

7. LO 10.3 _____ is the act of using another company to provide goods or services that your company requires.
   A. Allocating
   B. Outsourcing
   C. Segmenting
   D. Leasing

8. LO 10.3 Which of the following is a disadvantage of outsourcing?
   A. freeing up capacity
   B. freeing up capital
   C. transferring production and technology risks
   D. limiting ability to upsize or downsize production

9. LO 10.3 Which of the following is *not* a qualitative decision that should be considered in an outsourcing decision?
   A. employee morale
   B. product quality
   C. company reputation
   D. relevant costs

10. LO 10.4 Which of the following is one of the two approaches used to analyze data in the decision to keep or discontinue a segment?
   A. comparing contribution margins and fixed costs
   B. comparing contribution margins and variable costs
   C. comparing gross margin and variable costs
   D. comparing total contribution margin under each alternative

11. LO 10.4 When should a segment be dropped?
   A. only when the decrease in total contribution margin is less than the decrease in fixed cost
   B. only when the decrease in total contribution margin is equal to fixed cost
   C. only when the increase in total contribution margin is more than the decrease in fixed cost
   D. only when the decrease in total contribution margin is less than the decrease in variable cost

12. LO 10.4 Youngstown Construction plans to discontinue its roofing segment. Last year, this segment generated a contribution margin of $65,000 and incurred $70,000 in fixed costs. Discontinuing the segment will allow the company to avoid half of the fixed costs. What effect is expected to occur to the company's overall profit?
   A. a decrease of $5,000
   B. a decrease of $30,000
   C. a decrease of $5,000
   D. an increase of $30,000

13. **LO 10.5** Mallory's Video Supply has changed its focus tremendously and as a result has dropped the selling price of DVD players from $45 to $38. Some units in the work-in-process inventory have costs of $30 per unit associated with them, but Mallory can only sell these units in their current state for $22 each. Otherwise, it will cost Mallory $11 per unit to rework these units so that they can be sold for $38 each. How much is the financial impact if the units are processed further?
   A. $5 per unit profit
   B. $16 per unit profit
   C. $3 per unit loss
   D. $12 per unit loss

14. **LO 10.6** A company produces two products, E and F, in batches of 100 units. The production and cost data are:

	Product E	Product F
Contribution margin per batch	$450	$340
Machine set-ups needed per batch	25	20

The company can only perform 12,000 set-ups each period yet there is unlimited demand for each product. What is the differential profit from producing product E instead of product F for the year?
   A. $216,000
   B. $204,000
   C. $12,000
   D. $54,000

15. **LO 10.6** When operating in a constrained environment, which products should be produced?
   A. products with the highest contribution margin per unit
   B. products with the highest contribution margin per unit of the constrained process
   C. products with the highest selling price
   D. products with the lowest allocated joint cost

Questions

1. **LO 10.1** Your roommate at school believes that all fixed costs are always avoidable. Do you agree? How would you explain your point of view to your roommate?

2. **LO 10.1** Explain how to differentiate short-term decisions from long-term decisions of a business and the changes in analyses that influence these decisions.

3. **LO** 10.1 Felipe's Restaurant and Pie Shop needs help defining the costs for his business. He also wants to know which costs are relevant or irrelevant to his decision. Identify each cost as relevant or irrelevant. Then identify the type of cost (sunk, fixed, variable, or opportunity).

Cost	Relevant or Irrelevant?	Sunk, Fixed, Variable, or Opportunity?
Rent		
Baker wages		
Felipe's culinary school tuition		
Berries for pies		
Painting dining area last year		
Felipe's decision not to attend graduate school		

4. **LO** 10.2 What factors must any company consider before accepting a special-order contract?

5. **LO** 10.2 What are some of the qualitative issues that a special order can create?

6. **LO** 10.3 In "The Trouble with Outsourcing," a Schumpeter column in *The Economist*, there is a statement of advice to companies, who outsource products or services: "they need to think harder about what is their core business, and what is peripheral."[5] What types of problems do you think they are talking about? In your answer, present at least five (5) problems that companies should consider when outsourcing products or services.

7. **LO** 10.3 Many outsourced jobs have resulted in "offshoring" jobs, rather than using domestic outsourcing. If a U.S. company wants to offshore a service like customer service, for example, what are some of their considerations? In your answer, address offshoring disadvantages as compared with domestic outsourcing.

8. **LO** 10.4 What type of qualitative issues should management consider if a quantitative analysis reveals that a segment should be dropped?

9. **LO** 10.4 In the decision by a grocery company that is trying to decide whether to keep or drop the bakery department in its grocery stores, what would the bakery manager's salary be in relationship to the decision if the manager will be laid off?

10. **LO** 10.5 What is of key importance for a company whose products can be processed further?

11. **LO** 10.5 What is a general rule to remember with respect to a sell-or-process-further environment, and what costs are irrelevant to the decision?

---

5 "The Trouble with Outsourcing." *The Economist*. July 30, 2011. https://www.economist.com/business/2011/07/30/the-trouble-with-outsourcing

Exercise Set A

EA1. **LO 10.1** Garrison Boutique, a small novelty store, just spent $4,000 on a new software program that will help in organizing its inventory. Due to the steep learning curve required to use the new software, Garrison must decide between hiring two part-time college students or one full-time employee. Each college student would work 20 hours per week, and would earn $15 per hour. The full-time employee would work 40 hours per week and would earn $15 per hour plus the equivalent of $2 per hour in benefits. Employees are given two polo shirts to wear as their uniform. The polo-shirts cost Garrison $10 each. What are the relevant costs, relevant revenues, sunk costs, and opportunity costs for Garrison?

EA2. **LO 10.1** Derek Dingler conducts corporate training seminars on managerial accounting techniques all around the country. An upcoming training seminar is to be held in Philadelphia. Just prior to that engagement, Derek will be in New York City. He plans to stay in Philadelphia the night of the seminar, as the next morning he plans to meet with clients about future training seminar possibilities. One travel option is to fly from New York to Philadelphia on the first flight on Friday morning, which will get him to Philadelphia two hours before the start of his seminar. The cost of that flight is $287. Uber fees for his time in Philadelphia will cost $68. His meal per diem is $40 for each full day and $25 for each half day. The hotel cost is $225 per night. His second option is the rent a car and drive the two hours to Philadelphia from New York City the afternoon before the seminar. The cost of the rental car including gas is $57 per day and the car will be needed for two full days. At the end of the meetings he will return to New York City. What are the relevant costs, relevant revenues, sunk costs, and opportunity costs that Derek Dingler has to consider in making the decision whether to fly or drive from New York City to Philadelphia?

EA3. **LO 10.1** Bridget Youhzi works for a large firm. Her alma mater has asked her to make a presentation to the upcoming accounting honor society's annual scholarship dinner. Her firm supports the presentation because it hopes to recruit more excellent employees like Bridget. The university is 196 miles from her office. In order to get to the dinner by 5:00 p.m., she will need to leave work at 1:00 pm. She can drive her personal car and be reimbursed $0.50 per mile. The dinner ends at 9:00 p.m. Company policy allows her to spend the night if the return trip is four hours or more. There is a student-run inn and conference center across the street from campus that charges $101 per night.

Instead of driving, she could catch a 3:00 p.m. flight that has a round-trip fare of $300. Flying would require her to rent a car for $39 per day and pay an airport parking fee of $25 for the day. The company pays a per diem of $35 for incidentals if the employee spends at least six hours out of town. (The per diem would be for one 24-hour period for either flying or driving.) As a manager, Bridget is responsible for recruiting within a budget and wants to determine which is more economical.

Use the information provided to answer these questions.

    A.   What is the total amount of expenses Bridget would include on her expense report if she drives?
    B.   What is the total amount of expenses she would include on her expense report if she flies?
    C.   What is the relevant cost of driving?
    D.   What is the relevant cost of flying?
    E.   What is the differential cost of flying over driving?
    F.   What other factors should Bridget consider in her decision between driving and flying?

EA4. **LO** 10.2 Zena Technology sells arc computer printers for $55 per unit. Unit product costs are:

Direct materials	$14
Direct labor	20
Manufacturing overhead	3
Total	$37

A special order to purchase 15,000 arc printers has recently been received from another company and Zena has idle capacity to fill the order. Zena will incur an additional $2 per printer for additional labor costs due to a slight modification the buyer wants made to the original product. One-third of the manufacturing overhead costs is fixed and will be incurred no matter how many units are produced. When negotiating the price, what is the minimum selling price that Zena should accept for this special order?

EA5. **LO** 10.2 Shelby Industries has a capacity to produce 45,000 oak shelves per year and is currently selling 40,000 shelves for $32 each. Martin Hardwoods has approached Shelby about buying 1,200 shelves for a new project and is willing to pay $26 each. The shelves can be packaged in bulk; this saves Shelby $1.50 per shelf compared to the normal packaging cost. Shelves have a unit variable cost of $27 with fixed costs of $350,000. Because the shelves don't require packaging, the unit variable costs for the special order will drop from $27 per shelf to $25.50 per shelf. Shelby has enough idle capacity to accept the contract. What is the minimum price per shelf that Shelby should accept for this special order?

EA6. **LO** 10.3 Reuben's Deli currently makes rolls for deli sandwiches it produces. It uses 30,000 rolls annually in the production of deli sandwiches. The costs to make the rolls are:

Materials	$0.24 per roll
Labor	0.40 per roll
Variable overhead	0.16 per roll
Fixed overhead	0.20 per roll

A potential supplier has offered to sell Reuben the rolls for $0.90 each. If the rolls are purchased, 30% of the fixed overhead could be avoided. If Reuben accepts the offer, what will the effect on profit be?

EA7. **LO** 10.3 Almond Treats manufactures various types of cereals that feature almonds. Acme Cereal Company has approached Almond Treats with a proposal to sell the company its top selling cereal at a price of $22,000 for 20,000 pounds. The costs shown are associated with production of 20,000 pounds of almond cereal:

Direct material	$13,000
Direct labor	5,000
Manufacturing overhead	7,000
Total	$25,000

The manufacturing overhead consists of $2,000 of variable costs with the balance being allocated to fixed costs. Should Almond Treats make or buy the almond cereal?

EA8. LO 10.4 Party Supply is trying to decide whether or not to continue its costume segment. The information shown is available for Party Supply's business segments. Assume that neither the Direct fixed costs nor the Allocated common fixed costs may be eliminated, but will be allocated to the two remaining segments.

	Costumes	Party Supplies	Floral Decorations
Sales	$160,000	$110,000	$210,000
Variable costs	84,000	50,000	120,000
Contribution margin	76,000	60,000	90,000
Direct fixed costs	50,000	20,000	25,000
Allocated common fixed costs	30,000	25,000	30,000
Net income	$ (4,000)	$ 15,000	$ 35,000

If costumes are dropped, what change will occur to profit?

EA9. LO 10.5 Underground Food Store has 4,000 pounds of raw beef nearing its expiration date. Each pound has a cost of $4.50. The beef could be sold "as is" for $3.00 per pound to the dog food processing plant, or roasted and sold in the deli. The cost of roasting the beef will be $2.80 per pound, and each pound could be sold for $6.50. What should be done with the beef, and why?

EA10. LO 10.5 Ralston Dairy gathered this data about the two products that it produces:

Product	Current Sales Value	Estimated Added Processing Costs	Sales Value If Processed Further
Frozen yogurt	$ 8,000	$2,000	$11,000
Ice cream	12,000	7,000	18,000

Which of the products should be processed further?

EA11. LO 10.6 Rough Stuff makes 2 products: khaki shorts and khaki pants for men. Each product passes through the cutting machine area, which is the chief constraint during production. Khaki shorts take 15 minutes on the cutting machine and have a contribution margin per pair of shorts of $16. Khaki pants take 24 minutes on the cutting machine and have a contribution margin per pair of pants of $32. If it is assumed that Rough Stuff has 4,800 hours available on the cutting machine to service a minimum demand for each product of 3,000 units, how much will profits increase if 100 more hours of machine time can be obtained?

EA12. LO 10.6 Rough Stuff makes 2 products: khaki shorts and khaki pants for men. Each product passes through the cutting machine area, which is the chief constraint during production. Khaki shorts take 15 minutes on the cutting machine and have a contribution margin per pair of shorts of $16. Khaki pants take 24 minutes on the cutting machine and have a contribution margin per pair of pants of $32. If it is assumed that Rough Stuff has 4,800 hours available on the cutting machine to service a minimum demand for each product of 3,000 units, how many of each product should be made?

Exercise Set B

EB1. LO 10.1 Ella Maksimov is CEO of her own marketing firm. The firm recently moved from a strip mall in the suburbs to an office space in a downtown building, in order to make the firm's employees more accessible to clients. Two new clients are interested in using Ella's advertising services but both clients are in the same line of business, meaning that Ella's company can represent only one of the clients. Pampered Pooches wants to hire Ella's firm for a one-year contract for web, newspaper, radio, and direct mail advertising. Pampered will pay $126,000 for these services. Ella estimates the cost of the services requested by Pampered Pooches to be $83,000. Delightful Dogs is interested in hiring Ella to produce mass mailings and web ads. Delightful will pay Ella $94,000 for these services and Ella estimates the cost of these services to be $47,000. Identify any relevant costs, relevant revenues, sunk costs, and opportunity costs that Ella Graham has to consider in making the decision whether to represent Pampered Pooches or Delightful Dogs.

EB2. LO 10.1 You are trying to decide whether to take a job after you graduate or go onto graduate school. Consider the following questions as you make your decision.
  A. Which of these costs, for the most part, would be relevant (R), and which would be irrelevant (IR)?
      - Cost of your undergraduate education
      - Salary with an undergraduate degree
      - Salary with both an undergraduate degree and a graduate degree
      - Rent
      - Car Insurance
      - Graduate school tuition and fees
      - Food costs
      - Moving expenses
  B. Which of these costs could have a differential amount that is relevant/irrelevant, depending upon the location and or policies of your new job?

EB3. LO 10.1 You are working for a large firm that has asked you to attend a career fair at a university that is 185 miles from your office. You need to be there at 9:00 a.m. on a Monday morning. You can drive your personal car and be reimbursed $0.55 per mile, but you would need to leave home at 5:30 a.m. to get to the event and set up on time. Company policy allows you to spend the night if you must leave town before 6:00 a.m. The hotel across the street from campus charges $85 per night. Instead of driving, you could catch a 7:00 a.m. flight with a round-trip fare of $260. Flying would require you to rent a car for $29 per day, and you would have an airport parking fee of $20 for the day. The company pays a per diem of $40 for incidentals if you spend at least 6 hours out of town. (The per diem would be for one 24-hour period for either flying or driving.) As a manager, you are responsible for recruiting within a budget and want to determine which is more economical.

Use the information provided to answer these questions.
  A. What is the total amount of expenses you would include on your expense report if you drive?
  B. What is the total amount of expenses you would include on your expense report if you fly?
  C. What is the relevant cost of driving?
  D. What is the relevant cost of flying?
  E. What is the differential cost of flying over driving?
  F. What other factors should you consider in your decision between driving and flying?

EB4. **LO** 10.2 Dimitri Designs has capacity to produce 30,000 desk chairs per year and is currently selling all 30,000 for $240 each. Country Enterprises has approached Dimitri to buy 800 chairs for $210 each. Dimitri's normal variable cost is $165 per chair, including $50 per unit in direct labor per chair. Dimitri can produce the special order on an overtime shift, which means that direct labor would be paid overtime at 150% of the normal pay rate. The annual fixed costs will be unaffected by the special order and the contract will not disrupt any of Dimitri's other operations. What will be the impact on profits of accepting the order?

EB5. **LO** 10.2 Aspen Enterprises makes award pins for various events. Budget information regarding the current period is:

Revenue (200,000 pins at $3.00)	$600,000
Direct materials	120,000
Direct labor	220,000
Variable manufacturing overhead	50,000
Fixed manufacturing overhead	70,000

A fraternity with which Aspen has a long relationship approached Aspen with a special order for 6,000 pins at a price of $2.75 per pin. Variable costs will be the same as the current production, and the special order will not impact the rest of the company's orders. However, Aspen is operating at capacity and will incur an additional $5,000 in fixed manufacturing overhead if the order is accepted. Based on this information, what is the differential income (loss) associated with accepting the special order?

EB6. **LO** 10.3 Country Diner currently makes cookies for its boxed lunches. It uses 40,000 cookies annually in the production of the boxed lunches. The costs to make the cookies are:

Materials	$0.30 per cookie
Labor	0.30 per cookie
Variable overhead	0.20 per cookie
Fixed overhead	0.10 per cookie

A potential supplier has offered to sell Country Diner the cookies for $0.85 each. If the cookies are purchased, 10% of the fixed overhead could be avoided. If Jason accepts the offer, what will the effect on profit be?

EB7. **LO** 10.3 Oat Treats manufactures various types of cereal bars featuring oats. Simmons Cereal Company has approached Oat Treats with a proposal to sell the company its top selling oat cereal bar at a price of $27,500 for 20,000 bars. The costs shown are associated with production of 20,000 oat bars currently.

Direct material	$14,000
Direct labor	6,000
Manufacturing overhead	8,000
Total	$28,000

The manufacturing overhead consists of $3,000 of variable costs with the balance being allocated to fixed costs. Should Oat Treats make or buy the oat bars?

EB8. LO 10.4 The Party Zone is trying to decide whether or not to continue its costume segment. The information shown is available for Party Supply's business segments. Assume that neither the Direct fixed costs nor the Allocated common fixed costs may be eliminated, but will be allocated to the two remaining segments.

	Costumes	Party Supplies	Floral Decorations
Sales	$160,000	$112,000	$215,000
Variable costs	94,000	52,000	125,000
Contribution margin	66,000	60,000	90,000
Direct fixed costs	50,000	22,000	28,000
Allocated common fixed costs	20,000	27,000	32,000
Net income	$ (4,000)	$ 11,000	$ 30,000

If costumes are dropped, what change will occur to profit?

EB9. LO 10.5 Beretti's Food Mart has 6,000 pounds of raw pork nearing its expiration date. Each pound has a cost of $5.50. The pork could be sold "as is" for $2.50 per pound to the dog food processing plant, or it could be made into custom Italian sausage and sold in the meat department. The cost of the sausage making is $3.00 per pound and each pound could be sold for $7.50. What should be done with the pork and why?

EB10. LO 10.5 Balcom Dairy gathered this data about the two products that it produces:

Product	Current Sales Value	Estimated Added Processing Costs	Sales Value If Processed Further
Cream	$ 9,000	$3,000	$14,000
Milk	14,000	9,000	20,000

Which of the products should be processed further?

EB11. LO 10.6 Power Corp. makes 2 products: blades for table saws and blades for handsaws. Each product passes through the sharpening machine area, which is the chief constraint during production. Handsaw blades take 15 minutes on the sharpening machine and have a contribution margin per blade of $15. Table saw blades take 20 minutes on the sharpening machine and have a contribution margin per blade of $35. If it is assumed that Power Corp. has 5,000 hours available on the sharpening machine to service a minimum demand for each product of 4,000 units, how much will profits increase if 200 more hours of machine time can be obtained?

EB12. LO 10.6 Power Corp. makes 2 products: blades for table saws and blades for handsaws. Each product passes through the sharpening machine area, which is the chief constraint during production. Handsaw blades take 15 minutes on the sharpening machine and have a contribution margin per blade of $15. Table saw blades take 20 minutes on the sharpening machine and have a contribution margin per blade of $35. If it is assumed that Power Corp. has 5,000 hours available on the sharpening machine to service a minimum demand for each product of 4,000 units, how many of each product should be made?

Problem Set A

PA1. LO 10.1 Artisan Metalworks has a bottleneck in their production that occurs within the engraving department. Jamal Moore, the COO, is considering hiring an extra worker, whose salary will be $55,000 per year, to solve the problem. With this extra worker, the company could produce and sell 3,000 more units per year. Currently, the selling price per unit is $25 and the cost per unit is $7.85. Using the information provided, calculate the annual financial impact of hiring the extra worker.

Direct materials	$3.50
Direct labor	1.10
Variable overhead	0.45
Fixed overhead (primarily depreciation of equipment)	2.80
Total	$7.85

PA2. LO 10.1 Syntech makes digital cameras for drones. Their basic digital camera uses $80 in variable costs and requires $1,500 per month in fixed costs. Syntech sells 100 cameras per month. If they process the camera further to enhance its functionality, it will require an additional $45 per unit of variable costs, plus an increase in fixed costs of $1,000 per month. The current price of the camera is $160. The marketing manager is positive that they can sell more and charge a higher price for the improved version. At what price level would the upgraded camera begin to improve operational earnings?

PA3. LO 10.2 Marcotti Cupcakes bakes and sells a basic cupcake for $1.25. The cost of producing 600,000 cupcakes in the prior year was:

Revenues	$750,000
Direct materials	330,000
Direct labor	66,000
Manufacturing overhead (fixed)	132,000
Manufacturing overhead (variable)	84,000

At the start of the current year, Marcotti received a special order for 15,000 cupcakes to be sold for $1.10 per cupcake. To complete the order, the company must incur an additional $700 in total fixed costs to lease a special machine that will stamp the cupcakes with the customer's logo. This order will not affect any of Marcotti's other operations and it has excess capacity to fulfill the contract. Should the company accept the special order? (Show your work.)

PA4. 10.2 Ken Owens Construction specializes in small additions and repairs. His normal charge is $400/day plus materials. Due to his physical condition, David, an elderly gentleman, needs a downstairs room converted to a bathroom. Ken has produced a bid for $5000 to complete the bathroom. He did not provide David with the details of the bid. However, they are shown here.

Ken's Bid Detail Dollars	
Direct material	$2200
Direct labor	1600
Variable overhead	200
Fixed overhead	600
Profit	400
	$5000

A. The town's social services has asked Ken if he could reduce his bid to $4000. Should Ken accept the counter offer?

	Current Bid	New Bid
Direct material	$2200	$2200
Direct labor	1600	1600
Variable overhead	200	200
Fixed overhead	600	
Profit	400	
	5000	4000

B. How much would his income be reduced?
C. If the town's social services guaranteed him another job next month at his normal price, could he accept this job at $4000?

PA5. LO 10.3 Boston Executive, Inc., produces executive limousines and currently manufactures the mini-bar inset at these costs:

	Cost per Unit
Variable costs:	
Direct material	$ 950
Direct labor	650
Variable overhead	300
Total variable costs	$1,900
Fixed costs:	
Depreciation of equipment	500
Depreciation of building	200
Supervisor salaries	300
Total fixed costs	1,000
Total cost	$2,900

The company received an offer from Elite Mini-Bars to produce the insets for $2,100 per unit and supply 1,000 mini-bars for the coming year's estimated production. If the company accepts this offer and shuts down production of this part of the business, production workers and supervisors will be reassigned to other areas. Assume that for the short-term decision-making process demonstrated in this problem, the company's total labor costs (direct labor and supervisor salaries) will remain the same if the bar inserts are purchased.

The specialized equipment cannot be used and has no market value. However, the space occupied by the mini-bar production can be used by a different production group that will lease it for $55,000 per year. Should the company make or buy the mini-bar insert?

PA6. LO 10.3 Gent Designs requires three units of part A for every unit of A1 that it produces. Currently, part A is made by Gent, with these per-unit costs in a month when 4,000 units were produced:

Direct materials	$4.00
Direct labor	1.50
Manufacturing overhead	1.30
Total	$6.80

Variable manufacturing overhead is applied at $1.00 per unit. The other $0.30 of overhead consists of allocated fixed costs. Gent will need 6,000 units of part A for the next year's production.

Cory Corporation has offered to supply 6,000 units of part A at a price of $7.00 per unit. If Gent accepts the offer, all of the variable costs and $1,200 of the fixed costs will be avoided. Should Gent Designs accept the offer from Cory Corporation?

PA7. LO 10.4 Trifecta Distributors has decided to discontinue manufacturing its X Plus model. Currently, the company has 4,600 partially completed X Plus models on hand. The government has put a recall on a particular part in the X Plus model, so each base model must now be reworked to accommodate the style of the new part. The company has spent $110 per unit to manufacture these X Plus models to their current state. Reworking each X Plus model will cost $20 for materials and $20 for direct labor. In addition, $7 of variable overhead and $32 of allocated fixed overhead (relating primarily to depreciation of plant and equipment) will be allocated per unit. If Trifecta completes the X Plus models, it can sell them for $160 per unit. On the other hand, another manufacturer is interested in purchasing the partially completed units for $104 each and converting them into Z Plus models. Prepare a differential analysis per unit to determine if Trifecta should complete the X Plus models or sell them in their current state.

PA8. LO 10.4 Extreme Sports sells logo sports merchandise. The company is contemplating whether or not to continue its custom embroidery service. All of the company's direct fixed costs can be avoided if a segment is dropped. This information is available for the segments.

	Custom Embroidery	Logo Apparel
Sales	$60,000	$250,000
Variable costs	30,000	110,000
Contribution margin	30,000	140,000
Direct fixed costs	22,000	40,000
Allocated common fixed costs	12,000	50,000
Net income	$(4,000)	$ 50,000

A. What will be the impact on net income if the embroidery segment is dropped?
B. Assume that if the embroidery segment is dropped, apparel sales will increase 10%. What is the impact on the contribution margin and net income solely for the apparel?
C. Identify one cost that is not relevant in this analysis.

PA9. LO 10.4 Hong Publishing has purchased Lang Publishing. After reviewing titles from both companies, a decision must be made to determine what titles must be dropped. The following information is available to make the decision.

	Title X	Title Y	Title Z
Sales	$100,000	$150,000	$200,000
Variable cost	50,000	75,000	100,000
Contribution margin	50,000	75,000	100,000
Direct fixed cost	20,000	30,000	40,000
Allocated common fixed cost	10,000	15,000	20,000
Net income	20,000	30,000	40,000

A. What is the total income if all titles were produced?
B. If Title X was dropped, what would be the effect on Net Income?
C. How much did Title X Contribute to Fixed Costs?
D. Determine the cost and the amount that will remain even if Title X is dropped?
E. Which costs and amount will be eliminated if Title X is dropped?

PA10. LO 10.5 Calcion Industries produces two joint products, Y and Z. Prior to the split-off point, the company incurred costs of $36,000. Product Y weighs 25 pounds and product Z weighs 75 pounds. Product Y sells for $150 per pound and product Z sells for $125 per pound. Based on a physical measure of output, allocate joint costs to products Y and Z.

PA11. LO 10.5 Quality Clothing, Inc., produces skorts and jumper uniforms for school children. In the process of cutting out the cloth pieces for each product, a certain amount of scrap cloth is produced. Quality has been selling this cloth scrap to Jorge's Scrap Warehouse for $3.25 per pound. Last year, the company sold 40,000 lb. of scrap, which would be enough to make 10,000 teddy bears that the management of Quality is now interested in producing. Their processes would need some reprogramming, particularly in the cutting and stitching processes, but it would require no additional worker training. However, new packaging would be needed. The total variable cost to produce the teddy bears $3.85. Fixed costs would increase by $95,000 per year for the lease of the packaging equipment and Quality estimates it could produce and sell 10,000 teddy bears per year. Finished teddy bears could be sold for $18.00 each. Should Quality continue to sell the scrap cloth or should Quality process the scrap into teddy bears to sell?

PA12. LO 10.6 At Gems in the Rough, a jewelry company, the engraving department is a bottleneck. The company is considering hiring an extra worker, whose salary will be $56,000 per year, to ease the problem. Using the extra worker, the company will be able to engrave 8,000 more units per year. The selling price per unit is $16. The cost per unit currently is $11.85 as shown:

Direct material	$ 4.50
Direct labor	2.10
Variable overhead	1.45
Fixed overhead (primarily depreciation of equipment)	3.80
Total	$11.85

What is the annual financial impact of hiring the extra worker for the bottleneck process?

PA13. LO 10.6 Sports Specialists makes baseballs and softballs in a three-step process. Unfortunately, the sewing machine process has been identified as a bottleneck. Each softball has a contribution margin of $6.00 and each baseball has a contribution margin of $2.00. The sewing machine can make 10 softballs or 25 baseballs in one hour.
  A. If demand for both products is unlimited and the sewing machine capacity cannot be expanded, which product should be produced?
  B. If demand for each ball is limited to 6,000 balls and there are 800 hours available on the machine, how many of each product should be produced?

Problem Set B

PB1. LO 10.1 Variety Artisans has a bottleneck in their production that occurs within the engraving department. Arjun Naipul, the COO, is considering hiring an extra worker, whose salary will be $45,000 per year, to solve the problem. With this extra worker, the company could produce and sell 3,500 more units per year. Currently, the selling price per unit is $18 and the cost per unit is $5.85. Using the information provided, calculate the annual financial impact of hiring the extra worker.

Direct materials	$2.50
Direct labor	1.10
Variable overhead	0.45
Fixed overhead (primarily depreciation of equipment)	1.80
Total	$5.85

PB2. LO 10.1 Mortech makes digital cameras for drones. Their basic digital camera uses $80 in variable costs and requires $1,500 per month in fixed costs. Mortech sells 200 cameras per month. If they process the camera further to enhance its functionality, it will require an additional $45 per unit of variable costs, plus an increase in fixed costs of $1,000 per month. The current price of the camera is $200. The marketing manager is positive that they can sell more and charge a higher price for the improved version. At what price level would the upgraded camera begin to improve operational earnings?

PB3. LO 10.2 Cinnamon Depot bakes and sells cinnamon rolls for $1.75 each. The cost of producing 500,000 rolls in the prior year was:

Revenues	$875,000
Direct materials	425,000
Direct labor	75,000
Manufacturing overhead (fixed)	125,000
Manufacturing overhead (variable)	90,000

At the start of the current year, Cinnamon Depot received a special order for 18,000 rolls to be sold for $1.50 per roll. The company estimates it will incur an additional $1,000 in total fixed costs in order to lease a special machine that forms the rolls in the shape of a heart per the customer's request. This order will not affect any of its other operations. Should the company accept the special order? (Show your work.)

PB4. LO 10.2 Myrna White is a mobile housekeeper. The price for a standard house cleaning is $150 and takes 5 hours. Each worker is paid $25/hour, uses $15 of materials and $0.50 per mile to use their own vehicle to travel from job to job. The average job is 5 miles. Arniz Meyroyan has a family reunion at her house and needs her house freshened up. She offers $75 for this emergency tidy-up service. This service includes vacuuming and cleaning floors, dusting, and cleaning the bathrooms. Only $5 of materials would be used.
  A. Prepare an Excel spread sheet to determine the differential income if the emergency tidy-up service is priced at $75. The tidy-up service will take 2 hours.
  B. If a $25 surcharge was included to make the price of $100 how would the differential income change?
  C. If the hourly worker rate increased to $30/hour, how would net income change?
  D. What other issue would you need to consider?

PB5. LO 10.2 Blake Cohen Painting Service specializes in small paint jobs. His normal charge is $350/day plus materials. Moesha needs her basement painted. Blake has produced a bid for $1500 to complete the basement painting. Blake completed a cost estimate for his service as shown.

Direct material	$200
Direct labor	700
Variable overhead	50
Fixed overhead	60
Profit	100
	$1,110

  A. Moesha mentions that she can't pay the $1500. She is a widow and you feel an obligation to take care of widows but can't lose money. How much would you charge and still be able to make a profit?
  B. Moesha has asked you to paint the rest of her house. Could you continue to give her the same deal?

PB6. LO 10.3 Regal Executive, Inc., produces executive motor coaches and currently manufactures the tent awnings that accompany them at these costs:

	Cost per Unit
Variable costs:	
Direct material	$1,250
Direct labor	750
Variable overhead	500
Total variable costs	$2,500
Fixed costs:	
Depreciation of equipment	500
Depreciation of building	400
Supervisor salaries	300
Total fixed costs	1,200
Total cost	$3,700

The company received an offer from Saied Tents to produce the awnings for $3,200 per unit and supply 1,000 awnings for the coming year's estimated production. If the company accepts this offer and shuts down production of this part of the business, production workers and supervisors will be reassigned to other areas. Assume that for the short-term decision-making process demonstrated in this problem, the company's total labor costs (direct labor and supervisor salaries) will remain the same if the bar inserts are purchased.

The specialized equipment cannot be used and has no market value. However, the space occupied by the awning production can be used by a different production group that will lease it for $60,000 per year. Should the company make or buy the awnings?

PB7. LO 10.3 Remarkable Enterprises requires four units of part A for every unit of A1 that it produces. Currently, part A is made by Remarkable, with these per-unit costs in a month when 4,000 units were produced:

Direct materials	$4.80
Direct labor	2.00
Manufacturing overhead	2.10
Total	$8.90

Variable manufacturing overhead is applied at $1.60 per unit. The other $0.50 of overhead consists of allocated fixed costs. Remarkable will need 8,000 units of part A for the next year's production.

Altoona Corporation has offered to supply 8,000 units of part A at a price of $8.00 per unit. If Remarkable accepts the offer, all of the variable costs and $2,000 of the fixed costs will be avoided. Should Remarkable accept the offer from Altoona Corporation?

PB8. LO 10.3 Colin O'Shea has a carpentry shop that employs 4 carpenters. Colin received an order for 1,000 coffee tables. The coffee tables have a round table top and four decorative legs. An offer for $500 per table was received. Colin found an unfinished round table top that he could buy for $50 each.
  A. Using this quantitative cost data to make the table top, should Colin buy the table top or make it?

Direct materials	$10
Direct labor	35
Variable overhead	10
Fixed overhead	7

  B. What qualitative factors would be included in your decision.

B. Can the vendor make it to the same quality standards? Can it be completed on time? Is there idle capacity in the factory that could be used?

PB9. LO 10.4 ZZOOM, Inc., has decided to discontinue manufacturing its Z Best model. Currently, the company has 4,600 partially completed Z Best models on hand. The government has put a recall on a particular part in the Z Best model, so each base model must now be reworked to accommodate the style of the new part. The company has spent $110 per unit to manufacture these Z Best models to their current state. Reworking each Z Best model will cost $22 for materials and $25 for direct labor. In addition, $9 of variable overhead and $34 of allocated fixed overhead (relating primarily to depreciation of plant and equipment) will be allocated per unit. If ZZOOM completes the Z Best models, it can sell them for $180 per unit. On the other hand, another manufacturer is interested in purchasing the partially completed units for $105 each and converting them into Z Plus models. Prepare a differential analysis per unit to determine if ZZOOM should complete the Z Best models or sell them in their current state.

PB10. LO 10.4 Cable paper company produces many colors of paper. The current popular color is grey. To increase the production of grey paper, a decision must be made to determine what color must be dropped. The following information is available to make the decision.

	Custom Embroidery	Logo Apparel
Sales	$60,000	$275,000
Variable costs	20,000	115,000
Contribution margin	40,000	160,000
Direct fixed costs	22,000	50,000
Allocated common fixed costs	22,000	50,000
Net income	$(4,000)	$ 60,000

  A. What is the total income if all colors were produced?
  B. If Peach was dropped, what would be the effect on Net Income?
  C. How much did Peach paper contribute to Fixed Costs?
  D. Determine the cost and the amount that will remain even if Peach is dropped?
  E. Which costs and amount will be eliminated if Peach is dropped?

PB11. LO 10.5 Strawberry Sweet Company makes a variety of jams and jellies. During June, 55,000 gallons of strawberry mash was processed at a joint cost of $40,000. This produced 42,000 gallons of preserve-grade mix and 4,000 gallons of strawberry juice for jelly. The juice could be processed further into energy drinks, and the preserve mix could be processed further into ice cream flavoring. Information on these items is shown:

Product	Sales Value at Split-Off Point	Estimated Further Processing Cost	Sales Value after Processing
Preserve mix	$104,500	$ 8,000	$125,000
Juice for jelly	50,500	40,000	70,000

A. Assume that the joint cost is allocated to the products based on the physical quantity of output of each product. How much joint cost should be assigned to each product?
B. How much joint cost should be assigned to each product if the relative sales value allocation method is used?
C. Which products should be processed further?

PB12. LO 10.5 Laramie Industries produces two joint products, H and C. Prior to the split-off point, the company incurred costs of $66,000. Product H weighs 44 pounds and product C weighs 66 pounds. Product H sells for $250 per pound and product C sells for $295 per pound.

Based on a physical measure of output, allocate joint costs to products H and C.

PB13. LO 10.5 Jamboree Outfitters, Inc., produces pocket knives and fillet knives for outdoor sporting. In the process of making the knives, some irregularities occur and no further work is performed on the blades. Jamboree has been selling these irregular blades to scrap dealers for $5.00 per pound. Last year, the company sold 50,000 lbs. of scrap. The company found that Amazon will buy the irregular knives for $12 each provided Jamboree finishes producing the knives into sellable form and also assuming there are enough irregular blades to make 50,000 completed knives. Jamboree's processes would not need reprogramming, particularly in the shaping and sharpening processes. However, this would require one additional worker, and new packaging would be needed. The total variable cost to produce the irregulars is $4.85. Fixed costs would increase by $175,000 per year for the lease of the packaging equipment and the new worker. Jamboree estimates it could produce and sell 50,000 knives per year. Should Jamboree continue to sell the scrap blades or should Jamboree process the irregulars to sell to Amazon?

PB14. LO 10.5 Daisy Hernandez sells girls christening dresses through the online store, Etsy. Her customers have asked if she has necklaces that could be included with the dress. Daisy found white glossy ceramic hearts from another Etsy vendor for $20. Daisy has the talent and already has a fully depreciated kiln to make these hearts.

A. Using the provided quantitative cost data to make the heart, should Daisy buy from her fellow Etsy vendor or make it herself?

Direct materials	$3
Direct labor	5
Variable overhead	2
Fixed overhead	7

B. What qualitative factors would be included in your decision.

PB15. LO 10.5 Dr. Detail is a mobile car wash. The price for a standard wash is $35 and takes half an hour. Each worker is paid $20/hr, uses $5 of materials and $0.50 per mile to use their own vehicle to travel from job to job. The average job is 5 miles.

Ernest Kuhn's son got sick in the car, and Ernest Kuhn has asked Dr. Detail to detail his car instead of doing a simple wash and vacuum.

A. Determine the differential income if $100 was charged to detail the car. Each car detail will take 2 hours. The materials used by the worker is three times that of a standard car wash.
B. If the price is raised to $150, what is the differential income change?
C. Keeping the price at $150, if the worker rate per hour would increase to $20/hr how would the differential income change? Prepare an Excel spreadsheet.
D. What other issues would you need to consider?

PB16. LO 10.6 At Stardust Gems, a faux gem and jewelry company, the setting department is a bottleneck. The company is considering hiring an extra worker, whose salary will be $67,000 per year, to ease the problem. Using the extra worker, the company will be able to produce and sell 9,000 more units per year. The selling price per unit is $20. The cost per unit currently is $15.85 as shown:

Direct material	$ 5.50
Direct labor	3.10
Variable overhead	2.45
Fixed overhead (primarily depreciation of equipment)	4.80
Total	$15.85

What is the annual financial impact of hiring the extra worker for the bottleneck process?

PB17. LO 10.6 Sports Buffs makes basketballs and footballs in a three-step process. Unfortunately, the stem insertion process has been identified as a bottleneck. Each basketball has a contribution margin of $15.00 and each football has a contribution margin of $4.00. The stem insertion equipment can make 10 basketballs or 30 footballs in one hour.

A. If demand for both products is unlimited and the stem insertion machine capacity cannot be expanded, which product should be produced?
B. If demand for each ball is limited to 9,000 balls and there are 4,000 hours available on the machine, how many of each product should be produced?

Thought Provokers

TP1. LO 10.2 Seda Sarkisian makes wedding cakes from her home. A customer has requested two duplicate wedding cakes: one for the wedding and one to be frozen for their anniversary. The couple has offered $400 for both cakes instead of $500 ($250 each). The cost information to make one cake is shown.

One Cake	
Direct materials	$ 50
Direct labor	100
Variable overhead	25
Fixed overhead	10

A. What is the cost for the first cake?
B. What cost would not be included in the second cake?
C. What is the cost of the second cake?
D. What would be the total cost of this order if the offer was accepted?
E. How much profit will Seda be recording for this special order?
F. If your company policy is to always have a 15% profit on all order, would you still accept this order?
G. If you would not accept the order, what price would you negotiate?

TP2. LO 10.3 You are a management accountant for Time Treasures Company, whose company has recently signed an outsourcing agreement with Spotless, Inc., a janitorial service company. Spotless will provide all of Time Treasures' janitorial services, including sweeping floors, hauling trash, washing windows, stocking restrooms, and performing minor repairs. Time Treasures will be billed at an hourly rate based on the type of service performed. The work of common laborers (sweeping, hauling trash) is to be billed at $8 per hour. More skilled (repairs) and more dangerous work (washing outside windows on the 23rd floor) are to be billed at $18 per hour. Supervisory time is to be billed at $20 per hour. Spotless will submit monthly invoices, which will show the number and types of hours for which Time Treasures is being charged. The outsourcing contract is simple and straightforward.

A. What are some of the internal control problems you foresee as a result of outsourcing the janitorial service with this contract?
B. Explain recommendations to control risk that would you suggest after reviewing the contract.

TP3. LO 10.5 Brindi's Babysitting Center currently rents a 1200 sq foot facility for her 20-child facility. Her business has gotten five stars on Yelp, which has prompted more applications. She has to make a decision between expanding her operations to an 1,800 sq foot facility or staying in the current facility. Shown is the cost data of the options:

	Expand	Stay
Children served	30	20
Annual rent	$1,500	$1,000
Utilities	$ 500	$ 300
Food and materials	$2,100	$1,400
Direct labor	$6,000	$4,000
Moving cost	$5,000	

What is the differential cost of the two alternatives: A) move to a larger facility or B) stay in current facility?

TP4. LO 10.6 Akimoto's Bicycle Co assembles three types of bicycles: Charger, Sublime, Kidde. Due to their residential location they operate with one 8 hour shift, 5 days per week, 50 weeks a year. Balancing the bikes is the bottleneck. The information about production time and costs for these three bicycles are:

	Charger	Sublime	Kidde
Hours to produce	2	1.75	0.5
Selling price	$600	$300	$200
Direct material	$100	$75	$50
Direct labor	$150	$100	$75
Variable overhead	$50	$25	$25
Fixed overhead	$25	$25	$20

A. How many of each bicycle should be produced to maximize profits?
B. What qualitative factors would you need to consider?

11 Capital Budgeting Decisions

Figure 11.1 Milling Manufacturing. Long-term project investment requires careful capital budgeting analysis. (credit: modification of "Parts for CNC Machine" by Andy Malmin/Flickr, CC BY 2.0)

Chapter Outline

LO 11.1 Describe Capital Investment Decisions and How They Are Applied

LO 11.2 Evaluate the Payback and Accounting Rate of Return in Capital Investment Decisions

LO 11.3 Explain the Time Value of Money and Calculate Present and Future Values of Lump Sums and Annuities

LO 11.4 Use Discounted Cash Flow Models to Make Capital Investment Decisions

LO 11.5 Compare and Contrast Non-Time Value-Based Methods and Time Value-Based Methods in Capital Investment Decisions

Why It Matters

Jerry Price owns Milling Manufacturing, a production facility geared toward entrepreneurial product development. Initially, Jerry purchased several milling machines, but after seven years, the machines have become obsolete due to technological advances. Jerry must purchase new machines to continue business growth, and there are several options available. How does he choose the best machines for his business? What factors must he consider before purchase?

Jerry must consider several important factors—both financial and non-financial—as he makes this decision. First, he needs to consider the commitment of his initial capital investment. He also needs to compare differences between options such as warranties, the production capacities of different machines, and maintenance and repair costs. Another factor is the useful life of the new equipment—in other words, both its physical and the technological life. He will also consider how long it will take to recoup the cost of the investment, the impact on cash flow, and how the passage of time affects the value of the asset to the organization—it's monetary value that considered depreciation to determine what the asset is actually worth to the organization in terms of dollars (i.e., "what could we sell it for?"). Jerry will consider the value of the dollar invested today in purchasing the machine as opposed to the value of the dollar in the future that might be better spent on another project. This last factor is significant because the new equipment will probably provide part of his down payment on future replacement equipment. There are also nonfinancial factors to consider, such as changes to customer satisfaction and employee morale.

Jerry knows this equipment choice goes well beyond color or price preferences. The decision has a long-lasting influence on company direction and opportunity, and he needs to utilize capital budgeting analysis to help him make this decision.

11.1 Describe Capital Investment Decisions and How They Are Applied

Assume that you own a small printing store that provides custom printing applications for general business use. Your printers are used daily, which is good for business but results in heavy wear on each printer. After some time, and after a few too many repairs, you consider whether it is best to continue to use the printers you have or to invest some of your money in a new set of printers. A capital investment decision like this one is not an easy one to make, but it is a common occurrence faced by companies every day. Companies will use a step-by-step process to determine their capital needs, assess their ability to invest in a capital project, and decide which capital expenditures are the best use of their resources.

Fundamentals of Capital Investment Decisions

Capital investment (sometimes also referred to as capital budgeting) is a company's contribution of funds toward the acquisition of long-lived (long-term or capital) assets for further growth. Long-term assets can include investments such as the purchase of new equipment, the replacement of old machinery, the expansion of operations into new facilities, or even the expansion into new products or markets. These capital expenditures are different from operating expenses. An **operating expense** is a regularly-occurring expense used to maintain the current operations of the company, but a capital expenditure is one used to grow the business and produce a future economic benefit.

Capital investment decisions occur on a frequent basis, and it is important for a company to determine its project needs to establish a path for business development. This decision is not as obvious or as simple as it may seem. There is a lot at stake with a large outlay of capital, and the long-term financial impact may be unknown due to the capital outlay decreasing or increasing over time. To help reduce the risk involved in capital investment, a process is required to thoughtfully select the best opportunity for the company.

The process for capital decision-making involves several steps:

1. Determine capital needs for both new and existing projects.
2. Identify and establish resource limitations.
3. Establish baseline criteria for alternatives.
4. Evaluate alternatives using screening and preference decisions.
5. Make the decision.

The company must first determine its needs by deciding what capital improvements require immediate attention. For example, the company may determine that certain machinery requires replacement before any new buildings are acquired for expansion. Or, the company may determine that the new machinery and building expansion both require immediate attention. This latter situation would require a company to consider how to choose which investment to pursue first, or whether to pursue both capital investments concurrently.

> ## CONCEPTS IN PRACTICE
>
> ### Brexit
>
> The decision to invest money in capital expenditures may not only be impacted by internal company objectives, but also by external factors. In 2016, Great Britain voted to leave the European Union (EU) (termed "Brexit"), which separates their trade interests and single-market economy from other participating European nations. This has led to uncertainty for United Kingdom (UK) businesses.
>
> Because of this instability, capital spending slowed or remained stagnant immediately following the Brexit vote and has not yet recovered growth momentum.[1] The largest decrease in capital spending has occurred in the expansions of businesses into new markets. The UK is expected to separate from the EU in 2019.

The second step, exploring resource limitations, evaluates the company's ability to invest in capital expenditures given the availability of funds and time. Sometimes a company may have enough resources to cover capital investments in many projects. Many times, however, they only have enough resources to invest in a limited number of opportunities. If this is the situation, the company must evaluate both the time and money needed to acquire each asset. Time allocation considerations can include employee commitments and project set-up requirements. Fund limitations may result from a lack of capital fundraising, tied-up capital in non-liquid assets, or extensive up-front acquisition costs that extend beyond investment means (Table 11.1). Once the ability to invest has been established, the company needs to establish baseline criteria for alternatives.

Resource Limitations

Time Considerations	Money Considerations
• Employee commitments • Project set-up • Time-frame necessary to secure financing	• Lack of liquidity • Tied up in non-liquid assets • Up-front acquisition costs

Table 11.1 When resources are limited, capital budgeting procedures are needed.

Alternatives are the options available for investment. For example, if a company needs to purchase new printing equipment, all possible printing equipment options are considered alternatives. Since there are so many alternative possibilities, a company will need to establish baseline criteria for the investment. Baseline criteria are measurement methods that can help differentiate among alternatives. Common measurement methods include the payback method, accounting rate of return, net present value, or internal rate of return.

---

1   G. Jackson "UK Business Investment Stalls in Year since Brexit Vote." *The Financial Times*. August 24, 2017. https://www.ft.com/content/daff3ffe-88ac-11e7-8bb1-5ba57d47eff7

These methods have varying degrees of complexity and will be discussed in greater detail in Evaluate the Payback and Accounting Rate of Return in Capital Investment Decisions and Explain the Time Value of Money and Calculate Present and Future Values of Lump Sums and Annuities

To evaluate alternatives, businesses will use the measurement methods to compare outcomes. The outcomes will not only be compared against other alternatives, but also against a predetermined rate of return on the investment (or minimum expectation) established for each project consideration. The rate of return concept is discussed in more detail in Balanced Scorecard and Other Performance Measures. A company may use experience or industry standards to predetermine factors used to evaluate alternatives. Alternatives will first be evaluated against the predetermined criteria for that investment opportunity, in a screening decision. The **screening decision** allows companies to remove alternatives that would be less desirable to pursue given their inability to meet basic standards. For example, if there were three different printing equipment options and a minimum return had been established, any printers that did not meet that minimum return requirement would be removed from consideration.

If one or more of the alternatives meets or exceeds the minimum expectations, a preference decision is considered. A **preference decision** compares potential projects that meet screening decision criteria and will rank the alternatives in order of importance, feasibility, or desirability to differentiate among alternatives. Once the company determines the rank order, it is able to make a decision on the best avenue to pursue (Figure 11.2). When making the final decision, all financial and non-financial factors are deliberated.

Figure 11.2 Select Between Alternatives. Screening and preference decisions can narrow alternatives in making a selection. (attribution: Copyright Rice University, OpenStax, under CC BY-NC-SA 4.0 license)

ETHICAL CONSIDERATIONS

Volkswagen Diesel Emissions Scandal

Sometimes a company makes capital decisions due to outside pressures or unforeseen circumstances. The *New York Times* reported in 2015 that the car company Volkswagen was "scarred by an emissions-cheating scandal," and "would need to cut its budget next year for new technology and research—a reversal after years of increased spending aimed at becoming the world's biggest carmaker."[2] This was a huge setback for Volkswagen, not only because the company had budgeted and planned to become the largest car company in the world, but also because the scandal damaged its reputation and set it back financially.

> Volkswagen "set aside about 9 billion euros ($9.6 billion) to cover costs related to making the cars compliant with pollution regulations;" however, the sums were "unlikely to cover the costs of potential legal judgments or other fines."[3] All of the costs related to the company's unethical actions needed to be included in the capital budget, as company resources were limited. Volkswagen used capital budgeting procedures to allocate funds for buying back the improperly manufactured cars and paying any legal claims or penalties. Other companies might take other approaches, but an unethical action that results in lawsuits and fines often requires an adjustment to the capital decision-making process.

Let's broadly consider what the five-step process for capital decision-making looks like for Melanie's Sewing Studio. Melanie owns a sewing studio that produces fabric patterns for wholesale.

1. Determine capital needs for both new and existing projects.
   Upon review of her future needs, Melanie determines that her five-year-old commercial sewing machine could be replaced. The old machine is still working, but production has slowed in recent months with an increase in repair needs and replacement parts. Melanie expects a new sewing machine to make her production process more efficient, which could also increase her current business volume. She decides to explore the possibility of purchasing a new sewing machine.
2. Identify and establish resource limitations.
   Melanie must consider if she has enough time and money to invest in a new sewing machine. The Sewing Studio has been in business for three years and has shown steady financial growth year over year. Melanie expects to make enough profit to afford a capital investment of $50,000. If she does purchase a new sewing machine, she will have to train her staff on how to use the machine and will have to cease production while the new machine is installed. She anticipates a loss of $20,000 for training and production time. The estimation of the $20,000 loss is based on the downtime in production for both labor and product output.
3. Establish baseline criteria for alternatives.
   Melanie is considering two different sewing machines for purchase. Before she evaluates which option is a better investment, she must establish minimum requirements for the investment. She determines that the new machine must return her initial investment back to her in three years at a rate of 20%, and the initial investment cost cannot exceed her future earnings. This established a baseline for what she considers reasonable for this type of investment, and she will not consider any investment alternative that does not meet these minimum criteria.
4. Evaluate alternatives using screening and preference decisions.
   Now that she has established minimum requirements for the new machine, she can evaluate each of these machines to see if they meet or exceed her criteria. The first sewing machine costs $45,000. She is expected to recoup her initial investment in two-and-a-half years. The return rate is 25%, and her future earnings would exceed the initial cost of the machine.
   The second machine will cost $55,000. She expects to recoup her initial investment in three years. The return rate is $18%, and her future earnings would be less than the initial cost of the machine.
5. Make the decision.

---

2   Jack Ewing and Jad Mouawad. "VW Cuts Its R&D Budget in Face of Costly Emissions Scandal." *New York Times*. November 20, 2015. https://www.nytimes.com/2015/11/21/business/international/volkswagen-emissions-scandal.html
3   Jack Ewing and Jad Mouawad. "VW Cuts Its R&D Budget in Face of Costly Emissions Scandal." *New York Times*. November 20, 2015. https://www.nytimes.com/2015/11/21/business/international/volkswagen-emissions-scandal.html

Melanie will now decide which sewing machine to invest in. The first machine meets or exceeds her established minimum requirements in cost, payback, return rate, and future earnings compared to the initial investment. For the second machine, the $55,000 cost exceeds the cash available for investment. In addition, the second machine does not meet the return rate of 20% and the anticipated future earnings does not compare well to the value of the initial investment. Based on this information, Melanie would choose to purchase the first sewing machine.

These steps make it seem as if narrowing down the alternatives and making a selection is a simple process. However, a company needs to use analysis techniques, including the payback method and the accounting rate of return method, as well as other, more sophisticated and complex techniques, to help them make screening and preference decisions. These techniques can assist management in making a final investment decision that is best for the company. We begin learning about these various screening and preference decisions in Evaluate the Payback and Accounting Rate of Return in Capital

LINK TO LEARNING

More and more companies are using capital expenditure software in budgeting analysis management. One company using this software is Solarcentury, a United Kingdom-based solar company. Read this case study on Solarcentury's advantages to capital budgeting resulting from this software investment (https://openstax.org/l/50Solarcentury) to learn more.

11.2 Evaluate the Payback and Accounting Rate of Return in Capital Investment Decisions

Many companies are presented with investment opportunities continuously and must sift through both viable and nonviable options to identify the best possible expenditure for business growth. The process to select the best option requires careful budgeting and analysis. In conducting their analysis, a company may use various evaluation methods with differing inputs and analysis features. These methods are often broken into two broad categories: (1) those that consider the time value of money, or the fact that a dollar today differs from a dollar in the future due to inflation and the ability to invest today's money for future growth, and (2) those analysis methods that do not consider the time value of money. We will examine the non-time value methods first.

Non-Time Value Methods

Non-time value methods do not compare the value of a dollar today to the value of a dollar in the future and are often used as screening tools. Two non-time value evaluative methods are the payback method and the accounting rate of return.

Fundamentals of the Payback Method

The **payback method (PM)** computes the length of time it takes a company to recover their initial investment.

In other words, it calculates how long it will take until either the amount earned or the costs saved are equal to or greater than the costs of the project. This can be useful when a company is focused solely on retrieving their funds from a project investment as quickly as possible.

Businesses do not want their money tied up in capital assets that have limited liquidity. The longer money is unavailable, the less ability the company has to use these funds for other growth purposes. This extended length of time is also a concern because it produces a riskier opportunity. Therefore, a company would like to get their money returned to them as quickly as possible. One way to focus on this is to consider the payback period when making a capital budget decision. The payback method is limited in that it only considers the time frame to recoup an investment based on expected annual cash flows, and it doesn't consider the effects of the time value of money.

The payback period is calculated when there are even or uneven annual cash flows. **Cash flow** is money coming into or out of the company as a result of a business activity. A **cash inflow** can be money received or cost savings from a capital investment. A **cash outflow** can be money paid or increased cost expenditures from capital investment. Cash flow will estimate the ability of the company to pay long-term debt, its liquidity, and its ability to grow. Cash flows appear on the statement of cash flows. Cash flows are different than net income. Net income will represent all company activities affecting revenues and expenses regardless of the occurrence of a cash transaction and will appear on the income statement.

A company will estimate the future cash inflows and outflows to be generated by the capital investment. It's important to remember that the cash inflows can be caused by an increase in cash receipts or by a reduction in cash expenditures. For example, if a new piece of equipment would reduce the production costs for a company from $120,000 a year to $80,000 a year, we would consider this is a $40,000 cash inflow. While the company does not actually receive the $40,000 in cash, it does save $40,000 in operating costs giving it a positive cash inflow of $40,000.

Cash flow can also be generated through increased production volume. For example, a company purchases a new building costing $100,000 that will allow them to house more space for production. This new space allows them to produce more product to sell, which increases cash sales by $300,000. The $300,000 is a new cash inflow.

The difference between cash inflows and cash outflows is the net cash inflow or outflow, depending on which cash flow is larger.

$$\text{Net annual cash flows = Cash Inflows – Cash Outflows}$$

Annual net cash flows are then related to the initial investment to determine a payback period in years. When the expected net annual cash flow is an even amount each period, payback can be computed as follows:

$$\text{Payback Period} = \frac{\text{Initial Investment}}{\text{Net Annual Cash Flow}}$$

The result is the number of years it will take to recover the cash made in the original investment. For example, a printing company is considering a printer with an initial investment cost of $150,000. They expect an annual net cash flow of $20,000. The payback period is

$$\text{Payback Period} = \frac{\$150{,}000}{\$20{,}000} = 7.5 \text{ years}$$

The initial investment cost of $150,000 is divided by the annual cash flow of $20,000 to compute an expected payback period of 7.5 years. Depending on the company's payback period requirements for this type of investment, they may pass this option through the screening process to be considered in a preference decision. For example, the company might require a payback period of 5 years. Since 7.5 years is greater than 5 years, the company would probably not consider moving this alternative to a preference decision. If the company required a payback period of 9 years, the company would consider moving this alternative to a preference decision, since the number of years is less than the requirement.

When net annual cash flows are uneven over the years, as opposed to even as in the previous example, the company requires a more detailed calculation to determine payback. Uneven cash flows occur when different amounts are returned each year. In the previous printing company example, the initial investment cost was $150,000 and even cash flows were $20,000 per year. However, in most examples, organizations experience uneven cash flows in a multiple-year ownership period. For example, an uneven cash flow distribution might be a return of $10,000 in year one, $20,000 in years two and three, $15,000 in years four and five, and $20,000 in year six and beyond.

Year	Yearly Cash Flow	Outflow or Inflow	Remaining to Recoup	Number of Years	Cumulative Number of Years for Repayment
0	$150,000	Outflow	$150,000		
1	10,000	Inflow	140,000	1	1
2	20,000	Inflow	120,000	1	2
3	20,000	Inflow	100,000	1	3
4	15,000	Inflow	85,000	1	4
5	15,000	Inflow	70,000	1	5
6	20,000	Inflow	50,000	1	6
7	20,000	Inflow	30,000	1	7
8	20,000	Inflow	10,000	1	8
9	20,000	Inflow	$\left(\frac{10,000}{20,000}\right)$	0.5	8.5

In this case, then, the payback period is 8.5 years.

In a second example of the payback period for uneven cash flows, consider a company that will need to determine the net cash flow for each period and figure out the point at which cash flows equal or exceed the initial investment. This could arise in the middle of a year, prompting a calculation to determine the partial year payback.

$$\text{Partial Year Payback} = \frac{\text{Initial Investment Outstanding}}{\text{Net cash flow for current period}}$$

The company would add the partial year payback to the prior years' payback to get the payback period for uneven cash flows. For example, a company may make an initial investment of $40,000 and receive net cash flows of $10,000 in years one and two, $5,000 in year three and four, and $7,500 for years five and beyond.

Year	Cash Flow	Outflow or Inflow	Remaining to Recoup	Number of years
0	(40,000.00)	Outflow	40,000.00	
1	10000	Inflow	30,000.00	1
2	10000	Inflow	20,000.00	1
3	5000	Inflow	15,000.00	1
4	5000	Inflow	10,000.00	1
5	7500	Inflow	2,500.00	1
6	7500	Inflow	(5,000.00)	0.33
				5.33

Figure 11.3 Cash Flow. (attribution: Copyright Rice University, OpenStax, under CC BY-NC-SA 4.0 license)

We know that somewhere between years 5 and 6, the company recovers the money. In years one and two they recovered a total of $20,000 (10,000 + 10,000), in years three and four they recovered and additional $10,000 (5,000 + 5,000), and in year five they recovered $7,500, for a total through year five of $37,500. This left an outstanding balance after year five of $2,500 (40,000 – 37,500) to fully recover the costs of the investment. In year six, they had a cash flow of $7,500. This is more than they needed to recoup their initial investment. To get a more specific calculation, we need to compute the partial year's payback.

$$\text{Partial Year Payback} = \frac{\$2,500}{\$7,500} = 0.33 \text{ years (rounded)}$$

Therefore, the total payback period is 5.33 years (5 years + 0.33 years).

Demonstration of the Payback Method

For illustration, consider Baby Goods Manufacturing (BGM), a large manufacturing company specializing in the production of various baby products sold to retailers. BGM is considering investment in a new metal press machine. The payback period is calculated as follows:

$$\text{Payback Period} = \frac{\$50,000}{\$15,000} = 3.33 \text{ years}$$

We divide the initial investment of $50,000 by the annual inflow of $15,000 to arrive at a payback period of 3.33 years. Assume that BGM will not allow a payback period of more than 7 years for this type of investment. Since this computed payback period meets their initial screening requirement, they can pass this investment opportunity on to a preference decision level. If BGM had an expected or maximum allowable payback period of 2 years, the same investment would not have passed their screening requirement and would be dropped from consideration.

To illustrate the concept of uneven cash flows, let's assume BGM shows the following expected net cash flows instead. Recall that that the initial investment in the metal press machine is $50,000.

Year	Net Cash Flow	Outstanding Initial Investment	Calculations
0	($50,000)	($50,000)	Initial Investment
1	$10,000	$(40,000)	50,000 – 10,000
2	5,000	(35,000)	40,000 – 5,000
3	7,000	(28,000)	35,000 – 7,000
4	3,000	(25,000)	28,000 – 3,000
5	10,000	(15,000)	25,000 – 10,000
6	10,000	(5,000)	15,000 – 5,000
7	10,000	5,000	10,000 – 5,000

Between years 6 and 7, the initial investment outstanding balance is recovered. To determine the more specific payback period, we calculate the partial year payback.

$$\text{Payback Period} = \frac{\$5,000}{\$10,000} = 0.5 \text{ years}$$

The total payback period is 6.5 years (6 years + 0.5 years).

THINK IT THROUGH

Capital Investment

You are the accountant at a large firm looking to make a capital investment in a future project. Your company is considering two project investments. Project A's payback period is 3 years, and Project B's payback period is 5.5 years.

Your company requires a payback period of no more than 5 years on such projects. Which project should they further consider? Why? Is there an argument that can be made to advance either project or neither project? Why? What other factors might be necessary to make that decision?

Fundamentals of the Accounting Rate of Return Method

The **accounting rate of return (ARR)** computes the return on investment considering changes to net income. It shows how much extra income the company could expect if it undertakes the proposed project. Unlike the payback method, ARR compares income to the initial investment rather than cash flows. This method is useful because it reviews revenues, cost savings, and expenses associated with the investment and, in some cases, can provide a more complete picture of the impact, rather than focusing solely on the cash flows produced. However, ARR is limited in that it does not consider the value of money over time, similar to the payback method.

The accounting rate of return is computed as follows:

$$\text{Accounting Rate of Return} = \frac{\text{Incremental Revenues} - \text{Incremental Expenses}}{\text{Initial Investment}}$$

Incremental revenues represent the increase to revenue if the investment is made, as opposed to if the investment is rejected. The increase to revenues includes any cost savings that occur because of the project.

Incremental expenses show the change to expenses if the project is accepted as opposed to maintaining the current conditions. Incremental expenses also include depreciation of the acquired asset. The difference between incremental revenues and incremental expenses is called the incremental net income. The initial investment is the original amount invested in the project; however, any salvage (residual) value for the capital asset needs to be subtracted from the initial investment before obtaining ARR.

The concept of salvage value was addressed in Long-Term Assets (http://cnx.org/content/m67894/latest/) . Basically, it is the anticipated future fair market value (FMV) of an asset when it is to be sold or used as a trade-in for a replacement asset. For example, assume that you bought a commercial printer for $40,000 five years ago with an anticipated salvage value of $8,000, and you are now considering replacing it. Assume that as of the date of replacement after the five-year holding period, the old printer has an FMV of $8,000. If the new printer has a purchase price of $45,000 and the seller is going to take the old printer as a trade-in, then you would owe $37,000 for the new printer. If the printer had been sold for $8,000, instead being used as a trade-in, the $8,000 could have been used as a down payment, and the company would still owe $37,000. This amount is the price of $45,000 minus the FMV value of $8,000.

$$\text{Accounting Rate of Return (ARR)} = \frac{\text{Incremental Net Income}}{\text{Initial Investment} - \text{Salvage Value}}$$

There is one more point to make with this example. The fair market value is not the same as the book value. The book value is the original cost less the accumulated depreciation that has been taken. For example, if you buy a long-term asset for $60,000 and the accumulated depreciation that you have taken is $42,000, then the asset's book value would be $18,000. The fair market value could be more, less, or the same as the book value.

For example, a piano manufacturer is considering investment in a new tuning machine. The initial investment will cost $300,000. Incremental revenues, including cost savings, are $200,000, and incremental expenses, including depreciation, are $125,000. ARR is computed as:

$$\text{ARR} = \frac{(\$200{,}000 - \$125{,}000)}{\$300{,}000} = 0.25 \text{ or } 25\%$$

This outcome means the company can expect an increase of 25% to net income, or an extra 25 cents on each dollar, if they make the investment. The company will have a minimum expected return that this project will need to meet or exceed before further consideration is given. ARR, like payback method, should not be used as the sole determining factor to invest in a capital asset. Also, note that the ARR calculation does not consider uneven annual income growth, or other depreciation methods besides straight-line depreciation.

Demonstration of the Accounting Rate of Return Method

Returning to the BGM example, the company is still considering the metal press machine because it passed the payback period method of less than 7 years. BGM has a set rate of return of 25% expected for the metal press machine investment. The company expects incremental revenues of $22,000 and incremental expenses of $12,000. Remember that the initial investment cost is $50,000. BGM computes ARR as follows:

$$\text{ARR} = \frac{(\$20{,}000 - \$5{,}000)}{\$50{,}000} = 0.3 \text{ or } 30\%$$

The ARR in this situation is 30%, exceeding the required hurdle rate of 25%. A **hurdle rate** is the minimum required rate of return on an investment to consider an alternative for further evaluation. In this case, BGM would move this investment option to a preference decision level. If we were to add a salvage value of $5,000 into the situation, the computation would change as follows:

$$\text{ARR} = \frac{(\$20{,}000 - \$5{,}000)}{\$50{,}000 - \$5{,}000} = 0.33 \text{ or } 33\% \text{ (rounded)}.$$

The ARR still exceeds the hurdle rate of 25%, so BGM would still forward the investment opportunity for further consideration. Let's say BGM changes their required return rate to 35%. In both cases, the project ARR would be less than the required rate, so BGM would not further consider either investment.

YOUR TURN

Analyzing Hurdle Rate

Turner Printing is looking to invest in a printer, which costs $60,000. Turner expects a 15% rate of return on this printer investment. The company expects incremental revenues of $30,000 and incremental expenses of $15,000. There is no salvage value for the printer. What is the accounting rate of return (ARR) for this printer? Did it meet the hurdle rate of 15%?

Solution

ARR is 25% calculated as ($30,000 – $15,000) / $60,000. 25% exceeds the hurdle rate of 15%, so the company would consider moving this alternative to a preference decision.

Both the payback period and the accounting rate of return are useful analytical tools in certain situations, particularly when used in conjunction with other evaluative techniques. In certain situations, the non-time value methods can provide relevant and useful information. However, when considering projects with long lives and significant costs to initiate, there are more advanced models that can be used. These models are typically based on time value of money principles, the basics of which are explained here.

YOUR TURN

Analyzing Investments

Your company is considering making an investment in equipment that will cost $240,000. The equipment is expected to generate annual cash flows of $60,000, provide incremental cash revenues of $200,000, and provide incremental cash expenses of $140,000 annually. Depreciation expense is included in the $140,000 incremental expense.

Calculate the payback period and the accounting rate of return.

Solution

$$\text{Payback Period} = \frac{\$240{,}000}{60{,}000} = 4 \text{ years}$$

$$\text{ARR} = \frac{(\$200{,}000 - \$140{,}000)}{240{,}000} = 25\%$$

11.3 Explain the Time Value of Money and Calculate Present and Future Values of Lump Sums and Annuities

Your mother gives you $100 cash for a birthday present, and says, "Spend it wisely." You want to purchase the latest cellular telephone on the market but wonder if this is really the best use of your money. You have a choice: You can spend the money now or spend it in the future. What should you do? Is there a benefit to spending it now as opposed to saving for later use? Does time have an impact on the value of your money in the future? Businesses are confronted with these questions and more when deciding how to allocate investment money. A major factor that affects their investment decisions is the concept of the time value of money.

Time Value of Money Fundamentals

The concept of the **time value of money** asserts that the value of a dollar today is worth more than the value of a dollar in the future. This is typically because a dollar today can be used now to earn more money in the future. There is also, typically, the possibility of future inflation, which decreases the value of a dollar over time and could lead to a reduction in economic buying power.

At this point, potential effects of inflation can probably best be demonstrated by a couple of examples. The first example is the Ford Mustang. The first Ford Mustang sold in 1964 for $2,368. Today's cheapest Mustang starts at a list price of $25,680. While a significant portion of this increase is due to additional features on newer models, much of the increase is due to the inflation that occurred between 1964 and 2019.

Similar inflation characteristics can be demonstrated with housing prices. After World War II, a typical small home often sold for between $16,000 and $30,000. Many of these same homes today are selling for hundreds of thousands of dollars. Much of the increase is due to the location of the property, but a significant part is also attributed to inflation. The annual inflation rate for the Mustang between 1964 and 2019 was approximately 4.5%. If we assume that the home sold for $16,500 in 1948 and the price of the home in 2019 was about $500,000, that's an annual appreciation rate of almost 5%.

Today's dollar is also more valuable because there is less risk than if the dollar was in a long-term investment, which may or may not yield the expected results. On the other hand, delaying payment from an investment may be beneficial if there is an opportunity to earn interest. The longer payment is delayed, the more available earning potential there is. This can be enticing to businesses and may persuade them to take on the risk of deferment.

Businesses consider the time value of money before making an investment decision. They need to know what the future value is of their investment compared to today's present value and what potential earnings they could see because of delayed payment. These considerations include present and future values.

Before you learn about present and future values, it is important to examine two types of cash flows: lump sums and annuities.

Lump Sums and Annuities

A **lump sum** is a one-time payment or repayment of funds at a particular point in time. A lump sum can be either a present value or future value. For a lump sum, the present value is the value of a given amount today. For example, if you deposited $5,000 into a savings account today at a given rate of interest, say 6%, with the goal of taking it out in exactly three years, the $5,000 today would be a present value-lump sum. Assume for simplicity's sake that the account pays 6% at the end of each year, and it also compounds interest on the interest earned in any earlier years.

In our current example, interest is calculated once a year. However, interest can also be calculated in numerous ways. Some of the most common interest calculations are daily, monthly, quarterly, or annually. One concept important to understand in interest calculations is that of compounding. **Compounding** is the process of earning interest on previous interest earned, along with the interest earned on the original investment.

Returning to our example, if $5,000 is deposited into a savings account for three years earning 6% interest compounded annually, the amount the $5,000 investment would be worth at the end of three years is $5,955.08 ($5,000 × 1.06 – $5,300 × 1.06 – $5,618 × 1.06 – $5,955.08). The $5,955.08 is the future value of $5,000 invested for three years at 6%. More formally, **future value** is the amount to which either a single investment or a series of investments will grow over a specified time at a given interest rate or rates. The initial $5,000 investment is the present value. Again, more formally, **present value** is the current value of a single future investment or a series of investments for a specified time at a given interest rate or rates. Another way to phrase this is to say the $5,000 is the present value of $5,955.08 when the initial amount was invested at 6% for three years. The interest earned over the three-year period would be $955.08, and the remaining $5,000 would be the original deposit of $5,000.

As shown in the example the future value of a lump sum is the value of the given investment at some point in the future. It is also possible to have a series of payments that constitute a series of lump sums. Assume that a business receives the following four cash flows. They constitute a series of lump sums because they are *not all* the same amount.

December 31, 2019	$12,000
December 31, 2020	12,000
December 31, 2021	11,500
December 31, 2022	12,000

The company would be receiving a stream of four cash flows that are all lump sums. In some situations, the cash flows that occur each time period are the same amount; in other words, the cash flows are even each period. These types of even cash flows occurring at even intervals, such as once a year, are known as an **annuity**. The following figure shows an annuity that consists of four payments of $12,000 made at the end of each of four years.

December 31, 2019	$12,000
December 31, 2020	12,000
December 31, 2021	12,000
December 31, 2022	12,000

The nature of cash flows—single sum cash flows, even series of cash flows, or uneven series of cash flows—have different effects on compounding.

Compounding

Compounding can be applied in many types of financial transactions, such as funding a retirement account or college savings account. Assume that an individual invests $10,000 in a four-year certificate of deposit account that pays 10% interest at the end of each year (in this case 12/31). Any interest earned during the year will be retained until the end of the four-year period and will also earn 10% interest annually.

Year	Interest Earned	Investment Balance
0		$10,000
1	($10,000 × 10%) $1,000	11,000
2	(11,000 × 10%) 1,100	12,100
3	(12,100 × 10%) 1,210	13,310
4	(13,310 × 10%) 1,331	14,641
Total Interest Earned	4,641	

Through the effects of compounding—earning interest on interest—the investor earned $4,641 in interest from the four-year investment. If the investor had removed the interest earned instead of reinvesting it in the account, the investor would have earned $1,000 a year for four years, or $4,000 interest ($10,000 × 10% = $1,000 per year × 4 years = $4,000 total interest). Compounding is a concept that is used to determine future value (more detailed calculations of future value will be covered later in this section). But what about present value? Does compounding play a role in determining present value? The term applied to finding present value is called discounting.

Discounting

Discounting is the procedure used to calculate the present value of an individual payment or a series of payments that will be received in the future based on an assumed interest rate or return on investment. Let's look at a simple example to explain the concept of discounting.

Assume that you want to accumulate sufficient funds to buy a new car and that you will need $5,000 in three years. Also, assume that your invested funds will earn 8% a year for the three years, and you reinvest any interest earned during the three-year period. If you wanted to take out adequate funds from your savings account to fund the three-year investment, you would need to invest $3,969.16 today and invest it in the account earning 8% for three years. After three years, the $3,969.16 would earn $1,030.84 and grow to exactly the $5,000 that you will need. This is an example of discounting. Discounting is the method by which we take a future value and determine its current, or present, value. An understanding of future value applications and calculations will aid in the understanding of present value uses and calculations.

Future Value

There are benefits to investing money now in hopes of a larger return in the future. These future earnings are possible because of interest payments received as an incentive for tying up money long-term. Knowing what these future earnings will be can help a business decide if the current investment is worth the long-term potential. Recall, the **future value (FV)** as the value of an investment after a certain period of time. Future value considers the initial amount invested, the time period of earnings, and the earnings interest rate in the calculation. For example, a bank would consider the future value of a loan based on whether a long-time client meets a certain interest rate return when determining whether to approve the loan.

To determine future value, the bank would need some means to determine the future value of the loan. The bank could use formulas, future value tables, a financial calculator, or a spreadsheet application. The same is true for present value calculations. Due to the variety of calculators and spreadsheet applications, we will present the determination of both present and future values using tables. In many college courses today, these tables are used primarily because they are relatively simple to understand while demonstrating the material. For those who prefer formulas, the different formulas used to create each table are printed at the top of the corresponding table. In many finance classes, you will learn how to utilize the formulas. Regarding the use of a financial calculator, while all are similar, the user manual or a quick internet search will provide specific directions for each financial calculator. As for a spreadsheet application such as Microsoft Excel, there are some common formulas, shown in Table 11.2. In addition, Appendix C provides links to videos and tutorials on using specific aspects of Excel, such as future and present value techniques.

Excel Formulas

Time Value Component	Excel Formula Shorthand	Excel Formula Detailed
Present Value Single Sum	=PV	=PV(Rate, N, Payment, FV)
Future Value Single Sum	+FV	=FV(Rate, N, Payment, PV)
Present Value Annuity	=PV	=PV(Rate, N, Payment, FV, Type)
Future Value Annuity	=FV	=FV(Rate, N, Payment, PV, Type)
Net Present Value	=NPV	=NPV(Rate, CF2, CF3, CF4) + CF1
Internal Rate of Return	=IRR	=IRR(Invest, CF1, CF2, CF3)
Rate = annual interest rate		
N = number of periods		
Payment = annual payment amount, entered as a negative number, use 0 when calculating both present value of a single sum and future value of a single sum		
FV = future value		
PV = current or present value		
Type = 0 for regular annuity, 1 for annuity due		
CF = cash flow for a period, thus CF1 – cash flow period 1, CF2 – cash flow period 2, etc.		
Invest = initial investment entered as a negative number		

Table 11.2

Since we will be using the tables in the examples in the body of the chapter, it is important to know there are four possible table, each used under specific conditions (Table 11.3).

Time Value of Money Tables

Situation	Table Heading
Future Value – Lump Sum	Future Value of $1

Table 11.3

Time Value of Money Tables

Situation	Table Heading
Future Value – Annuity (even payment stream)	Future Value of an Annuity
Present Value – Lump Sum	Present Value of $1
Present Value – Annuity (even payment stream)	Present Value of an Annuity

Table 11.3

In the prior situation, the bank would use either the Future Value of $1 table or Future Value of an Ordinary Annuity table, samples of which are provided in Appendix B. To use the correct table, the bank needs to determine whether the customer will pay them back at the end of the loan term or periodically throughout the term of the loan. The Future Value of $1 table is used if the customer will pay back at the end of the period; if the payments will be made periodically throughout the term of the loan, they will use the Future Value of an Annuity table. Choosing the correct table to use is critical for accurate determination of the future value. The application in other business matters is the same: a business needs to also consider if they are making an investment with a repayment in one lump sum or in an annuity structure before choosing a table and making the calculation. In the tables, the columns show interest rates (i) and the rows show periods (n). The interest columns represent the anticipated interest rate payout for that investment. Interest rates can be based on experience, industry standards, federal fiscal policy expectations, and risk investment. Periods represent the number of years until payment is received. The intersection of the expected payout years and the interest rate is a number called a future value factor. The future value factor is multiplied by the initial investment cost to produce the future value of the expected cash flows (or investment return).

Future Value of $1

A lump sum payment is the present value of an investment when the return will occur at the end of the period in one installment. To determine this return, the Future Value of $1 table is used.

For example, you are saving for a vacation you plan to take in 6 years and want to know how much your initial savings will yield in the future. You decide to place $4,500 in an investment account now that yields an anticipated annual return of 8%. Looking at the FV table, n = 6 years, and i = 8%, which return a future value factor of 1.587. Multiplying this factor by the initial investment amount of $4,500 produces $7,141.50. This means your initial savings of $4,500 will be worth approximately $7,141.50 in 6 years.

Future Value of $1 Table Factor = $(1 + i)^n$					
	Rate (i)				
Period (n)	1%	2%	3%	5%	8%
1	1.010	1.020	1.030	1.050	1.080
2	1.020	1.040	1.061	1.103	1.166
3	1.030	1.061	1.093	1.158	1.260
4	1.041	1.082	1.126	1.216	1.360
5	1.051	1.104	1.159	1.276	1.469
6	1.062	1.126	1.194	1.340	**1.587**

Future Value of an Ordinary Annuity

An **ordinary annuity** is one in which the payments are made at the end of each period in equal installments. A future value ordinary annuity looks at the value of the current investment in the future, if periodic payments were made throughout the life of the series.

For example, you are saving for retirement and expect to contribute $10,000 per year for the next 15 years to a 401(k) retirement plan. The plan anticipates a periodic interest yield of 12%. How much would your investment be worth in the future meeting these criteria? In this case, you would use the Future Value of an Ordinary Annuity table. The relevant factor where n = 15 and i = 12% is 37.280. Multiplying the factor by the amount of the cash flow yields a future value of these installment savings of (37.280 × $10,000) $372,800. Therefore, you could expect your investment to be worth $372,800 at the end of 15 years, given the parameters.

Future Value of an Ordinary Annuity Table

$$\text{Factor} = \frac{[(1 + i)^n - 1]}{i}$$

Period (n)	Rate (i)						
	1%	2%	3%	5%	8%	10%	12%
1	1.000	1.000	1.000	1.000	1.000	1.000	1.000
2	2.010	2.020	2.030	2.050	2.080	2.100	2.120
3	3.030	3.060	3.091	3.153	3.246	3.310	3.374
4	4.060	4.122	4.184	4.310	4.506	4.641	4.779
5	5.101	5.204	5.309	5.526	5.867	6.105	6.353
6	6.152	6.308	6.468	6.802	7.336	7.716	8.115
7	7.214	7.434	7.662	8.142	8.923	9.487	10.089
8	8.286	8.583	8.892	9.549	10.637	11.436	12.300
9	9.369	9.755	10.159	11.027	12.488	13.579	14.776
10	10.462	10.950	11.464	12.578	14.487	15.937	17.549
11	11.567	12.169	12.808	14.207	16.645	18.531	20.655
12	12.683	13.412	14.192	15.917	18.977	21.384	24.133
13	13.809	14.680	15.618	17.713	21.495	24.523	28.029
14	14.947	15.974	17.086	19.599	24.215	27.975	32.393
15	16.097	17.293	18.599	21.579	27.152	31.772	**37.280**

Let's now examine how present value differs from future value in use and computation.

YOUR TURN

Determining Future Value

Determine the future value for each of the following situations. Use the future value tables provided in Appendix B when needed, and round answers to the nearest cent where required.

A. You are saving for a car and you put away $5,000 in a savings account. You want to know how much your initial savings will be worth in 7 years if you have an anticipated annual interest rate of 5%.

B. You are saving for retirement and make contributions of $11,500 per year for the next 14 years to your 403(b) retirement plan. The interest rate yield is 8%.

Solution

A. Use FV of $1 table. Future value factor where $n = 7$ and $i = 5$ is 1.407. 1.407 × 5,000 = $7,035. B. Use FV of an ordinary annuity table. Future value factor where $n = 14$ and $i = 8$ is 24.215. 24.215 × 11,500 = $278,472.50.

Present Value

It is impossible to compare the value or potential purchasing power of the future dollar to today's dollar; they exist in different times and have different values. **Present value (PV)** considers the future value of an investment expressed in today's value. This allows a company to see if the investment's initial cost is more or less than the future return. For example, a bank might consider the present value of giving a customer a loan before extending funds to ensure that the risk and the interest earned are worth the initial outlay of cash.

Similar to the Future Value tables, the columns show interest rates (i) and the rows show periods (n) in the Present Value tables. Periods represent how often interest is compounded (paid); that is, periods could represent days, weeks, months, quarters, years, or any interest time period. For our examples and assessments, the period (n) will almost always be in years. The intersection of the expected payout years (n) and the interest rate (i) is a number called a present value factor. The present value factor is multiplied by the initial investment cost to produce the present value of the expected cash flows (or investment return).

> **Present Value = Present Value Factor × Initial Investment Cost**

The two tables provided in Appendix B for present value are the Present Value of $1 and the Present Value of an Ordinary Annuity. As with the future value tables, choosing the correct table to use is critical for accurate determination of the present value.

Present Value of $1

When referring to present value, the lump sum return occurs at the end of a period. A business must determine if this delayed repayment, with interest, is worth the same as, more than, or less than the initial investment cost. If the deferred payment is more than the initial investment, the company would consider an investment.

To calculate present value of a lump sum, we should use the Present Value of $1 table. For example, you are interested in saving money for college and want to calculate how much you would need put in the bank today to return a sum of $40,000 in 10 years. The bank returns an interest rate of 3% per year during these 10 years. Looking at the PV table, $n = 10$ years and $i = 3\%$ returns a present value factor of 0.744. Multiplying this factor by the return amount of $40,000 produces $29,760. This means you would need to put in the bank now approximately $29,760 to have $40,000 in 10 years.

Present Value of $1 Table Factor = $\frac{1}{(1+i)^n}$

Period (n)	Rate (i) 1%	2%	3%	5%
1	0.990	0.980	0.971	0.952
2	0.980	0.961	0.943	0.907
3	0.971	0.942	0.915	0.864
4	0.961	0.924	0.888	0.823
5	0.952	0.906	0.863	0.784
6	0.942	0.888	0.837	0.746
7	0.933	0.871	0.813	0.711
8	0.924	0.853	0.789	0.677
9	0.914	0.837	0.766	0.645
10	0.905	0.820	0.744	0.614
11	0.896	0.804	0.722	0.585

As mentioned, to determine the present value or future value of cash flows, a financial calculator, a program such as Excel, knowledge of the appropriate formulas, or a set of tables must be used. Though we illustrate examples in the text using tables, we recognize the value of these other calculation instruments and have included chapter assessments that use multiple approaches to determining present and future value. Knowledge of different approaches to determining present and future value is useful as there are situations, such as having fractional interest rates, 8.45% for example, in which a financial calculator or a program such as Excel would be needed to accurately determine present or future value.

Annuity Table

As discussed previously, annuities are a series of equal payments made over time, and ordinary annuities pay the equal installment at the end of each payment period within the series. This can help a business understand how their periodic returns translate into today's value.

For example, assume that Sam needs to borrow money for college and anticipates that she will be able to repay the loan in $1,200 annual payments for each of 5 years. If the lender charges 5% per year for similar loans, how much cash would the bank be willing to lend Sam today? In this case, she would use the Present Value of an Ordinary Annuity table in Appendix B, where n = 5 and i = 5%. This yields a present value factor of 4.329. The current value of the cash flow each period is calculated as 4.329 × $1,200 = $5,194.80. Therefore, Sam could borrow $5,194.80 now given the repayment parameters.

Present Value of an Ordinary Annuity Table Factor = $\frac{[1 - 1/(1+i)^n]}{i}$

Period (n)	Rate (i) 1%	2%	3%	5%
1	0.990	0.980	0.971	0.952
2	1.970	1.942	1.913	1.859
3	2.941	2.884	2.829	2.723
4	3.902	3.808	3.717	3.546
5	4.853	4.713	4.580	**4.329**

Our focus has been on examples of *ordinary* annuities (annuities due and other more complicated annuity examples are addressed in advanced accounting courses). With **annuities due**, the cash flow occurs at the start of the period. For example, if you wanted to deposit a lump sum of money into an account and make monthly rent payments starting today, the first payment would be made the same day that you made the deposit into the funding account. Because of this timing difference in the withdrawals from the annuity due, the process of calculating annuity due is somewhat different from the methods that you've covered for ordinary annuities.

YOUR TURN

Determining Present Value

Determine the present value for each of the following situations. Use the present value tables provided in Appendix B when needed, and round answers to the nearest cent where required.

a. You are saving for college and you want to return a sum of $100,000 in 12 years. The bank returns an interest rate of 5% after these 12 years.
b. You need to borrow money for college and can afford a yearly payment to the lending institution of $1,000 per year for the next 8 years. The interest rate charged by the lending institution is 3% per year.

Solution

a. Use PV of $1 table. Present value factor where $n = 12$ and $i = 5$ is 0.557. 0.557 × $100,000 = $55,700. b. Use PV of an ordinary annuity table. Present value factor where $n = 8$ and $i = 3$ is 7.020. 7.020 × $1,000 = $7,020.

LINK TO LEARNING

For a lucky few, winning the lottery can be a dream come true and the option to take a one-time payout or receive payments over several years does not seem to matter at the time. This lottery payout calculator (https://openstax.org/l/50LotteryCalc) shows how time value of money may affect your take-home winnings.

11.4 Use Discounted Cash Flow Models to Make Capital Investment Decisions

Your company, Rudolph Incorporated, has begun analyzing two potential future project alternatives that have passed the basic screening using the non–time value methods of determining the payback period and the accounting rate of return. Both proposed projects seem reasonable, but your company typically selects only one option to pursue. Which one should you choose? How will you decide? A discounted cash flow model can assist with this process. In this section, we will discuss two commonly used time value of money–based options: the net present value method (NPV) and the internal rate of return (IRR). Both of these methods are based on the discounted cash flow process.

Fundamentals of the Discounted Cash Flow Model

The **discount cash flow model** assigns a value to a business opportunity using time-value measurement tools. The model considers future cash flows of the project, discounts them back to present time, and compares the outcome to an expected rate of return. If the outcome exceeds the expected rate of return and initial investment cost, the company would consider the investment. If the outcome does not exceed the expected rate of return or the initial investment, the company may not consider investment. When considering the discounted cash flow process, the time value of money plays a major role.

Time Value-Based Methods

As previously discussed, time value of money methods assume that the value of money today is worth more now than in the future. The payback period and accounting rate of return methods do not consider this concept when performing calculations and analyzing results. That is why they are typically only used as basic screening tools. To decide the best option between alternatives, a company performs preference measurement using tools, such as net present value and internal rate of return that do consider the time value of money concept. **Net present value (NPV)** discounts future cash flows to their present value at the expected rate of return and compares that to the initial investment. NPV does not determine the actual rate of return earned by a project. The **internal rate of return (IRR)** shows the profitability or growth potential of an investment at the point where NPV equals zero, so it determines the actual rate of return a project earns. As the name implies, net present value is stated in dollars, whereas the internal rate of return is stated as an interest rate. Both NPV and IRR require the company to determine a rate of return to be used as the target return rate, such as the minimum required rate of return or the weighted average cost of capital, which will be discussed in Balanced Scorecard and Other Performance Measures.

A positive NPV implies that the present value of the cash inflows from the project are greater than the present value of the cash outflows, which represent the expenses and costs associated with the project. In an NPV calculation, a positive NPV is typically considered a potentially good investment or project. However, other extenuating circumstances should be considered. For example, the company might not wish to borrow the necessary funding to make the investment because the company might be anticipating a downturn in the national economy.

An IRR analysis compares the calculated IRR with either a predetermined rate of return or the cost of borrowing the money to invest in the project in order to determine whether a potential investment or project is favorable. For example, assume that the investment or equipment purchase is expected to generate an IRR of 15% and the company's expected rate of return is 12%. In this case, similar to the NPV calculation, we assume that the proposed investment would be undertaken. However, remember that other factors must be considered, as they are with NPV.

When considering cash inflows—whether using NPV or IRR—the accountant should examine both profits generated or expenses reduced. Investments that are made may generate additional revenue or could reduce production costs. Both cases assume that the new product or other type of investment generates a positive cash inflow that will be compared to the cost outflows to determine whether there is an overall positive or negative net present value.

Additionally, a company would determine whether the projects being considered are mutually exclusive or not. If the projects or investment options are mutually exclusive, the company can evaluate and identify more than one alternative as a viable project or investment, but they can only invest in one option. For example, if a company needs one new delivery truck, it might solicit proposals from five different truck dealers and conduct NPV and IRR evaluations. Even if all proposals pass the financial requirements of the NPV and IRR methods, only one proposal will be accepted.

Another consideration occurs when a company has the ability to evaluate and accept multiple proposals. For example, an automobile manufacturer is considering expanding its number of dealerships in the United States over the next ten-year period and has allocated $30,000,000 to buy the land. They could purchase any number of properties. They conduct NPV and IRR analyses of fifteen properties and determine that four meet their required standards and market feasibility needs and then purchase those four properties. The opportunities were not mutually exclusive: the number of properties purchased was driven by research and expansion projections, not by their need for only one option.

CONTINUING APPLICATION AT WORK

Capital Budgeting Decisions

Gearhead Outfitters has expanded to many locations throughout its twenty-plus years in business. How did company management decide to expand? One of the financial tools a business can use is capital budgeting, which addresses many different issues involving the use of current cash flow for future return. As you've learned, capital outlay decisions can be evaluated through payback period, net present value, and methods involving rates of return.

With this in mind, think about the capital budgeting issues Gearhead's management might have faced. For example, in deciding to expand, should the company buy a building or lease one? What method should be used to evaluate this? Purchasing a building might require more initial outlay, but the company will retain an asset. How will such a decision affect the bottom line? With respect to equipment, Gearhead could maintain a fleet of vehicles. Should the vehicles be purchased or leased? What will need to be considered in the process?

In developing and maintaining its strategy for sustainability, a business must not only consider day-to-day operations, but also address long-term decisions. Common capital budgeting items like equipment purchases to increase efficiency or reduce costs, decisions about replacement versus repair, and expansion all involve significant cash outlay. How will these items be evaluated? How long will recouping the initial investment take? How much revenue will be generated (or costs saved) through capital outlay? Does the company require a minimum rate of return before it moves forward with investment? If so, how is that return determined? Considering Gearhead's decision to expand, what are some specific capital budgeting decisions important for the company to consider in their long-term strategy?

Basic Characteristics of the Net Present Value Model

Net present value helps companies choose between alternatives at a particular point in time by determining which produces the higher NPV. To determine the NPV, the initial investment is subtracted from the present value of cash inflows and outflows associated with a project at a required rate of return. If the outcome is positive, the company should consider investment. If the outcome is negative, the company would forgo investment.

We previously discussed the calculation for present value using the present value tables, where n is the number of years and *i* is the expected interest rate. Once the present value factor is determined, it is multiplied by the expected net cash flows to produce the present value of future cash flows. The initial investment is subtracted from this present value calculation to determine the net present value.

> **Net present value = Sum of Present Value of net cash flows − Initial Investment**

Recall that the Present Value of $1 table is used for a lump sum payout, whereas the Present Value of an Ordinary Annuity table is used for a series of equal payments occurring at the end of each period. Taking this distinction one step further, NPV requires use of different tables depending on whether the future cash flows are equal or unequal in each time period. If the cash flows each period are equal, the company uses the Present Value of an Ordinary Annuity table, where the present value factor is multiplied by the cash flow amount for one period to get the present value. If the cash flows each period are unequal, the company uses the Present Value of $1 table, where the total present value is the sum of each of the unequal cash flows multiplied by the appropriate present value factor for each time period. This concept is discussed in the following example.

Assume that your company, Rudolph Incorporated, is determining the NPV for a new X-ray machine. The X-ray machine has an initial investment of $200,000 and an expected cash flow of $40,000 each period for the next 10 years. The expected $40,000 cash flows from the new X-ray machine can be attributed to either additional revenue generated or cost savings realized by more efficient operations of the new machine. Since these annual cash flows of $40,000 are the same amount in each period over the ten-years this will be a stream of annuity amounts received. The required rate of return on such an investment is 8%. The present value factor (*i* = 8, *n* = 10) is 6.710 using the Present Value of an Ordinary Annuity table. Multiplying the present value factor (6.710) by the equal cash flow ($40,000) gives a present value of $268,400. NPV is found by taking the present value of $268,400 and subtracting the initial investment of $200,000 to arrive at $68,400. This is a positive NPV, so the company would consider investment.

		Present Value of an Ordinary Annuity Table				
		Rate (*i*)				
		1%	2%	3%	5%	8%
Period (*n*)	1	0.990	0.980	0.971	0.952	0.926
	2	1.970	1.942	1.913	1.859	1.783
	3	2.941	2.884	2.829	2.723	2.577
	4	3.902	3.808	3.717	3.546	3.312
	5	4.853	4.713	4.580	4.329	3.993
	6	5.795	5.601	5.417	5.076	4.623
	7	6.728	6.472	6.230	5.786	5.206
	8	7.652	7.325	7.020	6.463	5.747
	9	8.566	8.162	7.786	7.108	6.247
	10	9.471	8.983	8.530	7.722	**6.710**

If there are two investments that have a positive NPV, and the investments are mutually exclusive, meaning only one can be chosen, the more profitable of the two investments is typically the appropriate one for a company to choose. We can also use the profitability index to compare them. The profitability index measures the amount of profit returned for each dollar invested in a project. This is particularly useful when projects being evaluated are of a different size, as the profitability index scales the projects to make them comparable. The profitability index is found by taking the present value of the net cash flows and dividing by the initial investment cost.

$$\text{Profitability index} = \frac{\text{Present value of cash flows}}{\text{Initial investment cost}}$$

For example, Rudolph Incorporated is considering the X-ray machine that had present value cash flows of $268,400 (not considering salvage value) and an initial investment cost of $200,000. Another x-ray equipment option, option B, produces present value cash flows of $290,000 and an initial investment cost of $240,000. The profitability index is computed as follows.

$$\text{Option A:} \frac{\$268{,}400}{\$200{,}000} = 1.342$$

$$\text{Option B:} \frac{\$290{,}000}{\$240{,}000} = 1.208$$

Based on this outcome, the company would invest in Option A, the project with a higher profitability index of 1.342.

If there were unequal cash flows each period, the Present Value of $1 table would be used with a more complex calculation. Each year's present value factor is determined and multiplied by that year's cash flow. Then all cash flows are added together to get one overall present value figure. This overall present value figure is used when finding the difference between present value and the initial investment cost.

For example, let's say the X-ray machine information is the same, except now cash flows are as follows:

Year	Cash Flow Amount
1	$20,000
2	25,000
3	20,000
4	40,000
5	40,000
6	60,000
7	30,000
8	35,000
9	25,000
10	45,000

To find the overall present value, the following calculations take place using the present value of $1 table.

Year	Cash Flow Amount	Present Value Factor ($i = 8$, n = specific year)	Present Value
1	$ 20,000	($i = 8$, $n = 1$) = 0.926	0.926 × $20,000 = $18,520
2	25,000	($i = 8$, $n = 2$) = 0.857	0.857 × 25,000 = 21,425
3	20,000	($i = 8$, $n = 3$) = 0.794	0.794 × 20,000 = 15,880
4	40,000	($i = 8$, $n = 4$) = 0.735	0.735 × 40,000 = 29,400
5	40,000	($i = 8$, $n = 5$) = 0.681	0.681 × 40,000 = 27,240
6	60,000	($i = 8$, $n = 6$) = 0.630	0.630 × 60,000 = 37,800
7	30,000	($i = 8$, $n = 7$) = 0.583	0.583 × 30,000 = 17,490
8	35,000	($i = 8$, $n = 8$) = 0.540	0.540 × 35,000 = 18,900
9	25,000	($i = 8$, $n = 9$) = 0.500	0.500 × 25,000 = 12,500
10	45,000	($i = 8$, $n = 10$) = 0.463	0.463 × 45,000 = 20,835
Total	$340,000		$219,990

The Present Value of $1 table is used because, each year, a new "lump sum" cash flow is received, so the cash flow in each period is different. The cash flows are treated as one-time lump sum payouts during that year. The present value for each period looks at each year's present value factor at an interest rate of 8%. All the PVs are added together for a total present value of $219,990. The initial investment of $200,000 is subtracted from the $219,990 to arrive at a positive NPV of $19,990. In this case, the company would consider investment since the outcome is positive. (More complex considerations, such as depreciation, the effects of income taxes, and inflation, which could affect the overall NPV, are covered in advanced accounting courses.)

YOUR TURN

Analyzing a Postage Meter Investment

Yellow Industries is considering investment in a new postage meter system. The postage meter system would have an initial investment cost of $135,000. Annual net cash flows are $40,000 for the next 5 years, and the expected interest rate return is 10%. Calculate net present value and decide whether or not Yellow Industries should invest in the new postage meter system.

Solution

Use the Present Value of an Ordinary Annuity table. Present value factor at $n = 5$ and $i = 10\%$ is 3.791. Present value = 3.791 × $40,000 = $151,640. NPV = $151,640 − $135,000 = $16,640. In this case, Yellow Industries should invest since the NPV is positive.

Calculation and Discussion of the Results of the Net Present Value Model

To demonstrate NPV, assume that a company, Rayford Machining, is considering buying a drill press that will have an initial investment cost of $50,000 and annual cash flows of $10,000 for the next 7 years. Assume that Rayford expects a 5% rate of return on such an investment. We need to determine the NPV when cash flows are equal. The present value factor ($i = 5$, $n = 7$) is 5.786 using the Present Value of an Ordinary Annuity table. We multiply 5.786 by the equal cash flow of $10,000 to get a present value of $57,860. NPV is found by taking the present value of $57,860 and subtracting the initial investment of $50,000 to arrive at $7,860. This is a positive NPV, so the company would consider the investment.

Present Value of an Ordinary Annuity Table				
	Rate (i)			
Period (n)	1%	2%	3%	5%
1	0.990	0.980	0.971	0.952
2	1.970	1.942	1.913	1.859
3	2.941	2.884	2.829	2.723
4	3.902	3.808	3.717	3.546
5	4.853	4.713	4.580	4.329
6	5.795	5.601	5.417	5.076
7	6.728	6.472	6.230	**5.786**

Let's say Rayford Machining has another option, Option B, for a drill press purchase with an initial investment cost of $56,000 that produces present value cash flows of $60,500. The profitability index is computed as follows.

$$\text{Option A:} \frac{\$57,860}{\$50,000} = 1.157$$

$$\text{Option B:} \frac{\$60,500}{\$56,000} = 1.080$$

Based on this outcome, the company would invest in Option A, the project with a higher profitability potential of 1.157.

Now let's assume cash flows are unequal. Unequal cash flow information for Rayford Machining is summarized here.

Year	Net Cash Flow
1	$10,000
2	5,000
3	7,000
4	3,000
5	10,000
6	10,000
7	10,000

To find the overall present value, the following calculations take place using the Present Value of $1 table.

Year	Cash Flow Amount	Present Value Factor ($i = 5$, n = specific year)	Present Value
1	$10,000	($i = 5$, $n = 1$) = 0.952	0.952 × $10,000 = $9,520
2	5,000	($i = 5$, $n = 2$) = 0.907	0.907 × 5,000 = 4,535
3	7,000	($i = 5$, $n = 3$) = 0.864	0.864 × 7,000 = 6,048
4	3,000	($i = 5$, $n = 4$) = 0.823	0.823 × 3,000 = 2,469
5	10,000	($i = 5$, $n = 5$) = 0.784	0.784 × 10,000 = 7,840
6	10,000	($i = 5$, $n = 6$) = 0.746	0.746 × 10,000 = 7,460
7	10,000	($i = 5$, $n = 7$) = 0.711	0.711 × 10,000 = 7,110
Total	$55,000		$44,982

The present value for each period looks at each year's present value factor at an interest rate of 5%. All individual year present values are added together for a total present value of $44,982. The initial investment of $50,000 is subtracted from the $44,982 to arrive at a negative NPV of $5,018. In this case, Rayford Machining would not invest, since the outcome is negative. The negative NPV value does not mean the investment would be unprofitable; rather, it means the investment does not return the desired 5% the company is looking for in the investments that it makes.

Basic Characteristics of the Internal Rate of Return Model

The internal rate of return model allows for the comparison of profitability or growth potential among alternatives. All external factors, such as inflation, are removed from calculation, and the project with the highest return rate percentage is considered for investment.

IRR is the discounted rate (interest rate) point at which NPV equals zero. In other words, the IRR is the point at which the present value cash inflows equal the initial investment cost. To consider investment, IRR needs to meet or exceed the required rate of return for the investment type. If IRR does not meet the required rate of return, the company will forgo investment.

To find IRR using the present value tables, we need to know the cash flow number of return periods (n) and the intersecting present value factor. To calculate present value factor, we use the following formula.

$$\text{Present Value Factor} = \frac{\text{Initial Investment Cost}}{\text{Annual Net Cash Flows}}$$

We find the present value factor in the present value table in the row with the corresponding number of periods (n). We find the matching interest rate (i) at this present value factor. The corresponding interest rate at the number of periods (n) is the IRR. When cash flows are equal, use the Present Value of an Ordinary Annuity table to find IRR.

For example, a car manufacturer needs to replace welding equipment. The initial investment cost is $312,000 and each annual net cash flow is $49,944 for the next 9 years. We need to find the internal rate of return for this welding equipment. The expected rate of return for such a purchase is 6%. In this case, $n = 9$ and the present value factor is computed as follows.

$$\text{Present Value Factor} = \frac{\$312{,}000}{\$49{,}944} = 6.247 \text{ (rounded)}$$

Looking at the Present Value of an Ordinary Annuity table, where $n = 9$ and the present value factor is 6.247, we discover that the corresponding return rate is 8%. This exceeds the expected return rate, so the company would typically invest in the project.

Present Value of an Ordinary Annuity Table

Period (n)	Rate (i)					
	1%	2%	3%	5%	8%	10%
1	0.990	0.980	0.971	0.952	0.926	0.909
2	1.970	1.942	1.913	1.859	1.783	1.736
3	2.941	2.884	2.829	2.723	2.577	2.487
4	3.902	3.808	3.717	3.546	3.312	3.170
5	4.853	4.713	4.580	4.329	3.993	3.791
6	5.795	5.601	5.417	5.076	4.623	4.355
7	6.728	6.472	6.230	5.786	5.206	4.868
8	7.652	7.325	7.020	6.463	5.747	5.335
9	8.566	8.162	7.786	7.108	**6.247**	5.759

If there is more than one viable option, the company will select the alternative with the highest IRR that exceeds the expected rate of return.

Our tables are limited in scope, and therefore, a present value factor may fall in between two interest rates. When this is the case, you may choose to identify an IRR range instead of a single interest rate figure. A spreadsheet program or financial calculator can produce a more accurate result and can also be used when cash flows are unequal.

Calculation and Discussion of the Results of the Internal Rate of Return Model

Assume that Rayford Machining wants to know the internal rate of return for the new drill press. The drill press has an initial investment cost of $50,000 and an annual cash flow of $10,000 for each of the next seven years. The company expects a 7% rate of return on this type of investment. We calculate the present value factor as:

$$\text{Present Value Factor} = \frac{\$50{,}000}{\$10{,}000} = 5.000$$

Scanning the Present Value of an Ordinary Annuity table reveals that the interest rate where the present value factor is 5 and the number of periods is 7 is between 8 and 10%. Since the required rate of return was 7%, Rayford would consider investment in this metal press machine.

Present Value of an Ordinary Annuity Table

		\multicolumn{6}{c}{Rate (i)}					
		1%	2%	3%	5%	8%	10%
Period (n)	1	0.990	0.980	0.971	0.952	0.926	0.909
	2	1.970	1.942	1.913	1.859	1.783	1.736
	3	2.941	2.884	2.829	2.723	2.577	2.487
	4	3.902	3.808	3.717	3.546	3.312	3.170
	5	4.853	4.713	4.580	4.329	3.993	3.791
	6	5.795	5.601	5.417	5.076	4.623	4.355
	7	6.728	6.472	6.230	5.786	**5.206**	**4.868**
	8	7.652	7.325	7.020	6.463	5.747	5.335
	9	8.566	8.162	7.786	7.108	6.247	5.759

Consider another example using Rayford, where they have two drill press purchase options. Option A has an IRR between 8% and 10%. The other option, Option B, has an initial investment cost of $60,500 and equal annual net cash flows of $13,256 for the next seven years. We calculate the present value factor as:

$$\text{Present Value Factor} = \frac{\$60{,}500}{\$13{,}256} = 4.564 \text{ (rounded)}$$

Scanning the Present Value of an Ordinary Annuity table reveals that, when the present value factor is 4.564 and the number of periods is 7, the interest rate is 12%. This not only exceeds the 7% required rate, it also exceeds Option A's return of 8% to 10%. Therefore, if resources were limited, Rayford would select Option B over Option A.

Present Value of an Ordinary Annuity Table

		1%	2%	3%	5%	8%	10%	12%
Period (n)	1	0.990	0.980	0.971	0.952	0.926	0.909	0.893
	2	1.970	1.942	1.913	1.859	1.783	1.736	1.690
	3	2.941	2.884	2.829	2.723	2.577	2.487	2.402
	4	3.902	3.808	3.717	3.546	3.312	3.170	3.037
	5	4.853	4.713	4.580	4.329	3.993	3.791	3.605
	6	5.795	5.601	5.417	5.076	4.623	4.355	4.111
	7	6.728	6.472	6.230	5.786	5.206	4.868	**4.564**

Final Summary of the Discounted Cash Flow Models

The internal rate of return (IRR) and the net present value (NPV) methods are types of discounted cash flow analysis that require taking estimated future payments from a project and discounting them into present values. The difference between the two methods is that the NPV calculation determines the project's estimated return in dollars and the IRR provides the percentage rate of return from a project needed to break even.

When the NPV is determined to be $0, the present value of the cash inflows and the present value of the cash outflows are equal. For example, assume that the present value of the cash inflows is $10,000 and the present value of the cash outflows is also $10,000. In this example, the NPV would be $0. At a net present value of zero, the IRR would be exactly equal to the interest rate that was used to perform the NPV calculation. For example, in the previous example, where both the cash inflows and the cash outflows have present values of $10,000 and the NPV is $0, assume that they were discounted at an 8% interest rate. If you were to then calculate the internal rate of return, the IRR would be 8%, the same interest rate that gave us an NPV of $0.

Overall, it is important to understand that a company must consider the time value of money when making capital investment decisions. Knowing the present value of a future cash flow enables a company to better select between alternatives. The net present value compares the initial investment cost to the present value of future cash flows and requires a positive outcome before investment. The internal rate of return also considers the present value of future cash flows but considers profitability stated in terms of percentage of return on the investment or project. These models allows two or more options to be compared to eliminate bias with raw financial figures.

THINK IT THROUGH

Choosing Investments

Companies are presented with viable alternatives that sometimes produce nearly identical results and profitability goals. If they have the ability to invest in both alternatives, they may do so. But what about when resources are constrained? How do they choose which investment is best for their company?

Consider this: you have two projects that met the payback period and accounting rate of return screenings identically. Project 1 produced an NPV of $45,000 and had an IRR between 5% and 8%. Project 2 produced a NPV of $35,000 and had an IRR of 10%. This leaves you with a difficult choice, since each alternative has a measurement that exceeds the other and the other variables are the same. Which project would you invest in and why?

11.5 Compare and Contrast Non-Time Value-Based Methods and Time Value-Based Methods in Capital Investment Decisions

When an investment opportunity is presented to a company, there are many financial and non-financial factors to consider. Using capital budgeting methods to narrow down the choices by removing unviable alternatives is an important process for any successful business. The four methods for capital budgeting analysis—payback period, accounting rate of return, net present value, and internal rate of return—all have their strengths and weaknesses, which are discussed as follows.

Summary of the Strengths and Weaknesses of the Non-Time Value-Based Capital Budgeting Methods

Non-time value-based capital budgeting methods are best used in an initial screening process when there are many alternatives to choose from. Two such methods are payback method and accounting rate of return. Their strengths and weaknesses are discussed in Table 11.4 and Table 11.5.

The payback method determines the length of time needed to recoup an investment.

Payback Method

Strengths	Weaknesses
• Simple calculation • Screens out many unviable alternatives quickly • Removes high-risk investments from consideration	• Does not consider time value of money • Profitability of an investment is ignored • Cash flows beyond investment return are not considered

Table 11.4

Accounting rate of return measures incremental increases to net income. This method has several strengths and weaknesses that are similar to payback period but include a deeper evaluation of income.

Accounting Rate of Return

Strengths	Weaknesses
• Simple calculation • Screens out many unviable options quickly • Considers the impact on income rather than cash flows only (profitability)	• Does not consider the time value of money • Return rates for the entire lifespan of the investment is not considered • External factors, such as inflation, are ignored • Return rates override the risk of investment

Table 11.5

Because of the limited information each of the non-time value-based methods give, they are typically used in conjunction with time value-based capital budgeting methods.

Summary of the Strengths and Weaknesses of the Time Value-Based Capital Budgeting Methods

Time value-based capital budgeting methods are best used after an initial screening process, when a company is choosing between few alternatives. They help determine the best of the alternatives that a company should pursue. Two such methods are net present value and internal rate of return. Their strengths and weaknesses are presented in Table 11.6 and Table 11.7.

Net present value converts future cash flow dollars into current values to determine if the initial investment is less than the future returns.

Net Present Value

Strengths	Weaknesses
• Considers the time value of money • Acknowledges higher risk investments • Comparable future earnings with today's value • Allows for a selection of investment	• Requires a more difficult calculation than non-time value methods • Required return rate is an estimate, thus any changes to this condition and the impact that has on earnings are unknown • Difficult to compare alternatives that have varying investment amounts

Table 11.6

Internal rate of return looks at future cash flows as compared to an initial investment to find the rate of return on investment. The goal is to have an interest rate higher than the predetermined rate of return to consider investment.

Internal Rate of Return

Strengths	Weaknesses
• Considers the time value of money • Easy to compare different-sized investments, removes dollar bias • A predetermined rate of return is not required • Allows for a selection of investment	• Does not acknowledge higher risk investments because the focus is on return rates • More difficult calculation than non-time value methods, and outcome may be uncertain if not using a financial calculator or spreadsheet program • If the time for return on investment is important, IRR will not place more importance on shorter-term investments

Table 11.7

After a time-value based capital budgeting method is analyzed, a company can be move toward a decision on an investment opportunity. This is of particular importance when resources are limited.

Before discussing the mechanics of choosing the NPV versus the IRR method for decision-making, we first need to discuss one cardinal rule of using the NPV or IRR methods to evaluate time-sensitive investments or asset purchases: If a project or investment has a positive NPV, then it will, by definition, have an IRR that is above the interest rate used to calculate the NPV.

For example, assume that a company is considering buying a piece of equipment. They determine that it will cost $30,000 and will save them $10,000 a year in expenses for five years. They have decided that the interest rate that they will choose to calculate the NPV and to evaluate the purchase IRR is 8%, predicated on current loan rates available. Based on this sample data, the NPV will be positive $9,927 ($39,927 PV for inflows and $30,000 PV for the outflows), and the IRR will be 19.86%. Since the calculations require at least an 8% return, the company would accept the project using either method. We will not spend additional time on the calculations at this point, since our purpose is to create numbers to analyze. If you want to duplicate the calculations, you can use a software program such as Excel or a financial calculator.

CONCEPTS IN PRACTICE

Solar Energy as Capital Investment

A recent capital investment decision that many company leaders need to make is whether or not to invest in solar energy. Solar energy is replacing fossil fuels as a power source, and it provides a low-cost energy, reducing overhead costs. The expensive up-front installation costs can deter some businesses from making the initial investment.

Businesses must now choose between an expensive initial capital outlay and the long-term benefits of solar power. A capital investment such as this would require an initial screening and preference process to determine if the cost savings and future benefits are worth more today than the current capital expenditure. If it makes financial sense, they may look to invest in this increasingly popular energy source.

Now, we return to our comparison of the NPV and IRR methods. There are typically two situations that we want to consider. The first involves looking at projects that are not mutually exclusive, meaning we can consider more than one possibility. If a company is considering non-mutually exclusive opportunities, they will generally consider all options that have a positive NPV or an IRR that is above the target rate of interest as favorable options for an investment or asset purchase. In this situation, the NPV and IRR methods will provide the same accept-or-reject decision. If the company accepts a project or investment under the NPV calculation, then they will accept it under the IRR method. If they reject it under the NPV calculation, then they will also reject under the IRR method.

The second situation involves mutually exclusive opportunities. For example, if a company has one computer system and is considering replacing it, they might look at seven options that have favorable NPVs and IRRs, even though they only need one computer system. In this case, they would choose only one of the seven possible options.

In the case of mutually exclusive options, it is possible that the NPV method will select Option A while the IRR method might choose Option D. The primary reason for this difference is that the NPV method uses dollars and the IRR uses an interest rate. The two methods may select different options if the company has investments with major differences in costs in terms of dollars. While both will identify an investment or purchase that exceeds the required standards of a positive NPV or an interest rate above the target interest rate, they might lead the company to choose different positive options. When this occurs, the company needs to consider other conditions, such as qualitative factors, to make their decision. Future cost accounting or finance courses will cover this content in more detail.

Final Comparison of the Four Capital Budgeting Options

A company will be presented with many alternatives for investment. It is up to management to analyze each investment's possibilities using capital budgeting methods. The company will want to first screen each possibility with the payback method and accounting rate of return. The payback method will show the company how long it will take to recoup their investment, while accounting rate of return gives them the profitability of the alternatives. This screening will typically get rid of non-viable options and allow the company to further consider a select few alternatives. A more detailed analysis is found in time-value methods, such as net present value and internal rate of return. Net present value converts future cash flows into today's valuation for comparability purposes to see if an initial outlay of cash is worth future earnings. The internal rate of return determines the minimum expected return on a project given the present value of cash flow expectations and the initial investment. Analyzing these opportunities, with consideration given to time value of money, allows a company to make an informed decision on how to make large capital expenditures.

ETHICAL CONSIDERATIONS

Barclays and the LIBOR Scandal

As discussed in Volkswagen Diesel Emissions Scandal, when a company makes an unethical decision, it must adjust its budget for fines and lawsuits. In 2012, Barclays, a British financial services company, was caught illegally manipulating LIBOR interest rates. LIBOR sets the interest rate for many types of loans. As CNN reported, "LIBOR, which stands for London Interbank Offered Rate, is the rate at which banks lend to each other, and is used globally to price financial products, such as mortgages, worth hundreds of trillions of dollars."[4]

While Volkswagen decided to cover the costs related to fines and lawsuits by reducing its capital budget for technology and research, Barclays took a different approach. The company chose to "cut or claw back of about 450 million pounds ($680 million) of pay from its staff" and from past pay packages "another 140 million pounds ($212 million)."[5] Instead of reducing other areas of its capital budget, Barclays decided to cover its fines and lawsuits by cutting employee compensation.

The LIBOR scandal involved a number of international banks and rocked the international banking community. An independent review of Barclays reported that "if Barclays is to achieve a material improvement in its reputation, it will need to continue to make changes to its top levels of pay so as to reflect talent and contribution more realistically, and in ways that mean something to the general public."[6] Previously, as described by the company website, "Barclays has been a leader in innovation; funding the world's first industrial steam railway, naming the UK's first female branch manager and introducing the world's first ATM machine."[7] The positive reputation Barclays built over 300 years was tarnished by just one scandal, and demonstrates the difficulty of calculating just how much unethical behavior will cost a company's reputation.

---

4   Charles Riley. "Remember the Libor Scandal? Well It's Coming Back to Haunt the Bank of England." CNN. April 10, 2017. https://money.cnn.com/2017/04/10/investing/bank-of-england-libor-barclays/index.html

5   Steve Slater. "Barclays to Cut Pay by $890 Million over Scandals: Source." Reuters. February 27, 2013. https://www.reuters.com/article/us-barclays-libor-pay/barclays-to-cut-pay-by-890-million-over-scandals-source-idUSBRE91Q0SD20130227

6   Anthony Salz. *Salz Review: An Independent Review of Barclays' Business Practices.* April 3, 2018. https://online.wsj.com/public/resources/documents/SalzReview04032013.pdf

7   "Our History." Barclays. n.d. https://www.banking.barclaysus.com/our-history.html

LINK TO LEARNING

A popular television show, *Shark Tank*, explores the decision-making process investors use when considering ownership in a new business. Entrepreneurs will pitch their business concept and current position to the "sharks," who will evaluate the business using capital budgeting methods, such as payback period and net present value, to decide whether or not to invest in the entrepreneur's company. Learn more about Shark Tank's concept and success stories (https://openstax.org/l/50SharkTank) on the web.

Key Terms

accounting rate of return (ARR) return on investment considering changes to net income

alternatives options available for investment

annuities due equal installments paid at the beginning of each payment period within the series

annuity series of equal payments made over time

capital investment company's contribution of funds toward long-term assets for further growth; also called *capital budgeting*

cash flow cash receipts and cash disbursements as a result of business activity

cash inflow money received or cost savings from a capital investment

cash outflow money paid or increased cost expenditures from capital investment

compounding earning interest on previous interest earned, along with the interest earned on the original investment

discounted cash flow model assigns a value to a business opportunity using time-value measurement tools

discounting process that determines the present value of a single payment or stream of payments to be received

future value (FV) value of an investment after a certain period of time

hurdle rate minimum required rate of return on an investment to consider an alternative for further evaluation

internal rate of return method (IRR) calculation to determine profitability or growth potential of an investment, expressed as a percentage, at the point where NPV equals zero

lump sum one-time payment or repayment of funds at a particular point in time

net present value method (NPV) discounts future cash flows to their present value at the expected rate of return, and compares that to the initial investment

non-time value methods analysis that does not consider the comparison value of a dollar today to a dollar in the future

operating expenses daily operational costs not associated with the direct selling of products or services

ordinary annuities equal installments paid at the end of each payment period within the series

payback method (PM) calculation of the length of time it takes a company to recoup their initial investment

preference decision process of comparing potential projects that meet screening decision criteria, and will rank order of importance, feasibility, and desirability to differentiate among alternatives

present value (PV) future value of an investment expressed in today's value

screening decision process of removing alternatives from the decision-making process that would be less desirable to pursue given their inability to meet basic standards

time value of money assertion that the value of a dollar today is worth more than the value of a dollar in the future

Summary

11.1 Describe Capital Investment Decisions and How They Are Applied

- Capital investment decisions select a project for future business development. These projects typically require a large outlay of cash, provide an uncertain return, and tie up resources for an extended period of time.
- Having a large number of alternatives requires a careful budgeting and analysis process. This process includes determining capital needs, exploring resource limitations, establishing baseline criteria for

alternatives, evaluating alternatives using screening and preference decisions, and making the decision.
- Screening decisions help eliminate undesirable alternatives that may waste time and money. Preference decisions rank alternatives emerging from the screening process to help make the final decision. Both decision avenues use capital budgeting methods to select between alternatives.

11.2 Evaluate the Payback and Accounting Rate of Return in Capital Investment Decisions
- The payback method determines how long it will take a company to recoup their investment. Annual cash flows are compared to the initial investment but the time value of money is not considered and cashflows beyond the payback period are ignored.
- The accounting rate of return considers incremental net income as it compares to the initial investment. Time value of money is not considered with this method.
- Incremental net income determines the net income expected if the company accepts the investment opportunity, as opposed to not investing. Incremental net income is the difference between incremental revenues and incremental expenses.

11.3 Explain the Time Value of Money and Calculate Present and Future Values of Lump Sums and Annuities
- A dollar is worth more today than it will be in the future. This is due to many reasons including the power of investment in today's economy, market inflation, and the ability to use the money in the present to make more money in the future, with interest.
- Present value expresses the future value of a dollar in today's (present) value. Present value tables, showing the present value factor intersection of periods and interest rate, are used to multiply by the final payout amount to compute today's value.
- The future value shows what the value of an investment will be after a certain period of time. Future value tables, showing the future value factor intersection of periods and interest rate, are used to multiply by the initial investment amount to compute future value.
- A lump sum is a one-time payment after a certain period of time, whereas an ordinary annuity involves equal installments in a series of payments over time. A business can use lump sum or ordinary annuity calculations for present value and future value calculations.

11.4 Use Discounted Cash Flow Models to Make Capital Investment Decisions
- The discounted cash flow model assigns values to a project's alternatives using time value of money and discounts future rates back to present value. Two measurement tools are used in discounted cash flows: net present value and internal rate of return.
- Net present value considers an expected rate of return, converts future cash flows into present value, and compares that to the initial investment cost. If the outcome is positive, the company would look to invest in the project.
- Internal rate of return shows the profitability of an investment, where NPV equals zero. If the corresponding interest rate exceeds the expected rate of return, the company would invest in the project.

11.5 Compare and Contrast Non-Time Value-Based Methods and Time Value-Based Methods in Capital Investment Decisions
- The payback method uses a simple calculation, removes unviable alternatives quickly, and considers investment risk. However, it disregards the time value of money, ignores profitability, and does not consider cash flows after recouping the investment.
- The accounting rate of return uses a simple calculation, considers profitability, and removes unviable options quickly. However, it disregards the time value of money, values return rates more than risk, and ignores external influential factors.

- Net present value considers the time value of money, ranks higher risk investments, and compares future earnings in today's value. However, it cannot easily compare dissimilar investment opportunities, it uses a more difficult calculation, and it has limitations with the estimation of an expected rate of return.
- Internal rate of return considers the time value of money, removes the dollar bias, and leads a company to a decision, unlike non-time value methods. However, it has a bias toward return rates instead of higher risk investment consideration, it is a more difficult calculation, and it does not consider the time it will take to recoup an investment.

Multiple Choice

1. LO 11.1 Capital investment decisions often involve all of the following *except* _____.
   A. qualitative factors or considerations
   B. short periods of time
   C. large amounts of money
   D. risk

2. LO 11.1 Preference decisions compare potential projects that meet screening decision criteria and will be ranked in their preference order to differentiate between alternatives with respect to all of the following characteristics *except* _____.
   A. political prominence
   B. feasibility
   C. desirability
   D. importance

3. LO 11.1 The third step for making a capital investment decision is to establish baseline criteria for alternatives. Which of the following would *not* be an acceptable baseline criterion?
   A. payback method
   B. accounting rate of return
   C. internal rate of return
   D. inventory turnover

4. LO 11.3 You are explaining time value of money factors to your friend. Which factor would you explain as being larger?
   A. The future value of $1 for 12 periods at 6% is larger.
   B. The present value of $1 for 12 periods at 6% is larger.
   C. Neither one is larger because they are equal.
   D. There is not enough information given to answer this question.

5. LO 11.3 If you are saving the same amount each month in order to buy a new sports car when the new models are released, which of the following will help you determine the savings needed?
   A. future value of one dollar ($1)
   B. present value of one dollar ($1)
   C. future value of an ordinary annuity
   D. present value of an ordinary annuity

6. LO 11.3 You want to invest $8,000 at an annual interest rate of 8% that compounds annually for 12 years. Which table will help you determine the value of your account at the end of 12 years?
   A. future value of one dollar ($1)
   B. present value of one dollar ($1)
   C. future value of an ordinary annuity
   D. present value of an ordinary annuity

7. LO 11.3 Using the information provided, what transaction represents the best application of the present value of an annuity due of $1?
   A. Falcon Products leases an office building for 8 years with annual lease payments of $100,000 to be made at the beginning of each year.
   B. Compass, Inc., signs a note of $32,000, which requires the company to pay back the principal plus interest in four years.
   C. Bahwat Company plans to deposit a lump sum of $100,000 for the construction of a solar farm in 4 years.
   D. NYC Industries leases a car for 4 yearly annual lease payments of $12,000, where payments are made at the end of each year.

8. LO 11.3 Grummet Company is acquiring a new wood lathe with a cash purchase price of $80,000. The Wood Master Industries (the manufacturer) has agreed to accept $23,500 at the end of each of the next 4 years. Based on this deal, how much interest will Grummet pay over the life of the loan?
   A. $94,000
   B. $80,000
   C. $23,500
   D. $14,000

9. LO 11.3 The process that determines the present value of a single payment or stream of payments to be received is _____.
   A. compounding
   B. discounting
   C. annuity
   D. lump-sum

10. LO 11.3 The process of reinvesting interest earned to generate additional earnings over time is _____.
   A. compounding
   B. discounting
   C. annuity
   D. lump-sum

11. LO 11.4 The NPV method assumes that cash inflows associated with a particular investment occur when?
   A. only at the time of the initial investment
   B. only at the end of the year
   C. only at the beginning of the year
   D. at any of these times

12. LO 11.4 Which of the following does *not* assign a value to a business opportunity using time-value measurement tools?
    A. internal rate of return (IRR) method
    B. net present value (NPV)
    C. discounted cash flow model
    D. payback period method

13. LO 11.4 Which of the following discounts future cash flows to their present value at the expected rate of return, and compares that to the initial investment?
    A. internal rate of return (IRR) method
    B. net present value (NPV)
    C. discounted cash flow model
    D. future value method

14. LO 11.4 This calculation determines profitability or growth potential of an investment, expressed as a percentage, at the point where NPV equals zero
    A. internal rate of return (IRR) method
    B. net present value (NPV)
    C. discounted cash flow model
    D. future value method

15. LO 11.5 The IRR method assumes that cash flows are reinvested at _____.
    A. the internal rate of return
    B. the company's discount rate
    C. the lower of the company's discount rate or internal rate of return
    D. an average of the internal rate of return and the discount rate

16. LO 11.5 When using the NPV method for a particular invenstment deicision, if the present value of all cash inflows is greater than the present value of all cash outflows, then _____.
    A. the discount rate used was too high
    B. the investment provides an actual rate of return greater than the discount rate
    C. the investment provides an actual rate of return equal to the discount rate
    D. the discount rate is too low

Questions

1. LO 11.1 What are the steps involved in the process for capital decision-making?

2. LO 11.1 Why does a company evaluate both the money allocated to a project and the time allocated to the project?

3. LO 11.1 What is the next thing a company needs to do after it establishes investment criteria?

4. LO 11.1 What is the screening decision?

5. LO 11.1 Your supervisor is on the company's capital investment decision team that is to decide on alternatives for the acquisition of a new computer system for the company. The supervisor says, "The book value of the existing computer system for the firm that we are considering replacing is nothing but an accounting amount and as such is irrelevant in the capital expenditure analysis." Does this reasoning make sense? Why or why not?

6. LO 11.1 Ekon owns a small tow-truck business that responds to state patrol requests to tow cars involved in wrecks, as well as to private business requests from customers at various auto repair shops and individuals with stalled autos. Ekon's business is open 24/7 for 365 days a year. He is starting to see too many repairs on his three trucks, which either means that he loses business or must divert a truck from another area. He is now trying to consider whether it is best to continue use of the current trucks or whether he needs to invest some money in new trucks.

Using the steps for the process of capital decision-making, create an outline with sub-steps that include questions Ekon can use to guide his investigation or considerations of buying new trucks.

7. LO 11.2 What is the payback method used to determine?

8. LO 11.2 What are one advantage and one disadvantage of the payback method?

9. LO 11.2 What are one advantage and one disadvantage of the accounting rate of return method?

10. LO 11.2 What is the equation to calculate the payback period?

11. LO 11.2 What is the equation to calculate the accounting rate of return?

12. LO 11.3 What is future value and what is one example where it might be used?

13. LO 11.3 Why do businesses consider time value of money before making an investment decision?

14. LO 11.3 What determines the anticipated interest rate payout for an investment?

15. LO 11.3 To calculate present value of a lump sum, which table would be used?

16. LO 11.3 What is the definition of *present value*?

17. LO 11.4 What is the difference between the discount rate used for net present value and the internal rate of return methods?

18. LO 11.4 Briefly explain how NPV is computed and interpreted.

19. LO 11.4 What is the basic benefit of using IRR?

20. LO 11.4 How is the IRR determined if there are uneven cash flows?

21. LO 11.5 A fellow student studying managerial accounting says, "The net present value (NPV) weighs early receipts of cash much more heavily than more distant receipts of cash." Do you agree or disagree? Why?

22. LO 11.5 What are the strengths and weaknesses of NPV?

23. LO 11.5 What are the strengths and weaknesses of IRR?

24. LO 11.5 How does the size of the initial investment affect the internal rate of return on the net present value models?

Exercise Set A

EA1. LO 11.1 Bob's Auto Repair has determined that it needs new lift equipment to acquire more business opportunities. However, one or more alternatives meet or exceed the minimum expectations Bob has for the new lift equipment. As a result, what type of decision should Bob make for his company?

EA2. LO 11.1 In practice, external factors can impact a capital investment. Give a current external factor that may currently impact or cause instability of capital spending either here or abroad.

EA3. LO 11.2 If a copy center is considering the purchase of a new copy machine with an initial investment cost of $150,000 and the center expects an annual net cash flow of $20,000 per year, what is the payback period?

EA4. LO 11.2 Assume a company is going to make an investment of $450,000 in a machine and the following are the cash flows that two different products would bring in years one through four. Which of the two options would you choose based on the payback method?

Option A, Product A	Option B, Product B
$190,000	$150,000
190,000	180,000
60,000	60,000
20,000	70,000

EA5. LO 11.2 If a garden center is considering the purchase of a new tractor with an initial investment cost of $120,000, and the center expects a return of $30,000 in year one, $20,000 in years two and three, $15,000 in years four and five, and $10,000 in year six and beyond, what is the payback period?

EA6. LO 11.2 The management of Kawneer North America is considering investing in a new facility and the following cash flows are expected to result from the investment:

Year	Cash Outflow	Cash Inflow
1	$1,900,000	$100,000
2	550,000	200,000
3		360,000
4		480,000
5		510,000
6		600,000
7		590,000
8		300,000
9		250,000
10		250,000

A. What is the payback period of this uneven cash flow?
B. Does your answer change if year 10's cash inflow changes to $500,000?

EA7. LO 11.2 A mini-mart needs a new freezer and the initial investment will cost $300,000. Incremental revenues, including cost savings, are $200,000, and incremental expenses, including depreciation, are $125,000. There is no salvage value. What is the accounting rate of return (ARR)?

EA8. LO 11.3 You put $250 in the bank for 5 years at 12%.
  A. If interest is added at the end of the year, how much will you have in the bank after one year? Calculate the amount you will have in the bank at the end of year two and continue to calculate all the way to the end of the fifth year.
  B. Use the future value of $1 table in Appendix B and verify that your answer is correct.

EA9. LO 11.3 If you invest $12,000 today, how much will you have in (for further instructions on future value in Excel, see Appendix C):
  A. 10 years at 9%
  B. 8 years at 12%
  C. 14 years at 15%
  D. 19 years at 18%

EA10. LO 11.3 You have been depositing money into an account yearly based on the following investment amounts, rates and times, what is the value of that investment account at the end of that period?

Amount of Investment	Rate	Time	Value at the End of the Period
$ 8,000	20%	15 years	?
12,000	15%	10 years	?
15,500	12%	5 years	?
35,500	10%	2 years	?

EA11. LO 11.3 How much would you invest today in order to receive $30,000 in each of the following (for further instructions on present value in Excel, see Appendix C):
  A. 10 years at 9%
  B. 8 years at 12%
  C. 14 years at 15%
  D. 19 years at 18%

EA12. LO 11.3 Your friend has a trust fund that will pay her the following amounts at the given interest rate for the given number of years. Calculate the current (present) value of your friend's trust fund payments. For further instructions on future value in Excel, see Appendix C.

Amount of Yearly Receipt	Rate	Time	Current Value
$ 6,200	10%	5 years	?
12,200	12%	10 years	?
18,000	15%	15 years	?
22,500	20%	20 years	?

EA13. LO 11.3 Julio Company is considering the purchase of a new bubble packaging machine. If the machine will provide $20,000 annual savings for 10 years and can be sold for $50,000 at the end of the period, what is the present value of the machine investment at a 9% interest rate with savings realized at year end?

EA14. LO 11.3 How much must be invested now to receive $30,000 for 10 years if the first $30,000 is received one year from now and the rate is 8%?

EA15. LO 11.4 Project A costs $5,000 and will generate annual after-tax net cash inflows of $1,800 for five years. What is the NPV using 8% as the discount rate?

EA16. LO 11.4 Project B cost $5,000 and will generate after-tax net cash inflows of $500 in year one, $1,200 in year two, $2,000 in year three, $2,500 in year four, and $2,000 in year five. What is the NPV using 8% as the discount rate? For further instructions on net present value in Excel, see Appendix C.

EA17. LO 11.4 Gardner Denver Company is considering the purchase of a new piece of factory equipment that will cost $420,000 and will generate $95,000 per year for 5 years. Calculate the IRR for this piece of equipment. For further instructions on internal rate of return in Excel, see Appendix C.

EA18. LO 11.4 Consolidated Aluminum is considering the purchase of a new machine that will cost $308,000 and provide the following cash flows over the next five years: $88,000, 92,000, $91,000, $72,000, and $71,000. Calculate the IRR for this piece of equipment. For further instructions on internal rate of return in Excel, see Appendix C.

EA19. LO 11.4 Redbird Company is considering a project with an initial investment of $265,000 in new equipment that will yield annual net cash flows of $45,800 each year over its seven-year life. The company's minimum required rate of return is 8%. What is the internal rate of return? Should Redbird accept the project based on IRR?

EA20. LO 11.5 Towson Industries is considering an investment of $256,950 that is expected to generate returns of $90,000 per year for each of the next four years. What is the investment's internal rate of return?

EA21. LO 11.5 Cinemar Productions bought a piece of equipment for $55,898 that will last for 5 years. The equipment will generate net operating cash flows of $14,000 per year and will have no salvage value at the end of its life. What is the internal rate of return?

Exercise Set B

EB1. LO 11.1 Margo's Memories, a company that specializes in photography and creating family and group photo portfolios, has 50 stores in major malls around the U.S. The company is considering an online business, which will require a substantial investment in web design, security, payment processing, and technology in order to launch successfully. What potential advantages or disadvantages will be difficult to quantify from a capital investment standpoint?

EB2. LO 11.1 Boxer Production, Inc., is in the process of considering a flexible manufacturing system that will help the company react more swiftly to customer needs. The controller, Mick Morrell, estimated that the system will have a 10-year life and a required return of 10% with a net present value of negative $500,000. Nevertheless, he acknowledges that he did not quantify the potential sales increases that might result from this improvement on the issue of on-time delivery, because it was too difficult to quantify.

If there is a general agreement that qualitative factors may offer an additional net cash flow of $150,000 per year, how should Boxer proceed with this investment?

EB3. LO 11.2 A restaurant is considering the purchase of new tables and chairs for their dining room with an initial investment cost of $515,000, and the restaurant expects an annual net cash flow of $103,000 per year. What is the payback period?

EB4. LO 11.2 Assume a company is going to make an investment in a machine of $825,000 and the following are the cash flows that two different products would bring. Which of the two options would you choose based on the payback method?

Option A, Product A	Option B, Product B
$245,000	$225,000
195,000	345,000
295,000	250,000
245,000	225,000

EB5. LO 11.2 A grocery store is considering the purchase of a new refrigeration unit with an initial investment of $412,000, and the store expects a return of $100,000 in year one, $72,000 in years two and three, $65,000 in years four and five, and $38,000 in year six and beyond, what is the payback period?

EB6. LO 11.2 The management of Ryland International is considering investing in a new facility and the following cash flows are expected to result from the investment:

Year	Cash Outflow	Cash Inflow
1	$ 700,000	$200,000
2	2,100,000	400,000
3		260,000
4		360,000
5		260,000
6		800,000
7		480,000
8		400,000
9		420,000
10		420,000

A. What is the payback period of this uneven cash flow?
B. Does your answer change if year 6's cash inflow changes to $920,000?

EB7. LO 11.2 An auto repair company needs a new machine that will check for defective sensors. The machine has an initial investment of $224,000. Incremental revenues, including cost savings, are $120,000, and incremental expenses, including depreciation, are $50,000. There is no salvage value. What is the accounting rate of return (ARR)?

EB8. LO 11.3 You put $600 in the bank for 3 years at 15%.
   A. If interest is added at the end of the year, how much will you have in the bank after one year? Calculate the amount you will have in the bank at the end of year two and continue to calculate all the way to the end of the third year.
   B. Use the future value of $1 table in Appendix B and verify that your answer is correct.

EB9. LO 11.3 If you invest $15,000 today, how much will you have in (for further instructions on future value in Excel, see Appendix C):
   A. 20 years at 22%
   B. 12 years at 10%
   C. 5 years at 14%
   D. 2 years at 7%

EB10. LO 11.3 You have been depositing money into an account yearly based on the following investment amounts, rates and times. What is the value of that investment account at the end of that period?

Amount of Investment	Rate	Time	Value at the End of the Period
$ 4,000	12%	14 years	?
6,000	15%	10 years	?
13,500	10%	8 years	?
22,250	20%	6 years	?

EB11. LO 11.3 How much would you invest today in order to receive $30,000 in each of the following (for further instructions on present value in Excel, see Appendix C):

A. 20 years at 22%
B. 12 years at 10%
C. 5 years at 14%
D. 2 years at 7%

EB12. LO 11.3 Your friend has a trust fund that will pay her the following amounts at the given interest rate for the given number of years. Calculate the current (present) value of your friend's trust fund payments. For further instructions on present value in Excel, see Appendix C.

Amount of Yearly Receipt	Rate	Time	Current Value
$ 5,000	10%	5 years	?
7,500	12%	10 years	?
14,000	15%	15 years	?
25,000	20%	20 years	?

EB13. LO 11.3 Conestoga Plumbing plans to invest in a new pump that is anticipated to provide annual savings for 10 years of $50,000. The pump can be sold at the end of the period for $100,000. What is the present value of the investment in the pump at a 9% interest rate given that savings are realized at year end?

EB14. LO 11.3 How much must be invested now to receive $50,000 for 8 years if the first $50,000 is received in one year and the rate is 10%?

EB15. LO 11.4 Project X costs $10,000 and will generate annual net cash inflows of $4,800 for five years. What is the NPV using 8% as the discount rate?

EB16. LO 11.4 Project Y cost $8,000 and will generate net cash inflows of $1,500 in year one, $2,000 in year two, $2,500 in year three, $3,000 in year four and $2,000 in year five. What is the NPV using 8% as the discount rate?

EB17. LO 11.4 Caduceus Company is considering the purchase of a new piece of factory equipment that will cost $565,000 and will generate $135,000 per year for 5 years. Calculate the IRR for this piece of equipment. For further instructions on internal rate of return in Excel, see Appendix C.

EB18. LO 11.4 Garnette Corp is considering the purchase of a new machine that will cost $342,000 and provide the following cash flows over the next five years: $99,000, $88,000, $92,000, $87,000, and $72,000. Calculate the IRR for this piece of equipment. For further instructions on internal rate of return in Excel, see Appendix C.

EB19. LO 11.4 Wallace Company is considering two projects. Their required rate of return is 10%.

	Project A	Project B
Initial investment	$170,000	$48,000
Annual cash flows	$41,352	$12,022
Life of the project	6 years	5 years

Which of the two projects, A or B, is better in terms of internal rate of return?

EB20. LO 11.5 Taos Productions bought a piece of equipment for $79,860 that will last for 5 years. The equipment will generate net operating cash flows of $20,000 per year and will have no salvage value at the end of its life. What is the internal rate of return?

Problem Set A

PA1. LO 11.2 Your company is planning to purchase a new log splitter for its lawn and garden business. The new splitter has an initial investment of $180,000. It is expected to generate $25,000 of annual cash flows, provide incremental cash revenues of $150,000, and incur incremental cash expenses of $100,000 annually.

What is the payback period and accounting rate of return (ARR)?

PA2. LO 11.2 Jasmine Manufacturing is considering a project that will require an initial investment of $52,000 and is expected to generate future cash flows of $10,000 for years 1 through 3, $8,000 for years 4 and 5, and $2,000 for years 6 through 10. What is the payback period for this project?

PA3. LO 11.3 Use the tables in Appendix B to answer the following questions.
   A. If you would like to accumulate $2,500 over the next 4 years when the interest rate is 15%, how much do you need to deposit in the account?
   B. If you place $6,200 in a savings account, how much will you have at the end of 7 years with a 12% interest rate?
   C. You invest $8,000 per year for 10 years at 12% interest, how much will you have at the end of 10 years?
   D. You win the lottery and can either receive $750,000 as a lump sum or $50,000 per year for 20 years. Assuming you can earn 8% interest, which do you recommend and why?

PA4. LO 11.3 Ralston Consulting, Inc., has a $25,000 overdue debt with Supplier No. 1. The company is low on cash, with only $7,000 in the checking account and does not want to borrow any more cash. Supplier No. 1 agrees to settle the account in one of two ways:

Option 1: Pay $7,000 now and $23,750 when some large projects are finished, two years from today.

Option 2: Pay $35,000 three years from today, when even larger projects are finished.

Assuming that the only factor in the decision is the cost of money (8%), which option should Ralston choose?

PA5. LO 11.4 Falkland, Inc., is considering the purchase of a patent that has a cost of $50,000 and an estimated revenue producing life of 4 years. Falkland has a cost of capital of 8%. The patent is expected to generate the following amounts of annual income and cash flows:

	Year 1	Year 2	Year 3	Year 4
Net income	$ 5,100	$ 6,500	$ 6,300	$ 3,000
Operating cash flows	17,050	18,450	18,250	14,850

A. What is the NPV of the investment?
B. What happens if the required rate of return increases?

PA6. LO 11.4 There are two projects under consideration by the Rainbow factory. Each of the projects will require an initial investment of $35,000 and is expected to generate the following cash flows:

	Year 1	Year 2	Year 3	Total
Alpha Project	$32,000	$22,500	$ 5,000	$59,500
Beta Project	7,500	23,500	28,000	59,000

If the discount rate is 12%, compute the NPV of each project.

PA7. LO 11.4 There are two projects under consideration by the Rainbow factory. Each of the projects will require an initial investment of $35,000 and is expected to generate the following cash flows:

	Year 1	Year 2	Year 3	Total
Alpha Project	$32,000	$22,500	$ 5,000	$59,500
Beta Project	7,500	23,500	28,000	59,000

Use the information from the previous exercise to calculate the internal rate of return on both projects and make a recommendation on which one to accept. For further instructions on internal rate of return in Excel, see Appendix C.

PA8. LO 11.4 Pompeii's Pizza has a delivery car that it uses for pizza deliveries. The transmission needs to be replaced and there are several other repairs that need to be done. The car is nearing the end of its life, so the options are to either overhaul the car or replace it with a new car. Pompeii's has put together the following budgetary items:

	Present Car	New Car
Purchase cost new		$31,000
Transmission and other repairs	$ 8,500	
Annual cash operating cost	12,500	10,000
Fair market value now	5,000	
Fair market value in five years	500	5,000

If Pompeii's replaces the transmission of the pizza delivery vehicle, they expect to be able to use the vehicle for another 5 years. If they sell the old vehicle and purchase a new vehicle, they will use that vehicle for 5 years and then trade it in for another new pizza delivery vehicle. If they trade for the new delivery vehicle, their operating expenses will decrease because the new vehicle is more gas efficient and the maintenance on a new car is less. This project is analyzed using a discount rate of 12%. What should Pompeii's do?

PA9. LO 11.4 Pitt Company is considering two alternative investments. The company requires a 12% return from its investments. Neither option has a salvage value.

	Project X	Project Y
Initial investment	$180,000	$118,000
Net cash flows anticipated:		
Year 1	82,000	35,000
Year 2	59,000	55,000
Year 3	92,000	72,000
Year 4	81,000	68,000
Year 5	76,000	27,000

Compute the IRR for both projects and recommend one of them. For further instructions on internal rate of return in Excel, see Appendix C.

PA10. LO 11.5 The Ham and Egg Restaurant is considering an investment in a new oven that has a cost of $60,000, with annual net cash flows of $9,950 for 8 years. The required rate of return is 6%. Compute the net present value of this investment to determine whether or not you would recommend that Ham and Egg invest in this oven.

PA11. LO 11.5 Gallant Sports is considering the purchase of a new rock-climbing facility. The company estimates that the construction will require an initial outlay of $350,000. Other cash flows are estimated as follows:

Year 1	($ 60,000)
Year 2	$140,000
Year 3	$210,000
Year 4	$130,000

Assuming the company limits its analysis to four years due to economic uncertainties, determine the net present value of the rock-climbing facility. Should the company develop the facility if the required rate of return is 6%?

Problem Set B

PB1. LO 11.2 A bookstore is planning to purchase an automated inventory/remote marketing system, which includes an upgrade to a more sophisticated cash register system. The package has an initial investment cost of $360,000. It is expected to generate $144,000 of annual cash flows, reduce costs and provide incremental cash revenues of $326,000, and incur incremental cash expenses of $200,000 annually.

What is the payback period and accounting rate of return (ARR)?

PB2. LO 11.2 Markoff Products is considering two competing projects, but only one will be selected. Project A requires an initial investment of $42,000 and is expected to generate future cash flows of $6,000 for each of the next 50 years. Project B requires an initial investment of $210,000 and will generate $30,000 for each of the next 10 years. If Markoff requires a payback of 8 years or less, which project should it select based on payback periods?

PB3. LO 11.3 Use the tables in Appendix B to answer the following questions.
  A. If you would like to accumulate $4,200 over the next 6 years when the interest rate is 8%, how much do you need to deposit in the account?
  B. If you place $8,700 in a savings account, how much will you have at the end of 12 years with an interest rate of 8%?
  C. You invest $2,000 per year, at the end of the year, for 20 years at 10% interest. How much will you have at the end of 20 years?
  D. You win the lottery and can either receive $500,000 as a lump sum or $60,000 per year for 20 years. Assuming you can earn 3% interest, which do you recommend and why?

PB4. LO 11.3 Chang Consulting, Inc., has a $15,000 overdue debt with Supplier No. 1. The company is low on cash, with only $4,000 in the checking account and does not want to borrow any more cash. Supplier No. 1 agrees to settle the account in one of two ways:

Option 1: Pay $4,000 now and $18,750 when some large projects are finished, two years from today.

Option 2: Pay $25,000 three years from today, when even larger projects are finished.

Assuming that the only factor in the decision is the cost of money (8%), which option should Clary choose?

PB5. LO 11.4 Mason, Inc., is considering the purchase of a patent that has a cost of $85,000 and an estimated revenue producing life of 4 years. Mason has a required rate of return that is 12% and a cost of capital of 11%. The patent is expected to generate the following amounts of annual income and cash flows:

	Year 1	Year 2	Year 3	Total
Net income	$ 6,900	$ 9,600	$ 3,000	$ 6,300
Operating cash flows	19,500	18,700	20,250	15,900

  A. What is the NPV of the investment?
  B. What happens if the required rate of return increases?

PB6. LO 11.4 There are two projects under consideration by the Rainbow factory. Each of the projects will require an initial investment or $28,000 and is expected to generate the following cash flows:

	Year 1	Year 2	Year 3	Total
Alpha Project	22,000	23,500	5,000	50,500
Beta Project	12,700	22,000	15,800	50,500

If the discount rate is 5% compute the NPV of each project and make a recommendation of the project to be chosen.

PB7. LO 11.4 Use the information from the previous exercise to calculate the Internal Rate of Return on both projects and make a recommendation regarding which one to accept.

PB8. LO 11.4 D&M Pizza has a delivery car that is uses for pizza deliveries. The transmission needs to be replaced, and there are several other repairs that need to be done. The car is nearing the end of its life, so the options are to either overhaul the car or replace it with a new car. D&M's has put together the following budgetary items:

	Present Car	New Car
Purchase cost new		$30,000
Transmission and repairs	$6,500	
Annual cash operating cost	8,500	7,500
Fair market value now	6,000	
Fair market value in five years	1,000	6,000

If D&M replaces the transmission of the pizza delivery vehicle, they expect to be able to use the vehicle for another 5 years. If they purchase a new vehicle, they will sell the existing one and use the new vehicle for 5 years and then trade it in for another new pizza delivery vehicle. If they trade for the new delivery vehicle, their operating expenses will decrease because the new vehicle is more gas efficient. This project is analyzed using a discount rate of 15%. What should D&M do?

PB9. LO 11.4 Joliet Company is considering two alternative investments. The company requires an 18% return from its investments.

	Project X	Project Y
Initial investment	$108,000	$98,000
Net cash flows anticipated:		
Year 1	36,000	25,000
Year 2	39,000	45,000
Year 3	32,000	42,000
Year 4	34,000	28,000
Year 5	25,000	17,000

Compute the IRR for both Projects and recommend one of them. For further instructions on internal rate of return in Excel, see Appendix C.

PB10. LO 11.5 Bouvier Restaurant is considering an investment in a grill that costs $140,000, and will produce annual net cash flows of $21,950 for 8 years. The required rate of return is 6%.

Compute the net present value of this investment to determine whether Bouvier should invest in the grill.

 Thought Provokers

TP1. LO 11.1 What is the benefit(s) of the accountant's involvement in the capital investment decision?

TP2. LO 11.1 Austin's cell phone manufacturer wants to upgrade their product mix to encompass an exciting new feature on their cell phone. This would require a new high-tech machine. You are excited about his new project and are recommending the purchase to your board of directors. Here is the information you have compiled in order to complete this recommendation:

Unit selling price	$ 45
Unit variable cost	$ 25
Fixed costs	$200,000
Deprecation costs	$ 35,000
Expected sales	10,000 units per year

According to the information, the project will last 10 years and require an initial investment of $800,000, depreciated with straight-line over the life of the project until the final value is zero. The firm's tax rate is 30% and the required rate of return is 12%. You believe that the variable cost and sales volume may be as much as 10% higher or lower than the initial estimate. Your boss understands the risks but asks you to explain the alternatives in a brief memo to the board. Write a memo to the Board of Directors objectively weighing out the pros and cons of this project and make your recommendation(s).

TP3. LO 11.3 Would you rather have $7,500 today or at the end of 20 years after it has been invested at 15%? Explain your answer.

The following are independent situations. For each capital budgeting project, indicate whether management should accept or reject the project and list a brief reason why.

TP4. LO 11.4 Midas Corp. evaluated a potential investment and determined the NPV to be zero. Midas Corp.'s required rate of return is 9.1% and its cost of capital is 6.4%.

TP5. LO 11.4 Giorgio Co. is looking at an investment project with an internal rate of return of 10.8%. The initial outlay for the investment is $90,000. The hurdle rate or minimum acceptable rate of return is 10.2%.

TP6. LO 11.4 Dinaro Inc. is looking at an investment project that has an NPV of ($5,000). The hurdle rate is 8%.

TP7. LO 11.4 You begin a new job at Cabrera Medical Supplies. The company is considering a new accounting system, with an initial investment of about half a million dollars for new software and hardware. You are excited for the opportunity to apply your managerial accounting skills regarding screening and preference methods to decide on the best system for the company. Your boss is a little old-school, and when you mention some of the things you learned in managerial accounting, he says, "Discounted cash flow methods are not the only way to approach this. I have more of a gut reaction approach that blows most managers out of the water when they become absorbed by discounted cash flow methods (DCF)."

How would you react and what would you discuss with your boss?

TP8. **LO 11.5** Fenton, Inc., has established a new strategic plan that calls for new capital investment. The company has a 9.8% required rate of return and an 8.3% cost of capital. Fenton currently has a return of 10% on its other investments. The proposed new investments have equal annual cash inflows expected. Management used a screening procedure of calculating a payback period for potential investments and annual cash flows, and the IRR for the 7 possible investments are displayed in image. Each investment has a 6-year expected useful life and no salvage value.

	Payback Period	IRR	Investment Cost
Project A1	4.2	10.5%	$130,000
Project B2	5.9	5.1%	67,000
Project C3	5.0	13.4%	83,000
Project D4	4.8	7.4%	61,000
Project E5	3.2	12.1%	115,000
Project F6	4.0	9.9%	65,000
Project G7	6.3	9.8%	76,000

A. Identify which project(s) is/are unacceptable and briefly state the conceptual justification as to why each of your choices is unacceptable.

B. Assume Fenton has $330,000 available to spend. Which remaining projects should Fenton invest in and in what order?

C. If Fenton was not limited to a spending amount, should they invest in all of the projects given the company is evaluated using return on investment?

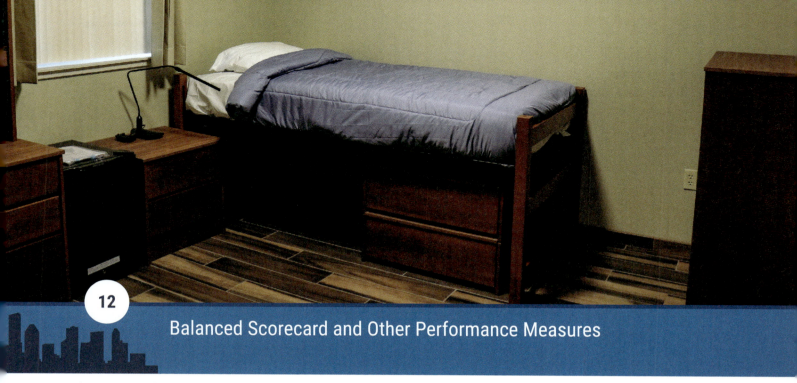

12 Balanced Scorecard and Other Performance Measures

Figure 12.1 Clean Room. A dorm room tidied up by Passing Inspection Cleaning and Organizing. (credit: modification of "170203-A-IE537-004" by U.S. Army Corp of Engineers's photostream/Flickr, CC BY 2.0)

Chapter Outline

- **LO 12.1** Explain the Importance of Performance Measurement
- **LO 12.2** Identify the Characteristics of an Effective Performance Measure
- **LO 12.3** Evaluate an Operating Segment or a Project Using Return on Investment, Residual Income, and Economic Value Added
- **LO 12.4** Describe the Balanced Scorecard and Explain How It Is Used

Why It Matters

A friend comes to you in a panic. His parents are coming to visit, and his apartment is a complete mess. Although he and his roommates frequently say they should clean, now the apartment has gotten so messy that they don't even know where to begin. He knows your place always looks clean and orderly, so he is seeking your help. You offer to help your friend, and, in the process, come up with a business idea.

To address the needs of students like your friend, you create a company—Passing Inspection Cleaning and Organizing—that will clean and/or organize dorm rooms and apartments. You set up a list of ten standard cleaning tasks that will be performed for a flat fee, and put together a list of à la carte services, such as laundry, closet organization, and refrigerator cleaning. Four students sign on with you as employees. Because it is important for your company to have a good reputation, you want to motivate your employees to perform their tasks to a high standard. You also want your employees to solicit additional business whenever possible by handing out flyers or business cards to nearby rooms and apartments when on a cleaning assignment.

How can you motivate your employees to perform to your standards so that your company goals are met? Will an hourly wage be sufficient? Should you pay per task or per job? What motivation will they have to sell your company's services to others? How will you know if they are performing the tasks in the manner you set forth? To answer these questions, you will need to be aware of the goals of your company, such as increasing the number of clients, as well as the goals of your employees, such as receiving raises, bonuses, or promotions. Armed with this knowledge, you will be able to design relevant evaluation measures and tie those measures to appropriate performance rewards so that both your goals and the goals of your employees are met. This same need—to measure the performance of a business and its employees so that each party's goals are met—is an issue that affects all businesses, regardless of size or type.

12.1 Explain the Importance of Performance Measurement

As you learned in Responsibility Accounting and Decentralization, as a company grows, it will often decentralize to better control operations and therefore improve decision-making. Remember, a decentralized organization is one in which the decision-making is spread among various managers throughout the organization and does not solely rest with the chief executive officer (CEO). However, with this dispersion of decision-making comes an even greater need to monitor the results of the decisions made by the many managers at the various levels of the organization to ensure that the overall goals of the organization are still being met.

ETHICAL CONSIDERATIONS

Ethical Evaluation of Performance Measures

To evaluate whether decisions made by management are both effective and ethical, performance is measured through responsibility accounting. This is a double-layer ethical analysis that requires some thought to establish and implement, as the evaluation system must also operate in an ethical fashion, just as the decision-making process itself does. In most organizations, the overall results of choices made by management, not just the resulting profit, need to be examined to determine whether or not the decisions are ethical.

When an organization's customers and other stakeholders are happy, and the corporate assets are in good condition, these are indicators that the customers, stakeholders, and assets are being treated ethically. Evaluation of customer and stakeholder satisfaction should come directly from the customer, such as through surveys or other direct questionnaires. Proper treatment of organizational assets can be determined by viewing the physical condition of such assets, or the loss rates and productivity of equipment. Customer satisfaction and positive results in the utilization of corporate assets typically indicate ethical decision-making and behavior, while negative results typically indicate the opposite. An organization with a satisfied group of stakeholders and customers, as well as assets that operate efficiently, is often more profitable in the long term.

Managerial accountants therefore must design a framework of **responsibility accounting** in which the evaluation system is based on criteria for which a manager is responsible. The framework should be structured to encourage managers to make decisions that will meet the goals of the company as well as their own professional goals. In your study of managerial accounting, you have learned about company goals such as increasing market share, increasing revenues, decreasing costs, and decreasing defects. Managers and employees have their own goals. These goals can be work related such as promotions or awards, or they can be more personal such as receiving raises, receiving bonuses, the privilege of telecommuting, or shares of company stock. This aligning of goals between a corporation's strategy and a manager's personal goals is known as **goal congruence**. Managers should make the best decisions for the benefit of the corporation, and the best way to motivate a manager to make those decisions is to link a reward system to performance results. To accomplish this, a business establishes performance evaluation measures that align the decisions made by management with the goals of the corporation and the professional goals of the manager.

Fundamentals of Performance Measurement

Performance measurement is used to motivate managers to make decisions that benefit the corporation and themselves. Therefore, the key to good performance measurement techniques is to set goals that are realistic and that incorporate decisions over which the manager has control. Then, the company can evaluate the manager based on **controllable factors**, which are the components of the organization for which the manager is responsible and that the manager can control, such as revenues, costs and procurement of long-term assets, and other possible factors. Recall that in Responsibility Accounting and Decentralization, you learned about responsibility centers, which are a means by which an organization can be divided based on factors that the manager can control. This makes it easier to align the goals of the manager with those of the organization and to design effective performance measures. The four types of responsibility centers are revenue centers, cost centers, profit centers, and investment centers.

In a **revenue center**, the manager has control over the revenues that are generated for the corporation but not over the costs of the organization. For example, the reservations department of an airline is a revenue center because the reservationists can control revenues by selling customers upgrades such as meals or first-class seating, by selling trip insurance, or by trying to keep customers from going to another airline. However, reservationists cannot control the costs of the flights the airline is offering and reserving because the reservation department cannot control the cost of the planes, airport space rental, or jet fuel. Therefore, the manager of the reservation department should have performance evaluations measures closely related to revenue generation.

In a **cost center**, the manager has control over costs but not over revenues. An example of a cost center would be the accounting department of a grocery store chain. The manager can control the types of people hired, the wages that are paid, and the hours that are worked within that department, and each of these costs contributes to the total cost of the department. However, the manager of the accounting department has no control over the generation of revenues.

In a **profit center**, the manager has control over both revenues and costs. An example would be a single location of Best Buy. The manager at that store has control over both revenues and costs; therefore, one component of evaluation for that manager will be store profits.

An **investment center** is a component of a business for which the manager has control over revenues, costs, and capital assets. This means the manager not only can make decisions regarding generating revenues and controlling costs but also has authority to make decisions regarding assets, such as buying new machines, expanding facilities, or selling old assets. With each of these types of centers, designing the appropriate performance measures begins with evaluating management based on which business areas they oversee.

Using the previous revenue center example, the manager of the reservation department should be evaluated on how well his team generates revenues. The proper incentives will motivate the team to perform better at their jobs. Evaluating a manager on the outcome of decisions over which he or she has no control, or **uncontrollable factors**, will be demotivating and does not promote goal congruence between the organization and the manager. The reservations manager has no control over fuel costs, plane maintenance costs, or pilot salaries. Thus, it would not be logical to evaluate the manager on flight costs.

A good **performance measurement system** is one that utilizes appropriate **performance measures**, which are performance metrics used to evaluate a specific attribute of a manager's role, to evaluate management in a way that will link the goals of the corporation with those of the manager. A **metric** is simply a means to measure something. For example, high school grade point average is a metric used by colleges when considering admission of prospective students, as it is considered a measure of prior academic success. In the business environment, individuals who design the performance measurement system must have extensive knowledge of the corporate strategic plan and the overall goals set by the organization, and a clear understanding of the job descriptions, responsibilities of each manager, and trends in rewards and compensation.

THINK IT THROUGH

Motivating Dental Industry Employees

As a dentist and owner of your own practice, you are considering ways to both reward and motivate your staff. The obvious choice is to simply give each employee a raise. However, you have heard that many businesses are compensating their employees for meeting various goals that are beneficial to the business. What types of goals might the dental practice have? What are several ideas for ways to motivate the staff, which consists of a receptionist, dental assistants, and dental hygienists? What are possible rewards for meeting goals?

Advantages Derived from Performance Measurement

Every business has a **strategic plan**, or a broad vision of how it will be in the future. This plan leads to goals that must be achieved to fulfill that vision. As shown in Figure 12.2, a business will use the strategic plan to determine the goals needed to achieve the strategic vision. Once goals are determined, the business will decide on the appropriate actions necessary to meet the goals. Then, the business will implement, review, and adjust the goals as needed. Properly designed performance measures will help move the company toward meeting the goals of its strategic plan. Advantages of a good performance management system include increased employee retention and loyalty, better communication between the various levels of management, increased productivity, and increased efficiencies. In addition, a well-designed performance plan should lead to improved job satisfaction for the manager and increased personal wealth if the rewards are monetarily based. In summary, a company needs to first identify and create a strategy and then set the necessary goals, which will lead to actions, and finally to an applicable evaluation process.

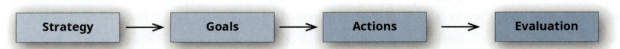

Figure 12.2 Strategy-to-Action Sequence. (attribution: Copyright Rice University, OpenStax, under CC BY-NC-SA 4.0 license)

YOUR TURN

Measuring Employee Performance

All companies need ways to measure the performance of employees. These measures should be designed in a way that the rewards for performance will motivate the employees to make decisions that are good for the business. Reflecting on the Why It Matters scenario, if this were your company, what are five goals you would have for your business? What are some measures you could use to see if you are meeting those goals? What types of incentives could you offer to motivate your employees to help meet these goals? Use Table 12.1 for your answers.

Motivating Employees toward Business Goals

Five Business Goals	Measures to Meet Goals	Incentives to Motivate Employees toward Goals

Table 12.1

Solution

Answers will vary. Sample answer:

Motivating Employees toward Business Goals

Five Business Goals	Measures to Meet Goals	Incentives to Motivate Employees toward Goals
Grow customer base	Number of new customers	Give a gift card to employees for each new customer they get
Increase company name recognition	Number of "likes" on Facebook, number of reviews on Google	Host a party or take employees to dinner after certain number of likes or positive reviews occur
Grow revenue each quarter	Percent change in revenue from prior quarter	Have a bonus pool that is shared after a targeted percentage increase in revenue is reached

Motivating Employees toward Business Goals		
Five Business Goals	**Measures to Meet Goals**	**Incentives to Motivate Employees toward Goals**
Lower cost of supplies used per job	Compare supplies used to a standard for each type of job	Provide a paid day off for suggestions that successfully reduce cost of supplies per job by 5%
Decrease time at each job/ increase efficiency	Measure time on job using a call-in system of entering and leaving the job	Pay a flat additional amount for each time the employee performs a job within the allotted time and that customer satisfaction is a 5/5

Potential Limitations of Traditional Performance Measurement

What types of measures are used to evaluate management performance? Historically, performance measurement systems have been based on accounting or other quantitative numbers. One reason for this is that most accounting-based measures are easy to use due to their availability, since many accounting measures can be found in or generated from a company's financial statements. Although this type of information is readily available, it does not mean the use of accounting numbers as performance measures is the best or only way to measure performance. One issue is that some accounting numbers can be affected by the actions of managers, and this may result in distorted performance results.

For example, as shown in Figure 12.3, if a retail company uses a last-in, first-out (LIFO) inventory system and the manager of the retail store is evaluated based on either cost containment or profit, the manager can postpone a decision to purchase inventory at the end of the year until the beginning of the next fiscal year if prices of the inventory have risen. This decision will postpone the effect of that purchase and, in turn, the higher costs associated with that inventory, until the next accounting cycle. As you can see, in either scenario, the company ordered 500,000 units of inventory but the timing of those orders, given the changing prices of the inventory, has a significant effect on income from operations. This scenario is an example of the possibility of an unintended conflict of interests between procurement and production decisions by an individual manager or department and the overall best interests of the company. A well-designed performance measurement system should eliminate these potential conflicts, as much as possible.

		Number of Units		(A) Decision to Avoid Purchase of Inventory at End of Accounting Period	(B) Decision to Purchase Inventory at End of Accounting Period	Difference	
		(A) 500,000	(B) 500,000				
Sales ($20.00 per unit)				$10,000,000	$10,000,000	$ 0	
Orders Placed for Inventory							
Aug. 1	($ 9.00 per unit)	100,000					
Sep. 1	($10.00 per unit)	100,000	100,000	$ 900,000	$ 0		
Oct. 1	($12.00 per unit)	200,000	200,000	$ 1,000,000	$ 1,000,000		
Nov. 1	($11.00 per unit)	50,000	50,000	$ 2,400,000	$ 2,400,000		
Dec. 1	($12.00 per unit)	50,000	50,000	$ 550,000	$ 550,000		
Dec. 31	($14.00 per unit)		100,000	$ 600,000	$ 600,000		
Total units ordered		500,000	500,000	$ 0	$ 1,400,000		
Cost of goods sold (LIFO)				$ (5,450,000)	$ (5,950,000)	$ 500,000	increase
Gross profit				$ 4,550,000	$ 4,050,000	$(500,000)	decrease
Selling and administrative expenses				$ (2,000,000)	$ (2,000,000)	$ 0	
Income from operations				$ 2,550,000	$ 2,050.000	$(500,000)	decrease

Figure 12.3 Effects on Income of Delaying Inventory Order. If LIFO is being used and inventory prices are rising, when inventory is ordered has an impact on income. (attribution: Copyright Rice University, OpenStax, under CC BY-NC-SA 4.0 license)

Accounting numbers are often affected by economic conditions, but these economic effects are beyond the control of the manager. For example, if the parts used in a manufacturing process are ordered from another country, the manager cannot control the exchange rate that occurs between the two currencies, yet this can impact the cost of the components to the manager and thus affect the cost of the product the company is producing.

Some management decisions affect multiple periods, or the decision being made will have the greatest impact in a future period. For example, capital budgeting decisions affect not only the current but future periods as well. This may compel a manager to have a short-term focus, because increasing his immediate remuneration, or compensation, is often his goal. Many long-term decisions, such as capital budgeting decisions, maintenance on equipment, or advertising campaigns, may most significantly affect future accounting numbers and, in turn, the compensation of the manager in future periods. If a manager cannot see himself reaping the rewards of that decision in future years, the decision becomes less attractive. If a performance measurement system is not designed properly, it can lead to managers having a short-term focus or making decisions that have the greatest impact on their individual goals (such as reaching a bonus goal), even if these decisions are not in the best long-term interest of the corporation. Last, a manager focused solely on accounting numbers may miss opportunities for future benefits because making the decision will have a negative impact on accounting measures in the current period. For example, spending money to build a potential customer database may decrease income in the current year. If the manager's performance is measured based on the profitability of his division, he may avoid spending the money to create the customer database. However, that database may result in a significant increase in profitability in future years if the potential customers become actual customers.

Is there a way to prevent these issues associated with using accounting measures as performance measures? The use of nonaccounting measures in conjunction with accounting-based measures can help mitigate the problems of using accounting-based measures alone. Therefore, most performance measurement systems today use a combination of accounting-based measures and non-accounting-based measures, short-term or long-term indicators, or quantitative and qualitative components. Let's first look at the use of accounting-based measures, and then we'll consider a methodology that also incorporates non-accounting-based measures.

> ### THINK IT THROUGH
>
> **Balancing Customer Needs with Company Needs**
>
> Noah Barnes just graduated from college and took a position as production supervisor for Morgensen Machines, who manufactures sewing machine and vacuum cleaner parts. On his first day at work, one of Morgensen's sales managers asked Noah if it would be OK to rearrange his manufacturing job schedule so that a special order from a new customer could be pushed to the front of the line. This new customer requires fast turnarounds; unfortunately, this also means running the production equipment for all three shifts at maximum output for at least one week, possibly more. This would completely prohibit the schedule that management told Noah to implement. Noah does not want to make the sales manager angry at him, but he also does not want to lose his job in the first month out of college. He knows that the manager is focused on landing this new customer, who could reward the company with a needed increase in overall sales and plant output. The problems, as Noah sees them, are that (1) current jobs will be delayed; (2) there will be greater demand on the machines during all three shifts, increasing the possibility that they will fail; (3) there will not be time for needed maintenance; and (4) eventually all of these factors will snowball into significant delays for the new customer, as well as extensive delays for the previously scheduled orders.
>
> How should Noah handle this problem? What managerial principles would you advise him to use from his college studies to help him develop better policies for future events like this?

12.2 Identify the Characteristics of an Effective Performance Measure

It is important to identify the characteristics that make a performance measure a good assessment of goal congruence. A good performance measurement system will align the goals of management with the goals of the corporation, and both parties will benefit. A lack of goal congruence in a performance measurement system can be detrimental to a business in many ways. Without proper performance measures, goal congruence is almost impossible to achieve and will likely lead to lost profits and dissatisfied employees.

A good performance measurement system should have the following characteristics:

- It should be based on activities over which managers have control or influence.
- It should be measurable.
- It should be timely.
- It should be consistent in its application.
- When appropriate, the actual results should be compared with the budgeted results, standards, or past

performance.
- The measurements must not favor the manager over the goals of the entire organization. Often, managers have the ability to make decisions that favor their individual units but that may be detrimental to the overall performance of the organization.

As you've learned, it is important that the activities on which managers are evaluated are within that manager's control. In addition, it is very important for the information that is used in the performance measurement system be gathered, evaluated, and presented in a timely manner. Performance measurement systems provide an indication of how well the evaluated managers are doing their jobs. Remember, the organization wants managers to make decisions that are in the best interest of the organization as a whole, and hence the need for the performance management system. If managers do not receive appropriate feedback in a timely manner, they will not know which decisions they should continue to make in the same manner and which are less effective. The same is true from the corporation's perspective. Timely information allows the evaluation team to determine the effects of individual management decisions on the corporation as a whole.

In addition to being timely, performance measures need to be applied or measured consistently. The accounting variables or other measures that are used to evaluate a manager should be measured the same way from period to period. For example, if a performance measure includes some form of income, such as operating income, then that measure should be used each time and not replaced with another income measure for the current measurement cycle (usually one year). If, upon further analysis, it seems that net income is a better measure to use in the evaluation of a manager, then the new measure can be implemented during the next measurement cycle. When measures are changed, it is imperative that the manager being evaluated is aware of the measurement change, as this may affect his or her decision-making. The idea is to keep the targets stable for a period. Otherwise, the measurements might be inconsistent, and thus misleading. A good performance measurement plan would include the manager's input in the design discussion. Not only does this help to ensure that the plan is clear to all parties involved in the process, it also helps to motivate managers. Rather than being told what goals are to be met, managers will be more motivated to achieve the goals if they have input into the process, the goals to be reached, and the measurements or metrics being used.

Performance measures are only useful if there is a baseline against which to compare the measured results. For example, students often evaluate how well they performed on a test by comparing their grade to the average for the test. If a student scored 65 out of 100 on a test, the initial response may be that this is a less than stellar grade unless that score is compared to the average. Suppose the average on that particular test was a 50. Obviously, in this example, the student performed above average on this test, but this could not be interpreted correctly until the score was compared to a baseline. In evaluating performance measures, a standard, baseline, or threshold is typically used as a basis against which to compare the actual results of the manager.

A company has both short- and long-term goals. Short-term goals include reducing costs of production by a certain percentage for the current year or increasing year-over-year sales by a certain percentage. Long-term goals may include expanding into new territories or adding new products. Employees also have short- and long-term goals. Short-term goals can include a beach vacation, and long-term goals can include saving for retirement or college. A good performance measurement system will include both short- and long-term measures in order to motivate managers to make decisions that will fulfill both the corporations and their own short- and long-term goals.

You've learned about the human factor that causes managers to make what is typically the best decision for themselves rather than the best decision for the overall good of the corporation, especially if the decision that benefits the corporation is not beneficial to the manager. Again, this means the performance measurement system must attempt to prevent the manager from benefitting without the corporation also benefitting. This is one of the trickiest parts of performance measurement system design.

For example, suppose the manager of the used car department at an automobile dealership is responsible for the profit he makes selling used cars that were taken as trade-ins on new car sales. Some of these used cars need a few repairs to prepare them for sale. The manager has the option of getting the cars fixed using the service department at the dealership or outsourcing the repairs to another company. If the manager can get the repairs completed at a lower cost at another repair shop, and if he is evaluated and receives a bonus based on his profit, then he is likely to use the outside repair shop. Is this a good thing to do? Obviously, it is good for the manager of the used car department who will have fewer costs getting the used car ready to sell and therefore will make more of a profit from the sale of that car. Higher profits for the used car department mean a higher bonus for the manager. But what about for the dealership? Was outsourcing the repairs the right decision?

It depends on several factors, but here are points to ponder. What if the dealership's service department is more expensive because it provides higher-quality parts and the mechanics are certified? Does the reputation of the quality of the used cars sold by the dealership affect more than just the used car department? What if the service department could have completed the work at cost? As you can tell by these questions, without further information, we do not know whether or not the used car manager should outsource the repairs. But we do know that his decision was based on his bonus being tied to his profitability and not linked to other factors such as dealership profitability or dealership reputation (customer satisfaction). Therefore, it is important that the performance management system not promote decisions that only benefit the manager to the detriment of the corporation.

CONCEPTS IN PRACTICE

Performance Measures at NASA[1]

Nearly twenty years ago, the National Aeronautics and Space Administration (NASA) along with five NASA contractors undertook a project to derive performance measures. As a result, they developed a series of five models for measures. These measures included effectiveness, quantity, quality, value, and change, and are as follows:

- Effectiveness was measured as projected/actual. An example was number of tests completed/number of tests planned.
- Quantity was measured as process or product unit/sources of cost. An example was total number of wind tunnel tests run/facilities management cost.
- Quality was measured as indicators of error or loss/process or product unit. An example of quality measures is mistakes in work packages issued/work packages issued in total.
- Value was measured as desirability/source of cost. An example of value measures is savings from suggestion program/man hours to review suggestions.
- Change was measured as the information provided by the indexes that are developed by tracking the same performance measures over time. An example would be the improvement measures, like
  ◦ Reduction by X percent in downtime of facilities/tests accomplished or attempted or
  ◦ Increase by X percent of documents prepared/procurement clerk

These measures have some distinct advantages but also may be met with some resistance from employees and contractors. Advantages likely included a better understanding of their processes as well as an understanding of the amount of time wasted and value emulating from these processes. Development and implementation become an opportunity to discover what may be wrong with processes, to start a dialogue concerning ongoing change and improvement, and to communicate and brainstorm about organizational inefficiencies. Networking involved in development of the performance measures can become an equalizer among processes that break down silos and complexity.

Resistance would likely come from the measurements being too time consuming and the processes too complex to be charted for these measurement objectives. How can upper management judge the complex progress on projects if they have little to no involvement? If these measures were so important, then NASA would have already developed them in an organization that was started around 1960. Resistance like this develops as one where the prior absence of these measures becomes the primary resistance toward developing them.

LINK TO LEARNING

General Electric is changing their performance measurement practices to more closely align with the goals of millennials. Read the Impraise blog on GE Performance Reviews (https://openstax.org/l/50GE_perform) for more details.

12.3 Evaluate an Operating Segment or a Project Using Return on Investment, Residual Income, and Economic Value Added

There are three performance measures commonly used when a manager has control over investments, such as the buying and selling of inventory and equipment: return on investment, residual income, and economic value added. These measures use financial accounting data to evaluate how well a manager is meeting certain goals.

Introduction to Return on Investment, Residual Income, and Economic Value Added as Evaluative Tools

One of the primary goals of a company is to be profitable. There are many ways a company can use profits. For example, companies can retain profits for future use, they can distribute them to shareholders in the form of dividends, or they can use the profits to pay off debts. However, none of these options actually contributes to the growth of the company. In order to stay profitable, a company must continuously evolve. A fourth option for the use of company profits is to reinvest the profits into the company in order to help it grow. For example, a company can buy new assets such as equipment, buildings, or patents; finance research and development; acquire other companies; or implement a vigorous advertising campaign. There are many options that will help the company to grow and to continue to be profitable.

One way to measure how effective a company is at using its invested profits to be profitable is by measuring

---

1   D. Kinlaw. "Developing Performance Measures with Aerospace Managers." *National Productivity Review*. December 1, 1986.

its **return on investment (ROI)**, which shows the percentage of income generated by profits that were invested in capital assets. It is calculated using the following formula:

$$\text{ROI} = \frac{\text{Income}}{\text{Average Capital Assets}}$$

Capital assets are those tangible and intangible assets that have lives longer than one year; they are also called *fixed assets*. ROI in its basic form is useful; however, there are really two components of ROI: sales margin and asset turnover. This is known as the *DuPont Model*. It originated in the 1920s when the DuPont company implemented it for internal measurement purposes. The DuPont model can be expressed using this formula:

$$\text{ROI} = \text{Sales Margin} \times \text{Asset Turnover}$$

Sales margin indicates how much profit is generated by each dollar of sales and is computed as shown:

$$\text{Sales Margin} = \frac{\text{Income}}{\text{Sales Revenue}}$$

Asset turnover indicates the number of sales dollars produced by every dollar invested in capital assets—in other words, how efficiently the company is using its capital assets to generate sales. It is computed as:

$$\text{Asset Turnover} = \frac{\text{Sales Revenue}}{\text{Average Capital Assets}}$$

Using ROI represented as Sales Margin × Asset Turnover, we can get another formula for ROI. Substituting the formulas for each of these individual ratios, ROI can be expressed as:

$$\text{ROI} = \left(\frac{\text{Operating Income}}{\text{Sales Revenue}}\right) \times \left(\frac{\text{Sales Revenue}}{\text{Average Capital Assets}}\right)$$

To visualize this ROI formula in another way, we can deconstruct it into its components, as in Figure 12.4.

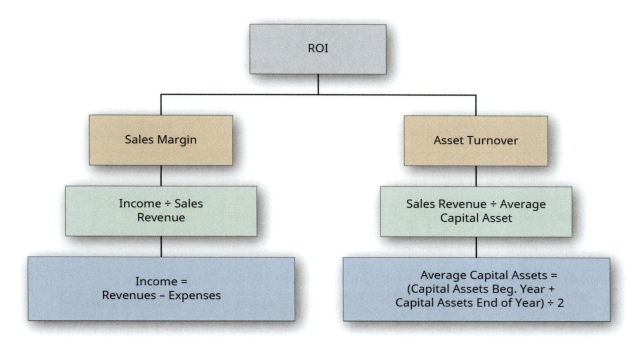

Figure 12.4 Decomposition of ROI into the Components Sales Margin and Asset Turnover. (attribution: Copyright Rice University, OpenStax, under CC BY-NC-SA 4.0 license)

When sales margin and asset turnover are multiplied by each other, the sales components of each measure will cancel out, leaving

$$ROI = \frac{Income}{Average\ Capital\ Assets}$$

ROI captures the nuances of both elements. A good sales margin and a proper asset turnover are both needed for a successful operation. As an example, a jewelry store typically has a very low turnover but is profitable because of its high sales margin. A grocery store has a much lower sales margin but is successful because of high turnover. You can see it is important to understand each of these individual components of ROI.

Calculation and Interpretation of the Return on Investment

To put these concepts in context, consider a bakery called Scrumptious Sweets, Inc., that has three divisions and evaluates the managers of each of these decisions based on ROI. The following information is available for these divisions:

	Donut Division	Bagel Division	Brownie Division
Income	$1,000,000	$2,500,000	$1,300,000
Sales Revenue	5,000,000	8,500,000	5,500,000
Assets Jan. 1	2,800,000	5,950,000	4,850,000
Assets Dec. 31	2,900,000	5,950,000	4,820,000

This information can be used to find the sales margin, asset turnover, and ROI for each division:

	Donut Division	**Bagel Division**	**Brownie Division**
Sales Margin	$\frac{\$1,000,000}{\$5,000,000} = 20\%$	$\frac{\$2,500,000}{\$8,500,000} = 29\%$	$\frac{\$1,300,000}{\$5,500,000} = 24\%$
Asset Turnover	$\frac{\$5,000,000}{\$2,850,000^*} = 1.75$ times	$\frac{\$8,500,000}{\$5,950,000^{**}} = 1.43$ times	$\frac{\$5,500,000}{\$4,835,000^{***}} = 1.14$ times
ROI	$\frac{\$1,000,000}{\$2,850,000^*} = 35\%$	$\frac{\$2,500,000}{\$5,950,000^{**}} = 42\%$	$\frac{\$1,300,000}{\$4,835,000^{***}} = 27\%$

*The average capital assets for donuts are $\frac{(2,800,000 + 2,900,000)}{2} = 2,850,000$.

**The average capital assets for bagels are $\frac{(5,950,000 + 5,950,000)}{2} = 5,950,000$.

***The average capital assets for brownies are $\frac{(4,850,000 + 4,820,000)}{2} = 4,835,000$.

Alternatively, ROI could have been calculated by multiplying Sales Margin × Asset Turnover:

	Donut Division	**Bagel Division**	**Brownie Division**
ROI	20% × 1.75 times = 35%	29% × 1.43 times = 42%	24% × 1.14 times = 27%

ROI measures the return in a percentage form rather than in absolute dollars, which is helpful when comparing projects, divisions, or departments of different sizes. How do we interpret the ROIs for Scrumptious Sweets? Suppose Scrumptious has set a target ROI for each division at 30% in order to share in the bonus pool. In this case, both the donut division and the bagel division would participate in the company bonus pool. What does the analysis regarding the brownie division show? By looking at the breakdown of ROI into its component parts of sales margin and asset turnover, it is apparent that the brownie division has a higher sales margin than the donut division, but it has a lower asset turnover than the other divisions, and this is affecting the brownie division's ROI. This would provide direction for management of the brownie division to investigate why their asset turnover is significantly lower than the other two divisions. Again, ROI is useful if there is a benchmark against which to compare, but it cannot be judged as a stand-alone measure without that comparison.

Managers want a high ROI, so they strive to increase it. Looking at its components, there are certain decisions managers can make to increase their ROI. For example, the sales margin component can be increased by increasing income, which can be done by either increasing sales revenue or decreasing expenses. Sales revenue can be increased by increasing sales price per unit without losing volume, or by maintaining current sales price but increasing the volume of sales. Asset turnover can be increased by increasing sales revenue or decreasing the amount of capital assets. Capital assets can be decreased by selling off assets such as equipment.

For example, suppose the manager of the brownie division has been running a new advertising campaign and is estimating that his sales volume will increase by 5% over the next year due to this ad campaign. This increase in sales volume will lead to an increase in income of $140,000. What does this do to his ROI? Division income will increase from $1,300,000 to $1,440,000, and the division average assets will stay the same, at $4,835,000. This will lead to an ROI of 30%, which is the ROI that must be achieved to participate in the bonus pool.

Another factor to consider is the effect of depreciation on ROI. Assets are depreciated over time, and this will reduce the value of the capital assets. A reduction in the capital assets results in an increase in ROI. Looking at the bagel division, suppose the assets in that division depreciated $500,000 from the beginning of the year to the end of the year and that no capital assets were sold and none were purchased. Look at the effect on ROI:

Bagel Division	Original ROI	ROI with Increased Depreciation
	$\dfrac{\$2,500,000}{\$5,950,000^*} = 42\%$	$\dfrac{\$2,500,000}{\$5,700,000^{**}} = 44\%$

*The original average capital assets for bagels are $\dfrac{(5,950,000 + 5,950,000)}{2} = 5,950,000$.

**The new average capital assets for bagels are $\dfrac{(5,950,000 + 5,450,000)}{2} = 5,700,000$.

Notice that depreciation helped to improve the division's ROI even though management made no new decisions. Some companies will calculate ROI based on historical cost, while others keep the calculation based on depreciated assets with the idea that the manager is efficiently using the assets as they age. However, if depreciated values are used in the calculation of ROI, as assets are replaced, the ROI will drop from the prior period.

One drawback to using ROI is the potential of decreased goal congruence. For example, assume that one of the goals of a corporation is to have ROI of at least 15% (the cost of capital) on all new projects. Suppose one of the divisions within this corporation currently has a ROI of 20%, and the manager is evaluating the production of a new product in his division. If analysis shows that the new project is predicted to have a ROI of 18%, would the manager move forward with the project? Top management would opt to accept the production of the new product. However, since the project would decrease the division's current ROI, the division manager may reject the project to avoid decreasing his overall performance and possibly his overall compensation. The division manager is making an intentional choice based on his division's ROI relative to corporate ROI.

In other situations, the use of ROI can unintentionally lead to improper decision-making. For example, look at the ROI for the following investment opportunities faced by a manager:

	Income	Average Capital Assets	ROI
Investment Opportunity 1	$ 500	$ 1,000	50%
Investment Opportunity 2	20,000	75,000	27%

In this example, though investment opportunity 1 has a higher ROI, it does not generate any significant income. Therefore, it is important to look at ROI among other factors in order to make an informed decision.

Calculation and Interpretation of the Residual Income

Another performance measure is **residual income (RI)**, which shows the amount of income a given division (or project) is expected to earn in excess of a firm's minimum return goal. Every company sets a **minimum required rate of return** on projects and investments, representing the minimum return, usually in percentage form, that a project or investment must produce in order for the company to be willing to undertake it. This return is used as a basis for evaluating investments so that the firm may meet its targets and goals, and ensures that only profitable projects will be accepted. (You will learn the theory and mechanics behind establishing a minimum required rate of return in advanced accounting courses.)

Think about this concept in your own life. If you plan to invest in stocks, bonds, a work of art, precious stones, a graduate degree, or a business, you would want to know what your expected return would be before you made that investment. Most people shy away from investing time or money in things that do not provide a certain return, whether that return is money, happiness, or satisfaction. A company has to make similar decisions and decide where to spend its money and does not want to spend it in areas that will not return a minimum profit to the company and its shareholders. Companies will determine a minimum required rate of return as a basis against which to compare investment opportunities to aid in the decision of whether or not to accept a project. This minimum required rate of return is used to calculate residual income, which uses this formula:

> **RI = Project Profit − (Project Invested Capital × Minimum Required Rate of Return)**

Suppose the donut division of Scrumptious Sweets is considering acquiring new machinery to speed up the production of donuts and make the donuts more uniform in shape and size. The cost of the machine is $1,500,000, and it is expected to generate a profit of $250,000. Scrumptious has a corporate policy of a required minimum rate of return on projects of 18%. Based on residual income, should the donut division move forward on this project?

$$RI = \$250{,}000 - (\$1{,}500{,}000 \times 0.18)$$
$$RI = -\$20{,}000$$

A project will be accepted as long as the RI is a positive number, because that implies the project is earning more than the minimum required by the company. Therefore, the manager of the donut division would not accept this project based on RI alone. Note that RI is measured in absolute dollars. This makes it almost impossible to compare firms of different sizes or projects of different sizes to one another. Both ROI and RI are useful, but as shown, both tools have drawbacks. Therefore, many companies will use a combination of ROI and RI (as well as other measures) to evaluate performance.

Calculation and Interpretation of Economic Value Added

Economic value added (EVA) is similar to RI but is a measure of shareholder wealth that is being created by a project, segment, or division. Companies want to maximize shareholder wealth, and to do that, they have to generate enough income to cover their cost of debt and their cost of equity, but also to have income available to shareholders. Just as in residual income, the goal is a positive EVA. A positive EVA indicates management has effectively used its capital assets to increase the value of the firm and thus the wealth of shareholders. EVA is computed as shown:

> **EVA = After-Tax Income − (Invested Capital × Weighted Average Cost of Capital)**

After-tax income is the income reduced by tax expenses. The **weighted average cost of capital (WACC)** is the cost that the company expects to pay on average to finance assets and growth using either debt or equity. WACC is based on the proportion of debt and equity held by a company and the costs of each of those. For example, if a company has a total of $1,000,000 in debt and equity, consisting of $400,000 in debt and $600,000 in stock, then the proportion of the company's capital structure that is debt is 40% ($400,000/$1,000,000), and the proportion that is equity is 60% ($600,000/$1,000,000).

What about the cost component for each? A company raises capital (money) in three primary ways: borrowing (debt), issuing stock (equity), or earning it (income). The cost of debt is the after-tax interest rate associated with borrowing money. The cost of equity is the rate associated with what the shareholders expect the corporation to earn in order for that shareholder to maintain ownership in the company. For example, shareholders of Apple stock may on average expect the company to earn a return of 10% per year; otherwise, they will sell their stock.

Sometimes the weighted average cost of capital and the required rate of return are the same for some companies, but often they will differ. Suppose Scrumptious Sweets, for example, has both debt capital and equity capital. Table 12.2 lists the cost of each type of capital as well as what proportion of the capital is made up of each of the two types. Notice that debt makes up 45% of the capital of Scrumptious Sweets and that the cost of debt is 8%. Equity makes up the other 55% of the capital structure of Scrumptious and the cost of equity is 9.8%. The weighted average cost of capital is the sum of each of the weighted cost of each type of capital. Thus, the weighted cost of debt is 0.08 × 0.45 = 0.036 or 3.6% and the weighted cost of equity is 0.098 × 0.55 = 0.054 or 5.4%. This results in a weighted average cost of capital of 3.6% plus 5.4%, or 9%.

Scrumptious Sweets' Weighted Average Cost of Capital

Type of Capital	A Cost of Capital	B Proportion of Total Capital	A × B Weighted Cost
Debt	8%	45%	3.6%
Equity	9.8%	55%	5.4%
Weighted Average Cost of Capital			9%

Table 12.2

Reconsidering the new machine the donut division wants to buy, and using EVA to evaluate the project decision, would the decision change? Remember, the cost of the machine is $1,500,000, and it is expected to generate a profit of $250,000. Assume the tax rate for Scrumptious is 40%. To calculate EVA for the project, we need the following:

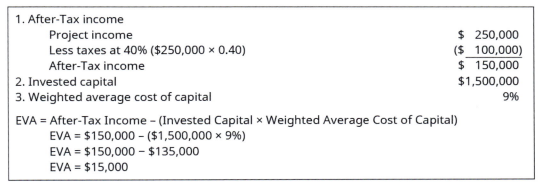

The positive EVA of $15,000 indicates that the project is generating income for the shareholders and should be accepted.

As you can see, though RI and EVA look similar, they can lead to different decisions. This difference stems from two sources. First, RI is calculated based on management's choice for the required rate of return, which can be determined from many different variables, whereas the weighted average cost of capital is based on the actual cost of debt and the estimated cost of equity, weighted by the actual percentages of both components. Second, when used to evaluate unit managers, RI often is based on pretax income, whereas EVA is based on after-tax income to the company itself. EVA and RI do not always lead to different decisions, but it is important that managers understand the components of both measures to ensure they make the best decision for the company.

Considerations in Using the Three Evaluative Tools

One of the most challenging aspects of using ROI, RI, and EVA lies in the determination of the variables used to calculate these measures. Income and invested capital are factors in the ROI, RI, and EVA performance models, and each can be defined in several ways. **Invested capital** can be defined as fixed assets, productive assets, or operating assets. **Fixed assets** typically include only tangible long-term assets. **Productive assets** typically include inventory plus the fixed assets. **Operating assets** include productive assets plus intangible assets, and current assets. One problem is determining which assets the manager can control with his or her decision-making authority. Each definition of invested capital will have a different impact on the performance measure, whether that measure is ROI, RI, or EVA. Deciding how to define invested capital is further complicated when combined with the additional decision of whether to use net book value (depreciated value) or gross book value (nondepreciated value) of long-lived assets. Net book value is the historical cost of an asset minus any accumulated depreciation, whereas gross book value is merely the historical cost of the asset. Obviously at the time of acquisition of an asset, these two numbers are the same, but over time, net book value will decrease for any given asset, while gross book value will stay the same for that asset. Using gross book value will result in a higher value for invested capital than using net book value. Remember, net book value will vary based on the depreciation method employed—straight line versus double declining balance, for example. Thus, gross book value removes the effect of choosing different depreciation methods. Despite this, most companies use net book value in the computation of ROI since net book value aligns with their financial reporting of capital assets on the balance sheet at their net value. Assets can also be measured at fair value, also known as market value. This is the value at which the assets could be sold. Fair value is only used in special cases of computing ROI such as in computing ROI for a real estate investment. The reason fair value is not typically used for ROI is that the fair or market value is rarely known or determinable with certainty and is often very subjective, whereas both gross and book value are readily known and determinable.

The second major component of these performance measures involves which income measure to use. First and foremost, no matter how a company measures income, the most important point is that the income the company uses as a measure should be controllable income if the performance model is to be a motivator and if the company uses responsibility accounting. Income, sometimes referred to as earnings, can be measured in many ways, and there are often common acronyms given for some of the these measures. Common ways to measure income are **operating income** (income before taxes); earnings before interest and taxes (EBIT); earnings before interest, taxes, and depreciation (EBITDA); net income (income after taxes); or return on funds employed (ROFE), which adds working capital to any of the other income measures. Companies must decide which income measure they want to use in their determination of these various performance metrics. They must consider how the metric is being used, who they are evaluating by that metric, and whether the income and capital asset chosen capture the decision-making authority of the individual or division whose performance is being evaluated.

YOUR TURN

SkyHigh Superball Decisions

The manager of the SkyHigh division of Superball Corp. is faced with a decision on whether or not to buy a new machine that will mix the ingredients used in the SkyHigh superball produced by the SkyHigh division. This ball bounces as high as a two-story building upon first bounce and is so popular that the

SkyHigh division barely keeps up with demand. The manager is hoping the new machine will allow the balls to be produced more quickly and therefore increase the volume of production within the same time currently being used in production. The manager wants to evaluate the effect of the purchase of the machine on his compensation. He receives a base salary plus a 25% bonus of his salary if he meets certain income goals. The information he has available for the analysis is shown here:

Cost of the machine	$2,000,000
Income to be generated by the machine	$1,000,000
Income without the new machine	$7,000,000
Beginning of the year capital assets (without the machine)	$8,000,000
End of the year capital assets (without the machine)	$8,400,000
Tax rate	30%
Minimum required rate of return	15%
Weighted average cost of capital	9%
Sales revenue without the machine	$18,000,000
Sales revenue with the machine	$19,400,000

The manager is looking at several different measures to evaluate this decision. Answer the following questions:

1. What is the sales margin without the new machine?
2. What is the asset turnover without the new machine?
3. What is ROI without the new machine?
4. What is RI without the new machine?
5. What is EVA without the new machine?
6. What is the sales margin with the new machine?
7. What is the asset turnover with the new machine?
8. What is ROI with the new machine?
9. What is RI with the new machine?
10. What is EVA with the new machine?
11. Should the manager buy the new machine? Why or why not?
12. How would ROI be affected if the invested capital were measured at gross book value, and the gross book values of the beginning and end of the year assets without the new machine were $11,000,000 and $11,800,000, respectively?

Solution

1. Income/Sales: $7,000,000/$18,000,000 = 39%
2. Sales/Average Assets: $18,000,000/[($12,000,000 + $12,400,000)/2] = 1.48 times
3. Income/Average Assets: $7,000,000/[($12,000,000 + $12,400,000)/2] = 58%
   Or #1 × #2: 39% × 1.48 = 58%
4. Income − (Invested Capital × Minimum Required Rate of Return)
   $7,000,000 − ($12,200,000 × 0.15) = $5,170,000
5. After-Tax Income − (Invested Capital × Weighted Average Cost of Capital)
   [$7,000,000 × (1 − 0.30)] × ($12,200,000 × 0.09) = $3,802,000
6. Income/Sales: $8,000,000/$19,400,000 = 41%
7. Sales/Average Assets: $19,400,000/[($12,000,000 + $12,400,000)/2] = 1.59 times
8. Income/Average Assets: $8,000,000/[($12,000,000 + $12,400,000)/2] = 66%

> Or #7 × #8: 41% × 1.59 = 66%
> 9. Income − (Invested Capital × Minimum Required Rate of Return)
> $8,000,000 − (12,200,000 × 0.15) = $6,170,000
> 10. After-Tax Income − (Invested Capital × Weighted Average Cost of Capital)
>   [$8,000,000 × (1 − 0.30)] − ($12,200,000 × 0.09) = $4,502,000
> 11. The manager of the SkyHigh division of Superball Corp. should accept the project, as the project improves all of his performance measures.
> 12. Income/Average Assets: $8,000,000/[($13,000,000 + $13,800,000)/2] = 60% This shows that the choice used as the measure of assets can affect the analysis.

12.4 Describe the Balanced Scorecard and Explain How It Is Used

The performance measures considered up to this point have relied only on financial accounting measures as the means to evaluate performance. Over time, the trend has become to incorporate both quantitative and qualitative measures and short- and long-term goals when evaluating the performance of managers as well as the company as a whole. One approach to evaluating both financial and nonfinancial measures is to use a balanced scorecard.

History and Function of the Balanced Scorecard

Suppose you work in retail and your compensation consists of an hourly wage plus a bonus based on your sales. You have excellent interpersonal skills, and customers appreciate your help and often seek you out when they come to the store. Some of your customers will return on a different day, even making an extra trip to the store to make sure you are the employee who helps them. Sometimes these customers buy items and other times they do not, but they always come back. Your compensation does not include any acknowledgment of your attention to customers and your ability to keep them returning to the store, but consider how much more you could earn if this were the case. However, in order for compensation to include nonfinancial, or qualitative, factors, the store would need to track nonfinancial information, in addition to the financial, or quantitative, information already tracked in the accounting system. One way to track both qualitative and quantitative measures is to use a **balanced scorecard**.

The idea for using a balanced scorecard to evaluate employees was first suggested by Art Schneiderman of Analog Devices in 1987 as a means to improve corporate performance by using metrics to measure improvements in areas in which Analog Devices was struggling, such as in a high number of defects. Schneiderman went through different iterations of a balanced scorecard design over several years, but the final design chosen measured three different categories: financial, customer, and internal. The financial category included measures such as return on assets and revenue growth, the customer category included measures such as customer satisfaction and on-time delivery, and the internal category included measures such as reduced defects and improved throughput time. Eventually, Robert Kaplan and David Norton, both Harvard University faculty, expanded upon Schneiderman's ideas to create the current concept of the balanced scorecard and four general categories for evaluation: financial perspective, customer perspective, internal perspective, and learning and growth. These categories are sometimes modified for particular industries.

Therefore, a balanced scorecard evaluates employees on an assortment of **quantitative factors**, or metrics based on financial information, and **qualitative factors**, or those based on nonfinancial information, in several significant areas. The quantitative or financial measurements tend to emphasize past results, often based on their financial statements, while the qualitative or nonfinancial measurements center on current results or activities, with the intent to evaluate activities that will influence future financial performance.

ETHICAL CONSIDERATIONS

Use of a Balanced Scorecard Leads to Ethical Decision-Making

Managers and employees generally strive to create and work in an ethical environment. In order to develop such an environment, employees need to be informed of the organization's ethical standards and values and have an understanding of the laws and regulations under which the organization operates. If employees do not know the standards by which they will be measured, they might not be aware if their behavior is ethical. A balanced scorecard allows employees to understand their organization's obligations, and to evaluate their own obligations in the workplace.

To evaluate their ethical environment, organizations can hold meetings that use ethical analysis metrics. Kaplan and Norton, leaders in balanced scorecard use, explain the use of the balanced scorecard in the context of strategy review meetings: Companies conduct strategy review meetings to discuss the indicators and initiatives from the unit's Balanced Scorecard and assess the progress of and barriers to strategy execution.[2] In such meetings, the metrics analyzed should include, but not be limited to, the availability of a hotline; employee participation in ethics training; satisfaction of customers, employees, and other stakeholders; employee turnover rate; regulation compliance; community involvement; environmental awareness; diversity; legal expenses; efficient asset usage; condition of assets; and social responsibility.[3] Metrics should be tailored to an organization's values and desired operational results. The use of a balanced scorecard helps lead to an ethical environment for employees and managers.

Four Components of a Balanced Scorecard

To create a balanced scorecard, a company will start with its strategic goals and organize them into key areas. The four key areas used by Kaplan and Norton were financial perspective, internal operations perspective, customer perspective, and learning and growth (Figure 12.5).

---

2   Alistair Craven. *An Interview with Robert Kaplan & David Norton* (Emerald Publishing, 2008). http://www.emeraldgrouppublishing.com/learning/management_thinking/interviews/kaplan_norton.htm
3   Paul Arveson. *The Ethics Perspective* (Balanced Scorecard Institute, Strategy Management Group, 2002). https://www.balancedscorecard.org/The-Ethics-Perspective

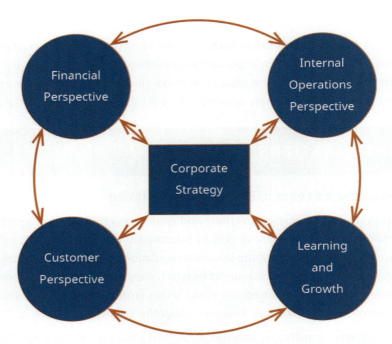

Figure 12.5 Four Key Areas of a Balanced Scorecard. (attribution: Copyright Rice University, OpenStax, under CC BY-NC-SA 4.0 license)

These areas were chosen by Kaplan and Norton because the success of a company is dependent on how it performs financially, which is directly related to the company's internal operations, how the customer perceives and interacts with the company, and the direction in which the company is headed. The use of the balanced scorecard allows the company to take a stakeholder perspective as compared to a stockholder perspective. **Stockholders** are the owners of the company stock and often are most concerned with the profitability of the company and thus focus primarily on financial results. **Stakeholders** are people who are affected by the decisions made by a company, such as investors, creditors, managers, regulators, employees, customers, suppliers, and even laypeople who are concerned about whether or not the company is a good world citizen. This is why social responsibility factors are sometimes included in balanced scorecards. To understand where these types of factors might fit in a balanced scorecard framework, let's look at the four sections or categories of a balanced scorecard.

Financial Perspective

The financial performance section of a balanced scorecard retains the types of metrics that have historically been set by companies to evaluate performance. The particular metric used in the scorecard will vary depending on the type of company involved, who is being evaluated, and what is being measured. You've learned that ROI, RI, and EVA can be used to evaluate performance. There are other financial measures that can be used as well, for example, earnings per share (EPS), revenue growth, sales growth, inventory turnover, and many others. The type of financial measures used should capture the components of the decision-making tasks of the person being evaluated. Financial measures can be very broad and general, such as sales growth, or they can be more specific, such as seat revenue. Looking back at the Scrumptious Sweets example, financial measures could include baked goods revenue growth, drink revenue growth, and product cost containment.

Internal Business Perspective

A successful company should operate like a well-tuned machine. This requires that the company monitor its internal operations and evaluate them to ensure they are meeting the strategic goals of the corporation. There are many variables that could be used as internal business measures, including number of defects produced, machine downtime, transaction efficiency, and number of products completed per day per employee, or more refined measures, such as percent of time planes are on the ground, or ensuring air tanks are well stocked for a scuba diving business. For Scrumptious Sweets, internal measures could include time between production and sale of the baked goods or amount of waste.

Customer Perspectives

All businesses have customers or clients—a business will cease to operate without them—thus, it is important for a company to measure how well it is doing with respect to customers. Examples of common variables that could be measured include customer satisfaction, number of repeat customers, number of new customers, number of new customers from customer referrals, and market share. Variables that are more specific to a particular business include factors such as being ranked first in the industry by customers and providing a safe diving environment for scuba diving. Customer measures for Scrumptious Sweets might include customer loyalty, customer satisfaction, and number of new customers.

Learning and Growth

The business environment is a very dynamic one and requires a company to constantly evolve in order to survive, let alone grow. To reach strategic targets such as increased market share, management must focus on ways to grow the company. The learning and growth measures are a means to assess how the employees and management are working together to grow the company and to help the employees grow within the company. Examples of measures in this category include the number of employee suggestions that are adopted, turnover rates, hours of employee training, scope of process improvements, and number of new products. Scrumptious Sweets may use learning and growth measures such as hours of customer service training and hours on workforce relationship training.

Combining the Four Components of a Balanced Scorecard

Balanced scorecards can be created for any type of business and can be used at any level of the organization. An effective and successful balanced scorecard will start with the strategic plan or goals of the organization. Those goals are then restated based on the level of the organization to which the balanced scorecard pertains. A balanced scorecard for an entire organization will be broader and more general in terms of goals and measures than a balanced scorecard designed for a division manager. Balanced scorecards can even be created at the individual employee level either as an evaluation mechanism or as a means for the employee to set and monitor individual goals. Once the strategic goals of the organization are stated for the appropriate level for which the balanced scorecard is being created, then the measures for each of the categories of the balanced scorecard should be defined, being sure to consider the areas over which the division or individual does or does not have control. In addition, the variables have to be obtainable and measurable. Last, the measures must be useful, meaning that what is actually being measured must be informative, and there must be a basis of comparison—either company standards or individual targets. Using both quantitative and nonquantitative performance measures, along with long- and short-term measurements, can be very beneficial, as they can serve to motivate an employee while providing a clear framework of how that employee fits into the company's strategic plan.

As an example, let's examine several balanced scorecards for Scrumptious Sweets. First, Figure 12.6 shows an overall organizational balanced scorecard, the broadest and most general balanced scorecard.

SCRUMPTIOUS SWEETS, INC. Corporate Balanced Scorecard				
Mission: Provide customers with superior-quality traditional and innovative baked goods				
		Business Objectives	**Measures**	**Target**
Financial		Increase Revenue	Sales Revenues	Increase revenue 5%
		Lower Costs	Operating Costs	Decrease costs 3%
		Increase Profits	Net Income	Increase income 6%
Customer		Increase Customer Satisfaction	Customer satisfaction surveys	95% customer satisfaction rating
		Improve Customer Loyalty	Number of repeat customers	90% retentions of existing customers
		Grow Market Share	Number of new customers	10% increase in market share
Internal		Improve Production Processes	Reduce time from production to customer	10% decrease in production-to-customer time
		Reduce Waste on Products Produced	Units of waste per production process	10% decrease in waste generated per production process
		Reduce Carbon Footprint	Factory effluents and exhaust measured in PPM (parts per million)	5% decrease in both effluents and exhaust pollutants (PPM)
Learning & Growth		Improve Product & Service Innovation	Implemented employee suggestions	40% increase in number of employee suggestions made
		Increase Motivation and Empowerment	Management training course certificates awarded	20% incerase in number of employees completing management training courses
		Improve Employee Retention	Employee satisfaction surveys	90% rating on overall employee satisfaction

Figure 12.6 Scrumptious Sweets, Inc. Corporate Balanced Scorecard. (attribution: Copyright Rice University, OpenStax, under CC BY-NC-SA 4.0 license)

Notice that this scorecard starts with the overall corporate mission. It then contains very broad goals and measures in each of the four categories: financial, customer, internal, and learning and growth. In this scorecard, there are three general goals for each of these four categories. For example, the goals related to customers are to improve customer satisfaction, improve customer loyalty, and increase market share. For each of the goals, there is a general measure that will be used to assess if the goal has been met. In this example, the goal to improve customer satisfaction will be assessed using customer satisfaction surveys. But remember, measures are only useful as a management tool if there is a target to work toward. In this case, the goal is to achieve an overall 95% customer satisfaction rating. Obviously, the goals on this scorecard and the associated measures seem almost vague due to their general nature. However, these goals match with the overall corporate strategy and provide guidance for management at lower levels to begin dissecting these goals to more specific ones that pertain to their particular area or division. This allows them to create more detailed balanced scorecards that will allow them to help meet the overall corporate goals laid out in the corporate scorecard. Figure 12.7 shows how the corporate balanced scorecard previously presented could be further detailed for the manager of the brownie division.

SCRUMPTIOUS SWEETS, INC.			
Brownie Division Balanced Scorecard			
Corporate Mission: Provide customers with superior-quality traditional and innovative baked goods			
	Business Objectives	**Measures**	**Target**
Financial	Increase revenues through improved sales mix	Sales mix revenues	Increase revenues 10% through better sales mix utilization
	Lower production costs	Production costs	Decrease production costs by 4% through order and production efficiencies
	Increase divisional profits	Divisional profit	Increase divisional profit by 12%
Customer	Meet customer unique needs	Number of customer suggestions or special requests	Meet 95% of customer special requests and track customer suggestions implemented
	Brand recognition	Number of repeat customers and number and variety of best selling-products	95% retention of existing customers; 10% increase in sales of best sellers
	Customer referrals	Number of customer referrals	15% increase in referral cards received
Internal	Reduce time from production to customer/storefront	Time from packaging to delivery or display	10% decrease in time from production to customer access
	Reduce product waste through improved uniformity of product and better timing of orders and production	Units of waste per production process, uniformity of product and inventory control	10% decrease in production waste; 5% improvement in inventory turnover
	Increase environmental protection efforts	Number of energy-efficient bulbs replaced; paperless efforts measure	75% use of energy-efficient bulbs; 5% decrease in water usage; 80% paperless work environment
Learning & Growth	New or improved product or process ideas	Number of new products introduced; number of improved products	10% increase in new products produced; improvements to 5% of products or processes
	Increase employee motivation and empowerment	Management training course certificates awarded	20% increase in number of employees completing management training courses
	Improve employee retention	Employee satisfaction surveys	90% rating on overall employee satisfaction; 50% increase in employees using open-door policy

Figure 12.7 Scrumptious Sweets, Inc. Brownie Division Balanced Scorecard. (attribution: Copyright Rice

University, OpenStax, under CC BY-NC-SA 4.0 license)

As you can see from the balanced scorecard for the brownie division, the same corporate mission is included, as are the same four categories; however, the divisional goals are more specific, as are the measures and the targets. For example, related to the overall corporate goal to increase customer satisfaction, the divisional goal is to meet customers' unique needs. The division will assess how well they are accomplishing this goal by tracking the number of customer suggestions and customer special requests, such as when a customer requests a special flavor of brownie not normally produced by the brownie division. The target set by the management of the brownie division is to meet 95% of customer special requests and to track the number of customer suggestions that are implemented by the division. The idea is that if the division is meeting customer needs and requests, this will result in high customer satisfaction, which is an overriding corporate goal. The success of the division will be based on each employee doing his or her best at his or her specific job. Therefore, it is useful to see how the balanced scorecard can be used at an individual employee level.
Figure 12.8 shows a balanced scorecard for the brownie division's employees who work in the front end or store portion of the division.

SCRUMPTIOUS SWEETS, INC.
Brownie Division Storefront Employees Balanced Scorecard

Corporate Mission: Provide customers with superior-quality traditional and innovative baked goods

	Objectives	Measures	Target
Financial Initiatives	Increase Sales • Offer additional products to each customer • Promote mobile ordering	Same store sales	10% increase
		Mobile sales	20% increase in mobile orders
	Lower Costs • Follow safety rules • Reduce waste • Follow drink recipes exactly	Safety reports/claims	5% reduction in number of reports filed
		Inventory turnover	5% improvements in inventory turnover
Customer Initiatives	Improve Customer Experience • Clean and well-stocked store • Polite, friendly interaction • Offering to carry/load products	Customer satisfaction surveys	95% customer satisfaction rating
		Mystery customer reports	Average rating of A on all 10 dimensions measured
	Customer Retention and Growth • Promote frequent buyer awards • Promote referral incentives	Frequent buyer rewards redeemed	5% increase in rewards redeemed
		Customer referral cards redeemed	20% increase in rewards redeemed
Internal Initiatives	Improve Product Delivery Efficiency • Follow order queuing/filling • Order taking accuracy • Correct errors quickly	Order queuing reports	100% accuracy in order queuing
		Customer surveys and mystery customer reports	100% accuracy in order taking
	Reduce Carbon Footprint • Avoid order errors • Minimize waste • Turn off lights in unused rooms	Pounds of trash	10% reduction in trash generated
		Utility charges	5% reduction in utility costs
Learning and Growth Initiatives	Expand Employee Mentoring Program and Expand Business Improvements • Meet with mentor regularly • Take advantage of open-door policy • Making suggestions	Mentor meeting log	100% quarterly employee/mentor meetings
		Employee suggestions implemented	20% increase in number of viable suggestions by employees
	Actively Participate in Corporate Training opportunities • Management training courses • College tuition program	Training certifications	100% of employees completing quarterly training

Figure 12.8 Scrumptious Sweets, Inc. Brownie Division Store Front Employees Balanced Scorecard. (attribution: Copyright Rice University, OpenStax, under CC BY-NC-SA 4.0 license)

In this balanced scorecard the same categories are used, but there is more detail about each of the business objectives, and each objective has more refined measures than the prior two scorecards. Again in the customer category, one of the objectives of the storefront employees is to improve the customer experience. Notice that there are three initiatives listed to help drive this goal. The measures that would be used to evaluate the success of these initiatives as well as their specific targets are detailed. Again, the idea is that if the employees who work in the store portion of the brownie division make the customer experience great, this will translate into high scores on the customer satisfaction surveys and help the company meet its overriding goal to increase customer satisfaction. In order to ensure that this occurs, the specific goals and metrics are created. As previously expressed, it is best if these objectives, measures, and targets are determined by a process that includes management and the employees. Without employee input, employees may feel resentful of targets over which they had no input. But, the employees alone cannot set their own goals and targets, as there could be a tendency to set easy targets, or the employee may not be aware of how his or her efforts affect the division and overall corporation. Thus, a collaborative approach is best in creating balanced scorecards.

The three scorecards presented show that the process of creating appropriate and viable scorecards can be quite complicated and challenging. Determining the appropriate qualitative and quantitative measures can be a daunting process, but the results can be extremely beneficial. The scorecards can be useful tools at all levels of the organization if they are adequately thought out and if there is buy-in at all levels being evaluated by a scorecard. Next, we'll consider how the use of the balanced scorecard and performance measures are not mutually exclusive and can work well together.

CONTINUING APPLICATION AT WORK

Balanced Scorecard

Let's revisit Gearhead Outfitters in the context of their operating results, internal processes, growth, and customer satisfaction. Recall that the company was founded as a single store in 1997 and grew to multiple locations mainly in the southern United States. How did Gearhead get there? How did the company gather information to make expansion decisions? Now that Gearhead has expanded, should it keep all current locations open? Is the company meeting the desires of its customers?

Questions such as these are addressed through performance measures detailed in a balanced scorecard. Financial metrics such as return on investment and residual income give Gearhead information on whether or not dollars invested have translated into additional income, and if current income can support needed cash flow for current and future operations. While financial measures are important, they are only one aspect of evaluating the effectiveness of a company's strategy. Value provided to customers should also be considered, as well as the success of internal processes, and whether or not the company adequately provides growth opportunities for employees. Sales from new products, employee turnover, and customer satisfaction surveys can also provide valuable data for measuring success. The idea of a balanced scorecard is to give a business both financial and nonfinancial information to use in its strategic decisions.

The Our Story page of Gearhead's website reads: "Gearhead Outfitters exists to create a positive shopping experience for our guests. Gearhead is known for its relaxed environment, specialized inventory and customer service for those pursuing an active lifestyle. True to our local roots, we employ local residents of each city we operate in, support local organizations, and strive to build relationships within our communities."[4]

Given how Gearhead describes itself, and the performance measures discussed previously, what other information might the company want to gather for its balanced scorecard?

Final Summary of Quantitative and Quantitative Performance Measurement Tools

As the business environment changes, one thing stays the same: businesses want to be successful, to be profitable, and to meet their strategic goals. With these changes in the business environment come more varied responsibilities placed on managers. These changes occur due to an increased use of technology along with ever-increasing globalization. It is very important that an organization can appropriately measure whether employees are meeting these various responsibilities and reward them accordingly.

You've learned about some common performance measures such as ROI, RI, EVA, and the balanced scorecard. The more accurately and efficiently a company can monitor and measure its decision-making processes at all levels, the more quickly it can respond to change or problems, and the more likely the company will be able to meet its strategic goals. Most companies will use some combination of the quantitative and nonquantitative measures described. ROI, RI, and EVA are typically used to evaluate specific projects, but ROI is sometimes used as a divisional measure. These measures are all quantitative measures. The balanced scorecard not only has quantitative measures but adds qualitative measures to address more of the goals of the organization. The combination of these different types of quantitative and qualitative measures—project-specific measures, employee-level measures, divisional measures, and corporate measures—enables an organization to more adequately assess how it is progressing toward meeting short- and long-term goals. Remember, the best performance measurement system will contain multiple measures and consist of both quantitative and qualitative factors, which allows for better assessment of managers and better results for the corporation.

THINK IT THROUGH

Nonfinancial Measurements of Success

For each of the following businesses, what are four nonfinancial measures that might be useful for helping management evaluate the success of its strategies?

- Grocery store
- Hospital
- Auto manufacturer
- Law office
- Coffee shop
- Movie theater

---

4   Gearhead Outfitters. "Our Story." https://www.gearheadoutfitters.com/about-us/our-story/

Key Terms

after-tax income income reduced by tax expenses

asset turnover measure of how efficiently a company is using its capital assets to generate revenues

balanced scorecard tool used to evaluate performance using qualitative and nonqualitative measures

capital asset tangible or intangible asset that has a life longer than one year

controllable factor component of the organization for which the manager is responsible and that the manager can control

cost center part of an organization in which management is evaluated based on the ability to contain costs; the manager primarily has control only over costs

economic value added (EVA) measure of shareholder wealth that is being created by a project, segment, or division

fixed asset tangible long-term asset

goal congruence integration of multiple goals, either within an organization or across multiple components or entities; congruence is achieved by aligning goals to achieve an anticipated mission

invested capital fixed assets, productive assets, or operating assets

investment center organizational segment in which a manager is accountable for profits (revenues minus expenses) and the invested capital used by the segment

metric means to measure something such as a goal or target

minimum required rate of return minimum return, usually in a percentage form, that a project or investment must produce in order for the company to be willing to undertake it

operating asset product asset plus intangible asset and current asset

operating income income before considering interest and taxes

performance measure metric used to evaluate a specific attribute of a manager's role

performance measurement system evaluates management in a way that will link the goals of the corporation with those of the manager

productive asset fixed asset plus inventory

profit center organizational segment in which a manager is responsible for and evaluted on both revenues and costs

qualitative factor component of a decision-making process that cannot be measured numerically

quantitative factor component of a decision-making process that can be measured numerically

residual income (RI) amount of income a given division (or project) is expected to earn in excess of a firm's minimum return goal

responsibility accounting method of encouraging goal congruence by setting and communicating the financial performance measures by which managers will be evaluated

return on investment (ROI) measure of the percentage of income generated by profits that were invested in capital assets

revenue center part of an organization in which management is evaluated based on the ability to generate revenues; the manager's primary control is only revenues

sales margin measure of how much profit is generated by each sales dollar

stakeholder someone affected by decisions made by a company; may include an investor, creditor, employee, manager, regulator, customer, supplier, and layperson

stockholder owner of stock, or shares, in a business

strategic plan broad vision of how a company will be in the future

uncontrollable factor decision or outcome over which a manager does not have control

weighted average cost of capital cost that the company expects to pay on average to finance assets and growth using either debt or equity

 Summary

12.1 Explain the Importance of Performance Measurement
- Well-designed performance measurement systems help businesses achieve goal congruence between the company and the employees.
- Managers should be evaluated only on factors over which they have control.
- Performance measures can be based on financial measures and/or nonfinancial measures.
- Performance measurement systems should help the company meet its strategic goals while helping the employee meet his or her professional goals.

12.2 Identify the Characteristics of an Effective Performance Measure
- A good performance measurement system uses measures over which a manager has control, provides timely and consistent feedback, compares the measures to standards of some form, has both short- and long-term measures, and puts the goals of the business and the individual on an equal level.

12.3 Evaluate an Operating Segment or a Project Using Return on Investment, Residual Income, and Economic Value Added
- Three common performance measures based on financial numbers are return on investment, residual income, and economic value added.
- Return on investment measures how effectively a company generates income using its assets.
- ROI can be broken into two separate measures: sales margin and asset turnover.
- Residual income measures whether or not a project or a division is exceeding a minimum return that has been determined by management.
- Economic value added is used to measure how well a project or division is contributing to shareholder wealth.
- A big challenge with ROI, RI, and EVA is determining which value of income and assets to use in calculating these measures.

12.4 Describe the Balanced Scorecard and Explain How It Is Used
- Balanced scorecards use both financial and nonfinancial measures to evaluate employees.
- The four categories of a balanced scorecard are financial perspective, internal business perspective, customer perspective, and learning and growth perspective.
- Financial perspective measures are usually traditional measures, based on financial statement information such as EPS or ROI.
- Internal business perspective measures are those that evaluate management's operational goals, such as quality control or on-time production.
- Customer perspective measures are those that evaluate how the customer perceives the business and how the business interacts with customers.
- Learning and growth perspective measures are those that evaluate how effectively the company is growing by innovating and creating value. This is often done through employee training.
- Well-designed balanced scorecards can be very effective at goal congruence through the utilization of both financial and nonfinancial measures.

Multiple Choice

1. LO 12.1 Components of the organization that are demotivating for purposes of performance management are known as _____.
   A. business goals
   B. strategic plans
   C. uncontrollable factors
   D. incentives

2. LO 12.1 When managerial accountants design an evaluation system that is based on criteria for which a manager is responsible, and it is structured to encourage managers to make decisions that will meet the goals of the company as well as their own personal job goals, the framework used is _____.
   A. a controllable factors framework
   B. an uncontrollable factors framework
   C. a strategic plan framework
   D. a responsibility accounting framework

3. LO 12.1 Goal congruence in well-designed performance measurement systems best explains a congruence between _____.
   A. employees and the company
   B. strategic plans and the future
   C. decisions and outcomes
   D. feedback and measurement

4. LO 12.1 Responsibility accounting holds managers responsible for _____.
   A. all costs charged to their subunit
   B. all costs charged to their subunit plus a share of company-wide fixed costs
   C. only the costs that they can control
   D. only the costs that they have personally approved

5. LO 12.1 Performance measures are only useful if _____.
   A. there are both controllable and uncontrollable factors to evaluate managers
   B. manager reward systems are designed by the chief financial officer prior to implementation
   C. all of the measures used are accounting numbers
   D. there is a baseline against which to compare the measured results

6. LO 12.2 Which of the following is *not* a characteristic of a good performance measurement system?
   A. timely
   B. consistent
   C. based on activities over which managers have no control or influence
   D. uses both long- and short-term performances and standards

7. LO 12.2 A good performance measurement system will align the goals of management with _____.
   A. the goals of the city manager and the mayoral staff
   B. the goals of the corporation, and both parties will benefit
   C. the priorities of the stockholders as listed at the annual meeting
   D. the investment department's response to the annual audit

8. LO 12.2 What should an organization do if performance measures change?
   A. Make sure that the manager being evaluated is aware of the measurement change, as this may affect his or her decision-making.
   B. Make sure that the manager benefits without the corporation also benefitting.
   C. Make sure that there are significant overriding opportunities for each manager, if the manager is unaware of the change.
   D. Obtain customer surveys on the change before communicating the change to the manager.

9. LO 12.2 A good performance measurement system will include which of the following?
   A. short-term goals
   B. long-term goals
   C. short-term and long-term goals
   D. no goals at all

10. LO 12.2 Without proper performance measures, goal congruence is almost impossible to achieve and will likely lead to _____.
    A. more stable targets
    B. decreased defects
    C. lost profits
    D. employees satisfied with the status quo

11. LO 12.3 Dixon Construction Materials has collected this information:

Net operating profit before tax	$300,000
Tax rate	30%
Invested capital	$2,500,000
Weighted average cost of capital	8%

    Based on this information, what is the EVA for the project?
    A. $100,000
    B. $10,000
    C. $450,000
    D. ($110,000)

12. LO 12.3 The cost of equity is _____.
    A. the interest associated with debt
    B. the rate of return required by investors to incentivize them to invest in a company
    C. the weighted average cost of capital
    D. equal to the amount of asset turnover

13. LO 12.3 Which of the following measures the profitability of a division relative to the size of its investment in capital assets?
    A. residual income (RI)
    B. sales margin
    C. return on investment (ROI)
    D. economic value added (EVA)

14. LO 12.3 The capital structure of Ridley Enterprises is: Debt 40%, Equity 60%. The cost of debt is 13%, and the cost of equity is 16.5%. What is the weighted average cost of capital for Ridley Enterprises?
   A. 14.4%
   B. 15.1%
   C. 16.2%
   D. 13.8%

15. LO 12.3 Calculate the ROI for Gardner Chemical given the following information:

Income	$ 6,000
Revenue	$24,000
Average assets	$10,000

   A. 25%
   B. 24%
   C. 60%
   D. 40%

16. LO 12.4 Which of the following statements is *false*?
   A. The four dimensions of performance that are considered in a balanced scorecard are financial, customer, internal process, and learning and growth
   B. A balanced scorecard will include qualitative and quantitative measures.
   C. Stakeholders cannot include stockholders.
   D. A balanced scorecard is the compatibility between personal goals and the goals of the organization.

17. LO 12.4 The metrics based on nonfinancial information are known as _____.
   A. quantitative factors
   B. qualitative factors
   C. stakeholders
   D. stockholders

18. LO 12.4 The metrics based on financial numbers produced by the accounting system are _____.
   A. quantitative factors
   B. qualitative factors
   C. stakeholders
   D. stockholders

19. LO 12.4 People affected by decisions made by a company, including investors, creditors, employees, managers, regulators, customers, suppliers, and laypeople, are known as _____.
   A. quantitative factors
   B. qualitative factors
   C. stakeholders
   D. stockholders

20. LO 12.4 The owners of company stock are _____.
   A. quantitative factors
   B. qualitative factors
   C. stakeholders
   D. stockholders

Questions

1. LO 12.1 Why might a manager focused solely on accounting numbers miss opportunities for future benefits?

2. LO 12.1 Is there a way to prevent managers from focusing on accounting measures as performance measures?

3. LO 12.1 Should an organization focus on controllable or uncontrollable factors to effectively implement a successful performance measurement system? Explain your answer.

4. LO 12.1 What are the components of a strategic plan? Find one of these components for the company you work for and share (if you are not currently employed, use the college you attend).

5. LO 12.1 What are the four types of centers and their corresponding responsibilities?

6. LO 12.2 What would be wrong with using two points of data in a performance measurement system to tell a company whether the amount of variation is normal or abnormal?

7. LO 12.2 Compare and contrast short- and long-term goals for a company. Give an example of each, and explain why they are important for performance measurement systems.

8. LO 12.2 Can a short-term goal also be a long-term goal? Where is the division, and why is it important for an employee to understand whether the goal is short or long term?

9. LO 12.2 What does *goal congruence* mean? Provide an example with your explanation.

10. LO 12.2 What are the six characteristics of a good performance measurement system?

11. LO 12.3 What is EVA and why is it superior to other performance measures?

12. LO 12.3 What are the drawbacks to ROI? Give examples of each.

13. LO 12.4 Describe the history and purpose of the balanced scorecard.

14. LO 12.4 What are the characteristics of successful balanced scorecards?

Exercise Set A

EA1. LO 12.1 For the following situations, identify whether the description is probably a centralized or decentralized organization.
  A. Seaside Furniture, a small builder of side tables managed solely by its sole proprietor
  B. Harbor Marketing, which wants Advertising Team Leaders to be able to respond quickly to needs of potential clients so Team Leaders have the authority to make decisions about advertising and pricing
  C. Couture's Creations, with a single owner who manages the production, accounting, engineering, sales, and other administrative functions
  D. British Navy
  E. McDonalds franchise #3101 in Canton, Ohio
  F. United States Army

EA2. LO 12.1 For the following descriptions state whether the cost is controllable or uncontrollable by responsibility center managers.
  A. property tax of an existing manufacturing facility
  B. research and development of a product
  C. advertising of a product
  D. insurance cost of the existing manufacturing facility
  E. design of a product

EA3. LO 12.1 Identify the type of responsibility center (revenue center, cost center, profit center, or investment center) for each of the following situations.
  A. the accounting department for Tubelite Inc.
  B. the Best Buy in Traverse City, Michigan
  C. the reservation department of Allegiant airlines
  D. the sales department of Four Winns
  E. the Kohl's store in Mount Pleasant, Michigan
  F. The Hershey Company
  G. Procter and Gamble
  H. the shoe department in the Kohl's store in Mount Pleasant, Michigan

EA4. LO 12.2 Sara has just taken a job as the middle school assistant principal for an area school district. Prior to this, she was a teacher. She has received the following performance measurements for her first administrative job. Her first order of business is to determine if these performance measurements are short-term goals or long-term goals based on her individual situation. She has completed her administrative degree but has not yet worked as an administrator. Identify each of the following goals as short term or long term.
  A. Conduct teacher walk-throughs/observations/evaluations for teachers of grades 6 and 7.
  B. Assist the district's mission in seeking to educate all youth in the school district.
  C. Train to become a building instructional leader. Act as building administrator in the absence of the principal.
  D. Attend meetings with building principals and the administrative team when called to do so.
  E. Engage all students in a meaningful way, and support teachers and staff in providing rigor and relevance. Success of school-wide discipline and attendance policies and enforcement depends on a combination of creativity and sound pedagogy while adhering to district, state, and federal law, guidelines, and regulations.
  F. Facilitate and supervise all federal- and state-mandated drills (fire, lockdowns, tornado, others).
  G. Dress professionally.
  H. Assist the building principal in all job duties and responsibilities.

EA5. LO 12.3 During the current year, Sokowski Manufacturing earned income of $350,000 from total sales of $5,500,000 and average capital assets of $12,000,000. What is the sales margin?

EA6. LO 12.3 During the current year, Sokowski Manufacturing earned income of $350,000 from total sales of $5,500,000 and average capital assets of $12,000,000.
  A. Based on this information, calculate asset turnover.
  B. Using the sales margin from the previous exercise, what is the total ROI for the company during the current year?

EA7. LO 12.3 Assume Skyler Industries has debt of $4,500,000 with a cost of capital of 7.5% and equity of $5,500,000 with a cost of capital of 10.5%. What is Skyler's weighted average cost of capital?

EA8. LO 12.3 Why do managers want a high ROI, and how would they strive to increase their ROI?

EA9. LO 12.4 Classify each of the following performance measures into the balanced scorecard perspective to which it relates: financial perspective, internal operations perspective, learning and growth perspective, or customer perspective.
   A. Number of improved products
   B. Time from packaging to delivery or display
   C. Production costs
   D. Number of customer suggestions
   E. Sales mix revenues
   F. Number of repeat customers

Exercise Set B

EB1. LO 12.1 For the following situations identify whether the description is a centralized or decentralized organization.
   A. the United States Navy
   B. Farah's Domino's franchise store
   C. Domino's Pizza
   D. Middie's Furniture, which is divided into separate operating units, such as living room, kitchen, flooring
   E. the local community college, which has a single payroll department, a single administrative headquarters, and a single human resources department since it "flattened" its organization structure
   F. Conner Corporation, which promotes managers from within the organization whenever possible and which has formal training programs for lower-level managers

EB2. LO 12.1 For the following descriptions, state whether the cost is controllable or uncontrollable by responsibility center managers.
   A. advertising for a merchandiser
   B. corporate income taxes
   C. office supplies for a merchandiser
   D. donations to the Salvation Army
   E. insurance for delivery vehicles

EB3. LO 12.1 Identify the type of responsibility center (revenue center, cost center, profit center, or investment center) for each of the following situations.
   A. the legal department for Avon Manufacturing
   B. the Macy's store in Mansfield, Ohio
   C. the food and beverage division of the Best Western
   D. the marketing department of the Hershey Company
   E. the Walmart #5030 on Central Avenue in Toledo, Ohio
   F. Apple's Braeburn Capital Inc., where most of Apple's billions of dollars are invested
   G. Zappo's department store
   H. the men's clothing department in the Walmart #5030 in Toledo, Ohio

EB4. LO 12.2 Padma completed her doctoral degree and has taken a position as an assistant professor at a local university. She was given the following performance measures for her new position. Identify whether these goals are long or short term.
   A. Interact in a fair and impartial way with students.
   B. Promote and access student academic achievement.
   C. Counsel students within the norms of society and the regulations of the college.
   D. Motivate students.
   E. Effectively plan and organize lectures and labs in accordance with the college course outlines.
   F. Report class attendance in accordance with the college policy and procedure.
   G. Serve on academic committees as assigned.
   H. Make progress toward tenure necessary at her university.

EB5. LO 12.3 During the current year, Plainfield Manufacturing earned income of $845,000 from total sales of $9,350,000 and average capital assets of $13,500,000. What is the sales margin?

EB6. LO 12.3 During the current year, Plainfield Manufacturing earned income of $845,000 from total sales of $9,350,000 and average capital assets of $13,500,000. Using the sales margin from the previous exercise, what is the total ROI for the company during the current year?

EB7. LO 12.3 Assume Plainfield Manufacturing has debt of $6,500,000 with a cost of capital of 9.5% and equity of $4,500,000 with a cost of capital of 11.5%. What is Tyler's weighted average cost of capital?

EB8. LO 12.3 Though a high ROI is desired, what are some reasons that might lead to a low or decreased ROI?

EB9. LO 12.4 Classify each of the following performance measures into the balanced scorecard perspective to which it relates: financial perspective, internal operations perspective, learning and growth perspective, or customer perspective.
   A. Employee satisfaction surveys
   B. Units of waste per production process, uniformity of products and inventory control
   C. Number of energy-efficient bulbs replaced
   D. Management training course certificates awarded
   E. Divisional profit
   F. Number of customer referrals

Problem Set A

PA1. **LO** 12.1 Match each of the following with its appropriate term.

A. Controllable factors	i. This is the part of an organization in which management is evaluated based on the ability to contain costs; the manager primarily has control only over costs.
B. Cost center	ii. This means to align the goals of the business with the personal goals of the manager.
C. Metric	iii. These components of the organization are components for which the manager is responsible and can control.
D. Goal congruence	iv. This is the means to measure something such as a goal or target.
E. Investment center	v. This is a system that evaluates management in a way that will link the goals of the corporation with those of the manager.
F. Performance measurement system	vi. For this center, management is responsible for revenues, costs, and assets and is evaluated based on these three components.

PA2. **LO** 12.1 Florentino Allers is the production manager of Electronics Manufacturer. Due to limited capacity, the company can only produce one of two possible products:

- An industrial motherboard with a 75% probability of making a profit of $1 million and a 25% probability of making a profit of $150,000
- A regular motherboard with a 100% chance of making a profit of $710,000

Florentino will get a 20% bonus from his department. Florentino has the responsibility to choose between the two products and is more of a risk-taker, more so than most of the top management at Electronics Manufacturer.

A. Which option is Florentino more likely to choose and why?
B. Which option would the company be more likely to choose and why?
C. What changes should the company make to Florentino's compensation to avoid unnecessary risks?

PA3. **LO** 12.3 Macon Mills is a division of Bolin Products, Inc. During the most recent year, Macon had a net income of $40 million. Included in the income was interest expense of $2,800,000. The company's tax rate was 40%. Total assets were $470 million, current liabilities were $104,000,000, and $72,000,000 of the current liabilities are noninterest bearing. What are the invested capital and ROI for Macon?

PA4. **LO** 12.3 Jefferson Memorial Hospital is an investment center as a division of Hospitals United. During the past year, Jefferson reported an after-tax income of $7 million. Total interest expense was $3,200,000, and the hospital tax rate was 30%. Total assets totaled $70 million, and non-interest-bearing current liabilities were $22,800,000. The required rate of return established by Jefferson is equal to 18% of invested capital. What is the residual income of Jefferson Memorial Hospital?

PA5. LO 12.4 Crawford's Books and Things has a traditional bookstore housed downtown Charlotte. The store has been there forty years, and many customers love the fact that they can hold the books in their hands and browse the offerings. Crawford's just started an online book division for people who like to order books online.

EVA for the Charlotte store is about $13 million, while EVA for the online division shows a value of −$2.2 million.

   A. Explain why it might be better to evaluate the online division using a balanced scorecard.
   B. Suggest two measures for the customer dimension that would be appropriate for the online division and two measures for the internal processes dimension of the balanced scorecard that would be appropriate for the online division.

PA6. LO 12.4 Coral Creations has strategic plans that call for rapid growth, a limited number of units for each design to enhance exclusivity, designs for the perfect fit, on-time delivery to customers, retention of highly trained employees with innovative skills, and excellent inventory control.
   A. Suggest one performance measure for each dimension of the balanced scorecard for Coral Creations.
   B. Take one of your measures and discuss the linkage it has to multiple strategies in Coral's plan.

Problem Set B

PB1. LO 12.1 Match each of the following with its appropriate term:

A. Performance measures	i. The decisions and outcomes over which a manager does not have control
B. Profit center	ii. That part of an organization in which management is evaluated based on the ability to generate revenues; the manager primarily has control only over revenues
C. Responsibility accounting	iii. The part of an organization in which management is evaluated based on the ability to generate profits because the manager has control over both revenues and costs
D. Revenue center	iv. A broad vision of how a company will be in the future
E. Strategic plan	v. A system that collects and reports data for which a manager has responsibility
F. Uncontrollable factors	vi. The metrics used to evaluate a specific attribute of a manager's role

PB2. LO 12.1 Oleg Markov is the production manager of NASA Solvents. Due to limited capacity, the company can only produce one of two possible products:
- an industrial concentrated solvent with a 15% probability of making a profit of $1 million and an 85% probability of making a profit of $200,000
- a household diluted solvent with a 100% chance of making a profit of $310,000

Oleg will get a 20% bonus from his department. Oleg has the responsibility to choose between the two products and is more risk averse than most of the top management at NASA Solvents.

A. Which option is Oleg more likely to choose and why?
B. Which option would the company be more likely to choose and why?
C. What changes should the company make to Oleg's compensation to encourage managers to take appropriate risks

PB3. LO 12.3 Evaluate the two departments for Moxie Products.

	Department 1	Department 2
Total assets	$138,000,000	$46,000,000
Non-interest-bearing liabilities	$9,000,000	$4,600,000
Net operating income after taxes	$24,000,000	$11,800,000
Required rate of return	12%	11%

Compare the year's performance of the two departments in terms of ROI and RI. Which department has created the most wealth for Moxie shareholders in the past year?

PB4. LO 12.3 Banyan Industries has two divisions, a tax rate of 30%, and a minimum rate of return of 20%. Division A has a weighted average cost of capital of 9.5% and is looking at a new project that will generate a profit of $1,200,000 from a machine that costs $4,000,000. Division B has a weighted average cost of capital of 9.5% and is looking at a new project that will generate a profit of $1,350,000 from a machine that costs $5,000,000.

A. Calculate the EVA for each of Banyan's divisions.
B. Calculate the RI for each of Banyan's division.
C. If Banyan uses EVA to evaluate the projects, which division has the better project and by how much?
D. If Banyan uses RI, which division has the better project and by how much?
E. What are some of the reasons for the similarity or difference that you found in the use of EVA versus RI?

PB5. **LO** 12.4 Forty years ago, Vinfen was founded as a nonprofit company by psychiatrists and social workers at the Massachusetts Mental Health Center and Harvard Medical School to help people with psychiatric conditions transition to group homes for community living. Vinfen's strategy map for fiscal 2006 shows how it is building from its mission to accelerating organizational learning and elevating agency performance through its balanced scorecard perspectives to bring value to the customer supported by operational excellence.[5] The following are elements in the balanced scorecard and the four key perspectives. Match the elements with the correct perspectives.

A. Improve organizational trust and teamwork	i. Financial perspective
B. Strengthen government engagement	ii. Learning and growth perspective
C. Deliver quality services to special populations	iii. Internal perspective
D. Achieve financial stability	iv. Customer perspective
E. Increase public awareness and visibility	
F. Contribute to human services research and innovation	
G. Improve efficiency and effectiveness of contracting process	
H. Build professional competencies that support strategy	
I. Develop and implement an integrated information system	
J. Deliver services consistent in value and quality	

Thought Provokers

TP1. **LO** 12.1 What combination of quantitative factors and qualitative factors would you like your potential employer to use as a performance management system? Explain your answer.

TP2. **LO** 12.2 Josh O'Shea is the manager of the Cardiovascular/Respiratory Laboratory. This department is responsible for measuring blood gases, performing respiratory treatments, and distributing automated IV equipment. As a manager, Josh hires and trains personnel, prepares his departmental budget, and maintains the personnel schedule. Josh recommends equipment needs for the department, but he may be overruled in the acquisition process. Josh and his departmental personnel are paid for the professional credentials they hold, earn, and maintain and are reimbursed by the hospital for any approved training or professional credentials they acquire. Josh must use the equipment, reagents, and supplies provided to him from central purchasing. Based on this information, what incentives do you see as those that will motivate Josh as part of the hospital team, and why? Which incentives will be demotivating, and why?

---

5   https://www.vinfen.org

TP3. LO 12.2 Kanye Achebe just became the operations manager of Weston Transportation. Weston transports large crates for online companies and transports containers overseas.

Kanye would like to evaluate each divisional manager on a basis similar to segmental reporting required by generally accepted accounting principles (GAAP) financial statements contained in annual reports. These data include a presentation of net sales, operating profit and loss before and after taxes, total identifiable assets, and depreciation for segment reported. Kanye thinks that evaluating business division managers by the same criteria as the total company is appropriate.

    A. Explain why you think the chief financial officer (CFO) disagrees and tells Kanye that publicly reporting information might demotivate managers.
    B. For better evaluation of the managers, what type of information should Kanye propose that the CFO might accept?

TP4. LO 12.3 Which of the performance measures—ROI, RI, or EVA—is best, and why? Explain your answer thoroughly.

13 Sustainability Reporting

Figure 13.1 Choices. Choices about where to invest and even where to work can be difficult if you can only evaluate options on the financial information they provide. (credit: modification of "Girl Crossroads Choice" by "Pixource"/Pixabay, CC0)

Chapter Outline

13.1 Describe Sustainability and the Way It Creates Business Value

13.2 Identify User Needs for Information

13.3 Discuss Examples of Major Sustainability Initiatives

13.4 Future Issues in Sustainability

Why It Matters

Gina studies supply chain management at a local university. Last summer, she worked at a manufacturing plant for a major auto manufacturer. She enjoyed her experience and learned quite a bit about the manufacturing and supply chain process, and she spent a significant amount of time on the production floor learning how the supply chain process affects the assembly of the vehicles. Gina felt she was well paid and she liked her colleagues. This summer, she has a comparable position and compensation with a different auto manufacturer. She is curious to see how the two companies compare.

One of the first things Gina notices is the number of reminders posted around the plant to save and conserve energy. There are procedures in place to save energy when machines are idle, and sensors that turn off lights when no one is in the offices or break room. Gina also heard fellow employees talking about taking paid time off to volunteer at local charities. Her supervisor has asked her to be one of the speakers at presentations given throughout the year at local schools as part of a project to promote school-age girls entering technical fields. She also visited the company's research and development symposium and learned how the company is trying to improve fuel efficiency and move away from cars that use fossil fuels.

Gina never noticed initiatives like these at her position the prior summer. And though she enjoyed that job, she feels better about the current manufacturer because she realizes the company is trying to accomplish goals in addition to making money for its shareholders. Her current employer takes steps to promote the well-being of its employees, the community, and the environment. When Gina asks one of her professors about the difference, she learns that her current employer is more involved in corporate social responsibility and the company's sustainability reports will provide more information. Gina decides to learn more about sustainability reporting.

13.1 Describe Sustainability and the Way It Creates Business Value

A primary goal of any business is to maximize shareholder or owner wealth and thus continue operating into the future. However, in making decisions to be profitable and to remain in business into the future, companies must think beyond their own organization and consider other stakeholders. This approach is a major goal of **sustainability**, which is meeting the needs of the present generation without compromising the ability of future generations to meet their own needs.[1] Another concept that is sometimes associated with sustainability is **corporate social responsibility** (CSR), which is the set of actions that firms take to assume responsibility for their impact on the environment and social well-being. CSR can be used to describe the actions of an individual company or in comparing the actions of multiple corporations.

Just as individuals often make conscious decisions to recycle, reuse items and reduce their individual negative effect on the environment, so too do most businesses. Corporations affect the world on many different levels—economic, environmental and social—and many corporations have realized that being good stewards of the world can add value to their business. Companies increase their value, both financial and nonfinancial, in the eyes of consumers and shareholders by heralding their efforts to be good citizens of the globe and the results of those efforts. It is important to note that a corporation's social and environmental influence is often affected by government policy, both local and federal, and sometimes even internationally through agreements and treaties. The global effort to limit climate change is an example of this influence.

In December 2015, 196 nations adopted the **Paris Climate Agreement**, a historic plan to work together to limit the increase of global temperatures to 1.5 °C. The Agreement aims to help delay or avoid some of the worst consequences of climate change within a system of transparency and accountability in which each nation can evaluate the progress of the others.

In June 2017, President Trump announced his intention that the United States withdraw from the Agreement. Five months later, Syria ratified the Agreement, leaving the United States as the only non-participating country in the world.

By November 2017, however, a coalition of 20 U.S. states and 50 cities, led by California governor Jerry Brown and former New York City Mayor Michael Bloomberg, had formed (Figure 13.2). During the 23rd UN Climate Change Conference in Germany, the members of this coalition pledged to continue supporting the Agreement. They aim to do this by reducing their **carbon output**, which is a measure of their carbon dioxide and other greenhouse gas emissions into the atmosphere.

In addition to these commitments at the local, state and national level, many U.S. companies have also committed to reducing their carbon output, including Walmart, Apple, Disney, Tesla, and Facebook.

---

1 Brundtland Commission. *Our Common Future*. 1987.

Figure 13.2 Governor Jerry Brown on Climate Change. California Governor Jerry Brown speaks at the UN Climate Change Conference in Paris, France in 2015. (credit: modification of "Jerry Brown, Gouverneur de Californie sur le Pavillon France" by COP PARIS/Wikimedia Commons, CC0)

The fact that these companies and others are run by CEOs whose primary objective is to make a profit does not mean they live in a vacuum, unaware of their effects on the larger world. As mentioned, responsible companies today are concerned not only about their economic performance, but also about their effects on the environment and society. Recall, corporate social responsibility (CSR) is the set of steps that firms take to bear responsibility for their impact on the environment and social well-being. Even if some managers are not personally guided by these motivations, good corporate citizenship makes good business sense.

Historically, companies disclosed financial information in their annual reports to allow investors and creditors to assess how well managers have allocated their economic resources. The public usually learned little about a company's hiring practices, environmental impact, or safety record unless a violation occurred that was serious enough to make the news. Companies that did not make the news were simply assumed to be doing the right thing.

Today, however, as a consequence of social media platforms such as Facebook and Twitter, the public is more aware of corporate behavior, both good and bad. Investors and consumers alike can make financial decisions about firms that align with their own values and beliefs. Management decisions perceived to be detrimental to society can quickly put companies in a bad light and affect sales and profitability for many years. Thus, users of financial reports increasingly want to know whether businesses are making appropriate decisions not only to increase shareholder wealth, but also to sustain the business, and minimize any future negative effects on the environment and the citizens of the world. This management goal is called **business sustainability**. The number of companies reporting sustainability outcomes has grown over the last two decades. This growth has made this non-financial component of reporting increasingly important to accountants.

Sustainability Reporting

A **sustainability report** presents the economic, environmental and social effects that a corporation or organization was responsible for during the course of everyday business. Sustainability reporting aims to respond to the idea that companies can be held accountable for sustainability. In 1987, the former Norwegian Prime Minister, Gro Harlem Brundtland, chaired a World Commission on Environment and Development to both formulate proposals and increase understanding of and commitment to environment and development. The resulting **Brundtland Commission Report** laid the groundwork for the concept of **sustainable development** (Figure 13.3). This was defined as "development that meets the needs of the present without compromising the ability of future generations to meet their own needs."[2]

Figure 13.3 Sustainable Energy. Sustainable development means meeting the needs of the present without compromising the ability of future generations to meet their own needs. (credit: modification of "Shepherds Flat Wind Farm 2011" by Steve Wilson/Wikimedia Commons, CC BY 2.0)

With that in mind, the early adopters of sustainability reporting attempted to construct a framework that could convey the good stewardship of companies, primarily their social and environmental effects. Since then, sustainability reporting has evolved to include the ways in which sustainability practices of the company benefit its profitability and longevity.

Indeed, adopting sustainable business practices may benefit business in many ways. Companies can:

- save money by using less water and energy and reducing or recycling business waste
- reduce insurance costs by limiting their exposure to environmental risks
- attract investors who prefer to work with businesses that are environmentally and socially responsible
- reduce social risks, such as racial or gender discrimination
- improve customer sales and loyalty by enhancing reputation and brand value
- reduce the possibility of potentially costly regulation by proactively undertaking sustainability initiatives
- attract and retain employees who share similar values
- strengthen their relationship with the community
- contribute to improving environmental sustainability

In short, sustainability reporting has evolved to describe both how the company's practices contribute to the social good and how they add value to the company, which ultimately provides better returns to its investors.

The need for improved reporting by corporations on sustainability developed over time. The Union Carbide,

---

2 NGO Committee on Education. "Report of the World Commission on Environment and Development: Our Common Future." *UN Documents: Gathering a Body of Global Agreements*. August 4, 1987. http://www.un-documents.net/wced-ocf.htm

Nestlé, and Johnson and Johnson cases are examples of corporate crises that contributed to the development of better sustainability reporting. And though each of these cases involved a negative public response toward the company, this led to a broader shift in business practices, changing how other corporations handle similar challenges.

Historical Drivers of Contemporary Sustainability Reporting

Much of the drive to adopt sustainability reporting has resulted from the publicity surrounding corporate responses to specific crises. The three featured cases, on Union Carbide, Nestlé, and Johnson & Johnson, look at events that had such an impact on communities and the social conscience that they have contributed to shaping modern sustainability reporting and what society's expectations of corporations are today. We first look at Union Carbide, whose actions, or lack of action, resulted in the deaths of thousands of impoverished Indians who lived in the shanty communities next to a facility of the U.S.-owned conglomerate. This case highlighted the power disparity between corporations and poor individuals and became a stark emblem of corporate disregard for the human toll of the quest for profit. We then consider the long running campaign against Nestlé Corporation, ongoing since the early 1980s. We will examine what Nestlé has attempted to do to mitigate the perception of exploitation which, some activists argue, is still a superficial response. Finally, we look at the reaction by Johnson & Johnson to the Tylenol poisoning crisis, which, while not of their making, is seen as a rapid and responsible response to ensure the well-being of the community, even if it initially came at considerable financial cost to the company.

Union Carbide

A few hours before midnight on December 2, 1984, at the Union Carbide pesticide plant in Bhopal India, pressure and heat built up in a tank that stored methyl isocyanate (MIC). Within two hours, approximately 27 tons[3],[4] of MIC had escaped into the surrounding community, exposing more than 600,000[5] people to the deadly gas cloud. By the next day, 1,700 people were dead. The official toll eventually rose to 3,598 dead[6] and another 42,000 injured, although some accounts estimate that the incident was responsible for 16,000–20,000 deaths.[7]

Though the plant had ceased production a couple of years earlier, the plant still contained vast quantities of dangerous chemicals. There was still 60 tons of deadly MIC in tanks at the plant, and proper maintenance of the tanks and the containment systems was necessary. It was later discovered that all the safety systems put into place failed due to lack of maintenance after the plant closed.[8]

Within days of the explosion, Warren Anderson, the CEO of Union Carbide, arrived in India, was arrested and released, and then immediately flew out of the country. Although he was subsequently charged with manslaughter, he never returned to India to face trial.[9] Some of the criticisms of Union Carbide's handling of

---

3   The Bhopal Medical Appeal. "Union Carbide's Disaster." n.d. http://bhopal.org/what-happened/union-carbides-disaster/
4   Paul Cullinan. "Case Study of the Bhopal Incident." *Environmental Toxicology and Human Health, Vol. I. Encyclopedia of Life Support Systems*. n.d. https://www.eolss.net/sample-chapters/C09/E4-12-02-04.pdf
5   Alan Taylor. "Bhopal: The World's Worst Industrial Disaster, 30 Years Later." *The Atlantic*. December 2, 2014. https://www.theatlantic.com/photo/2014/12/bhopal-the-worlds-worst-industrial-disaster-30-years-later/100864/
6   Paul Cullinan. "Case Study of the Bhopal Incident." *Environmental Toxicology and Human Health, Vol. I. Encyclopedia of Life Support Systems*. n.d. https://www.eolss.net/sample-chapters/C09/E4-12-02-04.pdf
7   The Bhopal Medical Appeal. "Basic Facts & Figures, Numbers of Dead and Injured, Bhopal Disaster." n.d. http http://bhopal.org/basic-facts-figures-numbers-of-dead-and-injured-bhopal-disaster/
8   The Bhopal Medical Appeal. "Union Carbide's Disaster." n.d. http://bhopal.org/what-happened/union-carbides-disaster/

matters, both before and after the disaster, are:

- A safety audit two years before had noted numerous problems at the plant, including several implicated in the accident.[10]
- Before the incident, staff were routinely ordered to deviate from safety regulations and fined if they refused to do so.[11]
- Employees discovered the leak around 11:30pm on December 2. However, they then decided to take a tea break and did not deal with the leak until two hours later.[12]
- Two of the plant's main safety systems were out of action at the time of the accident; one of them had been inoperable for several weeks.[13]
- Staffing had been cut from 12 operators a shift to six. Kamal K. Pareek, a chemical engineer employed by the plant later argued that it was not possible to safely run the closed plant with only six people.[14]
- There were no public education programs to inform the surrounding community about what to do in an emergency,[15] and on the night of the leak, there was no public warning of the disaster. An external alarm was turned on at 12:50am but ran for only a minute before it was turned off.
- Beginning at 1:15am, workers denied to local police that they were aware of any problems. They restarted the public warning siren at 2:15am and then contacted police to report the leak.[16]

Union Carbide asserts that a disgruntled employee sabotaged the plant by mixing water with the methyl isocyanate to create a reaction. Some employees claimed that a worker lacking proper training was ordered by a novice supervisor to wash out a pipe that had not been properly sealed. Although it was against plant rules, this action may have started the reaction.[17]

Union Carbide's disgruntled-employee theory appeared to many to be an effort to deflect blame and deny responsibility. Ultimately, the company agreed to pay the Indian Government $470 million in compensation to be distributed to Bhopal residents,[18] and seven former employees were jailed for two years. In 2001, the company was bought by Dow Chemical Company. Though Dow Chemical obtained the financial liabilities of Union Carbide, Dow maintains that it did not assume legal responsibility for the prior actions of Union Carbide.[19] More than thirty years later, many victims are still awaiting the compensation they were promised, after having paid doctors and lawyers to prove their injuries. "In a way, they were fighting their own government for adequate compensation, whereas the state should have fought with them against Union

---

9   Douglas Martin. "Warren Anderson, 92, Dies; Faced India Plant Disaster." *New York Times*. October 30, 2014. https://www.nytimes.com/2014/10/31/business/w-m-anderson-92-dies-led-union-carbide-in-80s-.html
10 Juanita Stuart. "Union Carbide Bhopal Chemical Plant Explosion." *Worksafe*. 2015. https://worksafe.govt.nz/data-and-research/research/role-of-information-management-disaster-prevention/#If-doc-34129
11 Juanita Stuart. "Union Carbide Bhopal Chemical Plant Explosion." *Worksafe*. 2015. https://worksafe.govt.nz/data-and-research/research/role-of-information-management-disaster-prevention/#If-doc-34129
12 Stuart Diamond. "The Bhopal Disaster: How It Happened." *New York Times*. January 28, 1985. http://www.nytimes.com/1985/01/28/world/the-bhopal-disaster-how-it-happened.html?pagewanted=all
13 Stuart Diamond. "The Bhopal Disaster: How It Happened." *New York Times*. January 28, 1985. http://www.nytimes.com/1985/01/28/world/the-bhopal-disaster-how-it-happened.html?pagewanted=all
14 Stuart Diamond. "The Bhopal Disaster: How It Happened." *New York Times*. January 28, 1985. http://www.nytimes.com/1985/01/28/world/the-bhopal-disaster-how-it-happened.html?pagewanted=all
15 Stuart Diamond. "The Bhopal Disaster: How It Happened." *New York Times*. January 28, 1985. http://www.nytimes.com/1985/01/28/world/the-bhopal-disaster-how-it-happened.html?pagewanted=all
16 "The Bhopal Disaster." Chapter 8 in *Health*. n.d. http://cseindia.org/userfiles/THE%20BHOPAL%20DISASTER.pdf
17 Stuart Diamond. "The Bhopal Disaster: How It Happened." *New York Times*. January 28, 1985. http://www.nytimes.com/1985/01/28/world/the-bhopal-disaster-how-it-happened.html?pagewanted=all
18 Business and Human Rights Resources Centre. "Union Carbide/Dow Lawsuit (re Bhopal)." n.d. https://business-humanrights.org/en/union-carbidedow-lawsuit-re-bhopal
19 Dow. "Dow and the Bhopal Tragedy." n.d. https://www.dow.com/en-us/about-dow/issues-and-challenges/bhopal/dow-and-bhopal

Carbide," says a representative of the one of the groups fighting for the victims' rights.[20]

Nestlé

Nestlé is the target of one of the longest-running consumer boycotts in modern history. Founded and headquartered in Switzerland, the company recently became the largest food company in the world. While there have been boycotts against a number of its products over the years, none has lasted as long as the baby formula boycott.

The origins of the boycott go back to the mid-1970s, when consumer concerns arose about Nestlé's use of aggressive marketing tactics to sell its baby formula in developing countries in Asia, Africa, and Latin America. Initially new mothers were provided with free samples of formula to feed their babies, a common practice in many hospitals throughout the world. But in developing countries, this led to two negative consequences for mothers and their babies. First, once bottle feeding begins, the demand on the mother's body is reduced and breast milk begins to dry up. Mothers in developing countries were often living in poverty and unable to afford the cost of artificial infant food. Action groups argued that, in Nigeria, the cost of bottle feeding a three-month-old infant was approximately 30% of the minimum wage, and by the time the child reached six months old, the cost was 47%.[21]

A second consequence arose from the fact that preparation of infant formula required sterilized equipment and clean water. Both clean water and sterilization were difficult to guarantee in developing nations where mothers may not have understood the requirements for sterilization or may have lacked the fuel or electricity to boil water. Lapses in preparing the formula led to increased risks of infections, including vomiting and diarrhea that, in some cases, proved fatal. UNICEF estimated that formula-fed infants were 14 times more likely[22] to die of diarrhea and four times more likely to die of pneumonia than breast-fed children. Advocacy groups also argued that dehydration could result if mothers used too much formula and malnutrition could occur if they used too little in an effort to save money.[23]

An active campaign against Nestlé ensued, and the company endures a backlash even today. One group distributed a report, *Nestlé Toten Babies* ("Nestlé Kills Babies"), which a Swiss court found to be libelous. Nonetheless, the judge warned Nestlé that perhaps it should change the way it did business if it did not want to face such accusations.[24]

The boycott and negative publicity precipitated a long-running campaign by Nestlé to improve its image. The company now explicitly states on its packaging that breastfeeding is best for babies and supports the World Health Organization's recommendation that babies should be breastfed exclusively for at least the first six months of life. It distributes educational materials for healthcare professionals and parents on the benefits of breastfeeding and holds seminars on breastfeeding for the medical community. Nestlé established a global Maternity Protection Policy that provides its own employees with extended maternity leave (up to six months) and flexible work arrangements. It opened 945 breastfeeding rooms in India and another 1,500 in China in a partnership with several public and private organizations, and it developed a breastfeeding room locator app

---

20 Nita Bhalla. "Victims Call for Justice 30 Years after Bhopal Disaster." *Reuters*. December 3, 2014. https://www.reuters.com/article/us-india-bhopal-anniversary/victims-call-for-justice-30-years-after-bhopal-disaster-idUSKCN0JH1L620141203
21 Mike Muller. "The Baby Killer." *War on Want*. March 1974. http://archive.babymilkaction.org/pdfs/babykiller.pdf
22 Unicef. "Improving Breastfeeding, Complementary Foods, and Feeding Practices." May 1, 2018. https://www.unicef.org/nutrition/index_breastfeeding.html
23 E. Ziegler. "Adverse Effects of Cow's Milk in Infants." Nestlé Nutrition Workshop Senior Pediatric Program. 2007 (60): 185–199. https://www.ncbi.nlm.nih.gov/pubmed/17664905
24 Mike Muller. "Nestlé Baby Milk Scandal Has Grown Up but Not Gone Away." *The Guardian*. February 13, 2013. https://www.theguardian.com/sustainable-business/nestle-baby-milk-scandal-food-industry-standards

for mothers.[25] In those countries considered to be at higher risk for infant mortality and malnutrition, Nestlé applies its own stringent policies, which they believe are stricter than national code and which were derived from the World Health Organization's International Code of Marketing of Breast-Milk Substitutes.[26] Meanwhile, debate about whether Nestlé is a good corporate citizen continues.

Johnson & Johnson

At 6:30 in the morning on Wednesday, September 29, 1982, twelve-year-old Mary Kellerman woke up feeling sick. Her parents gave her some Tylenol and decided to keep her home from school. Within an hour Mary had collapsed, and she was pronounced dead at 9:24. Within 24 hours another six people were dead, poisoned, like Mary, by cyanide capsules in Tylenol bottles.

In the early 1980s, Tylenol was the leader in over-the-counter pain relief, and during the first three quarters of 1982 the product was responsible for 19% of Johnson & Johnson's profits. Then an unknown person replaced Tylenol Extra-Strength capsules with cyanide-laced capsules and deposited the bottles on the shelves of at least a half-dozen stores across Chicago.

On learning of the deaths, Johnson & Johnson reacted swiftly. CEO James Burke formed a seven-member strategy team charged with answering two questions: "How do we protect the people?" and "How do we save the product?" The first step was to immediately warn consumers through a national announcement not to consume any type of Tylenol product until the extent of the tampering could be determined. All Tylenol capsules in Chicago were withdrawn, and upon discovering two more compromised bottles, Johnson & Johnson ordered a nationwide withdrawal of all Tylenol products. Less than a week had passed.

At the same time, the company established a toll-free number for consumers and another one for news organizations that provided daily recorded updates about the crisis. Within two months, Tylenol was re-launched with three-way tamper-proof packaging (Figure 13.4). The carton was securely glued, the cap was wrapped with a plastic seal, and the bottle carried a foil seal. The company also began an extensive media campaign emphasizing trust. In addition, other companies, not only in the pharmaceutical industry but in other industries such as food production and packaging, began to implement the use of tamper proof or double sealed packaging after the Tylenol incident.

---

25 Nestlé. "Supporting Breastfeeding." n.d. https://www.nestle.com/csv/impact/healthier-lives/baby-milk
26 Nestlé. "The Nestlé Policy and Procedures for Implementation of the WHO International Code of Marketing and Breast Milk Substitutes." September 2017. https://www.nestle.com/asset-library/documents/creating%20shared%20value/nutrition/nestle_policy_who_code_en.pdf

Figure 13.4 Tamper-Proof Packaging. Johnson & Johnson introduced tamper-proof packaging in an effort to mitigate the impact of problems from the cyanide-laced pills scare of fall 1982. To date, the killer has not been caught. (credit: "14418" by Debora Cartagena/CDC, Public Domain)

Since the crisis, the company's response has been lauded in business case studies and has formed the basis of crisis communications strategies developed by researchers.[27] Ultimately, Johnson & Johnson spent more than $100 million on the recall, an amount that might cripple some companies. Yet its share price returned to its previous high within six weeks.[28] In fact, if you had invested $1,000 in Johnson & Johnson in September 1982, it would have been worth almost $50,000 by late 2017. Today, the company ranks 35th in the Fortune 500, with revenues of almost $76 million.[29]

These are three early examples of the impact on businesses of decisions made by management that had unintended consequences or circumstances brought about by others that the company did not foresee happening. Each of these instances weakened the sustainability of the corporation, at least temporarily. These examples, as well as others, helped contribute to the CSR movement. Companies are concerned about the effects of their products and practices on all stakeholders from a moral and ethical standpoint and want to be socially responsible in addition to maintaining sustainability of their business. Certainly, there have been many more examples of company responses to social and environmental impacts that have been either positively or negatively received by **stakeholders** or those who have an interest or concern in the business. Nonetheless, the cases examined demonstrate a range of the types of events and company responses that can affect both the company's reputation and the society in which they operate in, sometimes for decades.

Initial Sustainability Reports

Following the Brundtland Report, financial statement preparers began to ask how they might communicate not just the financial status of a company's operations but the social and environmental status as well. The

---

27 Department of Defense. "Case Study: The Johnson & Johnson Tylenol Crisis." n.d. https://www.ou.edu/deptcomm/dodjcc/groups/02C2/Johnson%20&%20Johnson.htm
28 Judith Rehak. "Tylenol Made a Hero of Johnson & Johnson: The Recall That Started Them All." *New York Times*. March 23, 2002. http://www.nytimes.com/2002/03/23/your-money/tylenol-made-a-hero-of-johnson-johnson-the-recall-that-started.html
29 Fortune. "Fortune 500 Full List." n.d. http://fortune.com/fortune500/list/

concept of a **triple bottom line**, also known as TBL or 3BL, was first proposed in 1997 by John Elkington to expand the traditional financial reporting framework so as to capture a firm's social and environmental performance. Elkington also used the phrase *People, Planet, Profit* to explain the three focuses of triple bottom line reporting. By the late 1990s, companies were becoming more aware of triple bottom line reporting and were preparing sustainability reports on their own social, environmental, and economic impact. Another innovation was **life-cycle** or **full-cost accounting**. This reporting method took a "cradle to grave" approach to costing that put a price on the disposal of products at the end of their lives and then considered ways to minimize these costs by making adjustments in the design phase. This method also incorporated potential social, environmental, and economic costs (*externalities* in the language of economics) to attempt to identify all of the costs involved in production. For example, one early adopter of life-cycle accounting, Chrysler Corporation, considered all costs associated with each design phase and then made adjustments to the design. When its engineers developed an oil filter for a new vehicle, they estimated the material costs and hidden manufacturing expenses and also looked at liabilities associated with disposal of the filter. They found that the option with the lowest direct costs had hidden disposal costs that meant it was not the cheapest alternative.[30]

Much of the early sustainability reporting movement was driven by stakeholder concerns and protests. For example, throughout the 1990s, Nike drew accusations from consumers that its employees and subcontractors' employees in developing countries were being subjected to inhumane working conditions. The "sweatshop" charge has since been made against many companies that use off-shore manufacturing, and some now pre-emptively respond by producing sustainability reports to assure stakeholders that they are maintaining a good track record in human rights.

One of the earliest adopters of social reporting was The Body Shop, which released its first social report in 1995 based on surveys of stakeholders. BP (formerly British Petroleum) took a different approach, with a series of case studies in social impact assessment and releasing its social report in 1997.

Early study into the *hows* of sustainability reporting led researchers[31] to suggest that some performance indicators could be quantified. Figure 13.5 shows the sustainable product indicators identified by Fiksel and colleagues with suggestions on how each element of economic output might also be measured from an environmental or societal stance.

---

30 J. Fiksel, J. McDaniel, and D. Spitzley. "Measuring Product Sustainability." *The Journal of Sustainable Product Design* July, no. 6 (1998): 7–18.
31 J. Fiksel, J. McDaniel, and D. Spitzley. "Measuring Product Sustainability." *The Journal of Sustainable Product Design* July, no. 6 (1998): 7–18.

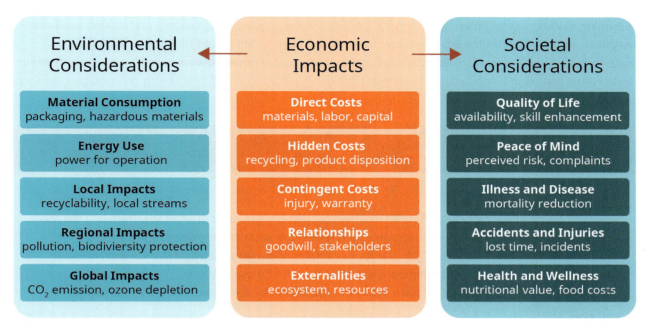

Source: Fiksel, J., J. McDaniel, and D. Spitzley. "Measuring Product Sustainability." The Journal of Sustainable Product Design. July 1998 (6): 7–18.

Figure 13.5 Sustainable Product Indicators. There are a number of approaches to dealing with economic costs from an environmental and/or social impact perspective. (attribution: Copyright Rice University, OpenStax, under CC BY-NC-SA 4.0 license)

Fiskel's research suggests that different elements can be categorized as *economic*, *environmental,* or *societal*. The study demonstrates how each element may have quantifiable costs or indicators that can be measured and reported so that users will be able to consider how those inputs and outputs contribute to the entire life cycle of a product. Although Fiskel's model is rarely reported today, the creation of quantifiable and measurable social and environmental standards is the basis of the Sustainability Accounting Standards Board, which uses an approach similar to Fiskel's model.

Current Examples of Sustainability in Business

The environment, human rights, employee relations, and philanthropy are all examples of topics on which corporations often report. When you think of sustainability in business, environmental sustainability might be the first area that comes to mind. **Environmental sustainability** is defined as rates of resource exploitation can be continued indefinitely without permanently depleting those resources. If these resources cannot be exploited indefinitely at the current rate, then the rate is not considered sustainable. A recent focus of environmental sustainability is **climate change** impacts. This focus has developed over the past three decades (although some contributors to climate change, such as pollution, have been a concern for much longer.). Climate change, in the context of sustainability, is a change in climate patterns caused by the increased levels of carbon dioxide (CO_2) in the atmosphere attributed mainly to use of fossil fuels. Companies are increasingly expected to measure and reduce their **carbon footprint**, the amount of CO_2 and other greenhouse gases they generate, in addition to adopting policies that are more environmentally friendly. For example, according to the sustainability report for Coca-Cola, in 2016 the company reduced the amount of CO_2 embedded in the containers that hold their beverages by 14%.[32] Such corporate policies to reduce their carbon footprint can include reducing waste, especially of resources like water; switching to paperless record-keeping systems;

designing environmentally friendly packaging; installing low-energy lighting, heating, and cooling in offices; recycling; and offering flexible working hours to minimize the time employees sit in traffic adding auto emissions to the environment. Industries that use or produce **non-renewable resources** as sources of energy, such as coal and oil, are significantly challenged to stay relevant in an era of new energy technologies like solar and wind power.

> ## YOUR TURN
>
> ### Mars Inc.
>
> Read this article (https://openstax.org/l/11caa) by Stephen Badger, chair of Mars Inc. Then visit the Mars Inc. website (https://openstax.org/l/50global) and review the sustainability discussion under "Sustainable in a Generation Plan." Discuss four examples of sustainability that Mars is implementing. What type of cost outlays might a company expend for each of these examples? Can you explain what type of savings the company might have, now or in the future, by these investments and outlays?
>
> **Solution**
>
> Mars is implementing a number of endeavors. In their "Healthy Planet" category, they identify climate action, water stewardship, land use, and waste reduction. In "Thriving People," they identify endeavors toward increasing income, respecting human rights, and increasing opportunities for women. In their "Nourishing Wellbeing" category, they identify product improvement, responsible marketing, and food safety and security. The company might make significant expenses or investments into each of the sustainability measures in the short term. Responses should provide examples of the type of programs that the company implements. For example, under Climate Plans, Mars discusses GHG emissions reductions targets of 67% by 2050 from 2015 levels. In reducing emissions, the company also explains that by improving raw material production practices, they can increase their efficiencies which should eventually lower costs. The company may make substantial savings by investments into energy reduction or water management.

The concept of sustainability in business also applies to a company's human rights and employee relations records. From an employee relations perspective, businesses that are willing to demonstrate that they are good corporate citizens endeavor to maintain sound working conditions to ensure their workplaces are safe, ergonomically appropriate, and healthy even if this means going above and beyond the rules and regulations set by local authorities. For example, good corporate citizens choose not to use child labor even in countries where it is accepted and choose to provide a working environment that exceeds local minimum standards for safety and cleanliness. Also, issues such as pay and job promotion fairness across genders, race and religion, otherwise known as **equity issues**, are also examined to ensure there are no inequities. For example, gender equity would exist when women are paid the same as men if they are performing the same duties. By other equity measures, a person would not be denied employment or equal pay simply because of their race or religion.

Firms may also implement parental leave policies and flexible or remote work hours to improve the morale and productivity of employees with families. A number of organizations also offer health and wellness groups

---

32   The Coca-Cola Company. "Infographic: 2016 Sustainability Highlights." n.d. https://www.coca-colacompany.com/stories/2016-sustainability-highlights-infographic

and healthy vending and cafeteria options for employees.

Companies may also promote sustainability through philanthropic endeavors, or charitable giving. While charitable giving is responsible, it is only sustainable if the money given improves or alleviates the underlying issue for which the money is being given. Otherwise, the money is not being spent productively, and that goes against sustainable business practices. To enhance the amount given to charities, many companies offer matching programs wherein they will match charitable contributions made by employees. Some companies also offer from two to five paid work days per year for employees to perform volunteer work. Many companies also go further and contribute a portion of company earnings to charitable causes. Investors may not always approve of the manner in which charitable funds are spent as they may prefer either that (1) the money be given to different charitable causes than the ones chosen by the company or (2) may feel the money could be more effective if applied to expansion and growth of the company. However, as most shareholders realize, corporations take a significant role in funding charitable organizations, and many of these not-for-profit organizations could not perform the services they provide without corporate funding. Table 13.1 provides an example of philanthropic contributions by several public corporations. Table 13.2 shows a few of the best places to work if you are looking for an employer that gives back to the community.

Examples of Corporate Charitable Giving

Corporation	Amount Donated	Primary Causes Supported
Gilead Sciences	$446.7 million	HIV/AIDS, liver diseases
Walmart	$301 million	Worker economic mobility, Feed America – anti-hunger campaign
Wells Fargo	$281.3 million	Part to local charities and part to national charities such as Neighborworks
Goldman Sachs	$276.4 million	Their own projects called 10,000 Women and 10,000 Small Businesses
Exxon Mobil	$268 million	Education, malaria prevention, and economic opportunity for women

Table 13.1 These companies were the top five charitable giving corporations in 2015.[33]

Top Places to Work That Give Back

Company	Amount Given	Matches Employee Giving	Gives Paid Days to Do Charitable Work
Salesforce	$137 million	Yes	56 hours

Table 13.2 These companies are considered the top five to work for if an employee is interested in community involvement and charitable contributions.[34]

---

33 Caroline Preston. "The 20 Most Generous Companies of the Fortune 500." *Fortune*. June 22, 2016. http://fortune.com/2016/06/22/fortune-500-most-charitable-companies/

34 Fortune. "The 50 Best Workplaces for Giving Back." February 9, 2017. http://fortune.com/2017/02/09/best-workplaces-giving-back/

Top Places to Work That Give Back

Company	Amount Given	Matches Employee Giving	Gives Paid Days to Do Charitable Work
NuStar Energy	$8.5 million	Yes	50 hours
Veterans United Home Loan	$7.1 million	Yes	40 hours
Intuit	$42 million	Yes	32 hours
Autodesk	$20.4 million	Yes	48 hours

Table 13.2 These companies are considered the top five to work for if an employee is interested in community involvement and charitable contributions.

Coca-Cola Corporation has a program designed to empower female entrepreneurs through e-learning programs. The company launched the 5by20 initiative that aims to empower 5 million women entrepreneurs across the company's value chain of producers, distributors, recyclers, and retailers around the world by 2020. By the end of 2016, the program had enabled 1.75 million women through the program in 64 countries globally.

Many corporations offer corporate giving programs by which employees are encouraged to participate in volunteerism or match with in-kind donations. Companies such as Intel, Pacific Gas and Electric Company, GE, General Mills, Intuit, Autodesk, and Salesforce have corporate giving programs that match dollar for dollar the amounts contributed by their employees. For example, if an employee wishes to support their local school, it is a registered tax exempt 501(c) (3) charity, and the employee donates $200, then the employer will match their contribution. Additionally, companies may give their employees paid volunteer time. For example, Intuit gives each of its employees 32 paid hours to help out at local organizations.

These volunteer hours can be used for many things, such as going to work in the local food bank for a few hours, volunteering for a fundraiser they believe in, or even something as simple as allowing an employee to participate in their child's school. These programs tend to be most effective when employees have input into where they will donate, or how they will dedicate their time.

Business decisions that affect the environment, human rights, employee relations, and philanthropic activities represent actions that are, hopefully, responsible and, at the same time, contribute to business sustainability, which in turn adds value to the business.

Creating Business Value

In the past, firms increased business value by increasing revenue or reducing expenses. However, managers now are realizing that some consumers are willing to pay more to support a company whose philosophy aligns with their own values. If they believe a company is making a greater effort to reduce its carbon emissions than its competitors are or that it looks after its workers and their communities, consumers will pay more for the product or invest in the company because they believe the company is doing the right thing by the environment or society. Many investors demonstrate these same principles. Companies have many ways to inform investors and customers of their efforts to improve the three P's—planet, people and profit—as you learned about in the discussion about the triple bottom line in the Initial Sustainability Reports section. While not every company officially reports a triple bottom line, many companies report their efforts to improve their impact on the planet and on people through various avenues such as in a formal corporate social responsibility report, on their website, or even through their advertising. It is often difficult to translate the effects of these efforts on the profits of the corporation; nonetheless, a company can often quantify the effects of their actions to help the planet, employees, and communities in other ways. Next, let's examine efforts by a few such companies and the results they have achieved.

Patagonia

For more than 30 years, the outdoor-clothing maker Patagonia has donated 1% of its annual sales or 10% of its pre-tax profits, whichever is greater, to environmental organizations. In 2010, the company helped found the Sustainable Apparel Coalition, whose members measure and score their environmental impact and then report the results in the Higgs Index. The Higgs Index is a social and environmental performance index that clothing industry executives use to make more sustainable decisions when sourcing materials and to protect the well-being of factory workers, local communities, and the environment.[35]

In 2012, Patagonia became one of California's first B corporations. A B corporation is a benefit corporation, which, although profit motivated, aims to make a positive impact on society, workers, the community, and the environment.

LINK TO LEARNING

This website on B Corporations (https://openstax.org/l/50Bcorp) will help you learn more.

In 2013, Patagonia's founder, Yvon Chouinard, launched the $20 Million and Change fund, now called Tin Shed Ventures,[36] which aimed to help start-up companies bring about positive benefit to the environment.[37] In late 2017, Patagonia sued the U.S. government and President Donald Trump for the decision to undo federal protections of public lands in Utah's Bears Ears and Grand Staircase-Escalante national monuments. The company temporarily turned its homepage into a single graphic reading, "The President Stole Your Land."

Patagonia claims that it holds itself to a single cause: "Using business to help solve the environmental crisis." The company has encountered some criticism from animal rights groups over its use of live-plucked feathers and mulesing (a controversial surgical process to help prevent parasitic infection) of sheep, but it appears to have taken action quickly to source down and wool according to strict animal welfare and land use standards.[38]

Walmart's Greenhouse Gas Reduction Goals

In February 2010, Walmart announced its aim to eliminate 20 million metric tons of greenhouse gas (GHG) emissions from its global supply chain within five years. Environmentally, this would be equal to taking more

---

35 Sustainable Apparel Coalition. "The Higg Index." n.d. https://apparelcoalition.org/the-higg-index/
36 Tin Shed Adventures. "About." n.d. http://www.tinshedventures.com/about/
37 Yvon Chouinard. "Introducing Patagonia Works, A New Kind of Holding Company." Patagonia. May 6, 2013. http://www.patagoniaworks.com/#index
38 Patagonia "Our Wool Restart." July 26, 2018. https://www.patagonia.com/blog/2016/07/our-wool-restart/; Patagonia. "Patagonia Traceable Down." n.d. https://www.patagonia.com/traceable-down.html

than 3.8 million cars off the road for a year.[39] By 2015 the company announced that they had surpassed that goal and had achieved a 28-million-ton reduction.

In April 2017, the company went several steps further and launched Project Gigaton, inviting their suppliers to commit to reducing GHG emissions by a billion tons by 2030. This would be the equivalent of taking more than 211 million passenger vehicles off the roads for a year.[40] To do this, the company has initiated a number of endeavors to achieve reduced GHG emissions. These include sourcing 25% of their total energy for operations from **renewable energy** sources (energy that is not depleted when used) and aiming to increase this to 50% by 2025.

The company also aims to achieve zero waste to landfill in key markets by 2025; by 2015, 75% of their global waste was already diverted from landfills.[41]

Walmart has gone to great lengths to measure the environmental implications of its supply chains, which has also saved the company money. One very simple example is the company's focus on selling more concentrated detergents so that they can reduce the number of ships bringing the detergent from China to the United States.[42]

Gravity Payments

Productivity, or the amount of output or income generated by an average hour of work, has improved 22% from 2000 to 2014 in the US. Yet, during the same time, median wages rose only 1.8%, adjusted for inflation.[43] CEOs have reaped more of the benefits of productivity gains and now earn about 271 times more than typical workers (up from 59 times more in 1989).[44] CEO pay has been a controversial topic for many years. As leaders of their organizations, CEOs affect not only the culture of the company but the direction as well. For example, unethical CEOs can result in significant loss of shareholder wealth, which happened to Enron, Hewlett-Packard, and Merrill Lynch.[45] Ethical CEOs can help guide the company to greater wealth by being cognizant of the role they play within their corporation as well as in the world.

In April 2015, Dan Price, the co-founder and CEO of Seattle-based credit-card processing firm Gravity Payments, decided to take a different path from other CEOs. Price announced he was slashing his own million-dollar salary to $70,000 and raising the minimum salary for all his 120 employees, in stages, to $70,000 a year.[46] After a few minor bumps in the road, mostly resulting from the attendant publicity, in the year after his announcement, profits doubled, the firm's employee turnover reached a record low, and another 50 employees were added to deal with the increased business. Team members were able to afford to move closer

---

39 Walmart. "Walmart Announces Goal to Eliminate 20 Million Metric Tons of Greenhouse Gas Emissions from Global Supply Chain." February 25, 2010. https://corporate.walmart.com/_news_/news-archive/2010/02/25/walmart-announces-goal-to-eliminate-20-million-metric-tons-of-greenhouse-gas-emissions-from-global-supply-chain

40 Walmart. "Walmart Launches Project Gigaton to Reduce Emissions in Company's Supply Chain." April 19, 2017. https://news.walmart.com/2017/04/19/walmart-launches-project-gigaton-to-reduce-emissions-in-companys-supply-chain

41 Walmart. "Walmart Offers New Vision for the Company's Role in Society." November 4, 2016. https://news.walmart.com/2016/11/04/walmart-offers-new-vision-for-the-companys-role-in-society

42 M.P. Vandenbergh and J.M. Gilligan. *Beyond Politics: The Private Governance Response to Climate Change*. (Cambridge, 2017), 198; Walmart. "Walmart Completes Goal to Sell Only Concentrated Liquid Laundry Detergent." May 29, 2008. https://corporate.walmart.com/_news_/news-archive/2008/05/29/wal-mart-completes-goal-to-sell-only-concentrated-liquid-laundry-detergent

43 Josh Bivens and Lawrence Mishel. "Understanding the Historic Divergence between Productivity and a Typical Worker's Pay." *Economic Policy Institute*. September 2, 2015. http://www.epi.org/publication/understanding-the-historic-divergence-between-productivity-and-a-typical-workers-pay-why-it-matters-and-why-its-real/

44 Economic Policy Institute. "Top CEOs Took Home 271 Times More Than the Typical Worker in 2016." July 20, 2017. https://www.epi.org/press/top-ceos-took-home-271-times-more-than-the-typical-worker-in-2016/

45 Tomas Chamorro-Premuzic. "Are CEOs Overhyped and Overpaid?" *Harvard Business Review*. November 1, 2016. https://hbr.org/2016/11/are-ceos-overhyped-and-overpaid

46 Gravity Payments. "$70K Minimum Wage Initial Results." n.d. https://gravitypayments.com/thegravityof70k/

to their workplace, reducing commute time and the stress associated with it.[47]

Part of Price's motivation was a conversation with a friend who was worried about a $200 rent increase. He remembered reading a 2010 study by Princeton behavioral economist Daniel Kahneman noting that people were decidedly unhappier the less they earned below $75,000.[48] After the pay increase, Gravity saw employee happiness, in terms of overall work place satisfaction levels increase significantly, although this tapered off somewhat to average levels in the year after (Figure 13.6). Almost three years on, the company is still going strong. Time will tell whether the "Price of Gravity" is a continued success.

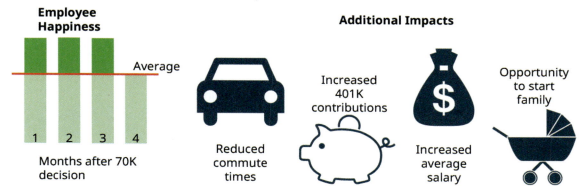

Source: "$70K Minimum Wage Initial Results." Gravity Payments. https://gravitypayments.com/thegravityof70k/#infographic-1

Figure 13.6 Employee Happiness. Gravity Payments noticed an immediate spike in employee happiness after employees' salaries were raised to at least $70,000 in 2015. Happiness settled at "average" levels in the months afterward. (attribution: Copyright Rice University, OpenStax, under CC BY-NC-SA 4.0 license)

Grameen Bank

In 1974, Muhammad Yunus, then an Economics Professor in Bangladesh, began to lend small sums of money at minimal or no interest to a few dozen local women who were basket weavers. Eliminating the high interest charged by traditional lenders allowed the women to make enough profit to enlarge their businesses into income-generating activities and lift themselves out of poverty.

Yunus continued helping poor entrepreneurs, usually women, and ultimately formalized his simple micro-lending system by forming Grameen Bank in 1983. The bank now has 8.9 million borrowers, most often women, across 81,399 villages[49] and has distributed more than US$19.6 billion in loans since its inception; more than $17.9 billion has been repaid. The bank claims a rate of recovery of 99.25%.[50] Its profits are loaned to other borrowers or go to fund local development to enrich the lives of the community (Figure 13.7).

---

47 Gravity Payments. "$70K Minimum Wage Initial Results." n.d. https://gravitypayments.com/thegravityof70k/
48 Paul Keegan. "Here's What Really Happened at That Company That Set a $70,000 Minimum Wage." *Inc*. November 2015. https://www.inc.com/magazine/201511/paul-keegan/does-more-pay-mean-more-growth.html
49 Grameen Bank. "Introduction." January 2018. http://www.grameen.com/introduction/
50 Grameen Bank. "Monthly Report: 2017-11 Issue 455 in BDT." December 5, 2017. http://www.grameen.com/data-and-report/monthly-report-2017-11-issue-455-in-bdt/

Figure 13.7 Grameen Bank Model. (attribution: Copyright Rice University, OpenStax, under CC BY-NC-SA 4.0 license)

The average household income of Grameen's members is about 50% higher than that of a target group in a control village, and 25% higher than that of non-members. While 56% of non-Grameen members live below the poverty line, the bank's micro-financing efforts have meant that only 20% of members now live below that line.[51]

Although it has not avoided controversy, the bank has won many awards, including the World Habitat Award of 1997 and the 2006 Nobel Peace Prize (awarded jointly to the bank and to Yunus) for efforts to create economic and social development through microcredit so that small entrepreneurs could break from the cycle of poverty.

LINK TO LEARNING

You can learn more about the corporate social reporting of these companies online:

- Patagonia corporate social reporting (https://openstax.org/l/50PatagoniaCSR)
- Walmart corporate social reporting (https://openstax.org/l/50WalmartCSR)
- Gravity Payments corporate social reporting (https://openstax.org/l/50GravityPayCSR)
- Grameen Bank corporate social reporting (https://openstax.org/l/50GrameenCSR)

---

51   Arjun Bhaskar. "Microfinance in South India: A Case Study." *Wharton Research Scholars, Scholarly Commons, Penn Libraries*. April 2015 https://repository.upenn.edu/wharton_research_scholars/122/

> ### THINK IT THROUGH
>
> **Do Friedman's Ideas Stand the Test of Time?**
>
> In a 1970 New York Times Magazine (https://openstax.org/l/50business) article, economist Milton Friedman argued that for a manager acting as an agent of the business owner (principal), "there is one and only one social responsibility of business—to use its resources and engage in activities designed to increase its profits so long as it stays within the rules of the game, which is to say, engages in open and free competition without deception or fraud."
>
> Given what we have learned about Earth's environment since this article was published, do you think Friedman's statement that the "sole purpose of business is to make profits" is valid? Explain your answer.

13.2 Identify User Needs for Information

The concept of the triple bottom line expanded the role of reporting beyond shareholders and investors to a broader range of stakeholders – that is, anyone directly or indirectly affected by the organization, including employees, customers, government entities, regulators, creditors, and the local community. Naturally, companies may feel their first obligation is to their present and potential investors. But it also makes good business sense to consider other stakeholders who can affect the company's livelihood. Let's examine the various users of sustainability reports and their particular information needs. Primary users would be considered shareholders and investors, whereas secondary users would be customers, suppliers, the community and regulators.

Shareholders

Many consider the company's shareholders to be its primary information user group. These equity investors may be small single investors or they may be part of an institutional investment fund charged with investing on behalf of its members. As shareholders they concern themselves with the future viability of the company and want profits to be sustained or increased over the long term. Shareholders often use financial ratios, such as earnings per share (EPS), return on investment (ROI), and the price/earnings ratio to evaluate the financial health and the sustainability of financial growth of the company. Shareholders not only evaluate whether there is current value in owning stock of the company but also whether there will continue to be value in owning that company's stock. Otherwise the shareholder is likely to divest of their ownership interest.

One ratio that shareholders often use to measure the value of the company's stock relative to the company's earnings is the price-earnings ratio, or **P/E ratio**. In the P/E ratio, the market price of the stock is divided by the earnings per share of the company's stock. This ratio indicates the amount an investor is willing to pay for one dollar of the company's earnings. For example, if a stock is trading at a P/E of 30, then this indicates investors are willing to pay $30 for $1 of current earnings. A high P/E ratio indicates investors expect high future earnings. A low P/E ratio has several interpretations but could indicate a company is undervalued. Many investors use the P/E ratio as a measure of whether or not a stock should be purchased, but no single metric should be used alone. In addition, the P/E ratio is only useful when comparing changes across time for a single company to see trends or lack of trends. The P/E ratio is most useful if compared across companies within a given industry sector. Most often, growth will vary widely between different sectors but will be more similar within a particular sector. Investors buy and sell stock for many reasons, both financial and non-financial. They can sell a stock due to lack of current growth in value or an expected drop in future earnings. They can also buy a stock because the company participates in activities that the shareholder values, such as fair wages and greenhouse emission reductions even if the company has a low P/E ratio. Let's look at an example of an investment driven by more than just the company's current financial situation.

In 2008, Warren Buffett's MidAmerican Energy Company, a subsidiary of Berkshire Hathaway, bought a $230m stake in BYD, a Chinese battery maker about to begin auto production.[52] Although the auto industry initially ridiculed Buffet's investment in such a little- known company, he may well have the last laugh. Since 2008, the company has evolved into the world's leading producer of electric cars, and its shares now trade at almost 10 times what MidAmerican paid for them. This increase in value reflects the market's optimism about the future of the company based on the Chinese government's commitment to speeding up the phasing out of fossil fuels.

The new ethical investing movement focuses on eliminating investments that conflict with shareholders' values, such as dependence on environmentally damaging fossil fuels. The movement is growing each year. In 2016, ethical investments topped $8.7 trillion, up 33% from 2014, and they now account for 20% of all investment under professional management.[53] Ethical investors are increasingly avoiding polluters, weapon manufacturers, and tobacco companies as well as companies with a poor track record on human rights or philosophies that do not align with a fund's religious tenets. Pension funds, such as the New York City Pension Fund[54] have announced a move away from investing in companies in the fossil fuel industry, a move that will put substantial pressure on these companies to seek out alternatives to the non-renewables business model. On the opposite side of the country, the California Public Employees' Retirement System announced that it had divested from most of its holdings in thermal coal stock.[55]

Investors are also increasingly looking to the future to evaluate whether a firm's stock price is sustainable. Consider that, as the cost of renewable energy alternatives become cheaper, non-renewable resources become less able to compete. That is, the price of the non-renewable commodity falls to a point where the costs of extraction become greater than the price that can be obtained for the asset, and so the non-renewable resource remains in the ground.[56] At this point, the value of the asset, the mine, is impaired, which leads to a reduced share price.

For example, in mid-2017, Coal India, the largest coal-mining company in the world, announced that it would close 96[57] of its 394 mines[58] by March 2018 because they would be no longer economically viable after the

---

52   Keith Bradsher. "Buffet Buys Stake in Chinese Battery Manufacturer." *New York Times*. September 29, 2008. https://www.nytimes.com/2008/09/30/business/worldbusiness/30battery.html
53   Matt Whittaker. "Ethical Investing Continues to Grow." *U.S. News and World Report*. January 27, 2017. https://money.usnews.com/investing/articles/2017-01-27/ethical-investing-continues-to-grow
54   William Neuman. "To Fight Climate Change, New York City Takes on Oil Companies." *New York Times*. January 10, 2018. https://www.nytimes.com/2018/01/10/nyregion/new-york-city-fossil-fuel-divestment.html?
55   Randy Diamond. "CalPERS Reveals It Divested from Most Thermal Coal Companies." *Pensions & Investments*. August 7, 2017. http://www.pionline.com/article/20170807/ONLINE/170809876/calpers-reveals-it-divested-from-most-thermal-coal-companies
56   M.K. Linnenluecke, J. Birt, J. Lyon, and B.K. Sidhu. "Planetary Boundaries: Implications for Asset Impairment." *Accounting & Finance* 55, no. 4 (2015).
57   IANS. "Coal India Could Close 53 Underground Mines This Fiscal." *The Economic Times*. September 12, 2018. https://economictimes.indiatimes.com/industry/indl-goods/svs/metals-mining/coal-india-could-close-53-underground-mines-this-fiscal/articleshow/65783526.cms

Indian Government announced it would cut its commitments to purchase coal after 2022.[59]

Investors, including ethical investors, must look to the future of their investments, buying shares that are sustainable for the long term to provide better returns. A recent Harvard Business Review study showed that socially responsible companies post higher profits and stock performance than those that were not focused on social responsibility.[60] This result is supported by a Deutsche Bank analysis of more than 2,000 studies dating back to the 1970's, 90% of which suggested that socially responsible investing gives better returns than passive investing.[61]

ETHICAL CONSIDERATIONS

Millennials Are Demanding Sustainable Investments

According to the Forum for Sustainable and Responsible Investment, a U.S.-based membership organization, "sustainable, responsible and impact investing is an investment discipline that considers environmental, social and corporate governance criteria to generate long-term competitive financial returns and positive societal impact."[62] Demand for this type of sustainable investments is being driven in a large part by millennials who prefer that their investments align with their personal beliefs and values. Ethical companies are seeing value in the millennial investors because "millennials are poised to receive more than $30 trillion of inheritable wealth."[63] Forward-looking companies need to develop an awareness of millennial values.

Forward-looking companies and investment advisor companies also need to adapt to a sustainable investment environment. This changes the perspective of accounting because managers will need to look to other factors besides profits to guide management's business decisions. Management and accountants will need to look beyond just numbers, and this will require a change in culture, technology, and operational and financial reporting to investors, potential investors and stakeholders.

Lenders

Sustainability reports provide useful information for lenders. Lenders want to know that the company borrowing from them does not have any going-concern risks that could affect its ability to repay the loan (Figure 13.8). They want to know the company will not be sued for human rights violations at home or abroad,

---

58   Coal India. *Annual Report and Accounts 2016–2017*. n.d. https://www.coalindia.in/DesktopModules/DocumentList/documents/Annual_Report_&_Accounts_2016_17_Deluxe_English_07112017.pdf
59   Harriet Agerholm. "World's Biggest Coal Company Closes 37 Mines as Solar Power's Influence Grows." *Independent*. June 21, 2017. http://www.independent.co.uk/news/world/asia/coal-india-closes-37-mines-solar-power-sustainable-energy-market-influence-pollution-a7800631.html
60   MoneyShow. "Socially-Responsible Investing: Earn Better Returns from Good Companies." *Forbes*. August 16, 2017. https://www.forbes.com/sites/moneyshow/2017/08/16/socially-responsible-investing-earn-better-returns-from-good-companies/#7f73a8a1623d
61   MoneyShow. "Socially-Responsible Investing: Earn Better Returns from Good Companies." *Forbes*. August 16, 2017. https://www.forbes.com/sites/moneyshow/2017/08/16/socially-responsible-investing-earn-better-returns-from-good-companies/#7f73a8a1623d
62   US SIF. "SRI Basics." n.d. https://www.ussif.org/sribasics
63   Ernst & Young. *Sustainable Investing: The Millennial Investor*. 2017. https://www.ey.com/Publication/vwLUAssets/ey-sustainable-investing-the-millennial-investor-gl/$FILE/ey-sustainable-investing-the-millennial-investor.pdf

be unable to repay its loans because consumer boycotts have hurt its cash flow, or that they maintain valuable property assets in high-risk areas. For example, after the 2017 Houston floods, a number of Houston-based banks were examined to find that they had a high level of exposure in commercial real estate in Houston.[64] This type of investment concentration in a single geographic area can be risky for lenders as a single disaster can have a more damaging effect than on a portfolio spread over a broader geographical area.

Figure 13.8 Sustainable Investment. Lenders appreciate sustainable investment because it gives them assurance that their loans will be repaid. (credit: modification of "Money Coin Investment" by "nattanan23"/Pixabay, CC0)

Employees

Employees and potential employees want to know that the company they work for is concerned about their safety and is an ethical organization. They want assurance that they will be fairly compensated and that all employees have equal rights and opportunities, regardless of gender, race, religion, or sexual orientation.

Recent studies show that employees increasingly want to work for companies that align with their own values and will be more loyal to those organizations. In 2016, 76% of millennials said that a company's social and environmental commitments were considerations in employment, with 64% of millennials indicating that they would not work for a company that did not have strong corporate social responsibility practices.[65]

Employees also report higher levels of satisfaction when their employers engage in corporate giving programs that are aligned with employee values or are chosen by employees.[66] For example, Intel will donate $10 to an educational institution, environmental program, or other community organization for every hour an employee volunteers there. More than 40% of Intel's U.S. employees have donated time that totals hundreds of

---

64 Ely Razin. "As Harvey Leaves Houston Reeling, These Banks Are More Exposed Than Others." *Forbes*. August 31, 2017. https://www.forbes.com/sites/elyrazin/2017/08/31/as-harvey-leaves-houston-reeling-these-banks-are-more-exposed-than-others/#423dcb5e6355
65 Cone Communications (Whitney Dailey). "Three-Quarters of Millennials Would Take a Pay Cut to Work for a Socially Responsible Company, According to the Research from Cone Communications." November 2, 2016. http://www.conecomm.com/news-blog/2016-cone-communications-millennial-employee-engagement-study-press-release
66 America's Charities. "Facts and Statistics on Workplace Giving, Matching Gifts, and Volunteer Programs." n.d. https://www.charities.org/facts-statistics-workplace-giving-matching-gifts-and-volunteer-programs

thousands of volunteer hours.[67] Other firms have corporate giving programs that match employee's charitable donations dollar for dollar.

Customers

Customers often have many choices about where to spend their hard-earned dollars. They want to know the companies to which they give that money reflect their own values and beliefs. If a company is seen to be uncaring about an issue, then customers may arrange campaigns to boycott the company (see the Nestlé story for an example of such consumer activism).

A 2016 study by Unilever showed that 33% of consumers buy from brands they believe are doing social or environmental good and that this presents a €966 billion (over 1.1 trillion $USD) opportunity for brands. As such, it is important for a company to demonstrate their commitment to CSR, and sustainability reporting offers a medium to do this.[68]

Governments and Regulators

Governments and regulators want to be able to see that a company is behaving responsibly. If they are confident that it is, there is less need to design laws and regulations that might restrict the company even more than if it undertook best-practice measures on its own. Many companies form industry alliance groups that aim to implement best practices in trade, social responsibility, or environmental initiatives.

Community

The community at large also wants to know that the organization is behaving at the level of society's expectations. This reflects the existence of a **social contract**, the expectation that companies will hold to an unwritten contract with society as a whole. If a firm is undertaking actions that might harm society or that reject its general values, community backlash may cost the firm dearly.

In summary, a company's accountability to a wider group of users is an element of stakeholder theory. This theory presents a view that asserts a corporation has an obligation to groups beyond just its shareholders.

YOUR TURN

Identifying Stakeholders

Locate the sustainability report of a Fortune 500 company and read the management discussion in it. Explain who you think the company considers its primary and secondary users. What information about itself and its operations does the company attempt to convey to each audience? Do you think its choices meet the information needs of these two groups of stakeholders? Why or why not?

Solution

---

67 Intel. "Giving Back: How Our Employees Make a Difference." n.d. https://www.intel.com/content/www/us/en/jobs/life-at-intel/usa/giving-back.html

68 Unilever. "Report Shows a Third of Consumers Prefer Sustainable Brands." May 5, 2017. https://www.unilever.com/news/Press-releases/2017/report-shows-a-third-of-consumers-prefer-sustainable-brands.html

Invariably, the primary users will be shareholders and creditors. Secondary users would be customers, employees, environmental groups, the community and regulators. The strength or relevance of each user will be dependent on the type of business discussed in the response.

ETHICAL CONSIDERATIONS

Public Benefit Corporations

Traditionally, standard American corporations consider their ultimate purpose as maximizing the profits of the shareholders. In the United States, directors of for-profit corporations recognize that one of their major goals is to maximize shareholder value. While corporations generally have the ability to engage in any legal activities, including those that are socially responsible, corporate decision-making must be justified in terms of creating shareholder value. Mission driven and other socially conscious businesses, impact investors, and social entrepreneurs are constrained by this inflexible legal framework that does not accommodate for-profit entities whose mission and impact is central to their business model.

In response, the benefit corporation model has emerged, which "broadens the perspective of traditional corporate law by incorporating concepts of purpose, accountability and transparency with respect to all corporate stakeholders, not just stockholders."[69] Public benefit corporations expand the obligations of boards, requiring them to consider environmental and social factors, as well as the financial interests of shareholders. This gives directors and managers the legal protection to pursue a mission other than maximizing profit and consider the impact their business has on society and the environment.

13.3 Discuss Examples of Major Sustainability Initiatives

In 2017, a KPMG report noted that 93% of the world's 250 largest companies by revenue produced corporate responsibility reports. When looking at the top 100 companies in each of 49 countries, the report found an underlying trend of 75% of companies that reported corporate responsibility and this was up from 18% only 15 years ago.[70] Given these figures, sustainability reporting is clearly responding to a need by investors, lenders and other stakeholders to provide information beyond what financial reports can produce.

However, for these reports to be comparable and useful, there needs to be a standard that users can rely on. Just as financial statements are produced using GAAP or IFRS, there is a need for some type of uniformity within corporate social responsibility reporting. The non-mandatory nature of CSR reporting has made the emergence of a single set of standards a challenge.

Three of the most well-known reporting frameworks are the Global Reporting Initiative (GRI), the Sustainability Accounting Standards Board (SASB), and Integrated Framework. Each framework relies on **materiality** (how significant an event or issue is to warrant its inclusion or discussion) as its basis of reporting, but each describes it slightly differently.

---

69   Morris, Nicols, Arsht & Tunnel. "Understanding Delaware's Benefit Corporation Governance Mode." *The Public Benefit Corporation Guidebook*. May 2016. http://news.mnat.com/rv/ff00272e4c8b3699806e25d24c48a286df5bf926
70   KPMG. *The Road Ahead: The KPMG Survey of Corporate Responsibility Reporting 2017*. 2017. https://assets.kpmg.com/content/dam/kpmg/xx/pdf/2017/10/kpmg-survey-of-corporate-responsibility-reporting-2017.pdf

Global Reporting Initiative (GRI)

In 1997, a not-for-profit organization called the Global Reporting Initiative (GRI) was formed with the goal of increasing the number of companies that create sustainability reports as well as to provide those companies with guidance about how to report and establish some consistency in reporting (such as identifying common themes and components for reports). The idea is that as companies begin to create these reports, they become more aware of their impact on the sustainability of our world and are more likely to make positive changes to improve that impact. According to GRI, 92% of the Global 250 produced sustainability reports in 2016.

Although businesses have been preparing reports using GRI standards for some time, in 2016, the GRI produced its first set of global reporting standards,[71] which have been designed as modular, interrelated standards. Every organization that produces a GRI sustainability report uses three universal standards: foundation, general disclosures, and management approach (Figure 13.9). The foundation standard (GRI 101) is the starting point and introduces the 10 reporting principles and explains how to prepare a report in accordance with the standards. General Disclosures (GRI 102) is for reporting contextual information about the organization and its reporting practices. Management Approach (GRI 103) is used to report how a firm manages each of its material topics. Applying the materiality principle, the organization identifies its material topics, explains why each is material, and then shows where the impacts occur. Then, it selects topic-specific standards most significant to its own stakeholders.

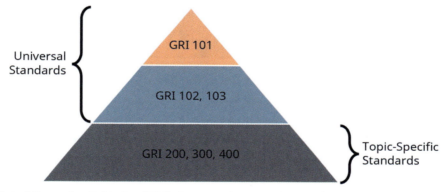

Figure 13.9 Global Reporting Initiative (GRI). Every entity reporting under GRI must use three universal standards, covering foundations, general disclosures, and the firm's management approach. Then topic-specific standards are chosen. (attribution: Copyright Rice University, OpenStax, under CC BY-NC-SA 4.0 license)

Though the GRI has provided a framework, a firm's decision about what to report rests on its definition of materiality. GRI defines materiality in the context of a sustainability report as follows: "The report should cover Aspects that: Reflect the organization's significant economic, environmental and social impacts; or substantively influence the assessments and decisions of stakeholders."[72] In its 2016 report, Coca-Cola listed these areas as its primary sustainability goals:

- Agriculture
- Human and Workplace Rights
- Climate Protection

---

71 Global Reporting Initiative (GRI). "GRI Standards." n.d. https://www.globalreporting.org/standards
72 Global Reporting Initiative (GRI). "G4 Sustainability Reporting Guidelines. *Reporting Principles and Standard Disclosures*. 2013.

- Giving Back
- Water Stewardship
- Packaging and Recycling
- Women's Economic Development[73]

Dow Chemical issues a different type of report and lists these categories:

- Who We Are—Strategy and Profile
- Why We Do It—Global Challenges
- What We Do—Our Products and Solutions
- How We Do It—Our People and Operations
- Awards and Recognitions[74]

Sustainability reporting is not confined to manufacturing or merchandising. Service organizations report as well. For example, Bank of America states in its 2016 sustainability report: "At Bank of America, we are guided by a common purpose to help make financial lives better through the power of every connection. We deliver on this through a focus on responsible growth and environmental, social and governance leadership. Through these efforts, we are driving growth—investing in the success of our employees, helping to create jobs, develop communities, foster economic mobility and address society's biggest challenges—while managing risk and providing a return to our clients and our business."[75] For more information about the GRI (https://openstax.org/l/50GRI2) can be found on the web.

CONCEPTS IN PRACTICE

Sustainability in Mobile Telecommunications

With more than 460,000 employees, China Mobile Limited is the largest mobile telecommunications company in the world. The company published their first GRI report in 2006, and, since then, the company has been able to review and disclose key sustainability performance indicators. Wen Xuelian, responsible for CSR reporting and management told GRI that sustainability reporting has helped the company to keep track of material sustainability issues and to improve overall performance each year. Xuelian notes that "at China Mobile we have built our CSR management systems by combining elements of the GRI framework with the operational infrastructure that we already had in place."[76]

Another challenge, Xuelian explains, was quantifying costs and benefits of the company's sustainability efforts. "Over the years of reporting, we have gradually built up relevant systems and incorporated social and environmental impact assessments into the early stage of business development and introduced external assessment methods for better evaluation."[77]

The company addressed material issues such as network connectivity, information security, using information to benefit society, energy conservation, GHG emissions, reduction of poverty, employee development and anti-corruption efforts and sustainability reporting helped them to be more

---

73 Coca-Cola Company. "2016 Sustainability Report: Women's Economic Empowerment." August 17, 2017. https://www.coca-colacompany.com/stories/2016-womens-economic-empowerment

74 Dow Chemical Company. *Redefining the Role of Business in Society: 2016 Sustainability Report*. 2017. http://storage.dow.com.edgesuite.net/dow.com/sustainability/highlights/Dow_2016_Sustainability_Report.pdf

75 Bank of America. "Responsible Growth." n.d. https://about.bankofamerica.com/en-us/what-guides-us/driving-responsible-growth.html

transparent in their operations. In the 10 years since implementation, they have reduced their electricity consumption per unit of business volume by 94%, built over 13,000 new energy base stations, reduced timber usage in packaging by over 600,000 cubic meters and introduced smart digital solutions for community emissions reductions.[78]

LINK TO LEARNING

Visit the GRI website (https://openstax.org/l/50GRI) and select one of the companies in the featured reports. Locate the company's sustainability report on their website and then locate their oldest sustainability report publication available. How has the company improved their corporate social responsibility performance since they implemented GRI reporting?

Sustainability Accounting Standards Board (SASB)

GRI standards were targeted at a variety of stakeholders, from the community at large to investors and lenders. This meant that the scope of disclosure encouraged by the GRI standards was perhaps too broad for companies that were primarily focused on reporting to investors in routine terms. Investors have their own unique needs related to sustainability information. Their concerns are related to the price and value of the organization, whereas other stakeholders are interested in how the company might affect them specifically. This effect may not even be financial; it could be whether the company pollutes in its local community, or it could be how a firm treats its workers.

For this reason, the Sustainability Accounting Standards Board (SASB) was established in 2011. SASB's mission is to help businesses around the world identify, manage and report on the sustainability topics that matter most to their investors. The SASB develops standards for disclosure of material sustainability information to investors, which can meet the disclosure requirements for known trends and uncertainties in the Management Discussion and Analysis section filed with the Securities Exchange Commission. SASB's version of materiality differs somewhat from the GRI's version.

Whereas the GRI viewed materiality as the inclusion of information that reflects an organization's significant economic, environmental, and social impacts or its substantial influence on the assessments and decisions of stakeholders, SASB adopted the US Supreme Court's view that information is material if there is "a substantial likelihood that the disclosure of the omitted fact would have been viewed by the reasonable investor as having significantly altered the 'total mix' of information made available".[79] It is up to the firms to determine

---

76 Xuelian, Wen. "China Mobile: Helping Build a Robust Sustainability Reporting Community in China." GRI. Nov. 7, 2017. https://www.globalreporting.org/information/news-and-press-center/Pages/China-Mobile-Helping-build-a-robust-sustainability-reporting-community-in-China.aspx
77 Xuelian, Wen. "China Mobile: Helping Build a Robust Sustainability Reporting Community in China." GRI. Nov. 7, 2017. https://www.globalreporting.org/information/news-and-press-center/Pages/China-Mobile-Helping-build-a-robust-sustainability-reporting-community-in-China.aspx
78 Xuelian, Wen. "China Mobile: Helping Build a Robust Sustainability Reporting Community in China." GRI. Nov. 7, 2017. https://www.globalreporting.org/information/news-and-press-center/Pages/China-Mobile-Helping-build-a-robust-sustainability-reporting-community-in-China.aspx

whether something is material and needs reporting, and this determination would begin with the initial questions "Is the topic important to the total mix of information?" and "Would it be of interest to the reasonable investor.[80]

The SASB standards, available for 79 industries across 10 sectors, help firms disclose material sustainability factors that are likely to affect financial performance. For example, a company that has operations in a developing nation may need to disclose its employment practices in that country to inform users of the risks to which the company is exposed because of its operations. SASB Standards and Framework (http://openstaxcollege.org/l/50SASBFramework) to see the current SASB conceptual framework.

Integrated Reporting

Even though companies were reporting through a range of mechanisms—sustainability reports, triple bottom line, and CSR reports—these methods of reporting were seen as fragmented and not integrating the financial and non-financial information into one report (Figure 13.10).[81] Also, the methods "failed to make the connection between the organization's strategy, its financial performance and its performance on environmental, social and governance issues."[82]

In response to these criticisms, the International Integrated Reporting Council (IIRC) was formed in 2010, touting Integrated Reporting as a solution to the shortfalls of financial reporting. Its intent is to act as a catalyst for behavioral change and long-term thinking,[83] bringing together financial, social, environmental and governance information in a clear, concise, consistent and comparable format.[84]

The goals of Integrated Reporting are to:

- improve the quality of information provided to investors and lenders
- communicate the full range of factors that materially affect the ability of an organization to create value over time by using a more cohesive and efficient approach to corporate reporting which draws on different reporting strands.
- enhance accountability and stewardship for the broad base of six capitals (financial, manufactured, intellectual, human, social and relationship, natural) and promote understanding of their interdependencies.
- support integrated thinking, decision-making and actions so as to create value[85].

As outlined, the Integrated Reporting framework identifies six broad categories of capital used by organizations which are: financial, manufactured, intellectual, human, social and relationship, and natural.

Whether information should be prepared and presented, that is, whether it is material in its inclusion is

---

79   *TSC Indus. v. Northway, Inc.* (426 U.S. 438, 449 (1976)).
80   The explanation of SASB's interpretation of "total mix" can be viewed on their website. Sustainability Accounting Standards Board (SASB). *SASB's Approach to Materiality for the Purpose of Standards Development* (Staff Bulletin No. SB002-07062017). July 6, 2017. http://library.sasb.org/wp-content/uploads/2017/01/ApproachMateriality-Staff-Bulletin-01192017.pdf?hsCtaTracking=9280788c-d775-4b34-8bc8-5447a06a6d38%7C2e22652a-5486-4854-b68f-73fea01a2414—Ed.
81   Wendy Stubbs, Colin Higgins, and Markus Milne. "Why Do Companies Not Produce Sustainability Reports?" November 12, 2012. *Business Strategy and the Environment* 22(7): 456–470.
82   Harold P. Roth. "Is Integrated Reporting in the Future?" April 22, 2014. *CPA Journal* 84(3): 62-67. https://insurancenewsnet.com/oarticle/Is-Integrated-Reporting-in-the-Future-a-493109#.XC6i GGm1vpw
83   Stathis Gould. "Integrated Reporting <IR> Longs for Finance Professionals." *International Federation of Accountants (IFAC)*. February 2, 2017. https://www.ifac.org/global-knowledge-gateway/business-reporting/discussion/integrated-reporting-longs-finance
84   International Federation of Accountants. "A4S and GRI Announce Formation of the IIRC." August 2, 2010. https://www.ifac.org/news-events/a4s-and-gri-announces-formation-iirc-0
85   International Integrated Reporting Council (IIRC). *The International Integrated Reporting Framework*. 2013. http://integratedreporting.org/wp-content/uploads/2013/12/13-12-08-THE-INTERNATIONAL-IR-FRAMEWORK-2-1.pdf

determined by:

- Identifying relevant matters based on their ability to affect value creation—that is how it increases, decreases or transforms the capitals caused by the organization's activities. This may be value created for the organization itself or for stakeholders, including society itself.
- Evaluating the importance of relevant matters in terms of their known or potential effect on value creation. This includes evaluating the magnitude of a occurrence's effect and its likelihood of occurrence.
- Prioritizing those matters based on their relative importance so as to focus on the most important matters when determining how they should be reported.
- Determining what information to disclose about material matters. This may require some judgment and discussion with stakeholders to ensure that the report meets its primary purpose.[86]

Integrated Reporting has been adopted by a number of companies throughout the world and is mandatory for listed companies in South Africa and Brazil. So far, it has been slow to take hold in the U.S., however, a number of companies have implemented Integrated Reporting, including Clorox, Entergy, General Electric, Jones Lang LaSalle, PepsiCo, Prudential Financial, and Southwest Airlines.

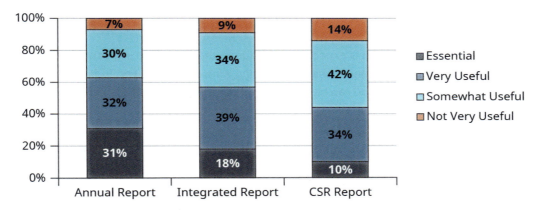

Source: Nelson, Matthew. "The Importance of Nonfinancial Information to Investors." Harvard Law School Forum on Corporate Governance and Financial Regulation. Apr. 25, 2017. https://corpgov.law.harvard.edu/2017/04/25/the-importance-of-nonfinancial-performance-to-investors/

Figure 13.10 Most Useful Non-Financial Information Sources for Investment Decisions. Although Integrated Reporting does not have mandatory status in many countries, an Ernst & Young survey of Global Investors found that integrated reports ranked second after annual reports in importance for decision-making. (attribution: Copyright Rice University, OpenStax, under CC BY-NC-SA 4.0 license)

You can find out more information about the IR framework by visiting the Integrated Reporting (https://openstax.org/l/50Reporting) website.

13.4 Future Issues in Sustainability

Sustainability reporting is still relatively new and its use is not yet mandatory. But from the standpoint of materiality, companies should disclose information if it has become important enough to influence the

---

86 International Integrated Reporting Council (IIRC). *The International Integrated Reporting Framework*. 2013. http://integratedreporting.org/wp-content/uploads/2013/12/13-12-08-THE-INTERNATIONAL-IR-FRAMEWORK-2-1.pdf

decisions of users of financial information.

The focus on sustainability has led to some notable innovation. For example, Tesla Corporation has become the United States' premier electric car manufacturer and is planning an electric semi-trailer to compete with diesel semi-trailers. The company has also made huge strides in the development of economically viable battery and solar technologies, and developing affordable attractive glass solar tiles that can provide all the electricity necessary for the typical home. The Tesla Gigafactory, located in Sparks, Nevada, expects to be able to produce more lithium ion batteries in one year than were produced in globally in 2013.

If industries reduce carbon emissions and improve social responsibility, what issues remain to guide the quest for sustainability in the future? One possibility is the need for security against cyberattacks, which not only harm the company's functioning but also dent consumer confidence. Another issue will be whether companies can continue to become or remain global in their operations, as political winds shift and the potential arises for backlash against the resulting economic changes in industrialized nations.

A third issue is the role of artificial intelligence (AI). As AI gains prominence and robots become more capable of undertaking complex tasks, white-collar workers of the 21st century may find themselves losing jobs like their 20th-century manufacturing counterparts did. This result will raise a number of ethical questions, such as whether corporations have a greater responsibility to society than to shareholders, and whether the use of robots should be taxed in order for governments to provide retraining to displaced workers and a universal basic income[87].

AI can herald positive change as well. It is expected, for instance, that 10 million self-driving cars will be on the road by 2020,[88] most of them electric and rechargeable using wind or solar power. In fact, you may not even need to own a vehicle at all! Instead, you can be taken to work in a driverless car that will drop you off and then collect other passengers.

These changes are examples of what some call the technological revolution.[89] To maintain relevance, today's worker must learn to be multi-skilled, more innovative, and have a good analytical mind that is able to think critically and creatively. These types of shifts can increase stress for employees and means that the business will be subject to high degrees of scrutiny by stakeholders. As a result, stakeholders will demand that companies be more accountable than simply providing financial reports.

THINK IT THROUGH

Robot Tax

In 2017, Microsoft founder, Bill Gates called for a "robot tax" to be introduced to offset the inequality expected to result from automation.[90] He called for the robot tax to finance a Universal Basic Income (UBI). A universal basic income is the concept by which citizens would receive a regular and unconditional amount of money from the government that is sufficient to meet basic needs. Another similar concept is that of a Universal Basic Dividend (UBD) by which a portion of the initial public offerings (IPOs) of a company would go into a public trust that generates an income stream to pay the UBD.[91]

---

87   Catherine Clifford. "Automation Could Kill 2× More Jobs Than the Great Depression—so San Francisco Lawmaker Pushes for Bill Gates' 'Robot Tax.'" *CNBC*. August 24, 2017. https://www.cnbc.com/2017/08/24/san-francisco-lawmaker-pushes-forward-bill-gates-robot-tax.html
88   Business Insider Intelligence. "10 Million Self-Driving Cars Will Be on the Road by 2020." *Business Insider*. June 15, 2016. http://www.businessinsider.com/report-10-million-self-driving-cars-will-be-on-the-road-by-2020-2015-5-6
89   Klaus Schwab. "Are You Ready for the Technological Revolution?" *World Economic Forum*. February 19, 2015. https://www.weforum.org/agenda/2015/02/are-you-ready-for-the-technological-revolution/

- What are the costs to society of increased automation?
- How might a robot tax be calculated and implemented?

The discussion of the environmental and social responsibility in this chapter only touched on some of the issues that affect our world. Sustainability reporting allows companies to not only report what they are doing to be good global citizens, it also makes them more aware of areas in which they need to improve. Awareness of the areas that need improvement allows companies to create a plan to continually improve their role in society. In addition, as more and more companies assess their own social responsibility and move to improve their sustainability, it draws attention to unreported sustainability issues as well as to companies that are not being socially aware. Social responsibility reporting has moved us a long way from merely reporting the financial results of businesses. It provides a foundation that links all businesses to all citizens, whether they are shareholders or not, and it helps bind us all in a way that says we are all truly part of a single, global environment that is determined by the actions of both businesses and citizens.

---

90   Yanis Varoufakis. "Robot Taxes and Universal Basic Income." *Acuity*. June 16, 2017. https://www.acuitymag.com/technology/robot-taxes-and-universal-basic-income

91   Yanis Varoufakis. "Robot Taxes and Universal Basic Income." *Acuity*. June 16, 2017. https://www.acuitymag.com/technology/robot-taxes-and-universal-basic-income

Key Terms

Brundtland Commission Report report issued after the 1987 World Commission on Environment and Development that laid the groundwork for the concept of sustainable development

business sustainability actions taken to sustain the business so that it survives and thrives well into the future

carbon footprint measure of the amount of CO_2 generated by an individual, group or organization

carbon output measure of carbon dioxide emissions into the atmosphere

climate change change in climate patterns due to the increased levels of carbon dioxide in the atmosphere which is attributed mainly to the usage of fossil fuels

corporate social responsibility (CSR) actions that firms take to assume responsibility for their impact on the environment and social well-being

environmental sustainability situation in which rates of resource use can be continued indefinitely without permanently depleting those resources

equity issues related to the fairness of pay and job promotions, regardless of gender, sexual orientation, race or religion

full-cost accounting accounting that recognizes all costs related to the provision of a product or service; this includes all economic, environmental and social costs

life-cycle accounting similar to full-cost accounting, this assesses all costs related to the production of a product from the extraction of raw materials used to the final disposal of the product at the end of its life

materiality how significant an event or issue is to warrant its inclusion or discussion

non-renewable resources resources that, once used, are depleted, and not able to be used again

P/E ratio company's stock price divided by the company's earnings per share and indicates the amount investors are willing to pay for one dollar of earnings

Paris Climate Agreement 2015 agreement between 196 nations to strive to limit the increase of global temperatures to 1.5 degrees Celsius

renewable energy energy that is not depleted once used, for example, tidal energy, wind energy or solar power

social contract expectation that companies will hold to an unwritten contract with society as a whole

stakeholder person or group with an interest or concern in some aspect of the organization

sustainability meeting the needs of the present generation without compromising the ability of future generations to meet their own needs by being aware of current economic, social, and environmental impacts

sustainability report report that presents the economic, environmental or social impacts that a corporation or organization was responsible for

sustainable development development that meets the needs of the present without compromising the ability of future generations to meet their own needs

triple bottom line (TBL) expansion of traditional reporting that is focused on economic performance, to include social and environmental performance

Summary

13.1 Describe Sustainability and the Way It Creates Business Value

- Users of financial reports want to know whether businesses are making appropriate decisions not only to increase shareholder wealth, but also to sustain the business, and the world around it, into the future.

This management goal is called business sustainability.
- Although the U.S. has pulled out of the Paris Climate Agreement, many companies have announced their own commitment to maintain the spirit of the Agreement.
- Early ventures into sustainability practices and reporting often arose in response to negative events and even tragedies as communities demanded more accountability by companies that operated within those communities.
- Many businesses have chosen to develop sustainable business practices because they realize doing so can provide positive benefits, not just to society and the environment, but also to the long-term viability of their own business.

13.2 Identify User Needs for Information
- Users of sustainability reporting information are not just primary users such as shareholders and lenders but can also be secondary users such as employees, customers, the community, governments, and regulators.
- Shareholders concern themselves with the future viability of the company and want profits to be sustained or increased over the long term.
- Lenders want to know the company borrowing from them does not have any going-concern risks that could affect its ability to repay the loan.
- Employees and potential employees want assurance that they will be fairly compensated, that the workplace is safe and the employer ethical, and that all employees have equal rights and opportunities, regardless of gender, race, religion, or sexual orientation.
- Customers want to know the companies to which they give their money reflect their own values and beliefs.
- Governments and regulators want to be able to see that a company is behaving responsibly.
- Communities want to know the organization is behaving at the level of society's expectations. This information need reflects the existence of a social contract, the expectation that companies will hold to an unwritten contract with society as a whole.

13.3 Discuss Examples of Major Sustainability Initiatives
- Materiality describes how significant an event or issue is to warrant its inclusion or discussion.
- The not-for-profit Global Reporting Initiative (GRI) provides companies with guidance about how to report sustainability and identifies common themes and components for reports and in 2016 produced its first set of global reporting standards. According to GRI, 92% of the Global 250 produced sustainability reports in 2016.
- The Sustainability Accounting Standards Board (SASB) was established in 2011 to develop standards for disclosure of material sustainability information to investors. SASB adopted the view of materiality taken by the US Supreme Court, that information is material if there is "a substantial likelihood that the disclosure of the omitted fact would have been viewed by the reasonable investor as having significantly altered the 'total mix' of information made available."[92] SASB standards are available for 79 industries across 10 sectors.
- The International Integrated Reporting Council (IIRC) was formed in 2010 to improve the quality of information provided to investors and lenders, promote a more cohesive and efficient approach to corporate reporting which draws on different reporting strands, enhance accountability and stewardship for six types of capital (financial, manufactured, intellectual, human, social and relationship, and natural), and support integrated thinking, decision-making and actions so as to create value.

---

92   Sustainability Accounting Standards Board (SASB). *Hardware: Sustainability Accounting Standard*. Aprril 2014. https://www.sasb.org/wp-content/uploads/2014/04/SASB_Standard_Hardware_Provisional.pdf

13.4 Future Issues in Sustainability

- Innovation, security risks, and globalization mean that businesses must adapt quickly or risk becoming obsolete.
- Artificial intelligence is predicted to significantly change our lives in the future. Some of those changes may threaten the stability of employment for white collar workers. Workers must learn to be multi-skilled, more innovative and possess a good analytical mind.

Multiple Choice

1. **LO** 13.1 Which agreement did 196 nations adopt in December 2015?
   A. Oslo Accord
   B. Paris Climate Agreement
   C. Kyoto Agreement
   D. Copenhagen Accord

2. **LO** 13.1 The 2015 Paris Agreement on Climate Change aimed to limit the increase of global temperatures to _____.
   A. 0.5 °C
   B. 1.0 °C
   C. 1.5 °C
   D. 2.0 °C

3. **LO** 13.1 Good corporate citizenship _____.
   A. is expensive to implement and does not guarantee returns
   B. must have management's sincere convictions behind it in order to succeed
   C. is more relevant in countries with less regulation.
   D. makes good business sense

4. **LO** 13.1 According to the World Commission on Environment and Development, how is sustainable development defined?
   A. It meets the needs of the future without compromising the ability of the present generations to meet their own needs.
   B. It applies the fairness doctrine that no generation, present or future, will be disadvantaged in their ability to meet their own needs.
   C. It meets the needs of the present without compromising the ability of future generations to meet their own needs.
   D. none of the above

5. **LO** 13.1 Sustainability reporting can incorporate which of the following?
   A. environmental reporting
   B. social reporting
   C. business viability reporting
   D. all of the above

6. LO 13.1 What caused Union Carbide's deadly gas leak in Bhopal, India, which killed 3,000 and injured 42,000?

   A. a combination of low staff levels, corruption, pay-offs to employees to keep quiet, and the manager going on vacation the day before the leak
   B. diversion of funds and resources to a Northern India project that also took staff from the Bhopal plant, plus many safety issues, including fines imposed on community members who camped too close to the plant
   C. employees' deciding to have lunch before dealing with the pressure buildup inside the tank and bribes paid to the government employees who inspected the plant
   D. a combination of low staff levels, numerous safety issues, and a lack of immediate employee attention to the problem as pressure built up inside the tank

7. LO 13.1 Nestlé's reputation was damaged when the company was accused of which of the following?
   A. forcing mothers to buy baby formula within days of delivering their babies
   B. promoting inadequate nutrition in developing countries
   C. providing cheap formula to mothers in developing countries, but more expensive to mothers in developed countries
   D. selling poor quality bottled water to developing countries

8. LO 13.1 Which form of energy is renewable?
   A. solar
   B. oil
   C. coal
   D. nuclear

9. LO 13.1 Which of the following types of reporting does the Triple Bottom Line *not* incorporate?
   A. management
   B. social
   C. environmental
   D. economic

10. LO 13.2 Which of the following best defines *stakeholders*?
   A. investors and lenders
   B. environmental groups
   C. anyone directly or indirectly affected by the organization
   D. groups or individuals financially impacted by the organization

11. LO 13.2 Which of the following statements is most often the case?
   A. Socially responsible businesses tend to post higher profits than those not focused on social responsibility.
   B. Companies that are not socially responsible will have better profits, but have a moral obligation to society.
   C. Socially responsible investing gives poorer returns than non-socially responsible investing.
   D. Investors are more short termed focus and so socially responsible investing should not be a factor in their investment portfolio.

12. LO 13.3 Which standards are considered universal under the GRI?
   A. economic, environmental, social
   B. foundation, general disclosures, management approach
   C. foundation, economic, general disclosures
   D. management approach, economic, social

13. LO 13.3 The SASB view on materiality has been adapted from which of the following?
   A. the U.S. Executive branch
   B. the GRI definition
   C. a determination by U.S. Congress
   D. the U.S. Supreme Court

14. LO 13.3 The fundamental tenets of SASB's Approach are considered _____.
   A. evidence-based, industry-specific, and market-informed
   B. industry-specific, interest-based, and value creating
   C. consensus-based, industry-specific, and actionable
   D. interest-based, value creating, and market-informed

15. LO 13.3 How many broad categories of capital are identified by the Integrated Reporting Framework?
   A. 2
   B. 4
   C. 6
   D. 8

Questions

1. LO 13.1 What is sustainability and how might corporations incorporate sustainability practices into their business?

2. LO 13.1 What is the value of triple bottom line reporting to users? What is the cost to the company to provide this extra information?

3. LO 13.1 What type of information do you think an oil company should include in their sustainability report? What about a car manufacturer? A large retailer?

4. LO 13.2 Identify four different stakeholders in need of sustainability information and show how their actions might affect a business.

5. LO 13.2 How might a business interact with each of the four different stakeholders you identified in the previous exercise?

6. LO 13.2 Contrast the investment risk potentials of an electric vehicle manufacturer whose shares have a PE ratio of 10:1 and a coal company whose stock has a PE ratio of 2.5 to 1.

7. LO 13.2 There are currently no formal mandatory environmental accounting standards firms must adhere to. Given the lack of regulation, should accountants even bother with preparing sustainability reports? Why or why not?

8. LO 13.3 Explain the role and purpose of the Global Reporting Initiative

9. LO 13.3 Explain the role and purpose of the Sustainability Accounting Standards Board.

10. **LO** 13.3 Explain the role and purpose of the Integrated Reporting Framework.

 Thought Provokers

TP1. **LO** 13.2 Obtain the 2016/2017 sustainability report for Ford Motor Company. Prepare a report that addresses the following issues:
- A. How do the vision and mission statement on the company's website relate to its definition of sustainability, if at all?
- B. Who are Ford's stakeholders? Do you think that the company has addressed the information needs of each stakeholder group?
- C. What type of governance processes are in place to ensure that the Board of Directors' values are aligned with sustainability?
- D. How does Ford tie sustainability to its risk-management system? What potential risks does Ford face that could harm the company, the environment, or the community?

A | Financial Statement Analysis

Financial Statement Analysis

Financial statement analysis reviews financial information found on financial statements to make informed decisions about the business. The income statement, statement of retained earnings, balance sheet, and statement of cash flows, among other financial information, can be analyzed. The information obtained from this analysis can benefit decision-making for internal and external stakeholders and can give a company valuable information on overall performance and specific areas for improvement. The analysis can help them with budgeting, deciding where to cut costs, how to increase revenues, and future capital investments opportunities.

When considering the outcomes from analysis, it is important for a company to understand that data produced needs to be compared to others within industry and close competitors. The company should also consider their past experience and how it corresponds to current and future performance expectations. Three common analysis tools are used for decision-making; horizontal analysis, vertical analysis, and financial ratios.

For our discussion of financial statement analysis, we will use Banyan Goods. Banyan Goods is a merchandising company that sells a variety of products. Figure A.1 shows the comparative income statements and balance sheets for the past two years.

BARRY'S SUPERSTORE Comparative Year-End Income Statements			BARRY'S SUPERSTORE Comparative Year-End Balance Sheets		
	Prior Year	Current Year		Prior Year	Current Year
Net Sales	$100,000	$120,000	Assets:		
Cost of Goods Sold	50,000	60,000	Cash	$90,000	$110,000
Gross Profit	50,000	60,000	Accounts Receivable	20,000	30,000
			Inventory	35,000	40,000
Rent Expense	5,000	5,500	Short-Term Investments	15,000	20,000
Depreciation Expense	2,500	3,600	Total Current Asstes	160,000	200,000
Salaries Expense	3,000	5,400	Equipment	40,000	50,000
Utility Expense	1,500	2,500	Total Assets	$200,000	$250,000
Operating Income	38,000	43,000	Liabilities:		
			Accounts Payable	$ 60,000	$ 75,000
Interest Expense	3,000	2,000	Unearned Revenue	10,000	25,000
Income Tax Expense	5,000	6,000	Total Current Liabilities	70,000	100,000
Net Income	$ 30,000	$ 35,000	Notes Payable	40,000	50,000
			Total Liabilities	110,000	150,000
			Stockholder Equity		
			Common Stock	75,000	80,000
			Ending Retained Earnings	15,000	20,000
			Total Stockholder Equity	90,000	100,000
			Total Liabilities and Stockholder Equity	$200,000	$250,000

Figure A.1 Comparative Income Statements and Balance Sheets.

Keep in mind that the comparative income statements and balance sheets for Banyan Goods are simplified for our calculations and do not fully represent all the accounts a company could maintain. Let's begin our analysis discussion by looking at horizontal analysis.

Horizontal Analysis

Horizontal analysis (also known as trend analysis) looks at trends over time on various financial statement line items. A company will look at one period (usually a year) and compare it to another period. For example, a company may compare sales from their current year to sales from the prior year. The trending of items on these financial statements can give a company valuable information on overall performance and specific areas for improvement. It is most valuable to do horizontal analysis for information over multiple periods to see how change is occurring for each line item. If multiple periods are not used, it can be difficult to identify a trend. The year being used for comparison purposes is called the base year (usually the prior period). The year of comparison for horizontal analysis is analyzed for dollar and percent changes against the base year.

The dollar change is found by taking the dollar amount in the base year and subtracting that from the year of analysis.

Dollar Change = Year of Analysis Amount − Base Year Amount

Using Banyan Goods as our example, if Banyan wanted to compare net sales in the current year (year of analysis) of $120,000 to the prior year (base year) of $100,000, the dollar change would be as follows:

$$\text{Dollar change} = \$120{,}000 - \$1000{,}000 = \$20{,}000 \tag{A1}$$

The percentage change is found by taking the dollar change, dividing by the base year amount, and then multiplying by 100.

$$\text{Percent Change} = \left(\frac{\text{Dollar Change}}{\text{Base Year Amount}}\right) \times 100$$

Let's compute the percentage change for Banyan Goods' net sales.

$$\text{Percentage change} = \left(\frac{\$20{,}000}{\$100{,}000}\right) \times 100 = 20\% \tag{A2}$$

This means Banyan Goods saw an increase of $20,000 in net sales in the current year as compared to the prior year, which was a 20% increase. The same dollar change and percentage change calculations would be used for the income statement line items as well as the balance sheet line items. Figure A.2 shows the complete horizontal analysis of the income statement and balance sheet for Banyan Goods.

BARRY'S SUPERSTORE Comparative Year-End Income Statements Horizontal Analysis				
	Prior Year	Current Year	Dollar Change	% Change
Net Sales	$100,000	$120,000	$20,000	20%
Cost of Goods Sold	50,000	60,000	$10,000	20%
Gross Profit	50,000	60,000	$10,000	20%
Rent Expense	5,000	5,500	$ 500	10%
Depreciation Expense	2,500	3,600	$ 1,100	44%
Salaries Expense	3,000	5,400	$ 2,400	80%
Utility Expense	1,500	2,500	$ 1,000	67% *
Operating Income	38,000	43,000	$ 5,000	13% *
Interest Expense	3,000	2,000	($ 1,000)	(33%)*
Income Tax Expense	5,000	6,000	$ 1,000	20%
Net Income	$ 30,000	$ 35,000	$ 5,000	17% *

*Rounded to nearest whole percent

BARRY'S SUPERSTORE Comparative Year-End Balance Sheets Horizontal Analysis				
	Prior Year	Current Year	Dollar Change	% Change
Assets:				
Cash	$90,000	$110,000	$20,000	22%*
Accounts Receivable	20,000	30,000	$10,000	50%
Inventory	35,000	40,000	$ 5,000	14%*
Short-Term Investments	15,000	20,000	$ 5,000	33%*
Total Current Asstes	160,000	200,000	$40,000	25%
Equipment	40,000	50,000	$10,000	25%
Total Assets	$200,000	$250,000	$50,000	25%
Liabilities:				
Accounts Payable	$ 60,000	$ 75,000	$15,000	25%
Unearned Revenue	10,000	25,000	$15,000	150%
Total Current Liabilities	70,000	100,000	$30,000	43%*
Notes Payable	40,000	50,000	$10,000	25%
Total Liabilities	110,000	150,000	$40,000	36%*
Stockholder Equity				
Common Stock	75,000	80,000	$ 5,000	7%*
Ending Retained Earnings	15,000	20,000	$ 5,000	33%*
Total Stockholder Equity	90,000	100,000	$10,000	11%*
Total Liabilities and Stockholder Equity	$200,000	$250,000	$50,000	25%

*Rounded to nearest whole percent

Figure A.2 Income Statements and Horizontal Analysis.

Depending on their expectations, Banyan Goods could make decisions to alter operations to produce expected outcomes. For example, Banyan saw a 50% accounts receivable increase from the prior year to the current year. If they were only expecting a 20% increase, they may need to explore this line item further to determine what caused this difference and how to correct it going forward. It could possibly be that they are extending credit more readily than anticipated or not collecting as rapidly on outstanding accounts receivable. The company will need to further examine this difference before deciding on a course of action. Another method of analysis Banyan might consider before making a decision is vertical analysis.

Vertical Analysis

Vertical analysis shows a comparison of a line item within a statement to another line item within that same statement. For example, a company may compare cash to total assets in the current year. This allows a company to see what percentage of cash (the comparison line item) makes up total assets (the other line item) during the period. This is different from horizontal analysis, which compares across years. Vertical analysis compares line items within a statement in the current year. This can help a business to know how much of one item is contributing to overall operations. For example, a company may want to know how much inventory contributes to total assets. They can then use this information to make business decisions such as preparing the budget, cutting costs, increasing revenues, or capital investments.

The company will need to determine which line item they are comparing all items to within that statement and then calculate the percentage makeup. These percentages are considered *common-size* because they make businesses within industry comparable by taking out fluctuations for size. It is typical for an income statement to use net sales (or sales) as the comparison line item. This means net sales will be set at 100% and all other line items within the income statement will represent a percentage of net sales.

On the balance sheet, a company will typically look at two areas: (1) total assets, and (2) total liabilities and stockholders' equity. Total assets will be set at 100% and all assets will represent a percentage of total assets. Total liabilities and stockholders' equity will also be set at 100% and all line items within liabilities and equity will be represented as a percentage of total liabilities and stockholders' equity. The line item set at 100% is considered the base amount and the comparison line item is considered the comparison amount. The formula to determine the common-size percentage is:

$$\text{Common-Size Percentage} = \left(\frac{\text{Comparision Amount}}{\text{Base Amount}}\right) \times 100$$

For example, if Banyan Goods set total assets as the base amount and wanted to see what percentage of total assets were made up of cash in the current year, the following calculation would occur.

$$\text{Common-size percentage} = \left(\frac{\$110{,}000}{\$250{,}000}\right) \times 100 = 44\% \tag{A3}$$

Cash in the current year is $110,000 and total assets equal $250,000, giving a common-size percentage of 44%. If the company had an expected cash balance of 40% of total assets, they would be exceeding expectations. This may not be enough of a difference to make a change, but if they notice this deviates from industry standards, they may need to make adjustments, such as reducing the amount of cash on hand to reinvest in the business. Figure A.3 shows the common-size calculations on the comparative income statements and comparative balance sheets for Banyan Goods.

BARRY'S SUPERSTORE
Comparative Year-End Income Statements
Vertical Analysis

	Prior Year	Current Year	Common Size* Prior Year	Common Size* Current Year
Net Sales	$100,000	$120,000	100%	100%
Cost of Goods Sold	50,000	60,000	50%	50%
Gross Profit	50,000	60,000	50%	50%
Rent Expense	5,000	5,500	5%	5%
Depreciation Expense - Eq.	2,500	3,600	3%	3%
Salaries Expense	3,000	5,400	3%	5%
Utility Expense	1,500	2,500	2%	2%
Operating Income	38,000	43,000	38%	36%
Interest Expense	3,000	2,000	3%	2%
Income Tax Expense	5,000	6,000	5%	5%
Net Income	$ 30,000	$ 35,000	30%	29%

BARRY'S SUPERSTORE
Comparative Year-End Balance Sheets
Vertical Analysis

	Prior Year	Current Year	Common Size Prior Year	Common Size Current Year
Assets:				
Cash	$90,000	$110,000	45%	44%
Accounts Receivable	20,000	30,000	10%	12%
Inventory	35,000	40,000	17.5%	16%
Short-Term Investments	15,000	20,000	7.5%	8%
Total Current Asstes	160,000	200,000	80%	80%
Equipment	40,000	50,000	20%	20%
Total Assets	$200,000	$250,000	100%	100%
Liabilities:				
Accounts Payable	$ 60,000	$ 75,000	30%	30%
Unearned Revenue	10,000	25,000	5%	10%
Total Current Liabilities	70,000	100,000	35%	40%
Notes Payable	40,000	50,000	20%	20%
Total Liabilities	110,000	150,000	55%	60%
Stockholder Equity				
Common Stock	75,000	80,000	37.5%	32%
Ending Retained Earnings	15,000	20,000	7.5%	8%
Total Stockholder Equity	90,000	100,000	45%	40%
Total Liabilities and Stockholder Equity	$200,000	$250,000	100%	100%

*Some figures rounded to the nearest whole percent, which may alter the total percentage to +/− 1% of 100%

Figure A.3 Income Statements and Vertical Analysis.

Even though vertical analysis is a statement comparison within the same year, Banyan can use information from the prior year's vertical analysis to make sure the business is operating as expected. For example, unearned revenues increased from the prior year to the current year and made up a larger portion of total liabilities and stockholders' equity. This could be due to many factors, and Banyan Goods will need to examine this further to see why this change has occurred. Let's turn to financial statement analysis using financial ratios.

Overview of Financial Ratios

Financial ratios help both internal and external users of information make informed decisions about a company. A stakeholder could be looking to invest, become a supplier, make a loan, or alter internal operations, among other things, based in part on the outcomes of ratio analysis. The information resulting from ratio analysis can be used to examine trends in performance, establish benchmarks for success, set budget expectations, and compare industry competitors. There are four main categories of ratios: liquidity, solvency, efficiency, and profitability. Note that while there are more ideal outcomes for some ratios, the industry in which the business operates can change the influence each of these outcomes has over stakeholder decisions. (You will learn more about ratios, industry standards, and ratio interpretation in advanced accounting courses.)

Liquidity Ratios

Liquidity ratios show the ability of the company to pay short-term obligations if they came due immediately with assets that can be quickly converted to cash. This is done by comparing current assets to current liabilities. Lenders, for example, may consider the outcomes of liquidity ratios when deciding whether to extend a loan to a company. A company would like to be liquid enough to manage any currently due obligations but not too liquid where they may not be effectively investing in growth opportunities. Three common liquidity measurements are working capital, current ratio, and quick ratio.

Working Capital

Working capital measures the financial health of an organization in the short-term by finding the difference between current assets and current liabilities. A company will need enough current assets to cover current liabilities; otherwise, they may not be able to continue operations in the future. Before a lender extends credit, they will review the working capital of the company to see if the company can meet their obligations. A larger difference signals that a company can cover their short-term debts and a lender may be more willing to extend the loan. On the other hand, too large of a difference may indicate that the company may not be correctly using their assets to grow the business. The formula for working capital is:

$$\text{Working Capital} = \text{Current Assets} - \text{Current Liabilities}$$

Using Banyan Goods, working capital is computed as follows for the current year:

$$\text{Working capital} = \$200,000 - \$100,000 = \$100,000 \tag{A4}$$

In this case, current assets were $200,000, and current liabilities were $100,000. Current assets were far greater than current liabilities for Banyan Goods and they would easily be able to cover short-term debt.

The dollar value of the difference for working capital is limited given company size and scope. It is most useful to convert this information to a ratio to determine the company's current financial health. This ratio is the current ratio.

Current Ratio

Working capital expressed as a ratio is the current ratio. The current ratio considers the amount of current assets available to cover current liabilities. The higher the current ratio, the more likely the company can cover its short-term debt. The formula for current ratio is:

$$\text{Current Ratio} = \left(\frac{\text{Current Assets}}{\text{Current Liabilities}}\right)$$

The current ratio in the current year for Banyan Goods is:

$$\text{Current ratio} = \left(\frac{\$200{,}000}{\$100{,}000}\right) = 2 \text{ or } 2{:}1 \tag{A5}$$

A 2:1 ratio means the company has twice as many current assets as current liabilities; typically, this would be plenty to cover obligations. This may be an acceptable ratio for Banyan Goods, but if it is too high, they may want to consider using those assets in a different way to grow the company.

Quick Ratio

The quick ratio, also known as the acid-test ratio, is similar to the current ratio except current assets are more narrowly defined as the most liquid assets, which exclude inventory and prepaid expenses. The conversion of inventory and prepaid expenses to cash can sometimes take more time than the liquidation of other current assets. A company will want to know what they have on hand and can use quickly if an immediate obligation is due. The formula for the quick ratio is:

$$\text{Quick Ratio} = \left(\frac{\text{Cash + Short-Term Investments + Accounts Receivable}}{\text{Current Liabilities}}\right)$$

The quick ratio for Banyan Goods in the current year is:

$$\text{Quick ratio} = \left(\frac{\$110{,}000 + \$20{,}000 + \$30{,}000}{\$100{,}000}\right) = 1.6 \text{ or } 1.6{:}1 \tag{A6}$$

A 1.6:1 ratio means the company has enough quick assets to cover current liabilities.

Another category of financial measurement uses solvency ratios.

Solvency Ratios

Solvency implies that a company can meet its long-term obligations and will likely stay in business in the future. To stay in business the company must generate more revenue than debt in the long-term. Meeting long-term obligations includes the ability to pay any interest incurred on long-term debt. Two main solvency ratios are the debt-to-equity ratio and the times interest earned ratio.

Debt to Equity Ratio

The debt-to-equity ratio shows the relationship between debt and equity as it relates to business financing. A company can take out loans, issue stock, and retain earnings to be used in future periods to keep operations running. It is less risky and less costly to use equity sources for financing as compared to debt resources. This is mainly due to interest expense repayment that a loan carries as opposed to equity, which does not have this requirement. Therefore, a company wants to know how much debt and equity contribute to its financing. Ideally, a company would prefer more equity than debt financing. The formula for the debt to equity ratio is:

$$\text{Debt-to-Equity Ratio} = \left(\frac{\text{Total Liabilities}}{\text{Total Stockholder Equity}}\right)$$

The information needed to compute the debt-to-equity ratio for Banyan Goods in the current year can be found on the balance sheet.

$$\text{Debt-to-equity ratio} = \left(\frac{\$150,000}{\$100,000}\right) = 1.5 \text{ or } 1.5:1 \tag{A7}$$

This means that for every $1 of equity contributed toward financing, $1.50 is contributed from lenders. This would be a concern for Banyan Goods. This could be a red flag for potential investors that the company could be trending toward insolvency. Banyan Goods might want to get the ratio below 1:1 to improve their long-term business viability.

Times Interest Earned Ratio

Time interest earned measures the company's ability to pay interest expense on long-term debt incurred. This ability to pay is determined by the available earnings before interest and taxes (EBIT) are deducted. These earnings are considered the operating income. Lenders will pay attention to this ratio before extending credit. The more times over a company can cover interest, the more likely a lender will extend long-term credit. The formula for times interest earned is:

$$\text{Times Interest Earned} = \left(\frac{\text{Earnings before Interest and Taxes}}{\text{Interest Expense}}\right)$$

The information needed to compute times interest earned for Banyan Goods in the current year can be found on the income statement.

$$\text{Times interest earned} = \left(\frac{\$43,000}{\$2,000}\right) = 21.5 \text{ times} \tag{A8}$$

The $43,000 is the operating income, representing earnings before interest and taxes. The 21.5 times outcome suggests that Banyan Goods can easily repay interest on an outstanding loan and creditors would have little risk that Banyan Goods would be unable to pay.

Another category of financial measurement uses efficiency ratios.

Efficiency Ratios

Efficiency shows how well a company uses and manages their assets. Areas of importance with efficiency are management of sales, accounts receivable, and inventory. A company that is efficient typically will be able to generate revenues quickly using the assets it acquires. Let's examine four efficiency ratios: accounts receivable turnover, total asset turnover, inventory turnover, and days' sales in inventory.

Accounts Receivable Turnover

Accounts receivable turnover measures how many times in a period (usually a year) a company will collect cash from accounts receivable. A higher number of times could mean cash is collected more quickly and that credit customers are of high quality. A higher number is usually preferable because the cash collected can be reinvested in the business at a quicker rate. A lower number of times could mean cash is collected slowly on these accounts and customers may not be properly qualified to accept the debt. The formula for accounts receivable turnover is:

$$\text{Accounts Receivable Turnover} = \left(\frac{\text{Net Credit Sales}}{\text{Average Accounts Receivable}}\right)$$

$$\text{Average Accounts Receivable} = \left(\frac{\text{Beginning Accounts Receivable + Ending Accounts Receivable}}{2}\right)$$

Many companies do not split credit and cash sales, in which case net sales would be used to compute accounts receivable turnover. Average accounts receivable is found by dividing the sum of beginning and ending accounts receivable balances found on the balance sheet. The beginning accounts receivable balance in the current year is taken from the ending accounts receivable balance in the prior year.

When computing the accounts receivable turnover for Banyan Goods, let's assume net credit sales make up $100,000 of the $120,000 of the net sales found on the income statement in the current year.

$$\text{Average accounts receivable} = \frac{\$20{,}000 + \$30{,}000}{2} = \$25{,}000 \tag{A9}$$

$$\text{Accounts receivable turnover} = \frac{\$100{,}000}{\$25{,}000} = 4 \text{ times}$$

An accounts receivable turnover of four times per year may be low for Banyan Goods. Given this outcome, they may want to consider stricter credit lending practices to make sure credit customers are of a higher quality. They may also need to be more aggressive with collecting any outstanding accounts.

Total Asset Turnover

Total asset turnover measures the ability of a company to use their assets to generate revenues. A company would like to use as few assets as possible to generate the most net sales. Therefore, a higher total asset turnover means the company is using their assets very efficiently to produce net sales. The formula for total asset turnover is:

$$\text{Total Asset Turnover} = \left(\frac{\text{Net Sales}}{\text{Average Total Assets}}\right)$$

$$\text{Average Total Assets} = \left(\frac{\text{Beginning Total Assets + Ending Total Assets}}{2}\right)$$

Average total assets are found by dividing the sum of beginning and ending total assets balances found on the balance sheet. The beginning total assets balance in the current year is taken from the ending total assets balance in the prior year.

Banyan Goods' total asset turnover is:

$$\text{Average total assets} = \frac{\$200{,}000 + \$250{,}000}{2} = \$225{,}000 \tag{A10}$$

$$\text{Total assets turnover} = \frac{\$120{,}000}{\$225{,}000} = 0.53 \text{ times (rounded)}$$

The outcome of 0.53 means that for every $1 of assets, $0.53 of net sales are generated. Over time, Banyan Goods would like to see this turnover ratio increase.

Inventory Turnover

Inventory turnover measures how many times during the year a company has sold and replaced inventory.

This can tell a company how well inventory is managed. A higher ratio is preferable; however, an extremely high turnover may mean that the company does not have enough inventory available to meet demand. A low turnover may mean the company has too much supply of inventory on hand. The formula for inventory turnover is:

$$\text{Inventory Turnover} = \left(\frac{\text{Cost of Goods Sold}}{\text{Average Inventory}}\right)$$

$$\text{Average Inventory} = \left(\frac{\text{Beginning Inventory} + \text{Ending Inventory}}{2}\right)$$

Cost of goods sold for the current year is found on the income statement. Average inventory is found by dividing the sum of beginning and ending inventory balances found on the balance sheet. The beginning inventory balance in the current year is taken from the ending inventory balance in the prior year.

Banyan Goods' inventory turnover is:

$$\text{Average inventory} = \frac{\$35,000 + \$40,000}{2} = \$37,500 \tag{A11}$$

$$\text{Inventory turnover} = \frac{\$60,000}{\$37,500} = 1.6 \text{ times}$$

1.6 times is a very low turnover rate for Banyan Goods. This may mean the company is maintaining too high an inventory supply to meet a low demand from customers. They may want to decrease their on-hand inventory to free up more liquid assets to use in other ways.

Days' Sales in Inventory

Days' sales in inventory expresses the number of days it takes a company to turn inventory into sales. This assumes that no new purchase of inventory occurred within that time period. The fewer the number of days, the more quickly the company can sell its inventory. The higher the number of days, the longer it takes to sell its inventory. The formula for days' sales in inventory is:

$$\text{Days' Sales in Inventory} = \left(\frac{\text{Ending Inventory}}{\text{Cost of Goods Sold}}\right) \times 365$$

Banyan Goods' days' sales in inventory is:

$$\text{Days' sales in inventory} = \left(\frac{\$40,000}{\$60,000}\right) \times 365 = 243 \text{ days (rounded)} \tag{A12}$$

243 days is a long time to sell inventory. While industry dictates what is an acceptable number of days to sell inventory, 243 days is unsustainable long-term. Banyan Goods will need to better manage their inventory and sales strategies to move inventory more quickly.

The last category of financial measurement examines profitability ratios.

Profitability Ratios

Profitability considers how well a company produces returns given their operational performance. The company needs to leverage its operations to increase profit. To assist with profit goal attainment, company revenues need to outweigh expenses. Let's consider three profitability measurements and ratios: profit margin, return on total assets, and return on equity.

Profit Margin

Profit margin represents how much of sales revenue has translated into income. This ratio shows how much of each $1 of sales is returned as profit. The larger the ratio figure (the closer it gets to 1), the more of each sales dollar is returned as profit. The portion of the sales dollar not returned as profit goes toward expenses. The formula for profit margin is:

$$\text{Profit Margin} = \left(\frac{\text{Net Income}}{\text{Net Sales}}\right)$$

For Banyan Goods, the profit margin in the current year is:

$$\text{Profit margin} = \left(\frac{\$35,000}{\$120,000}\right) = 0.29 \text{ (rounded) or } 29\% \quad (A13)$$

This means that for every dollar of sales, $0.29 returns as profit. If Banyan Goods thinks this is too low, the company would try and find ways to reduce expenses and increase sales.

Return on Total Assets

The return on total assets measures the company's ability to use its assets successfully to generate a profit. The higher the return (ratio outcome), the more profit is created from asset use. Average total assets are found by dividing the sum of beginning and ending total assets balances found on the balance sheet. The beginning total assets balance in the current year is taken from the ending total assets balance in the prior year. The formula for return on total assets is:

$$\text{Return on Total Assets} = \left(\frac{\text{Net Income}}{\text{Average Total Assets}}\right)$$

$$\text{Average Total Assets} = \left(\frac{\text{Beginning Total Assets} + \text{Ending Total Assets}}{2}\right)$$

For Banyan Goods, the return on total assets for the current year is:

$$\text{Average total assets} = \frac{\$200,000 + \$250,000}{2} = \$225,000 \quad (A14)$$

$$\text{Return on total assets} = \frac{\$35,000}{\$225,000} = 0.16 \text{ (rounded) or } 16\%$$

The higher the figure, the better the company is using its assets to create a profit. Industry standards can dictate what is an acceptable return.

Return on Equity

Return on equity measures the company's ability to use its invested capital to generate income. The invested capital comes from stockholders investments in the company's stock and its retained earnings and is leveraged to create profit. The higher the return, the better the company is doing at using its investments to yield a profit. The formula for return on equity is:

$$\text{Return on Equity} = \left(\frac{\text{Net Income}}{\text{Average Stockholder Equity}}\right)$$

$$\text{Average Stockholder Equity} = \left(\frac{\text{Beginning Stockholder Equity} + \text{Ending Stockholder Equity}}{2}\right)$$

Average stockholders' equity is found by dividing the sum of beginning and ending stockholders' equity balances found on the balance sheet. The beginning stockholders' equity balance in the current year is taken from the ending stockholders' equity balance in the prior year. Keep in mind that the net income is calculated after preferred dividends have been paid.

For Banyan Goods, we will use the net income figure and assume no preferred dividends have been paid. The return on equity for the current year is:

$$\text{Average stockholder equity} = \frac{\$90{,}000 + \$100{,}000}{2} = \$95{,}000 \tag{A15}$$

$$\text{Return on equity} = \frac{\$35{,}000}{\$95{,}000} = 0.37 \text{ (rounded) or } 37\%$$

The higher the figure, the better the company is using its investments to create a profit. Industry standards can dictate what is an acceptable return.

Advantages and Disadvantages of Financial Statement Analysis

There are several advantages and disadvantages to financial statement analysis. Financial statement analysis can show trends over time, which can be helpful in making future business decisions. Converting information to percentages or ratios eliminates some of the disparity between competitor sizes and operating abilities, making it easier for stakeholders to make informed decisions. It can assist with understanding the makeup of current operations within the business, and which shifts need to occur internally to increase productivity.

A stakeholder needs to keep in mind that past performance does not always dictate future performance. Attention must be given to possible economic influences that could skew the numbers being analyzed, such as inflation or a recession. Additionally, the way a company reports information within accounts may change over time. For example, where and when certain transactions are recorded may shift, which may not be readily evident in the financial statements.

A company that wants to budget properly, control costs, increase revenues, and make long-term expenditure decisions may want to use financial statement analysis to guide future operations. As long as the company understands the limitations of the information provided, financial statement analysis is a good tool to predict growth and company financial strength.

B | Time Value of Money

Present Value of $1 Table

Present Value of $1 Table

$$\text{Factor} = \frac{1}{(1+i)^n}$$

Rate (i)

Period (n)	1%	2%	3%	5%	8%	10%	12%	15%	20%
1	0.990	0.980	0.971	0.952	0.926	0.909	0.893	0.870	0.833
2	0.980	0.961	0.943	0.907	0.857	0.826	0.797	0.756	0.694
3	0.971	0.942	0.915	0.864	0.794	0.751	0.712	0.658	0.579
4	0.961	0.924	0.888	0.823	0.735	0.683	0.636	0.572	0.482
5	0.952	0.906	0.863	0.784	0.681	0.621	0.567	0.497	0.402
6	0.942	0.888	0.837	0.746	0.630	0.564	0.507	0.432	0.335
7	0.933	0.871	0.813	0.711	0.583	0.513	0.452	0.376	0.279
8	0.924	0.853	0.789	0.677	0.540	0.467	0.404	0.327	0.233
9	0.914	0.837	0.766	0.645	0.500	0.424	0.361	0.284	0.194
10	0.905	0.820	0.744	0.614	0.463	0.386	0.322	0.247	0.162
11	0.896	0.804	0.722	0.585	0.429	0.350	0.287	0.215	0.135
12	0.888	0.788	0.701	0.557	0.397	0.319	0.257	0.187	0.112
13	0.879	0.773	0.681	0.530	0.368	0.290	0.229	0.163	0.093
14	0.861	0.758	0.661	0.505	0.340	0.263	0.205	0.141	0.078
15	0.861	0.743	0.642	0.481	0.315	0.239	0.183	0.123	0.065
16	0.853	0.728	0.623	0.458	0.292	0.218	0.163	0.107	0.054
17	0.844	0.714	0.605	0.436	0.270	0.198	0.146	0.093	0.045
18	0.836	0.700	0.587	0.416	0.250	0.180	0.130	0.081	0.038
19	0.828	0.686	0.570	0.396	0.232	0.164	0.116	0.070	0.031
20	0.820	0.673	0.554	0.377	0.215	0.149	0.104	0.061	0.026

Figure B.1 Present Value of $1 Table.

Present Value of an Ordinary Annuity Table

	Future Value of an Ordinary Annuity Table $$\text{Factor} = \frac{[1 - 1/(1+i)^n]}{i}$$ Rate (i)								
	1%	2%	3%	5%	8%	10%	12%	15%	20%
1	0.990	0.980	0.971	0.952	0.926	0.909	0.893	0.870	0.833
2	1.970	1.942	1.913	1.859	1.783	1.736	1.690	1.626	1.528
3	2.941	2.884	2.829	2.723	2.577	2.487	2.402	2.283	2.106
4	3.902	3.808	3.717	3.546	3.312	3.170	3.037	2.855	2.589
5	4.853	4.713	4.580	4.329	3.993	3.791	3.605	3.352	2.991
6	5.795	5.601	5.417	5.076	4.623	4.355	4.111	3.785	3.326
7	6.728	6.472	6.230	5.786	5.206	4.868	4.564	4.160	3.605
8	7.652	7.325	7.020	6.463	5.747	5.335	4.968	4.487	3.837
9	8.566	8.162	7.786	7.108	6.247	5.759	5.328	4.772	4.031
10	9.471	8.983	8.530	7.722	6.710	6.145	5.650	5.019	4.192
11	10.368	9.787	9.253	8.306	7.139	6.495	5.938	5.234	4.327
12	11.255	10.575	9.954	8.863	7.536	6.814	6.194	5.421	4.439
13	12.134	11.348	10.635	9.394	7.904	7.103	6.424	5.583	4.533
14	13.004	12.106	11.296	9.899	8.244	7.367	6.628	5.725	4.611
15	13.865	12.849	11.938	10.380	8.559	7.606	6.811	5.847	4.675
16	14.718	13.578	12.561	10.838	8.851	7.824	6.974	5.954	4.730
17	15.562	14.292	13.166	11.274	9.122	8.022	7.120	6.047	4.775
18	16.398	14.992	13.754	11.690	9.372	8.201	7.250	6.128	4.812
19	17.226	15.678	14.324	12.085	9.604	8.365	7.366	6.198	4.844
20	18.046	16.351	14.877	12.462	9.818	8.514	7.469	6.259	4.870

Period (n)

Figure B.2 Present Value of an Ordinary Annuity Table.

Future Value of $1 Table

Future Value of $1 Table
Factor = $(1 + i)^n$

Period (n)	1%	2%	3%	5%	8%	10%	12%	15%	20%
1	1.010	1.020	1.030	1.050	1.080	1.100	1.120	1.150	1.200
2	1.020	1.040	1.061	1.103	1.166	1.210	1.254	1.323	1.440
3	1.030	1.061	1.093	1.158	1.260	1.331	1.405	1.521	1.728
4	1.041	1.082	1.126	1.216	1.360	1.464	1.574	1.749	2.074
5	1.051	1.104	1.159	1.276	1.469	1.611	1.762	2.011	2.488
6	1.062	1.126	1.194	1.340	1.587	1.772	1.974	2.313	2.986
7	1.072	1.149	1.230	1.407	1.714	1.949	2.211	2.660	3.583
8	1.083	1.172	1.267	1.477	1.851	2.144	2.476	3.059	4.300
9	1.094	1.195	1.305	1.551	1.999	2.358	2.773	3.518	5.160
10	1.105	1.219	1.344	1.629	2.159	2.594	3.106	4.046	6.192
11	1.116	1.243	1.384	1.710	2.332	2.853	3.479	4.652	7.430
12	1.127	1.268	1.426	1.796	2.518	3.138	3.896	5.350	8.916
13	1.138	1.294	1.469	1.886	2.720	3.452	4.363	6.153	10.699
14	1.149	1.319	1.513	1.980	2.937	3.797	4.887	7.076	12.839
15	1.161	1.346	1.558	2.079	3.172	4.177	5.474	8.137	15.407
16	1.173	1.373	1.605	2.183	3.426	4.595	6.130	9.358	18.488
17	1.184	1.400	1.653	2.292	3.700	5.054	6.866	10.761	22.186
18	1.196	1.428	1.702	2.407	3.996	5.560	7.690	12.375	26.623
19	1.208	1.457	1.754	2.527	4.316	6.116	8.613	14.232	31.948
20	1.220	1.486	1.806	2.653	4.661	6.727	9.646	16.367	38.338

Figure B.3 Future Value of $1 Table.

Future Value of an Ordinary Annuity Table

Future Value of an Ordinary Annuity Table

$$\text{Factor} = \frac{[(1 + i)^n - 1]}{i}$$

Rate (i)

Period (n)	1%	2%	3%	5%	8%	10%	12%	15%	20%
1	1.000	1.000	1.000	1.000	1.000	1.000	1.000	1.000	1.000
2	2.010	2.020	2.030	2.050	2.080	2.100	2.120	2.150	2.200
3	3.030	3.060	3.091	3.153	3.246	3.310	3.374	3.473	3.640
4	4.060	4.122	4.184	4.310	4.506	4.641	4.779	4.993	5.368
5	5.101	5.204	5.309	5.526	5.867	6.105	6.353	6.742	7.442
6	6.152	6.308	6.468	6.802	7.336	7.716	8.115	8.754	9.930
7	7.214	7.434	7.662	8.142	8.923	9.487	10.089	11.067	12.916
8	8.286	8.583	8.892	9.549	10.637	11.436	12.300	13.727	16.499
9	9.369	9.755	10.159	11.027	12.488	13.579	14.776	16.786	20.799
10	10.462	10.950	11.464	12.578	14.487	15.937	17.549	20.304	25.959
11	11.567	12.169	12.808	14.207	16.645	18.531	20.655	24.349	32.150
12	12.683	13.412	14.192	15.917	18.977	21.384	24.133	29.002	39.581
13	13.809	14.680	15.618	17.713	21.495	24.523	28.029	34.352	48.497
14	14.947	15.974	17.086	19.599	24.215	27.975	32.393	40.505	59.196
15	16.097	17.293	18.599	21.579	27.152	31.772	37.280	47.580	72.035
16	17.258	18.639	20.157	23.657	30.324	35.950	42.753	55.717	87.442
17	18.430	20.012	21.762	25.840	33.750	40.545	48.884	65.075	105.930
18	19.615	21.412	23.414	28.132	37.450	45.599	55.750	75.836	128.120
19	20.811	22.841	25.117	30.539	41.446	51.159	63.440	88.212	154.740
20	22.019	24.297	26.870	33.066	45.762	57.275	72.052	102.440	186.690

Figure B.4 Future Value of an Ordinary Annuity Table.

C Suggested Resources

The resources listed provide further information on several topics: financial statements from real-world companies, accounting software and tools, personal finance, accounting organizations, and exams and professional certifications for accountants.

Sample Financial Statements

The following income statements and balance sheets show the finances of companies representing the manufacturing, retail, and service industries.

Manufacturing Company: General Motors

- Income statement: https://www.nasdaq.com/symbol/gm/financials?query=income-statement
- Balance sheet: https://www.nasdaq.com/symbol/gm/financials?query=balance-sheet

Retail Company: Costco Wholesale

- Income statement: https://www.nasdaq.com/symbol/cost/financials
- Balance sheet: https://www.nasdaq.com/symbol/cost/financials?query=balance-sheet

Service Company: Prudential

- Income statement https://www.marketwatch.com/investing/stock/pru/financials
- Balance sheet: https://www.marketwatch.com/investing/stock/pru/financials/balance-sheet

Accounting Software and Tools

The resources listed offer a variety of tutorials, training videos, and practice activities using software and tools common in accounting.

QuickBooks

- QuickBooks tutorials: https://quickbooks.intuit.com/tutorials/

Peachtree/Sage 50

- Peachtree 2011 guide: https://www.perdisco.com/peachtreeLearning/quickReferenceGuide/2011.aspx
- Sage 50 training course with videos: https://www.freebookkeepingaccounting.com/single-post/Sage-50-Accounts-Training-Course-Part-1

Microsoft Excel

- Excel tutorials, video guides, trainings, and worksheets: https://chandoo.org/wp/welcome/
- YouTube channel with accounting-specific video tutorials: https://www.youtube.com/user/ExcelIsFun

Financial Calculators

- HP10B setup video guide: https://www.youtube.com/watch?v=lmMdRfKre44
- HP10BII video introduction and examples: https://www.youtube.com/watch?v=fTqkkeG1xlw
- HP10B and HP12C time value of money calculations video guides: https://www.youtube.com/user/mssuprof/videos

Personal Finance

These resources can assist you with personal financial planning.

Earnings

- Current starting salaries for recent college graduates for various majors and degrees: https://careers.kennesaw.edu/employers/docs/2018-nace-salary-survey-winter.pdf
- Accounting-specific salaries and positions: https://www.roberthalf.com/blog/salaries-and-skills/the-rise-of-the-accountant-salary-and-10-top-accounting-jobs

Take-Home Pay

- Salary calculator that determines your net pay—the amount you'll take home in your paycheck that you need to plan your budget around. In addition to calculating state and federal taxes, this resource allows you to input other withholdings such as health insurance or 401K contributions: https://www.paycheckcity.com/

Saving and Retirement Planning

Determining how much your savings will grow and how much you will have in retirement are very important components of personal financial planning. These links will help you better plan for those aspects of saving.

- This basic savings growth calculator includes graphs that provide helpful visuals of the impact of changing any assumptions such as the timing or amount of contributions or the interest rate earned: https://smartasset.com/investing/investment-calculator
- To estimate retirement savings growth, use this calculator that allows you to see the impact of saving now (enter your current age) versus saving later (enter a future age): https://www.daveramsey.com/smartvestor/investment-calculator
- This calculator lets you more accurately plan how your retirement savings will grow by allowing you to input any matching amounts contributed by employers: https://nb.fidelity.com/public/nb/401k/tools/calculators/contributioncalculator

Budgeting

- A well-planned budget is the cornerstone of personal financial planning. Using the salary, pay and savings numbers obtained from the resources above, this calculator will help you create a detailed financial budget: https://www.clearpoint.org/tools/budget-calculator/

Debt Reduction

- Whether it is student loans, credit cards, car loans or any other kind of debt, it is always beneficial to understand the impact of differing payments on paying off debt. This resource will help you see the impact of changing the amount paid on the payoff timing and interest paid on the debt: https://www.money-zine.com/calculators/loan-calculators/debt-reduction-calculator/

Accounting-Related Organizations

A number of organizations are dedicated to regulating and supporting the variety of work undertaken in the discipline of accounting.

- Governmental Accounting Standards Board (GASB): https://www.gasb.org
- Financial Accounting Standards Board (FASB): https://www.fasb.org
- U.S. Securities and Exchange Commission (SEC): https://www.sec.gov
- Association of Chartered Certified Accountants (ACCA): https://www.accaglobal.com
- Institute of Management Accountants (IMA): https://www.imanet.org

Accounting Exams and Certificates

These sites provide information on exams and professional certifications.

Certified Public Accountant (CPA)

- American Institute of Certified Public Accountants (AICPA): https://www.aicpa.org/content/aicpa/
- National Association of State Boards of Accountancy (NASBA): https://nasba.org/
- This Way to the CPA: https://thiswaytocpa.com/

Certified Management Accountant (CMA)

- Institute of Management Accountants (IMA): https://www.imanet.org/cma-certification?ssopc=1

Certified Internal Auditor (CIA)

- Institute of Internal Auditors (IIA)-Global: https://global.theiia.org/Pages/globaliiaHome.aspx
- Institute of Internal Auditors (IIA)-North America: https://na.theiia.org/Pages/IIAHome.aspx

Certified Fraud Examiner (CFE)

- Association of Certified Fraud Examiners (ACFE): http://www.acfe.com/default.aspx

Chartered Financial Analyst (CFA)

- CFA Institute: https://www.cfainstitute.org/Pages/index.aspx

Certified Financial Planner (CFP)

- Certified Financial Planners (CFP) Board: https://www.cfp.net/home

Answer Key

Chapter 1

Multiple Choice
1. D
3. A
5. A
7. A
9. C
11. A
13. C
15. C
17. C
19. B
21. D
23. D
25. D
27. C

Questions
1. Answers will vary but should include that cost analysis, branding, pricing, and competition all fall under positioning, and this information comes from the managerial accounting staff. It is used to plan for future processes.
3. Answers will vary but should include the following: Managers must determine what modifications and changes need to be made to operations to get back on track to meet the stated goals and objectives. Managers need to decide if stated goals and objectives should continue to be pursued as they are, or if they should be modified or completely scrapped. Examples may include revising inventory controls to include antitheft tags that trigger an alarm when inventory is moved from an approved location in order to reduce inventory losses; installing more cameras in more strategic locations to further reduce theft from shoplifting; revising the financial metrics such as ratios or other performance measurements to provide more meaningful and timely insight to help determine how to get back on track; investigating why market share has not changed as expected by talking to the sales force and analyzing market data; evaluating same-store sales to understand how to expand sales in accordance with goals and objectives; and investigating why a production process has experienced a bottleneck and how to relieve the pressure in that specific area, such as making sure appropriate raw materials are available in a timely manner to avoid machine shutdowns waiting on materials to arrive.
5. Reports generated from financial accounting are a compilation of a company's various transactions and contain aggregated information for the entire company in the form of financial statements. For publicly traded companies, these reports follow the rules set forth by the Financial Accounting Standards Board (FASB). In addition, the financial statements are verified by external auditors. Reports generated by managerial accounting are varied in nature because they are driven by the questions that need to be addressed by management. Different companies and different questions require different reports. Managerial accounting reports are therefore on a more detailed level, such as on a product or division level. There are no specific rules guiding the creation of these reports, and they are usually unaudited.
7. The primary users of information gathered by managerial accountants are internal users, including management, employees, and officers.
9. Six qualities a managerial accountant should exhibit are commercial awareness, collaboration, effective communication, strong technology skills, analytical skills, and ethics.
11. The chain of command for someone being hired into an organization as a staff managerial accounting is: Management accounting supervisor → Controller → CFO → CEO → Board of Directors
13. Specialization areas for management accountants includes budget analyst, financial analyst, accounting manager, controller, chief financial officer.
15. Professional business organizations that have a code of ethics include the American Institute of Public Accountants, the Association of Certified Fraud Examiners, the Financial Executives Institute, the American Marketing Association, and National Society of Professional Engineers.
17. Several accounting scandals involving publicly traded companies (Enron, WorldCom, and Arthur Andersen) led to the act. It was aimed particularly at public accounting organizations that performed audits of publicly traded corporations.

Chapter 2

Multiple Choice
1. C
3. A
5. A
7. D
9. D
11. B
13. D
15. D
17. C

Questions
1. Answers will vary but should include merchandising, service, and manufacturing businesses.
3. Answers will vary but should include a discussion of operating costs such as salaries and wages, advertising, rent, and office expenses.
5. Answers will vary but must include direct materials, direct labor, and manufacturing overhead.
7. Answers will vary but should include that fixed costs remain fixed in total across the relevant range, bounded by a minimum and maximum activity level.
9. Answers will vary but should include that prime costs are the direct material and direct labor costs, and conversion costs are direct labor and general factory overhead combined.
11. Answers will vary.

Chapter 3

Multiple Choice
1. A
3. C
5. B
7. C
9. D
11. B
13. C
15. C
17. C
19. D
21. C
23. D

Questions
1. Answers will vary. Responses should include that per-unit contribution margin is the amount by which a product's selling price exceeds it total variable cost per unit.
3. Answers will vary. Responses should include that contribution income statements express total contribution margin for a given level of activity and can be useful in making decisions about product pricing and optimal levels of activity.
5. Answers will vary. Responses should include the fact that the contribution margin ratio represents the percentage of every sales dollar available to cover fixed expenses. Businesses can use this ratio when projecting profit at various levels of sales revenue.
7. Answers will vary. Responses should include a description of how the CVP analysis information can be brought into a projected income statement that takes into account additional revenues and expenses of the business to create a "big picture" of what happens as a result of a change in cost, volume, and profit
9. Answers will vary. Responses should include the definition of sales mix as the relative proportions in which a company's products are sold as well as a description of how products within the sales mix have unique sales prices, variable costs, and contribution margins.
11. Answers will vary. Responses should include an explanation of how margin of safety allows the business to operate at a level where the risk of falling to or below the break-even point is low. There should also be some mention of the usefulness of the margin safety as an "alarm" for companies, such that when sales fall to the margin of safety level, action may be warranted.

Chapter 4

Multiple Choice
1. B
3. B
5. C
7. A
9. A
11. D
13. A
15. C
17. D

Questions
1. The company should use process costing. Since there are many similar items, process costing is a better fit than job order costing.
3. The conversion cost is $72,000: the sum of direct labor, factory depreciation expense, and utility expense.
5. The expense recognition principle requires that expenses follow the revenue. Product costs are assigned to the product because they are associated with the revenue from the sale of the product. The cost is transferred from inventory to cost of goods sold when the item is sold. This matches the revenue from the sale with the cost of the item being sold. Period costs are expensed when incurred because they are not related to a specific product but are instead related to the time period in which revenue is earned.
7. B, D, C, A.
9. Management uses the activity considered to be the cost driver and multiplies that rate by the activity for each specific job. The result is the amount of overhead applied to that specific job.
11. Expenses normally have a debit balance, and the manufacturing overhead account is debited when expenses are incurred to recognize the incurrence. When the expenses are allocated to the asset, the work in process inventory, the expense account manufacturing overhead is credited. This is in accordance with the expense recognition principle. The timing of the expense follows the revenue, and when the costs are allocated to inventory, they become a part of the product's cost and are recognized when the asset is sold.
13. direct materials

Chapter 5

Multiple Choice
1. C
3. A
5. D
7. A
9. C
11. B
13. C
15. C
17. C
19. C

Questions
1.
Answers will vary but should include the following:

Area	Process	Job Order
Types of jobs	Identical	Custom order
Quantity within each job	Large volume	Small volume
Cost accumulation	In each department	In each job

3. The weighted-average method assigns the beginning inventory and the costs added during the period. The weighted-average method does not differentiate between the beginning inventory and the units started in production. This is different from the FIFO method that accounts for the beginning inventory differently and separately from current period costs.

5. Prime costs and conversion costs both include labor. Prime costs are the direct costs, other than equipment, used in manufacturing and therefore are direct material and direct labor. Conversion costs are the costs involved in converting the direct material into the product and therefore are direct labor and manufacturing overhead.

7. Job order costing and process costing are the accounting systems used to record the costs expended to produce a product. Conversion costs are the direct labor and manufacturing overhead involved in the production process and exist regardless of the accounting system used.

9. While conversion typically occurs evenly throughout the process, materials are not typically added evenly, so the ending work in process can be different. For example, when materials are added at the beginning of the process, materials can be 100% complete and conversion can be 50% complete. Different completion percentages result in different equivalent units.

11. Step 1: Determine the units to which costs are assigned. Step 2: Compute the equivalent units of production. Step 3: Determine the cost per equivalent unit. Step 4: Allocate the costs to the units transferred out and the units partially completed.

13. The costs transferred in are treated in the same way as direct material that is added to production at the beginning of the process.

15. A. iv; B. ii; C. vi; D. vii; E. iii; F. v; G. i; H. viii.

17. Prior to the new year, a company computes the estimates of the annual overhead per department divided by the estimated driver for that department. A driver is the measure that increases the cost of overhead and is commonly direct labor hours, direct labor cost, or machine hours. The result is the predetermined overhead rate. Costs are accumulated in an account called *manufacturing overhead*. At the end of each period, the overhead is removed from the overhead account and applied to the department.

Chapter 6

Multiple Choice
1. B
3. B
5. C
7. A
9. C
11. B
13. B
15. C
17. A
19. C

Questions
1. The predetermined overhead rate is the amount of manufacturing overhead that is estimated to be applied to each product or department depending on the cost system used (job order costing or process costing). It typically is estimated at the beginning of each period by dividing the estimated manufacturing overhead by an activity base. While it is most commonly a year, the period can be a year, quarter, or month as determined by management. In traditional allocation systems, that base is typically direct labor hours, direct labor dollars, or machine hours. In activity-based costing systems, the activity base is one or more cost drivers.

3. Non-value-added costs can often be eliminated since they are rarely essential, and identifying them helps managers reduce their costs.

5. Answers may vary but should be similar to the following: A. number of orders; B. number of customers; C. number of meals; D. number of material requisitions received.

7. Activity-based costing has multiple cost drivers and focuses on the overhead-related activities performed during manufacturing. Traditional allocation has a single unit-level base for allocating overhead and focuses on the units of production.

9. Estimated overhead costs are first allocated to activity cost pools. Then, an allocation rate is determined based on the estimated usage of the cost driver for that pool. Then the costs are allocated to each product based on that product's cost driver usage.

11. The traditional method of applying overhead does not allocate overhead as precisely as with the ABC method. Management relies on the costing information when setting selling prices and bidding on service jobs. If the costing method is not accurate, some products may be considered profitable under traditional allocation, when those products are actually operating at a loss.

13. While variable costing is not acceptable for financial reporting purposes, some managers prefer variable costing because they believe fixed costs are period costs and do not change during the period. Variable costing separates variable and fixed manufacturing overhead, and using only variable costs allows them to make decisions based on the more reliable variations in unit costs.

15. Yes, as long as the system computes the amount of fixed manufacturing overhead per unit. The total amount can be expensed under variable costing and assigned to overhead produced during absorption costing. This will allow a portion to be included in ending inventory for absorption costing and not included for variable costing.

Chapter 7

Multiple Choice

1. D
3. A
5. B
7. D
9. C
11. C
13. C
15. A
17. C

Questions

1. A budget is a written financial plan for a set period, which is typically a year. There are several different types of budgets including the master budget, operating budget, financial budget, flexible budget, and operating budget.

3. This approach begins at the lowest levels of management. These managers know the details involved with their departments. This allows for more accurate budget estimates when management understands how their department contributes to the company's goals. Disadvantages include that this type of budgeting takes time, which leads to more labor costs, and when management doesn't fully understand how it contributes to the company goals, the budget may support the department and not the company.

5. Operating budgets plan the primary operations of the business and need accurate information in order to provide accurate planning. Assumptions such as sales in units, sales price, desired ending inventory in units, manufacturing costs per unit, which include direct material needed per unit, desired direct materials ending inventory, amount of direct labor hours and rate, and the overhead required for production and managing the company.

7. The budgeted income statement includes the estimated revenue and expenses for the company. Using historical data on cash collections helps plan when the cash will be received and is used to develop the cash collections schedule. The company applies its payment policies on its purchases and other items requiring cash expenditures. This creates the cash payments schedule. Information from the cash collections schedule, cash payments schedule, and the capital expense budget are combined to develop the cash budget. The information from the cash budget and the ending balance sheet from the preceding year are used to develop the budgeted balance sheet.

9. A. cash budget; B. cash receipts budget; C. production budget; D. cash payments schedule; E. capital assets budget

11. This budget is the plan for the purchase and disposal of plant assets and lists the estimated dollar amounts for each.

13. Before the time period begins, the organization's goals should be defined so the budget can be set to achieve the goals. During the time period, the results should be properly measured and reported so necessary changes can be made during the year. Then, the results of the operations can be evaluated and compared to

the original budget and organization's goals.

Chapter 8

Multiple Choice

1. A
3. A
5. A
7. C
9. C
11. A
13. C
15. B
17. A
19. B
21. C
23. A
25. B

Questions

1. The expected price of materials per unit and the expected quantity usage are needed to help determine a standard.
3. Fixed overhead and variable overhead should be considered.
5. Paying more or less than the standard price
7. Buying a different quality level of material; good or bad purchasing/negotiation
9. A direct labor rate variance is the actual rate paid being different from the standard rate.
11. Employees have a different level of experience than standards; the labor market is tighter or looser than expected; contract renegotiation.
13. Total direct labor variance = (Actual hours × Actual rate) – (Standard hours × Standard rate) or the total direct labor variance is also found by combining the direct labor rate variance and the direct labor time variance.
15. The difference between the actual and standard amounts of the allocation base cause variable overhead efficiency variance.
17. It is caused by paying or using less than the standard amount.
19. It may not be a good outcome when buying substandard material or hiring substandard employees.
21. Causes may include substandard material, quantity discount, negotiated better price, quantity discount, or price drop.
23. Causes may include higher-quality material, better-qualified employees, or a change in manufacturing process.
25. Causes may include less-qualified employees or a change in quality level of employees due to a change in process.
27. Causes may include better material, higher-quality employees, or a change in process.

Chapter 9

Multiple Choice

1. B
3. A
5. C
7. C
9. A
11. C
13. B
15. D
17. D
19. B

Questions

1. A management control system allows management to establish, implement, and monitor the organization's achievement of strategic goals. Once the goals are developed, goals must be communicated throughout the organization and activities of the organization should align to achieve the strategic goals. The control system

must also provide feedback and allow for alterations, as necessary, to the organization's strategic goals.

3. Centralized organizations reserve decision-making authority for top management. Decentralized organizations disperse decision-making throughout the organization. Companies of all sizes may exhibit tendencies for both centralized and decentralized decision-making. For example, while Apple might give its stores great latitude to meet customer needs, the company will reserve research and development activities for the highest levels of the organization.

5. Daily decisions are frequent and usually have a short-term impact. Strategic decisions are infrequent and usually have a long-term impact. Daily decisions impact the operational effectiveness and efficiency of the organization while strategic decisions address the long-term aspect of the business. For example, daily decisions for a grocery store might relate to signage, displays, and inventory levels to maintain. Strategic decisions for a grocery store might include whether or not to offer online ordering or leasing in-store space to other businesses such as a coffee shop, nail salon, or bank.

7. These activities represent a significant cost to the organization, require specialization, relate to strategic and quality goals, and allow for benefits related to buying power. Also, there is the possibility that without centralizing some of these costs, they might experience a significant cost overrun. For example, the company might want to finance capital improvements, and they often can do so less expensively, in terms of interest rates, by packaging bonds into one issue. Similar cost savings and improvements in operational efficiencies could probably be identified in the other examples listed.

9. Answers will vary. Sample answer: McDonald's might have a policy that all stores must sell items at a price set by the company. The purpose of this is to prevent stores from competing with each other based on price and causing confusion or frustration with customers.

11. Answers will vary. Responses should include factors relating to establishing a competitive pay rate based on the local economy, hiring experienced workers, investing in training, and other factors necessary to ensure the store's success.

13.

Netflix has three segments: Domestic Streaming, International Streaming, and Domestic DVD. Responses should present the following information:

Domestic Streaming	2017	2016	2015
Paid memberships	54,750	47,905	43,401
Revenues	$6,153,025	$5,077,307	$4,180,339
Contribution profit/(loss)	$2,280,454	$1,838,686	$1,375,500
International Streaming	**2017**	**2016**	**2015**
Paid memberships	62,832	41,185	27,438
Revenues	$5,089,191	$3,211,095	$1,953,435
Contribution profit/(loss)	$226,589	($308,521)	($333,386)
Domestic DVD	**2017**	**2016**	**2015**
Paid memberships	3,380	4,029	4,787
Revenues	$450,497	$542,267	$645,737
Contribution profit/(loss)	$249,972	$279,525	$321,829

Responses may note that Domestic Streaming memberships, revenues, and contribution profit are all increasing. International streaming is experiencing significant increases in memberships and revenues, but the contribution loss continues (the loss decreased from 2016 to 2017). The Domestic DVD segment is experiencing declining memberships, revenues, and contribution profit.

15. Answers will vary. Responses should include an organizational chart for a decentralized structure that

includes three divisions: residential, corporate, and nonprofit. Under each of these divisions would be the mowing, trimming, and landscaping activities. Alternative responses may present three divisions: mowing, trimming, and landscaping activities with the client categories (residential, corporate, and nonprofit) below each. This is less desirable due to inefficiency. The advantage of this approach is the speed of decision-making and responding to clients. Lavell would need to ensure the quality of the services remains at a high standard.

17. Answers will vary. One example is the transportation division in a school system. The goal of the transportation division is to manage costs while maintaining safety in transporting students.

19. Answers will vary. The benefits of an ROI structure include consideration for the segment's investment and evaluation of management's ability to generate profitability. In addition, this framework incentivizes management to undertake value-added investments. A disadvantage is that the segment may prioritize the segment over company financial goals.

21. Answers will vary. Managers can influence controllable costs but have little or no ability to influence uncontrollable costs. While it is common to include uncontrollable (including allocated) costs in the financial information of the responsibility center, managers should be evaluated only on controllable costs.

23. Answers will vary. An advantage of a market-based approach is that the company remains up-to-date on current cost levels. This allows the business to compare its current cost structure to the market and to identify areas where changes are necessary. A disadvantage is this approach is that it requires a significant investment of time and resources on the part of the business.

25. Answers will vary. An advantage of a negotiated approach is that the responsibility center management must be actively involved in the process of establishing the transfer price. This approach may encourage managers to remain attentive to opportunities for cost improvements. A disadvantage would include the possibility of significant disagreements between responsibility center managers.

Chapter 10

Multiple Choice
1. B
3. D
5. B
7. B
9. D
11. A
13. A
15. B

Questions

1. Primarily disagree, but there are a few times where fixed costs can be avoided or partially avoided. Variable costs are avoidable costs since variable costs do not exist if the product is no longer made, or if the portion of the business (such as a segment or division) that generated the variable costs ceases to operate. Fixed costs, on the other hand, may be unavoidable, partially unavoidable, or avoidable only in certain circumstances. When a company discontinues a product or service, certain fixed costs may not be required.

3.

Cost	Relevant or Irrelevant	Sunk, Fixed, Variable, or Opportunity?
Rent	Relevant	Fixed
Baker wages	Relevant	Variable
Felipe's culinary school tuition	Irrelevant	Sunk
Berries for pies	Relevant	Variable
Painting dining area last year	Irrelevant	Sunk
Felipe's decision not to attend graduate school	Irrelevant	Opportunity

5. One issue is the concern for how existing customers will feel if they discover that the company offered a lower price to the special-order customer for the same goods or services. If the goods in the special order are modified, and thus cheaper for that reason, current customers may prefer the modified, cheaper version of the product. The company would need to determine if selling the new version of the project would hurt profitability or the company's reputation.

7. First and foremost, customer service quality is a consideration, followed closely by the ability of the offshore personnel to speak clearly in English and to understand the customer's needs. Chief operating officers should also make sure that the call centers are adequately staffed and run in an ethical manner, similar to the main company contracting with the outsourced service. Offshoring disadvantages should be weighed against domestic outsourcing in the areas of time zone problems, politically correct labor choices, rising labor costs abroad, as well as culture and language.

9. The bakery manager's salary would be avoidable and therefore differential in the analysis.

11. In general, if the differential revenue from processing further is greater than the differential costs, then it will be profitable to process a joint product after the split-off point. Any costs incurred prior to the split-off point are irrelevant to the decision to process further, as those are sunk costs, and only future costs are relevant costs. Joint product costs are common costs that are incurred simultaneously to produce a variety of end products. Even though they are common costs, they are routinely allocated to the joint products.

Chapter 11

Multiple Choice
1. B
3. D
5. C
7. A
9. B
11. D
13. B
15. A

Questions
1. The process for capital decision-making involves five steps: 1. Determine capital needs. 2. Explore resource limitations. 3. Establish baseline criteria for alternatives. 4. Evaluate alternatives using screening and preference decisions. 5. Make the decision.

3. The company then needs to establish alternatives, which are options available for investment, and evaluate the options using common measurement methods, including the payback method, accounting rate of return, net present value, and internal rate of return.

5. From the standpoint of the decision to replace the asset, the book value of an existing asset is irrelevant. Book value is just the historical cost (or value) of the asset less the total depreciation calculated to date. A gain or loss situation often happens when the asset is sold for more or less than its book value, respectively. It is only at that point that the company truly realizes whether they have extra value or not enough value in the assets. This difference can provide either a gain or a loss to the company that will impact the taxes at year-end. Therefore, gains or losses affecting tax payments, plus cash flows, are important, since cash-flow effects are relevant in capital investment decisions.

7. It is used to determine the length of time needed for a long-term project to recapture or pay back the initial investment in the project.

9. Advantage: The ARR compares income to the initial investment rather than to cash flows; thus, incremental revenues, cost savings, and incremental expenses associated with the investment are reviewed and provide a more complete picture than payback, which uses cash flows. Disadvantage: ARR is limited in that it does not consider the value of a dollar over time.

11. Accounting Rate of Return = (Incremental revenues − Incremental expenses) ÷ Initial Investment

13. They need to know what the future value is of their investment compared to today's present value, and what potential earnings they could see because of delayed payment.

15. The Present Value of $1 table.

17. For NPV computations, a minimum required rate of return or discount rate is used as a screening tool to determine whether or not a capital investment decision meets a predetermined set of criteria. If the net present value of an investment is positive, then the capital investment generates an actual return greater than the discount rate and the project will be deemed acceptable. The discount rate, however, is not the actual rate of return earned by the project.
The internal rate of return determines the actual rate of return that a project earns.

19. The internal rate of return (IRR) shows the profitability or growth potential of an investment. All external factors are removed from calculation, such as inflation concerns, and the project with the highest return rate percentage is considered for investment. A company may have several viable alternatives that need a differentiating factor. IRR gives a solid differentiation, presented as a percentage rather than a dollar figure, as

seen in NPV. This removes bias from projects with dissimilar NPVs and is a way to compare more than one option.
21. Answers will vary but should include something like the following: the NPV weighs the early receipt of cash more heavily because when the receipts come in earlier, the discount is closer to 100%; however, the interest rate also impact the NPV.
23. Strengths: It considers the time value of money, removes the dollar bias, and allows for a company to make a decision, unlike non-time value methods. Weaknesses: It has a bias toward return rates instead of higher risk investment consideration, uses a more difficult calculation, and does not consider the time it will take to recoup an investment.

Chapter 12

Multiple Choice
1. C
3. A
5. A
7. B
9. C
11. B
13. C
15. C
17. B
19. C

Questions
1. Answers will vary. Responses may focus on the short-term view versus long-term views and include examples such as: managers focusing on only profitability might avoid spending the money for long-term assets to fuel the future; managers may miss other opportunities like funding the expense for creation of a customer database, if profitability is the focus in the short term; managers may avoid research and development costs that would be used to create the next generation of their product to achieve profitability in the short term.
3. Controllable. Responses will vary based on students' prior experiences.
5. Revenue center—the manager has control over the revenues that are generated for the corporation but not over the costs of the organization. Cost center—the manager has control over costs but not over revenues. Profit center—the manager has control over both revenues and costs. Investment center— the manager has control over revenues, costs, and capital assets.
7. Short-term goals include goals such as reducing costs of production by a certain percentage for the current year or increasing year-over-year sales by a certain percentage. Long-term goals may include goals such as expanding into new territories or adding new products over the next five years. A good performance measurement system will include both short- and long-term measures in order to motivate managers to make decisions that will fulfill both the corporations and their own short- and long-term goals.
9. Answers will vary and should lead to discussions. Goal congruence means aligning the goals of the business with the personal goals of the manager. For example, when a company has a goal to significantly improve sales of a certain product, the regional sales manager will have an increased sales goal as a result.
11. EVA is residual income adjusted for accounting distortions. Like residual income, it encourages managers to make appropriate levels of investment. In addition, it treats items such as research and development costs as having a long-term benefit to the company.
13. Answers may vary but should include some of these ideas. The idea for using both quantitative and qualitative measures in the form of a balanced scorecard was first suggested by Art Schneiderman of Analog Devices in 1987 and was later added to by Kaplan and Norton. The resulting design incorporated various performance measures grouped under four categories: financial perspective, internal operations perspective, customer perspective, and learning and growth. These areas were chosen because the success of a company is dependent on how it performs financially, which is directly related to the company's internal operations, how the customer perceives and interacts with the company, and the direction in which the company is headed.

Chapter 13

Multiple Choice
1. B
3. D

Answer Key

5. D
7. B
9. A
11. A
13. D
15. C

Questions

1. Sustainability is meeting the needs of the present generation without compromising the ability of future generations to meet their own needs. Corporations can incorporate sustainability practices into their businesses a variety of ways; through the reduction of greenhouse gas emissions, efficient use of water and scarce resources, by ensuring that employees have access to a safe working environment, adequate health care and that they are not exploited with an imbalance of power between the employer and employee. Responses may include a variety of suggestions.

3. An oil company might include measures as to how they would sequester excess carbon emissions in their production phase, they may also include information about both environmental and employee safety measures implemented. The company may also provide information on how they have improved the communities in which they operate. A car manufacturer might include a good deal of information on employee well-being as well as community outreach and philanthropy. The company may also provide information on moves toward more environmentally sustainable new automobiles. A large retailer might provide information on GHG reductions through improved energy in their value chain as well as employee well-being programs. The company might also demonstrate its community outreach, and that products are sourced from ethically sustainable suppliers. For example, Walmart has announced that they will no longer sell cage eggs, selling only barn laid and free-range eggs.

5. With the exception of lenders and major shareholders, the majority of these stakeholders are not able to command tailor made sustainability information and so are reliant upon disclosures by the organization. At present there is little legal requirement of non-financial disclosures related to sustainability unless there are material factors which may affect the investment decision-making of a user. (See SASB discussion on materiality)

7. This is a difficult question. Without a mandatory framework for sustainability disclosures, companies can produce "boilerplate reports" that look attractive and say a lot without saying too much of real substance. However, there is increasing evidence that investors are looking for more than just financial reports and they want to know an organization's environmental philosophy and strategy.

9. The SASB is a private sector Sustainability Accounting Standards body that aims to enhance capital market efficiency by encouraging high-quality disclosure of material sustainability information that meets user needs.

Index

A

absorption costing, 313, 323
accounting rate of return (ARR), 574, 600
activity base, 296, 323
activity-based costing, 294, 323
Activity-based costing, 302
After-tax income, 634
after-tax income, 649
allocated costs, 482, 490, 530, 541
Alternatives, 567
alternatives, 600
annuities due, 584, 600
annuity, 578, 600
Asset turnover, 630
asset turnover, 649
attainable standard, 407, 438
Automation, 45
automation, 55
Average fixed cost (AFC), 87
average fixed cost (AFC), 110
Average variable cost (AVC), 88
average variable cost (AVC), 110
avoidable cost, 517, 541

B

balanced scorecard, 55, 638, 649
balanced scorecard (BSC), 50
Baseline criteria, 567
batch-level cost, 302, 323
board of directors, 31, 55
bottleneck, 536, 541
break-even point, 136, 166
bribery, 42, 55
Brundtland Commission Report, 666, 694
budget, 350, 383
budget analyst, 33, 55
budgeted balance sheet, 371, 383
budgeted income statement, 364, 383
business sustainability, 665, 694
business value, 676

C

capital asset, 649
capital asset budget, 366, 383
Capital assets, 630
capital budgeting, 566
capital expenditure budget, 366
Capital investment, 566
capital investment, 600
carbon footprint, 673, 694
carbon output, 664, 694
cash budget, 366, 383
cash collections schedule, 367, 383
Cash flow, 571
cash flow, 600
cash inflow, 571, 600
cash outflow, 571, 600
cash payments schedule, 367, 383
cash-management accountant, 33, 55
Centralization, 460
centralization, 490
Certified Financial Analyst (CFA), 37, 55
Certified Fraud Examiner (CFE), 37, 55
Certified Government Auditing Professional (CGAP), 38, 55
Certified Internal Auditor (CIA), 37, 55
Certified Management Accountant (CMA), 37, 55
Certified Public Accountant (CPA), 36, 55
charitable giving, 675
chief executive officer (CEO), 31, 55
chief financial officer (CFO), 31, 55
Chili's, 186
CITGO, 188
climate change, 673, 694
Collaboration, 28
collaboration, 55
Commercial awareness, 28
commercial awareness, 55
Common fixed costs, 318
common fixed costs, 323
composite unit, 155, 166
Compounding, 578
compounding, 600
constraint, 536, 541
Continuous improvement, 47
continuous improvement, 55
Contribution margin, 128
contribution margin, 166
contribution margin income statement, 132
contribution margin per unit, 129
contribution margin ratio, 130, 166
Controllable costs, 481
controllable costs, 490
controllable factor, 649
controllable factors, 621
controller, 31, 55
Controlling, 17
controlling, 55
conversion cost, 276
conversion costs, 96, 110, 191, 229
Conversion costs, 255
corporate social responsibility, 664
Corporate social responsibility (CSR), 52
corporate social responsibility (CSR), 55, 694
cost accountant, 56
cost accountants, 33
cost approach, 485, 490
cost behaviors, 83
cost center, 468, 490, 621, 649
cost driver, 85, 110, 205, 229, 299, 323
cost equation, 101
cost of goods manufactured, 209, 229
cost of goods sold, 210, 229
cost per unit, 308
cost pool, 304, 323
cost-volume-profit (CVP) analysis, 135
costs of goods sold, 255

D

Decentralization, 460
decentralization, 490
differential analysis, 516, 541
differential cost, 516, 541
differential revenue, 516, 541
Direct labor, 77, 200, 295
direct labor, 110, 196, 229, 323
direct labor budget, 361, 383
direct labor rate variance, 417, 438
direct labor time variance, 418, 438

direct labor variance, 416, 438
Direct material, 295
Direct materials, 77, 196
direct materials, 110, 196, 229, 323
direct materials budget, 360, 383
direct materials price variance, 411, 438
direct materials quantity variance, 413, 438
direct materials variance, 411, 438
discount cash flow model, 586
discounted cash flow model, 600
Discounting, 579
discounting, 600
discretionary cost center, 470, 490
Dow, 188

E
Economic value added (EVA), 634
economic value added (EVA), 649
effective communication, 28, 56
Enrolled Agent (EA), 37, 56
enterprise resource planning (ERP), 44, 56
Environmental sustainability, 673
environmental sustainability, 694
equity issues, 674, 694
equivalent units, 258, 276
estimated activity base, 215, 229
ethics, 39
Evaluating, 18
evaluating, 56
expense recognition principle, 194, 229, 257, 276, 314, 323
external user, 56
external users, 23

F
factory-level cost, 302, 323
favorable variance, 408, 438
financial accounting, 21
Financial Accounting Standards Board (FASB), 21, 56
financial analyst, 33, 56
financial budget, 354, 383
finished goods inventory, 207, 210
fixed asset, 649
Fixed assets, 636
fixed cost, 83, 110
Fixed costs, 123, 517
fixed factory overhead variance, 428, 438

flexible budget, 374, 383, 422, 438
flow of goods through production, 189
Foreign Corrupt Practices Act (FCPA), 42, 56
full-cost accounting, 672, 694
future value, 578
future value (FV), 579, 600

G
GAAP, 38, 313
generally accepted accounting principles (GAAP), 21, 56
Global Reporting Initiative (GRI), 687
globalization, 51, 56
goal, 56
goal congruence, 483, 490, 621, 649
goals, 16
Government agencies, 33
government agency, 56

H
H&R Block, 186
high-low method, 107, 110
hurdle rate, 575, 600

I
ideal standard, 407, 438
Incremental expenses, 575
incremental net income, 575
Incremental revenues, 574
indirect labor, 96, 110, 229, 296, 323
Indirect labor, 203
indirect material, 96
Indirect material, 296
indirect materials, 110, 229, 323
Indirect materials, 203
initial investment, 575
Institute of Management Accountants (IMA), 38, 56
intangible good, 56, 110
intangible goods, 43
intangible products, 80
Integrated Reporting, 690
internal auditor, 33, 56
internal rate of return (IRR), 586
internal rate of return method (IRR), 600
internal user, 56
internal users, 23

inventory account, 208
Invested capital, 636
invested capital, 649
investment center, 475, 490, 621, 649
irrelevant cost, 516, 541
irrelevant revenue, 516, 541

J
job cost sheet, 194, 218, 229
job order cost system, 217
Job order costing, 187
job order costing, 188, 193, 229
joint costs, 532, 541
Just-in-time (JIT) manufacturing, 47
just-in-time (JIT) manufacturing, 56

K
Kaizen, 48
kaizen, 56
Kellogg's, 188

L
lean business model, 47, 56
Lean Six Sigma (LSS), 48, 56
life-cycle, 672
life-cycle accounting, 694
loss leader, 196, 229
Lower-level management, 459
lower-level management, 490
lump sum, 577, 600

M
management control system, 458, 490
Managerial accounting, 12
managerial accounting, 21, 56
manufacturing, 70
manufacturing costs, 191, 229, 276
Manufacturing costs, 255
manufacturing organization, 74, 110
Manufacturing overhead, 77, 203
manufacturing overhead, 110, 204, 229
manufacturing overhead budget, 362, 383
manufacturing overhead costs, 295, 323
margin of safety, 158, 166

market price approach, 485, 490
Marshalls, 186
master budget, 354, 383
materiality, 686, 694
materials requisition form, 197, 229
merchandising, 70
merchandising firm, 71, 110
metric, 622, 649
metrics, 638
Mid-level management, 459
mid-level management, 490
minimum required rate of return, 633, 649
mission statement, 15, 57
Mixed costs, 88
mixed costs, 110
monetary accounting information, 26, 57
multi-product environment, 154, 166
multiplier effect, 162, 166

N
negotiated price approach, 486, 490
Net present value (NPV), 586
net present value method (NPV), 600
non-renewable resources, 674, 694
Non-time value methods, 570
non-time value methods, 600
nonmonetary accounting information, 27, 57
nonprofit (not-for-profit) organization, 57
Nonprofit (not-for-profit) organizations, 34
normal capacity, 521, 541

O
objective, 57
objectives, 16
operating asset, 649
Operating assets, 636
operating budget, 354, 383
Operating budgets, 357
operating expense, 566
operating expenses, 600
operating income, 636, 649
Operating leverage, 160

operating leverage, 166
operating overhead, 227, 229
opportunity costs, 520, 541
ordinary annuities, 600
ordinary annuity, 582
organizational chart, 30, 464, 490
Outsourcing, 46, 524
outsourcing, 57, 541
overapplied overhead, 221, 229
overhead, 196, 204
overhead costs, 192
overhead rate, 213
overhead variances, 421

P
P/E ratio, 681, 694
Paris Climate Agreement, 664, 694
payback method (PM), 570, 600
performance measure, 649
performance measurement system, 622, 649
performance measures, 622
period cost, 192
Period costs, 94
period costs, 110, 229, 255, 276
Pet Smart, 186
planning, 16, 57
predetermined overhead allocation rate, 213
predetermined overhead rate, 296
preference decision, 568, 600
present value, 578
Present value (PV), 583
present value (PV), 600
price-earnings ratio, 681
Primary users, 681
Prime costs, 96, 255
prime costs, 110, 191, 229, 276
process costing, 188, 188, 276
Process costing, 252
Product costs, 93
product costs, 110, 255, 276
product-level cost, 302, 323
production budget, 359, 383
production cost report, 267, 276
productive asset, 649
Productive assets, 636
profit center, 470, 490, 621, 649
profit margin percentage, 476

Q
qualitative factor, 516, 541, 649
qualitative factors, 639
quantitative factor, 516, 541, 649
quantitative factors, 638

R
radio-frequency identification (RFID), 46, 57
raw materials inventory, 199, 207, 208
relevant cost, 516, 541
relevant range, 90, 110, 128, 166, 521, 541
relevant revenue, 516, 541
renewable energy, 678, 694
reporting, 22, 24, 25
Residual income (RI), 479
residual income (RI), 490, 633, 649
Responsibility accounting, 467
responsibility accounting, 490, 620, 649
responsibility centers, 467, 490
Return on investment, 477
return on investment (ROI), 490, 630, 649
revenue center, 470, 490, 621, 649
Robinson-Patman Act, 522
rolling budget, 353, 383

S
sales budget, 358, 383
Sales margin, 630
sales margin, 649
sales mix, 154, 166
Sarbanes-Oxley Act (SOX), 57
Sarbanes-Oxley Act of 2002 (SOX), 41
scatter graph, 105, 110
screening decision, 568, 600
SEC, 38
secondary users, 681
segment, 490, 528, 541
segments, 464
Selling and administrative (S&A) expenses, 257
selling and administrative (S&A) expenses, 276
Selling and administrative costs, 192
selling and administrative expense budget, 363, 383

sensitivity analysis, 147, 166
service, 70
service industries, 227
service organization, 80, 110
Sherwin Williams, 188
short-term decision analysis, 515, 541
social contract, 685, 694
Sony, 227
special order, 541
special orders, 521
split-off point, 532, 541
spoilage, 265, 276
stakeholder, 649, 694
Stakeholders, 640
stakeholders, 671
standard, 406, 438
standard cost, 406, 438
static budget, 375, 383
stepped cost, 90, 110
stockholder, 649
Stockholders, 640
strategic goals, 458
strategic plan, 622, 649
strategic planning, 16, 57
sunk cost, 518, 541
sustainability, 52, 57, 664, 694
Sustainability Accounting Standards Board (SASB), 689
sustainability report, 665, 694
sustainable development, 666, 694

T
tangible good, 57, 110
tangible goods, 43
tangible products, 80
target pricing, 148, 166
technology, 44
theory of constraints (TOC), 49, 57
time ticket, 229
time tickets, 201
time value of money, 577, 600
Titleist, 188
total contribution margin, 131, 166
total cost, 85, 110
total direct labor variance, 419, 438
total direct materials cost variance, 414, 438

total fixed costs, 85, 110
Total quality management (TQM), 47
total quality management (TQM), 57
total variable costs, 85, 110
total variable overhead cost variance, 426, 438
Traditional allocation, 295
traditional allocation, 311, 323
transfer pricing, 483, 491
treasurer, 31, 57
triple bottom line, 672
triple bottom line (TBL), 694
Turkey Hill, 188

U
unavoidable cost, 517, 541
Uncontrollable costs, 482
uncontrollable costs, 491
uncontrollable factor, 649
uncontrollable factors, 621
underapplied overhead, 221, 229
unfavorable variance, 408, 438
unit contribution margin, 129, 536, 541
unit contribution margin per production restraint, 536, 541
unit-level cost, 302, 323
Upper management, 459
upper management, 491

V
variable cost, 85, 110
Variable costing, 313
variable costing, 323
Variable costs, 128, 517
variable overhead efficiency variance, 425, 438
variable overhead rate variance, 423, 438
variance, 406, 438
Variance analysis, 378
variance analysis, 429

W
weighted average cost of capital, 650
weighted average cost of capital (WACC), 634
whistleblower, 57
Whistleblowers, 41

work in process inventory, 195, 199, 207, 209

Z
Zero-based budgeting, 351
zero-based budgeting, 383